D0845655

Alexander Pope & the Arts of Georgian England

Pope's Villa, attributed to Charles Knapton, *c.* 1750.

His House, embosom'd in the Grove,
Sacred to social Life and social Love,
Shall glitter o'er the pendent green,
Where Thames reflects the visionary Scene.

Pope, *Imitations of Horace*, Od. IV. i. 21–4

Alexander Pope & the Arts of Georgian England

MORRIS R. BROWNELL

OXFORD
AT THE CLARENDON PRESS

Oxford University Press, Walton Street, Oxford OX2 6DP

OXFORD LONDON GLASGOW NEW YORK
TORONTO MELBOURNE WELLINGTON CAPE TOWN
IBADAN NAIROBI DAR ES SALAAM LUSAKA
KUALA LUMPUR SINGAPORE JAKARTA HONG KONG TOKYO
DELHI BOMBAY CALCUTTA MADRAS KARACHI

British Library Cataloguing in Publication Data

Brownell, Morris R.
Alexander Pope & the Arts of Georgian England
1. Pope, Alexander 2. Art, English—History
I. Title
709'.42 N6766
ISBN 0-19-817338-5

Printed in Great Britain
at the University Press, Oxford
by Vivian Ridler
Printer to the University

FOR

BERTRAND H. BRONSON

Preface and Acknowledgements

THIS book is dedicated to Professor Bertrand Bronson, who suggested the subject for a dissertation in English at the University of California. In revising it for publication I have attempted to deal with Pope's career as a virtuoso in the Renaissance tradition, an artist intimately involved in contemporary life of the arts, who took the unity of the arts for granted, and assumed a responsibility to revive taste in the arts of his time. This required a study of Pope's career in relation to the art history of the Georgian period. The publication of modern editions of Pope's *Correspondence* (1956) and Spence's *Anecdotes* (1966) has provided the primary sources to do justice to Pope's interest in the non-literary arts, a subject which has been prejudiced by the romantic misconception that the eighteenth-century artist was somehow deficient in aesthetic sensibility. This book sets out to discredit the persistent but mistaken notions that Pope was a dilettante in painting, inadequately responsive to landscape, a trifler in his grotto, ignorant of architecture, and insensible to music. It makes the claim that the major poet of the period was endowed with an aesthetic sensibility of his own.

This study can be distinguished from the recent exemplary treatment of Pope and the arts in Maynard Mack's *The Garden and the City* (1969) by its attempt to give a comprehensive account of Pope's career as a virtuoso in its biographical and art-historical context. It amounts to a history of the arts of the Georgian period in the light of Pope's career. My approach has been empirical and inductive, descriptive rather than normative, in the effort to account for the dynamics of Pope's taste in the arts. Since the evidence is often fragmentary I have practised a kind of literary archaeology, collecting enough shards of circumstantial evidence to determine the facts, and to reveal the pattern of Pope's artistic sensibility and influence. I have supplied documentation full enough to allow the reader to follow my tracks through the circumstantial maze.

Apart from my primary debt to Bertrand Bronson, next I am indebted to Maynard Mack for reading large parts of this book from the earliest to the latest draft, for penetrating commentary which has spared me many errors, and for generous support, advice, and encouragement. Other readers who have contributed to whatever may be valuable in the book include Professors Wayne Shumaker, John Traugott, and Karl Aschenbrenner of the University of California; James Sutherland, and the late Geoffrey Tillotson of the University of London; Meyer Abrams, Sanford Budick, Donald Eddy, Scott Elledge, and Robert Hume of Cornell University; and Graham Midgley, of St. Edmund Hall, Oxford.

The staff of many libraries, museums, galleries, and sale rooms have ably assisted the research, and collection of illustrations for this book: Thomas Agnew & Sons, Ltd.; Art Institute, Chicago; Avery Architectural Library, Columbia University; M. Bernard, London; Bodleian Library; British Library; Christie, Manson & Woods; Cornell University Library; Courtauld Institute of Art; Guildhall General Library; Houghton Library; Huntington Library; Metropolitan Museum of Art; National Museum, Stockholm; National Portrait Gallery, London; New York Public Library; Pierpont Morgan Library; Royal Academy of Arts; Scottish National Portrait Gallery; Sotheby & Co.; Tate Gallery; Arthur Tooth & Sons Ltd.; Victoria and Albert Museum; Royal Library, Windsor Castle; and Yale University Library.

For the answers to importunate questions, all kinds of expert assistance, and generous hospitality I am grateful to E. J. Adsett, the Marquess of Ailesbury, Allen Earl Bathurst, Christopher Lennox Boyd, Martin Butlin, Mrs. Richard D. Butterfield, Beverly Carter, George B. Clarke, J. E. C. Clarke, E. A. Clough, J. Peter W. Cochrane, G. L. Conran, Mrs. S. V. Christie-Miller, T. Cottrell-Dormer, Clare Crick, G. B. Dawson, Peter Day, Mrs. J. H. Dent-Brocklehurst, Simon Wingfield Digby, Robert O. Dougan, R. Q. Drayson, Michael R. Dudley, W. A. Eden, J. J. Eyston, Mary Isabel Fry, F. W. Greenacre, Ernst Gombrich, John Harris, William Edward Viscount Harcourt, Maurice Heckscher, L. F. Herbert, P. A. Howe, John Jacob, Derek Jones, Richard Kingzett, Susan Le Roux, W. S. Lewis, Charles John Lyttelton,

Viscount Cobham, Sir John Molesworth-St. Aubyn, Sir John Murray, James M. Osborn, Peter Pagan, J. M. Paterson, P. S. Peberdy, P. A. S. Pool, A. R. Rawlence, C. J. Rawson, William Rees-Mogg, Richard E. Sandell, Dudley Snelgrove, Dorothy Stroud, Sir John Summerson, Elinor McD. Thomson, Gilbert Turner, Lady Mary Waldegrave, Robert R. Wark, Ellis K. Waterhouse, Reginald Williams, Richard G. Williams, Peter Willis, Rudolf Wittkower, T. S. Wragg, and Marjorie G. Wynne.

For financial support of this project at different stages I am indebted to the Board of Foreign Scholarships, The Committee on International Exchange of Persons, and The United States–United Kingdom Educational Commission for Fulbright graduate student fellowships, 1966–8; the Humanities Faculty Research Grants Committee at Cornell for research awards in 1968, 1973, and a travel grant; finally, the Hull Memorial Publication Fund Committee at Cornell for a subvention.

Dorothy G. Pearson expertly typed a long, sometimes indecipherable draft. My editors at the Clarendon Press, James Raimes, John S. Nicoll, and Jon Stallworthy have been constantly helpful. Lastly, my profound gratitude to Ann, Kate, and Amanda, who waited for me to finish, and sustained me until I did.

Oxford University
March 1976

Contents

PART III. ARCHITECTURE

PART IV. SCULPTURE

APPENDICES

List of Plates

List of Figures

Abbreviations

Correspondence: *The Correspondence of Alexander Pope*, ed. George Sherburn (5 vols., Oxford, 1956). Volume and page numbers cited in the text refer to the *Correspondence*.

Colvin: Howard M. Colvin, *A Biographical Dictionary of British Architects, 1660–1830* (London, 1954).

D.N.B.: *Dictionary of National Biography*.

E.C.: Whitwell Elwin and W. J. Courthope, ed., *The Works of Alexander Pope* (10 vols., London: John Murray, 1871–89).

Griffith: Reginald Harvey Griffith, *Alexander Pope, A Bibliography* (2 vols., Austin, Texas, 1922–7). Citations from the reprint (2 vols., London: The Holland Press, 1968).

H.M.C.: Reports of the Historical Manuscripts Commission.

'Inventory': Annotated reprint in Mack, appendix B, pp. 249–58, of F. G. [Colonel Francis Grant], 'Inventory of Pope's Goods Taken after His Death', *Notes and Queries*, 6th s., 5 (1882), 363–5.

Mack: Maynard Mack, *The Garden and the City: Retirement and Politics in the Later Poetry of Pope 1731–1743* (Toronto: At the University Press, 1969).

O.E.D.: *Oxford English Dictionary*.

Portraits: William Kurtz Wimsatt, *The Portraits of Alexander Pope* (New Haven: Yale University Press, 1965). References to 'Wimsatt' are to types in the catalogue.

Prose: *The Prose Works of Alexander Pope 1711–1720*, ed. Norman Ault (Oxford: Shakespeare Head Press, 1936).

Spence: Joseph Spence, *Observations, Anecdotes, and Characters of Books and Men*, ed. James M. Osborn (2 vols., Oxford: Clarendon Press, 1966). Numbers cited in the text refer to anecdotes in this edition.

TE: The Twickenham Edition of Pope's *Poetical Works* (vols. i–vi: the original poems, London, 1938–61; vols. vii–x: the Homer translations, London, 1967).

Vertue: George Vertue, *Note Books*, Walpole Society (7 vols., Oxford: Oxford University Press, 1930–55).

Walpole, *Anecdotes*: Horace Walpole, *Anecdotes of Painting in England*, ed. Ralph N. Wornum (3 vols., London, 1876).

Walpole, *Correspondence*: *The Correspondence of Horace Walpole*, ed. Wilmarth S. Lewis (New Haven, 1937–   ).

Walpole, *History of Gardening*: 'The History of the Modern Taste in Gardening', ed. Isabel Wakelin Urban Chase, in *Horace Walpole: Gardenist*, pp. 3–40 (Princeton: At the University Press, 1943).

Introduction

IN 1724, when Pope referred to himself and the leading professional landscape gardener, Charles Bridgeman, as men 'of the Virtuoso-class' (ii. 264) he was using a loaded word. In a pejorative sense current since the end of the seventeenth century it referred to the 'pedantic throng' of scholars, antiquarians, collectors, and natural scientists whom Pope himself satirized throughout his career. From the *Essay on Criticism* (1711) to the *Dunciad* (1742), and in writings for the Scriblerus Club, he ridiculed the 'false tastes in learning' of virtuosi, the injudicious dipping into every art and science, the snobbish cult of the strange, rare, and exotic, the vanity of studies contrary to common sense which failed 'to proceed beyond Trifles, to any useful or extensive views of Nature, or of the Author of Nature'.[1]

Obviously Pope did not mean to include himself or his friend, even facetiously, in this discredited and misguided group whose ideals were antithetical to his own. He is referring instead to an uncorrupted ideal of the virtuoso defined by Johnson as 'a man studious of painting, statuary, or architecture'.[2] It was Shaftesbury who early in the eighteenth century 'attempted to rescue the word "virtuoso" from contempt; to broaden the old ideal, purified of scientific contamination; to revive the middle group [between the pedant and the fashionable illiterate]; and once again to unite the courtier with the scholar'.[3]

Shaftesbury began with the encouraging assertion in *Characteristics* (1711) that 'every one is a virtuoso of a higher or lower degree' because of the

[1] See cancelled lines in the *Essay on Criticism*, *TE* i. 242, n. 25; *Spence*, No. 135; 'The Argument', *Dunciad* IV, *TE* v. 338. The Virtuosi-scientists are compared to a devouring plague of locusts in the *Dunciad* IV, l. 397, and the Queen of Dulness confers degrees on those who 'Impale a Glow-worm, or Vertù profess,/Shine in the dignity of F.R.S.' (IV, ll. 569–70).

[2] See Johnson's *Dictionary*, s.v. virtuoso. Cf. H. Bunker Wright and Henry C. Montgomery, 'The Art Collection of a Virtuoso in Eighteenth-Century England', *Art Bulletin*, 27 (Sept. 1945), 195.

[3] Walter Houghton, 'The English Virtuoso in the Seventeenth Century (II)', *Journal of the History of Ideas*, 3 (Apr. 1942), 218–19.

universal love of beauty.[4] He carefully distinguishes between 'inferior virtuosi . . . in love with rarity for rareness' sake', and the true virtuosi, who study the liberal arts and sciences in a broadly humanistic spirit (ii. 252, 255). Shaftesbury conceives of the virtuoso above all as a man of taste, who knows that the pursuit of the beautiful is the pursuit of the good, and understands that aesthetic and moral values are roughly equivalent: 'the science of virtuosi and that of virtue itself become, in a manner, one and the same' (i. 217). He is persuaded that 'to be a *virtuoso* (so far as befits a gentleman) is a higher step towards the becoming a man of virtue and good sense than the being what in this age we call a scholar' (i. 214–15).

It has been implied that Shaftesbury's attempted revival of the virtuoso ideal was a failure, which never won wide support, and that by 1700 'the golden age of the virtuosi was over'.[5] Nevertheless, the career of Pope and many of his fellow artists and patrons indicates that Shaftesbury's ideals of the virtuoso were potent influences in the early eighteenth century. To be sure, Pope had the humanist's awareness of mankind's limitations—'One *Science* only will one *Genius* fit;/So *vast* is Art, so *narrow* Human Wit'[6]—and he could not share Shaftesbury's condescending attitude towards the artist or his contempt for the 'virtuoso tribe' in which he included himself and his closest friends. Nor could he conform to Shaftesbury's aristocratic ideal of the gentleman-virtuoso, with his attitudes of hauteur, distaste for practical execution, and reserve—all of which characterize the outlook of men like Chesterfield and Walpole to some degree.

Pope wittily caricatured himself as a false virtuoso when he imagined himself a part of Lady Mary's retinue during her tour of the Orient in 1717—'Allow me but to sneak after you in your train, to fill my pockets with Coins, or to lug an old Busto behind you, & I shall be proud beyond Expression' (i. 440)—but he earnestly studied throughout his career to become a true virtuoso, and pursued his interest in the arts in the spirit of the Renaissance ideals of virtu, the unity of the arts, and the responsibility of the artist to cultivate his own taste in the fine arts and to refine the national taste. He believed with

[4] Anthony Ashley Cooper, Earl of Shaftesbury, *Characteristics of Men, Manners, Opinions, Times*, ed. John M. Robertson, 2 vols. (London, 1900), i. 92. Citations in the text hereafter from this edition.

[5] Walter Houghton, 'The English Virtuoso', p. 219.

[6] *Essay on Criticism*, ll. 60–1.

Pliny that the artist alone is the true critic,[7] and he sought from the beginning of his career to become such a critic of the arts of his time. The measure of his success may be judged from the reputation he had acquired even before the publication of the *Epistle to Burlington* (1731) as an arbiter of taste.[8] After the *Epistle to Burlington* Pope's enemies, smarting from the *Dunciad*, mocked him as 'Mr. Alexander Taste', and pictured him as the dictator of taste.[9] Throughout the eighteenth century Pope was widely regarded by admirers as the epitome of the man of taste in the arts, and M. M'Dermot expressed the view which still prevails today when he wrote of Pope in 1823: 'Perhaps no writer, ancient or modern, possessed a more elegant taste than Pope.'[10]

The purpose of this book is to give a comprehensive account of Pope's 'virtuosoship' and taste in the arts, a neglected chapter of his biography,[11] and a subject which has frequently been misunderstood and misrepresented. A full account could not have been written before the publication of Pope's *Correspondence* (1956) and the complete edition of Spence's *Anecdotes* (1966). Another essential condition for the writing of this study has been the gradual illumination of an obscure period in English art history by the publication of George Vertue's *Note Books* (1930–55), a large number of specialized studies, and some excellent general histories of the arts in the period. A fair treatment of the subject would have been difficult as long as serious misconceptions about Pope and the arts of his time prevailed: myths about the insensibility of Pope

[7] See Pope's reference to Pliny ('De Pictore, Sculptore, Fictore, nisi artifex judicare non potest') in the note to the *Essay on Criticism*, l. 15, *TE* i. 240: 'Let such teach others who themselves excell.'

[8] See Norman Ault, *New Light on Pope* (1949; rpt. New York, 1967), p. 100; James Lees-Milne, *Earls of Creation* (London, 1962), p. 14; Basil Williams, *The Life of William Pitt* (London, 1913), i. 53.

[9] See the play attributed to Mrs. Eliza Heywood, *Mr. Taste, the Poetical Fop* (Apr. 1732); Matthew Concanen, *A Miscellany on Taste* (15 Jan. 1732); *Mr. Taste's Tour* (31 May 1733); and Joseph Dorman, *The Rake of Taste: A Poem, Dedicated to Alexander Pope, Esq.* (Nov. 1735). The first three are discussed by J. V. Guerinot, *Pamphlet Attacks on Alexander Pope 1711–1744* (London, 1969), pp. 217–18, 207, 236. For *The Rake of Taste*, see D. F. Foxon, *English Verse 1701–1750, A Catalogue of Separately Printed Poems*, 2 vols. (Cambridge, 1975), D. 409. For the satirical engraving, Taste, see below, chapter X.

[10] *A Critical Dissertation on the Nature and Principles of Taste* (London, 1823), p. 217.

[11] This is not to overlook useful studies directed to different ends: Robert J. Allen's analysis of Pope's imagery, 'Pope and the Sister Arts', in *Pope and His Contemporaries*, ed. James L. Clifford and Louis A. Landa (Oxford, 1949), pp. 78–88; Maynard Mack's study of the making of Twickenham as 'an act of the mythopoeic imagination', *The Garden and the City: Retirement and Politics in the Later Poetry of Pope 1731–1743* (Toronto, 1969), p. 9; and Arthur James Sambrook's summary article, 'Pope and the Visual Arts', in *Writers and Their Background: Alexander Pope*, ed. Peter Dixon (London, 1972), pp. 143–71.

and his age to the arts; unbalanced accounts of the role of the amateur; a general attitude that the visual arts of the period are beneath contempt; and a scepticism about the validity of the doctrine of the sister arts.

This study begins with a consideration of painting, chronologically the earliest of Pope's interests in the arts, and probably the most influential on his sensibility and imagination. It includes, first, an account of his relationships with contemporary artists, and his activity as a collector and connoisseur, and second, an exploration of the significance of painting in his criticism and poetry in the light of Lessing's attack on him in the *Laokoön* for confusing the arts. Pope's concept of the landscape garden derives from painting, and an analysis of his sensibility to landscape introduces a discussion of his theory and practice of gardening, the most important of his interests in the arts to which about half the book is devoted: comprising his idea of garden design, its sources, relation to contemporary theory, and influence; the character and influence of his own garden design at Twickenham; finally, the nature and extent of his collaboration with professional and amateur garden designers, and his influence on the development of the landscape garden. His subordinate but collateral interest in architecture involves a discussion of his garden-Gothic designs including the Twickenham grotto, his connection with the Palladian movement, and the strain of architectural satire in his poetry of the 1730s. A chapter on sculpture deals with Pope's concern for funerary monuments, particularly his contribution to the establishment of Poets' Corner in Westminster Abbey. A brief discussion of the myth of Pope's insensibility to music is contained in an appendix.

The study of Pope's 'virtuosoship' affords an insight into his life as an artist, and his relationships with contemporary artists and patrons—Kneller, Richardson, Bridgeman, Vanbrugh, Burlington, Handel, and others. It illuminates some obscure episodes in the art history of the period, and explores the interrelations of the arts at a time when the doctrine of the sister arts was one of the supreme fictions of the age. It examines an important area of allusion in Pope's poetry, the way 'images reflect from art to art', supplies an intellectual background to one of his major poems, the *Epistle to Burlington*, and throws new light on Pope's sensibility which results in a reinterpretation of the evolution of eighteenth-century taste.

Even today there are those who would not disagree with Horace Walpole's estimate of Georgian England as 'the period in which the arts were sunk to the lowest ebb in Britain'.[12] To those who come to it from the high Italian Renaissance, or even from the preceding era of the English Baroque of Wren, Lely, and Vanbrugh, it may be found wanting. But it was the period when taste was discovered in England, the beginning of a Renaissance in appreciation and connoisseurship if not in the arts themselves—the age of the Spectator. But the culture which produced the English novel, the finest satire in the language, the landscape garden, the country house, and the English oratorio cannot be dismissed as negligible. The study of Pope's contribution to this achievement helps to discredit the view of the Georgian period as a 'winter of the imagination'.[13]

[12] *Anecdotes*, ii. 259. [13] Kenneth Clark, *Landscape into Art* (1949; rpt., Boston, 1961), p. 52.

Part I. Painting

1. William III. After Kneller, 1701.

2. Hercules Farnese. By Kneller. *c.* 1719.

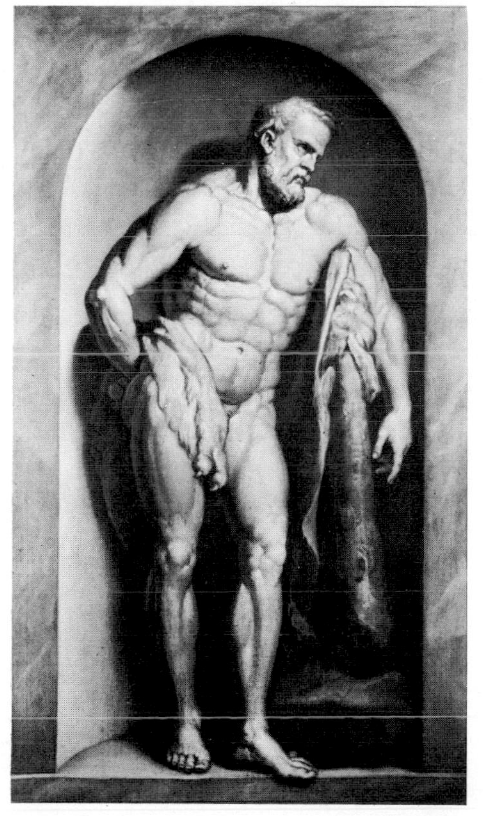

3. Lady Mary Wortley Montagu. By Kneller. 1720.

4. Jonathan Richardson the elder. Self-portrait. 1732.

1. *Amateur, Sitter, and Connoisseur*

DURING his infatuation with Lady Mary Wortley Montagu Pope began a letter to her in 1717 by saying that she had made him indifferent to the arts, including painting: 'how meanly I thought of the pleasure of Italy, without the qualification of your Company . . . Meer Statues & pictures are not more cold to me, than I to them' (i. 407). But by the autumn of the same year he was expressing his passion in the picturesque manner: 'I lye dreaming of you in Moonshiny Nights exactly in the posture of Endymion gaping for Cynthia in a Picture' (i. 439). These playful histrionics conceal the interest Pope had for an art which gave him, he told Joseph Spence in 1730 (No. 110), as much enjoyment as poetry.

Painting has particular importance in Pope's career as virtuoso: it was the first non-literary art seriously to engage his attention; it bears a closer relation to his literary work than any of the other arts; and it had an important effect on his sensibility and poetic imagination. Painting is at the root of his aesthetics, and the source of principles he applied to the landscape garden, architecture, and even sculpture. He was an amateur painter of some competence, a friend of many of the important painters of his time, and probably the most frequently portrayed person of his generation.[1] He made extensive use of the analogy to painting in literary criticism, particularly in the notes to Homer, and critics since the eighteenth century have found his poetry pervasively pictorial.

The nature and extent of Pope's interest in the art of painting can best be indicated by a study of his relationship with three painters: Charles Jervas, Godfrey Kneller, and Jonathan Richardson Sr. All three were portrait painters, and all are representative of an age that has been called by the modern historian of painting 'the most drab in the history of British painting'.[2] The age was

[1] *Portraits*, p. xv.

[2] Ellis K. Waterhouse, *Painting in Britain 1530–1790* (London, 1953), p. 98.

characterized by a radical conflict between popular and academic taste in painting. Popular taste was for portraiture, a demand which attracted to London the foreign artists who dominated the native school until the latter half of the century, and resulted in studios organized like the 'factory' of Kneller. The taste for portraiture triumphed in spite of the attempts of virtuosi to reform it according to the academic standards of classical idealism and the high Italian Renaissance.[3] The hallmark of academic taste was the preference for history painting, which was ranked above portraiture, landscape, and still-life in a strict hierarchy of genres. The influence of academic taste can be observed in the attempts of native artists (Thornhill, Kent, and even Hogarth) to emulate Italian Renaissance painting, and to compete with rival foreign artists in covering rich men's walls and ceilings with classical and biblical scenes; and in the popularity of connoisseurship, the activity of collectors, the currency of engravings, the formation of the Academy, and establishment of societies of artists.

i. POPE AND CHARLES JERVAS (*c.* 1695–1739)

Pope's friendship with Charles Jervas introduces all the significant aspects of his interest in the art of painting: most important, his career as a student of painting and amateur artist; his activity as a sitter for portraits; and finally his early interest in connoisseurship. The study of painting Pope pursued for a year or more while he lived in the London studio of Jervas at Bridgewater House in Cleveland Court appears to have been the culmination of a childhood interest in the art. The interest may have been inspired by the example of the poet's uncle, Samuel Cooper (1609–72), the portrait miniaturist who had a European reputation as the '*Van-Dyke* in *little*' when Pope was a boy, and whose pictures and books he inherited by delayed bequest.[4] The family had associations with painters and would have done nothing to discourage the love of drawing which was one of his childhood amusements, according to his biographers.[5] In 1705 he sent a book of 'Rudiments of Drawing' (i. 4) to a

[3] See Charles Mitchell, 'Benjamin West's "Death of General Wolfe" and the Popular History Piece', *Journal of the Wartburg and Courtauld Institute*, 7 (1944), 23.

[4] George Sherburn, *The Early Career of Alexander Pope* (Oxford, 1934), p. 102. For Samuel Cooper, see Basil S. Long, *British Miniaturists* (London, 1929; repr. 1966), p. 82.

[5] See William Ayre, *Memoirs of the Life and Writings of Alexander Pope* (London, 1745) i. 4; and Ault, pp. 68–9.

lady, telling her in a gallant letter that he had been attempting unsuccessfully for three days to copy her portrait after Kneller. This has disappeared with the rest of his juvenilia: a fan painting censured by Reynolds, and a Madonna

FIG. 1. Figure drawing by Pope, 1708–11.

presented to the John Carylls at Christmas 1710. Only a figure drawing has survived among his letters to Cromwell, variously described as a self-portrait 'reading his poems aloud', and 'some classical figure'.[6]

It is unlikely that Pope had professional ambitions when he followed the Carylls' advice to study painting; but it was not the childish amusement or mere pastime that it has been thought to be. He was applying himself with

[6] See Charles Robert Leslie and Tom Taylor, *Life and Times of Sir Joshua Reynolds* (London, 1865), i. 25; and *Correspondence*, i. 115. *Summary Catalogue of Western MSS. in the Bodleian Library*, 14978; *Portraits*, p. 8 n.

some diligence when he told John Caryll in April 1713 that he was 'almost every day employed in following your advice in learning to paint . . . obliged to Mr. Gervase [Jervas], who gives me daily instructions and examples' (i. 174), and in June that 'I generally employ the mornings this way' (i. 177). The extent of his interest in the art is suggested by the remark in August that he is 'so entirely immersed in the designing art, (the only sort of designing I shall ever be capable of) that I have not heard a rhyme of my own gingle this long time. My eyes have so far got the better of my ears' (i. 189). One must allow for exaggeration, but his enthusiasm is proved by the number of his productions.

A letter to Gay (August 1713) from the frustrated student of painting turned iconoclast indicates that he was concentrating on portraiture in Jervas's studio:

> I have thrown away three Dr. *Swift's*, each of which was once my Vanity, two Lady *Bridgwaters*, a Dutchess of *Montague*, besides half a dozen Earls, and one Knight of the Garter. I have crucify'd *Christ* over-again in effigie, and made a *Madona* as old as her mother St. Anne. (i. 187)

Later he confided to Caryll that 'I find my hand most successful in drawing of friends . . . my masterpieces have been one of Dr Swift, and one Mr Betterton' (i. 189). Spence recorded other works by Pope which he must have seen hanging at Twickenham: 'a grave old Chaucer from Occleve, a Betterton, Lucius Verus (large profile), two Turkish heads, [a] Janizary from the life, Antinous, St. John praying, etc.' (No. 108). From these references we can infer Pope had tried his hand at copying a variety of portraits sacred and profane: classical busts, old masters, fashionable society portraits of women (after Jervas), portraits of his friends (after Kneller), and one exotic study *ad vivum* of a Turkish soldier.[7] Only the portrait of Betterton survives, once thought to be too good for Pope, but now accepted as a competent copy of Kneller's portrait.[8]

All this does not amount to much in itself, but Pope's painting lessons resulted

[7] Ault, pp. 73–5.

[8] For the sceptical view see William T. Whitley, *Artists and Their Friends in England 1700–1799* (London, 1928), i. 42, but Sherburn (*Early Career*, p. 103 n.) observes that 'Whitley much underestimates the time Pope gave to painting.' See frontispiece and 'Pope's Portrait of Betterton', Appendix A of Benjamin Boyce, *The Character-Sketches in Pope's Poems* (Durham, N.C., 1962), pp. 131–2; and David Piper, *Catalogue of Seventeenth-Century Portraits in the National Portrait Gallery 1625–1714* (Cambridge, 1963), pp. 27–8.

in the first of many close friendships with painters, a life-long love of the painter's studio, an apparent preference for practice over theory in art, and a delight in the technicalities of the arts.[9] He acquired a competence in painting and drawing which he applied later to landscape design and architecture, an insight into physiognomy, a sensitivity to colour, light, and design which is conspicuous in his poetry; and perhaps most important, that sharpening of perception characteristic of all students of painting which is apparent in a letter to Gay (1713) when he speaks of becoming

> by Mr. J—s's [Jervas's] help, *Elegans Formarum Spectator*. I begin to discover Beauties that were till now imperceptible to me. Every corner of an Eye, or Turn of a Nose or Ear, the smallest degree of Light or Shade on a Cheek, or in a dimple, have charms to distract me. (i. 187)

It is no exaggeration to say that this heightening of aesthetic perception was a crucial influence on the development of Pope's imagination as an artist.[10]

The warm tribute Pope pays in the *Epistle to Jervas* to the painter who appears so feeble to the modern art historian[11] cannot be scrutinized as sober art criticism. The poem reflects the admiration of an enthusiastic student of painting for a gifted teacher and friend, as it appears from lines in an early version of the poem:

> Nature to thee has all her Graces shown
> And gave thee words to make those Graces known
> If Raphael writ or if Leandro [Leonardo] wrought
> The Verse is perishd or the Piece forgot.
> Evn Fresnoy painted wth unfruitful pains
> The artist Lost, ye Critic yet remains
> Of Jervas only future Times shall tell
> None practisd better, none explaind so well
> Thou only sawst wt others coud not know;
> Or if they saw it, only thou canst show.[12]

Pope regarded Jervas as a teacher whose precept and example in the studio

[9] See 'Pope and the Technicalities of the Arts', *The Spectator*, 123 (20 Sept. 1919), 364–5.

[10] See Ault, p. 73, and Marjorie Nicolson and G. S. Rousseau, '*This Long Disease, My Life*': *Alexander Pope and the Sciences* (Princeton, 1968), p. 233.

[11] Waterhouse, *Painting in Britain*, pp. 101–2.

[12] Transcribed by Ault (pp. 72–3) from a draft in the Homer MSS. in the British Museum (Add. MS. 4807, f. 128b).

excelled the academic instruction of Du Fresnoy, whose treatise inspired the poem:

> How finish'd with illustrious toil appears
> This small, well-polish'd gem, the work of years!
> Yet still how faint by precept is exprest
> The living image in the Painter's breast?
> Thence endless streams of fair ideas flow,
> Strike in the sketch, or in the picture glow;
> Thence beauty, waking all her forms, supplies
> An Angel's sweetness, or *Bridgewater's* eyes. (39–46)[13]

Both Pope and Jervas had an editorial share in the second English edition of Du Fresnoy's *Art of Painting*, the standard work on painting of the French Academy.[14]

Pope preferred to the book apparently the livelier introduction to the subject he received in the studio of the artist from the study of Jervas's large collection:

> Here thy well-study'd Marbles fix our eye;
> A fading Fresco here demands a sigh:
> Each heav'nly piece unweary'd we compare,
> Match *Raphael*'s grace, with thy lov'd *Guido*'s air,
> *Caracci*'s strength, *Correggio*'s softer line,
> *Paulo*'s free stroke, and *Titian*'s warmth divine. (33–8)

This warmly humanistic attitude to the art of the high Italian Renaissance is far from the didactic scholasticism of Du Fresnoy. 'Unweary'd comparison' is the essence of the 'Science of a Connoisseur' introduced by Jonathan Richardson Sr., which encouraged a greater freedom of taste and independence of judgement than academic canons.[15]

Pope's point of view is always that of the artist, and this attitude helps to explain the earnest appeal which interrupts a letter full of raillery and banter from Pope to Jervas written in 1716:

I long to see you a History Painter. You have already done enough for the Private, do something for the Publick; and be not confined, like the rest, to draw only such silly

[13] *TE* vi. 157.

[14] See William Guild Howard, 'Ut Pictura Poesis', *PMLA*, 24 (Mar. 1900), 42–3, and Luigi Salerno, 'Seventeenth-Century English Literature on Painting', *Journal of the Warburg and Courtauld Institute*, 14 (1951), 251.

[15] Salerno, 'English Literature on Painting', pp. 255–6.

stories as our own faces tell of us. The Ancients too expect you should do them right; those Statues from which you learned your beautiful and noble Ideas, demand it as a piece of Gratitude from you, to make them truly known to all nations, in the account you intend to write of their *Characters*. I hope you think more warmly than ever of that noble design. (i. 377)

This repeats commonplaces about history painting to be found in Du Fresnoy, but it would be a mistake to dismiss Pope's appeal as cant or flattery because it is not merely academic. It springs from an ambition to revive the arts in his own age such as can be found in Shaftesbury's call for a national taste in *A Letter Concerning Design* (1712). Pope wants to enlist Jervas in the common pursuit, to summon him from portraiture to the kind of enterprise he was pursuing in the translation of Homer: 'It is my employment to revive the old of past ages to the present, as it is yours to transmit the young of the present, to the future' (i. 239). His motive is the reform of national taste; he dreams of a Renaissance of the arts.

It is true, however, that Pope's concern for the public had little influence on his own private taste, and no effect on the demands he made on Jervas to paint portraits of his friends and of himself. His preference for portraiture reflects the discrepancy referred to above between the aspirations and actualities of eighteenth-century taste. Jervas specialized in portraits of fashionable women and Pope's collection appears to have included his portraits of Elizabeth Hamilton, Henrietta Howard, the Blount sisters, and a crayon drawing of Judith Cowper.[16]

Our concern is with portraits of Pope himself by Jervas where we encounter for the first time that aspect of his interest in painting throughout his career, which has been documented by William Wimsatt, who remarks on 'the importance to him of having an adequate image of himself made public, and his apparently persistent efforts toward that end'.[17] According to Joseph Spence (No. 9) it was Jervas who inserted a laurel branch in the hand of the poet represented in a childhood portrait by an unknown artist (Wimsatt 1). His own portraits of Pope have the same intimate connection with Pope's literary career. The first known type by Jervas (Wimsatt 2. 1), painted by the autumn of 1714, appears to have been intended to coincide with the publication of the

[16] These portraits are listed in the 'Inventory', pp. 250, 252, 254.

[17] *Portraits*, p. xv.

first volume of the *Iliad* (Books I–IV, 6 June 1715), and was later used as frontispiece to Pope's *Works* (1717).[18] It was engraved by George Vertue under the watchful eye of the painter (i. 310). 'A Print of Mr. Alexander Pope, done from the original painting of Mr. Jervasi, by Mr. Vertue' (Wimsatt 2. 2) was advertised by Lintot with Pope's Homer,[19] but it is not at all the portrait of the English Homer which Kneller was soon to provide. This engraving, subscribed in one version with the legend 'Alexander Pope, Armiger', presents the image of himself Pope wanted to present to the readers of the *Works* (1717), the picture of 'the modish modern Author' he speaks of in the *Correspondence* (i. 243).[20] Curll quickly found another use for this elegant, bewigged, and debonair image of Pope: he planned 'to hang him up in effigy for a sign to all spectators of his falsehood and my own veracity'.[21]

Jervas's second portrait of Pope (Wimsatt 3. 1, 3. 2), also dated about 1715, appears to have an allegorical significance which links it more intimately to the translation of Homer than the first. The picture showing Pope between the bust of Homer and a woman traditionally thought to be Martha Blount can be interpreted as an attempt to dramatize Pope's state of mind when he was beginning his translation of Homer, preoccupied with the difficulty of the task and the sacrifices it would entail. In letters to Martha Blount at the time he repeatedly refers to the hard choice between perfecting his life or his work:

> if I could have seen you every day, and imagin'd my company cou'd have every day pleas'd you, I shou'd scarce have thought it worth my while to please the world. How many verses cou'd I gladly have left unfinish'd . . . had I been permitted to pass all those hours more pleasingly? Whatever some may think, Fame is a thing I am much less covetous of, than your Friendship; for that I hope will last all my life, the other I cannot answer for. (i. 280)

In another letter the same year he puts the conflict more wittily:

> if ever I could have any merit with you, it is in writing to you at a time when I am studying to forget every Creature I ever lov'd or esteemed . . . When I am to be entertain'd only with that Jade whom every body thinks I love, as a Mistress, but whom in

[18] For Jervas's connection with Pope's Homer, see *Correspondence*, i. 243–4, 262; *TE* ix, pl. 6 and Notes on the Plates, pp. xiii–xiv; 'Inventory', pp. 249, 253.

[19] *Portraits*, p. 18.

[20] Critics have found this portrait of Pope 'sentimental', 'romantic', and 'sweet'. See Walpole, *Anecdotes*, ii. 260; R. K. Root, *The Poetical Career of Alexander Pope* (Princeton, 1938), pp. 104–5; and R. M. Schmitz, rev. of *Portraits*, *Philological Quarterly*, 45 (July 1966), 580.

[21] *Portraits*, p. 19.

reality I hate as a Wife, my Muse. Pitty me, Madam, who am to lye in of a Poetical Child for at least two Months [volume ii of the *Iliad*]. (i. 293)

References to 'sleep and musing' (i. 239), and to his deep 'Rêverie' (i. 243) in letters to Jervas at the outset of his translation perfectly correspond to the hypnagogic state in which he is depicted in the portrait. A letter of 1712 practically supplies the pose, when he describes himself 'lolling on an Arm Chair, nodding . . . like the picture of January in an old Salisbury Primer' (i. 163).

These letters invite the speculation that the painting represents the poet smiling at the moment when he has been distracted from thoughts of the translation of the *Iliad*, as symbolized by the dark, lifeless, brooding bust of Homer. This significantly occupies the margin of the picture, enveloped in shadow, while a woman usually identified with Martha Blount—idealized, sensuous, Titianesque, whose image conveys a 'shade of anonymity and allegorization'[22]—is significantly putting away a book on a shelf, which for this reading must be a volume of the *Iliad*. Thus Jervas has painted a portrait of the artist as a young man, whose mind is divided by the conflicting demands of fame and friendship, who has been obliged to bid the 'dear, damn'd, distracting Town' of London farewell:

> Let *Jervase* gratis paint. . . .
> Why should I stay? Both Parties rage;
> My vixen Mistress squalls;
> The Wits in envious Feuds engage;
> And *Homer* (damn him!) calls. (21–4)[23]

If this reading has any validity, Jervas has managed to preserve more than Pope's face in this portrait, making a statement which is a close counterpart in paint to the mood of 'wistful retrospect' of Pope's own *Epistle to Jervas*, in which he nostalgically celebrates his friendship with the painter:

> Smit with the love of Sister-arts we came,
> And met congenial, mingling flame with flame;
> Like friendly colours found them both unite,
> And each from each contract new strength and light. (13–16)[24]

[22] *Portraits*, pp. 22–3.
[23] 'A Farewell to London' (1715), *TE* vi. 129.
[24] *Portraits*, p. 12; *TE* vi. 156.

ii. POPE AND SIR GODFREY KNELLER (1649?–1723)

Kneller's portraits of Pope exist in a different world from the elegant and 'sentimental' likenesses of Jervas. They belong to the most crucial phase in the poet's long campaign to illustrate his fame with 'an adequate image of himself': the image of the English Homer after he had emerged as champion in the contest with his rival translator of the *Iliad*, Thomas Tickell. Kneller's portraits were painted for the new audience he had gained of subscribers to the *Iliad* and later the *Odyssey*, whose subscriptions gave him a lifetime of financial independence. Kneller was the inevitable choice of artist for the job. He had succeeded Lely as the dominant court painter and had been for five reigns the *roi soleil* of face painting, the painter of 'nearly everybody in England of rank, wealth, or accomplishment'.[25]

In the 1716 type (Wimsatt 5. 1) Pope is no longer the periwigged spark of Jervas's frontispiece; now he appears dignified but informal, like the portraits of artists in the Kit-Kat series (*c.* 1700–21), at three-quarter length, coat unbuttoned, in *négligé* cap against an outdoor background, leaning on a table as he turns the page of a Greek quarto of the *Iliad*, exposing the Greek letters of the opening lines of Book IX (in his translation volume iii, published June 1717), the conspicuous Greek letters perhaps a pointed rejoinder to his detractors' claim that he was ignorant of the original. Versions of this portrait were owned by some half a dozen subscribers,[26] and it would appear that the portrait was plainly intended by artist and subject to be available to them to hang in their libraries, despite Pope's facetious advice to one of them, Robert Harley, Earl of Oxford, to keep his picture 'at a convenient distance from the Library [the famous Harleian library at Wimpole], not to be of ill Example to those who shall come to study there' (iii. 115).

Kneller's next portrait of Pope (1721, Wimsatt 6. 1) may be considered the apotheosis of Pope, after he had been triumphantly welcomed home from Greece by Kneller among others in John Gay's poem, 'Mr. Pope's Welcome

[25] *Portraits*, p. 28.

[26] Wimsatt lists types in the possession of Robert Harley, Earl of Oxford (5. 1), Allan Apsley, Earl Bathurst (5. 2), John Boyle, Earl of Orrery (5. 4), Thomas Stoner (5. 5), Brigadier James Dormer (5. 6), and the fourth Earl of Chesterfield (5. 7), all of whom subscribed to Pope's *Iliad*. See 'The Names of the Subscribers' in Pope's *Iliad*, vol. i (1715), Griffith 38.

from Greece' (1720).[27] Now he appears not of an age but for all time in 'the bardic role a poet could yet assume and an audience accept when Pope wrote'.[28] Kneller's chalk model (Wimsatt 6. 1) from which copies of this type were reproduced, shows Pope in profile, crowned with ivy, clad in toga, in a medallic frame circumscribed by the uroboros, the iconographic symbol of eternity—'a highly stylized exploitation of numismatic motifs', which can be related to Pope's poem, 'To Mr. Addison, Occasioned by his Dialogues on Medals' (1720), in which the question is asked:

> Oh when shall Britain, conscious of her claim,
> Stand emulous of Greek and Roman fame? (53–4)
>
> . . .
>
> Or in fair series laurell'd Bards be shown,
> A Virgil there, and here an Addison. (61–2)[29]

Not to mention a Pope. Curll had it engraved by Parr as frontispiece for his pirated edition of *Mr. Pope's Literary Correspondence* (1735) with the subscription, appropriate in the decade of the *Imitations of Horace*: 'Mr Pope /*Horatius Anglicanus*' (Wimsatt 6. 13).

In Kneller's last portrait of Pope (1722, Wimsatt 7. 1) we return from effigy to another document of the English Homer. He now appears 'as old as Nestor' (ii. 118), pensive, profound, and lugubrious,[30] holding a quarto copy of his own *Iliad*, no longer the Greek original. Significant facts about this portrait can be learned from Pope's letter to Simon Viscount Harcourt, a subscriber to the *Iliad* to whom he wrote in 1723: 'I came to Town yesterday, & got admission to Sir Godfrey Kneller, who assur'd me that the original was done for Your Lordship, & that You, & no man but You, shoud have it' (ii. 193). A letter of 1725 indicates that Harcourt got the picture from Kneller in exchange

[27] *The Poetical Works of John Gay*, ed. G. C. Faber (London, 1926), p. 167, st. xvi:

> *Kneller* amid the triumph bears his part,
> Who could (were mankind lost) anew create:
> What can th'extent of his vast soul confine?
> A painter, critick, engineer, divine! (125–8)

[28] Maynard Mack, *TE* x. xii.

[29] For descriptions of this portrait, see *Portraits*, p. 50, and J. D. Stewart, *Sir Godfrey Kneller*, National Portrait Gallery Catalogue (London, 1971), p. 9. For Pope's lines, see *TE* vi. 204.

[30] For descriptions of this portrait see David Piper, *The English Face* (London, 1957), p. 147; and *Portraits*, pp. 68, 92, 329.

for 'another picture which you had long before, from Him [Kneller] & not from me, & of which he took the honour' (ii. 307). From this it appears that the painting was not commissioned by Harcourt or by Pope, but by Kneller himself who had apparently prevailed upon the poet to sit for a third likeness when he was just beginning his translation of the *Odyssey*. Thus Kneller shrewdly anticipated the demand for a portrait which was frequently reproduced in his studio after his death, and became one of the best-known portraits of Pope in the nineteenth century.[31]

From this account it can be inferred that the basis of the relationship between Pope and Kneller was a mutually advantageous association between painter and client: Pope obtained from Kneller the image of himself as the English Homer and modern classic which was accepted by his subscribers, and, multiplied in copies and engravings, became the official painted image of Pope; Kneller acquired a client of extraordinary value to his studio, perhaps the person most frequently portrayed throughout the eighteenth century. When Voltaire observed of the Englishman's love of painting in *Lettres philosophiques* (1728) that 'the picture of the prime minister hangs over the chimney of his own closet, but . . . that of Mr. Pope in twenty noblemen's houses',[32] he was in all likelihood referring to Kneller types.

The professional nature of this relationship needs to be emphasized because of the persistent and distorted view of it as a story of moral depravity, as Pope's relations with his contemporaries have so often been interpreted. According to this view Pope had contempt for Kneller's art and character, flattered him while he lived, mocked and ridiculed him after his death in 1723. This is difficult to reconcile with the satisfactory relationship between client and sitter just described, and it turns out to be based on anecdote and a basic misunderstanding of Pope's attitude to the artist.

It is a mistake to suppose that Pope shared the view of many of his contemporaries—Shaftesbury, Walpole, even Jervas, Kneller's former student—who believed that Kneller had become a degenerate artist in the reign of George I, and that he was a fool of overweening vanity.[33] The popularity of

[31] *Portraits*, p. 62.

[32] *Portraits*, pp. xv, xvii.

[33] John Vanbrugh spoke of Kneller as a 'fool'. See Lord Killanin, *Sir Godfrey Kneller and His Times, 1646–1723* (London, 1948), p. 79. Cf. Anthony Ashley Cooper, *Second Characters*, ed. Benjamin Rand

Kneller's portraits of him would have caused Pope to question such opinions about Kneller's art and character: 'I have reason to say', he wrote to the painter in 1718, 'I have seen the least of mankind appear one of the greatest under your hands' (i. 466). It is true that Kneller's vanity about his monument and epitaph caused Pope some annoyance and inconvenience (see chapter 13), and he had no illusions about Kneller's character as he gave it to the younger Richardson: 'Sir Godfrey was very covetous . . . very vain, and a great glutton.'[34] But despite his faults Pope valued Kneller as a friend, and sincerely regarded him as the greatest painter in the England of his time—a judgement that has not been challenged to this day. He did not write a flattering epistle to Kneller as many of his contemporaries did, or such as he had written to Jervas, but he 'preserv'd his name' in tributes which cannot be dismissed as flattery. Pope's portrait of Kneller is idealized, but it is a far cry from the caricature we have been asked to accept.

The source of much confusion about Pope's attitude to Kneller is the epitaph 'Imitated from the famous Epitaph on Raphael', inscribed on his monument in Westminster Abbey (1730), which Pope had promised the painter he would write:

> Kneller, by Heav'n and not a Master taught,
> Whose Art was Nature, and whose Pictures thought;
> Now for two ages having snatch'd from fate
> Whate'er was Beauteous, or whate'er was Great,
> Lies crown'd with Princes Honours, Poets Lays,
> Due to his Merit, and brave Thirst of Praise.
> Living, great Nature fear'd he might outvie
> Her works; and dying, fears herself may die.[35]

When Pope described the 'scene of vanity' at Kneller's deathbed to Spence in 1735 and his unwillingness to write the epitaph he stated that it was 'the worst thing I ever wrote in my life' (No. 115), but it is unlikely that he was ashamed of the implied comparison with Raphael in the last two lines, which his note

(Cambridge, 1914), p. 131; Walpole, *Anecdotes* ii. 259; and Jervas to Pope (31 July 1715), *Correspondence*, i. 310.

[34] *Richardsoniana* (London, 1776), quoted by Samuel W. Singer, ed., *Joseph Spence's Observations . . . Collected from the Conversation of Mr. Pope* (London, 1820), p. 181.

[35] *TE* vi. 312.

in the published version makes explicit.[36] Walpole considered the lines outrageous flattery: 'as high a compliment as even poetry could be allowed to pay to the original; a silly hyperbole when applied to the modern'.[37] But Pope did not share Walpole's reserve in his admiration of Raphael, and he uses the implied comparison to express a genuine admiration for Kneller as a painter in the Renaissance tradition. It is more likely that Pope's dissatisfaction with the epitaph refers to recognized deficiencies of the original Latin epitaph thought to be prolix, or to faults in his versification noted by Johnson, coloured by the memory of his tomb trouble with Kneller.[38]

Pope's praise of Kneller in the epitaph is consistent with all the statements he made about him during the lifetime of the artist. In his testimonial to Kneller at the end of the *Observations on the Shield of Achilles* (1720), appended to Book XVIII of the *Iliad*, Pope acknowledges Kneller as the one contemporary painter equal to the sublime subject of Homer:

> I ought not to end this Essay, without vindicating myself from the Vanity of treating of an Art [painting], which I love so much better than I understand: But I have been very careful to consult both the best Performers and Judges in Painting. I can't neglect this occasion of saying, how happy I think myself in the Favour of the most distinguish'd Masters of that Art. Sir *Godfrey Kneller* in particular allows me to tell the World, that he entirely agrees with my Sentiments on this Subject: And I can't help wishing, that he who gives this Testimony to *Homer*, would ennoble so great a Design by his own Execution of it. *Vulcan* never wrought for *Thetis* with more readiness and Affection than Sir *Godfrey* has done for me: And so admirable a Picture of the whole Universe could not be a more agreeable Present than he has oblig'd me with, in the Portraits of some of those Persons who are to me the dearest Objects in it.[39]

The discrepancy between academic and personal taste appears even more clearly here than in the similar appeal to Jervas, when he encourages Kneller to paint history in the same breath with his public expression of gratitude for

[36] See *TE* vi. 313: 'Imitated from the famous Epitaph on Raphael:

—Raphael, timuit quo sospite, vinci
Rerum magna parens, & moriente, mori.'

[37] *Anecdotes*, ii. 208.

[38] See Jonathan Richardson, *An Account of Some of the Statues, Bas-reliefs, Drawings and Pictures in Italy, &c. with Remarks* (London, 1722), pp. 261–2; Samuel Johnson, *Life of Pope* in *Lives of the English Poets*, ed. G. B. Hill (Oxford, 1905), iii. 264–5; Edith Sitwell, 'Troubles and Tombs', Chap. 15 of *Alexander Pope* (London, 1930).

[39] *TE* viii. 370.

portraits of himself and his friends. Nor can this be dismissed as a hollow appeal, since Pope expressed his admiration for Kneller as a history painter in the *Imitations of Horace* (Ep. II, i) when he praises Kneller's equestrian portrait of William III at Hampton Court (plate 1), an example of sublime historical portraiture which Pope considered the equal of Bernini's famous bust of Charles I:

> Charles, to late times to be transmitted fair,
> Assign'd his figure to Bernini's care;
> And great Nassau to Kneller's hand decreed
> To fix him graceful on the bounding Steed. (380–3)[40]

Furthermore, Pope had himself commissioned history paintings from Kneller for the decoration of his staircase at Twickenham. Kneller painted three grisaille panels of antique statuary in simulated niches which were hung along Pope's staircase (a legacy to Allen Bathurst, still to be seen at Cirencester).[41] The subjects were antique statues of the Hercules Farnese (plate 2), the Venus di Medici, and the Apollo Belvedere. Pope acknowledged the gift in lines 'To *Sir* Godfrey Kneller, On his painting for me the Statues of Apollo, Venus, and Hercules' (1719):

> What God, what Genius did the Pencil move
> When KNELLER painted These?
> Twas Friendship—warm as *Phoebus*, kind as Love,
> And strong as *Hercules*.[42]

It seemed to Walpole that Pope had paid for the pictures with flattery,[43] but the words pay tribute to Kneller's friendship as much as to his art.

Pope's supposed mocking and contemptuous flattery of Kneller has been grossly exaggerated.[44] It is absurd to regard the stories Pope related, doubtless with embellishment, for the entertainment of Spence and other friends, as cynical mockery. The flattery which has so alarmed critics is transparently part of a social game which all visitors to Kneller's studio played,[45] and which

[40] *TE* iv. 227.

[41] *Correspondence*, ii. 17–18, and n.

[42] *TE* vi. 212.

[43] *Anecdotes*, ii. 208.

[44] See William R. Halewood, rev. of *Portraits*, *Journal of Aesthetics and Art Criticism*, 25 (1966–7), 336–7; and Hans-Joachim Zimmermann, 'Gedanken zu den Porträts eines grossen Augusteers', rev. of *Portraits* in *Archiv*, 206 (1969), 120.

[45] Killanin, *Kneller*, p. 66.

Pope had mastered, as appeared from this characteristic anecdote Pope told Spence in 1736:

> As I was sitting by Sir Godfrey Kneller one day, whilst he was drawing a picture, he stopped and said, 'I can't do so well as I should do unless you flatter me a little; pray flatter me, Mr. Pope! You know I love to be flattered.' (No. 112)

Exactly the same spirit characterizes the only surviving letter from Pope to Kneller (Feb. 1717), which has been mistakenly described as 'sychophantic ecstasy' and 'fulsome flattery':[46]

> You will perceive Sir, that I am as much at [a loss] how to Express myself, as you pretend to be. [But] a Genius like yours never fails to Express it[self well] to all the world. And in the warmth with which [it is] agitated, let it but throw the Pen or [Pen]-cil with never so careless a dash, all peop[le would] see 'tis a noble Frenzy, a Vaghezza, like the *Foam* of a Great Master. (i. 466)

We miss the point of the flattery if we do not appreciate that Pope's letter has more to do with Kneller as a letter-writer than painter.[47] Pope is replying in kind to an extravagantly flattering letter from Kneller, phrased in the imperfect English which so delighted Pope: 'you raise me to such a degree . . . I think myself *paulò minus ab Angelis*' (i. 466). Kneller's vanity was a source of amusement to Pope, but he publicly acknowledged his fundamental respect for Kneller's character in the *Imitations of Horace* (Ep. II, ii) the year after he had retailed stories of Kneller's vanity in private to Spence. There Kneller appears as the type of the incorruptible magistrate, 'an eminent Justice of Peace [at Whitton, Middlesex], who decided much in the manner of Sancho Pança':

> I think Sir Godfry should decide the Suit;
> Who sent the Thief that stole the Cash, away,
> And punish'd him that put it in his way. (24–6)[48]

Pope's anecdotes about Kneller (Spence, Nos. 111–16) are testimony to friendship rather than flattery: they indicate the frequency of Pope's visits to Kneller's studio, his delight in Kneller's conversation, and his enjoyment in watching Kneller paint. The latter can be inferred from Kneller's invitation to Pope to play cards in 1718: 'I belive ther will be Card playrs enoug, and we

46 Halewood, rev. of *Portraits*, p. 337; Spence, No. 112 n.

47 See *Portraits*, p. 32.

48 *TE* iv. 167, and 166 n.

5. Belisarius. After Van Dyck(?). 1741.

6. Continence of Scipio. By Sebastiano Ricci. *c.* 1715.

7. The Death of Germanicus. After Poussin. 1663.

8. Raphael's Hampton Court Cartoons. Engraving by Simon Gribelin. 1720.

may do how we please. If you Come about 4:a Clock, you may see me paint' (ii. 9). A final indication of the friendship Pope repeatedly avowed for Kneller can be seen in the portraits in Pope's collection, a number of which were gifts from the painter, as implied by the *Iliad* acknowledgement (Wimsatt surmises he never paid for a painting).[49] The story of one of these, well documented in the correspondence, the portrait of Lady Mary Wortley Montagu, illustrates the nature of the friendship between poet and painter more clearly than any of the anecdotes.

Among the 'dearest objects' Pope had in mind when he wrote the *Iliad* acknowledgement to Kneller in 1720 was the portrait of Lady Mary which Kneller had painted for Pope after her return from the Orient in 1718 (plate 3). Sometime in the spring of 1719, after Pope had moved to Twickenham to become the neighbour of Kneller, the owner of Whitton Hall, he helped to arrange the lease of a house in Twickenham that Kneller had agreed to rent to the Wortley Montagus.[50] While Pope was serving in the unlikely capacity of estate agent, Kneller (perhaps as a gesture of gratitude) had offered to paint a portrait of Lady Mary for Pope's collection. Pope had remarked to Kneller earlier that 'I really believe . . . that even a Man in love woud think his Mistress improved by you' (i. 466), and he wrote to Lady Mary in 1719 imploring her to 'allow me as much of your Person as Sir Godfrey can help me to':

> Upon conferring with him yesterday, I find he thinks it absolutely necessary to draw the Face first, which he says can never be set right on the figure if the Drapery & Posture be finishd before. To give you as little trouble as possible, he proposes to draw your face with Crayons, & finish it up, at your own house in a morning; from whence he will transfer it to the Canvas, so that you need not go to sit at his house. This I must observe, is a manner in which they seldom draw any but Crown'd Heads; & I observe it with a secret pride & pleasure. (ii. 22)

Pope was up early at nine in the morning writing to tell her that Kneller had returned to Twickenham from London and was prepared to 'wait upon you

[49] *Portraits*, p. 62 n. 3. In addition to the stair paintings (*TE* vi. 213) Pope acknowledged several gifts of paintings from Kneller in the *Correspondence*: i. 417; ii. 307. Portraits by or after Kneller in his collection outnumbered those of any other artist: see 'Inventory' (pp. 244–50, 253–4), portraits of Craggs, Talbot, Walsh, Wycherley, Betterton, Mordaunt, Atterbury, Arbuthnot, Burlington, Bathurst, Garth, Lady Mary, Mary Churchill, and Robert or Edward Harley.

[50] *Correspondence*, ii. 6–7, and n.

this morning at twelve to take a sketch of you in your dress, if you'l give leave. He is really very good to me: I heartily wish you will be so too' (ii. 22), begging in an urgent postscript 'a single word in answer, because I am to send to Sir Godfrey accordingly' (ii. 23). No fit of immoderate laughter answered this proposal, and it must have been a triumph for Pope some time later to hang in the best room at Twickenham the picture which has been tentatively identified with the portrait of Lady Mary dated 1720, 'half-reclining, in Turkish head-dress, ermine cloak, and low-cut blue bodice', against a background of landscape containing a house (perhaps Saville House)—a memorial of his infatuation which survived their estrangement in its favoured place.[51] The portrait is testimony to an exchange of favours, to Pope's keen interest in Kneller's technical procedure, and above all, to a warm friendship between the poet and the greatest painter of the age.

iii. POPE AND JONATHAN RICHARDSON SR. (1665–1745)

In Pope's relationship with Jonathan Richardson Sr. throughout the 1730s, portraiture continues to be important, and his interest in connoisseurship, the new 'Science' introduced by Richardson, becomes more significant. Richardson's portraits of Pope are the most numerous and significant part of a continuing campaign after the death of Kneller to illustrate his fame, which reflects the change of direction in his literary career from translation to satire, and the necessity to counteract the humiliating caricatures of himself, like the simian frontispiece of *Pope Alexander's Supremacy Examin'd* (1729), which began to appear after the *Dunciad* (1728). The most celebrated image of Pope after Kneller, the portrait bust by Roubiliac (1738–41), inscribed in one version with the lines *Uni Aequis Virtuti atque eius Amicis* (Wimsatt, 59. 1), transforms the English Homer into the English Horace, the idealized but intensely life-like image of the poet who speaks to us in the *Imitations*. But the general movement in portraits of Pope during this time appears to be away from portraits of the 'Bard' or the poet, as in the unsatisfactory representation by Michael Dahl (1727, Wimsatt 10. 1) towards straightforward, even prosaic

[51] The description of the painting is Wimsatt's, *Portraits*, p. 33 n. Its location in Pope's house is established by the 'Inventory', p. 250.

images of the man, as we see him slightly feverish in William Kent's Chiswick portrait (Wimsatt 18), in morning *déshabillé* in William Hoare's attractive crayon (?1739–40, Wimsatt 63. 3a), and at full length in the famous surreptitious sketch (*c.* 1740, Wimsatt 64).

The portraits of Pope most characteristic and numerous in this decade are the portrait drawings and oils by Richardson himself. The large number of drawings executed between 1733 and 1741 belong to a 'familial and friendly cult of portrait drawing' of the Pope family by Richardson, which included sketches of his mother in 1703, and after her death in 1733, when Pope requested the painter take his sketch 'before this Winter-flower is faded' (iii. 374), and of his father in 1717 on his deathbed.[52] The drawings of Pope were taken *ad vivum* during 'friendly & philosophical hours' (iii. 486) when Richardson visited Twickenham or when Pope was an 'Evening Visitant' (iv. 484) to the painter's studio in Great Ormond Street, in the years when their friendship was becoming more intimate. Varied in pose—profile, full-face, wigged, laureated, bare-headed—some are clearly studies for etchings and oil portraits; others, like the drawings of Pope asleep or the interesting composite profiles of Pope as Chaucer and Milton, appear to have been purely recreational. The laureated heads are not public tributes to the Bard, like Kneller's numismatic profile, but the friendly compliment of the painter who had pretensions to poetry himself, as indicated by the couplet subscribed on a pencil-on-vellum sketch dated 31 January 1734 (Wimsatt 23), showing Pope with a wreath of bay intermingled with ivy:

> Your Friend but gives the Bay you had before,
> Friendship wou'd fain, but Friendship Can no more.[53]

A group of etchings derived from these sketches enjoyed 'preferred status' with Pope's intimate circle of friends, and were used as memorials in made-up sets of his *Works*, and for the important role of title-page medallion in the authorized volume of his *Letters* brought out in quarto and folio in May

[52] See William Wimsatt, '"Amicitiae Causa", A Birthday Present from Curll to Pope', in *Restoration and Eighteenth-Century Literature*, ed. Carroll Camden (Chicago, 1963), p. 341; and *Portraits*, pp. 81, 140 and n., 150–1, 176 ex. 10.

[53] *Portraits*, p. 170. My account of Richardson's drawings relies on Wimsatt, pp. 148–78.

1737.[54] Two are inscribed *amicitiae causa*, the first a three-quarter profile bust with wig (Wimsatt 41), the second a profile medallion (Wimsatt 43. 1); the third (Wimsatt 48. 1) a profile inscribed in Greek with the words, 'This is the Man.' Speaking of the title-page vignette of the *Letters* Pope told Richardson in March 1737, 'that excellent Etching in My Titlepage . . . will be the most Valuable thing in the book' (iv. 58). He appears to have had Richardson's portrait sketches in mind when he wrote in the 'Preface' to the *Letters*:

> Had he [Pope] sate down with a design to draw his own picture, he could not have done it so truly; for whoever sits for it (whether to himself or another) will inevitably find his features more composed, than his appear in these letters. But if an author's hand like a Painter's, be more distinguishable in a slight sketch than in a finish'd picture, this very carelessness will make them the better known from such counterfeits, as have been and may be imputed to him, either thro a mercenary or a malicious design.[55]

Here Pope uses the analogy to sketching to justify the carelessness of 'talking on paper', and to emphasize the difference between originals and copies like Curll's piracies (it was a commonplace that sketches were closer to the artist's original idea than the finished picture). Richardson's portrait medallion suggests the kind of self-portrait Pope was sketching of himself in the *Letters*; it also characterizes the finished pictures of Pope by Richardson painted in oil throughout the decade.

Except for the laureated profile of Pope in the National Gallery (Wimsatt 54), Richardson's oil portraits of Pope are images of the man rather than the poet. They were all painted for friends to whom he was addressing his letters and verse epistles of the decade, and with whom he was exchanging portraits for his own collection: Burlington, Oxford, Bolingbroke, Mead, Lyttelton, Marchmont, Harcourt, and others.[56] One of these portraits stands out from what is at best a somewhat drab collection, the Hagley three-quarter length showing Pope with his dog Bounce, seated meditatively in a landscape setting holding a folio volume (Wimsatt 9. 1). Because of its association with Lyttelton and Hagley this is the only one which corresponds to Richardson's own

[54] *Portraits*, p. 182.

[55] *Works* (1737), i. xxxix.

[56] See *Portraits*, types owned by Lyttelton (9. 1), Harcourt (50), Burlington (51), Mead (52. 1, 52. 4), Horatio Walpole (52. 4), Marchmont (53. 6), and Jonathan Richardson Jr. (55. 1). For Oxford see Wimsatt, *Portraits*, pp. xviii, 349; for Bolingbroke, *Correspondence*, iv. 147–8.

ideal of the portrait as 'a sort of general history of the life of the person it represents'.[57]

The relationship between Pope and Richardson, like all his friendships with painters, transcended the formal relation between artist and sitter, and ripened in the 1730s into an intimacy despite a difference in age of twenty-seven years. Besides painting they had literature in common. Like Reynolds later in the century Richardson had literary aspirations, as can be observed in verses he subscribed to a laureated self-portrait drawing (plate 4):

> Yes Pope, yes Milton I am Bayes'd you see.
>
> . . .
>
> I am Pope, Milton, Virgil, Homer Here.[58]

The Richardsons were important literary associates of Pope: the father helped to collate Pope's Shakespeare in the 1720s; his son annotated and transcribed some of Pope's manuscripts in the next decade. Pope corrected the manuscript of *Explanatory Notes, and Remarks on Milton's Paradise Lost*, a book on Richardson's favourite poet written in collaboration with his son, published in 1734.[59] Richardson's literary pretensions and his work on Milton exposed him to ridicule from his contemporaries, including a practical joke by Pope (iv. 80), but his writings on painting were well received throughout the century. The contemporary influence of his works on painting published between 1715 and 1725 can be clearly illustrated by the example of Pope.

Richardson's essays belong to the tradition of Renaissance apologies for painting as a liberal art, grounded on the doctrine of *ut pictura poesis*.[60] His *Theory of Painting* (1715) is an eloquent version of this humanistic argument: 'Painting is a sort of Writing' (40). His other works pursue the same theme appropriately with quotations from the foremost contemporary writer: Pope's *Prologue* to Addison's *Cato* is quoted in *An Essay in the Whole Art of*

[57] *An Essay in the Whole Art of Criticism as it relates to Painting*, in *Works*, ed. Jonathan Richardson Jr. (London, 1773), p. 179. Page numbers in the text refer to this collected edition, cited in all cases except where passages have been omitted.

[58] *Portraits*, p. 157.

[59] On the literary relations between Pope and Richardson see *Correspondence*, ii. 100, 106 n., 177 n.; iii. 231, 240, 270, 330. John F. Kerslake discusses *Explanatory Notes* in 'The Richardsons and the Cult of Milton', *Burlington Magazine*, 96 (Jan. 1957), 23–4.

[60] See Lawrence Lipking, 'The Uncomplicated Richardson', ch. 5 in *The Ordering of the Arts in Eighteenth-Century England* (Princeton, 1970), pp. 109–26.

Criticism as it Relates to Painting (1719), to argue the equality of 'the most estimable modern tragedy' and the art of painting:

> 'To Wake the Soul by Tender Strokes of Art,
> To raise the genius and to mend the heart'
>
> is the business of painting as well as of Tragedy. Mr. Pope (178)

In the same discourse he applies Pope's lines on ideal imitation in the *Essay on Criticism* to painting (248), and in an 'Essay on the Sublime' added to the second edition of the *Theory* (1725) he misquotes a line from *Eloisa to Abelard* (130).

But Richardson does not dwell long on the high *a priori* road of criticism; the audience he has in mind is the same Addison had set out to educate in the *Spectator*. Like Addison, Richardson wrote to reform taste, and in *The Connoisseur, A Discourse on the Dignity, Certainty, Pleasure and Advantage, of the Science of a Connoisseur* (1719) Richardson presented to his readers 'a new Science of Pleasure' to which he gave the name, at the suggestion of Matthew Prior, 'Connoissance' (282). This essay, summarized as 'an attempt to show how to judge of the goodness of a Picture, to know hands, and to distinguish Copies from Originals',[61] was not the novelty Richardson claimed, but he did succeed in making the science of connoisseurship a fashionable one, and in his last book written in collaboration with his son, *An Account of some of the Statues, Bas Reliefs, Drawings and Pictures in Italy with Remarks* (1722) he applied the new science in a book which became the Baedecker of the grand tourist. It was the gift of this book Pope acknowledged in a letter to Richardson (1722):

> the agreeable present . . . worthy Mr. R. and his son,—worthy two such lovers of one another, and two such lovers of the fine arts. It will certainly be a most useful book to all such, and to me in particular a most delightful one. (ii. 140–1)

Pope's familiarity with Richardson's writings and his friendship with the 'Great Connoisseur', as he was known to his contemporaries, developed that interest in connoisseurship already apparent in his idyllic description of life in the studio of Charles Jervas. His frequent visits to Richardson's studio in Great Ormond Street would have acquainted him with a far greater collection than Jervas's, which had 'some good . . . amidst an infinite number of trash' accord-

[61] Richardson, 'Preface', *An Account*, p. 5.

ing to Vertue;[62] Richardson's has been described as the 'classic collection of Old Master drawings, worthy to rival . . . Lely's collection of paintings and drawings of the century before'.[63] In 1735 Pope wrote to Richardson to introduce a grand tourist setting out for Rome who would be 'ashamed not to be able to give some account of the drawings' (iii. 457).

Richardson's was only one of the distinguished collections known to Pope where he could have pursued his education as a connoisseur of painting.[64] Not to mention the superb collections in country houses like the Earl of Pembroke's Wilton where Pope intended a visit in 1722, and foreign collections he knew by catalogue or report, he was acquainted with a number of the great virtuoso collections. In 1716 he visited George Clarke's collection of architectural drawings, paintings, and sculpture at Oxford (i. 376). He may have had first-hand acquaintance with the collections he refers to in the *Epistle to Burlington*: Dr. Richard Mead's 'excellent Library', antiquities and paintings at Great Ormond Street; Sir Hans Sloane's natural curiosities in Chelsea, which he called 'the finest collection in Europe'; Richard Topham's 'judicious collection of Drawings' at Windsor; Sir Andrew Fountain's collection of pictures and antiquities at Narford in Norfolk he probably knew only by reputation.[65] In 1742 Pope was able to arrange for Richardson to visit Burlington's collection of paintings housed in his Palladian villa at Chiswick: 'I will . . . prepare your way . . . & you shall have your fill of the Pictures' (iv. 409).

His intimate friendships with artists and virtuoso collectors account for Pope's confident sense of himself as a connoisseur, which appears in his talk to Spence about 'schools of the painters' (No. 514) and paintings in Burlington's collection at Chiswick; his adamant refusal to speculate about the

[62] Vertue, iii. 103. On the sale catalogue of Jervas's collection, see *Portraits*, pp. 14–15.

[63] Waterhouse, *Painting in Britain*, p. 100. See Frits Lugt, *Les Marques de collections de dessins et d'estampes* (Amsterdam, 1921), pp. 406–47, for an account of Richardson's collection.

[64] See F. J. B. Watson, 'On the Early History of Collecting in England', *Burlington Magazine*, 85 (Sept. 1944), 223–8; and Frank Hermann, ed., *The English as Collectors* (London, 1972).

[65] See references to Pembroke and Clarke in *Correspondence*, ii. 240, i. 376. For references to collectors in the *Epistle to Burlington*, see *TE* iii. ii, 134 n., 136 n. On the collections of Thomas and Henry Herbert, 8th and 9th Earls of Pembroke, Topham, and Clarke, see Vertue, *Note Books*, and Lugt, *Collections de Dessins*. On Mead see Mary Webster, 'Taste of an Augustan Collector: The Collection of Dr. Richard Mead—I–II', *Country Life*, 147 (29 Jan. 1970), 249–51; and 148 (24 Sept. 1970), 765–7.

disputed authorship of Burlington's portrait of Belisarius (No. 595, plate 5); his categorical judgement about the portrait of a pontiff in the same collection by Carlo Maratta which he thought 'the best portrait in the world' (Nos. 596–7);[66] his statement at Lord Radnor's, his Twickenham neighbour, about Peter Tillemans (1684–1734) and John Wootton (1678?–1765), whom he considered 'the two best landscape painters in England' (No. 109); or the postscript in a letter to John Caryll, that 'your pictures are very pretty copies from Bassano' (i. 443). The same assurance appears in his remarks to Spence about the ignorance of others: the opinion that Bolingbroke was 'not deep either in pictures, statues, or architecture' (No. 280); the ribald epigram attributed to Pope on William Wyndham, a notorious philistine:

> W— be wise, let each man know his Part:
> Wield you the State, let Others judge of Art:
> What tho', by either Andrew often bitt,
> You scarce can tell a Jarvas from a Titt?
> Blush not, great Sir! You cannot know it less,
> Than We, G—d help us! if tis War or Peace?[67]

and the judgement that Charles Montagu, Earl of Halifax, was 'rather a pretender to taste than really possessed of it' (No. 204).[68]

All this suggests that Pope numbered himself among those 'chusing artists' mentioned in the opening lines of the *Epistle to Burlington*, those to whom it is strange that

> . . . the Prodigal should waste
> His wealth, to purchase what he ne'er can taste?
> Not for himself he sees, or hears, or eats;
> Artists must chuse his Pictures, Music, Meats. (3–6)[69]

In 1717 as steward of Charles Jervas's studio Pope was getting pictures

[66] Vertue stated in 1741 that he had seen 'the Famous picture of Pope Clement 9th [Giulio Rospigliosi, 1600–69] . . . painted by Carlo Marratti brought over into England by Jarvis and bought by Sr Robt Walpole K^t^ now Ld Orford—a half length setting on a chair . . . cost 200^ll^.' Osborn asserts that 'a portrait of Pope Clement IX by Carlo Maratta . . . painted for the Earl of Winchelsea, was in Lord Burlington's Collection'. See Vertue, vi. 122; Spence, No. 596 n.

[67] Among epigrams found in the Pope–Burlington MSS. Chatsworth (143. 76), 'perhaps by Pope', according to John Butt's annotation.

[68] For the Halifax collection, see Vertue, iv. 165; Lugt, *Collections de dessins*, p. 497.

[69] *TE* iii. ii, 134.

'fram'd and scour'd' (i. 416) for his friend John Caryll, and in the next decade he advised him on the decoration of his staircase at Ladyholt in the fashionable manner Kneller had painted his own at Twickenham, with the offer to draw a design.[70] In 1736 when Pope met Ralph Allen he became his arbiter of taste on gardening, sculpture, and painting in the building of Allen's house at Prior Park at Widcombe, near Bath. Long before the house was completed Allen was planning to decorate his hall with history painting with the assistance of Pope, who located subjects chosen by Allen in the collections of his friends, arranged to have them copied in the London studio of an obscure portrait painter, Johan Van Diest (*c.* 1680–1760), and supervised the artist's execution of them between 1736 and 1741.[71]

Pope's letters to Allen cast a revealing light on his activity as a 'chusing artist' and a student of the 'Science of a Connoisseur'. He writes to Allen about the paintings for his hall in 1736:

> I saw Mr Morice yesterday who has readily allowed Mr Vandiest to copy the Picture. I have enquired for the best Originals of those two Subjects which I found were Favorite ones with you, & well deserve to be so, the Discovery of Joseph to his Bretheren, and the Resignation of the Captive by Scipio. Of the latter my Lord Burlington has a fine one done by Ricci, & I am promis'd ye other in a Good Print from One of the chief Italian Painters. That of Scipio is of the exact Size one would wish for a Basso Relievo, in which manner in my opinion you would best ornament your Hall, done in Chiaro oscuro. (iv. 13)

Pope had arranged for Van Diest to copy a picture in the collection of his friend William Morice,[72] perhaps the same picture Pope refers to in a letter to Allen in July, in which he speaks of seeing Van Diest 'with that picture, in which I made a small Alteration' (iv. 23), one of several stolen strokes. Pope employed Van Diest at Twickenham 'to paint one or two things of a Grotesque kind' in the grotto (iv. 340), but the artist did not inspire his confidence, and he supervised his work for Allen closely. 'I would not neglect seeing him, to prevent any Errors' (iv. 247), he assured Allen on one occasion.

[70] *Correspondence*, iii. 402, 406.

[71] See Benjamin Boyce, 'The Poet and the Postmaster: The Friendship of Alexander Pope and Ralph Allen', *Philological Quarterly*, 45 (1966), 114–22, and *The Benevolent Man: A Life of Ralph Allen of Bath* (Cambridge, Mass., 1967), p. 68.

[72] On Morice's virtuosoship see Benjamin Boyce, 'Baroque into Satire: Pope's Frontispiece for the Essay on Man', *Criticism*, 4 (Winter 1962), 23–4.

In June 1736, Pope wrote to Allen again to announce that he had discovered a version of *The Resignation of the Captive* which he preferred to the one by Sebastian Ricci in the hall of Burlington House (plate 6):

> Since I wrote last, I have found on further Enquiry that there is another fine Picture on the Subject of Scipio & the Captive by Pietro da Cortona, which Sir Paul Methuen has a Sketch of: & I believe is more expressive than that of Ricci, as Pietro is famous for Expression: I have also met with a fine Print of the Discovery of Joseph to his Brethren a design which I fancy is of La Sueur, a noble painter, & will do perfectly well. (iv. 20)

Pope's preference for the sketch in the collection of Sir Paul Methuen (1672–1757), Secretary of State, and owner of a collection said by Vertue to contain many 'good pictures',[73] is of some interest because Cortona (1596–1669) was not 'famous for Expression' among Pope's contemporaries, but was considered something of a renegade from classical conventions of history painting.[74] Perhaps Pope's preference is an example of that freedom of taste which is characteristic of the connoisseur.

Pope's choice of the *Discovery of Joseph to his Brethren* after Eustache Le Sueur (1616–55) reflects his renown as a painter of religious history. In eighteenth-century France Le Sueur's reputation rivalled Nicolas Poussin's. He was praised for a 'certain *tendresse* which distinguished his work from that of his more heroic rival'.[75] It was one of Nicolas Poussin's heroic subjects that Pope recommended to Allen for Prior Park when he resumed his letter of 5 June 1736:

> For your two others, that of Jonathan with the Circumstance of shooting his Arrow, may easily be done (tho I do not know that it has been done except in a print in Blome's History of the Bible) And I could wish you pitchd on that admirable piece for Expression, the Death of Germanicus by Poussin, for the 4th since the Action of Scipio's drawing his Sword &c. will be very difficult to get well done, & has not (I am afraid)

[73] Vertue, iii. 10–11. See the catalogue of his collection in Thomas Martyn, *The English Connoisseur* (1766), i. 29, reprinted in Frank Hermann, ed., *The English as Collectors*, pp. 102–7.

[74] Rudolf Wittkower, *Art and Architecture in Italy 1600 to 1750* (Baltimore, 1958), Chap. 10, and pp. 171–3. Richard Graham writes in *A Short Account of the Most Eminent Painters both Ancient and Modern*, appended to Du Fresnoy's *Art of Painting*, 2nd edn. (London, 1716), p. 360: 'His [Cortona's] Talent lay in *Grand Ordonnances*: and tho' he was Uncorrect in his Design, Injudicious in his Expression, and Irregular in his Draperies, yet those Defects were . . . happily atton'd for.' Cortona, like Michelangelo and Shakespeare, was admired in spite of his faults.

[75] Anthony Blunt, *Art and Architecture in France*, 2nd edn. (London, 1957), p. 186.

ever been attempted by any good hand. You will thus have two of sacred, & two of prophane History. (iv. 20)

The *Death of Germanicus* was 'one of Poussin's most popular and most frequently copied compositions'; and the copy in Richardson's collection or the print by G. Chasteau (1663, plate 7) probably supplied Van Diest's model.[76] In the *Account* Richardson finds fault with the expression Pope admired in the picture, but he asserts that painters like Poussin can 'carry the imagination beyond . . . the Historian or Poet'.[77]

Pope's talk of expression has been dismissed as a 'sophomoric turn',[78] but it is unlikely that he used the term casually which is second to Invention in Richardson's rules for the Connoisseur's judgement of painting:

> The expression must be proper to the subject, and the character of the persons; it must be strong, so that the dumb-shew may be perfectly well, and readily understood. Every part of the picture must contribute to this end; colours, animals, draperies, and especially the actions of the figures, and above all the airs of the heads.[79]

At its lowest formalistic level expression is no more than decorum (Le Brun's psychophysical codes); in another sense it refers to the pathetic style, the painting of the passions, which Richardson calls the 'dumb-shew' (172); at its highest level it appears to refer to dramatic unity, the total expressive force with which a painting conveys an idea.[80] In reference to Poussin, and Cortona, Pope appears to be speaking at the highest level of generalization, Richardson to more specific matters of the pathetic style.

The crucial matter for Pope in the selection of the history paintings for Allen was the expression of ideas—of charity and friendship in the sacred histories of Joseph and Jonathan, of continence and stoic heroism in the profane histories of Scipio[81] and Germanicus—as he reveals in a passage of his letter to Allen in which he echoes Richardson's high claims for the value of history painting:

> A Man not only shews his Taste but his Virtue, in the Choice of such Ornaments:

[76] Anthony Blunt, *The Paintings of Nicolas Poussin: A Critical Catalogue* (London, 1966), pp. 113–14.

[77] *Works* (1773), pp. 250, 262.

[78] Benjamin Boyce, *The Benevolent Man*, p. 105.

[79] *Works*, p. 172.

[80] Rensselaer W. Lee, '*Ut Pictura Poesis*: The Humanistic Theory of Painting', *Art Bulletin*, 12 (1940), 197–269, rpt. (New York, 1967), pp. 23–32; Richardson, *Works*, pp. 48–63.

[81] On the eighteenth-century vogue of the continence of Scipio, see Boyce, *The Benevolent Man*, pp. 104–5.

And whatever Example most strikes us, we may reasonably imagine may have an influence upon others, so that the History itself (if wellchosen) upon a Rich-mans Walls, is very often a better lesson than any he could teach by his Conversation. In this sense, the Stones may be said to speak, when Men cannot, or will not. I can't help thinking (and I know you'l joyn with me, you who have been making an Altar-piece) that the Zeal of the first Reformers was ill placed, in removing *Pictures* (that is to say Examples) out of Churches, and yet suffering *Epitaphs* (that is to say, Flatteries and False History) to be the Burden of Church-Walls, & the Shame, as well as Derision, of all honest men. (iv. 13)

The importance to Pope of decorum and moral utility in religious history painting is indicated by his censure of the 'sprawling Saints' of Verrio and Laguerre in the *Epistle to Burlington*, his contempt for the obscene illustrations to the sonnets of Pietro Aretino by Giulio Romano, and finally his criticism of 'modern painters bad at allegory'.[82] His mention of an illustration from *The History of the Bible* by Richard Blome, a publisher whose illustrated books he satirizes in the *Dunciad*, as a model for one of Allen's sacred subjects suggests that he prizes moral utility above aesthetic value.[83]

Next to Pope's activity as a 'chusing artist' the most important index of his taste as connoisseur is to be found in his large collection of prints at Twickenham. Pope's '7 prints of Raphael's cartoons' indicate that he was an admirer of the undisputed master of history painting in the connoisseur's lexicon. Pope's prints were undoubtedly one of the numerous sets of engravings after the Hampton Court cartoons (plate 8).[84] In Richardson's *Theory* Raphael is the paradigm of excellence in all parts of painting, and the cartoons at Hampton

[82] *TE* iii. ii, ll. 145–6 and nn.; *TE* iv. 33 and n.; Spence, No. 541 n.

[83] *TE* v. 79 n.

[84] See 'Inventory', p. 247. The Hampton Court cartoons were seven out of the original ten designs for tapestry commissioned from Raphael by Leo X for the Sistine Chapel, which were purchased by James I in 1624, restored, and hung in a special gallery at Hampton Court at the end of the seventeenth century in frames designed by Christopher Wren. They are now in the Victoria and Albert Museum. The cartoons were first engraved about 1707 by Simon Gribelin (1661–1733), advertised in the *Tatler* (No. 69, 17 Sept. 1709), and 'sold mightily'. Between 1711 and 1719 Nicholas Dorigny (1658–1746) engraved them 'by Subscription of four guineas the Sett', and one of his assistants, Claude du Bosc (1682–1745?) 'undertook to grave the Cartoons . . . for print sellers' —apparently a piracy. See Vertue i. 56–7; iii. 7; vi. 186–8, and Ronald Paulson, *Hogarth: His Life, Art, and Times* (New Haven, 1971), i. 58, 61–3, 209–12. On the history of the cartoons in England see John Pope-Hennessy, *The Raphael Cartoons*, Victoria and Albert Museum booklet (London, 1966), pp. 5–7.

Court are said to display his 'stupendous works of art' (63) to better advantage than the Vatican:

> When a Man enters into that Awful Gallery at Hampton Court, he finds himself amongst a sort of People Superior to what he has ever seen, and very probably to what those Really were. Indeed this is the Principal Excellence of those wonderful Pictures, as it must be allow'd to be that Part of Painting which is preferable to all others. (96)

The Hampton Court cartoons are the best history pictures in the world (276):

> The Pictures at Hampton-Court, (bating some very few Exceptions) are perfectly well thought: Such Ideas are convey'd to our Minds, the Stories are so told, as tho' we had Read, and Consider'd em a thousand times, we might go from these Pictures with Clearer and Nobler Conceptions of those great Actions than ever we had before . . . because Words Cannot convey such ideas as Such a Pencil can. (254–5)

In the *Epistle to Jervas* (l. 36) the sublime epithet—'grace'—is reserved for Raphael.

For all the evidence of Pope's connoisseurship it must be admitted that his own collection of paintings is not at all the collection of a virtuoso. Except for Kneller's stair paintings, Pope's collection consisted entirely of paintings regarded by the connoisseur as lesser genres: a dozen landscape, four still-life (animal and fruit pieces), a 'rable' (perhaps a Dutch scene of low life),[85] and fifty-six or more portraits. The explanation for this is not simply that Pope could not afford histories and old masters. Another poet, Matthew Prior, with the advantage over Pope of residence abroad, acquired without wealth or inheritance a distinguished virtuoso collection including histories by Poussin and Veronese, portraits by Rembrandt, Holbein, Rubens, Tintoretto, and Titian.[86] The portraits in Pope's collection reflect the social activity of the man, not the taste of the virtuoso.

Portraits for Pope and his contemporaries were one of the sacraments of friendship, exchanged in much the same way as letters, and characterized by the same easy, familiar, and prosaic style—as much documents as works of art. Portraits of this kind have little in common with the grand-operatic historical

[85] For contemporary usage of the word, including Dryden's as an adjective ('Rabble-Scene'), see *OED*, s.v. 'Rabble'. Maynard Mack interprets 'Rable' as 'Probably a phonetic rendering of Rabelais': *The Garden and the City*, p. 252.

[86] See H. Bunker Wright and Henry C. Montgomery, 'The Art Collection of a Virtuoso in Eighteenth-Century England', *Art Bulletin*, 27 (Sept. 1945), 195–204.

portraits of Van Dyke; they were valued for their associations rather than their artistry. As Richardson remarks in the *Theory of Painting*, 'to sit for one's Picture, is to have an Abstract of one's Life written and published' (7). This is the rationalization for the countless exchanges of portraits, *amicitiae causa*, referred to in Pope's correspondence from 1711 until his death.[87]

Does the inconsistency between the taste of the collector and the taste of the virtuoso mean that Pope's talk about the sublime virtues of history painting should be dismissed as cant?[88] This would put him in the same category as the ignorant and fatuous connoisseurs, collectors, and art-dealers satirized by Hogarth. But Hogarth's own ambition was to paint history, to emulate the career of his father-in-law, James Thornhill; he was not attacking the ideal of history painting, but its perversion by the greed and snobbery of his contemporaries.[89] Pope and his mentor Richardson shared an idealism which distinguishes them from those whom Hogarth attacked; they did not aim to prescribe to the artist, to deceive the collector, or to legislate academic rules, but to encourage a Renaissance of taste in what Pope referred to in a letter to Richardson as 'That Obliging Art' (iii. 374).

87 *Correspondence*, i. 120, 417; ii. 78, 196, 204, 294; iii. 341; iv. 147–8, 500, 512.

88 See Waterhouse, *Painting in Britain*, p. 187.

89 See Ronald Paulson, 'The Presence of Sir James Thornhill', and 'The Bad Taste of the Town', chaps. 6 and 7 of *Hogarth*, i. 85–134.

2. *Parallels between Painting and Poetry*

WHEN Pope wrote his couplets on the relationship between painting and poetry in the *Epistle to Jervas* he was expressing critical commonplaces of his time. A manuscript version of the lines reads:

> Notions awake & Images renew
> From Art to Art ye pleasing Track pursue.[1]

The published version (1716):

> How oft' our slowly-growing works impart,
> While images reflect from art to art? (19–20)[2]

Shaftesbury's scepticism about such parallels, 'almost ever absurd . . . at best constrained, lame, or defective', remained unpublished.[3] Pope's confidence in the classical and Renaissance doctrine of *ut pictura poesis* which sanctioned parallels between the arts was entirely orthodox. In the important enterprise of annotating his translation of the *Iliad*, he uses the parallel with painting as the basis of his critical approach; and readers since the eighteenth century have testified to the importance of pictorialism in Pope's translation of Homer and his own poetry.

We cannot approach the study of the relationship between the arts in Pope with the assurance of eighteenth-century readers like Thomas Twining, who observes of the translation of Homer that 'the landscapes . . . are of Mr. Pope's painting',[4] or Joseph Warton, who exclaims over Claudes and Salvators in Pope's poetry, telling us that 'our author is never happier than in his allusions

[1] Ault, p. 73.

[2] *TE* vi. 156.

[3] Anthony Ashley Cooper, 'Plastics, An Epistolary Excursion in the Original, Progress, and Power of Designatory Art', in *Second Characters*, pp. 140–1. Elizabeth Manwaring points out in *Italian Landscape in Eighteenth-Century England* (Oxford, 1925), p. 19, that 'Shaftesbury treated conventionally of the relation between the arts in his first *Characteristicks*.'

[4] *Aristotle's Treatise on Poetry* (London, 1789), i. 31–3.

to painting, an art he so much admired and understood'.[5] Lessing's challenge to the parallel as a critical analogy, and his indictment of its damaging effect on poetic description in the *Laokoön* (1766), have been succeeded by the attacks of later writers like Irving Babbitt on the romantic confusion of the arts, or Rensselaer W. Lee on the fallacies of the idea in academic art criticism, leading to the demand recently made by Ralph Cohen on the literary critic to demonstrate precisely how reflection between the arts occurs in a literary work.[6] Lessing's little-known attack on Pope's use of the parallel as critic and poet supplies a convenient point of departure in considering the way images reflect from art to art in the literary work of a poet whose knowledge of the theory and practice of painting has already been demonstrated.

i. THE NOTES TO HOMER

In the *Laokoön* Lessing attacked Pope's use of the parallel with painting as a critical device in the commentary on Homer contained in the 'Observations on the Shield of Achilles' (1718) appended to Book XVIII of the *Iliad*. Pope's 'Observations' are a defence of Homer from his critics, a contribution to the quarrel between Ancients and Moderns, the kind of learned debate he tried to avoid elsewhere in the notes. It has recently been discovered that the first two parts of the essay answering attacks by French critics on Homer were translated almost verbatim by Pope without acknowledgement from André Dacier, and Jean Boivin,[7] but, because it can be assumed Pope endorsed their arguments, he will be designated the author in this discussion. Part I sets out to refute two arguments of Scaliger and others who attacked the manner and matter of Homer's description of the shield: first, the supposed impropriety of describing figures on the shield as living beings, of representing movement or

[5] *An Essay on the Genius and Writings of Pope*, 5th edn. (London, 1806), ii. 182.

[6] See Babbitt's *The New Laokoön* (Boston, 1910); Lee's *Ut Pictura Poesis: The Humanistic Theory of Painting*; and Ralph Cohen, 'The Scope of Critical Analogy: *Ut Pictura Poesis*', chap. 4 in *The Art of Discrimination* (Berkeley, 1964), p. 247.

[7] Fern Farnham, 'Achilles' Shield: Some Observations on Pope's Iliad', *PMLA*, 84 (Oct. 1969), 1571: 'Part I of Pope's essay is . . . simply lifted from note forty-seven to Chapter xxvi of Dacier's *Aristotle*' (*La Poetique*, traduite en François avec des Remarques Critiques par M. Dacier, Paris, 1692). In Part II 'Pope borrows not only the plate from [Jean] Boivin, but the Frenchman's account of the precise dimensions which could be allotted to each scene' (Jean Boivin, *Apologie d'Homère et Bouclier d'Achille*, Paris, 1715).

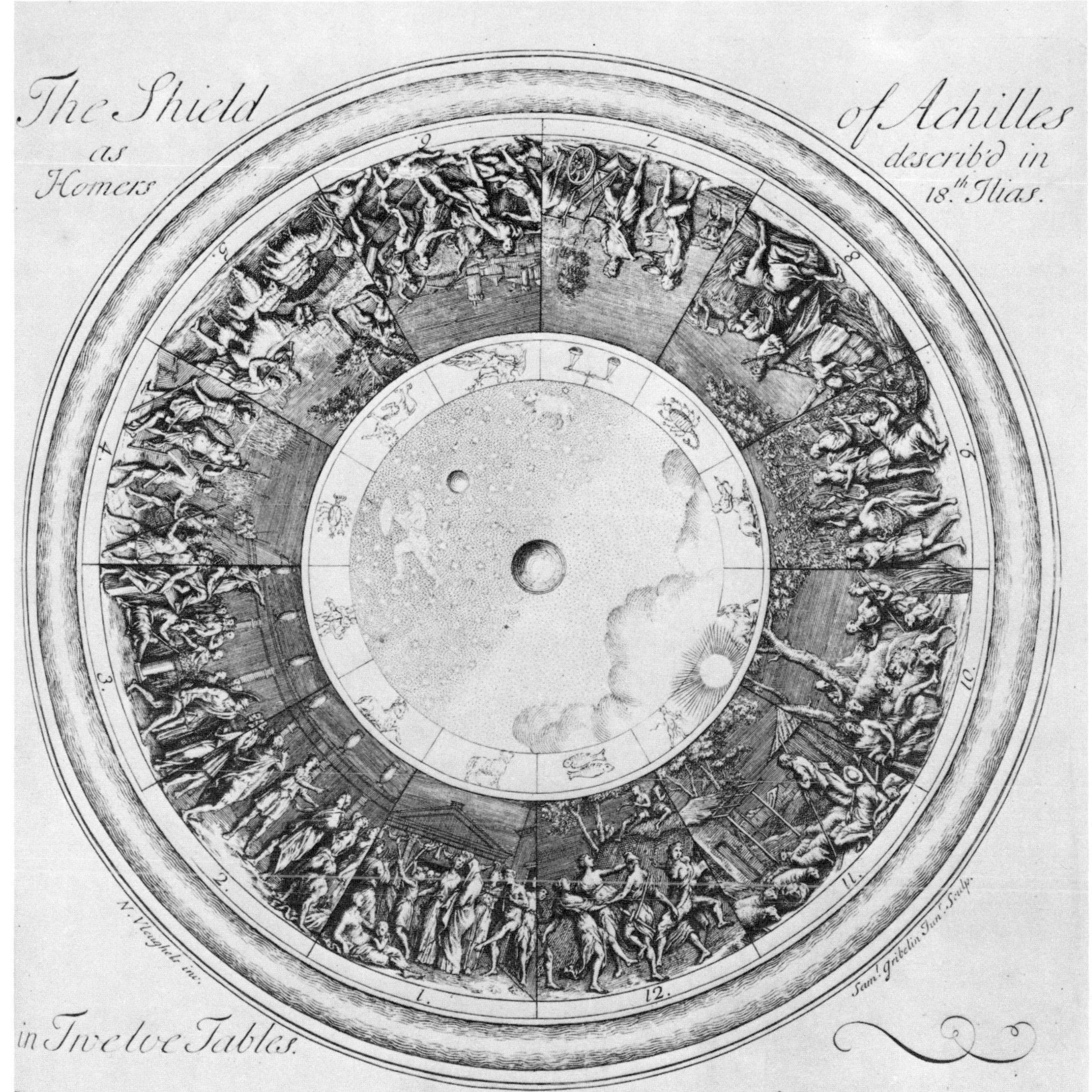

9. The Shield of Achilles. Engraved by Samuel Gribelin. 1720.

10. Raphael's School of Athens. Engraved by Pietro Aquila. *c.* 1683.

11. Raphael's Battle of Constantine. Engraved by Pietro Aquila. 1683.

animated figures on an artifact;[8] second, the impossibility of 'painting' so many figures on so small a surface (360–1).

The essay exposes the absurdity of each charge with admirable common sense. As for the impossibility of representing movement, it argues that it is ridiculous to suppose that Homer is speaking literally when he describes scenes depicted on the shield, and absurd to conjecture either that the shield must have been a marvel, the work of a God, or to concoct the far-fetched mechanistic explanation that the figures on the shield were moved by springs (359). Homer, according to Pope–Dacier, is speaking figuratively, describing figures on the shield *as if* they were alive. It is argued that when Homer describes actions—sequential actions like the 'Harangues of two Pleaders' (359), or simultaneous actions in the scenes of the ambuscade or dance (359–60)—he is interpreting the action suggested by the artist:

> Can we express ourselves otherwise of these two Arts, which tho' they are mute, yet have a Language? Or in explaining a Painting of *Raphael* or *Poussin*, can we prevent animating the Figures, in making them speak conformably to the Design of the Painter? . . . we can never speak of Painting if we banish those Expressions (359–60).

Pliny, it is pointed out, describes artifacts in this way, and even surpasses Homer when, in describing the painter Timanthes, he remarks 'that in all his Works there was something more understood than was seen' (360).

The essence of the Pope–Dacier argument on the issue of decorum is therefore that necessity and convention justify Homer's poetic licence; the assumption is clearly stated that 'there is a difference between the Work itself, and the Description of it' (359)—precisely what fundamentalist detractors of Homer failed to admit. In dealing with the second charge concerning the impossibility of representing so many figures on the shield, the argument follows Boivin exactly. It begins by making unexceptionable points that the shield is 'broader than the brims of a Hat' (360), that it is not a mere crowd of figures, but a deliberate design, an image 'design'd as a Representation of the Universe' (360). The argument cites the example of Virgil who improved on Homer in the description of the shield of Aeneas, which contained more than Achilles', even things unseen (prophecies of the future of Rome) without arousing the

[8] *TE* viii. 358–60. References to Pope's 'Observations', hereafter cited in the text, refer to page numbers in the Twickenham edition.

objections of critics (360–1). Finally in Part II Pope submits Boivin's ocular proof (a plate by Nicolas Vleughels reproduced here [plate 9], which Gribelin copied for Pope's folio edition) illustrating his plan of the way the shield could be divided into compartments geometrically to admit all that Homer describes.

It is at this point that Pope makes his own contribution to the discussion when in Part III he proposes 'to consider this Piece [the Shield] as a complete *Idea* of *Painting*, and a Sketch for what one may call an *universal Picture*' (363). 'This is certainly', he continues, 'the Light in which it is chiefly to be admired, and in which alone the Criticks have neglected to place it' (363). He proceeds to argue that the shield is not merely sculpture but painting; that the art of enamelling in colour flourished in Homer's time; furthermore (setting aside the evidence of Pliny that painting was not known at the time of the Trojan war) that Homer 'had, whether by Learning, or by Strength of Genius . . . a full and exact Idea of Painting in all its Parts' (364). Pope credits Homer with an understanding of all the artistry of high Renaissance painting: invention, composition, expression, observation of unities, and perspective—terms humanist critics applied interchangeably to painting and poetry. He concludes his essay by examining each of Boivin's compartments 'to shew with what exact order all that he [Homer] describes may enter into the Composition, according to the Rules of Painting' (366). In each instance Pope gives a prose paraphrase of Homer's description of a scene on the shield, followed by comments on the perspective, composition, and expression of the 'paintings', with references to Raphael, Rubens, and Giulio Romano.

Lessing objects to Pope's arguments at the point in the *Laokoön* when he considers Homer's shield as a possible exception to the distinction he had brilliantly drawn in chapter 16 between painting and poetry: that succession in time is the sphere of the poet, as space is that of the painter. 'And shall Homer nevertheless have fallen into those barren descriptions of material objects?', he asks of the Shield of Achilles.[9] Lessing wants to remove the objection that Homer himself, his idol as much as Pope's, had attempted to paint in poetry,

[9] G. E. Lessing, *Laokoön*, ed. Dorothy Reich (Oxford, 1965), chapter XVIII, p. 172. The translation quoted is by Ellen Frothingham (Boston, 1880, repr. New York, 1968), p. 109. Citations in my text refer to chapter and page number in Lessing, followed by the page number of the translation.

had confused the arts, and been guilty of *schilderungssucht* (mania for description). It would have been damaging to Lessing's boundaries (*grenzen*) between the arts if it could be said that Homer, the father of poetry, had sanctioned that confusion of the arts of painting and poetry which seemed to him the cause of the modern degeneracy of poetry, its mania for description and allegory. But Lessing finds Homer innocent of the charge of painting in poetry, because he 'does not paint the shield finished' but in the process of creation; he substituted 'progression for coexistence, and thus converted the tiresome description of an object into a graphic picture of an action. We see not the shield, but the divine master-workman employed upon it' (XVIII, 177, p. 114). By this somewhat desperate expedient Lessing is able to fit Homer's *ekphrasis* into his rigid categories.

To dispose of Boivin's ocular proof which tended to confuse the description with a real artifact, Lessing has only to point out that his divisions of the shield are arbitary (chapter 19). As for Pope's assertions about Homer's knowledge of painting, Lessing has no difficulty in proving his arguments unsound. He argues that the primary evidence of archaeology (remains of ancient paintings) and the secondary evidence of witnesses like Pliny prove that painting was in its infancy in Homer's time, and that perspective in particular was unknown. He dismisses Pope's proof of perspective with the statement that 'the mere representing of an object at a distance as smaller than it would be if nearer the eye, by no means constitutes perspective in a picture' (XIX, 186, p. 124). Moreover, Pope had confused 'aerial' with linear perspective; the former 'has nothing to do with the diminishing of the size according to the increased distance, but refers only to the change of color occasioned by the air or other medium through which the object is seen'. 'A man capable of this blunder', Lessing concludes in his characteristic role as prosecutor of careless critics, 'may justly be supposed ignorant of the whole subject' (XIX, 185–6 n., p. 233).

Lessing brilliantly exposes weaknesses in Pope's defence of the shield, but Pope's analogy to painting is a better defence of Homer than his own.[10]

[10] On the nature and limitations of Lessing's argument see William Guild Howard, 'Introduction', *Laokoön: Lessing, Herder, Goethe, Selections edited with an Introduction and Commentary* (New York, 1910); Lee, *Ut Pictura Poesis*, pp. 20–3; René Wellek, *A History of Modern Criticism: 1750–1950*, I, *The Later Eighteenth Century* (New Haven, 1955), pp. 159–67; and E. H. Gombrich, 'Lessing', Lecture on a Master Mind, *Proceedings of the British Academy*, 43 (1957), 133–56.

The arguments about Homer as a learned painter are specious, but they are designed to convince ignorant critics who really do not know or will not admit the difference between a thing and the description of it. It is obvious that Pope does, and that he regards the passage as a paradigm of Homer's poetic description, which can be illustrated by analogy to painting. Whatever the weaknesses of his arguments Pope's critical approach has the virtue of recognizing the passage for what it is, an *ekphrasis* (the poetic description of an artifact), the earliest example of iconic poetry.[11] Lessing struggles to transform *ekphrasis* into action on the basis of one or two verbs in order to redeem Homer from an imaginary sin—a desperate and pedantic expedient which leads him to condemn Virgil's shield simply because it is not the description of an action (XVIII, 177–80, pp. 114–17).

The most convincing appeal from Lessing's charge of ignorance and confusion is to be found in a consideration of the analogy to painting in the rest of Pope's *Iliad* commentary, in which notes on painting comprise an important line. These notes are perhaps the primary vehicle by which Pope achieves what he describes as the 'principal Design' of the Notes—'to illustrate the Poetical Beauties of the Author'—avoiding on the one hand the extremes of textual criticism, and, on the other, mere beauties or 'nosegays'.[12] It must be admitted that Pope often sounds in the notes like a curator escorting a distinguished guest or subscriber through the galleries of Homer's *musée imaginaire*: 'This is a fine Picture of the Grief of Achilles' (XVIII, 27); 'We have just seen at full length the Picture of the General of the Greeks: Here we see Hector beautifully drawn in Miniature' (XI, 83); 'There is scarce any Picture in Homer so much in the savage and terrible way, as this Comparison of the Myrmidons to Wolves: It puts one in mind of the Pieces of Spagnolett, or Salvator Rosa' (XVI, 194), and so on. But the insinuating voice of the curator is misleading; the analogy to painting, as Pope uses it, is not mere cant sanctioned by the shop-worn notion of *ut pictura poesis*.

Pope uses the analogy to painting to illustrate what he regards as Homer's

[11] See Jean Hagstrum, *The Sister Arts* (Chicago, 1958), pp. 19–22, and Murray Krieger, 'The Ekphrastic Principle and the Still Movement of Poetry; or *Laokoön* Revisited', in *The Play and Place of Criticism* (Baltimore, 1967), pp. 108–9.

[12] See *TE* vii. 82 (headnote, Book I); *TE* viii. 231 (Book XV, 890 n.). Subsequent references to Pope's Notes to Homer in the text are to book and line numbers in the Twickenham edition.

distinguishing excellence as a poet, the power of Invention or imagination which he describes in the opening passage of the 'Preface to the Iliad':

> Homer is universally allow'd to have had the greatest Invention of any Writer whatever. . . . It is to the Strength of this amazing Invention we are to attribute that unequal'd Fire and Rapture, which is so forcible in Homer. . . . What he writes is of the most animated Nature imaginable; every thing moves, every thing lives, and is put in Action. . . . The Course of his Verses resembles that of the Army he describes . . . *They pour along like a Fire that sweeps the whole Earth before it*. . . . It [his Fancy] grows in the Progress both upon himself and others, and becomes on Fire like a Chariot-Wheel, by its own Rapidity. . . . This Fire is discern'd in Virgil, but discern'd as through a Glass, reflected from Homer, more shining than fierce, but every where equal and constant: In Lucan and Statius, it bursts out in sudden, short, and interrupted Flashes: In Milton, it glows like a Furnace kept up to an uncommon ardor by the Force of Art: In Shakespear, it strikes before we are aware, like an accidental Fire from Heaven: But in Homer, and in him only, it burns every where clearly, and every where irresistibly.[13]

Throughout the notes Pope demonstrates by analogy to painting the nature and effect of this imaginative 'fire', how it suffuses the entire poem—its language, action, scene, and character.[14]

Ralph Cohen states that a crude 'picture theory of language' challenged by Burke underlies the doctrine of *ut pictura poesis* as it applies to figurative language.[15] However Pope may have rationalized the theory, he uses the analogy not to force identity but to illustrate the imaginative effect of figurative language. Thus he speaks of epithets as 'supernumerary Pictures of the Persons or Things to which they are join'd' (Preface, 10), images as 'Pictures of particular things', and similes are 'like Pictures, where the principal Figure has not only its proportion given agreeable to the Original, but is also set off with occasional Ornaments and Prospects'.[16]

Analogy to the theory and practice of painting even permits Pope to illustrate Homer's artistry in drawing character. Pope admires the way Homer

[13] *TE* vii. 3–5.

[14] See Douglas Knight, *Pope and the Heroic Tradition* (New Haven, 1951), pp. 31, 32 n. Knight argues that Pope is concerned not with 'specious similarities of technical procedure', but with the 'common fact of design', and the nature of a poetic illusion: 'Pope's constant use of parallels between poetry and painting as a critical context for his analysis of Homer's action is one of his chief ways of asserting the nature of this illusion.'

[15] *The Art of Discrimination*, p. 223.

[16] 'Preface', *TE* vii. 10; 'Index of Arts and Sciences', *TE* viii. 615; 'Preface', *TE* vii. 13.

combines the individual with the type, good likeness with idealization as treatises on painting prescribed. His characters have, as he remarks in the 'Preface', the distinctiveness of good portraits:

> No Author has ever drawn so many with so visible and surprizing a Variety, or given us such lively and affecting Impressions of them. Every one has something so singularly his own, that no Painter could have distinguish'd them more by their Features, than the Poet has by their Manners.[17]

Here, as often elsewhere in the notes, he compares the art of drawing character to the composition of portraits—miniatures, half and full-length, the full draught gradually revealed in sketches and added strokes. He remarks on how, in poetry as in painting, 'a small Action, or even a small Circumstance of an Action . . . will express the Character and Action of the Figure more than all the other Parts of the Design' (VI, 595); and he compares a speech of Nestor to a self-portrait, in which Nestor is 'very careful to draw his own Picture in the strongest Colours, and to shew it in the fairest Light' (XXIII, 719). Action and speech reveal 'the Lights and Shades of . . . Character', as he says of Achilles, 'which Homer has heighten'd and darken'd in Extreams' (I, 155).

The analogy is most illuminating, and least subject to merely rhetorical or conventional use, when Pope applies it to Homer's description and organization of scenes, books, even to entire epic poems. As he remarks in the 'Preface':

> If we observe his Descriptions . . . we shall find the Invention still predominant. To what else can we ascribe that vast Comprehension of Images of every sort, where we see each Circumstance of art and Individual of Nature summon'd together by the Extent and Fecundity of his Imagination; to which all things, in their various Views, presented themselves in an Instant, and had their Impressions taken off to Perfection at a Heat? Nay, he not only gives us the full Prospects of Things, but several unexpected Peculiarities and Side-Views, unobserv'd by any Painter but Homer.[18]

Here the activity of Homer's imagination is compared to a painter's brilliant sketch, and Pope constantly illustrates the power of the imagination to summon together, to compose scenes by analogy to painting: in selection of detail, 'Painting is to be consulted, and the whole regard had to those circumstances which contribute to form a full, and yet not a confused, idea of the

[17] *TE* vii. 7. [18] *TE* vii. 9.

thing';[19] in omission of circumstances, like the painter the poet 'drops . . . Particularities, and leaves them to be supply'd by the Imagination of the Reader' (X, 207); and in use of repetition, Homer 'has done like a great Painter, who does not think himself oblig'd to vary all his Pieces to that degree, as not one of them shall have the least Resemblance to another' (XIX, 197).

In an 'Essay on Homer's Battels' preceding Book V (1716) Pope compares Homer's composition of battle scenes, the most numerous and complex scenes in the poem, to history painting:

> It is worth taking Notice . . . what Use Homer every where makes of each little Accident or Circumstance that can naturally happen in a Battel, thereby to cast a Variety over his Action . . . [which] makes his Work resemble a large History-Piece, where even the less important Figures and Actions have yet some convenient Place or Corner to be shewn in.[20]

In a long note on the description of a battle scene in Book VIII Pope shows how 'all that he describes may enter into the composition as in painting':

> Here is a Battel describ'd with so much Fire, that the warmest Imagination of an able Painter cannot add a Circumstance to heighten the Surprize or Horror of the Picture. Here is what they call the *Fracas*, or Hurry and Tumult of the Action in the utmost Strength of Colouring, upon the Foreground; and the *Repose* or *Solemnity* at a distance, with great Propriety and Judgment. First, in the *Eloignement*, we behold Jupiter in golden Armour, surrounded with Glory, upon the Summit of Mount *Ida*; his Chariot and Horses by him, wrapt in dark Clouds. In the next Place below the Horizon, appear the Clouds rolling and opening, thro' which the Lightning flashes in the Face of the *Greeks*, who are flying on all sides; *Agamemnon* and the rest of the Commanders in the Rear, in Postures of Astonishment. Towards the middle of the Piece, we see Nestor in the utmost Distress, one of his Horses having a deadly Wound in the Forehead with a Dart, which makes him rear and writhe, and disorder the rest. Nestor is cutting the Harness with his Sword, while *Hector* advances driving full speed. *Diomed* interposes, in an action of the utmost Fierceness and Intrepidity: These two Heroes make the principal Figures and the Subject of the Picture. A burning Thunderbolt falls just before the feet of *Diomed*'s horses, from whence a horrid Flame of Sulphur rises. (VIII, 164)

We might easily imagine we are reading Pope's instructions to the engraver of his headpiece for Book VIII in the quarto *Iliad*[21] but the point of the analogy

[19] 'Postscript to the Odyssey', *TE* x. 387. [20] *TE* vii. 255.
[21] See notes on Plates 10–11, *TE* vii. xiii.

as it is used here is not to reduce the action to a static tableau, but to comment on the coherence and unity Homer's imagination has imparted to an intrinsically chaotic scene.[22]

When he wants to comment on the organization of emotion rather than action in a scene, Pope applies the doctrine of expression derived from painting to Homer's description. His 'Index' contains a long section entitled 'Descriptions of the Internal Passions, or of their visible Effects', which he illustrates in a comment on an encounter between Lycaon and Achilles in Book XXI:

> There is hardly any in the whole *Iliad* more proper to move Pity than this Circumstance of *Lycaon*, or to raise Terror, than this view of *Achilles*. It is also the finest Picture of them both imaginable: We see the different Attitude of their Persons, and the different Passions which appear'd in their Countenances: At first *Achilles* stands erect, with Surprize in his Looks, at the Sight of one whom he thought it impossible to find there; while *Lycaon* is in the Posture of a Suppliant, with Looks that plead for Compassion; with one Hand holding the Hero's Lance, and his Knee with the other: Afterwards, when at his Death he lets go the Spear and places himself on his Knees, with his Arms extended, to receive the mortal Wound, how lively and how strongly is this painted? I believe every one . . . allows that poetry (at least in *Homer*) is truly a speaking Picture. (XXI, 41)

Pope is emphasizing what Richardson calls the 'dumb-shew', the way everything in history paintings like the cartoons of Raphael, even the background, contributes to the unified dramatic expression of emotion.

The analogy to painting is used to illustrate the imaginative unity of an entire book of the *Iliad* in a concluding note to Book X, which is discussed below in relation to Pope's sensibility to landscape. In the 'Postscript' to the *Odyssey* Pope compares Homer's epics to paintings of Raphael (plates 10, 11) to demonstrate that each should be judged on its own merits as a unique integrated composition:

> The *Battle of* Constantine, and the *School of* Athens, are both pieces of *Raphael*: Shall we censure the School of *Athens* as faulty, because it has not the fury and fire of the other? or shall we say, that *Raphael* was grown grave and old, because he chose to represent the manners of old men and Philosophers? There is all the silence, tranquillity and composure in the one, and all the warmth, hurry and tumult in the other, which

[22] See Douglas Knight, *Pope and the Heroic Tradition*, p. 31.

the subject of either required: both of them had been imperfect, if they had not been as they are. And let the Painter or Poet be young or old, who designs or performs in this manner, it proves him to have made the piece at a time of life when he was master not only of his art, but of his discretion.[23]

The poems, like the paintings, are masterpieces of unified organization; what the poet and painter have in common is a mastery of design.

Commentary of this kind, which Pope applies to everything in Homer's description from an epithet to an entire epic, has led some critics to infer that he has a preference for static scenes, arrested action, and frozen tableaux.[24] Interpreted in this way the analogy flatly contradicts his sense of the fire and movement of Homer's imagination as expressed in the 'Preface'. But we should bear in mind that Pope's conception of painting does not correspond to that of Lessing, who 'unconsciously confused painting with sculpture'.[25] Pope's idea of painting is derived from a familiarity with the art of the high Italian Renaissance. For Pope it is as true of painting as of Homer that 'every thing moves, every thing lives, and is put in Action'.[26]

Lessing censures critics like Spence and Caylus who make 'the painter's color-stone the touchstone of the poet' (XVI, 159, p. 93), and who ignore 'one of the most detailed and graphic' pictures in Homer, the description of Pandarus drawing his bow.[27] Significantly Pope does comment on this passage in the notes (IV, 144), but the point of the comparison to painting is apparently to show how Homer's description of a sequential action produces in the reader's imagination an illusion of simultaneity. Pope's comment on Idomeneus evading the spear of Deiphobus makes in Book XIII the same point:

Nothing could paint in a more lively manner this whole Action, and every Circumstance of it, than the following Lines. There is the Posture of *Idomeneus* upon seeing the Lance flying toward him; the lifting of the Shield obliquely to turn it aside; the Arm discover'd in that Position; the Form, Composition, Materials, and Ornaments of the

[23] *TE* x. 384. Cf. Jonathan Richardson's remarks on the Battle of Constantine in *An Account*, p. 245: 'This Picture is indisputably the Foremost in the World in its Kind; when I am considering It, all Lesser Names of Battel-Painters appear Little Indeed; and I imagine my self reading a Description of a Battel in Homer.'

[24] D. R. Clark, 'Landscape Painting Effects in Pope's Homer', *Journal of Aesthetics and Art Criticism*, 22 (1963), 26; and Jean Hagstrum, *The Sister Arts*, pp. 230, 232.

[25] Rensselaer W. Lee, *Ut Pictura Poesis* (1967), p. 21.

[26] 'Preface', *TE* vii. 4.

[27] *Laokoön*, XV, 155–6, pp. 89–90.

Shield distinctly specify'd; the Flight of the Dart over it, the Sound of it first as it flew, then as it fell; and the Decay of that Sound on the Edge of the Buckler, which being thinner than the other Parts rather tinkled than rung, especially when the first Force of the Stroke was spent on the Orb of it. All this in the Compass of so few Lines, in which every word is an Image, is something more beautifully particular, than I remember to have met with any Poet. (XIII, 511)

Here Pope describes a series of pictures, a series of frames, as we would say, in a moving picture; the value of comparing the passage to a single painting of a 'whole action' appears to be not only the liveliness of the whole impression but the illusion of simultaneity. Moreover, Pope's emphasis on sound as a component of the 'picture' indicates that he understood exactly what Lessing defines as a legitimate 'poetical picture':[28]

A picture in poetry is not necessarily one which can be transferred to canvas. But every touch, or every combination of touches, by means of which the poet brings his subject so vividly before us that we are more conscious of the subject than of his words, is picturesque, and makes what we call a picture; that is, it produces that degree of illusion which a painted picture is peculiarly qualified to excite, and which we in fact most frequently and naturally experience in the contemplation of the painted canvas. (XIV, 154, p. 88)

We may conclude, therefore, that Lessing's strictures on Pope's blunders in the 'Observations on the Shield' do not do justice to his astute use of the analogy to painting elsewhere in his notes to Homer.

ii. HOW IMAGES REFLECT IN POPE'S POETRY

Lessing was one of the first critics to describe Pope's development as a poet in terms of his literary pictorialism, an interpretation derived from lines in the *Epistle to Arbuthnot*, where Pope asks who could take offence, 'While pure Description held the place of Sense'? (148), and where he draws the famous line of demarcation in his poetic career with the boast

That not in Fancy's Maze he wander'd long,
But stoop'd to Truth, and moraliz'd his song. (340–1)[29]

[28] *Laokoön*, XIV, 154, p. 88. [29] *TE* iv. 106, 120.

Lessing, paraphrasing Warburton's obtuse note on these lines, interprets them in the *Laokoön* as Pope's repudiation of pictorial description:

> Pope, when a man, looked back with Contempt on the descriptive efforts of his poetic childhood. He expressly enjoined upon every one, who would not prove himself unworthy the name of poet, to abandon as early as possible this fondness for description [Schilderungssucht]. A merely descriptive poem he declared to be a feast made up of sauces. (XVII, 170–1, p. 108)[30]

The inference is unwarranted because there is no trace of the prescriptive in Pope's lines (he enjoins nothing), and they cannot possibly be read in context as a straightforward description of his own career. On the contrary, his 'contempt' is deliberately rhetorical, part of an ironic apology for his career in which he adopts a self-deprecatory tone, and belittles his own early poetry as a harmless and innocent amusement, which he compares to the namby-pamby of Hervey's 'painted Mistress, or a purling Stream' (l. 150). Furthermore, it can be demonstrated that Pope's literary pictorialism, which has been recognized as an important feature of his poetry, is of a piece throughout, as 'pure' in the translation of Homer, the *Dunciad*, and the *Imitations of Horace* as in the *Pastorals*, nowhere consisting of that mania for description and allegory which Lessing condemns. In Pope's poetry, as in his use of the critical analogy, the connection between the arts is neither formal nor mimetic, but a transaction of the imagination where 'images reflect'.

The nature of Pope's literary pictorialism can most clearly be seen in passages of natural description, which are discussed below in connection with landscape gardening (Part II, chapter 3), but examples are plentiful throughout his poetry to illustrate how scrupulously he avoided the sins of Lessing's 'poet-painter'. He made his attitude to word-painting explicit in *Peri Bathous*

[30] Warburton's note on the *Epistle to Arbuthnot*, in *Works* (1751), iv. 19–20, is quoted (inaccurately) by Lessing in his notes to the *Laocoön*: 'Warburton's remark on this last line [*Epistle to Arbuthnot*, l. 148] may have the force of an explanation by the poet himself. "He [Pope] uses *pure* equivocally, to signify either chaste or empty; and has given in this line what he esteemed the true Character of descriptive poetry, as absurd as a feast made up of sauces. The use of a picturesque imagination is to brighten and adorn good sense; so that to employ it only in description, is like children's delighting in a prism for the sake of its gaudy colours, which, when frugally managed, and artfully disposed, might be made to represent and illustrate the noblest objects in nature." Both poet and commentator seem to have regarded the matter rather from a moral than an artistic point of view. But so much the better that this style of poetry seems equally worthless from whichever point it be viewed' (XVII, 171 n., pp. 230–1).

where he ridicules Blackmore's personification of Nature 'as a painter' in *Job* (1716):

> Sometimes the Lord of Nature in the Air,
> Spreads forth his Clouds, his sable Canvass, where
> His Pencil, dipped in heavenly Colour bright,
> Paints his fair Rain bow, charming to the Sight.[31]

It is rare to find in Pope's poetry the kind of allegorical history painting employed in a *Spectator* essay (No. 425) attributed to him, 'A Dream of the Seasons', describing the retinue of autumn:

> *Plenty* walk'd by his Side with an healthy fresh Countenance, pouring out from an Horn all the various Product of the Year. *Pomona* followed with a Glass of Cyder in her Hand, with *Bacchus* in a Chariot drawn by Tygres, accompanied by a whole Troop of Satyrs, Fauns, and Sylvans.[32]

More characteristic of the early poetry are figures of speech derived from the theory and practice of painting, where there is no pretence of imitation.

In the *Essay on Criticism* (1711) Pope compares the limits of human knowledge and critical myopia to prospect and perspective (225–32); conceits in false wit to ornate costume portraiture (240–7); the seeds of judgement to a painter's sketch (19–22), false learning to 'ill-colouring' (23–5), and mutability of language to fading colours (484–93). In the *Rape of the Lock* (1714) properties of painting considered as an artifact are used to characterize the figures of the sylphs as metaphors of female vanity.

Critics have seen 'pictures' in *Windsor Forest* (1713) since the eighteenth century, but the account they give of them tends to illustrate their own confusion rather than Pope's. Warton delights in the 'exquisite picture' of the pheasant:[33]

> Ah! what avail his glossie, varying Dyes,
> His Purple Crest, and Scarlet-circled Eyes,
> The vivid Green his shining Plumes unfold;
> His painted Wings, and Breast that flames with Gold? (115–18)

Norman Ault speaks of the passage describing the 'various Race' of fish as a

[31] *The Art of Sinking in Poetry: A Critical Edition*, ed. Edna Leake Steeves (New York, 1952), p. 22.
[32] *Prose*, p. 54.
[33] Joseph Warton, *Essay on Pope*, i. 32.

'still life, arranged and coloured with the precision and rapture of an old Dutch master':[34]

> The bright-ey'd Perch with Fins of Tyrian Dye,
> The silver Eel, in shining Volumes roll'd,
> The yellow Carp, in Scales bedrop'd with Gold,
> Swift Trouts, diversify'd with Crimson Stains. (142–5)

But it is misleading to call these animated descriptions pictures or still life as if poetic diction was equivalent to paint, and poetry to painting. The same assumption leads nineteenth-century critics to condemn the poetic diction of such passages. But the point of this vivid appeal to the visual imagination is to intensify the pathos of a dying creature, or to give, as Tillotson argues, a scientifically precise account of a species.[35] If Pope was looking at a picture, as Reuben Brower observes, it is 'a picture in language consecrated to such descriptive uses through literary tradition'.[36] And Jean Hagstrum points out that 'Pope does not luxuriate in these colors for their own sensuous sake. Though keeping his eye on the object, he has stylized the visual detail to make it intellectually and emotionally expressive.'[37]

The description of Father Thames in *Windsor Forest* is an example of what has been called a 'full-scale allegorical painting',[38] but Pope avoids the confusion of the arts Lessing condemns as the 'rage of allegorizing':

> In that blest Moment, from his Oozy Bed
> Old Father *Thames* advanc'd his rev'rend Head.
> His Tresses dropt with Dews, and o'er the Stream
> His shining Horns diffus'd a golden Gleam:
> Grav'd on his Urn appear'd the Moon, that guides
> His swelling Waters, and alternate Tydes;
> The figur'd Streams in Waves of Silver roll'd,
> And on their Banks *Augusta* rose in Gold. (329–36)

It is clear that Pope conceives of the figure of Father Thames as a monument reminiscent of the Baroque fountains of Bernini,[39] in his account of the throne

[34] Ault, p. 90.
[35] Geoffrey Tillotson, 'Correctness III. Language', *On the Poetry of Pope*, 2nd edn. (Oxford, 1950), pp. 63–104.
[36] *The Poetry of Allusion* (Oxford, 1959), p. 53. [37] *The Sister Arts*, p. 216. [38] Ibid., p. 217.
[39] See Reuben Brower, *The Poetry of Allusion*, p. 53. Pope's study of Roman fountains, particularly

of the River God with surrounding figures and the urn ornamented in relief. But the description is not categorical or enumerative, nor a static formalistic reduction of a work of art—in a word, it is not ekphrastic. The language merely suggests the monumental to invest the prophetic allegorical figure with authority, stature, and metaphorical significance at a crucial point in the poem. Significantly, the detail which Joseph Warton found 'highly picturesque' in the appearance of Father Thames is a description of movement:

> His Sea-green Mantle waving with the Wind (l. 350).[40]

One reason for the continuing popularity of Pope's *Eloisa to Abelard* (1717) was the appeal of its picturesque description, but once again we discover that the pictures are in the mind of the beholder. The description of the apotheosis of Abelard (337–42) reminded Warton of 'the death of St. Jerome . . . finely painted by Domenichino, with such attendant particulars', and he recommends other scenes in the poem as 'fine subject[s] for the pencil . . . worthy a capital painter'.[41] But none of these paintings are to be found in the text. The real analogy to painting in the poem is theoretical—the idea of expression, the common attempt to express the passions dramatically, as indicated by Pope's concluding line: 'He best can paint 'em, who shall feel 'em most' (l. 366).

Chronologically Pope's *Iliad* (1715–20) as much as *Eloisa to Abelard* (1717) belongs to the 'pure description' of 'Fancy's maze', and its pervasive pictorialism has been recognized since the eighteenth century.[42] Pope's Homer offers another striking example of the confusion of critics rather than Pope himself about the nature of literary pictorialism. Invariably where Pope's notes lead us to expect pictures of the kind Lessing condemned they are not to be found in the translation. Even in translating the description of Achilles' shield which he recognizes as an iconic description Pope makes no attempt to reproduce the hypothetical 'paintings' he comments on in the 'Observations'. For example, his translation of the description of 'A Town in War' (fourth Compartment of the shield) contains nothing of the careful composition of

Bernini's, is indicated by his annotations in a book of engravings now at Yale, Pieter Schenk (1660–1718/19), *Romae Novae Delineatio* (n.d.), plates 8 and 11.

[40] *Essay on Pope*, i. 24.

[41] *Essay on Pope*, i. 326, 323.

[42] *TE* vii. liii, lv n.

the scene into foreground and background perspective he had demonstrated in his analysis:

> Another Part (a Prospect differing far)
> Glow'd with refulgent Arms, and horrid War.
> Two mighty Hosts a leaguer'd Town embrace,
> And one would pillage, one wou'd burn the Place.
> Meantime the Townsmen, arm'd with silent Care,
> A secret Ambush on the Foe prepare:
> Their Wives, their Children, and the Watchful Band,
> Of trembling Parents on the Turrets stand.
> They march; by *Pallas* and by *Mars* made bold;
> Gold were the Gods, their radiant Garments Gold,
> And Gold their Armour: These the Squadron led,
> August, Divine, Superior by the Head! (XVIII, 591–602)

This is clearly not the ekphrastic description of a static scene or tableau, but of action; as Pope remarked in the 'Observations', the poet cannot 'prevent animating the figures'.[43] Pope leaves the composition of the scene to the reader's imagination, heightening its visual appeal by 'selected visual impressions'—'glow'd', 'refulgent', 'radiant', and 'gold' reiterated three times.[44]

Nevertheless critics have found a gallery of 'pictures' to praise and blame in Pope's Homer; a notorious example of the confusion of painting and poetry is the critical history of the famous nightpiece in Book VIII of the *Iliad*.[45] This is the simile comparing the Trojan camp fires on the field of Troy to the moon and stars, a comparison which Pope asserts in his note 'is inferior to none in Homer'.

> It is the most beautiful Nightpiece that can be found in Poetry. He presents you with a prospect of the Heavens, the Seas, and the Earth: The Stars shine, the Air is serene, the World enlighten'd, and the Moon mounted in Glory. (VIII, 687)

[43] *TE* viii. 359.

[44] Reuben Brower, *The Poetry of Allusion*, pp. 23, 134. Fern Farnham is misleading about Pope's pictorialism when she states ('The Shield of Achilles', p. 1574), that 'Pope . . . is creating a picture gallery'.

[45] See Geoffrey Tillotson, *Augustan Poetic Diction* (1961; repr. London, 1964), p. 29 and n.; Alfred C. Ames, 'Early Criticism of Pope's "Night Piece"', *Modern Language Notes*, 60 (1945), 265–7, and G. S. Rousseau, 'Seven Types of *Iliad*', *English Miscellany: A Symposium of History, Literature and the Arts*, ed. Mario Praz, 16 (Rome, 1965), 143–67.

This is Pope's translation:

The Troops exulting sate in order round,
And beaming Fires illumin'd all the Ground.
As when the Moon, refulgent Lamp of Night!
O'er Heav'ns clear Azure spreads her sacred Light,
When not a Breath disturbs the deep Serene;
And not a Cloud o'ercasts the solemn Scene;
Around her Throne the vivid Planets roll,
And Stars unnumber'd gild the flowing Pole,
O'er the dark Trees a yellower Verdure shed,
And tip with Silver ev'ry Mountain's Head;
Then shine the Vales, the Rocks in Prospect rise,
A Flood of Glory bursts from all the Skies:
The conscious Swains, rejoicing in the Sight,
Eye the blue Vault, and bless the useful Light.
So many Flames before proud *Ilion* blaze,
And lighten glimm'ring *Xanthus* with their Rays.
The long Reflections of the distant Fires
Gleam on the Walls, and tremble on the Spires.
A thousand Piles the dusky Horrors gild,
And shoot a shady Lustre o'er the Field.
Full fifty Guards each flaming Pile attend,
Whose umber'd Arms, by fits, thick Flashes send.
Loud neigh the Coursers o'er their Heaps of Corn,
And ardent Warriors wait the rising Morn. (685–708)

Most critics of this passage take their cue from Pope's note on the nightpiece, and proceed to regard it as painting rather than poetry. This is the premise of William Gilpin who can speak here for the eighteenth-century admirers of the passage, describing, according to Gilpin,

the effects of an illumination very picturesquely detailed. . . . Homer, however, has nothing to do with most of these picturesque images. They are only to be found in Pope's translation. Though it may be fashionable to depreciate this work, as a translation, it must at least be owned, that Pope, who was a painter, has enriched his original with many ideas of his art.[46]

Curiously, the same assumption underlies the judgements of the romantics

[46] *Observations on the Western Parts of England* (London, 1798), p. 210.

12. Classical Landscape.
By John Wootton. *c.* 1725.

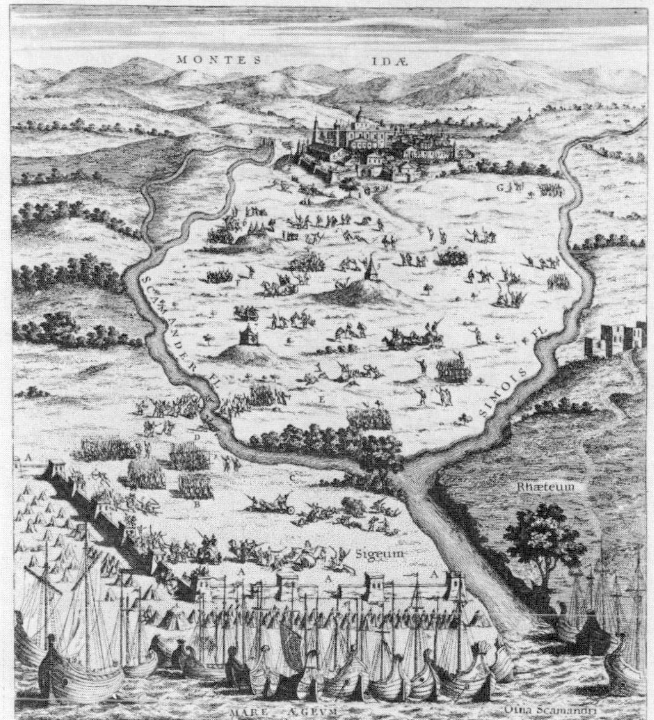

13. Map of Troy from Pope's
Homer. 1716.

14. The Shield of Achilles. Details showing compartments 8 and 11, 'Harvest' and 'Sheep'.

15. Netley Abbey. After William Bellers. 1774.

who unanimously condemned Pope's nightpiece for its 'pseudo-poetic diction', and a modern critic who argues that the 'static, spatial itemization' of Pope's description 'would probably deserve the censure of a Lessing as an artificial and imperfectly fused itemization of quasi-visual details'.[47] All these critics divorce the passage from its rhetorical context, and consider it in isolation as a piece of word-painting. Disgusted by Pope's poetic diction, and by his false picture of nature, they overlook the crucial fact that the nightpiece is a figure of speech, a simile duly listed in Pope's Poetical Index under 'Similes . . . From the Sun, Moon, Stars: The Moon and Stars in Glory, [compared] to the Brightness and Number of the Trojan Fires'.[48] Matthew Arnold alone among Victorian critics discriminates between the tenor and vehicle of Pope's comparison, but he nevertheless condemns Pope's translation as 'singularly and notoriously unfortunate', unable to appreciate the 'resemblance' which Pope values so highly in Homer's similes.[49]

Considered as a figure of speech, rather than as a sterile exercise in word painting or a set-piece of strained description—that is, as poetry rather than painting—the description can be criticized more fairly. The intense heightening of visual impressions, which constitutes the pictorial aspect of Pope's description, is not superfluous ornament. Douglas Knight has commented on the way the poetic diction serves to represent 'typical nature . . . transfigured by the moon-goddess', and shown how the magical transformation of the landscape by moonlight becomes a metaphor of the Trojan attitude to the war at this point, a mixture of hope and presentiment. Thus Pope's nightpiece can fairly be seen as a picture of the kind Lessing would approve, a good example of 'how much Pope owes to his power over metaphor'.[50]

In Pope's later poetry pictorialism does not disappear as Warburton and Lessing would have us believe because of Pope's repudiation of a contemptible mode of description. On the contrary the analogy to painting emerges most powerfully and characteristically in the satires of the 1730s in relation to the

[47] See Robert Southey, review of Chalmer's *English Poets*, *Quarterly Review*, 12 (Oct. 1814), 86–7; Wordsworth, 'Essay, Supplementary to the Preface' (1815) in *Literary Criticism of William Wordsworth*, ed. Paul M. Zall (Lincoln, Nebraska, 1966), pp. 173–4; Coleridge, *Biographia Literaria*, ed. J. Shawcross (Oxford, 1907), i. 26 n.; and Jean Hagstrum, *The Sister Arts*, p. 264.

[48] *TE* viii. 606.

[49] Matthew Arnold, *The Complete Prose Works*, ed. R. H. Super (Ann Arbor, 1960), i. 110–11; *TE* viii. 157 n.

[50] *Pope and the Heroic Tradition*, pp. 41–2, 46. Cf. Maynard Mack, *TE* vii. lv–lvi.

character portraits, where painting is 'a key metaphor',[51] and where Pope carries the comparison far beyond the conventional idea of parallels between poetry and painting. In his study of the character sketches Benjamin Boyce concludes that 'Pope does little with physical appearance', his portraits are 'psychological';[52] he never gives us the physical inventory of a Petrarchan sonneteer. Another critic, Robert Rogers, has argued that 'nearly all of Pope's characters reflect the influence of the analogy between poetry and painting', and he refers to the effect on the reader of 'a simultaneous rather than a sequential consciousness of meaning'.[53] The effect cannot be denied; perhaps Pope had it in mind when he told Arbuthnot that 'examples are pictures, and strike the senses'.[54] But it is difficult to demonstrate beyond the statement of Boyce that the 'most complex' of Pope's characters 'are unified by the poet's intensely emotional perception'.[55] It is possible, however, to show more precisely how 'images reflect' which are derived from the theory of painting, the practice of the artist, and the nature of the painting as an artifact.

Renaissance theory of painting, particularly ideas about the art of characterization, are clearly reflected in Pope's character sketches. Ideal imitation was the essence of academic doctrine, which applied to the portrait artist as much as the history painter. Richardson observes in the *Theory of Painting* that 'the Face, and Air, as well as our actions indicates the Mind' (50), and he requires that 'a portrait painter must understand mankind and enter into their characters, and express their minds as well as their faces' (12). Thus, the portrait painter needs to combine naturalism and idealization: 'To raise the Character', Richardson asserts, is 'the most difficult part of his Art' because 'in making Portraits we must keep Nature in View; if we launch out into the Deep we are lost'.[56]

One of Pope's early poems, *Of Her Picture, an Imitation of Waller* (1717), describes a portrait which appears to have been composed according to such a theory of imitation:

> The nymph her graces here express'd may find,
> And by this picture learn to dress her mind;

[51] Reuben Brower, *The Poetry of Allusion*, p. 269.
[52] *Character Sketches*, p. 97.
[53] Robert W. Rogers, *The Major Satires of Alexander Pope*, Illinois Studies in Language and Literature, 40 (Urbana, 1955), 60–1.
[54] *Correspondence*, iii. 423.
[55] *Character Sketches*, p. 128.
[56] 'Of Grace and Greatness', in *Theory of Painting* (1715), pp. 175, 179.

For here no frowns make tender love afraid,
Soft looks of mercy grace the flatt'ring shade,
And, while we gaze, the gracious form appears
T'approve our passion and forbid our fears.
Narcissus here a different fate had prov'd,
Whose bright resemblance by himself was lov'd;
Had he but once this fairer shade descry'd,
Not for his own, but hers, the youth had dy'd.[57]

This 'gracious form' recalls 'that perfect and excellent example of the mind' which Bellori describes as the proper object of the painter's imitation.[58] Similarly, in the *Epistle to Jervas* (1717) Pope praises Jervas's portraits of ladies for the brilliance of the 'ideas'—'the living image in the Painter's breast' (l. 42):

Thence endless streams of fair ideas flow,
Strike in the sketch, or in the picture glow;
Thence beauty, waking all her forms, supplies
An Angel's sweetness, or Bridgewater's eyes. (43–6)

In lines on 'Lady Mary Wortley Montagu's Portrait' (1719), written after Kneller had painted her portrait for Pope and perhaps a comment on it, he expresses some scepticism about Richardson's demand that the portrait painter 'must understand mankind, and enter into their characters, and express their minds as well as their faces'.

The play full smiles around the dimpled mouth
That happy air of Majesty and Youth.
So would I draw (but oh, 'tis vain to try
My narrow Genius does the power deny)
The Equal Lustre of the Heavenly mind
Where every grace with every Virtue's join'd
Learning not vain, and wisdom not severe
With Greatness easy, and with wit sincere.
With Just Description shew the Soul Divine
And the whole Princesse in my work should shine.[59]

57 *TE* vi. 9.
58 Quoted by Dryden in 'A Parallel of Poetry and Painting', in *Essays of John Dryden*, ed. W. P. Ker (Oxford, 1900), ii. 118.
59 *TE* vi. 211–12.

The poem implies that the artist has succeeded in drawing the face but not the 'Soul Divine'; and significantly it questions whether the poet can do more. This question is exactly the one that preoccupied Pope in his satires on the characters of men and women in the 1730s.

In the *Moral Epistles* and the *Essay on Man* Pope's scepticism about the Renaissance doctrine of ideal portraiture is implicit. He insists on the complexity of human nature, the difficulty of knowing it, or describing it—catching the manners as they fly. How is the painter or poet to know other men's minds when he cannot know himself? The famous injunction at the beginning of Epistle II of the *Essay on Man*, 'Know then thyself', is shown to be all but impossible for a being 'darkly wise' (l. 4). Self-knowledge is denied even to a Newton:

> Could he, whose rules the rapid Comet bind,
> Describe or fix one movement of his Mind? (II, 35–6)

'Our depths who fathoms, or our shallows finds,/Quick whirls, and shifting eddies, of our minds?', he asks in the *Epistle to Cobham* (ll. 29–30). Certainly not, Pope replies, the painter of ideal portraits.

The difficulty, Pope appreciated, was compounded by problems of perception, fallacies of the 'optics seeing' and the 'objects seen' (l. 23), which he describes in the *Epistle to Cobham*:

> That each from other differs, first confess;
> Next, that he varies from himself no less:
> Add Nature's, Custom's, Reason's, Passion's strife,
> And all Opinion's colours cast on life.
> Yet more; the diff'rence is as great between
> The optics seeing, as the objects seen.
> All Manners take a tincture from our own,
> Or come discolour'd thro' our Passions shown.
> Or Fancy's beam enlarges, multiplies,
> Contracts, inverts, and gives ten thousand dyes. (18–27)

The mind, acting as a prism, refracts clear ideas or images into the vari-coloured rays of opinion, half-truth, or outright falsehood. A sense of the vagaries of perception inevitably undermines faith in the ideal truth of the artist's image. The academic formulas of Le Brun, instructing the painter how to depict every shade of human psychology, simply beg the question.

The 'objects seen' had been proved similarly deceptive in the light of Newton's discoveries in the *Opticks*, which had the effect of rationalizing the Renaissance distrust of colour. Colour, which Du Fresnoy characterized as a deceiving harlot, had been defended in the seventeenth century by the Rubenists, but the prejudice remained.[60] In the *Essay on Criticism* Pope compares 'False Eloquence' to the 'gawdy colours' in the 'Prismatic Glass' (ll. 311–12). In the *Rape of the Lock* the sylphs are characterized in terms of Newtonian discoveries about colour.

> Transparent Forms, too fine for mortal Sight,
> Their fluid Bodies half dissolv'd in Light.
> Loose to the Wind their airy Garments flew,
> Thin glitt'ring Textures of the filmy Dew;
> Dipt in the richest Tincture of the Skies,
> Where Light disports in ever-mingling Dies,
> While ev'ry Beam new transient Colours flings,
> Colours that change whene'er they wave their Wings. (II, 61–8)

The volatile elements of colour and light are the 'airy substance' not only of sylphs, but of paintings considered as artifacts.

The clear, static appearance of the canvas is deceptive because the surface reflects the illusory properties of light and colour. In the literature, moreover, painting is invariably discussed in terms of contrast: of light and shade, line and mass, mixed and unmixed colour, foreground and background. Painting becomes, therefore, a valuable metaphor rich in suggestion, when Pope styles himself in the *Epistle on the Characters of Women* (1735) as a painter, handicapped by the peculiar limitations of perception, who attempts to portray in the medium of paint, itself a complex idiom of light and colour, the ambiguities of human character.

The painter who speaks in the poem is more than sceptical about the

[60] Charles A. Du Fresnoy, *The Art of Painting*, 2nd edn. (1716), p. 37. On the Renaissance distrust of colour, and seenteenth-century controversies, see Luigi Salerno, 'Seventeenth-Century English Literature on Painting', *Journal of the Warburg and Courtauld Institute*, 14 (1951), 255–8.

possibility of knowing women's characters; he accepts the Aristotelian idea that women are creatures of sensibility rather than character (*ethos*):[61]

> Nothing so true as what you once let fall,
> Most Women have no Characters at all
> Matter too soft a lasting mark to bear,
> And best distinguished by black, brown or fair. (1–4)

Women's nature is too soft a ground on which to draw the clear outlines of character, and the painter-poet ridicules the false, idealized images of historical portraiture:

> How many pictures of one Nymph we view,
> All how unlike each other, all how true!
> Arcadia's Countess, here, in ermin'd pride,
> Is there, Pastora by a fountain side:
> Here Fannia, leering on her own good man,
> Is there, a naked Leda with a Swan.
> Let then the Fair one beautifully cry,
> In Magdalen's loose hair and lifted eye,
> Or drest in smiles of sweet Cecilia shine,
> With simp'ring Angels, Palms, and Harps divine;
> Whether the Charmer sinner it, or saint it,
> If Folly grows romantic, I must paint it. (5–13)

The 'one certain Portrait' (ll. 181–6) of a woman, the Queen, is equally false because such royal portraits are devised according to decorum and academic prescription which belie the character of the subject.

But Pope's artist has none of the idealism of the academic artist. He does not paint the divine idea according to academic formula; he knows that

> Th' exactest traits of Body or of Mind,
> We owe to models of an humble kind. (191–2)

He attempts mere sketches, which connoisseurs prized above finished paintings:

> Come then, the colours and the ground prepare!
> Dip in the Rainbow, trick her off in Air,
> Chuse a firm Cloud, before it fall, and in it
> Catch, ere she change, the Cynthia of this minute. (17–20)

[61] Maynard Mack, ed., *The Augustans*, English Masterpieces, Vol. 5, 2nd edn. (Englewood Cliffs, 1961), p. 30.

He poses as one of 'those free Painters', to whom Homer is compared in the notes to the *Iliad*, 'who . . . had only made here and there a few very significant Strokes, that give Form and Spirit to all the Piece':[62]

> Pictures like these, dear Madam, to design,
> Asks no firm hand, and no unerring line;
> Some wand'ring touch, or some reflected light,
> Some flying stroke alone can hit 'em right:
> For how should equal Colours do the knack?
> Chameleons who can paint in white and black? (151–6)

This painter is all 'dash' and 'vaghezza', like Kneller in Pope's exuberant characterization (i. 466), or Reynolds later in the century, a painter of moments, not hours.

It is obvious that the portraits in Pope's poem, introduced as momentary sketches which emerge antithetically precise, as finished as any portraits in literature, cannot literally be compared to paintings. At the same time there is a significant metaphorical connection. In a note introducing his gallery of Beauties Pope describes them as 'instances of contrarieties, given even from such Characters as are most strongly mark'd and seemingly therefore most consistent'.[63] As we have seen, the painting considered as an artifact was defined as a system of contrasts; seeming consistency is a description of the medium of painting as well as the character of women. Paintings are thus useful vehicles for the concept of character illustrated by portraits of the 'affected', 'softnatured', 'Cunning and Artful', 'Whimsical', 'Lewd and Vicious', 'Witty and Refined', all culminating in the full-length prototypical portrait of Atossa, 'scarce once herself, by turns all Womankind' (116), who 'finds all her life one warfare on earth' (118).

In the *Essay on Man* (1733) Pope uses the metaphor of painting to suggest how this 'Chaos of Thought and Passion, all confus'd' (II, 13) can be restored to order. Man must form his own character like the artist, by composing the contrarieties of his nature, like the colours of the painter, into a harmonious design:

> Passions, like Elements, tho' born to fight,
> Yet, mix'd and soften'd, in his work unite:
>
> . . .

[62] *Iliad*, V. 116; *TE* vii. 272.

[63] *TE* iii. ii, 50, l. 21 n.

Love, Hope, and Joy, fair pleasure's smiling train,
Hate, Fear, and Grief, the family of pain;
These mix'd with art, and to due bounds confin'd,
Make and maintain the balance of the mind:
The lights and shades, whose well accorded strife
Gives all the strength and colour of our life. (II, 111–12; 117–22)

He suggests that reason composes the contrarieties of man's nature into a self-portrait:

This light and darkness in our chaos join'd,
What shall divide? The God within the mind.
Extremes in Nature equal ends produce,
In Man they join to some mysterious use;
Tho' each by turns the other's bound invade,
As, in some well-wrought picture, light and shade,
And oft so mix, the diff'rence is too nice
Where ends the Virtue, or begins the Vice. (II, 203–10)

Thus he achieves what Maynard Mack has aptly called 'creative equilibrium'.[64] Such is the equanimity of a woman like Martha Blount who is 'blest with Temper, whose unclouded ray/Can make to morrow chearful as to day' (*To a Lady*, 257–8), or of a man like Bathurst:

Oh teach us, Bathurst! yet unspoil'd by wealth!
That secret rare, between th'extremes to move
Of mad Good-nature, and of mean Self-love. (*To Bathurst*, 226–8)

iii. SISTER ARTS IN THE *EPISTLE TO JERVAS*

The *Epistle to Jervas* supplies a synthesis of Pope's ideas about the relationships between painting and poetry which is more profound than his brilliant paraphrase of the doctrine *ut pictura poesis* in the lines quoted at the beginning of this chapter. He compares the relationship between painting and poetry in the poem metaphorically to human friendship and to the interaction of complementary colours:

Smit with the love of Sister-arts we came,
And met congenial, mingling flame with flame;

[64] *TE* iii. i, lv.

Like friendly colours found them both unite,
And each from each contract new strength and light.

. . .

How oft' our slowly-growing works impart,
While images reflect from art to art? (13–16; 19–20)

'Friendly colours' signify either complementary colours disposed to unite, as Richardson says, or masses of colour composed in a picture.[65] The 'Union of Colours', one of the prized principles of painting explained by Du Fresnoy, depends upon the capacity of colour and light to 'reflect on each other, that which is naturally and properly their own'. Du Fresnoy further explains that 'objects in the same light . . . should participate of each others colours'.[66] Pope's metaphor implies both the integrity of each art and their disposition to unite like the temperaments of congenial friends.

But Pope's poem is not concerned with definition of the boundaries between the arts, but with larger concerns which unite all artists, painters, and poets, the life of the imagination, and a perennial theme of the Renaissance poet—the relationship of the artist to time, of his art to eternity. The question of the destiny of the artist is introduced in the opening lines of the poem, which urge Jervas in reading Du Fresnoy, to 'wish, like theirs [Du Fresnoy and Dryden], our fate and fame',

So mix'd our studies, and so join'd our name,
Like them to shine thro' long succeeding age,
So just thy skill, so regular my rage. (10–12)

The artist can be deluded into believing that he has nothing to fear from time. Three couplets each beginning with 'How oft' (ll. 17 ff.) give the reassuring sense that the artist exists outside time in the spacious world of the imagination. But the last one contains ominous overtones.[67]

How oft' in pleasing tasks we wear the day,
While summer suns roll unperceiv'd away? (17–18)

The passage of time is relentless, even if unperceived. Moreover, throughout the vision of '*Rome*'s pompous glories rising to our thought' (l. 24) we are

[65] 'Of Colouring', *Theory of Painting* (1715), p. 149. [66] *Art of Painting* (1716), p. 47.
[67] See Thomas Edwards, *This Dark Estate: A Reading of Pope* (Berkeley and Los Angeles, 1963), p. 2.

impressed simultaneously with the powers of the artist's imagination to re-create the past, and at the same time with the truth that these are only the 'flatt'ring scenes' of 'wand'ring fancy' (l. 23). The arts of a whole civilization have largely vanished, and more recent works are beginning to decay—'A fading Fresco here demands a sigh' (l. 34).

In the same visionary passage reference to the monuments of Raphael and Virgil reminds the artist of his mortality. It is some consolation that Raphael's art still lives to inspire artists like Pope and Jervas. Thus Pope consoles his friend for the loss of his favourite subject, the Countess of Bridgewater. He insists that Jervas's portraits of the Countess will make a monument more lasting than the marble of her tomb described in ll. 47–54:

> Yet still her charms in breathing paint engage;
> Her modest cheek shall warm a future age.
> Beauty, frail flow'r that ev'ry season fears,
> Blooms in thy colours for a thousand years.
> Thus *Churchill*'s race shall other hearts surprize,
> And other Beauties envy *Worsley*'s eyes,
> Each pleasing *Blount* shall endless smiles bestow,
> And soft Belinda's blush for ever glow. (55–62)

But the force of this consolation is qualified in the final verse paragraph in which Pope concedes that however the graces adorn Jervas's canvas and the Muses inspire his own numbers:

> Alas! how little from the grave we claim?
> Thou but preserv'st a Face and I a Name. (77–8)

Paint, Pope realized, was the most perishable of artistic mediums: the colours of paint, as we have observed, are symbolic of transience and mutability in his verse.[68] The metaphor in the *Essay on Criticism*, comparing the mutability of language to painting, precisely parallels Pope's meaning in the *Epistle to Jervas*:

> Our Sons their Fathers' failing Language see,
> And such as Chaucer is, shall Dryden be.
> So when the faithful Pencil has design'd
> Some bright Idea of the Master's Mind,

[68] See *Rape of the Lock*, *V*, 27–8, *TE* ii. 201; and *Windsor Forest*, ll. 307–8, *TE* i. 178.

Where a new World leaps out at his command,
And ready Nature waits upon his Hand;
When the ripe Colours soften and unite,
And sweetly melt into just Shade and Light,
When mellowing Years their full Perfection give,
And each Bold Figure just begins to Live;
The treach'rous Colours the fair Art betray,
And all the bright Creation fades away! (482–93)

Painting illustrates for Pope the exciting voyage of discovery of artistic creation, the colourful brilliance of the created artifact, and the bitter knowledge that art must decay. There is a simultaneous awareness in all Pope's references to painting of the sensuous brilliance of colour, and of its transience. Thus the allusions to Jervas's paintings 'Where life awakes, and dawns at ev'ry line' (l. 4), and the 'endless streams of fair ideas' which 'strike in the sketch, or in the picture glow' (l. 44) are richly ironic.

How little hope remains for the 'fate and fame' of the artists, painter or poet, to 'shine thro' long succeeding age' (l. 11), is expressed by Pope in the *Imitations of Horace* (Ep. I, vi), when he compares Time itself to a portrait painter:

Yet Time ennobles, or degrades each Line;
It brighten'd CRAG's, and may darken thine:
And what is Fame? The Meanest have their day,
The Greatest can but blaze, and pass away. (44–7)

Part II. Landscape Gardening

3. 'The Visionary Scene': Pope's Sensibility to Landscape

THE landscape garden, which began gradually to supplant gardens organized on formal, architectural principles early in the eighteenth century, was the product of a coincidence of the sister arts of painting and poetry—a striking illustration of the way images reflect from art to art in the age. It has recently been recognized that the landscape garden was the conception of men of letters, and, since the eighteenth century, that Pope was one of its founders. As John Summerson has remarked, early landscape gardeners were imitating in their designs 'the sensibility of the man of letters (especially Pope) to his surroundings'.[1] But Pope's contribution to the development of the landscape garden has remained obscure precisely because his sensibility to his surroundings has not been taken into account. His 'rules' of gardening in the *Epistle to Burlington* have rarely been distinguished from the ideas of an ever-lengthening line of prophets of the landscape garden extending from Evelyn to Addison. His practice, just now emerging from the obscurity which surrounds the whole subject, has been confusingly interpreted as consistent or inconsistent with a theory of natural gardening imperfectly understood.[2]

[1] *Architecture in Britain 1530–1830*, 5th edn. rev. (Baltimore, 1969), p. 204.

[2] Maren-Sofie Røstvig nominates Timothy Nourse, author of *Campania Felix* (1700), as a prophet of the picturesque in *The Happy Man: Studies in the Metamorphoses of a Classical Ideal* (Oslo, 1954–8), ii. 73; and A. J. Sambrook finds another early witness for irregularity in the description of Petersham in a letter from Samuel Molyneux (1713) in 'Pope's Neighbours: An Early Landscape Garden at Richmond', *Journal of the Warburg and Courtauld Institute*, 30 (1967), 444–6. In the debate about the consistency of Pope's theory and practice in gardening, B. Sprague Allen in *Tides in English Taste* (Cambridge, Mass., 1937), ii. 130–1, argues that Pope 'admirably illustrates the gap between theory and practice' and that Twickenham 'belied his own principles of naturalistic design'; the same view persists in Derek Clifford, *A History of Garden Design* (London, 1962), pp. 134–5; Pope's consistency is defended by A. Lynn Altenbernd, 'On Pope's "Horticultural Romanticism"', *Journal of English and Germanic Philology*, 54 (Oct. 1955),

Consequently, Pope's important part in the development of the landscape garden has not been adequately explained.[3]

Accordingly this study of Pope's contribution to the landscape garden begins with an investigation of his sensibility to landscape on the premiss that his 'Precepts' in gardening 'teach but what his Works inspire' (*Essay on Criticism*, l. 660). The following chapters attempt to demonstrate that descriptions of landscape in his poetry, translations, and prose reveal the strongest evidence yet encountered of his literary pictorialism, and indicate a complex response to picturesque landscape which had an important influence on the development of aesthetics later in the century; that his practice of gardening at Twickenham and elsewhere can be distinguished from that of his contemporaries by

470–7; Røstvig, *The Happy Man*, ii. 76–7; Edward Malins, *English Landscaping and Literature, 1660–1840* (Oxford, 1966), p. 37, and by H. F. Clark, in 'Lord Burlington's Bijou or Sharawaggi at Chiswick', *Architectural Review*, 95 (May 1944), 127, who observes that 'this gap between theory and practice is . . . more apparent than real'.

[3] Christopher Hussey, 'Introduction', Margaret Jourdain, *The Work of William Kent* (London, 1948), p. 15. Pope's biographers, who have considered his interest in gardening as a footnote to his literary career, make summary and sceptical acknowledgement of his influence: E.C., iii. 166–7, v. 182–3; Sherburn, *Early Career*, pp. 277–88; Bonamy Dobrée, *Alexander Pope* (London, 1951), pp. 69–71. Historians of gardening and intellectual history have not had the facts to make an adequate estimate of Pope's contribution to the landscape garden: see the summary notice of Pope in Elizabeth Manwaring, *Italian Landscape*, pp. 126–8; the low estimate of Pope's importance compared to Walpole in Isabella W. U. Chase, *Horace Walpole: Gardenist* (Princeton, 1943), pp. 106–9; and the serious and influential misrepresentation of Pope by Christopher Hussey in *The Picturesque, Studies in a Point of View* (1927; repr. London, 1967), pp. 30–1; Hussey has recently re-evaluated Pope in 'The Poet and the Painter', chap. 5 of *English Gardens and Landscapes 1700–1750* (London, 1967). Brief reviews of Pope's role in the history of gardening are found in recent histories by Ralph Dutton, *The English Garden* (New York, 1938), pp. 81–4; H. F. Clark, *The English Landscape Garden* (London, 1948), the best short history extant, and Osvald Sirén, 'Alexander Pope, Charles Bridgeman, and William Kent', chap. 4 of *China and the Gardens of Europe of the Eighteenth Century* (New York, 1950). A good historical evaluation of Pope's gardening is Miles Hadfield's 'The Landskip 1720–1780; Poet and Painter: Pope and Kent', chap. 5 of *Gardening in Britain* (London, 1960). Nikolaus Pevsner helps to correct Hussey's distorted view of Pope in 'The Genesis of the Picturesque', *Architectural Review*, 96 (Nov. 1944), 142–4. Peter E. Martin in 'Pope and the Garden: A Background, Biographical, and Critical Study' (Ph.D. dissertation, Syracuse University, 1968) discusses the seventeenth-century origins of Pope's ideas on gardening. Maynard Mack gives an excellent account of Pope's classical conception of garden design in *The Garden and the City* pp. 51–7. In a recent discussion of the development of the landscape garden Susan Lang steadfastly cleaves to Hussey's view, insisting that Pope's garden was not a 'true landscape garden', and that 'Pope's . . . gardening activity had nothing to do with landscape gardens'. 'The Genesis of the English Landscape Garden', in *The Picturesque Garden and its Influence Outside the British Isles*, ed. Nikolaus Pevsner, Dumbarton Oaks Colloquium on the History of Landscape Architecture, vol. 2 (Washington, 1974), 19–20.

16. Landscape sketch by Pope.

17. Map of Clifton, showing the Hotwells, St. Vincent's Rock, and Durdham Down.

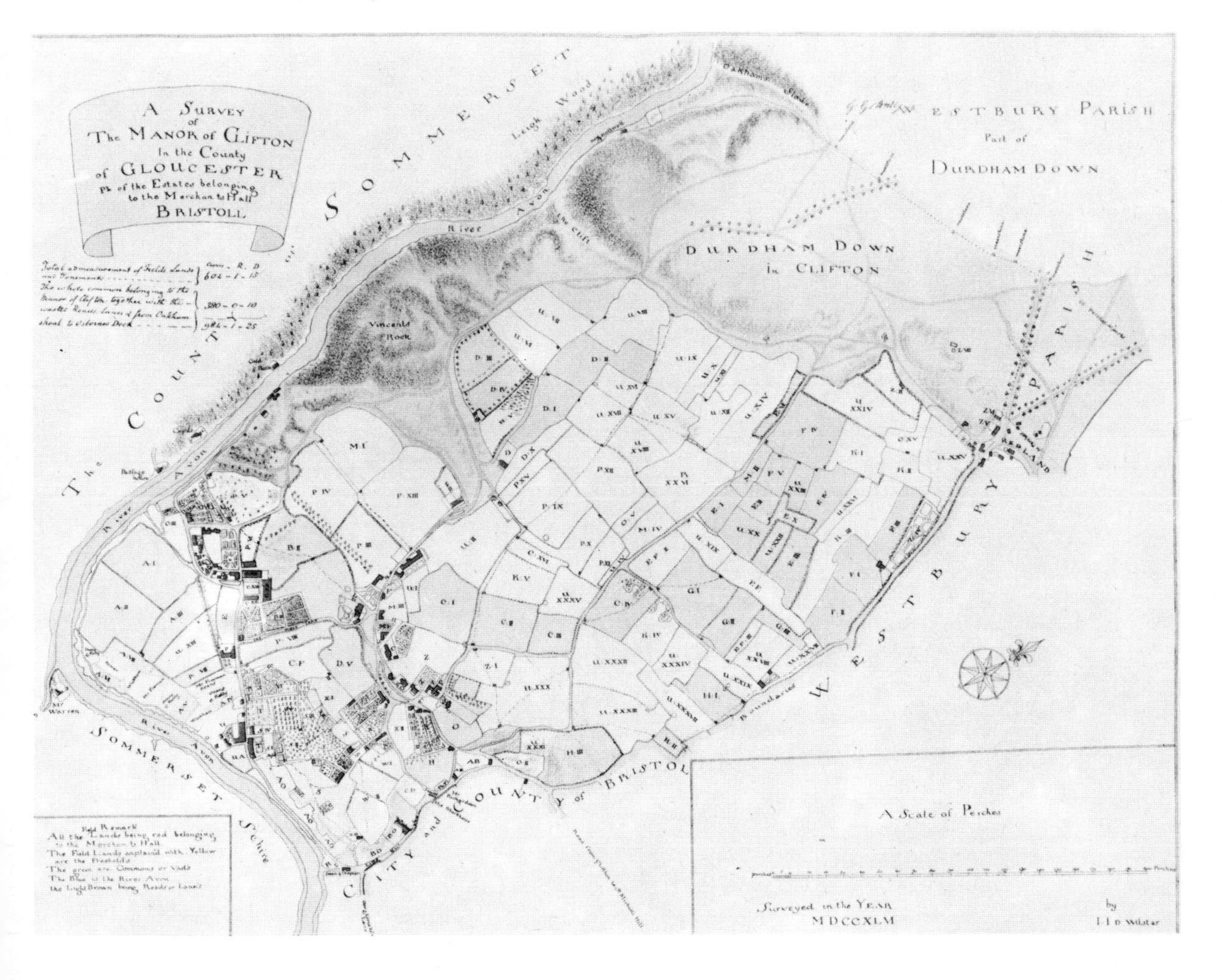

18. View of St. Vincent's Rock and the Hotwells at Clifton. By Thomas Smith. 1756.

19. Broad Quay, Bristol. *c.* 1725.

the application of picturesque principles of design; and finally, that his influence on professional and amateur designers of gardens recognized throughout the century as models of the landscape style is the result of his particular sensibility to the picturesque.

Contrary to the influential view of Christopher Hussey that 'Pope . . . had little appreciation of picturesque landscape', his poetry of natural description, limited as it is, contains evidence of a powerful pictorial imagination and an unusual sensibility to picturesque landscape. Hussey finds only 'crowds of personifications' and 'no visualization' in Pope's landscape, but he was looking for 'pictures', specifically paintings by Claude Lorrain and Gaspar Poussin, masters of the seventeenth-century tradition of ideal landscape, his touchstones of the picturesque. He claims to have found them in Thomson, who was helpful enough to allude to Claude in his descriptions, and accordingly he anoints Thomson the apostle of picturesque landscape in the eighteenth century. But Hussey's judgement, based on the same critical confusion of the arts which we observed in the last chapter, distorts the nature of Thomson's landscape, and completely overlooks the distinguishing mark of Pope's.[4]

Ironically Pope's contemporaries and a number of modern readers have discovered in Pope pictures of exactly the kind Hussey finds in Thomson. It is as plausible to look for a Claude in Pope as in Thomson, because the taste for that painter, it is now known, was widespread in England from the end of the seventeenth century, and Pope would have encountered examples in many of the collections he knew.[5] Pope was himself a collector of landscape paintings (plate 12). The landscape painters he most admired in the English school, Peter Tillemans (1684–1734) and John Wootton (1678?–1765), both exemplify the transition from topographical to ideal landscape in the early eighteenth century, the tendency of the strictly topographical view to yield to the style of Gaspar Poussin and stage design.[6] But taste in painting, the poet's

[4] *The Picturesque*, pp. 30–1. For Hussey's critics see below, nn. 62, 65.

[5] See Henry V. S. Ogden and Margaret S. Ogden, *English Taste in Landscape in the Seventeenth Century* (Ann Arbor, 1955), pp. 128, 162–4; Jonathan Richardson Sr. owned nearly sixty drawings by Claude, 'next to Chatsworth, the largest representation of his century', according to Marcel Roethlisberger, *Claude Lorrain: The Drawings* (Berkeley and Los Angeles, 1968), p. 71.

[6] On Tillemans and Wootton, see Vertue, i. 101, iii. 14; see also M. H. Grant, *A Chronological History of Old English Landscape Painters* (3 vols., London, 1925), i. 74, ii. 80–1; George E. Kendall,

or the critic's, is a poor index of poetic sensibility to landscape, and an inadequate basis for distinguishing between the character of landscape in Thomson and Pope.

This difference is indicated by a remark Pope made to Joseph Spence criticizing Thomson's natural description:

> 'Tis a great fault in descriptive poetry to describe everything [that is one fault in Thomson's *Seasons*]. The good ancients (but when I named them I meant Virgil) have no long descriptions, commonly not above ten lines, and scarce ever thirty. (No. 384)

Pope strictly adhered to a classical poetic of natural description which allowed him no 'long Descriptions', and permitted him no prospect poem, much less a *Seasons*.[7] Nevertheless, despite this constraint, perhaps because of it, Pope makes a powerful appeal to the pictorial imagination in the description of landscape. It might be argued that Pope is as much the poet of the picturesque as Thomson is of the sublime landscape.[8]

i. SCENE DESIGN IN THE *PASTORALS*

In the *Pastorals* (1709) we see clearly how Pope's sensibility to the picturesque modifies the classical idiom of natural description. The description of landscape in the *Pastorals* belongs to the classical tradition of ideal landscape,

'Notes on the Life of John Wootton', Walpole Society, vol. 21 (Oxford, 1933), 23–42; Deborah Howard, 'Some Eighteenth-Century English Followers of Claude', *Burlington Magazine*, iii (December, 1969), 726–33. According to the 'Inventory', Pope owned at least ten landscapes, including views of Twickenham and Richmond (pp. 254–5); 'a Landskip by Titeman' (probably Peter Tillemans, p. 253); 'a Ruen by Wooten' (p. 254), possibly the classical landscape now at Mapledurham; 'a Vew [*sic*] of Sr John St. Aubins House and Landskip' (p. 253), perhaps Clowance, Cornwall, plate xxii in William Borlase, *The Natural History of Cornwall* (Oxford, 1758), facing p. 219, or the house on St. Michael's Mount in Penzance owned by St. Aubin which 'he had restored from a ruined monastic cell to a comfortable dwelling-house'. See 'William Borlase, St. Aubyn, and Pope. MS. Collections at Castle Horneck, 1720–1772', *Quarterly Review*, 139 (July–Oct. 1875), 379; 'View of St. Michael's Mount in Cornwall', plate xxix, facing p. 351 in William Borlase, *Observations on the Antiquities Historical and Monumental, of the County of Cornwall* (Oxford, 1754); Christopher Hussey, 'St. Michael's Mount—I–II, Cornwall', *Country Life*, 56 (1 and 8 Nov. 1924), 679, 718.

[7] See Pope's ridicule of 'long Descriptions' in 'A Receit to Make an Epick Poem', *Guardian*, No. 78 (1713), in *Prose*, p. 117. Thomson presented Pope with a copy of the first collected edition of the *Seasons* illustrated by William Kent (1730), with an inscription on the flyleaf: C. R. Manning, 'Thomson's *Seasons*', *Notes & Queries*, 4th Ser., 11 (24 May 1873), 434.

[8] See *Portraits*, p. 7. Cf. Ault, pp. 89–90.

explicated by Ernst Curtius.[9] All the requisites of the *locus amoenus* can be found, with a distinct suggestion of the garden, in the idyllic descriptions of the variety of shady trees and flowers, murmuring springs, grassy banks, fountains, and groves. The landscape serves its traditional literary purpose as mirror of man's emotions:

> Thro' Rocks and Caves the Name of Delia sounds,
> Delia, each Cave and echoing Rock rebounds. (*Autumn*, 49–50)

And, as always in this tradition, it is alleged to be numinous with the presence of divinity:

> See what Delights in Sylvan Scenes appear!
> Descending Gods have found Elysium here. (*Summer*, 59–60)

Reuben Brower has given the best account of the way Pope's pictorial imagination colours this classical landscape. Pope transforms the Gods and *mythos* of Theocritus 'almost to mere picture'. He heightens the landscape of Virgil 'not photographically but in a painter's fashion, through selected visual impressions of light, shade, colour, and movement', endowing the landscape with extraordinary animation by the power of what Brower calls the 'mythological eye': 'what survives from the past and what we do believe in is the transformation of the landscape to the eye'.[10]

Another revealing indication of Pope's pictorial imagination in the *Pastorals*, which has not been commented on, is the analogy he appears to draw between landscape and stage scenery, explicit in the notes and implicit in the composition of the poems. In his *Discourse on Pastoral Poetry* (1717) he insists that each eclogue should 'contain some particular beauty in itself, and that it be different in every eclogue. Besides in each of them a design'd scene or prospect is to be presented to our view, which should likewise have its variety.'[11] The suggestion that the 'design'd scene' includes reference to painted scenery in the theatre is supported by the primary sense of the word 'scene' as used by Pope and his contemporaries 'with reference to the theatre'.[12] Still more indicative,

[9] 'The Ideal Landscape', chap. 10 in *European Literature and the Latin Middle Ages* (New York, 1953).

[10] *The Poetry of Allusion*, pp. 23–4, 26.

[11] *TE* i. 27–8.

[12] *OED*, s.v. 'Scene'. Cf. Pope's reference to the unities, and 'one unbroken Scene in each Eclogue' in his attack on Philips in the *Guardian* (No. 40, 1713), *Prose*, pp. 99–100.

the notes Pope added to the 1736 and succeeding editions of the poem are suggestive of stage directions:

Spring: The Scene of this Pastoral a Vally, the Time the Morning (l. 17 n.).
Summer: The Scene of this Pastoral by the River's side; suitable to the heat of the season; the Time, Noon (l. 3 n.).
Autumn: The Scene, a Hill; the Time, at Sun-set (headnote).
Winter: The Scene of this Pastoral lies in a grove, the Time at midnight (headnote).

The concluding lines of 'Winter' (88–92) recapitulate these scenes, as Pope observes in his note: 'These four last lines allude to the several Subjects of the four Pastorals, and to the several Scenes of them, particularized before in each.'

The notes were added later, and they are conventional in the literature of the time, but they confirm the impression that Pope attempted to compose a 'design'd scene' of observed landscape, distinct from the ideal landscape of the shepherd's complaint, in each of the pastorals. Only once, in 'Autumn', does he describe a landscape at length, but the scene is sharply evoked at the beginning and end of each eclogue, reinforced by a few pointed allusions in the complaints. For example in 'Spring', after the Exordium and apostrophe to Trumbull in the opening lines where the landscape description is generalized, the shepherd's debate is introduced by the following passage, a *compositio loci* of the scene indicated in the note—'a Vally, the Time the Morning':

Soon as the Flocks shook off the nightly Dews,
Two Swains, whom Love kept wakeful, and the Muse,
Pour'd o'er the whitening Vale their fleecy Care,
Fresh as the Morn, and as the Season fair:
The Dawn now blushing on the Mountain's Side,
Thus Daphnis spoke, and Strephon thus reply'd. (17–22)

A few more details of the scene are 'particularized' before the contest begins, introduced by adverbs contemporary readers regarded as hints of perspective[13] —'yon slow Oxen' (l. 30), 'yon' Lamb that near the Fountain plays' (l. 33), and including observations which show that Pope can speak of the 'bright Crocus and blue Vi'let' (l. 31) as well as Venus and Ceres (ll. 65–6). Once the singing contest begins the landscape reverts to the kind of unparticularized literary

[13] See Jean Hagstrum, *The Sister Arts*, p. 293.

landscape—allegorical, historical, and mythological—which dominates the poem.[14] Finally, after the conclusion of the contest, Pope reminds us once more of the 'scene' which frames the action by the emphatic summons to 'see!':

> Now rise, and haste to yonder Woodbine Bow'rs,
> A soft Retreat from sudden vernal Show'rs;
> The Turf with rural Dainties shall be Crown'd,
> While opening Blooms diffuse their Sweets around.
> For see! the gath'ring Flocks to Shelter tend,
> And from the Pleiads fruitful Show'rs descend. (97–102)

Again in 'Summer' and 'Winter' ideal landscape dominates the shepherds complaints, but vignettes of observed landscape are introduced at the beginning and end, with occasional allusions to particular features of the landscape. In 'Autumn' the pattern is varied when the initial *compositio* is reduced to a couplet, but an extended description of a prospect appropriate to the scene, 'a Hill at Sun-set', is introduced in the middle of this most rhetorically stylized complaint, 'Go gentle Gales, and bear my Sighs along':

> Resound ye Hills, resound my mournful Strain!
> Of perjur'd Doris, dying I complain:
> Here where the Mountains less'ning as they rise,
> Lose the low Vales, and steal into the Skies.
> While lab'ring Oxen, spent with Toil and Heat,
> In their loose Traces from the Field retreat;
> While curling Smokes from Village-Tops are seen,
> And the fleet Shades glide o'er the dusky Green. (57–64)

Here Pope produces a strong illusion of the pictorial, with the defined point of view in which the eye is led from background to foreground and then to mid-ground, with a suggestion of perspective, together with impressions of movement which animate the scene and charge the atmosphere.

The possibility that Pope's response to landscape in the *Pastorals*, and later to natural scenery and gardens, was influenced by scene design in the theatre is strengthened by his reaction to the stage spectacle of his time. Landscapes, some in the idealized tradition of history painting and the heroic play, others

[14] See l. 86, alluding to 'the Royal Oak, in which Charles the second had been hid from the pursuit after the battle of Worcester'. *TE* i. 69 n.

in the topographical tradition of London comedy, were an important part of the contemporary scene-painter's output. Moreover, such landscapes were enjoyed by audiences in the Georgian playhouse with all the exciting effects made possible by changeable scenery, the major technical innovation of the Restoration stage. Sliding flats moving in grooves horizontally across the stage allowed scenes to be suddenly 'opened' to view, or left partially open, cut-out, or staggered in a perspective of 'broken views'. Richard Southern emphasizes that this changing of scenes '*always took place under the eyes of the audience* and was part of the excitement and spectacle of the swiftly-moving show'.[15] The effect all this had on Pope is obvious from his exuberant satire of stage effects in the *Rape of the Lock* and the *Dunciad*.[16] As we will see, Pope's language of natural description and his idea of garden design appear to have been influenced by the stage.[17]

ii. LANDSCAPE IN POPE'S HOMER

Since the eighteenth century the picturesque landscape description in Pope's Homer has been admired, and it has been recognized that 'if we turn to the original, we shall seldom, or never, find these landscapes. They are of Mr. Pope's painting; sometimes suggested by a single epithet.'[18] Pope's Homer illustrates his sense of picturesque landscape more extensively than the *Pastorals*. And it was here that he began to write the notes on the 'scenes' which indicate his interest in topographical landscape. In the 'Argument' of Book II, for example, we are told 'The Scene lies in the Graecian-Camp and upon the Sea-

[15] *The Georgian Playhouse* (London, 1948), p. 21. See Southern's *Changeable Scenery: Its Origin and Development in the British Theatre* (London, 1952), pp. 17, 209, 272–81, and Allardyce Nicoll, *Restoration Drama 1660–1700*, 4th edn. rev. (Cambridge, 1952), i. 41–3.

[16] On Pope's interest in the theatre, see Malcolm Goldstein, *Pope and the Augustan Stage*, Stanford Studies in Language and Literature, 17 (Stanford, 1958).

[17] See Susan Lang, 'Genesis of the Landscape Garden', The Picturesque Garden and its Influence (1974), p. 27: she asserts that the 'influence of the theatre' was 'the decisive factor . . . in the earlier phases of the eighteenth century garden'.

[18] Thomas Twining, *Aristotle's Treatise on Poetry* (London, 1789), i. 31. Cf. Norman Ault, 'Mr. Alexander Pope: Painter', in *New Light on Pope*, pp. 91–5; Jean Hagstrum, *The Sister Arts*, pp. 229–33; Mario Praz, 'La Versione dell "Iliade" ', chap. 7 in *La poesia di Pope et le sue origini* (Rome, 1962), pp. 157–255; and D. R. Clarke, 'Landscape Painting Effects in Pope's Homer', *Journal of Aesthetics and Art Criticism*, 22 (1963), 25–8.

Shore; toward the end it removes to Troy.' In Book XIII where 'the Scene is between the Grecian Wall and the Sea-Shore', he reminds us that 'the Poet now shifts the Scene', and remarks how well the description is contrived so that 'the Reader might take notice of this Change of Place, and carry distinctly in his Mind each Scene of Action':

> As the Poet is so very exact in describing each Scene as in a Chart or Plan, the Reader ought to be careful to trace each Action in it; otherwise he will see nothing but Confusion in things which are in themselves very regular and distinct.[19]

To assist the reader Pope provides in the 'Essay on Battels', appended to Book IV of the *Iliad*, 'a short View of the Scene of War, the Situation of Troy, and those Places which Homer mentions, with the proper Field of each Battel', illustrated by a topographical engraving, *Troyja cum locis pertingentibus*, drawn by John Harris (plate 13), where the reader can find with the help of a key the Monument of Ilus or 'The Tomb of Æsyetes, [which] commanded the Prospect of the Fleet, and that Part of the Sea-coast'.[20]

An admirable example of Pope's ability to trace Homer's action as in a chart or plan occurs in a long note at the conclusion of Book X of the *Iliad*:

> I cannot conclude the Notes to this Book without observing, that what seems the principal Beauty of it, and what distinguishes it among all the others, is the Liveliness of its Paintings: The Reader sees the most natural Night-Scene in the World . . . . We see the very Colour of the Sky, know the Time to a Minute, are impatient while the Heroes are arming, our Imagination steals out after them, becomes privy to all their Doubts, and even to the secret Wishes of their Hearts sent up to *Minerva*. . . . We are perfectly acquainted with the Situation of all the Forces, with the Figure in which they lie, with the Disposition of *Rhesus* and the *Thracians*, with the Posture of his Chariot and Horses. The marshy Spot of Ground where *Dolon* is killed, the Tamarisk, or aquatick Plants upon which they hang his Spoils, and the Reeds that are heap'd together to mark the Place, are Circumstances the most Picturesque imaginable. And tho' it must be owned, that the human Figures in this Piece are excellent, and disposed in the properest Actions; I cannot but confess my Opinion, that the chief Beauty of it is in the Prospect, a finer than which was never drawn by any Pencil. (X, 677)

The passage is a striking illustration of Pope's pictorial imagination, his power to imagine an entire landscape which is scarcely suggested in the original. Even in Pope's translation there is not a single passage of natural description, only

[19] *TE* viii. 103, 146. [20] *TE* vii. 261–2, and plate 4, facing p. 252.

a few allusions to night, shade, reflected light (ll. 47, 113, 175), and four lines describing the approach of dawn (295–8)—nothing resembling a prospect. The night-scene is completely the product of his own imagination.

The most systematic pictorial analysis of Homer's description of landscape occurs in the 'Observations on the Shield of Achilles', where Pope paraphrases and comments on each of Homer's three descriptions of landscape on the shield —Tillage, Harvest, and Sheep (plate 14). Once again Pope reveals his own rather than Homer's pictorial imagination. For example, although his own paraphrase of Homer's description of 'Harvest' shows no sign of the pictorial, his commentary demonstrates in detail how the description might be composed into a painting:

> The Reapers on the Fore-ground, with their Faces towards the Spectators; the Gatherers behind, and the Children on the farther ground. The master of the Field, who is the chief Figure, may be set in the middle of the Picture with a strong Light upon him, in the Action of directing and pointing with his Scepter. The Oak, with the Servants under it, the Sacrifice, &c. on a distant Ground, would altogether make a beautiful Grouppe of great Variety.[21]

Elsewhere in the 'Observations' Pope commented on the detail in this description which he regarded as evidence of Homer's knowledge of aerial perspective: 'He tells us', Pope observes, 'that the Oak under which was spread the Banquet of the Reapers *stood apart*' (my italics).[22] Even less was required to inspire Pope in Homer's description of 'Sheep', which he envisions as 'an entire landscape without human figures', and proof of Homer's knowledge of perspective: 'What he says of the Valley sprinkled all over with Cottages and Flocks, appears to be a Description of a large Country in Perspective.'[23]

These 'Landscapes of a fine Country' referred to in the poetical index to the *Iliad*[24] and the prospects in his commentary are largely left to the imagination in Pope's translation. The way he appeals to the visual imagination of the reader can be illustrated by his translation of the catalogue, the landscape similes in the *Iliad*, and the 'prospects' of the *Odyssey*. In 'Observations on the

[21] *TE* viii. 369.

[22] *TE* viii. 365.

[23] *TE* viii. 365. Fern Farnham observes in 'Achilles' Shield', p. 1575: 'Pope has unmistakably visualized a landscape without a single human figure, such a landscape, moreover, as was hardly painted before the nineteenth century.'

[24] *TE* viii. 598.

Catalogue' appended to Book II of the *Iliad* Pope speaks of the alterations necessary to make it 'afford . . . Entertainment to an English Reader':

> There were but two things to be done to give it a chance to please him; to render the Versification very flowing and musical, and to make the whole appear as much a *Landscape* or *Piece of Painting* as possible. . . . For the latter Point I have ventured to open the Prospect a little, by the addition of a few Epithets or short Hints of Description to some of the Places mention'd; tho' seldom exceeding the Compass of half a Verse (the Space to which my Author himself generally confines these Pictures in Minature).[25]

Coleridge's view of Pope's Homer as 'the main source of our pseudo-poetic diction'[26] does not prepare us for what we find: not a gazetteer of arbitrary epithets, but diction derived from careful topographical and antiquarian research.

After complaining in a letter to Edward Blount (1714) of 'the negligence of the Geographers in their Maps of old Greece' (i. 246) Pope had a map of 'Graecia Homerica, Phrygia cum oris Maritimis' engraved for his quarto edition by John Senex (d. 1740) to accompany 'A Geographical Table of the Towns, &c. in Homer's Catalogue of Greece, with the Authorities for the Situation, as placed in this Map' in the 'Observations on the Catalogue'.[27] The manuscript of Pope's notes shows that he was not satisfied with the standard authorities on Homer, that he consulted a wide array of original sources on Homeric geography, and verified the situations of the place-names in his 'Geographical Table': 'The Table itself I thought but necessary to annex to the Map, as my Warrant for the Situations assign'd in it to several of the Towns.'[28] The landscape description which resulted from this research combines topographical accuracy with poetic significance. The historical and mythological allusions which epitomize the genius of each place give to Pope's short hints of description a higher specific gravity than Coleridge supposed.[29]

[25] *TE* vii. 176–7.

[26] *Biographia Literaria*, ed. Shawcross, i. 26 n.

[27] The map appears in Pope's quarto, vol. i, facing p. 184; for the 'Geographical Table' see *TE* vii. 177–85.

[28] *TE* vii. 177; Pope's study of geography in connection with the Homer commentary is discussed by Hans-Joachim Zimmermann, *Alexander Popes Noten zu Homer: Eine Manuskript-und Quellenstudie* (Heidelberg, 1966), pp. 38 ff., 50 n. 74, 103, 245.

[29] 'Mycalessia's ample Piny Plain' (l. 593), for example, is substantiated in the 'Table' on the authority of Strabo and Statius as a place 'famous for its Pine-trees'. 'Harma where Apollo's Prophet fell' (l. 595)

We have often been reminded that Pope's diction is 'unsuitable for the sweeps of landscape', and it is probably true that epithets are not sufficient to stimulate the imagination of modern readers accustomed to romantic descriptions of landscape.[30] But Pope and the eighteenth-century reader found them intensely stimulating to the visual imagination. Pope's readers would have seen in the catalogue as he did himself a 'universal picture' of landscape: 'pictures in miniature' in single epithets like 'Rocky Aulis' (590), or 'chalky Calydon' (776); and whole landscapes in a line when 'Titan hides his hoary Head in Snow' (894), or 'where Hills encircle Boebe's lowly Lake,/Where Pherae hears the neighb'ring Waters fall' (865–6).

Joseph Spence compliments Pope in *An Essay on Pope's Odyssey* (1726–7) for imitating the classical poetics of natural description: ''Tis by Epithets that the ancient Poets paint their *Elysian Groves*; and the Modern, their *Windsor-Forests*.'[31] Pope escaped his censure of contemporary writers who indulge in extensive description: 'Some fanciful Writers afford us nothing but Pictures and Descriptions: they continue Image after Image; and put one in Mind of those *Americans*, who, when first they were discover'd, are said to have us'd Painting instead of Writing' (ii. 164). Throughout the century readers responded imaginatively to Pope's hints of picturesque description, as Joseph Warton does when he declares lines in the *Imitations of Horace*, Ep. I, i, 'superior to the original' because 'a pleasing little landscape is added to the satire:

> Sir Job sail'd forth, the evening bright and still,
> "No place on earth (he cry'd), like Greenwich hill!"' (138–9)[32]

We have already discussed the sense in which Homer's similes are 'like pictures' in relation to the nightpiece in Book VIII. Elsewhere Pope's translation of Homer's similes illustrates the intensity of his pictorial response to

is the 'Town . . . near the Road from Thebes to Chalcis' where, according to Strabo, 'Amphiaraus was swallow'd by the Earth in his Chariot, from whence it receiv'd its Name.' *TE* vii. 177–8.

[30] John Traugott, 'Red'ning Phoebus', review of Geoffrey Tillotson, *Augustan Studies*, *Sewanee Review*, 72 (Winter, 1964), 167. Tillotson gives a sensitive account of the poetics of Pope's landscape description in his book, *On the Poetry of Pope*, p. 22, where he observes: 'In his mature work a landscape will often be allotted only a single couplet, sometimes two. But the space of those twenty syllables has the appearance of infinity. There is no other poet who habitually catches so much in a small glass.'

[31] 2 vols. (London, 1726–7, repr. 2 vols. in one, New York, 1972), ii. 18. Hereafter cited in the text.

[32] *Essay on Pope*, ii. 327.

landscape. He differs from 'all the Commentators' in his interpretation of the comparison between 'the present State of the Greeks, after Patroclus had extinguish'd the Flames' in Book XVI, and 'Jupiter dispersing a black Cloud which had cover'd a high Mountain, whereby a beautiful Prospect, which was before hid in Darkness, suddenly appears':[33]

> So when thick Clouds inwrap the Mountains Head,
> O'er Heav'ns Expanse like one black Cieling spread;
> Sudden, the Thund'rer, with a flashing Ray,
> Bursts thro' the Darkness, and lets down the Day:
> The Hills shine out, the Rocks in Prospect rise,
> And Streams, and Vales, and Forests strike the Eyes,
> The smiling Scene wide opens to the Sight,
> And all th'unmeasur'd Aether flames with Light. (XVI, 354–61)

Pope achieves this pictorial effect 'by increasing the "kinetic energy" of the scene', intensifying verbs and heightening the contrast of light and dark.[34]

Another illuminating example of a pictorial simile criticized by Joseph Spence occurs in Book XIV, the description of Nestor's reaction to the battle-field:

> Soon as the Prospect open'd to his View,
> His wounded Eyes the Scene of Sorrow knew;
>
> . . .
>
> As when old Ocean's silent Surface sleeps,
> The Waves just heaving on the purple Deeps;
> While yet th'expected Tempest hangs on high,
> Weighs down the Cloud, and blackens in the sky,
> The Mass of Waters will no Wind obey;
> Jove sends one Gust, and bids them roll away.
> While wav'ring Counsels thus his Mind engage,
> Fluctuates, in doubtful Thought, the Pylian Sage. (17–18; 21–8)

Spence objected that purple 'among us is confin'd to one colour, and that not very applicable to the Deep'.[35] Pope justifies his word by reference to painting and to observation of nature. In a note in the manuscript of Spence's *Essay on*

[33] *TE* viii. 256. [34] Reuben Brower, *The Poetry of Allusion*, p. 134.
[35] In Spence's manuscript of the *Essay*, *TE* x. 596 (Appendix H).

Pope's Odyssey he insists that 'the Sea is actually of a deep purple in many places, & in many views'.[36] In his note he defends the comparison from its critics by the aptness of the comparison that 'exactly represent[s] the State of an irresolute Mind' (XIV, 21).

These landscape similes in the *Iliad* reflect an interest in prospect which is even more conspicuous in the *Odyssey*, where opportunities for description of landscape, particularly coastal scenery, were more plentiful than in the *Iliad*, and where Pope reserved to himself for translation books containing the 'imaging and picturesque parts'.[37] Here we find the culmination of a fascination with prospect which can be observed throughout his early poetry.[38] In the *Essay on Pope's Odyssey* Joseph Spence dwells at length on Pope's 'Happiness in drawing Landscapes' (i. 64–8), praising particularly the succession of prospects of rocky coast, wood, city, and the gardens of Alcinous during Ulysses' adventures in Phaeacia (Books V–VII).

Spence admired still more Pope's masterful description of landscape as it appears to the observer in motion, 'this Idea of the Land seeming to sink and recede . . . very beautifully added [by Pope to Homer]' (i. 68–9) which is repeatedly experienced by Ulysses

> When lifted on a ridgy wave, he spies
> The land at distance, and with sharpen'd eyes. (*Od.* V, 504–5)

Throughout the *Odyssey* Pope makes an intense appeal to the visual imagination in his description of views of 'the dubious coast' (X, 180), 'sinking' and 'less'ning' (XIII, 95) 'upon our sight' (X, 33).[39]

Sometimes the effect of this picturesque vision of landscape is intensely

[36] *TE* x. 596. See 'Pope's Palette' in 'Mr. Alexander Pope: Painter', in Ault, pp. 82–100.

[37] *TE* ix. 26; *TE* x. 390, 'Postscript to the Odyssey'. For Pope's books of the *Odyssey*, see *TE* vii. ccii.

[38] See the 'design'd scene' of the *Pastorals*; the imagery of the *Essay on Criticism* with the Alpine prospect (ll. 219–32) that Johnson considered the finest comparison in literature; the winter-piece and 'Intellectual Scene' (ll. 11–20; 53–60) of the *Temple of Fame*; the opening lines of *Windsor Forest* (ll. 7–28), the 'inverted landscape' following the Lodona episode (ll. 211–14), and the moving landscape when 'The Youth rush eager to the Sylvan War', 'And Earth rolls back beneath the flying Steed' (ll. 148, 158).

[39] Cf. Book I, 76; III, 616, 628; V, 69, 357; VII, 354; X, 633; XIII, 95, 401–2. Cf. the account of Pope's 'picturesque' description in the *Iliad* by Mario Praz, 'La Verzione dell Iliade', chap. 7 of *La Poesia di Pope* (1962).

dramatic as in the description cited by Spence (i. 69–70) of Telemachus, when he sees

> The tow'rs of Pylos sink, its views decay,
> Fields after fields fly back, till close of day:
> Then sunk the Sun, and darken'd all the way.
>
> . . .
>
> Along the waving fields their way they hold,
> The fields receding as the chariot roll'd:
> Then slowly sunk the ruddy globe of light,
> And o'er the shaded landscape rush'd the night.
>
> (*Od.* III, 616–18; 627–30)

This is an evocative description of the changeable scenery of landscape with effects suggestive of stage lighting. Spence aptly calls landscapes like these in Pope's *Odyssey*, strongly appealing to the eye and the imagination, 'poetical Prospects' (i. 67). We encounter them again in Pope's experience as an observer of real prospects in the landscape.

iii. LANDSCAPE IN POPE'S LETTERS

As in Pope's poetry, the 'scene of Man' looms larger than landscape in his correspondence. Unlike the letters of Walpole, Shenstone, or Gray, Pope's letters contain few passages of extensive description of landscape or gardens. But what there is reveals in Pope a sensibility to picturesque landscape in natural scenery explicit enough to allow us to infer his adherence to something like an aesthetic of picturesque scenery: a taste for landscape visualized in terms of painting or stage design, containing the pictorial values of colour, light, and shade, organized according to perspective and 'a Picture for a point of Sight',[40] composed in terms of the painter's sense of ground, contrast, and balance, poetically significant and expressive of emotions which can be distinguished from sublime or romantic responses to landscape.

Among the correspondents who recognized Pope's interest in landscape and sent him descriptions of places they visited are John Gay, who described Dunster Castle near Minehead, Somersetshire, and the 'extensive view of the Bristol Channel' in a letter dated 1732 (iii. 322), and David Mallet, who gave

[40] *TE* viii. 366.

him an account of the 'delightfully romantic' seaport town of Tenby and Milford Haven in South Wales in 1734 (iii. 422). Long before, in 1717, Bishop Berkeley had written to Pope from Naples a long description of the island of Inarime (now called Ischia) he had recently visited, 'an Epitome of the whole Earth, containing within the compass of eighteen Miles, a wonderful variety of Hills, Vales; ragged Rocks, fruitful Plains, and barren Mountains, all thrown together in a most romantic Confusion' (i. 446), where from the top of the extinct volcano, Mount Epomeus, 'you have the finest Prospect in the World, surveying at one view, besides several pleasant Islands lying at your Feet, a tract of *Italy* about three hundred Miles in length, from the Promontory of *Antium*, to the Cape of Palinurus' (i. 446). It was an account which he knew would appeal to the author who had shown such a lively interest in classical topography, prospect, and landscape in the first volume of his *Iliad* (1715), one whom he evidently regarded as a landscape poet: 'this noble Landscape . . . would demand an Imagination as warm, and numbers as flowing as your own, to describe it' (i. 446).

It may be significant that nearly all of Pope's extended descriptions of landscape are addressed to a woman, his life-long friend Martha Blount.[41] Like Pope she had spent a childhood in the country in the picturesque situation of Mapledurham on the 'pretty windings of the Thames' (i. 308); she shared his taste for country life, for walks, for prospects and gardens, and undoubtedly had a higher tolerance for sentiment than Lady Mary who hilariously ridiculed Pope's sentimental account of a 'pastoral romance', the death of two rustic Devonshire lovers struck by lightning 'on a Haycock' (i. 495). Probably some of his descriptions are 'raised' to appeal to her but they provide us with a valuable insight into the aesthetic sensibility which created the landscape garden.

The most interesting of these letters to Martha Blount, recently released for publication,[42] establishes Pope as one of the first of a long line of picturesque tourists; he gives her an account which might rank as the archetype of the picturesque tour later cultivated by William Gilpin. He describes an excursion

[41] See Nicolson and Rousseau, *This Long Disease* (1968), pp. 209–19, for a discussion of Pope's letters to Martha Blount describing 'romantic' landscape.

[42] George S. Rousseau, ed., 'A New Pope Letter', *Philological Quarterly*, 45 (1966), 409–18. Page references in the text to this edition.

during the summer of 1734 in a yacht with his host Charles Mordaunt, Earl of Peterborough, down Southampton water to Netley Castle and Netley Abbey (plate 15). The letter recounts his amusing rivalry with his host, Peterborough, owner of Bevis Mount in Southampton, to choose the most picturesque spot for a picnic: hallooing to his companion in the thickets, straying into an impassable bog, overruled by Mordaunt on his choice—a regular grove of very high oaks which reminded him of the Mall in St. James's Park—following hungry and irritated in the footsteps of his 'Bold Leader', at last arriving at the Abbey, where he admits the prospect is striking (411, 413).

Throughout the description Pope's interest in architecture is subordinate to prospect and picturesque situation. This is conspicuous in the description (after disembarking), of the first view of Netley Castle:

When we came to the Shore, we were both struck with the beauty of it, a rising Hill very deeply hung with Woods, that fell quite in to the Water, & at the Edge of the Sea a very old min'd Castle. We were very hungry, but the aspect of the Towers, & the high crumbling Battlements, overgrown with Ivy, with a Square room in the middle out of which at three large arches you saw the Main Sea, & all the windings of the Coasts on the Side next us, provoked us first to look in, in order to chuse the best place to dine in. (411)

Here he shows that love of prospect, views of winding coastal landscape, framed in a picturesque manner by arches, which we would expect of the translator of the picturesque parts of the *Odyssey*. In his rambles in the vicinity the same fascination with picturesque prospect appears, when he sees objects in perspective relationships: a barn 'thro' a glade of Trees' (413), the sea 'by fits thro the trees' (413), a panoramic coastal landscape 'opening in a hundred broken views' (413), a reference to stage scenery, as will be seen below. He demonstrates his power to imagine the prospect from 'a large plain very highly seated' some distance above, 'from which I conclude the whole prospect of the Sea, the Isle of Wight on two sides, Southampton, & Two Rivers farther off, must undoubtedly be seen at once' (417).

Pope gives an animated account of Netley Abbey, the 'Ruin of a large Monastery' (413) he found 'very Extensive' (415):

the Shell . . . of a Church, not much less than the Body of that at Westminster, a whole side of windows entire, to the number of eight great arches; the End window over the Altar vastly high, & the whole wrought finely with old Gothic ornaments: one Part of the Roof, which seemed to have been under the Steeple, was yet standing, but lookd terribly, it was above 60 foot high, & hung like Net work, so thin & so fine, over our heads: No part of Westminster abby is more ornamented. (415)

In his enthusiastic comparison to Westminster Pope more than doubled the length of the Abbey (250 to 530 feet), although the modern architectural historian recognizes the similarity in decorative motif, and the possibility that the same mason was responsible for it.[43] But once again Pope's main concern is with the picturesque landscape beauty of the ruins, their situation and their picturesque aspect: 'a great number of Vaults & Rooms, coverd with Ivy and Weeds, & some Flowers ... the whole Quire of the Church ... fill'd with fallen Fretworks, & window frames of Stone, mixed with high heaps of Rubbish, & great Trees of Elder &c. growing among them' (415). Finally, his eagerness to sketch the ruins (415–16) is indicative of the picturesque tourist. Although Pope's sketches of Netley Abbey have disappeared, a pencil drawing of Twickenham village, an example of his landscape artistry, has survived on the flyleaf of one of his books (plate 16).[44]

It surprised Pope that Peterborough had 'never once heard mention of so remarkable a Monastery' (417), 'Ruins of the finest Abbey & Castle', Pope wrote to Oxford, 'I ever saw' (iii. 430). It seemed still odder to him that Camden said 'not a word of it' (417).[45] Of course it was not then unknown, as appears from the engraving of Nathaniel Buck, dated 1733. But Buck's neat, topographical view shows how far contemporary sensibility remained at that date from the picturesque sensibility of Pope, which is closer to the vision of William Bellers later in the century.[46] It was not then the picturesque resort it was soon to become, when visited by Walpole (1755), Gray (1764), and Gilpin (1798), but Pope's account is fully as sensitive to the picturesque

43 Nikolaus Pevsner and David Lloyd, *Hampshire and the Isle of Wight* (Harmondsworth, 1967), p. 345.

44 See Allen T. Hazen, *A Catalogue of Horace Walpole's Library*, 3 vols. (New Haven: Yale University Press, 1969), No. 2399, 2: 325; and Maynard Mack, *The Garden and the City*, plate 4, 'Notes to the Plates', p. 281.

45 Cf. *Correspondence*, iii. 430. William Camden's *Britannia* (1586) had been translated by Edmund Gibson in 1722, and reached a twelfth edition by 1734.

46 See 'The North View of Netley Abbey in Hampshire', S. & N. Buck *delin et sculp.*, 1733 and 'South-East View of Netley Abbey', William Bellers p x., Toms & Mason sc., 17 Jan. 1774.

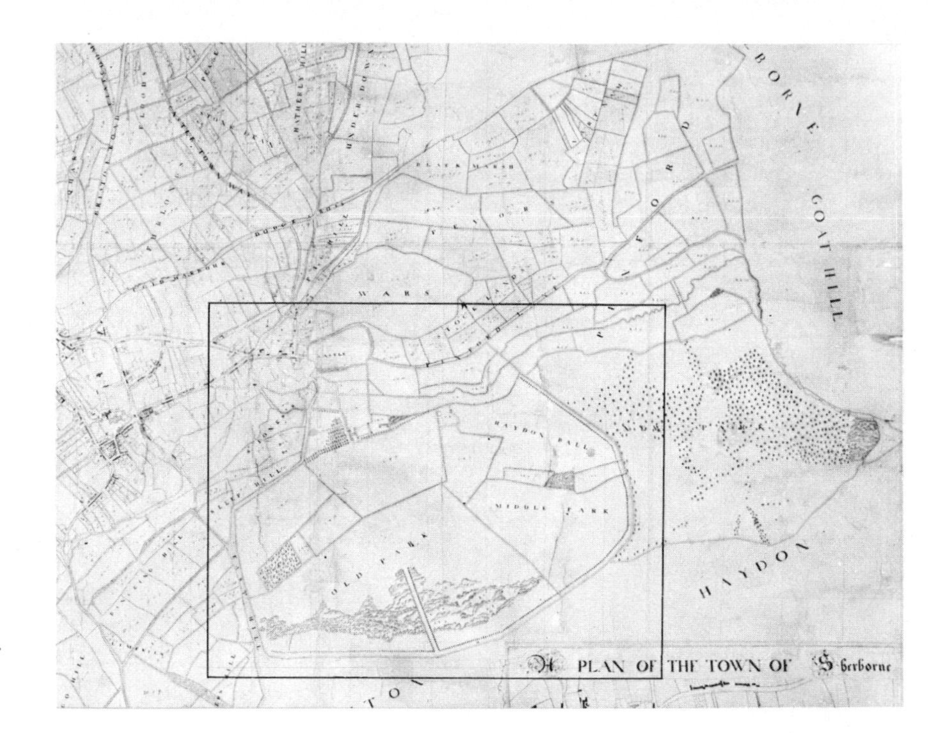

20. Sherborne, Dorset. Detail from a Map by T. Ladd. 1733.

21. Ruins of Sherborne Castle. Engraving by Philip Brannon. 1883.

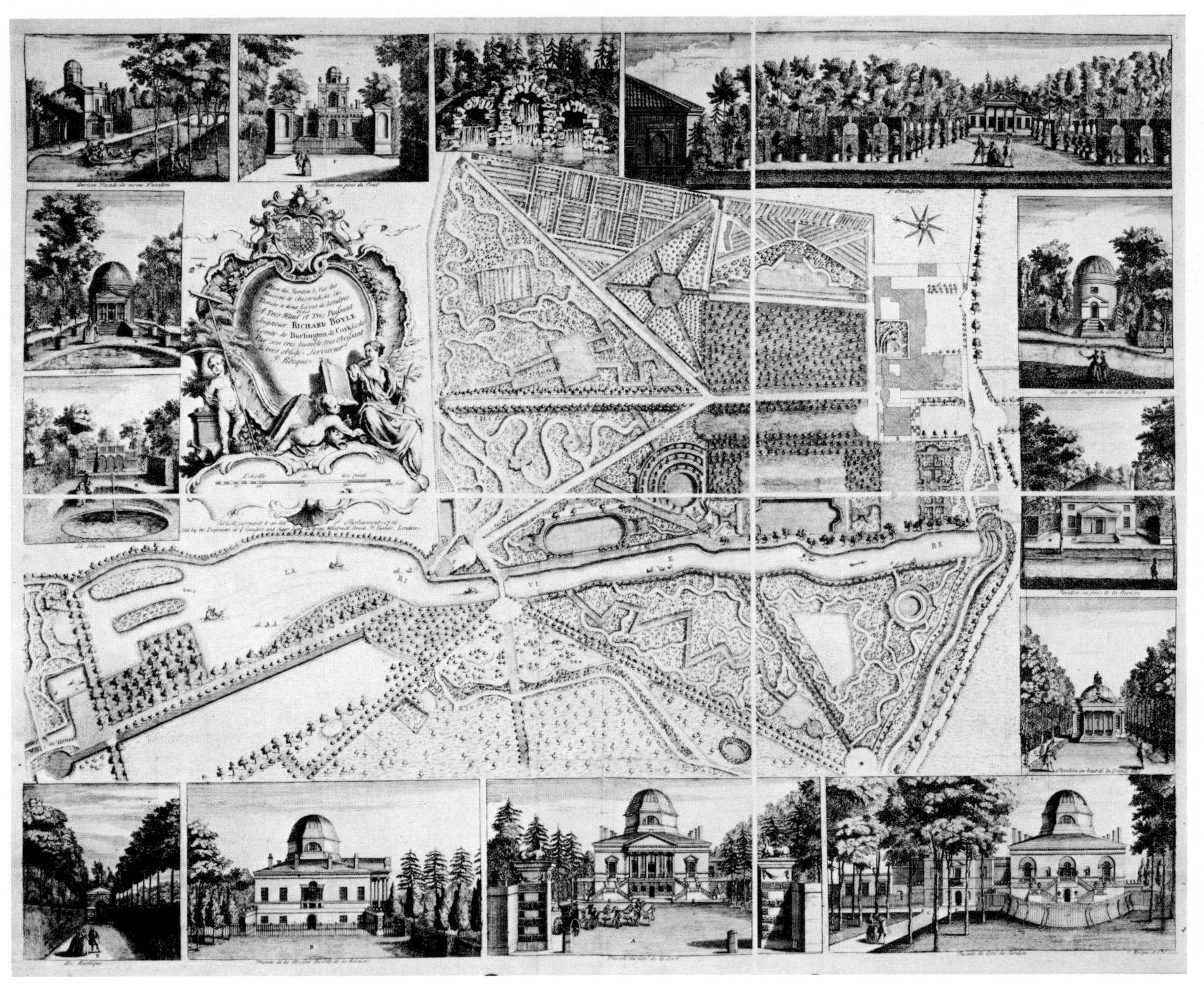

22. Plan of Chiswick, Middlesex. By John Rocque. 1736.

beauty of its situation as any of the later apostles of the picturesque cult.[47] The discovery Pope made at Netley Abbey was the picturesque. He can properly be called the first picturesque tourist of the eighteenth century.

Pope refers at the beginning of his Netley letter to Martha Blount's 'Romantick Taste' (410), which his description was calculated to satisfy, but the word 'romantic' appears to have little of the emotional energy usually associated with it. The description, which Pope calls 'an Adventure & Discovery' (410), and concludes with 'a Story, which is necessary to a Romance' (417), is romantic only in the sense that it self-consciously imitates the literary genre in this way. Even the exaggerated account of the size of the ruins, and reference to a collapsing roof which 'lookd terribly' (415) suggests more an awareness of than an indulgence in sublime or romantic sentiments. The way Pope's sensibility to the picturesque controls emotional response to landscape may be further illustrated by examining Pope's description of a landscape with sublime capabilities on the river Avon at Clifton near Bristol (plate 17) which he described in letters to Martha Blount dated 1739. 'I hardly knew what I undertook,' he wrote, 'when I said I would give you some Account of this place. Nothing can do it but a Picture, it is so unlike any Scene you ever saw' (iv. 201).

After commenting in an interesting way on perspectives in Bristol's urban landscape, he describes in detail St. Vincent's Rock (plate 18) and the prospect from the House of the Hot Well,[48] one mile west of the city along the Avon at Clifton:

[47] See Walpole to Richard Bentley (18 Sept. 1755), *The Letters of Horace Walpole*, ed. Paget Toynbee (Oxford, 1903), iii. 343; Gray to Brown (1 or 8 Oct. 1764), and Norton Nicholls (19 Nov. 1764), letters 392, 397 in *Correspondence of Thomas Gray*, ed. Paget Toynbee and Leonard Whibley (Oxford, 1935); and William Gilpin, *Observations on the Western Parts of England Relative Chiefly to Picturesque Beauty* (London, 1798), pp. 349, 351. The most recent account of Netley Abbey and the picturesque cult omits Pope and dates the vogue of Netley Abbey from Walpole and Gray 'whose writings first clearly crystallized the romantic appeal of Gothic ruins'. See A. J. Sambrook, 'Netley and Romanticism', in *Netley Abbey, Hampshire*, by A. Hamilton Thompson, Ministry of Public Building and Works Official Guide Book, revised ed. (London, 1969), p. 23.

[48] See John Latimer, 'Clifton in 1746', an address read 28 Nov. 1900, *Proceedings of the Clifton Antiquarian Club for 1900–1903*, ed. Alfred E. Hudd, 5 (Exeter, 1904), 25–34. Facing p. 28 he reproduces the facsimile of a plan dated 1746 (see plate 17), *A Survey of the Manor of Clifton in the County of Gloucester, . . . Estates belonging to the Merchants Hall, Bristol.* 'At the Hot Well itself, the Plan shows the pump room, a lodging house, and what was probably a room for billiards and other amusements, all of which are known

Passing still along by the River you come to a Rocky way on one Side, overlooking green Hills on the other; On that rocky way rise several white Houses, and over them red rocks, and as you go further, more Rocks above rocks, mixd with green bushes, and of different colourd stone. This at a Mile's end, terminates in the House of the Hot well, whereabouts lye several pretty Lodging Houses open to the River with Walks of Trees. When you have seen the Hills seem to shut upon you & to stop any further way, you go into the House & looking out of the Back door, a vast Rock of 100 foot high, of red, white, green, blue & yellowish Marbles, all blotch'd & variegated strikes you quite in the face, & turning on the left, there opens the River at a vast depth below, winding in & out, & accompanied on both sides with a Continued Range of Rocks up to the Clouds, of a hundred Colours, one behind another, & so to the end of the Prospect quite to the Sea. But the Sea nor the Severn you do not see, the Rocks & River fill the Eye, and terminate the View, much like the broken Scenes behind one another in a Playhouse. (iv. 201)

The suggestions encountered earlier in the *Pastorals* and the description of Netley Abbey of landscape viewed in terms of stage scenery find explicit confirmation here. 'Broken Scenes', like the 'broken views' mentioned at Netley, apparently derive from the painted flats arranged on stage to give the illusion of perspective. The 'design'd scene' Pope perceives in the river landscape of Clifton is unmistakably related to the stage scenery of the play house; and it will be seen below how he applied the analogy to scenes 'opened' in the landscape garden.[49]

That the same scene, with its 'vast depth', 'vast extent', and 'vast Rock', could be a pretext for sublime emotions in Addison's or Burke's sense appears from a sequel to the letter just quoted, in which Pope describes the view from Durdham Down above St. Vincent's Rock. 'Upon the top of those high Rocks by the Hotwell, which I've described to you, there runs on One side a large Down, of fine Turf, for about three miles. It looks too frightful to approach the brink, & look down upon the River' (iv. 204). This is perhaps as close as Pope comes to the brink of the sublime in landscape; even though

to have existed' (28). Cf. the description of 'an enchanting variety of moving pictures' from the Pump-room at Clifton by Lydia Melford in Smollett's *Humphry Clinker*, ed. Lewis M. Knapp (Oxford, 1966), p. 27.

[49] On the 'theatricality of nature' in the period see Samuel Monk, *The Sublime* (New York, 1935), p. 228; Elizabeth Manwaring, *Italian Landscape*, p. 96; and Nicolson and Rousseau, *This Long Disease*, p. 193. On Pope's terms of description for gardens and landscape, see A. D. Atkinson, 'A Prospect of Words', *Notes & Queries*, 197 (11 and 25 Oct. 1952), 452–4, 475–7.

he shows how well he conceives the idea in the 'Postscript to the *Odyssey*' (1725):

> The Odyssey is a perpetual source of Poetry: The stream is not the less full, for being gentle; tho' it is true (when we speak only with regard to the *Sublime*) that a river, foaming and thund'ring in cataracts from rocks and precipices, is what more strikes, amazes, and fills the mind, than the same body of water, flowing afterwards thro' peaceful vales and agreeable scenes of pasturage.[50]

Despite Pope's awareness of the terrible in ruined architecture and the frightful in landscape, his normal response to landscape is neither terror nor fright. Natural scenery interpreted as in painting, playhouse, or garden does not arouse turbulent emotion; it yields 'a delicious feeling about the heart', not the *tremor cordis* of the sublime.[51]

This sensibility is illustrated once again by Pope's descriptions of scenery between Bath and Bristol, a journey he made by land in 1739, and by water in 1743. The second journey made in the company of George Arbuthnot is mentioned briefly in a letter to Orrery, in which he remarks: 'We are both at Bristol, whither I came by water, thro the most Romantic Scene I could desire, to other Scenes here [Bristol and Clifton] of still higher beauty' (iv. 466). From a detailed description of the earlier trip by land in a letter to Martha Blount we can derive some idea of what Pope means by 'romantic' scenery:

> I hardly knew what I undertook when I said I would give you some Account of this place. Nothing can do it but a Picture, it is so unlike any Scene you ever saw. But I'll begin at least, & reserve the rest to my next letter. From Bath you go along the River [the Avon], or its Side, the Road lying generally in sight of it, on each Bank are steep rising Hills cloathd with Wood at top, and sloping toward the stream in Green Meadows, intermixt with white Houses, Mills & Bridges, this for 7 & 8 miles, then you come in sight of Bristol, the River winding at the bottom of steeper banks to the Town where you see twenty odd Pyramids smoking over the Town (which are Glasshouses) and a vast Extent of Houses red & white. You come first to Old Walls, & over a Bridge built on both Sides like London bridge, and as much crowded, with a strange mixture of Seamen, women, children, loaded Horses, Asses, & Sledges with Goods

[50] *TE* x. 386.

[51] Spence (No. 615) describing his reaction, shared by Pope, to Philip Southcote's landscape garden at Woburn Farm.

dragging along, all together, without posts to separate them. From thence you come to a Key along the old Wall with houses on both sides, and in the middle of the street, as far as you can see, hundreds of Ships, their Masts as thick as they can stand by one another, which is the oddest & most surprising sight imaginable. This street is fuller of them, than the Thames from London Bridge to Deptford, & at certain times only, the Water rises to carry them out; so that at other times, a Long Street full of ships in the Middle & Houses on both sides [plate 19] looks like a Dream. (iv. 201)

This is not the 'inchanted' landscape of romance, nor does it correspond to the other current sense of the word romantic, 'wild scenery'.[52] It approaches most nearly the idea of order in variety, pleasing confusion, and *discordia concors* in Pope's description of *Windsor Forest*, which is the sense of the word in his short account of the surroundings of the seat of Sir William Codrington at Durhams, near Bath, in a letter to Martha Blount (1728): 'Their house is pretty enough, the situation romantic, covered with woody hills tumbling upon one another confusedly, and the garden makes a valley betwixt them, with some mounts and waterfalls' (ii. 514). The whole tenor of Pope's description of the 'romantic' Bath–Bristol landscape, and even of his view of the city, is picturesque in its attention to colour, contrast, and surprise: 'the oddest & most surprising sight imaginable' (iv. 201). He explicitly compares it to a picture, and goes on to describe a succession of views of the city comparable to that series of prospects enjoyed by Ulysses approaching the city of Phaeacia. His pictorial vision is so intense that the city 'looks like a Dream'.

The vision of Bristol as an unreal city suggests psychological and emotional dimensions in Pope's response to landscape, sometimes labelled romantic or pre-romantic, which have been thought incompatible with the picturesque sensibility.[53] But the dissociated sensibility which is said to be so characteristic of the picturesque does not apply to Pope's response to landscape. Both

[52] See Johnson's *Dictionary*, s.v. 'romantick'; and Logan Pearsall Smith's discussion of 'romantic' in 'The Romantic History of Four Words', in *Society for Pure English*, 17 (Oxford, 1924), 3–17.

[53] See Mario Praz's discussion of the 'pre-romantic' passages in Pope's *Iliad, Poesia di Pope* (1962), pp. 174–5, 242, 252. In *The Sublime* (New York, 1935), p. 225, Samuel Monk asserts that the 'total ignoring of the emotive quality of landscape' was characteristic of the picturesque movement. Cf. Christopher Hussey, *The Picturesque* (1967), pp. 83–4, 245. Maynard Mack distinguishes Pope's interest in landscape from the romantics in *The Garden and the City*, p. 4. John Dixon Hunt discusses the psychological import of Pope's ideas on gardening in 'Gardening, and Poetry, and Pope', *The Art Quarterly*, 37 (Spring, 1974), pp. 1–30.

thought and feeling are involved in his reaction to picturesque landscape, but in a way which must be distinguished from the romantic sensibility with which it is usually confused. Locke's sensationist rather than romantic idealist philosophy accounts for a response like Pope's which involves a state of heightened self-consciousness instead of the romantic self-transcendence. Significantly, Locke refers to 'rêverie', the word which best describes Pope's psychological response to landscape, as one of the 'modes of thinking': 'when ideas float in our mind, without any reflection or regard of the understanding'. Happily Pope was able to find in Horace a classical sanction for the dream-like state of mind landscape inspired in him.[54]

The clearest example of this kind of response to landscape is contained in Pope's description of a journey from Binfield to Oxford in letters to the Blount sisters dated 1717. On the way he visited Stonor Park, Oxfordshire, the seat of a former Binfield neighbour and one of the Catholic gentry, a place Martha Blount had romantically described to him. At the end of one letter he describes his general impression of the journey: 'The Melancholy which my Wood [Binfield and Windsor Forest], and this Place [Oxford], have spread over me, will go near to cast a cloud upon the rest of my letter, if I don't make haste to conclude it here' (i. 429). He postponed a full description until the next letter, which he carefully revised in the attempt to describe a 'romantic' landscape:

> I came from Stonor (its Master [Thomas Stonor] not being at home) to Oxford the same night. Nothing could have more of that Melancholy which once us'd to please me, than that days journey: For after having Passd thro' my favorite Woods in the Forest [Windsor near Binfield], with a thousand Reveries of past pleasures; I rid over hanging hills, whose tops were edgd with Groves, & whose feet water'd with winding rivers, listening to falls of Cataracts below, & the murmuring of Winds above. The gloomy Verdure of Stonor succeeded to these, & then the Shades of the Evening overtook me, the Moon rose in the clearest Sky I ever saw, by whose solemn light I pac'd on slowly, without company, or any interruption to the range of my thoughts. About a mile before I reachd Oxford, all the Night bells toll'd, in different notes; the Clocks of every College answered one another; & told me some in a deeper, some in a softer voice, that it was eleven a clock. (i. 429–30)

[54] John Locke, *An Essay Concerning Human Understanding*, ed. Alexander C. Fraser (Oxford, 1894), i. 298 (Bk. II, chap. 19); Horace, *Odes*, III. iv. 5–8. See below, chap. 5.

The scene is romantic in the current sense of wildness, even sublime—hanging hills, murmuring winds, winding rivers, and cataracts—but Pope's response is reflective rather than emotional. Landscape inspires a 'range of . . . thoughts', 'a thousand Reveries of past pleasures', overcast by a mood of melancholy nostalgia. These are scenes like those in *Eloisa to Abelard*, which 'meditation aid' (l. 161), and which mirror emotion: verdure is 'gloomy', moonlight 'solemn'.

The reverie apparently was a favourite, consciously cultivated state of mind for the young poet,[55] and a remark to Parnell in a letter reminiscing about Binfield—'I have many an agreeable reverie, through those woods and downs, where we once rambled together' (i. 395)—suggests that this kind of dream vision was characteristic of his response to landscape. Even a garden as formal as Hampton Court could make him contemplative, as he told Lady Mary:

> No lone house in Wales with a Rookery, is more contemplative than Hampton Court; I walk'd there the other day by the Moon, and met no creature of any quality but the King, who was giving Audience, all alone, to the Birds under the Garden-Wall. (i. 470)

That his response to landscape comprised thought and feeling is evident from his remark on *Cooper's Hill* in the notes to the *Iliad*:

> The Descriptions of Places, and Images rais'd by the Poet, are still tending to some Hint, or leading into some Reflection, upon moral Life or political Institution: Much in the same manner as the real Sight of such Scenes and Prospects is apt to give the Mind a compos'd Turn, and incline it to Thoughts and Contemplations that have a Relation to the Object. (XVI. 466)

Pope spoke of the value of such chance reflections in a conversation with Swift related to Spence (No. 144): 'if a man was to take notice of the reflections that came into his mind on a sudden, as he was walking in the fields or sauntering in his study, there might be several of them perhaps as good as his most deliberate thoughts.'

'Thoughts and Contemplations that have a relation to the Object' could be studied and sententious, or personal and subjective in Pope's experience. He reported philosophical reflections, inspired perhaps by the lectures of William

[55] See *Correspondence*, i. 322–3, 344; iv. 371, 413.

Whiston, during another moonlight walk in St. James's Park in 1713 to John Caryll, the audience for some of his most sober reflections:

> I have been just taking a solitary walk by moonshine in St James's park, full of the reflections of the transitory nature of all human delights, and giving my thoughts a loose into the contemplation of those sensations of satisfaction which probably we may taste in the more exalted company of separate spirits, when we range the starry walks above, and gaze on this world at a vast distance, as now we do on those. (i. 190)

Another edifying 'thought' was prompted by a journey in Lord Cobham's coach through the Buckinghamshire downs in 1728:

> I passed by the door of my Lord Deloraine's, which is a neat stone-house, with a view of the Downs, but low situated. I can't help telling you one circumstance, that, as I travelled all alone, made me contemplative. I was drawn by a horse now employed by Lord C.[obham] in rolling the gardens [at Stowe], which was the same in former days on which the Earl of Derwentwater rid at Preston. It made me reflect, that man himself is as blind and unknowing of his fate, as the beast he bestrides: equally proud and prancing in his glory, and equally ignorant whither or to what he is running. (ii. 513)

But as the description of 'a thousand Reveries of past pleasures' associated with his childhood experience at Binfield shows, the thoughts were more frequently memories of his own experience associated with a particular place. Thus he writes to Thomas Dancastle in 1717, the manor Lord of Binfield: 'The Memory of our old neighbors yet lives in me; I often give a Range to my Imagination, & goe a strolling with one or other of you, up & down Binfield Wood, or over Bagshot Heath' (i. 393). He wrote a 'Hymn' to 'these [Binfield] Groves' ending with a 'deep Sigh' (i. 428) which he sent to the Blount sisters the same year:

> All hail! once pleasing, once inspiring Shade,
> Scene of my youthful Loves, and happier hours!
> Where the kind Muses met me as I stray'd,
> And gently pressd my hand, and said, Be Ours.
>
> Take all thou e're shalt have, a constant Muse:
> At Court thou may'st be lik'd, but nothing gain;
> Stocks thou may'st buy & sell, but always lose;
> And love the brightest eyes, but love in vain! (i. 429)

In 1734 he closes the description of Netley Abbey with a melancholy reflection about his return through Binfield: 'This may be the last time I shall see those Scenes of my past Life, where I have been so happy, & I look upon one of them in particular in this Light, since it was there I first knew you' (418). A similar association of landscape with a friend occurs in a letter to Swift:

> I shall never more think of Lord Cobham's, the woods of Ciceter [Cirencester], or the pleasing prospect of Byberry, but your Idea must be joined with 'em; nor see one seat in my own garden, or one room in my own house, without a Phantome of you, sitting or walking before me. (ii. 388)

All these associations—thoughts, memories, and reflections—are coloured by the same feeling of melancholy Pope cultivates so deliberately in the Stonor letter. It is an early sign, along with the figure of Black Melancholy in *Eloisa*, of what was to become a fashionable cult, soon to be given poetic expression by Edward Young, Robert Blair, and the moonlight school of poets. Tom Jones, we remember, wanted to climb Mazard Hill, 'for the solemn gloom which the moon casts on all objects is beyond expression beautiful, especially to an imagination which is desirous of cultivating melancholy ideas' (Book VIII, x). Pope had defined the kind of melancholy he enjoyed in landscape in an early letter to Caryll (1713):

> I have just now stolen myself from a tumult of acquaintance at Will's, into my chamber, to enjoy the pleasing melancholy of an hour's reflection alone. There is an agreeable gloominess which instead of troubling, does but refresh and ease the mind, and has an effect upon it not unlike the relief a sudden cloud sometimes gives the eye, when it has been aching, and too much distended with the glaring of a summer's day. (i. 172)

Here is an explicit statement of the emotion that charges the prospects in the *Odyssey*, and is characteristic of Pope's emotional response to picturesque landscape.

This kind of sensibility to landscape has been referred to by a recent critic as 'psychological picturesque', and related to Addison's theory of the pleasures of the imagination.[56] Indeed Addison's *Spectator* papers on the pleasures of the imagination illuminate Pope's response to landscape in the same way Cole-

[56] Wylie Sypher, 'Psychological Picturesque: Association and Reverie', Part Two, chap. iii of *Rococo to Cubism in Art and Literature* (New York, 1960).

ridge helps to explain Wordsworth. Landscape is a primary source for Addison of pleasures of the primary and secondary imagination. Addison's man of polite imagination wanders rapt through the landscape, his soul 'delightfully lost and bewildered in a pleasing Delusion . . . like the Enchanted Hero of a Romance'. 'We always find the Poet', Addison observes, 'in love with a Country-Life', and his reader of poetry travels through a landscape of 'Agreeable' emotions.[57] Pope feels more gloom than good cheer in landscape, but for Pope as for Addison landscape is a metaphor of the imagination which he applies to Homer in the *Preface to the Iliad*.[58]

We need not suppose, therefore, that Pope was handicapped in his sensibility to landscape. He responded fully and imaginatively to the possibilities of picturesque landscape, and it is fair to say that he is as much the poet of picturesque landscape as Thomson is of the sublime. He responds to it as an 'intellectual scene' like the cosmic prospect he describes in the opening lines of the *Temple of Fame*:

> A Train of Phantoms in wild Order rose,
> And, join'd, this Intellectual Scene compose.
> I stood, methought, betwixt Earth, Seas, and Skies;
> The whole Creation open to my Eyes:
> In Air self-ballanc'd hung the Globe below,
> Where Mountains rise, and circling Oceans flow;
> Here naked Rocks, and empty Wastes were seen,
> There Tow'ry Cities, and the Forests green:
> Here sailing Ships delight the wand'ring Eyes;
> There Trees, and intermingl'd Temples rise:
> Now a clear Sun the shining Scene displays,
> The transient Landscape now in Clouds decays. (9–20)

This scene more than any other in Pope invites comparison with Claude,[59] but this transient landscape, rich in poetic, intellectual, and emotional

[57] Joseph Addison, *The Spectator*, ed. D. F. Bond (Oxford, 1965), Nos. 413 (24 June 1712), 414 (25 June 1712), 417 (28 June 1712), iii. 546, 549, 562–6.

[58] Pope compares Homer's imagination in the *Preface to the Iliad* to 'the vast and various Extent of Nature' (*TE* vii. 3). Opposed to the 'uniform and bounded Walk of Art' in 'regular Gardens' (3) 'he [Homer] open'd a new and boundless Walk for his Imagination' (5). The *Iliad* is 'like a mighty Tree which rises from the most vigorous Seed, is improv'd with Industry, flourishes, and produces the finest Fruit' (17).

[59] See Elizabeth Manwaring, *Italian Landscape*, p. 97.

significance, is more than picture. It is the expression of the same poetic and picturesque sensibility which helped to create the 'visionary Scene' of the English landscape garden.[60]

iv. POPE AND THE PICTURESQUE

The unmistakable conclusion to be drawn from the evidence of Pope's sensibility to landscape and the idea of the landscape garden derived from it, is that the picturesque was for him a complex and meaningful aesthetic of natural scenery. Picturesque is a better word to describe the tendencies of this sensibility than romantic, the word so often associated with it. Romantic landscape was wilderness in Pope's time, or the enchanted ground of romance. The picturesque, on the other hand, defines the prevailing pictorial notion of the aesthetic values of landscape, and, at the same time conforms to the Lockean concept of imagination as a kind of sense-perception.[61] The concept of the picturesque accurately describes the kind of sensibility which sees in landscape both picture and vision—a 'visionary Scene'.

On the basis of this account of Pope's sensibility it is possible to modify, if not to discard, some earlier explanations of the dialectic of eighteenth-century taste. The validity of the idea that sensibility for the picturesque appeared 'suddenly' about 1740, coinciding with the taste in England for Thomson and Claude, has already been disputed, and the evidence presented here confirms the inadequacy of such an oversimplified view of eighteenth-century taste. But it can be argued further as a demonstration of the gradual evolution of English taste for the picturesque in the eighteenth century that Pope, far from having nothing to do with the cult of the picturesque in the latter half of the century, as generally believed,[62] adumbrates most of the important ideas which it developed and refined. In conclusion, without any attempt at

[60] See *Imitations of Horace*, Ode IV, i. l. 24, *TE* iv. 153.

[61] See Elizabeth Manwaring, *Italian Landscape*, p. 169; *The Spectator*, No. 413 (24 June 1712), ed. Bond, iii. 546; and Ernest Tuveson, *Imagination as a Means of Grace* (Berkeley and Los Angeles, 1960).

[62] See Elizabeth Manwaring, *Italian Landscape*, pp. 169–70; the *locus classicus* for this point of view, Christopher Hussey, *The Picturesque*; and Samuel Monk, *The Sublime*, p. 209. Jean Hagstrum challenges this view in *The Sister Arts*, pp. xvi–xvii; Mario Praz exposes its historical fallacies in *The Romantic Agony* (Oxford, 1933), pp. 18–21. But both Norman Ault (*New Light on Pope*, p. 81) and Jean Hagstrum (*The Sister Arts*, pp. 158–9), deny that Pope had anything to do with the cult of the picturesque.

exhaustiveness, a few ways in which Pope's sensibility to the picturesque was influential can be indicated.

Windsor Forest, in which we have observed the implicit ideal of picturesque landscape, rivalled Thomson's *Seasons* in its influence on eighteenth-century topographical poetry, a genre which reflects taste in garden design throughout the century. Both *Guardian* No. 173 and the *Epistle to Burlington* served as models later in the century for satire of folly in landscape design. The latter's inimitable ridicule of false taste, according to William Mason's 'Preface' to the *English Garden* (1773), 'seemed to preclude all other authors . . . from touching it after him'. Treatises on gardening by the landscape architect Stephen Switzer, published between 1715 and 1742, quote from *Windsor Forest*, the *Essay on Criticism*, the *Guardian*, and the *Epistle to Burlington* in support of new ideas of garden design. Handbooks by less daring writers like Batty Langley and Philip Miller show only slight influence of Pope, but by mid-century, when the new fashion for the picturesque had become entrenched, George Mason remarked of the *Epistle to Burlington* in an *Essay on Design in Gardening* (1768): 'The hints . . . are hardly sufficient for directions: but in vain might we have searched for better before the publication of Shenstone's *Unconnected Thoughts on Gardening*.' In the nineteenth century Richard Morris wrote that 'on the modern style of forming landscape scenery, Pope has given principles that may ever be acted upon'; and in our own time Nikolaus Pevsner has indicated the value of Pope's principles to the post-war city planning of London.[63]

Still more striking is Pope's influence on the writings, published and unpublished, and the *obiter dicta* of two of the most important mid-century gardeners, Philip Southcote and William Shenstone, who will be discussed below, and upon two popularizers of picturesque garden design, Joseph Spence and Horace Walpole. Spence learned the art of gardening in Pope's

[63] See Robert Aubin, *Topographical Poetry in Eighteenth-Century England* (New York, 1936), p. 124; Arthur Murphy's satire on gardening in *Three Weeks After Marriage* (1776), first performed as *What We Must All Come To* (1764); William Mason, *The English Garden*, ed. William Burgh (York, 1783), p. vii; Stephen Switzer, *Ichnographia Rustica* (1742), i. xx–xxi, xliv, 8–10, 343–4; George Mason, *Essay on Design in Gardening* (London, 1768), pp. 51–2; Richard Morris, *Essays on Landscape Gardening, and on Uniting Picturesque Effect with Rural Scenery* (London, 1825), pp. 49–50, 58; Pevsner, *The Englishness of English Art* (London, 1956), p. 168.

garden at Twickenham, and he became the devoted apostle of Pope s principles throughout an active career advising on garden design. Spence admits that the substance of sixteen rules of gardening he lists in a letter to the Reverend Mr. Wheeler (1751) 'and perhaps a great deal more, is included by Mr. Pope in two lines', and his unpublished treatise on gardening, entitled 'Tempe', also shows the decisive influence of Pope. Horace Walpole, neighbour and admirer of Pope's Twickenham garden, wrote the first and most influential history of garden design, a defence of the new taste for picturesque gardening, which attributes to Pope and his garden at Twickenham an important contribution to what has been called the 'reformed style of picturesque gardening'.[64]

Turning to the literature of the cult of the picturesque in the latter half of the eighteenth century it is surprising to discover explicit evidence of the influence of Pope, whom most of these writers never suspected of the sensibility they admired. William Gilpin, recognized as the founder of the cult, quotes *Windsor Forest* on the title-page of his *Dialogue Upon Stowe* (1748): 'Here Order in Variety we See/Where all things differ, yet where all agree', a couplet which might be called the epigraph of the picturesque school of landscape. The influence of Pope on Gilpin in the *Dialogue* and elsewhere is sufficient to support the statement of Gilpin's biographer, William Templeman, that Christopher Hussey was 'scarcely fair' in denying to Pope a sensibility for the picturesque.[65]

While there is no explicit evidence of borrowings from Pope in the writings of Uvedale Price, Richard Payne Knight, and Humphry Repton, who developed the systematic aesthetics of the picturesque, many of their ideas about picturesque landscape had been anticipated by Pope. When Price writes in *An Essay on the Picturesque*—'I am therefore persuaded that the two opposite qualities of roughness, and of sudden variation, joined to that of irregularity,

[64] See Austin Wright, *Joseph Spence: A Critical Biography* (Chicago, 1950), pp. 35–6, 116–19, 231 n. 16; Appendix to No. 1059, 'Spence's Letter to the Reverend Mr. Wheeler' (1751), Spence, ii. 650 and No. 1059, headnote; and S. W. Singer, 'Life of the Author', in Spence, *Anecdotes* (1820), pp. xxxi–xxxii.

[65] William Templeman, *The Life and Work of William Gilpin*, Illinois Studies in Language and Literature, 24 (Urbana, 1939), p. 124 n. The attribution of *A Dialogue Upon the Gardens of the Right Honourable the Lord Viscount Cobham, at Stowe in Buckinghamshire* (Buckingham, 1748) is established by Templeman, pp. 34–5.

are the most efficient causes of the picturesque'—he was refining ideas which appear in Pope, as will be seen in the next chapter. His identification of 'variety' and 'intricacy' as two of 'the most fruitful sources of human pleasure' is the expression of an aesthetic Pope shared. The source of Repton's statement that 'all rational improvement of grounds is, necessarily, founded on a due attention to the Character and Situation of the place to be improved', is a windy paraphrase of Pope's 'Genius of the Place'. The great quarrel between Price and Repton was on the proposition urged by Pope that 'all gardening is landscape-painting' (No. 606).[66]

All this is not to deny the manifest difference of sensibility and of landscape design between Pope and his successors. Pope's response to picturesque landscape comprised intellect and emotion, sense and sensibility; during the cult of the picturesque, sensibility was often 'dissociated' by indulgence in extremes: the 'O *altitudo*' of the sublime on the one hand, the mere scrapbook of picturesque views on the other, as satirized by William Combe in *Dr. Syntax*.[67] But differences have been stressed too often; what is remarkable is how prophetic Pope's eye for picturesque landscape was. Thus it appears that the picturesque, like every sensibility we encounter in art or literature,[68] is no sudden development; and if we must date its introduction into England as a significant aesthetic, we ought to date it from Pope.

[66] See Uvedale Price, *An Essay on the Picturesque*, 2 vols. (London, 1796–8), i. 61, 25; Humphry Repton, *Sketches and Hints on Landscape Gardening* (London, 1794), p. 39. On the controversy between Price, Repton, and Knight, see H. F. Clark, 'Eighteenth Century Elysiums: The Role of "Association" in the Landscape Movement', *Journal of the Warburg and Courtauld Institute*, 6 (1943), 187–9.

[67] *The Tour of Doctor Syntax, in Search of the Picturesque. A Poem* (London, 1812).

[68] See Mario Praz, '"Romantic", an Approximate Term', Introduction to *The Romantic Agony*.

4. *Pope's Concept of Garden Design*

POPE'S published statements on gardening—a satirical essay in the *Guardian* (No. 173, 1713) long attributed to Steele, lines in a verse satire, the *Epistle to Burlington* (1731), and scattered remarks in conversations with Spence only recently published in full—are not enough to constitute a 'theory' of gardening, or to make Pope a significant theorist of the art. In 1728 he had a hand in editing a French treatise on gardening, but his corrections were purely stylistic.[1] He once referred to the *Epistle to Burlington* as 'the gardening poem',[2] but the centre of gravity in the poem is architecture, and principles of gardening are subordinate to architecture. Joseph Spence's remark that 'Mr. Pope's ideas of *Windsor Forest* in 1704 [Spence's dating of lines 11–20 of the poem] like his ideas afterwards for gardening' (No. 605) has the virtue of shifting our attention from rules of gardening to the sensibility of the poet to landscape, a more fruitful source of his idea of the landscape garden. Pope's rules do not contain anything which cannot be found in the theory and practice of contemporary landscape architects: Stephen Switzer's 'surprise', Batty Langley's 'variety', and Charles Bridgeman's brilliant employment of the ha-ha, which served to conceal the bounds. The distinction of Pope's idea of the garden from that of a long line of prophets is to be found in his poetic sensibility to landscape and the way it informs his principles of garden design.

Spence recognized in *Windsor Forest* an expression of the poet's sensibility to the pictorial and poetic values of landscape from which his theory and

[1] James Gardiner's translation of René Rapin's *Hortorum Libri IV* (1665), *Of Gardens, A Latin Poem, in Four Books, English'd by Mr. Gardiner*, 3rd edn. (London, 1728), first appeared in 1709, and a second edition about 1718. Pope made minor stylistic revisions in Books I–II. See R. H. Griffith, 'Pope on the Art of Gardening', *Texas Studies in English*, 31 (1952), 52–6.

[2] Spence, No. 310; Osborn dismisses Griffith's contention that 'the gardening poem' refers to Rapin's *Of Gardens* in 'Which Gardening Poem?', Appendix A to No. 310, ii. 631.

practice of landscape architecture are derived. The opening lines compare Windsor Forest to Milton's garden of Eden, which had already become a paradigm of the new taste in gardening among contemporary writers:[3]

> Here Hills and Vales, the Woodland and the Plain,
> Here Earth and Water seem to strive again,
> Not Chaos-like together crush'd and bruis'd,
> But as the World, harmoniously confus'd:
> Where Order in Variety we see,
> And where, tho' all things differ, all agree.
> Here waving Groves a checquer'd Scene display,
> And part admit and part exclude the Day;
> As some coy Nymph her Lover's warm Address
> Nor quite indulges, nor can quite repress.
> There, interspers'd in Lawns and opening Glades,
> Thin Trees arise that shun each others Shades.
> Here in full Light the russet Plains extend;
> There wrapt in Clouds the blueish Hills ascend:
> Ev'n the wild Heath displays her Purple Dies,
> And 'midst the Desart fruitful Fields arise,
> That crown'd with tufted Trees and springing Corn,
> Like verdant Isles the sable Waste adorn. (11–28)

Pope transmutes the 'design'd scene' of the *Pastorals* into physico-theological terms. This is the perfect picturesque landscape which the gardener worked to restore when he confronted real landscapes where the maker's hand had trembled.[4]

Pope's idea of the landscape garden is unmistakably based upon the sensibility to picturesque landscape observed in the last chapter. It is a matter of some significance that Pope was one of the first English writers to use the word 'picturesque' (he is given credit for introducing it into the language from the French),[5] and almost always in reference to the language of natural

[3] Both *Windsor Forest* and *Paradise Lost* are quoted by Stephen Switzer: *Gardener's Recreation* (1715), pp. 260–2; *Ichnographia Rustica* (1742), i. 343–6.

[4] On the imitation of ideal nature in gardening see Christopher Hussey, 'The Aesthetic Background to the Art of William Kent', Introduction to *The Work of William Kent* by Margaret Jourdain, pp. 20–1; H. F. Clark, 'Sharawaggi at Chiswick', p. 127; and A. R. Humphreys, 'The Quest of the Sharawadgi', Part II of *William Shenstone, An Eighteenth-Century Portrait* (Cambridge, 1937).

[5] See Hussey, *The Picturesque*, p. 32; Manwaring, *Italian Landscape*, p. 167; Ault, *New Light on Pope*,

description in criticism of poetry, or directly applied to natural scenery. In a little anthology of 'beautiful winterpieces' which Pope quoted in a December letter to John Caryll (1712) he includes a couplet from Ambrose Philips's *Epistle to the Earl of Dorset from Copenhagen*—

> All hid in snow, in bright confusion lie,
> And with one dazling waste fatigue the eye—

lines which he observes 'seem to me what the French call very *picturesque*' (i. 167–8). Richard Steele used the word earlier in *The Tender Husband* (1703),[6] but Pope's is the first recorded application of the word in English to natural description.

Pope uses the word three times in the notes to the *Iliad*, and once in the 'Postscript to the Odyssey', always in connection with landscape: the note in Book X, quoted above, describing 'Circumstances the most Picturesque imaginable' (X, 677); the note in Book XIII on the comparison of Achilles shaking the plumes of his helmet, 'a very pleasing Image, and very much what the Painters call Picturesque' (XIII, 948); and the headnote to Book XVI on the 'lively and Picturesque . . . Attitude' of Patroclus in his appeal to Achilles:

> We see Patroclus touch'd with the deepest Compassion for the Misfortune of the *Greeks*, (whom the Trojans had forc'd to retreat to their Ships, and which Ships were on the Point of Burning) prostrating himself before the vessel of *Achilles*, and pouring out his Tears at his Feet. *Achilles*, struck with the Grief of his Friend, demands the Cause of it. *Patroclus*, pointing to the Ships, where the Flames already began to rise, tells him he is harder than the Rocks or Sea which lay in prospect before them, if he is not touch'd with so moving a Spectacle, and can see in cold Blood his Friends perishing before his Eyes. As nothing can be more natural and affecting than the Speech of *Patroclus*, so nothing is more lively and Picturesque than the Attitude he is here describ'd in.

The final instance in the Homer notes appears in the 'Postscript to the Odyssey' where Pope is discussing diction of natural description 'in the imaging and picturesque parts . . . the character of which is simplicity and purity'.[7]

In all these instances picturesque applied to the description of a scene or to the attitude of a figure against its background means graphic vividness,

p. 80; Walter J. Hipple, *The Beautiful, the Sublime, and the Picturesque in Eighteenth-Century British Aesthetic Theory* (Carbondale, Ill., 1957), pp. 185, 354 n; Paul Frankl, *The Gothic: Literary Sources and Interpretations through Eight Centuries* (Princeton, 1960), p. 433; and Spence, No. 613 n.

[6] Frankl, *The Gothic*, p. 432.

[7] *TE* x. 390–1.

enargeia, or suitability for painting.[8] Other references in the 1720s and 1730s show that Pope applied the same word to real landscapes, for example the remark preserved in Spence's cryptic note: 'At first blush, sombre (or the sombre) such a thing has a good effect, full, rich (of a prospect or view)—Mediocre, picturesque (of natural views)' (No. 614). In the summer of 1735 he mentioned to Spence 'Lord Peterborow's two hills by Southampton' apparently as an example of a picturesque view (No. 608 n.). Finally, about 1728, Pope made an important remark about the prospect from his own house at Twickenham:[9] 'That idea of "picturesque"—from the swan just gilded with the sun amidst the shade of a tree over the water on the Thames' (No. 613). Here we have an indication that the picturesque was a conceptual 'idea' for Pope, an aesthetic derived from immediate observation of natural scenery,[10] along with the suggestion that the scene described has emotional as well as pictorial meaning, that the tranquil mood of the scene is as much a part of the concept of the picturesque as the play of light and shade—all the implications of landscape we have observed in his poetry and prose, and which we encounter when we examine his explicit statements in the light of his sensibility to landscape.

In Pope's statements on garden design we discover the adaptation of a classical idea by a modern sensibility for the picturesque, a pattern entirely characteristic of his poetic imitations and translations. Unlike the speculative essays on gardening by Addison in the *Spectator* (Nos. 414, 477) the earliest statement, in the *Guardian* (No. 173, 1713), contains no tactful hints to gentlemen of polite imagination, no compliments on royal gardens and gardeners, and above all, no equivocation about the proper model for a garden. Addison entertains vague notions about French, Italian, and Chinese prototypes, but Pope's satire measures modern degeneracy manifested in topiary work derived from Dutch and French gardens by the standard of 'the Taste of the Ancients in their Gardens'.[11] Pope's essay can be seen as another skirmish

[8] See Walter Hipple, *The Beautiful, the Sublime, and the Picturesque*, p. 186.

[9] See Geoffrey Tillotson, *On the Poetry of Pope*, p. 26.

[10] See Paul Frankl, 'The Concept of the Picturesque', chap. 3 in *The Gothic*, p. 435, where he observes that 'important as it is to know the history of the word picturesque, it is even more important and interesting to see how the word gradually became associated with an appropriate concept'.

[11] *Prose*, p. 145.

in the Battle of the Books, in which Pope sides with the Ancients on gardening, invoking at one point the opinion of Sir William Temple on Homer's account of the Garden of Alcinous in the *Odyssey* (Book VII) that 'this Description contains all the justest Rules and Provisions which can go toward composing the best Gardens'.[12]

The 'Rules and Provisions' of a walled orchard and vineyard of about four acres which Pope finds relevant to eighteenth-century gardens are not formal principles of design but classical principles fundamental to all the arts—in particular, the virtues of simplicity and utility. Thus he praises the Garden of Alcinous for its modest size, conveniency, plantation of Standards ('trees suffered to grow to their full height'), and waterworks disposed to serve not only the gardens but 'the Town, for the Service of the Publick'. Virgil's description of the garden of the Old Corycian in the fourth Georgic, from which the epigraph of the essay is taken, is mentioned for its portrait of the gardener, who is the type of the happy man and the *beatus ille* ideal.

A more exact model of Pope's theory and practice of landscape garden design is the landscape ideal of the Roman villa invoked at the opening of the *Guardian* essay in the quotation from Martial's epigram:

> Baiana nostri Villa, Basse, Faustini,
> Non otiosis ordinata myrtetis,
> Viduaque platano, tonsilique buxeto,
> Ingrata lati spatia detinet campi,
> Sed *rure vero, barbaroque* laetatur. (III, lviii. 1–5)[13]

Rus verum barbarumque—this was the ideal which appears to have inspired the design of the Popes' rural retirement at Binfield; and it was the 'doctrine . . . Pope was to preach throughout his lifetime with reference to gardening'.[14]

The classical villa and its situation is clearly the model Pope had in mind

[12] *Prose*, p. 147; William Temple's remark is in his essay 'Upon the Gardens of Epicurus or, Of Gardening, in the Year 1685' in *Five Miscellaneous Essays by Sir William Temple*, ed. Samuel Holt Monk (Ann Arbor, 1963), p. 13.

[13] Translated in *Alexander Pope, Selected Poetry & Prose*, ed. William K. Wimsatt, 2nd edn. (New York, 1972), p. 36 n.: 'Bassus, the country seat of our friend Faustinus at Baia does not spread over the fields unfruitfully in rows of idle myrtle, vineless plane trees, plantations of fancy clipped boxwood. It rejoices in the true rustic, the untrimmed farm.'

[14] George Sherburn, *Early Career*, p. 278.

when he gave his fullest statement of the principles of gardening in the *Epistle to Burlington* (1731). The *ethos* of the poem is classical and humanistic, its dedicatee was the architect Earl of Burlington, who had sponsored a study of the classical villa and its garden design published in 1728,[15] and whose garden at Chiswick was the setting for a pseudo-Palladian villa. The poem is not a didactic essay on the rules of gardening, like the poem by René Rapin Pope helped to edit; nor is it a doctrinaire manifesto attacking the architectural formalism of Dutch and French seventeenth-century gardening. Pope deals with garden design in the context of a celebration of classical architecture, and it is here that we can observe the way his sensibility to picturesque landscape colours the classical ideal, the way he interprets classical principles according to his own taste.

The famous lines on the art of architecture and its situation culminate in precepts in which the idea of the picturesque is implicit:

> To build, to plant, whatever you intend,
> To rear the Column, or the Arch to bend,
> To swell the Terras, or to sink the Grot;
> In all, let Nature never be forgot.
> But treat the Goddess like a modest fair,
> Nor over-dress, nor leave her wholly bare;
> Let not each beauty ev'ry where be spy'd,
> Where half the skill is decently to hide.
> He gains all points, who pleasingly confounds,
> Surprizes, varies, and conceals the Bounds. (47–56)

Pope explained the implications of the last two lines in a Socratic conversation recorded by Spence in 1742:

P[ope]: All the rules of gardening are reducible to three heads: the contrasts, the management of surprises, and the concealment of the bounds.
S[pence]: Pray, what is it you mean by the contrasts?
P: The disposition of the lights and shades.
S: 'Tis the colouring then?
P: Just that.
S: Should not variety be one of the rules?

[15] Robert Castell, *The Villas of the Ancients Illustrated* (London, 1728).

P: Certainly, one of the chief, but that is included mostly in the contrasts. I have expressed them all in two verses (after my manner, in a very little compass), which are in imitation of Horace's *Omne tulit punctum*:

> He gains all points, who pleasingly confounds,
> Surprizes, varies, and conceals the Bounds. (No. 612)

Contrast, a primary principle of painting, is here made to embrace all the rules of gardening.

Still more significant, the genius of the place, Pope's application of Virgil's *genius Loci* (*Aeneid* V, 95) to gardening, turns out to be, among other things, a painter:

> Consult the Genius of the Place in all;
> That tells the Waters or to rise, or fall,
> Or helps th' ambitious Hill the heav'n to scale,
> Or scoops in circling theatres the Vale,
> Calls in the Country, catches opening glades,
> Joins willing woods, and varies shades from shades,
> Now breaks or now directs, th' intending Lines;
> Paints as you plant, and, as you work, designs. (57–64)[16]

The Genius of the Place can be best understood as the informing spirit of ideal nature—*natura naturans*—realizing in spite of accidents an ideal form, as the painter gives expression to the 'divine idea' in history painting. The result is a unified composition like the well-composed portrait described in the *Essay on Criticism*, a passage later applied by Stephen Switzer to gardening:[17]

> In Gard'ns [Pope wrote 'Wit'], as Nature, what
> affects our Hearts
> Is not th' Exactness of peculiar parts:
> 'Tis not a Lip, or Eye, we Beauty call,
> But the joint Force and full Result of all.
> . . .

[16] Isabel Chase interprets the genius of the place as 'study [of] the local topography' in *Horace Walpole: Gardenist*, pp. 108–9; H. F. Clark recognizes in it a 'spirit struggling for coherence, for fulfillment', in 'Sharawaggi at Chiswick', p. 127. R. W. Chapman observes of these lines that 'though Pope does not here use the word "picturesque", he does use the metaphor [painting] that was to exercise a dominant influence over the art' ('The Literature of Landscape Gardening', in *Johnsonian and other Essays and Reviews* [Oxford, 1953], p. 58); Jean Hagstrum quotes the lines to show that Pope 'conceived of gardening as closely analogous to painting' (*Sister Arts*, p. 212). Edward Malins remarks 'how much the poet and painter combine' in these lines in *English Landscaping and Literature*, p. 37.

[17] *Ichnographia Rustica* (1742), i. xxi.

No single Parts unequally surprize,
All comes united to th' admiring Eyes. (243–6; 249–50)

In the *Epistle to Burlington* the principle of unity in gardening is exemplified by Villario's perfect picturesque garden design:

Behold Villario's ten-years toil compleat;
His Quincunx darkens, his Espaliers meet,
The Wood supports the Plain, the parts unite,
And strength of Shade contends with strength of Light;
A waving Glow his bloomy beds display,
Blushing in bright diversities of day,
With silver-quiv'ring rills maeander'd o'er. (79–85)

The force of the painting metaphor is in the verbs—'supports' and 'unite'—and in the picturesque contention of light and shade.[18]

This brings us to the statement Pope made to Spence in 1734 which must be allowed primary significance in the development of the idea of the landscape garden. They were looking through the Roman triumphal arch built by the mason Nicholas Stone into the Physick Garden next to Magdalen College, Oxford, when Pope remarked that 'All gardening is landscape-painting. Just like a landscape hung up' (No. 606).[19] Thus the view of a formal botanical garden seen through the frame of an arch prompted the unequivocal statement of the radical principle which underlies his own practice and the art of landscape garden design in England.

The importance of Pope's statement has been overlooked because it belongs to an oral tradition (unpublished until 1820), but there is no doubt that it is the concept of the picturesque which distinguishes Pope's theory and practice of gardening from the seventeenth-century tradition and from his own contemporaries. The connection between painting and gardening is missing in seventeenth-century theory and practice. Painted architectural perspectives were sometimes 'added to walks in gardens and were painted outside the

[18] See *Epistle to Burlington*, l. 58 n., in *The Works of Alexander Pope*, ed. Joseph Warton (London, 1797), iii. 284.

[19] The garden and gates are depicted in a bird's-eye view of the *Hortus Botanicus*, a plate (no. viii) dedicated to Sarah Duchess of Marlborough in *Oxonia Depicta* (1733), Giuliemus Williams del., Bodleian, Gough Maps, fol. B. 33.

windows of rooms to feign an outlook which was non-existent',[20] but this is further evidence that architecture was the paradigm art in the seventeenth-century garden. William Temple in his influential essay *Upon the Gardens of Epicurus* (1685) admires Chinese irregularity, for which he coined the puzzling word, '*sharawadgi*', but he did not attempt to put it into practice himself at Moor Park, Farnham, Surrey, and advised others against it.[21] Timothy Nourse, author of *Campania Felix* (1700), speaks of prospect and the 'natural-artificial' garden, but says nothing of painting and gives no hint of the picturesque sensibility.[22] Elizabeth Manwaring has concluded that 'the books on gardening published in the seventeenth century . . . show that the interest was largely practical, and never picturesque'.[23]

The literature on gardening in the early eighteenth-century typically lags haltingly behind practice, tends to be practical rather than theoretical, and timid in broaching new ideas for fear of upsetting potential clients. French treatises, unequivocally committed to formal principles of gardening, continued to be influential.[24] The vast literature of handbooks on agriculture and horticulture appears to have had little influence on the development of taste in landscape gardening. Writers like Richard Bradley (1717) and George Agricola (1721) plod resolutely over familiar ground, offering a mixture of expert technical advice on the raising of trees and plants with scientific speculation about agriculture and botany.[25] A nurseryman like Pope's acquain-

[20] See Lily B. Campbell, *Scenes and Machines on the English Stage during the Renaissance* (Cambridge, 1923), p. 148. John Evelyn describes perspectives in French gardens in *The Diary of John Evelyn*, ed. E. S. de Beer (Oxford, 1955), ii. 112–13; see Peter Martin, 'Pope and the Garden', Ph.D. dissertation (Syracuse University, 1968), p. 20.

[21] 'Upon the Gardens of Epicurus', in *Five Miscellaneous Essays*, ed. Samuel Holt Monk, p. 30. Christopher Hussey discusses a recently discovered plan of Temple's garden in *English Gardens and Landscapes*, pp. 20–1. See Susan Lang and Nikolaus Pevsner, 'Sir William Temple and Sharawaggi', *Architectural Review*, 106 (Dec. 1949), 391–3.

[22] See Røstvig, *The Happy Man*, ii. 73.

[23] *Italian Landscape*, p. 122.

[24] *The Compleat Gard'ner*, John Evelyn's translation (1693) of Jean de la Quintinie's *Parfait Jardinier* (Paris and Geneva, 1692), appeared in a second edition in 1699 by the English royal gardeners, John London and Henry Wise. Dezallier d'Argenville's *La Theorie et la Pratique du Jardinage* (1709) was translated by John James in 1712. For Pope's part in the third edition of the translation of René Rapin's Latin poem, *Hortorum Libri IV* (1665), see n. 1.

[25] Richard Bradley, *New Improvements of Planting and Gardening* (London, 1717); Georg Andreas Agricola, *A Philosophical Treatise of Husbandry and Gardening*, trans. Richard Bradley (London, 1721). See the

tance Philip Miller, foreman of Chelsea Gardens, whose dictionaries began to appear in 1724, nods in the direction of 'diversity' and 'variety' but continues to speak the 'retrograde' language of parterre and bowling Green.[26] An opportunist like Batty Langley is prepared to declare with Addison in his *New Principles of Gardening* (1728) that there is nothing 'more *shocking* than a *stiff regular Garden*',[27] but his plates of rigid geometrical designs shows that what he has in mind is a tame variation on formal patterns.

Altogether the most important of these early writers is the neglected and still obscure figure of Stephen Switzer (1682–1745),[28] who is the one professional landscape architect of Pope's time who made a serious attempt to formulate in writing principles of landscape gardening, and whose theory of gardening can usefully be compared to Pope's. Switzer's *The Nobleman, Gentleman and Gardener's Recreation* (1715) appeared in the same year as Richardson's *Theory of Painting* and the first volume of Colen Campbell's *Vitruvius Britannicus*, and it contains something of the same mixture of idealism and professional opportunism. Most of the book is a technical horticultural treatise but the 'Preface' contains a genuine attempt to outline a new concept of landscape gardening, an 'imperfect Essay on Design' which he expanded in a subsequent book under the title *Ichnographia Rustica* (1718, 2nd edn., 1742).[29]

Switzer begins by distinguishing between horticulture, 'the cultivating Part

bibliography of works on gardening in English in Alicia Amherst, *A History of Gardening in England* (London, 1895).

[26] Ralph Dutton, *The English Garden* (London, 1938), p. 85. Miles Hadfield points out Miller's debt to d'Argenville in *Gardening in Britain*, p. 158. See Pope's letter to Miller, *Correspondence*, iii. 451.

[27] *New Principles of Gardening, or the Laying out and Planting Parterres* (London, 1728), p. iv (mispaged xi). See Nikolaus Pevsner, 'Genesis of the Picturesque', p. 146, and A. R. Humphreys, *William Shenstone* (1937), pp. 53–6.

[28] Switzer's career has been most recently discussed by Christopher Hussey, *English Gardens and Landscapes*, pp. 32–4. See B. Sprague Allen's characterization of Switzer as 'an incipient romanticist' in *Tides in English Taste*, ii. 126–9, and Maren-Sofie Røstvig's objection in *The Happy Man*, ii. 75–83, 101, 107–8. On his life and works see Ernest Clarke, *D.N.B.*, and Laurence Whistler, *The Imagination of Vanbrugh and his Fellow Artists* (London, 1954), pp. 62–3.

[29] See 'Preface', *The Nobleman, Gentleman, and Gardener's Recreation* (1715), p. xv; *Ichnographia Rustica ... containing directions for the general distribution of a country seat ... and a general system of Agriculture*, 3 vols. (London, 1718), 2nd edn. with additions, including an important appendix (London, 1742). Pevsner ignores the importance of Switzer's 'Preface' in his statement that 'The Nobleman's Recreation (1715) ... contains nothing of importance for the history of landscaping' ('Genesis of the Picturesque', 144).

of Gard'ning' (xii), and the subject of his proposed work 'under the General Title of *Icnographia Rustica*, by which is meant the general Designing and Distributing of Country Seats into Gardens, Woods, Parks, Padducks, &c. which I therefor call Forest, or in a more easy Stile, Rural Gard'ning' (xi). The art of 'Design' is introduced as a liberal art based 'on a noble and correct Judgment and Taste of Things', not a mere 'Observation and Experience'. He anticipates Pope by formulating classical principles, 'Theses' to direct 'the Pursuit of Design', in imitation of Horace's *Ars Poetica*:

> 'Utile qui dulci miscens, ingentia Rura,
> Simplex Munditiis ornans, punctum hic tulit omne.' (xii)

Throughout the *Gardener's Recreation* he appeals to the taste of his genteel audience, and dignifies his art by quotations from contemporary literature including Roscommon, Pope's *Guardian* translation of Homer's lines on the garden of Alcinous, his *Essay on Criticism*, and *Windsor Forest*, with additions in later editions from Milton, Cowley, Addison, Steele, and Blackmore.[30]

But Switzer's 'Preface' is not as bold as it appears. Timid subservience to his patrons and prospective clients is apparent in his assurance to the reader that he is not 'setting up new Schemes in Gard'ning, which may, till the Prints come out [in *Ichnographia Rustica*, 1718], cause divers Reflections, as the Readers are dispos'd to think' (xxviii). He reveals his loyalties in statements that the gardens of France 'out-do Italy' (30), in outspoken admiration for Versailles and the gardens of Louis XIV and in praise for Rapin's *Of Gardens* (34). Indeed his model for 'large prolated Gardens and Plantations' (xiii) is the French forest park and he encourages his readers to emulate French designs (xii), defining his classical principle of 'Ingentia rura' as what 'the French call La Grand Manier . . . opposed to those crimping, Diminutive and wretched Performances we every where meet with, so bad and withal so expensive' (xiii). The discussion in his later treatises emphasizes and the plates illustrate the surveying and laying out the interior parts of a garden into parterre and terraces which differ from the French designs mainly in the elimination of expensive broderie—economy is throughout one of the selling-points of his system of extensive gardening.

[30] *Gardener's Recreation* (1715), pp. xv–xvi, xxxiii–xxxiv, 7, 260–1, Index, s.v. Pope, 106.

Switzer was sympathetic to new ideas of landscape design,[31] and it may be that his practical influence on the early landscape movement was greater than we yet know. But he cannot claim credit, any more than any other contemporary professional landscape architect, for the radical change behind the landscape garden from architecture to painting as the paradigm art. Switzer suspects that gardening ought to have something to do with poetry, but he cannot translate his appreciation of Milton's Eden and Pope's *Windsor Forest* into garden design. He appreciates prospect, but appears to have no conception of the picturesque. He respects classical authority in the villas of Horace and Pliny, but in 1715 he had no real sense of the situation of the Roman villa. For the adaptation of a classical ideal and the translation of poetic and picturesque sensibility into garden design we must return to the theory and practice of Pope.

The best summary we have of Pope's theory of landscape gardening, and a convenient introduction to his practice, is the long letter to Martha Blount (*c.* 1722) describing the gardens at Sherborne, Dorset, the estate of his friend William Lord Digby. This letter, the only surviving discussion by Pope of the 'capabilities' of a specific garden, describes the manor house and its surroundings, speculates about improvements in which he had a hand, and gives us a unique insight into his ideas of gardening early in the first decade of the landscape movement, before he had finished laying out Twickenham. Sherborne was at this time in a state of transition, and the formal Italian gardens of the Tudor house were beginning to be transformed into the landscape garden which Capability Brown was consulted about in 1756.[32]

After a brief description of the house, Pope tells Martha that 'the Gardens

[31] See Pevsner, 'Genesis of the Picturesque', p. 144, who recognizes the importance of Switzer's book despite its equivocations: 'It shows that by 1718—that is, before Pope had bought his Twickenham estate—an enterprising gardener of thirty-six could risk to place before landowners some of the principles of landscape gardening and hope thereby to obtain their clientele' (145).

[32] See H. F. Clark, 'Eighteenth-Century Elysiums', p. 167: 'In this garden [Sherborne] are either suggested or actually constructed most of the elements of those landscapes which were to be the greatest achievements of the movement.' For a detailed analysis of Sherborne as Pope described it, reproducing what may be Pope's sketch plan, see Peter E. Martin, 'Intimations of the New Gardening: Alexander Pope's Reaction to the "Uncommon" Landscape at Sherborne', *Garden History*, The Journal of the Garden History Society, 4 (Spring 1976), 57–87. See also *An Inventory of the Historical Monuments in Dorset*, Royal Commission on Historical Monuments England (London, 1952), i (West Dorset), 66–70; and Dorothy Stroud, *Capability Brown* (London, 1950), p. 54.

are so Irregular, that tis very hard to give an exact idea of 'em but by a Plan' (ii. 237; plate 20). This is a surprising remark because he goes on to mention a great many regular features of the Italian garden which would not suggest irregularity to the modern eye.[33] But it is clear from a subsequent remark that Pope identifies the irregularity of the garden with his own sense of picturesque beauty. He explains that:

> Their beauty rises from this Irregularity, for not only the Several parts of the Garden itself make the better Contraste by these sudden Rises, Falls, and Turns of ground; but the Views about it are lett in, & hang over the Walls, in very different figures and aspects. (ii. 237)

Pope admires the irregular disposition of formal features, because it has introduced the picturesque: contrast within the garden, prospects without.

The picturesque corollaries of contrast—Pope's 'rules' of surprise, variety, and concealment of bounds—had been observed or were being introduced in planned improvements at Sherborne noticed by Pope: variety in the contrast between the serpentine course of the river Yeo, with its natural banks, and the T-shaped canal bounded by a slope wall; variety too in plantations of standard lime trees, groves of forest trees, and orchards of fruit trees; surprise in the 'sudden Rises, Falls, and Turns of ground' (237), and in the way 'a close high Arbour' gave way to 'a sudden open Seat' (238). Most impressive to Pope was the concealment of bounds by which the country was 'called into' the garden at Sherborne in a succession of picturesque views which were to become the soul of the landscape garden. He expresses his delight in the constantly changing views of the town of Sherborne and the surrounding country obtained from wilderness, terrace, and seats. He admires perspectives obtained where the 'Wall of the Garden [is] humourd so as to appear the Ruin of another Arch or two above the bridge' (238), suggesting the management of stage scenery. And he is particularly fascinated by 'several venerable Ruins of an Old Castle, with arches & broken views' (238).

Pope's reference is to the colossal ruins of Bishop's Castle (Sherborne Old

[33] These include a T-shaped canal, 'a little triangular wilderness', 'pyramid yews, & large round Honisuckles', 'a Semicircular Berceau', 'regular Groves of Horse chestnuts', 'five green Terras's hanging under each other', a Bowling-green, walls, and 'a hedge that makes a Colonnade' (ii. 237). Some of these are shown on 'A Map of the Right Honourable William Lord Digby's Manor of Sherborne in the County of Dorset', T. Ladd *mensuravit et delineavit*, 1733 (plate 20).

Castle) including a Norman Tower and keep, commanding the gardens 400 yards to the north of the house (plate 21).[34] Pope's idea for 'calling in' these ruins to the garden design and his suggestions for picturesque improvement contain the essence of his conception of the landscape garden. After describing a 'Deep Scene' (239) in the garden with ornaments in the 'ruinous taste', he discovers in the solemnity of the ruins of Bishop's Castle the genius of the place:

> On the left, full behind these old Trees, which make this whole Part inexpressibly awful & solemn, runs a little, old, low wall, beside a Trench, coverd with Elder Trees & Ivyes; which being crost by another bridge, brings you to the Ruins, to compleat the Solemnity of the Scene. (ii. 238)

Pope is clearly aware of the pleasing melancholy of this scene, in its solemnity and venerability, and he proposes to Digby that he 'cultivate' the ruins, do honour to his ancestors by raising an obelisk commemorating the defence of the castle in the Civil War, confident that he 'will not disgrace them, as most Modern Progeny do, by an unworthy Degeneracy, of principle, or of Practise' (ii. 239). Thus Pope is encouraging in gardening the kinds of poetic allusion he praised in John Denham's *Cooper's Hill*, which awaken 'thought and Contemplations that have a Relation to the Object'.[35]

Pope's proposals for the landscape embellishment of the ruins themselves are said to have 'belied his own principles of naturalistic design'.[36] But this is to misread his proposals:

> These venerable broken Walls, some Arches almost entire of 30 or 40 ft deep, some open like Portico's with fragments of pillars, some circular or inclosd on three sides, but exposd at top, with Steps which Time has made of disjointed Stones to climb to the highest point of the Ruin: These I say might have a prodigious Beauty, mixd with Greens & Parterres from part to part, and the whole Heap standing as it does on a round hill, kept smooth in green turf, which makes a bold Basement to show it. The open Courts from building to building might be thrown into Circles or Octagons of Grass or flowers, and even in the gaming Rooms you have fine trees grown, that might be made a natural Tapistry to the walls, & arch you over-head where time has uncoverd them to the Sky. (ii. 238)

[34] See *Inventory of Monuments in Dorset*, i. 64–6. From 1107 Sherborne Castle was the episcopal seat of the Bishop of Salisbury; it figured in the civil war after it was acquired by the Digbys in 1617.

[35] *Iliad*, XVI, 466 n.; *TE* viii. 261.

[36] Allen, *Tides in English Taste*, ii. 131.

The suggestions Pope makes here for octagons of grass, greens, parterres, and flowers do not violate principles of naturalistic design. They arise from an aesthetic of the picturesque, which does not preclude formality, but invites it according to the principle of contrast that has been described as the essential principle of picturesque design.[37]

In any event, these schemes of beautification are merely incidental to the potential of the ruins to afford picturesque prospect, Pope's central concern here as at Netley Abbey in the next decade, in his comments on the landscape situation of the ruins:

> You first see an old Tower penetrated by a large Arch, and others above it thro which the whole Country appears in prospect, even when you are at the top of the other ruins, for they stand very high, & the Ground slopes down on all sides. (ii. 238)

The purpose of his improvements is to conduct the visitor through a succession of picturesque prospects, exploiting the 'broken views':

> Little paths of earth, or sand, might be made, up the half-tumbled walls; to guide from one View to another on the higher parts; & Seats placd here and there, to enjoy those views, which are more romantick than Imagination can form them. (ii. 238–9)

Pope's genius for multiplying picturesque scenery, which impressed Walpole at Twickenham, is displayed here in such a way as to give us a clear idea of what he means by a 'romantic' view.

He proposes a temple situated on a 'neighbouring round Hill that is seen from all points of the Garden & is extremely pretty' (ii. 239), perhaps Jerusalem Hill (see Ladd's Map). It was intended to terminate a view from the 'Deep Scene' by the cascade, which he had described earlier as a place 'from whence you lose your eyes upon the glimmering of the Waters under the wood, & your ears in the constant dashing of the waves' (ii. 238). From here the temple would appear, as Pope imagined it, 'as in the clouds, between the tops of some very lofty Trees that form an Arch before it, with a great Slope downward to the end of the said river' (ii. 239). Pope's idea is a striking expression of the picturesque sensibility in gardening, a taste for the prospect of

[37] Nikolaus Pevsner, 'Picturesque England', chap. 7, *The Englishness of English Art* (1956). Pope's idea of the place is closer to the 'Ruins of the Ancient Castle at Sherborne', Philip Brannon *del. et sculp.*, in John Hutchins, *The History and Antiquities of the County of Dorset*, 3rd edn. (4 vols., London, 1873), iv, facing p. 274, than to Samuel and Nathaniel Buck's 'South View of Sherborne Castle' (1733). See plate 21.

a classical temple glimpsed through trees 'decay d' in clouds, as in the paintings of Claude. The description as a whole reveals at this early date Pope's 'prophetic eye of taste' for the picturesque.[38]

[38] *History of Gardening*, p. 14. Referring to Milton's description of Eden as an anticipation of the natural garden, Walpole observes: 'He seems with the prophetic eye of taste [as I have heard taste well defined] to have conceived, to have foreseen modern gardening.'

5. *Twickenham, Paradigm of the Picturesque Garden*

TWICKENHAM has always been recognized as a crucial document in the history of gardening, but there has been little agreement about its character, and hence about its historical significance in the development of the landscape garden. There is scarcely a word in the critical lexicon that has not been applied to the garden design—romantic, baroque, rococo, classical—and accordingly interpretation of its importance has varied widely.[1] Those who noticed a gap between Pope's theory and practice believed that Twickenham contradicted his own principles of naturalistic design and condemned it as reactionary: 'a complicated piece of mimicry of rural scenery of all sorts', 'as grotesque and fantastic a travesty of nature as anything that can be imagined'.[2] At the same time, Pope was regarded as 'something of a radical in his method of laying out a garden', and Twickenham has recently been described as 'probably the first of all "natural" gardens'.[3] The prevailing view which has emerged from these extremes is of Pope as a cautious

[1] The most important and influential essay on Pope's romantic taste in gardening is Frederick Bracher's article on 'Pope's Grotto: The Maze of Fancy', *Huntington Library Quarterly*, 12 (1949), 141–62; William Wimsatt mentions in passing Pope's 'baroque' taste in variegation in the 'Introduction' to *Alexander Pope: Selected Poetry and Prose*, 2nd edn. (New York, 1972), p. xvii; Nikolaus Pevsner ('Genesis of the Picturesque', p. 144) remarks of the garden that 'we would now probably call it Rococo more than anything else, with its wiggly paths, its minute mount, its cockle shells and minerals, and its effects of variety on a small scale'; H. F. Clark, in 'Sharawaggi at Chiswick', *Architectural Review*, 95 (1944), 126–7, argues for classical origins.

[2] B. Sprague Allen, *Tides in English Taste*, ii. 131; Alicia Amherst, *A History of Gardening in England* (London, 1896), p. 239; S. T. Prideaux, *Aquatint Engraving: A Chapter in the History of Book Illustration* (1909, repr. London, 1968), p. 168. On Pope's inconsistency see Isabel Chase, *Horace Walpole, Gardenist*, p. 171, and Derek Clifford, *A History of Garden Design*, p. 134.

[3] B. Sprague Allen, *Tides in English Taste*, ii. 133. The caption to Serle's *Plan* in Pevsner, 'Genesis of the Picturesque', p. 142.

reformer, and of Twickenham as 'eclectic' in style, and 'transitional' in importance.[4]

Much of the confusion about Twickenham is the result of the obscurity which surrounds the whole subject of the origins of the landscape garden. Taking into account the fact that Pope never gave a detailed description of the place or of his intentions (his often quoted letter to Blount is primarily a description of the grotto), that the garden no longer exists, and that very little documentary evidence survives, we are confronted with the conditions that everywhere face the historian of the landscape garden. Still, it is possible to find a way out of this labyrinth, and to demonstrate from an analysis of an unnoticed early description of the garden that Pope laid out at Twickenham what was probably the first, and certainly one of the most influential landscape gardens designed from the outset in accordance with picturesque principles of gardening. Contrary to the judgement of the leading historian of the garden, H. F. Clarke, that Twickenham was not picturesque,[5] it can be shown that Twickenham was a paradigm of picturesque principles of landscape design, and an eloquent expression of the pictorial and poetic sensibility we have described in the preceding chapters. Furthermore, it can be shown that Twickenham became a model of the picturesque garden for amateur and professional designers, as important in the history of landscape architecture as Lord Burlington's Chiswick in the history of English Palladian architecture.

Pope acquired Twickenham in the same year that Switzer published his expanded treatise on the idea of forest, rural, or extensive gardening which, as we have seen, was inspired by the idea of adapting to the English landscape a French ideal of magnificence. The inspiration of the garden at Twickenham, as Maynard Mack has recently suggested, was classical;[6] moreover the making of the Twickenham landscape was part of a classical architectural movement, the Palladian revival, of which Colen Campbell was prophet, Burlington

[4] Bracher states that 'Pope's taste in gardening was eclectic, beyond question', in 'Pope's Grotto', p. 154; Peter Willis maintains that 'Twickenham is a transitional garden' in 'A Poets' Gardener', *The Listener*, 72 (24 Dec. 1964), 1009. Cf. Christopher Hussey, 'Twickenham—I', *Country Life*, 96 (8 Sept. 1944), 420; Marie Luise Gothein, *A History of Garden Art*, trans. Mrs. Archer-Hind (London, 1928), ii. 282; Fiske Kimball, 'Romantic Classicism in Architecture', *Gazette des Beaux Arts*, 25 (Feb. 1944), 97; James Lees-Milne, *Earls of Creation* (London, 1962), p. 142.

[5] 'Eighteenth-Century Elysiums', p. 168.

[6] Mack, pp. 51–7.

executor, Robert Castell the scholar, and Robert Morris the expositor.[7] The origins of Twickenham, then, are to be discovered in this new initiative which combined architecture and garden in a harmony different from the traditional formalism of Renaissance Italian, French, and Dutch models.

The practical formulation of Pope's classical idea is undoubtedly related to the landscape of Whitehill House in Binfield, near Wokingham, Berkshire, where Pope's father, an enthusiastic gardener, retired between 1698 and 1701.[8] Whitehill House was surrounded by about seventeen acres of arable land, situated on a hill 'near the highest ground, which commands in every direction extensive and beautiful views' of Ascot, Windsor, Marlow, and the Thames valley.[9] It was one of the retreats of Catholic gentry disqualified by law from owning land near London, which included a number of friends of the Popes who made reputations in gardening: Sir Henry Englefield of Whiteknights, near Reading; Robert James Petre of Ingatestone Hall, Essex; the Southcote family of Albery Place, Surrey; the John Carylls of Ladyholt, Sussex; the Blounts of Mapledurham, Oxon.; and finally John Dancastle, the manor Lord of Binfield.[10]

The Dunces never tired of mocking Pope's father as a farmer and his son as the 'little Squire'.[11] The references in the *Imitations of Horace* (1734, 1738), to the 'Forest planted by a Father's hand' (Sat. II. ii. 135), and to 'A little House, with Trees a-row, /And like its Master, very low' (Ep. I. vii. 77–8), indicate that Pope remembered his father for 'forest' gardening, that is for extensive rural planting as well as horticulture. 'A row of noble Scotch firs' survived when Courthope wrote his description in the *Life* (1889); and a 'grove of beech trees known as Pope's Wood . . . about half-a-mile north-east of Whitehill, on the slope of a little hill from which a pleasant view is to be obtained', was perhaps part of the forest planted by a father's hand.[12] Fenton wrote to

7 See Chap. 11, 'Palladian Revival'.

8 Quoted by Sherburn, *Early Career*, p. 35.

9 W. J. Courthope, *Life of Pope*, Elwin–Courthope, v. 13. Cf. Lucius Fitzgerald, 'Pope at Binfield', *The Home Counties Magazine*, 2 (1900), 57.

10 On Catholic gardening gentry, see Walpole, *History of Gardening*, p. 33; Spence, 422, headnote and No. 603 n.; *Correspondence*, i. 123 n.

11 [Curll, Edmund and Elizabeth Thomas?], *Codrus: or, The Dunciad Dissected, Being the Finishing-Stroke. To Which is added, Farmer Pope and his Son. A Tale*, by Mr. Phillips (London, 1728), pp. 3, 11, 51. Guerinot No. 73.

12 W. J. Courthope, *Life of Pope*, Elwin–Courthope, v. 13–14; Fitzgerald, 'Pope at Binfield', p. 58.

23. The Imperial Gardens at Jehol. Engraving by Matteo Ripa. 1713.

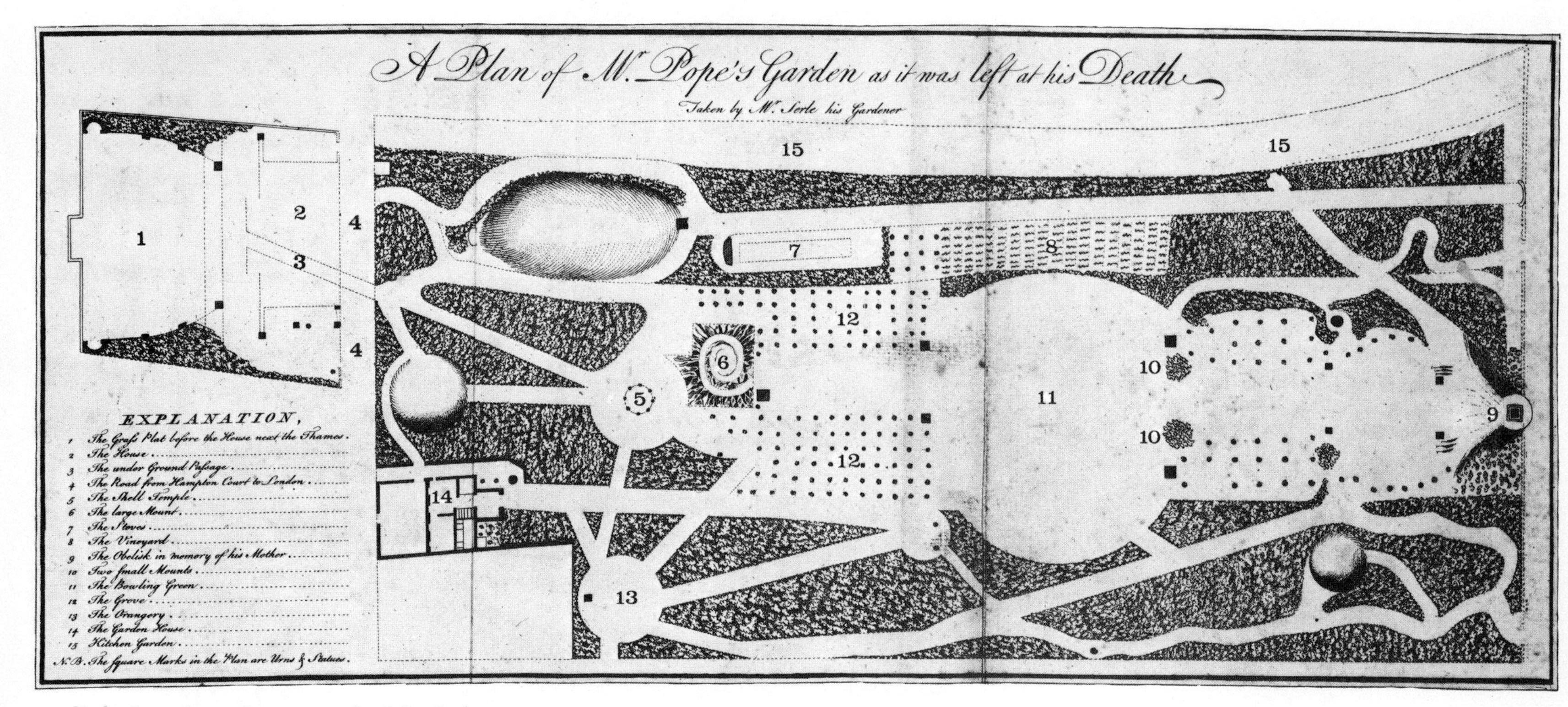

24. Plan of Pope's Garden. Drawn by John Serle. 1745.

EXPLANATION

1. The Grass Plat before the House next the Thames.
2. The House.
3. The underground Passage.
4. The Road from Hampton Court to London.
5. The Shell Temple.
6. The large Mount.
7. The Stoves.
8. The Vineyard.
9. The Obelisk in memory of his Mother.
10. Two small Mounts.
11. The Bowling Green.
12. The Grove.
13. The Orangery.
14. The Garden House.
15. Kitchen Garden.

N.B. The Square Marks in the Plan are Urns and Statues.

Broome (1724) that he was 'ready to have waited on you to Mr. Pope's old grove . . . to catch the Muse soft whispering through the trees, as Homer says' (ii. 233).

But the evidence most indicative of the character of Binfield is to be found in the beginning of Pope's gardening essay in the *Guardian* (173), in which the reference to 'my House in the country' where a visitor had discovered 'that Beauty which he always thought wanting in the most celebrated Seats, or if you will Villa's, of the Nation', has been plausibly interpreted as an allusion to a visit by Nicholas Rowe to Binfield in the same year.[13] As we have seen, the authority given for 'that Beauty' is a classical one, from Martial's Epigrams—*rus verum barbarumque*—which shows that Pope identified it with the classical ideal of the villa and rural wildness.

A second important antecedent of Twickenham is Chiswick House, Middlesex (plate 22), the Thames-side villa of Richard Boyle, Earl of Burlington, who became Pope's neighbour and friend when the Pope family moved from Binfield in 1716 to Mawson's New Buildings in Chiswick. Chiswick House is remembered more for its architecture than garden, but it was recognized by contemporaries and is regarded by historians now as a landmark in the history of garden design. Robert Dodsley mentions it as the first example of the landscape style when he traces with awful solemnity the progress of the Genius of Gardens in his poem *Public Virtue* (1753):

> And Lo! The progress of thy steps appears
> In fair improvements scatter'd round the land.
> Earliest in Chiswick's beauteous model seen. (426–8)[14]

It was not the first English garden to show variations from the formal style, but it has recently been shown by H. F. Clark that Chiswick illustrates a concept of the relationship between house and garden which was as studiously classical as the design of its architecture.[15] This is the idea of a 'certaine contrarietie betweene building and gardening' which is stated succinctly in Henry

[13] Pope, *Prose*, p. 145. See Sherburn, *Early Career*, pp. 277–8: 'The first paragraph of the essay seems to reflect this visit, and suggests the influence of modest, rural Binfield on Pope's conception of what a garden well might be.'

[14] *A Poem in Three Books* (London, 1753), 'Agriculture', Book the First, Canto the Second.

[15] 'Sharawaggi at Chiswick', pp. 125–6.

Wotton's *Elements of Architecture* (1624): 'For as Fabriques should bee *regular*, so gardens should bee *irregular*, or at least cast into a very Wilde *Regularitie*.'[16] The importance of Chiswick in the history of English landscape gardening is the application of this classical idea in the creation of a setting for the series of classical temples and pavilions, which culminated in the Palladian villa Burlington built between 1717 and 1724 to house his large collection of sculpture.[17]

Oriental was added to classical authority for the development of the landscape garden at Chiswick by Burlington's protégé, the architect Robert Castell, in a volume dedicated to his patron entitled *The Villas of the Ancients Illustrated* (1728) which reconstructs gardens and architecture of famous ancient villas from descriptions of classical writers, and illustrates them with 'plans'.[18] Castell concedes that the Romans had regular gardens, but distinguishes a middle kind between the 'rough Manner' and the 'regular and exact Taste', which he compares to the 'Accounts we have of the present Manner of Designing in *China*':

> whose Beauty consisted in a close Imitation of Nature; where, tho' the Parts are disposed with the greatest Art, the Irregularity is still preserved; so that their Manner may not improperly be said to be an artful Confusion, where there is no Appearance of that Skill which is made use of, their *Rocks*, *Cascades*, and *Trees*, bearing their natural Forms.[19]

The 'accounts we have . . . of China' by Temple and Addison had been recently supplemented by views of the Imperial Gardens at Jehol (plate 23), 150 miles north-east of Peking, engraved by the missionary Jesuit Father, Matteo Ripa (1682–1746), who visited London in 1724 when Burlington acquired what appear to be 'the first illustrations of Chinese landscape gardens to reach the West'.[20]

Thus Burlington and his circle were able to visualize Chinese 'Sharawadgi' (a generation before William Chambers returned from his visit to China)

[16] Ed. Frederick Hard (Charlottesville, Virginia, 1968), p. 109.

[17] See H. Avray Tipping, 'Chiswick House—I', *Country Life*, 43 (9 Feb. 1918), 130–7.

[18] 'Sharawaggi at Chiswick', p. 126; F. Saxl and Rudolf Wittkower, *British Art and the Mediterranean* (Oxford, 1948), p. 53.

[19] *Villas of the Ancients* (London, 1728), pp. 116–17.

[20] Rudolf Wittkower, 'English Neo-Palladianism, the Landscape Garden, China, and the Enlightenment', *L'Arte*, 2 (June 1969), 19, 28.

at precisely the moment the setting for the classical villa at Chiswick was being planned,[21] and sanctions were found for irregularity in gardening. Such authorities would have been sufficient for Pope to answer the author of a *Miscellany on Taste* (1732), who attacked his principles of gardening in the *Epistle to Burlington* (1731) with the argument that 'the best of all the gardens, as well as Fabricks of ancient times, were perfectly regular. And had Mr. Pope been the Designer of those, I dare almost venture to assert, he would have plann'd them out in a regular Form, or every good Judge would have condemned his Gothick Fancy.'[22] On the contrary, it was soon taken for granted by the *cognoscenti* that the gardens of the enlightened Ancients had been irregular. One commentator observed in 1740 that Horace in his Sabine villa 'had that taste for wild natural gardening which has obtained so much among us of late'.[23]

It may have been the example of Burlington's classical villa at Chiswick as much as expense which prompted Pope to refuse the Earl's offer of a town house in London, and to lease at the end of 1718 a house and grounds on the Thames at Twickenham. In the architecture of his house he followed Burlington explicitly, and the gardens are clearly derived from the classical ideals exemplified in the wildness of Binfield, and the irregularity of Chiswick. The classical ideal in the garden is apparent in the garden architecture, ornament, statuary, and inscriptions. The Twickenham Inventory lists various 'Deities' and 'Antike busttos'. Kent's drawing of the garden (plate 56) with its allusions to the 'Wild Paradise' of Homer suggests something of the classical *ethos* which was undoubtedly in Pope's mind. The ornament of sculpture and architecture Pope was planning to erect on the riverside in his garden the year before he died was an elaborate composition of classical iconography.[24]

[21] Basil Gray, 'Lord Burlington and Father Ripa's Chinese Engravings', *British Museum Quarterly*, 22 (1960), 42.

[22] [Concanen, Matthew], p. 13. Guerinot, No. 100.

[23] 'Mr. T's Notes on Horace', Appendix to No. 1448, Spence ii. 672.

[24] On the classical inspiration of Twickenham, see Mack, p. 57. On Kent's pen and sepia drawing, 'Pope's Garden at Twickenham' (B.M. Drawing 1872–11–9–878) see Laurence Binyon, *Catalogue of Drawings by British Artists . . . Preserved in the British Museum*, 4 vols. (London, 1898–1907), ii. 174; and Wimsatt 14, *Portraits*, pp. 119–22. For Pope's riverside ornament see Spence, No. 620, and Mack, pp. 37–40.

Notwithstanding the importance of classical inspiration, the garden design of Twickenham represents a departure from the uncompromising classicism of Chiswick's architecture and statuary.[25] Burlington has been remembered as an architect rather than a garden designer, and Chiswick was celebrated for its architecture. Twickenham became the model of the new taste in garden design, and its influence was as radical as Chiswick's in architecture.

H. F. Clark argues that at Twickenham 'Pope did not plan his garden according to the laws of picturesque composition but followed "the rules of the Ancients" as interpreted by Robert Castell.'[26] I would argue, on the contrary, that the distinguishing mark of the design at Twickenham from the outset was the picturesque. Pope adapted the classical idea of the garden exemplified at Binfield and Chiswick in accordance with his sensibility for picturesque landscape, much in the same way that he transformed Homer in his translation of the *Iliad*.

The rarity of reliable descriptions of Pope's gardens during his lifetime is a fundamental obstacle in the way of anyone who attempts to determine the character and trace the development of its design. Only one extended description by Pope himself survives, the often quoted letter to Edward Blount (1725), but this letter is primarily a description of the grotto, and is so entitled in Pope's *Letters* (1737).[27] Of the accounts published after Pope's death the text of the guidebook, *A Plan of Mr. Pope's Garden* (1745; plate 24), published by Pope's gardener, John Serle, is exclusively concerned with the grotto, and the only full description of the garden before it was altered beyond recognition by subsequent owners is the long report by a correspondent of the *Newcastle General Magazine*, published in 1748.[28] Except for the casual allusions of Pope and his visitors we have no description of the gardens during his

[25] On Chiswick's classicism see H. Avray Tipping, 'Chiswick House—I', *Country Life*, 43 (1918), p. 137; David Green, *Gardener to Queen Anne, Henry Wise (1653–1738) and the Formal Garden* (London, 1956), p. 155.

[26] 'Eighteenth Century Elysiums', p. 168.

[27] *Correspondence*, ii. 296–7 (2 June 1725). See *Letters of Mr. Alexander Pope, And Several of his Friends* (1737), where the letter (XCVI) is listed in the table of contents as 'A Description of a Grotto'.

[28] *A Plan of Mr. Pope's Garden as it was left at his Death: With a Plan and Perspective View of the Grotto* (London, 1745); 'An Epistolary Description of the late Mr. Pope's House and Gardens at Twickenham', *The Newcastle General Magazine, or Monthly Intelligencer*, i (Jan. 1748), reprinted in Mack, Appendix A, pp. 237–43, hereafter cited in the text. The desecration of Twickenham is reported by Horace Walpole in a letter to Horace Mann: Walpole, *Correspondence*, xxv. 177 (23 Aug. 1781).

lifetime. Hence the importance of the possibility hitherto unrecognized, strongly suggested by circumstantial evidence, that Joseph Spence's description of the gardens of Horatio in Part II of *An Essay on Pope's Odyssey* (August 1727) is a unique and substantially accurate account of Pope's garden at Twickenham during its first decade of existence.

It has been established that Pope and Spence became acquainted soon after the publication of Part I of Spence's *Essay* in June 1726 when Pope sought out and entered into a correspondence with the author.[29] Before publishing Part II Spence wrote to Pope '& desird [lea]ve to send the copy to him; [th]at I might not say anything [ag]st him in it, that might be ill-grounded'. The manuscript of Part II, which was in the press by February 1727, contains numerous marginal annotations in Pope's hand.[30] The results of this collaboration have been variously appraised. Austin Wright observes that Pope 'cannot be convicted of trying to alter the tone of the work significantly', but that 'the last two evenings [Part II] contain comparatively little adverse criticism and a larger share of praise'.[31] This reflects the awkward position Spence found himself in as he struggled to maintain impartiality as a critic, while anxious to ingratiate himself with a new and valued friend. Speaking of kind letters he had received from Pope, Spence wrote about his embarrassment to Christopher Pitt in February when Part II of the *Essay* was in the press:

> That Gentleman [Pope] is kinder in some particulars than I can express: and I verily think 'tis with him (as was said of the Prince of Orange) that 'If you had a mind to get into his friendship, you must do him an Injury.' I have tortur'd some of his lines and plagu'd the world with a String of Pedantick Rules—how unaccountable a way to so notable a reward![32]

It appears that Spence assuaged his conscience about his criticism of Pope's translation of the *Odyssey* by indirectly praising his gardens at Twickenham and

[29] See Austin Wright, *Joseph Spence* (Chicago, 1950), pp. 12–13, and 'The Beginning of Pope's Friendship with Spence', *Modern Language Notes*, 54 (May 1939), 359–61; and Spence, i. xxiii–vi.

[30] See Spence, i. xxiv; and Appendix H, 'Pope's Annotations in the Manuscript of Joseph Spence's *Essay on his Translation of the Odyssey*', *TE* x. 594.

[31] *Joseph Spence*, pp. 11, 25. Wright adds that 'however much Pope had to do with its final form, the second part of the *Essay* is beyond question more lavish of praise and more sparing of condemnation than the first had been' (p. 208, n. 11).

[32] Quoted by James Osborn, Spence, i. xxv.

his skill as a garden designer, pursuits Pope preened himself on as much as poetry, according to Philip Southcote.[33]

Spence's compliment to Pope's garden occurs in the setting of Evening the Fourth at the beginning of Part II of the *Essay*, where Spence introduces a new character into the dialogue and a change of scene. In Part I Spence followed the English and continental tradition, giving to the setting of the dialogue between the 'Greek' speakers, Philypsus and Antiphaus, a perfectly conventional treatment. We are told that the conversations take place at 'the Country-seat of . . . Philypsus. . . . a retirement every way agreeable'. The country-house setting is said to be derived from the 'maison de campagne fort jolie aux environs de Paris' where Dominique Bouhours sets his dialogue in *La Manière de bien penser dans les ouvrages d'esprit* (1687). But like Bouhours himself, and most French and English writers of dialogues, Spence does not further elaborate the setting after the initial *mise en scène*.[34]

Thus it is a surprising departure from literary convention and his own practice in Part I of the *Essay* when Spence changes the setting at the beginning of Part II in Evening the Fourth from the unparticularized location of a country-house to the gardens of a villa on the Thames near London, described in considerable detail, indeed in sufficient detail to suggest a particular place and a particular person. Philypsus proposes a change of scene to Antiphaus:

> ''Tis a fine Evening, says he; and if you please we will take a turn together in the Gardens of *Horatio*: since we cannot enjoy his Company, at least let us make use of that Liberty he has left with us. There we shall be retir'd from the Noise, and Bustle of the Town; and safe from every sort of Interruption.' (ii. 2)

The suggestion is agreeable and they proceed to the gardens of Horatio from town in a coach which sets them down 'at the Gates which lead into the Great-Walk of the Garden':

> After a turn or two there, they sat down by the side of a Fountain, full in sight of

[33] Spence, No. 603. Cf. Walpole, *History of Gardening*, p. 28: 'There was a little of affected modesty in the latter [Pope], when he said, of all his works he was most proud of his garden.'

[34] See Elizabeth Merrill, *The Dialogue in English Literature*, Yale Studies in English, vol. 42 (New York, 1911), chaps. 4–5; Joseph Spence, *An Essay on Pope's Odyssey* (2 vols., London, 1726–7. Repr. 2 vols. in 1, New York, 1972), i. 1 (page references hereafter in the text); Bouhours, *La Manière* (Amsterdam, 1688), p. 2; A. F. B. Clark, *Boileau and the French Classical Critics in England 1660–1830* (Paris, 1925), p. 267; and Austin Wright, *Joseph Spence*, pp. 27–8.

the *Thames*, which passes at the bottom of the Walk. The Walk itself makes a fine Visto in its Descent to the River: at a distance, you see the Fields and Hills; at first in an easy Ascent varied into Pasture and Arable, and then rising unequally, and cover'd here and there with Woods, till they are insensibly lost in a bluish Cast of the Clouds. The agreeableness of the Place made *Philypsus* forget himself for a few Moments: he was taken up wholly in wandering with his Eye, sometimes over those beautiful Gardens, and sometimes over the irregular Prospect that lay before them. (ii. 2–3)

This is obviously not a literally accurate topographical description of Pope's garden at Twickenham as we know it from various sources. The views described could not be obtained from the same vantage point, and the description might be said to be too generalized to be identified with any particular place. Nevertheless, the correspondences to the known characteristics of Pope's garden at this date are too striking to be ignored. Taking the apparent parallels in order, we know that Pope was accustomed throughout his residence at Twickenham to allow visitors (perhaps Spence himself by this time) the 'liberty' of his gardens during his absence.[35] The suburban situation of Pope's villa at Twickenham on the Thames, fifteen miles west of London on the Hampton Court road corresponds closely to Horatio's retirement away 'from the Noise, and Bustle of the Town'. Although we have no evidence of 'Gates which lead into the Great-Walk of the Garden' from the road at Twickenham, Serle's *Plan* indicates that entrances from the road did exist at the time of Pope's death, and he was building a 'triumphal arch' into the garden, perhaps through one of them, in 1733 (iii. 358). As for a 'Great-Walk', in 1721 Pope wrote to Lady Mary of the 'honour . . . to my Great Walk, that the finest Woman in this world, cou'd not stir from it. That Walk extremely well answerd the Intent of its Contriver,

[35] See Pope's letter to Lady Mary from Cirencester (15 Sept. 1721; ii. 82) acknowledging compliments to 'my Trees & Garden', which she had visited in his absence. Writing to Ralph Allen in 1736 Pope specifies what appears to have been his usual policy on admitting visitors: 'Mr Leake . . . was refused by my Servants to see the place, which I had myself invited him to: In general they never show the house (which you know is nothing) in my Absence; but the Garden I never hinder them to show, but when I have Company with me' (7 Apr. 1736; iv. 9). Thus Elizabeth Carter, visiting the garden in the summer of 1738 with a group that may have included Samuel Johnson, writes: 'At Twickenham we got a Sight of Mr. Pope's Gardens by the Interest of one of our Company with his celebrated man John' [John Serle, Pope's gardener, 'celebrated' in l. 1 of the *Epistle to Arbuthnot*, 1734]. See Elizabeth Carter's letter to Mrs. Underdown (July 1738) transcribed by G. Hampshire, 'Johnson, Elizabeth Carter, and Pope's Garden', *Notes & Queries*, 217 (June 1972), 221.

when it detaind her there' (ii. 82). Setting aside for the moment the apparent difference in location, Pope's 'Spring of the Clearest Water' (ii. 296) mentioned in the letter to Edward Blount corresponds roughly to the 'Fountain, full in sight of the Thames' in Horatio's garden. Moreover, Pope was contemplating the installation of a piece of fountain statuary with inscription in the same letter (ii. 297; 2 June 1725).

Granted that many of these features are conventional in contemporary gardens, it is nevertheless significant that Spence includes nothing in Horatio's gardens which could not be found in some form in Pope's. But this ignores the conspicuous discrepancies between the gardens' perspectives, and the prospects in Horatio's gardens—the 'fine Visto in its Descent to the River', and the 'irregular Prospect' of fields, hills, woods, and clouds—which would seem to be topographical impossibilities at Twickenham. Philypsus compares Horatio's garden unfavourably to these prospects when he recollects himself from a pleasing reverie:

> There is a difference (says he) in the agreeable Sense I feel at present from the delightful Views on all sides of us, which may partly confirm what we were talking of just before we sat down. Does not this Master-piece of Art [the gardens], with all its Symmetry and Justness of Proportions, strike the Mind in a feebler manner, than that Landskape of Nature in its infinite Irregularity? These measured Rises and Falls, in Slopes answering each other, Those Groves terminating every way in an exactness of figure, These Walks intercrossing without confusion, and uniting so happily, cannot fail of pleasing the Eye very much: Yet that Wildness and Variety abroad, the River, Lawn, Fields and Woods so beautifully interspers'd, compose a Scene much finer and more engaging. For my part, I shou'd be apt to prefer that single Grot yonder, and the hanging Precipice over it, to a whole Scenary of natural Objects laid out in the most regular order imaginable. (ii. 3–4)

The terms of this description, the preference for Nature to Art, are clearly derived from the aesthetics of Shaftesbury and Addision,[36] but 'that single Grot yonder', if not the 'hanging precipice over it', is another specific reference which corresponds to what was the most renowned feature of Pope's garden at the time. The quasi-formal features of 'Slopes', 'Groves', and 'Walks', common to most gardens of the period, can be established at Twicken-

[36] Cf. the 'lines [of a garden], intercrossing without confusion' in Shaftesbury, *Characteristics*, ed. Robertson, ii. 270 n.; and *Spectator*, No. 414.

ham by engravings, Serle's *Plan*, and allusions in the correspondence.[37] But what have prospects of the kind described by Philypsus to do with Pope's Twickenham, where topography and testimony of witnesses like Walpole about Pope's 'thick impenetrable woods', 'seeing nothing', would appear to make it impossible for any observer to find a vantage point that would allow him to see both the gardens and the opposite bank of the Thames simultaneously?[38]

Once again it must be insisted that while the correspondence is not exact the emphasis on prospect in the description of the gardens of Horatio gives us a valuable clue to the genius of the place at Twickenham when first laid out by Pope. Pope's description of the perspectives between the Shell Temple in his garden and the Thames in his letter to Edward Blount parallels Horatio's Walk which 'makes a fine Visto in its Descent to the River':

> From the River *Thames*, you see thro' my Arch up a Walk of the Wilderness to a kind of open Temple, wholly compos'd of Shells in the Rustic Manner; and from that distance under the Temple you look down thro' a sloping Arcade of Trees, and see the Sails on the River passing suddenly and vanishing, as thro' a Perspective Glass. (ii. 296)

Pope himself is shown holding a perspective glass in William Kent's sketch of the garden (plate 56), which illustrates the vista from the Shell Temple through the grotto to the river where a boat is dimly seen passing on the Thames. And while it is a manifest impossibility to reconcile this view, through a narrow underground cavern of sails on the Thames, with a simultaneous view of the countryside on the Surrey side, such views, it is clear, could be obtained from Pope's garden, and it may be fairly said that virtually every feature of his garden design, even the architecture of his house, was designed to take advantage of similar prospects.

The grotto, first of all, Pope explained to Edward Blount, had been contrived to function as a *camera obscura* 'on the Walls of which all the objects of the River, Hills, Woods, and Boats, are forming a moving Picture in their visible Radiations' (ii. 296). In addition, Pope included in his garden one

[37] 'Slopes' in Rysbrack's 'Exact Draught and View of Mr. Pope's House at Twickenham' (*c.* 1735); 'Groves' in *Correspondence*, ii. 24 (1720); 'quincunx groves' in Spence, No. 602; and 'intercrossing Walks' in the Newcastle correspondent's account.

[38] Walpole, *Correspondence*, xxi. 417 (20 June 1760).

feature of medieval and Elizabethan gardens still used in the early eighteenth century as a means of obtaining prospects. This was 'the large Mount' as indicated on Serle's *Plan* (no. 6 in the key) completed about 1725, when William Kent probably made the sketch of it now lost.[39] Spence later criticized its execution as 'stiff and bad', but admired 'the point of view at the top ... good and well chosen' (No. 602). Significantly for the comparison to the gardens of Horatio, it appears that extensive views within and without the garden could be obtained from this spot. The Newcastle correspondent gives the only detailed description of Pope's Mount and the views it afforded within the garden:

> Among the Hillocks on the upper Part of the open Area, rises a Mount much higher than the rest, and is composed of more rude and indigested Materials; it is covered with Bushes and Trees of a wilder Growth, and more confused Order, rising as it were out of Clefts of Rocks, and Heaps of rugged and mossy Stones; among which a narrow intricate Path leads in an irregular Spiral to the Top; where is placed a Forest Seat or Chair, that may hold three or four Persons at once, overshaded with the Branches of a spreading Tree. From this Seat we face the Temple [Shell Temple], and overlook the various Distribution of the Thickets, Grass-plots, Alleys, Banks, &c. (241)

In 1738 Elizabeth Carter testified to a 'broken view' of the Thames which could be obtained from Pope's Mount: 'A winding Ascent leads to the Top of a Mount surrounded by a Hedge of Yew & covered with Trees which thro' their Branches discover a Vista to the Thames.'[40] According to Nicholas Hardinge (1699–1758), the author of *Horti Popiani: Ode Sapphica*, Latin verses on Pope's garden dated 1743, and a visitor to Pope's garden, views of Sheen in Richmond could be seen from Pope's Mount:

> O who will put me back on the
> Height of the leafy hill [Pope's Mount], which overlooks
> The summits of Sheen adorned with villas
> And the glassy river broad.[41]

[39] First mentioned by Pope in 1721 (ii. 86). William Kent made a sketch of it, mistakenly called a design by Spence (No. 602). See chap 7. B. S. Allen comments on the garden history of the Mount in *Tides in English Taste*, ii. 251, n. 27. In the Pierpont Morgan MS. of the *Epistle to Burlington* (l. 35) the genius of the place 'Here bids ascend the future Mount'.

[40] G. Hampshire, 'Johnson, Elizabeth Carter, and Pope's Garden', *Notes & Queries*, 217 (June 1972), 221.

[41] My literal translation of the stanza from Item V in R. Dodsley, 'Verses on the Grotto at Twickenham by Mr. Pope Attempted in Latin and Greek to which is added Horti Popiani: Ode Sapphica, also

The importance of prospect to Pope in the initial layout of his estate is apparent in what may be one of his first thoughts for garden architecture at Twickenham, a crude sketch in the *Iliad* manuscript (*c.* 1719–20) labelled as

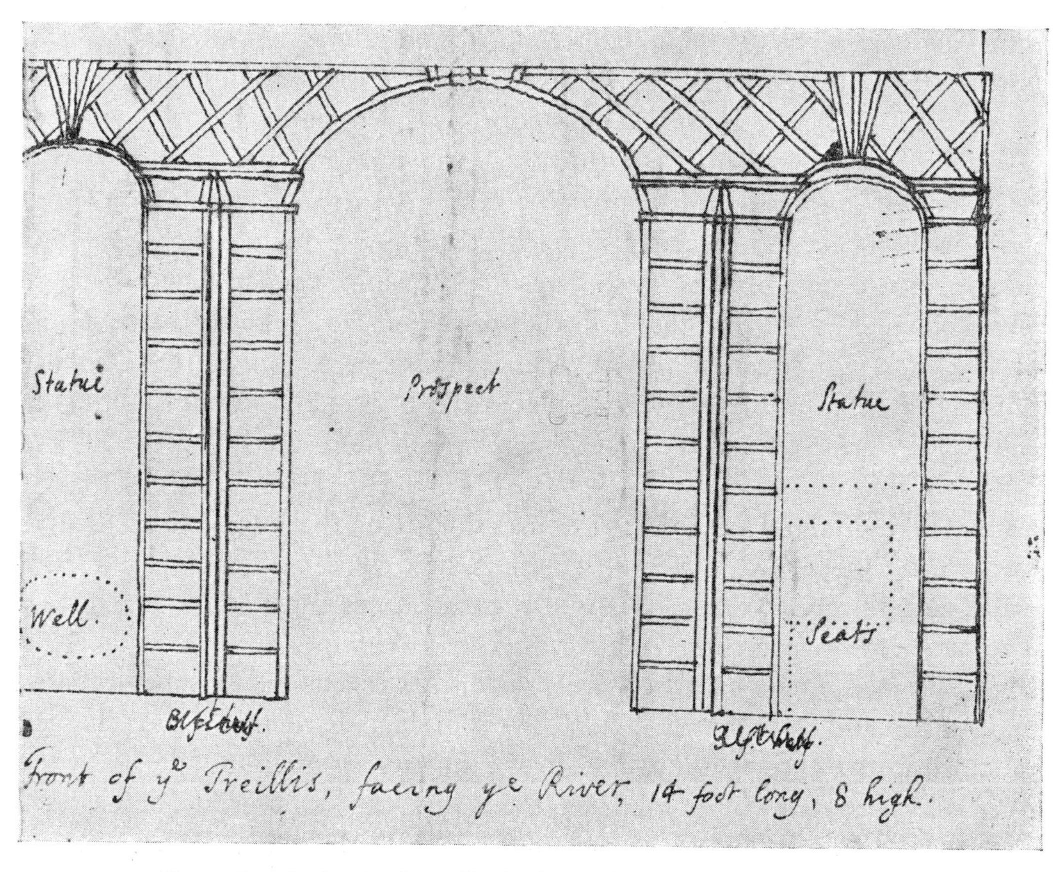

FIG. 2. Pope's sketch of a trellis for his garden at Twickenham. *c.* 1719.

a 'trellis, facing ye River, 14 foot long, 8 high' (fig. 2). Space was provided for statues in niches on either side of a central arch marked 'prospect', with indications for seats from which views of the river could be enjoyed.[42]

the Cave of Pope. A Prophecy' (London, 1743). Reprinted in Mack, Appendix E, p. 268. On the authorship of the *Ode*, printed anonymously by Dodsley and Mack, see Morris R. Brownell, 'Walter Harte, Nicholas Hardinge, and Pope's "Verses on the Grotto" ', *Notes & Queries* (June 1977).

[42] B.M. Add. 4808, f. 116v.

In 1743 Pope erected two stone summerhouses built on the bank of the Thames for a similar purpose which he described as 'the last Sacrifice I shall make to the Nymphs of the Thames'.[43] It may be that what we might by now call an obsession with prospect extended even to alterations of his villa. A crude ink plan in the *Odyssey* manuscript dated about 1722, possibly concerned with interior alterations to Pope's Twickenham villa, is accompanied by the autograph note: 'Window to ye 2nd floor, to reflect gardens.'[44]

All these improvements designed to call the country into the garden correlate with the importance of prospect in the gardens of Horatio, and suggest that prospect and the picturesque were guiding principles behind Pope's design. Picturesque prospect was one of the things that attracted Pope to Twickenham, where, he told William Broome in December of his first year of residence, 'the situation [is] so very airy, and yet so warm, that you will think yourself in a sort of heaven, where the prospect is boundless' (ii. 19), and where during a flood the following year he found 'the Prospect . . . prodigiously fine' (ii. 59).

His delight in the river landscape of his situation on the Thames is confirmed by his own sketch (see plate 16), paintings he owned of Twickenham landscape, and his repeated descriptions in verse of scenes reflected in the Thames. The same love of riverside scenery underlies his attempt to include the river landscape in the design of his gardens, which suggests he may have shared the 'judgement of a French taylor on a Villa and gardens by the Thames' ridiculed in the notes to the *Dunciad*: 'All this is very fine, but take away the river, and it is good for nothing.'[45] It was here on the riverside, as we have seen, that he commented to Spence on the 'idea of the picturesque' (No. 613) which was the controlling principle of his design.

Spence later recorded remarks of Pope dated about 1739 which prove that he carried out plantations in his garden in accordance with picturesque prin-

[43] See Spence, No. 356 n.; Pope, *Correspondence*, iv. 433. Niches or summer houses are indicated on Serle's *Plan*, and one is represented in the 'View of Mr. Pope's House at Twickenham', A. Heckell del. J. Mason sculp. (1749; plate 26).

[44] B.M. Add. 4809, f. 66^{v}.

[45] Testimonies of Authors, in *The Dunciad Variorum* (1729), *TE* v. 28. Pope's sketch is plate 4 in Mack; landscapes he owned are listed in the 'Inventory'; his fascination with the Thames' 'visionary scene' can be seen in the *Pastorals*, Spring, ll. 63–4; *Windsor Forest*, ll. 375–6; 'Lines to Mr. Gay' (1722), ll. 3–4 in *TE* vi. 225; *Imitations of Horace*, Ep. I, i (1737), ll. 140–2; and *Ode* IV, i (1737), ll. 21–4.

ciples. He told Spence during a visit to Twickenham that 'those clumps of trees are like the groups in pictures' (No. 607), explaining that 'The light and shades in gardening are managed by disposing the thick grove-work, the thin, and the openings in a proper manner, of which the eye generally is the properest judge' (No. 611). Referring in the same conversation to the plantations surrounding the monument to his mother, a focal point of his garden as shown on Serle's *Plan*, he told Spence that 'You may distance things by darkening them and by narrowing the plantation more and more toward the end, in the same manner as they do in painting, and as 'tis executed in the little cypress walk to that obelisk [Mrs. Pope's]' (No. 610). Thus the design of his own garden illustrates the principle Pope had stated to Spence in 1734: 'All gardening is landscape-painting' (No. 606). The 'master-piece of art' which Spence described in 1727 had become the paradigm of the picturesque landscape garden.

The concluding dialogue of Spence's *Essay*, Evening the Fifth, begins with idealized description of Horatio's gardens, introduces a piece of garden architecture which can be identified with Pope's Shell Temple, and later in the course of the dialogue makes an allusion to the designer which supplies compelling evidence for identifying Horatio with Pope. Having agreed that their next and last meeting 'shou'd be in the same place', Philypsus and Antiphaus 'set out for *Horatio*'s earlier than usual':

> When they alighted, Philypsus order'd his Servant before them to the *Dome* of *Apollo*, with a Book or two he had brought in the Coach; whilst He and *Antiphaus* walk'd on gently to enjoy the Freshness of the Air, and the Beauties of the Place. The Sun (which now began to be in its decline) as it shot thro' the Trees, made a thousand wavering Mixtures of Light and Shade: The Birds, on all sides were answering one another in their little natural Airs: every thing look'd Fresh about 'em; and every thing was Agreeable. (ii. 93–4)

This description of the gardens in terms of the *locus amoenus* and Addisonian pleasures of the imagination corresponds to similar accounts of Twickenham in Pope's correspondence (ii. 44, 1720), but it is too derivative to indicate any place in particular. As for the 'Dome of Apollo', Pope's Shell Temple was itself a Dome, an interesting variation of a classical rotunda; and it is particularly significant to discover that Pope had commented in detail on his ideas for such a piece of garden architecture in one of his earliest conversations with Spence.[46]

The last and most telling allusion to Horatio and his gardens occurs later in Evening the Fifth when Philypsus, speaking in Addisonian terms of 'great' and 'total' views of landscape, unexpectedly alludes to the gardens of Horatio and their designer in terms which point unmistakably to Pope:

> When I had the Pleasure of Conversing with the Gentleman, who design'd these Gardens, (as indeed the Finest in the Nation owe their Beauty to his Directions) I was very much pleas'd with a Maxim which he then mention'd; 'That as the greatest *fault* in a Prospect was Confinement; So the *meanest* thing too in a Design, was to have the Bounds and Restraint of it immediately visible.' (ii. 132–3)

Alluding to Philypsus' description of the gardens of Horatio in 1758, Spence adopted from it for his own the precept that 'Wildness [is] preferable to regularity in gardens' (No. 1092), clearly indicating that he identified himself with Philypsus in this context. The identity of his interlocutor, the speaker of the quoted remark, and the circumstances of the conversation are no less clear.

The 'Maxim' quoted with approval is an obvious paraphrase of Pope's principle of concealment of bounds, a principle Walpole noticed Pope had applied at Twickenham.[47] As for the statement about Horatio—'the finest [gardens] in the Nation owe their beauty to his Directions'—it applies more exactly to Pope at this date than to any person of Spence's acquaintance. By this time Twickenham was already famous, and Pope had established his reputation as a garden designer in a large number of important places including Cirencester, Richmond Lodge, Down Hall, Wimpole, Rousham, Stowe, and others. Swift had publicly spoke of him shortly before the publication of Part II of Spence's *Essay* as 'the Contriver of the Gardens' at the villa of his neighbour, Henrietta Howard, at Marble Hill.[48] Spence shrewdly paid his

[46] No. 619, dated 1728? by Osborn.

[47] Walpole, *Correspondence*, xxv. 177 (23 Aug. 1781, to Horace Mann). Spence, who was a frequent visitor to Twickenham from 1728, discussed the principle with Pope, and adopted it for his own treatise on gardening. See Spence, No. 602 headnote, quoting from Spence's MS. 'Heads for Garden Letters'; Spence, No. 612, and Appendix to No. 1059, 'Spence's Letter to the Reverend Mr. Wheeler', ii. 646–52. On the date of Spence's first meeting with Pope, see Osborn, Spence, i. xxiii, xxvi.

[48] 'Preface' to 'A Pastoral Dialogue between Richmond-Lodge and Marble-Hill' (June 1727), in *The Poems of Jonathan Swift*, ed. Harold Williams, 2nd edn. (Oxford, 1958), ii. 407. For Pope's gardening career see below, chaps. 7–8.

compliments on gardening to a man who was, according to Philip Southcote 'more fond of this sort of fame than any other' (No. 603).

To summarize, if the assumption can be granted that Spence attempted in the account of Horatio and his gardens in Part II of the *Essay* to introduce 'real Names' for his speakers and 'Action and Reality' to their conversation,[49] the circumstantial evidence overwhelmingly supports the identification of Pope's Twickenham with the gardens of Horatio. Considering Spence's rhetorical purpose to praise indirectly, the particularity of his description is very marked. He could not have given a literal 'translation' of Pope's gardens in the dialogue without violating decorum, but he did manage to give a faithful imitation, true to its essential character as it later developed. If I am right in identifying Pope's garden with Horatio's, it provides valuable evidence that Twickenham was not 'unapologetically regular', scarcely less formal than the gardens he attacked, as later charged, but laid out from the outset in accordance with his theory of picturesque design.[50] It also supplies additional evidence that by the mid-1720s Pope had established his reputation as a leading garden designer.

What little can be learned about Pope's early plantations at Twickenham confirms the impression derived from Spence that he was laying out a picturesque garden. Pope's orchard, vineyard, and kitchen garden, and his references to raising fruits and exotic vegetables throughout his correspondence indicate his interest in horticulture, but everything from the beginning was subordinate to the plantation of what Gilbert West referred to in his poem, *Stowe* (1732), as 'the care of thy own rising Wood'.[51]

Pope's determination to practise a version of Switzer's 'rural, extensive, or forest gardening' at Twickenham is apparent from numerous references to his wood and plantations of trees in his correspondence. His preference for 'Standards' stated in the *Guardian* essay on gardening has been quoted.[52]

[49] See the 'Preface', *Essay on Pope's Odyssey* (1726).

[50] Allen, *Tides of Taste*, ii. 132.

[51] *The Gardens of the Right Honourable Richard Lord Viscount Cobham. Address'd to Mr. Pope* (London, 1732), p. 2. Cf. Richard Savage, 'Epistle I. To Mr. Pope', in *A Collection of Pieces in Verse and Prose, Which have been Publish'd on Occasion of the Dunciad* (London, 1732), l. 1: 'Whilst you at *Twick'nam* plan the future Wood'.

[52] *Prose*, p. 148. Pope ordered from Bathurst about 1724 'all the limes which can possibly be spared' (ii. 263). See references to 'enchanted bowers' (ii. 19), an 'Arch of Trees' (ii. 297 and n.), 'a Grove' (ii. 328),

'A tree', he told Spence in their early conversations, 'is a nobler object than a prince in his coronation robes' (No. 616). Eighteenth-century expertise in plantation of trees makes plausible Pope's rapid transformation of a place where in 1718 'there were not Ten Sticks in the Ground', as John Serle described it to Curll, to a garden two years later whose trees 'like new Acquaintance brought happily together, are stretching their Arms to meet each other, and growing nearer and nearer every Hour' (ii. 44).[53]

The only detailed description of Pope's mature garden and its wood, published in the *Newcastle General Magazine* in January 1748 after his death, confirms its character as a 'forest garden'.[54] The Newcastle correspondent observes of Twickenham 'that a Wood or a Forest doth not deviate much more from Rule' (240). He admires the wildness and irregularity of the plantations, which include 'lofty Elms and other Forest Trees' (238), and the walk between the grotto and the Shell Temple 'over-arch'd with wild and interwoven Branches of Trees' (240). As we would expect in a garden of the author of the *Guardian* satire on topiary 'no Shear-work or tonsure is to be found in all the Scene' (241).

Pope's plantations at Twickenham were admired and his intentions understood by several knowledgeable visitors in addition to Joseph Spence and the anonymous Newcastle correspondent. Bolingbroke, owner and improver of Dawley Farm, referred to the 'multiplied scenes of your little garden' in a letter to Pope, a phrase which perfectly characterizes the intentions of its designer. Horace Walpole thought it 'a singular effort of art and taste to impress so much variety and scenery on a spot of five acres'. It was not, as he remembered it before its desecration by later owners, a rococo piece of variegation, wiggly paths, and puerilities, as later characterized, but a unified picturesque composition which 'appeared two or three sweet little lawns opening and opening beyond one another, and the whole surrounded with thick impenetrable woods'. He particularly admired the plantations around

'my Quincunx (*Imitations of Horace*, Sat. II, i, 130), 'the Garden shadow'd with trees' and his 'Laurel Circus' (iv. 170).

[53] Edmund Curll, *Mr. Pope's Literary Correspondence* (London, 1735), ii. 221–2. Reprinted by Mack, p. 308.

[54] Reprinted by Mack, Appendix A, pp. 237–43.

25. Pope's Villa. By Peter Tillemans. *c.* 1730.

26. Pope's Villa. After Augustin Heckell. 1749.

27. Pope's Villa. By Samuel Scott. *c.* 1759.

28. Pope's Villa. By Sawrey Gilpin. 1764. *Victoria and Albert Museum. Crown Copyright.*

the monument to Pope's mother, which Philip Southcote regarded as the model for 'distancing' in gardening:

> The passing through the gloom from the grotto to the opening day, the retiring and again assembling shades, the dusky groves, the larger lawn, and the solemnity of the termination at the cypresses that lead up to his mother's tomb, are managed with exquisite judgement.

These tributes by contemporary designers of important landscape gardens and by the historian of gardening who cites Twickenham as an important influence on the development of the picturesque garden, would not have been paid to a garden which was 'unapologetically regular'.[55] They realized that the genius of the place was the picturesque. It was the garden which prompted Philip Southcote to remark that 'Mr. Pope . . . [was] the first that practiced painting in gardening' (No. 603).

It needs to be emphasized in the remainder of this chapter that the garden design at Twickenham was as much the expression of a poet's as a painter's sensibility. The picturesque in Pope's garden was in no sense a purely visual aesthetic which ignored the emotive values of landscape, but part of the same sensibility observed in his descriptions of landscape. In conclusion, I would like to comment briefly on the psychological and emotional significance of the picturesque design Pope described memorably in the *Imitations of Horace*, Ode IV i:

> His House, embosom'd in the Grove,
> Sacred to social Life and social Love,
> Shall glitter o'er the pendent green,
> Where Thames reflects the visionary Scene. (21–4)[56]

[55] St. John, *Works* (1809), v. 80; Walpole, *History of Gardening*, pp. 28–9; Walpole, *Correspondence*, xxi. 417 (to Horace Mann, 20 June 1760). For Southcote, see Spence, No. 1133; 'unapologetical regularity', see B. S. Allen, *Tides in English Taste*, ii. 132. An interesting appreciation of Pope's garden by a later devotee of the sublime is to be found in a letter by Elizabeth Carter describing a visit to Twickenham in 1738. See G. Hampshire, 'Elizabeth Carter and Pope's Garden', *Notes & Queries*, 217 (June 1972), 221.

[56] In context these lines appear to be a description of 'Number five' (l. 9) King's Bench Walk in the Inner Temple, the town house designed by Christopher Wren, occupied in 1737 by William Murray, First Earl of Mansfield (1705–93), to whom the poem is addressed. Contemporary maps and the present location of the house far from the river establish that Murray's house, even before the construction of the embankment, could never have been reflected in the Thames. The description corresponds perfectly, however, to views of Pope's house at Twickenham, most of which show the house reflected in the river. Bowles's interpretation of the passage as an allusion 'to Mr. Murray's intention, at one time [1737?], of

Associations of a conventional kind were literally written into the landscape of Twickenham by means of the numerous statues, urns, and inscriptions indicated on Serle's *Plan*. Their utility to the landscape designer is indicated by Pope's remark in the 'Essay on Battels' where he compares Homer's repetitions to

> a skilful improver, who places a beautiful Statue in a well-disposed Garden so as to answer several Vistas, and by that Artifice one single figure seems multiply'd into as many Objects as there are Openings from whence it may be viewed.

At the same time Pope's garden statuary helped to make of Twickenham what Richard Savage, referring to Pope in another context, called 'one small, emblematic Landscape'. The value of garden statuary, is portentously explained by Stephen Switzer:

> 'Tis there also we hieroglyphically read the great Idea's of Valour and Renown, that particularly distinguished those Antients above the rest of their fellow-Creatures, and is of continual use and Amusement to the serious Beholders.

Joseph Warton compared the poet's 'unexpected insertion of such [moral] reflections' in a poem, to 'the . . . pleasure that we feel, when, in wandering through a wilderness or grove, we suddenly behold, in the turning of the walk, a statue of some VIRTUE or MUSE'. The metaphorical possibilities of garden statuary are suggested by the riverside ornament Pope was planning at the end of his life, an arrangement of sculpture which was to include statues of Homer, Virgil, Marcus Aurelius, and Cicero—an emblem of Pope's entire career as a poet, and 'a shrine to poetry's transforming power'.[57]

Pope censured the impropriety of placing a bust of Dr. Samuel Clarke in the Queen's Hermitage at Richmond, and his own choice of British Worthies in his garden indicates a more scrupulous regard for decorum. Edmund Curll's 'Description of Mr. Pope's House' informs us that Pope placed 'at the

taking the loan of Pope's house and grounds at Twickenham', seems plausible. See Elwin–Courthope, iii. 416 n.; John Rocque, *An Exact Survey of . . . London* (1746), Sheet D 2; Hugh Phillips, *The Thames about 1750* (London, 1951), figs. 79, 81; and Morris R. Brownell, '"His House" at Twickenham, and Pope's Imitation of Horace, Ode IV i', *Notes & Queries* (June 1977).

[57] Pope, *TE* vii. 255; Savage, 'The Wanderer', Canto I, l. 371, in *The Poetical Works of Richard Savage* (Cambridge, 1962), p. 107; Switzer, *Ichnographia Rustica* (1742), i. xiv–xv; Warton, *Essay on Pope*, i. 35. On Pope's statuary see Mack, pp. 28 n., 307–9, who discusses the riverside ornament Pope described to Spence (No. 620) in *The Garden and the City*, pp. 37–40, 76.

End of one Walk . . . a *Busto* of Sir *Isaac Newton*. And in a little Summer-House another of Mr. Dryden.' The choice of a natural philosopher was apt and significant, because 'much of that enthusiasm for the order and beauty of the Creation which pervades the early eighteenth century [and the idea of the landscape garden] was directly attributable to the influence of Newton's work'. Dryden, whose bust was also placed in Pope's library, and whose monument he helped to erect, is appropriately remembered in a poet's garden as one of 'the genii of the place'.[58]

Another important presence in the garden at Twickenham is Horace, who supplied Pope and his contemporaries not only with a doctrine of retirement, but also with a pattern for sensibility to landscape. Pope's imitation of Horace's sensibility is illustrated by his reflections on La Source, the garden in France on the Loire where Bolingbroke was spending his exile in 1724 with his French wife, when Pope, 'a poor Hermit on the banks of the Thames' had 'visions of her and of La Source':

—An me ludit amabilis
Insania, Audire et videor pios
Errare per lucos, amoenae
Quos et aquae subeunt et aurae.

What pleasing Phrensy steals away my Soul?
Thro' thy blest Shades (La Source) I seem to rove
I see thy fountains fall, thy waters roll
And breath the Zephyrs that refresh thy Grove
I hear what ever can delight inspire
Villete's soft Voice and St. John's silver Lyre.

—Seu voce nunc mavis acuta
Seu fidibus, cytharave Phoebi. (ii. 229)

Pope's vision of a garden he had never seen is a conscious imitation of the rapture of the poet in the *locus amoenus* described in Horace's *Ode* (III, iv, 5–8) which celebrates the poet's devotion to the Muses. The lines which

[58] For Curll's 'Description' see Mack, p. 308. On Newton's statue in Queen Caroline's hermitage at Richmond see Røstvig, *The Happy Man*, ii. 30. Matthew Green speaks of sculptures as 'genii of the place' in his poem on the Hermitage, 'The Grotto' (1732), in *The Poetical Works of Armstrong, Dyer, and Green*, ed. George Gilfillan (Edinburgh, 1858), p. 275.

Addison had used for the epigraph of his *Spectator* essay on gardening (No. 477, 1712), were favourites of Pope, who quoted them repeatedly in his correspondence,[59] and gave a free adaptation of them in *Windsor Forest* (1713):

> I seem thro' consecrated Walks to rove,
> I hear soft Musick dye along the Grove;
> Led by the Sound I roam from Shade to Shade,
> By God-like Poets Venerable made. (267–70)

The poet's reverie in the consecrated walks of Windsor Forest is a conscious imitation of Horace, a contemplative mood gardens like Twickenham were designed to evoke.

That Twickenham did evoke this kind of response in the minds of its visitors is indicated by the remarks of Pope's friends, like Robert Digby who wrote him a letter of thanks from Sherborne after a visit in 1723:

> I can't return from so agreeable an entertainment as yours in the country without acknowledging it. I thank you heartily for the new agreeable idea of life you there gave me; it will remain long with me, for it is very strongly impressed upon my imagination. I repeat the memory of it often, and shall value that faculty of the mind now more than ever, for the power it gives me of being entertained in your villa, when absent from it. . . . I have as you may guess, many philosophical reveries in the shades of Sir Walter Raleigh [whose house at Sherborne, Dorset, belonged to the Digbys], of which you are a great part. You generally enter there with me, and like a good Genius applaud and strengthen all my sentiments that have honour in them. (ii. 191–2)

Digby's references to memory, imagination, philosophical reverie, and sentiment characterize the psychological experience of the landscape garden which is summed up in Swift's remark after a similar visit in 1726 that Twickenham had taught him to 'dream' (ii. 393).

Pope's dream-vision of Twickenham, like that of La Source, was composed in large part of the memories of the friends who had visited it. To judge from his correspondence the garden was practically identified in his mind with his friends ('*Mihi & Amicis* would be the proper Motto over my Gate', iv. 34): the youngest daughters of Edward Blount, whom 'I still see . . . walking on

[59] Horace, *The Odes and Epodes*, trans. C. E. Bennett, Loeb Classical Library (Cambridge, Mass., 1960), 187. *Correspondence*, i. 168 (21 Dec. 1712, to John Caryll); iv. 371 (1741, to Warburton).

my Green at *Twickenham*, and gratefully remember (not only their green Gowns) but the Instructions they gave me how to slide down, and trip up the steepest Slopes of my Mount' (ii. 86); 'The three Yahoos of Twickenham . . . most excellent Triumvirs of Parnassus' (Gay, Arbuthnot, and Pope, ii. 383); '*The Suff'ring Triumvirate*' (Kent, Bolingbroke, and Pope, iv. 125); Jonathan Richardson and his son, whom he invited to 'enjoy my Groves . . . all this day & as much of the night as the fine moon now allows' (iv. 79); Bishop Atterbury, whom he wanted to 'carry . . . up a Mount, in a point of view to shew you the glory of my little kingdom' (ii. 109); William Broome, with whom he looked forward to 'roving the fields, sailing on the waters, and . . . lounging in the shades' during their collaboration on the *Odyssey* (ii. 231); Martha Blount, who 'so often walked' in the meadow opposite Pope's house on Ham Common (ii. 59); William Kent, sketching the garden palette in hand; Lord Burlington, approving his portico (iii. 322–3); Lord Pembroke, inquiring about his inscription in the grotto, *Secretum Iter*: 'Where the devil did you get this antique?' (Spence, No. 598); the Patriot opposition, convening in the grotto for the 'Feast of Reason and the Flow of Soul';[60] the Prince of Wales who conversed with Pope at his landing on the Thames (No. 591); the Talbot girl, who slipped as he was leading her to a boat 'from his own stairs . . . and pulled Mr. Pope after her' (iv. 28 n.); and finally, Joseph Spence, one of the last visitors to the garden, with whom Pope 'sat out . . . in the garden for three hours in his sedan but two days before he died' (No. 657a).

Thus Twickenham was inseparable from the memories of friends who inspired the same 'range of thoughts' and 'remembrance of a thousand past pleasures' which Pope experienced during his ride from Stonor to Oxford in a reverie of melancholy nostalgia. The Augustan imitation of the Horatian reverie in the *locus amoenus* was often coloured by melancholy. The Horatian ideal of retirement and the activity of gardening inevitably contributed to this state of mind. The line from Horace Pope inscribed over the entrance to the grotto—'*Secretum iter et fallentis semita vitae*'—is an appropriate epigraph for the theme of retirement at Twickenham,[61] but Pope entertained the ideal

[60] *Imitations of Horace*, Sat. II, i. 128.

[61] See Mack, p. 111, and Røstvig, *The Happy Man*, ii. 104.

with a simultaneous awareness of the impossibility, perhaps even the undesirability, of its realization. His villa was only intermittently 'a Scene where one finds no disappointments' (iii. 441). 'Alas! I live at *Twickenham*', he was complaining in 1723, where it was impossible to 'banish the World' (ii. 176), where unwanted guests invaded his grotto, and friends turned his house into the inn he compared it to. Pope was aware of the limitations of an ideal at war with his own social being: 'Tis time enough to like or affect to like, the Country,' he told Judith Cowper, 'when one is out of love with all but ones-self, & therfore studies to become agreeable or easy to oneself. Retiring into oneself is generally the *Pis-aller* of mankind' (ii. 141).

As for the activity of gardening, the vanity of works was one of the first lessons Pope learned in gardening, as he wrote to Robert Digby in 1720:

> The Moment I am writing this, I am surprized with the account of the Death of a Friend of mine; which makes all I have here been talking of, a meer Jest! Buildings, Gardens, Writings, Pleasures, Works, of whatever stuff Man can raise! None of them (God knows) capable of advantaging a Creature that is mortal, or of satisfying a Soul that is Immortal! (ii. 45)

He excused some of his 'Vanities' in gardening because friends had encouraged them, others because they were trifles, but he never escaped a sense of the aimlessness and futility of improvements, a recurring theme in his writing during the 1730s. In the manuscript of the *Epistle to Burlington* he refers to what may have been his own pointless project:

> To Thames's Shore who adds a creeping Rill
> This year may dig it, but ye next shall fill.[62]

And in the *Imitations of Horace* (Ep. I, i) the reference to gardening is a metaphor of the incoherence of his mind:

> One ebb and flow of follies all my Life
> I plant, root up, I build, and then confound,
> Turn round to square, and square again to round. (169–70)

He continued to improve his garden in the hope that 'my works . . . . will indeed out-live me . . . my Trees will afford Shade & Fruit to Others', despite the realization that 'no man finishes any View he has, or any Scheme he

[62] *Marginalia*, l. 35 of the Pierpont Morgan MS (MA 352).

projects, but by halves', with a prophetic awareness that his works could be destroyed by subsequent owners. This theme of the vanity of the arts is illustrated in the capriccio ruin-piece Pope composed for the frontispiece of the *Essay on Man*, showing the ruins of man's works—sculpture, architecture, even musical instruments—surrounding a sarcophagus inscribed *sic transit gloria mundi*, against a background of the ruins of the colosseum.[63]

Pope gave eloquent expression to both of these themes—the vanity of retirement and of works—in lines on his 'solitude and grotto' inspired by his troubling affair with Lady Mary, 'To Mr. Gay, Who wrote him a congratulatory Letter on the finishing his House' (1720):

> Ah friend, 'tis true—this truth you lovers know—
> In vain my structures rise, my gardens grow,
> In vain fair Thames reflects the double scenes
> Of hanging mountains, and of sloping greens:
> Joy lives not here; to happier seats it flies,
> And only dwells where WORTLEY casts her eyes.
>
> What are the gay parterre, the chequer'd shade,
> The morning bower, the ev'ning colonade,
> But soft recesses of uneasy minds,
> To sigh unheard in, to the passing winds?
> So the struck deer in some sequester'd part
> Lies down to die, the arrow at his heart;
> There, stretch'd unseen in coverts hid from day,
> Bleeds drop by drop, and pants his life away.[64]

In the absence of love and friendship the perfect environment of Twickenham provided 'soft recesses of uneasy minds' rather than the beatitudes of

[63] Frontispiece engraving ('A. Pope inv.', the name of the engraver indecipherable) in Warburton's editions of the *Essay on Man* (1745), Griffith, 607–8; fig. 1 in Benjamin Boyce, 'Baroque into Satire: Pope's Frontispiece for the *Essay on Man*', *Criticism*, 4 (Winter, 1962), 14–27. Boyce distinguishes three other versions (14–15): a red chalk drawing said to be by Pope 'not at present available to students', deriving from it (presumably) a sepia wash drawing, and an oil painting sometimes attributed to Pope, both reproduced by Mack, *TE* iii. i, plates I and II. See Mack's 'Note on the Illustrations' (xc), where it is stated that the wash drawing 'by Pope [is] evidently the original from which was engraved the traditional frontispiece to the *Essay on Man*'. Wimsatt questions the attribution of the painting to Pope in *Portraits*, p. 356.

[64] *TE* vi. 225–6. First printed in *The Works of Lady Mary Wortley Montagu*, iii. (1803). Pope enclosed lines 7–12 on 'my Solitude & Grotto' in a letter to Judith Cowper (5 Nov. 1722): *Correspondence*, ii. 142.

beatus ille. Similarly all the beauties of Bevis Mount could not satisfy Pope in the absence of their owner in 1723 (ii. 189–90). After Peterborough's death Pope described his emotions about 'the garden he [Peterborough] begun, & lived not to finish': 'It is a place that always made me Contemplative, & now Melancholy; but tis a Melancholy of that sort which becomes a Rational Creature, & an Immortal Soul' (iv. 34). This is the characteristic sentiment of the landscape gardener, who cultivated in the garden pleasures of melancholy.

The gardener's melancholy belongs to the elegiac tradition which Panofsky has traced in Virgil's conception of Arcadia in which 'human suffering and superhumanly perfect surroundings create a dissonance'. The attitude of Pope and the eighteenth century to the landscape garden resembles this Renaissance conception of Arcadia as a 'Utopia of bliss and beauty' distant in time (as distinct from the classical view of it as distant in space), 'an object of . . . nostalgia . . . a haven, not only from a faulty reality but . . . from a questionable present'.[65]

Two features in the garden at Twickenham clearly reflect this mood of elegiac melancholy. The first is the ruin Pope was planning to build in 1741 at the entrance to the grotto where the lines from Horace had been inscribed, a feature Pope told Ralph Allen would put the finishing touch on his garden: 'I told you my Grotto was finished, and now all that wants to the Completion of my Garden is the Frontispiece to it, of your rude Stones to build a sort of ruinous Arch at the Entry into it on the Garden side' (iv. 343). Serle's *Account* gives a description of Pope's arch, which appears unadorned in Kent's sketch, in the same ruinous taste he had admired at Sherborne:

> At the Entrance of the Grotto, next the Garden, are various sorts of Stones thrown promiscuously together, in imitation of an old Ruine; some full of Holes, others like Honey-combs, which came from Ralph Allen's, Esq; at Widcomb near Bath.

Thus Pope managed to introduce into his small garden at Twickenham the motif in the landscape garden which Oswald Spengler has called 'perhaps the most astonishing bizarrerie ever perpetrated, the artificial ruin'. In this

[65] Erwin Panofsky, 'Et in Arcadia Ego: Poussin and the Elegiac Tradition', chap. 7 in *Meaning in the Visual Arts* (New York, 1957), pp. 300, 303. Cf. A. R. Humphreys, *William Shenstone*, p. 101.

way he surrounds the marble inscription from Horace with the 'soft melancholy music' of ruins.[66]

Opposite the ruinous arch at the entrance to the grotto Pope designed and built a monument to his mother in 1735, 'a plain Stone Pillar resting upon a Pedestal' bearing a Latin inscription:

> Ah Editha!
> Matrum optima.
> Mulierum amantissima.
> Vale.

The monument figured in a painting of Pope by Jonathan Richardson, now lost, which is mentioned by William Kent in a letter to Burlington (1738): 'Pope in a mourning gown with a strange view of the garden to shew the obelisk as in memory to his mothers Death, the alligory seem'd Odde to me, but after I found, its to be in the next letters' (iv. 150). The valedictory inscription, and the solemnity of the cypresses leading up to her monument suggests that his mother is remembered in the garden as she is in the *Epistle to Arbuthnot* where he prayerfully writes, 'Be no unpleasing Melancholy mine' (l. 407). Death is dramatized in Pope's garden in the spirit of Virgil's elegy, or Poussin's painting *Et in Arcadia Ego* which 'no longer shows a dramatic encounter with Death but a contemplative absorption in the idea of mortality'. It is a part of the sadness of things—*lacrimae rerum*—observed in the spirit of 'ever-musing melancholy', the 'Divine oblivion of low-thoughted care'.[67]

[66] See Panofsky, 'Et in Arcadia Ego', p. 304; Serle, 'An Account of the Materials which Compose the Grotto', in *A Plan of Mr. Pope's Garden*, in Mack, p. 259; Spengler, *The Decline of the West* (New York, 1926), i. 254; Kenneth Clark, *The Gothic Revival* (Harmondsworth, 1964), p. 20; and Edward Malins, *English Landscaping and Literature*, p. ix.

[67] See 'An Epistolary Description' in Mack, p. 241, plates 11 and 19, and pp. 28–9; Panofsky, 'Et in Arcadia Ego', p. 313; and Pope, *Eloisa to Abelard*, ll. 3, 298.

6. *'Ascending Villa's': Pope's Influence on Twickenham Neighbours*

Behold! th' ascending *Villa's* on my Side
Project long Shadows o'er the Chrystal Tyde.
(*Windsor Forest*, 375–6)

AMONG his contemporaries and throughout the eighteenth century Pope enjoyed a reputation almost unchallenged as one of the founders of the landscape garden. He owed it to his topographical verse, particularly to the opening lines of *Windsor Forest*, to the precepts of the *Epistle to Burlington* (and later to the *Guardian* essay once it was recognized as Pope's), and finally, to the example of his garden at Twickenham, a garden cited by Walpole in his *History of Gardening* for its importance in the development of the picturesque landscape style. When charges were made in the latter part of the century about 'puerility in his practice' at Twickenham, Joseph Heely wrote an ardent defence of Pope, concluding that 'it is at once only doing justice to his genius to declare him the father of the modern taste'.[1]

These large claims for Pope's influence in gardening have remained essentially unexamined by garden historians and students of Pope. They could hardly be credited as long as Pope's ideas on gardening were regarded as scarcely distinguishable from those of his contemporaries, while the myth of

[1] On Pope's reputation in gardening, see Joseph Warton, *Essay on Pope*, ii. 179; William Lisle Bowles, ed., *Epistle to Burlington*, l. 23 n. in *The Works of Alexander Pope* (London, 1806), iii. 325; James Thomson, *The Complete Poetical Works of James Thomson*, ed. J. Logie Robertson (Oxford, 1961), p. 412; Walpole, *History of Gardening*, pp. 28–9; William Mason, *The English Garden*, ed. W. Burgh (1783), p. 210 (note VIII, verse 493); and Joseph Heely, *Letters on the Beauties of Hagley, Envil, and the Leasowes, with Critical Remarks: and Observations on the Modern Taste in Gardening*, 2 vols. (London, 1777), Letter III, 43. See H. F. Clark, 'Sharawaggi at Chiswick', p. 127.

his 'blindness' to nature survived, and while Twickenham was held to be 'a travesty of nature'.[2] Modern historians of the garden have generally rejected this reactionary view. Some have adopted Walpole's account of Pope's important role in a revolution of gardening taste, but most take an evolutionary view of the development of the garden, in which Pope emerges as a transitional figure. His ideas on gardening are seen as part of a gradual change in early eighteenth-century attitudes towards nature, his practice belongs to an 'irregular', 'rococo', 'poetic' phase in the development of the English garden from Dutch and French formal design towards the 'natural', 'informal', 'landscape' style.[3]

The prevailing view is fairer to Pope than the reactionary one it supplants, but it is still in many ways inadequate: it does not distinguish Pope's contribution from his contemporaries; it does not take into account the close link between the landscape movement and the Palladian revival, which cannot be construed as transitional; it is impossible to reconcile with the eighteenth-century view of Pope as one of the founders of the new taste in gardening; and, finally, it is not based on a review of available evidence. Consequently, it does nothing to answer the scepticism of George Sherburn about Walpole's claims for Pope's influence on gardening in the *History of Gardening*, or his doubts about Pope's gardening contemporaries 'whether they influenced him more than he them'.[4]

When the evidence is carefully examined it tends to substantiate the eighteenth-century view of Pope's reputation as the founder of the landscape garden, to indicate that Walpole, far from exaggerating, perhaps even underestimates

[2] S. T. Prideaux, *Aquatint Engraving* (1909), p. 168.

[3] See Sir Reginald Blomfield, *The Formal Garden in England* (London, 1892); Christopher Hussey, *The Picturesque* (1927), and *English Gardens and Landscapes* (1967); A. O. Lovejoy, 'On the Discrimination of Romanticisms' in *Essays in the History of Ideas* (Baltimore, 1948), pp. 240–1; Miles Hadfield, *Gardening in Britain* (1960); H. F. Clark, *The English Landscape Garden* (1948); Alicia Amherst, 'Dawn of Landscape Gardening', chap. 11 of *A History of Gardening in England* (London, 1896); Ralph Dutton, *The English Garden* (London, 1938); Laurence Whistler, *Sir John Vanbrugh, Architect and Dramatist 1664–1726* (New York, 1939), pp. 224–5; Isabel Chase, *Horace Walpole: Gardenist* (1943), p. 135; Nikolaus Pevsner, 'The Genesis of the Picturesque', *Architectural Review*, 96 (1944), 139–46; Maren Sophie Røstvig, 'The Happy Gardener', chap. 2 in *The Happy Man*, ii. (1958), pp. 65 f.; and Derek Clifford, 'The Great Revolution of Taste', chap. 6 in *A History of Garden Design* (1962).

[4] *Early Career*, p. 282. Cf. '"Timon's Villa" and Cannons', *Huntington Library Bulletin*, 8 (Oct. 1934), 132 n. 2.

Pope's influence on the development of the landscape garden. This conclusion emerges when the evidence is viewed in the light of two important considerations: the distinct picturesque and poetic character of Pope's garden just discussed, and the character of its designer. Pope's 'Poetical villa'[5] rapidly established itself as a model of garden design, which was as influential in gardening as Burlington's Chiswick in architecture. Walpole remarks in *Visits to Country Seats* that Pope laid out the garden of a house in Hampton for his friend Charles Jervas 'after his own' at Twickenham, and this was probably not an isolated instance.[6] Twickenham, as we have seen, was recognized by its contemporaries as the 'Muses' green retreat', a place where Pope 'first . . . practiced painting in gardening'[7]—the archetype of the poetic picturesque ideal. And it was constantly being visited throughout his lifetime not only by friends including the most distinguished amateur and professional designers, but by the general public since Pope followed the practice of opening the gardens to visitors during his absence.[8]

The considerable literature inspired by Twickenham indicates that Pope became during his lifetime, as he hoped, almost as famous for his garden as his poetry.[9] The fame of Twickenham extended from England to Ireland and the European continent. Even after Pope's death, when the house and garden had been altered beyond recognition, the garden continued to attract visitors who regarded it as a model. Thomas Jefferson studied and admired it; Richard Stockton visited it with an artist, and imitated it at his estate in Morven,

[5] This reference to Twickenham appears in an attack on Pope, *Gulliver Decypher'd* (1727?; Guerinot No. 53).

[6] *Journals of Visits to Country Seats*, ed. Paget Toynbee, Walpole Society, 16 (Oxford, 1928), p. 69: 'The House was Jervas's, & the garden seems to have been laid out by Pope after his own.'

[7] George Lyttelton, 'Verses, Written at Mr. Pope's House at Twickenham, which he had lent to Mrs. G—lle. In August, 1735', in *The Works of George Lord Lyttleton*, ed. George Edward Ayscough, 3rd edn. (London, 1776), iii. 126–7. Southcote's statement already quoted is in Spence, No. 603.

[8] *Correspondence*, iv. 9.

[9] Poems in whole or in part devoted to Pope's garden can be sampled in Mack, Appendix E. Others include George Lyttelton's verses 'Written at Mr. Pope's house at Twickenham', *Works*, ed. G. E. Ayscough, 3rd edn. (1776), iii. 126; Samuel Johnson's 'To Eliza plucking Laurel in Mr. Pope's Gardens', *Gentleman's Magazine* (Aug. 1738), in Samuel Johnson, *The Complete English Poems*, ed. J. D. Fleeman (Harmondsworth, 1971), p. 68; William Mason, *Musaeus: A Monody to the Memory of Mr. Pope, In Imitation of Milton*'s 'Lycidas' (London, 1747); and J. M. W. Turner, 'On the Demolition of Pope's House at Twickenham' (*c.* 1807), manuscript lines written to accompany his painting of the subject in *The Sunset Ship: The Poems of J. M. W. Turner*, ed. Jack Lindsay (London, 1966), pp. 78, 119.

Pennsylvania. In the nineteenth century a zealous estate agent was advertising it in 1878 as 'the most perfect example in England of landscape gardening'.[10]

Another important indication of the fame of Twickenham is the series of drawings, engravings, and paintings of Pope's house in its setting dating from about 1726 which established it as one of the picturesque beauties of Britain. It was painted by John Wootten, Peter Tillemans (plate 25), Augustin Heckell (plate 26), Sawrey Gilpin (plate 28), Charles Knapton (frontispiece), Elias Martin (plate 29), Samuel Scott (plate 27), William Westall (plate 31), John Martin (plate 32), and others including J. M. W. Turner (plate 30) who wrote an elegy 'On the Demolition of Pope's House at Twickenham' to accompany the exhibition of his painting of the house, which he imitated in the design of his own Twickenham villa, Sandycombe Lodge.[11] Pope's gardens, of all the notable ones in the vicinity of Twickenham, were the only ones identified by an inscription on John Rocque's map, and numerous engravings published from 1735 on kept it before the eyes of the public.[12]

The character of the gardener leads us to the same conclusion about Pope's reputation and influence in gardening. Pope can be distinguished from Addison and literary enthusiasts of gardening from Milton to Shaftesbury by 'potency in practice'. He accurately characterizes his *furor hortensis* in an epigram when he refers to himself as 'stark mad with Gardens', and refers to his indefatigable enthusiasm for gardening projects in a letter (1725) to Samuel Buckley, in which he writes 'to beg your View of my Gardens, & to take a view of yours, that we may put each other upon new projects, which

[10] See Mack, pp. 8, 267–8, 271; Desmond Fitz-Gerald, 'Irish Gardens of the Eighteenth Century, II. The Rococo', *Apollo*, 88 (Sept. 1968), 204; Isabel Chase, *Horace Walpole: Gardenist*, p. 257; and catalogue dated 1873 in *Sale Catalogues of Landed Estates*, Middlesex 2. K-7 [1868–83] B.M. Maps 137 a 11.

[11] See Appendix B. On Turner's elegy and house see Ann Livermore, 'J. M. W. Turner's Unknown Verse Book', *The Connoisseur Year Book 1957*, ed. L. G. G. Ramsey (London, 1957), pp. 78–86; and 'Sandycombe Lodge', *Country Life*, 110 (6 July, 1951), 40–2.

[12] *An Exact Survey of the City's of London, Westminster, ye Borough of Southwark and the Country near Ten Miles Round Begun in 1741 and Ended in 1745* (1746). The 'Proposals' for Rocque's *Survey* state that 'any gentleman may have his seat, and gardens as particularly inserted (in case they are not so already) upon terms which no gentleman, it is presumed, will think unreasonable'. Henry B. Wheatley, 'Rocque's Plan of London', *London Topographical Record*, 9 (London, 1914), 24; Hugh Phillips, 'John Rocque's Career', *London Topographical Record*, 20 (London, 1952), 9–25. See Mack, Notes pl. 20, p. 286. From 1735 into the nineteenth century scarcely a decade passed without the publication of an engraved view of Pope's House, even after his own villa had been demolished in 1807. See Appendix B.

I take to be the True Felicity of all Planters' (ii. 286). The extent of his ambition as a gardening projector is suggested by his willingness to undertake in all seriousness the project of the architect Dinocrates, described by Vitruvius, of forming Mount Athos into a statue of Alexander the Great:

> For my part, I have long since had an idea how that might be done, and if any body would make me a present of a Welsh mountain and pay the workmen, I would undertake to see it executed. I have quite formed it sometimes in my imagination.[13]

In his *History of Gardening* Walpole accuses Pope of 'a little of affected modesty . . . when he said, of all his works he was most proud of his garden', but it is borne out by Southcote's statement quoted earlier about Pope's fondness for fame in gardening, and by attacks as early as 1728 ridiculing him as 'a gardener . . . but no good Writer': 'If you'll believe himself, he is the best Gardiner in the Three Kingdoms.' Pope's influence on contemporary gardens is reflected in the elephantine irony of an attack on the *Epistle to Burlington* discussing line 13—'For what has Virro painted, built, and planted':

> What pity it is that Virro did not consult our Author, before he went to work? Had he done that, I dare vouch, all would have been well, tho' every Thing appear'd just as it does. But for want of this *Unum Necessarium*, for want of consulting this universal Genius, his Paintings are monstrous, his Buildings barbarous, his Planting ridiculous, and he has no Taste, or what's worse, an ill one.[14]

The study of Pope's influence on the landscape garden indicates that many of his contemporaries, including some of the most important garden designers amateur and professional, regarded Pope's advice on gardening as a necessary sanction for new undertakings.

It is not easy to document the importance of Pope's garden as a model when Twickenham and the places said to have imitated it have disappeared. The history of many important gardens and biographies of important professional landscape architects remain to be written. The early history of gardens like

[13] See Miles Hadfield, *Gardening in Britain* (London, 1960), p. 185; Pope, 'On lopping Trees in his Garden', *TE* vi. 385; Spence, No. 618. See Vitruvius, Introduction to Book II, *The Ten Books on Architecture*, trans. Morris Hicky Morgan (New York, 1960), pp. 35–6.

[14] Walpole, *History of Gardening*, p. 28. For Southcote, see Spence, No. 603. For attacks on Pope, see B.M. 116. 61–4, and Matthew Concanen, *A Miscellany on Taste* (London, 1732), p. 5. Guerinot, No. 100.

Chiswick, which puzzled informed contemporaries like Spence (who was able to consult gardeners who had worked there), remains obscure. Eighteenth-century landscape gardens are 'palimpsests upon which a succession of designers have written',[15] and now, when many are destroyed, all are transformed, and documentary evidence is scarce, fragmentary, and misleading, the historian often must depend upon hearsay, local tradition, and inference in writing the elusive history of the garden. But enough unexamined evidence is available, and enough new evidence has come to light relating to the history of important gardens and the work of contemporary landscape architects to allow us to evaluate Pope's contribution to the development of the garden more clearly than before. To do justice to the nature and extent of Pope's influence requires a recapitulation of the history of the early eighteenth-century garden between about 1715 and 1750. To reduce the subject to manageable proportions I will discuss first Pope's collaborations in the vicinity of Twickenham; second, his collaborations with professional designers; finally, his influence on the landscape of the country house.

Pope's influence as a gardener first appears, as we would expect, in the neighbourhood of Twickenham in the Thames valley. It is remarkable how rapidly he established himself here as a leading authority on taste in gardening. This can best be explained as a result of his friendship with Burlington and his association with the Palladian revival. From the time of his move to Chiswick in 1716, when he met Burlington, Pope was at the centre of the Earl's architectural revival, and it is important to remember that the Palladians regarded building as inseparable from landscape design, and that they advocated a classical idea of garden design compatible with classic architecture.[16] Burlington became the leading advocate of the new architecture, Chiswick a treasury of architectural ideas; there is good reason to believe that Pope and Twickenham played a similar role in gardening. The classical models of the villa, its ambience and situation, belonged to men of letters, Pliny and Horace; the modern instance was Pope's Twickenham.

There is a distinct possibility that Pope played a role in the layout of Burlington's gardens at Chiswick before he settled at Twickenham. In 1716, soon

[15] Margaret Jourdain, *The Work of William Kent, Artist, Painter, Designer and Landscape Gardener* (London, 1948), p. 78.

[16] See chap. 5.

after moving to Chiswick, Pope made friends with Burlington, was being entertained by 'Laborious Lobster-nights' at Burlington House in London,[17] visited his estates in Yorkshire (i. 370) and his gardens at Chiswick (plate 22), where John Gay pictures him in his Epistle 'To the Right Honourable the Earl of Burlington, A Journey to Exeter' (1716):

> While you, my Lord, bid stately piles ascend,
> Or in your *Chiswick* bow'rs enjoy your friend;
> Where *Pope* unloads the boughs within his reach,
> Of purple vine, blue plumb, and blushing peach;
> I journey far—— (1–5)[18]

Throughout his life-long friendship with Burlington Pope was a constant visitor to Chiswick, an admirer of the gardens, and intimately acquainted with improvements there. He found the gardens 'delightfull' (i. 338) and 'flourish-[ing]' (i. 347) in 1716, and told him in 1736, after years in which he had reserved Sundays for visits to Chiswick from Twickenham, unless 'the Wind full in my Teeth, & so chilling an East' (iii. 403) was blowing on the Thames —that 'Chiswick has been to me the finest thing this glorious Sun has shin'd upon' (iii. 313). They exchanged gardeners and gifts: a rhyme on a gate by Inigo Jones, the gift of Sir Hans Sloane, which was moved to Chiswick garden in 1738, has been attributed to Pope:

> I was brought from Chelsea last year
> Battered with Wind and weather.
> Inigo Jones put me together:
> Sir Hans Sloane let me alone;
> Burlington brought me hither.[19]

And his familiarity with improvements in the gardens until the end of his life is indicated by the mock 'tree petition' which he addressed with some

17 'A Farewell to London in the Year 1715', l. 45, *TE* vi. 130. On Pope and Burlington see James Osborn, 'Pope, the "Apollo of the Arts", and his Countess', in *England in the Restoration and Early Eighteenth Century, Essays in Culture and Society*, ed. H. T. Swedenberg, pp. 101–43 (Berkeley and Los Angeles, 1972).

18 *Works*, ed. G. C. Faber (London, 1926), p. 152. Vinton A. Dearing dates the poem 1716 in 'John Gay: Two Corrections', *The Scriblerian* 1 (Spring, 1969), 32.

19 'On an Old Gate Brought from Chelsea to Chiswick', among 'Poems of Doubtful Authorship', *TE* vi. 459. Cf. Chatsworth House MSS., Box 143. 34 for variant lines.

29. Pope's Villa.
By Elias Martin. 1773.

30. Pope's Villa.
By J. M. W. Turner. 1808.

31. Pope's Villa.
After William Westall. 1828.

32. Pope's Villa.
By John Martin. 1850.

33. Pope's Villa.
By W. Thewes. 1873.

friends to 'the Agent & Attorney of . . . Sathan [William Kent]', to prevent him from cutting down a tree (iv. 324).

These circumstances are sufficient to support Sherburn's conclusion that 'an interchange of ideas on gardening and building must have occurred' between Burlington and Pope at this time, and the inference of H. F. Clark that in the years before 1717 'the work had very possibly been carried out under the critical eye of Pope'. Some interesting new evidence adds support to this possibility. According to Philip Southcote, as recorded by Spence, he [Southcote] and Lord Petre had both helped to lay out 'the flower-garden by the Burlington summerhouse' (No. 1123). If Southcote's reference is to the New Bagnio or Casina which Colen Campbell describes in *Vitruvius Britannicus* (1725) as the 'first essay of his Lordship's happy invention' completed by 1717, this means that in the earliest stages Burlington was being assisted by members of that Catholic gardening circle mentioned in connection with Binfield. The inference would then be reasonable that Pope brought these gardening visitors to Chiswick, and that Burlington, hospitable to their designs, would not have been inhospitable to Pope's own.[20]

Pope was soon acquainted with a number of 'Gardening Lords' (iv. 459), as he called them, within '2 hours sail of Chiswick' (i. 418), many of whom were active in the early phase of the Whig building boom in London town houses, villas in the Thames valley, and country-houses all over England. Burlington's cousin, Henry Boyle, Lord Carleton, was owner of a villa opposite Twickenham described by John Macky in 1724:

> a pretty little Seat betwixt *Petersham* and *Ham*, with fine Gardens; and at the end of his green Walk [he] hath erected, upon an artificial Mount, a stately Banquetting House, to which you ascend by large Steps, or Stairs, its Portico supported by Pillars, from which you have a full View of *Richmond. Twittenham, Islesworth, Petersham, Ham*, the whole Tract of the River of *Thames*, and the adjacent Country.

Charles Talbot, another friend Pope was visiting at this time, had built 'a little Seat', at Isleworth, near Twickenham, where James Gibbs designed a villa in 1726 for his heir. Another person who had an 'indispensable claim' (i. 417) on Pope at this time was John Campbell, 2nd Duke of Argyll (1678–1743), who had purchased a house adjoining Petersham in 1714, replaced in

[20] Sherburn, *Early Career*, p. 279; H. F. Clark, *The English Landscape Garden*, p. 13.

1738 by a Palladian villa, Sudbrooke House, designed by Pope's architect James Gibbs. In 1716 Pope was visiting Jane Hyde, Countess of Rochester, a neighbour who lived in Richmond in a fine house with 'Gardens ascending the Hill in an artful confus'd manner'.[21]

When he moved to Twickenham in 1718 Pope found himself surrounded by gardening neighbours in what Christopher Hussey has well described as a 'forcing-bed of garden practice'. James Johnstone (1655–1737), the former Secretary of State for Scotland, who lived near Pope, was ranked 'amongst the first rate Gardeners in *England*', but his reputation was in horticulture and Pope ridiculed his gardens laid out in the French fashion. He was on better terms with Henry Robartes, 3rd Earl of Radnor, who lived between Twickenham village and Cross Deep in Radnor House, but Radnor was no serious rival to Pope's fame since he later earned the reputation of 'The Daemon Dire of Anti-Taste', perhaps because his house had acquired by 1750 a Gothic front and a Chinese summer house. Macky found the spacious gardens of another of Pope's neighbours and close friends, Thomas Wentworth, Earl of Strafford's Thames villa 'very glaring', but Pope admired his country-house, Wentworth Castle, Yorkshire, and said that he would 'as soon travel [to Yorkshire] to contemplate your Lordship's works, as the Queen of Sheba did to contemplate those of Solomon' (ii. 309).[22]

With another Twickenham neighbour, Archibald Campbell, Earl of Islay (1682–1761), and 3rd Duke of Argyll (1743), Pope was later to collaborate in

[21] John Macky, *A Journey Through England* (1724), i. 63, 192–3. For Pope's visit to Henry Boyle's Middleton, see *Correspondence*, i. 375. On Pope and Charles Talbot, Duke of Shrewsbury, see *Correspondence*, iv. 417, and a 'projected visit to his former estate' (iv. 347). On Talbot's houses see the anonymous *Life of Charles* [Talbot] *Duke of Shrewsbury* (London, 1718), pp. 18, 36, and Susan Reynolds, *A History of the County of Middlesex*, The Victoria History of the Counties of England (London, 1962), iii. 91. On Sudbrooke House, see Arthur T. Bolton, 'Petersham Surrey and its Houses—I. Sudbrook Park', *Country Life*, 44 (19 Oct. 1918), 332.

[22] See Christopher Hussey, 'Twickenham—II: Orleans House; The Octagon', *Country Life*, 96 (15 Sept. 1944), 465. For Johnstone, see *TE* vi. 45, Susan Reynolds, *History of Middlesex*, iii. 150, and John Macky, *A Journey Through England*, i. 61. Radnor is described as 'the Daemon of Anti-Taste' on the authority of James Thomson in notes to 'The Boat: An Imitation of the Dedicatio Phaeseli of Catullus', in *Recreations and Studies of a Country Gentleman: Being Selections from the Correspondence of the Reverend Thomas Twining*, ed. Richard Twining (London, 1882), p. 242 n. 5. For Radnor House, see Susan Reynolds, *History of Middlesex*, iii. 142–3. On Strafford House, see John Macky, *A Journey Through England*, i. 61; and H. Avray Tipping, 'Wentworth Castle—I–II, Yorkshire', *Country Life*, 56 (18 and 25 Oct., 1924), 588–96, 634–42.

the garden design of Marble Hill. His house near Twickenham, Whitton Place, was rebuilt by Roger Morris (1724–5), the grounds laid out with a lake, Gothic Tower, and parapets which inspired Walpole's ridicule. But he was an important botanical gardener to whom Walpole credits 'the introduction of foreign trees and plants . . . [which] contributed essentially to the richness of colouring so peculiar to our modern landscape'. He was the owner during Pope's lifetime of Caen Wood (now Kenwood), Middlesex, the 'soft Retreat' (iii. 123) in Hampstead, said to have been a favourite resort of Pope's during his lifetime.[23]

Many of the friends Pope made soon after his settlement at Twickenham figure in the story of his known collaborations in gardening to be described below. It is enough to point out here that in addition to country-houses most of them owned villas in or near London within easy reach of Twickenham where they could exchange visits with Pope. Henry Herbert's Whitehall House, designed in 1720 by Colen Campbell, is recognized as one of the prototypes of the Anglo-Palladian villa. At Parsons Green, Fulham, Charles Mordaunt, Earl of Peterborough, had a 'palace' on the riverside and a famous botanical garden.[24] Henry St. John, Lord Bolingbroke, became Pope's neighbour at Dawley, Middlesex, in 1726, and he was sharing an estate in Battersea, London, in 1743 with Hugh Hume, 3rd Earl of Marchmont, when Pope wrote to rally him with a remark of Lord Chesterfield's:

> He tells me your Lordship is got a-head of all the Gardening Lords, that you have distanc'd Lord Burlington & Lord Cobham in the true scientific part; but he is studying after you, & has here lying before him those Thesaurus's from which he affirms you draw all your knowledge, Millers Dictionaryes. But I informd him better, & told him your chief lights were from Joannes Serlius [Pope's gardener, John Serle]; whose Books he is now enquiring for, of Leake the Bookseller, who has writ for them to his Correspondents. (iv. 459)

23 On Whitton Place, see Walpole, *Correspondence*, xvii. 441 (to Horace Mann, 3 June 1742), and Susan Reynolds, *History of Middlesex*, iii. 144. On Archibald Campbell, see Horace Walpole, *History of Gardening*, p. 27, and Miles Hadfield, *Gardening in Britain*, p. 225. On Caen Wood, see John Summerson, *The Iveagh Bequest Kenwood, A Short Account of its History and Architecture*, Greater London Council Publication 48 (London, n.d.), p. 6.

24 On Whitehall House, see John Summerson, 'The Classical Country House in 18th-century England', *Journal of the Royal Society of Arts*, 107 (July 1959), 571–2. On Parson's Green, see John Macky, *A Journey Through England*, i. 210, and Miles Hadfield, *Gardening in Britain*, p. 137 n. Pope mentions a visit in 1732 (*Correspondence*, iii. 283).

Bathurst, Pope's most intimate gardening associate, had an estate outside London at Riskins, near Colnbrook, Buckinghamshire.

The earliest indication of Pope's reputation in gardening is found in Pope's letter to Allen Lord Bathurst, with whom he was already collaborating on the gardens at Cirencester, Gloucestershire (see chap. 8), which gives 'an account of a consultation lately held in my neighbourhood, about designing a princely garden'—the gardens of Frederick, Prince of Wales at Richmond Lodge in the Old Deer Park of Henry VII's Palace of Shene, north-west of Richmond Green as shown on Rocque's plan (plate 34), which had been granted to him by George I in 1722 after the forfeiture of the Duke of Ormonde.[25]

Several Criticks were of several opinions: One declar'd he would not have too much Art in it; for my notion (said he) of gardening is, that it is only sweeping Nature: Another told them that Gravel walks were not of a good taste, for all of the finest abroad were of loose sand: A third advis'd peremptorily there should not be one Lyme-tree in the whole plantation; a fourth made the same exclusive clause extend to Horse-chestnuts, which he affirm'd not to be Trees, but Weeds; Dutch Elms were condemn'd by a fifth; and thus about half the Trees were proscrib'd, contrary to the Paradise of God's own planting, which is expressly said to be planted with *all trees*. There were some who cou'd not bear Evergreens, and call'd them Never-greens; some, who were angry at them only when cut into shapes, and gave the modern Gard'ners the name of Evergreen Taylors; some who had no dislike to Cones and Cubes, but wou'd have 'em cut in Forest trees; and some who were in a passion against any thing in shape, even against clipt hedges, which they call'd green walls. These (my Lord) are our Men of Taste, who pretend to prove it by tasting little or nothing. Sure such a Taste is like such a stomach, not a good one, but a weak one. We have the same sort of Critics in poetry; one is fond of nothing but Heroicks, another cannot relish Tragedies, another hates Pastorals, all little Wits delight in Epigrams. Will you give me leave to add, there are the same in Divinity? where many leading Critics are for rooting up more than they plant, and would leave the Lord's Vineyard either very thinly furnish'd, or very oddly trimm'd.

I have lately been with my Lord—who is a zealous yet charitable Planter, and has so bad a Taste, as to like all that is good. (ii. 14–15)

The letter reveals Pope's contempt for narrow and doctrinaire principles of garden design in witty raillery reminiscent of the *Guardian* essay, his tactful

[25] H. E. Malden, ed., *The History of the County of Surrey*, The Victoria History of the Counties of England (London, 1911), iii. 536.

acknowledgment of the superiority of the taste of gardening Lords, and it suggests that Pope was being consulted about the design of a royal garden before he had finished laying out his own garden at Twickenham.

Very little can be determined about the improvements under way in the gardens at Richmond Lodge at this point, or about Pope's contribution to them. John Macky's description (1722) of 'the wood cut out into Walks' suggests that the 'perfect *Trianon*' of the Duke of Ormonde was beginning to be transformed in a more rural style, perhaps with Pope's encouragement.

> The late Duke of *Ormond* in Queen *Anne's* Reign, was Ranger and Keeper of this Park [Richmond Park], and his Lodge a perfect *Trianon*; but since his Forfeitures it hath been sold to the Prince of *Wales*, who makes his Summer Residence here. It does not appear with the Grandeur of a Royal Palace, but is very neat and pretty. There is a fine Avenue that runs from the Front of the House to the Town of *Richmond*, at half a Mile's distance one way, and from the other Front to the River-side, both inclosed with Balustrades of Iron.
>
> The Gardens are very spacious, and well kept. There is a fine Terrace towards the River. But above all, the Wood cut out into Walks with the plenty of Birds singing in it, makes it a most delicious Habitation.[26]

In 1726 Pope borrowed a detachment of workers from the Prince of Wales's gardens at Richmond to turf a 'Bridgmannick Theatre' in his garden at Twickenham (ii. 372), which suggests that an exchange of favours was occurring while these gardens were simultaneously being improved.

Another example of Pope's local influence on gardening which can be characterized more clearly than Richmond Lodge is his contribution to the garden design of Marble Hill, Middlesex (plate 35), the Twickenham villa a mile upstream from Richmond Lodge near Pope's, which the Prince of Wales built between 1724 and 1728 for his mistress, Henrietta Howard, Countess of Suffolk. Pope played a leading role in the layout of the garden which was a work of collaboration between some of the most distinguished amateur gardeners of the time, and the leading professional landscape architect of the day. Surviving evidence supports the statement of Jonathan Swift, an intimate friend of Lady Howard, in the 'Preface' to his burlesque country house poem, *A Pastoral Dialogue between Richmond-Lodge and Marble Hill* (1727), that 'Mr.

[26] See Christopher Hussey, 'Richmond Green, Surrey—I. Oak House and Old Palace Place', *Country Life*, 95 (5 May 1944), 772–5; and John Macky, *A Journey Through England*, i. 65–6.

Pope was the Contriver of the Gardens' at Marble Hill, which may be the principal basis of the statement by Spence published shortly afterwards in his *Essay on Pope's Odyssey* that 'the Finest [gardens] in the Nation owe their Beauty to his [Pope's?] Directions'.[27]

The contributions of two of Pope's friends, John Campbell, 2nd Duke of Argyll, Earl of Islay, and Henry Herbert, 9th Earl of Pembroke, seem to have been in connection with litigation about the site and the architecture of the house.[28] Two other gardening lords took a more active part in the garden design, and corresponded with Pope on the subject, but both appear to have worked 'to his directions'. Allan Apsley, first Earl Bathurst, appears to have delivered lime trees for Marble Hill on Pope's 'order' from his nurseries at Riskins (ii. 262–3). He was rewarded a year later with a facetious progress report from Pope: 'For the grass of Marbel hill springeth, yea it springeth exceedingly' (ii. 292). Charles Mordaunt, Earl of Peterborough, appears to have been the most energetic collaborator on the Marble Hill garden. In the summer of 1723 he asked Pope to have the grounds surveyed at night (perhaps because Lady Howard was trying to keep the whole project secret): 'You may have itt measured by moon light by a Ten foot Rod, or any body used to grounds will make a neer guess by pushing itt over' (ii. 183). Some time later he was impatient to know 'the issue of the affaire' from Pope: 'and what she intended for this autumn for no time is to be Lost either if she intends to build out houses or prepare for planting, I will send to morrow to know if you can give me any account, & will call upon you as soon as I am able that we may goe together to Mrs Howards' (ii. 197). This illustrates the initiative of Peterborough, and the role Pope was playing as intermediary between Lady Howard and her advisers. Later on, apparently, Peterborough believed he had lost influence in competition with his friends.[29]

27 See *The Poems of Jonathan Swift*, ed. Harold Williams, ii. 407; Spence, *An Essay on Pope's Odyssey*, ii. (1727), p. 132. See chap. 5.

28 See Marie P. G. Draper, and W. A. Eden, *Marble Hill House and its Owners* (1970), pp. 12, 15, 20, and chap. 3; and James Lees-Milne, *Earls of Creation*, p. 90. For Pope's involvement in litigation about Marble Hill, see *Correspondence*, ii. 259; v. 5, 19. The addressee of Pope's letter (1726) to Mr. B (2: 259) which Sherburn doubtfully assigns to George Berkeley is probably Robert Britiffe, Walpole's Norfolk lawyer and one of the trustees of the Prince of Wales's settlement.

29 See the undated letter from Peterborough to Lady Howard about his 'Rivalls' quoted by Marie Draper, *Marble Hill House*, p. 15: 'I hear I am to be Layed aside as an extravagant person fitt to build

Pope had the obvious advantage of proximity over his rivals, and his correspondence shows how seriously he took the responsibility of laying out the gardens at Marble Hill. At the end of his letter describing the gardens of Sherborne, Dorset (1722–4), he asked Martha Blount to reassure Lady Howard about his concern for her landscape design: 'don't let any Lady from hence [his interest in the improvements at Sherborne] imagine that my head is so full of any Gardens as to forget hers. The greatest proof I could give her to the contrary is, that I have spent many hours here in studying for hers, & in drawing new plans for her' (ii. 240). The layout of Marble Hill does have similarities to Sherborne, and it is possible that some of the crude marginal ink sketches of garden plans with measurements in the *Odyssey* manuscripts (*c.* 1723–4) are Pope's ideas for Lady Howard's gardens. On his way back from Sherborne, he was planning to stop at Lord Pembroke's Wilton House, Wiltshire—'I depend upon that for new matter' (ii. 240)—another place he may have studied for Marble Hill.[30]

Plans for Marble Hill were being executed by September 1724, when Pope wrote to his collaborator on the *Odyssey*, William Broome, that he was 'very busy in laying out of a garden, shall be busier next month in planting, but with all avocations, will proceed cheerfully through the version of the fourteenth book' (ii. 256); and told Fortescue that 'Mrs. Howard returns your services, and Marblehill waits only for its roof,—the rest finished. . . . My gardens improve more than my writings; my head is still more upon Mrs. Hd. [Howard] and her works, than upon my own' (ii. 257). Household accounts between September 1724 and June 1725 give glimpses of the works in the garden which were carried out subsequently under Pope's direction: payments are recorded for 'a Garden Roll . . . by the order of Mr. Pope', '120 ft. of Deale Railling Cross ye Bolling Green', and 'a grindstone, a trough pitch'd'; a meadow and yew hedge were being lined with railings, and work was in progress on 'ye Mount' and 'a Style & Steps at ye Thames side'.[31]

nothing but palaces . . . may every Tree prosper planted by whatever hand, may you ever be pleased & happy, what ever happens to your unfortunate Gardiner, & architect degraded, & turned of'.

[30] On similarities to Sherborne, see Marie Draper, *Marble Hill House*, p. 15; cf. *Marble Hill House, Twickenham, A Short Account of its History and Architecture* (London, Greater London Council Publication 64, 1966), pp. 6–7. For the *Odyssey* MS., see B.M. Add. MSS. 4809, 97^{v}.

[31] See Marie Draper, *Marble Hill House*, pp. 15, 36; and James Lees-Milne, *Earls of Creation*, p. 82.

At a rather late stage in the planning (September 1724), just before planting was to begin, the professional landscape architect Charles Bridgeman was called in to furnish a plan for Marble Hill. This may have been done at the suggestion of Pope; in any event a letter from Bridgeman to Pope dated 28 September 1724, the month before Pope intended to begin planting, alludes to a conference with Pope and Lady Howard at Twickenham, a 'kind Letter' (lost) from Pope to Bridgeman, and explains the delay in starting on a plan he was submitting to Pope:

> I came home on Fryday night & had your kind Letter[.] [O]n Saturday morning I begun on the plann, & have not [lef]t from that time to this so long as I could see, nor shall [I] leave it till 'tis finish'd which I hope will be about tomorrow Noon, but the affair I mention to You above will not let me move from Home this fortnight, so shall be glad if Your affairs call you to Towne on Tuesday or any other day this week that I may a little explain it to you, or if not I will Send it to You by my man on Wednesday morning. (ii. 261)

The nature of this plan (lost) is open to conjecture. At any rate it is clear evidence of collaboration, and a year later Pope's note to Bridgeman asking him 'to fix that matter with Mrs. Howard' (ii. 327) shows that Bridgeman continued to work to Pope's directions.

The product of this collaboration between Pope, Bridgeman, and the gardening Lords, in which Pope appears to have been the prime mover, was evidently something of a hybrid between formal and picturesque landscape design. The layout of the gardens on the riverside as shown in an engraving dated 1749—'a wide open lawn, bounded on either side by regular groves of trees, twice set back so as to reveal as wide a view as possible of the Thames'—resembles the plan Pope described at Sherborne where 'the Vally is layd level and divided into two regular Groves of Horse chestnuts, and a Bowling-green in the middle of about 180 foot . . . bounded behind with a Canall' (ii. 237).[32]

Like Sherborne and Twickenham, Marble Hill contained a number of formal or old-fashioned features in addition to its bowling green: an L-

[32] See Marie Draper, *A Short Account*, p. 7. Mrs. Draper makes the point that Pope's plans for Marble Hill 'owed much to Sherborne'. The engraving is by J. Mason after A. Heckell, 13 Feb. 1749: 'A View of the Countess of Suffolk's House near Twickenham'.

shaped plantation with walks which screened the house from the road to the North; and a Mount, which was criticized by Batty Langley in *New Principles of Gardening* (1728). He found the gardens 'stiff and regular', and objected to the 'low mean Manner' of terracing Mounts bare of shade, an 'Error' which he had observed 'in the Slopes of the Garden of the Honourable Mrs. Howard at Twickenham, being view'd at the River Thames'. But Langley is not an unimpeachable witness, and in the mind of another observer Marble Hill seems to have been the epitome of 'our Modern way of planning Gardens . . . far preferable to what was us'd 20 Years ago'. As John Summerson has pointed out, the architecture of Marble Hill corresponds very closely to the ideal house illustrated and discussed by Robert Morris in *An Essay in Defence of Ancient Architecture* (1728). There is reason to believe that the gardens of Marble Hill conformed to the corresponding ideal Morris describes in *Lectures on Architecture* (1734–6) where he resorts to Thomsonian blank verse to characterize the advantages of a riverside situation like Marble Hill's, affording 'fine Prospect', 'opening Lawns', and 'distant Views'.[33]

To us there is more Art than Nature in the situations Morris describes, and Marble Hill was a garden formal enough to entertain 'a greater court . . . than at Kensington' (iii. 478). At the same time it was sufficiently rural for Pope to characterize Lady Howard as 'a Pastoral Lady' (ii. 435), and 'poetick' enough to warrant the description of the garden and its designer in Swift's *Pastoral Dialogue* (1727).[34]

The recognition of Pope as 'Contriver of the Gardens' of Marble Hill did much to establish his reputation as a landscape designer, and his association with Chiswick, Richmond, and other places in the vicinity suggests that his local influence was greater than can now be documented in detail during the decade when he was often as much engrossed in gardening as literature. Few records of this activity survive besides indications of an exchange of visits, compliments, or favours which suggest that Pope was putting his friends upon

[33] See Marie Draper, *A Short Account*, p. 7; Batty Langley, *New Principles of Gardening* (London, 1728), p. vii; Robert Morris of Twickenham, *Lectures on Architecture Consisting of Rules Founded upon Harmonick and Arithmetical Proportions in Building . . . Read to a Society Establish'd for the Improvement of Arts and Sciences*, (London, 1734–36), pp. vi, 67, 88, 80, 86, 66, 215. On the conformity of Marble Hill to Morris's ideal of architecture, see John Summerson, 'The Classical Country House', pp. 572–3.

[34] Jonathan Swift, *Poems*, ed. Harold Williams, ii. 409–11.

new projects.[35] Something more can be said of his relationship with those whom he referred to in a letter to Thomas Wentworth, Earl of Strafford, as 'publick Professors of Gardening' (ii. 309).

[35] See *Correspondence*, ii. 129, 158, 425; iii. 225, 371.

7. *'Publick Professors of Gardening': Collaboration with Professional Landscape Architects*

i. POPE AND CHARLES BRIDGEMAN (d. 1738)

CHARLES BRIDGEMAN was an apprentice of Henry Wise (1653–1738) at the famous nursery in Brompton Park, 'one of His Majesty's Principall Gardiners' (1726), and successor to Wise as royal gardener (1728). Bridgeman's career includes work under Wise at Blenheim in association with Vanbrugh (1709–38), the great Whig designs at Eastbury (1725), Claremont (1729), and Houghton (1731), culminating in his masterpiece at Stowe (1714–38), along with works in the royal gardens of Hampton Court, Kensington, and Richmond between 1726 and 1738, and, among other private commissions, the design for the Queensberrys at Amesbury (1730–8).[1] Recent research into the obscure career of Bridgeman has not significantly altered Walpole's account of him as a transitional figure in the dawn of modern taste, who reformed and simplified the essentially French idiom of his master, and brilliantly exploited the possibilities of the French invention of the sunk fence or fossé, known in England as the ha-ha.[2]

[1] My account of Bridgeman's landscape architecture is derived from the annotated checklist by Peter Willis, 'The Work of Charles Bridgeman', *Amateur Historian*, 6 (Spring, 1964), 91–6. Willis's Ph.D. dissertation, 'Charles Bridgeman: Royal Gardener', 2 vols. (Cambridge University, 1961) is forthcoming from A. Zwemmer, London, under the title *Charles Bridgeman and the English Landscape Garden.* Christopher Hussey summarizes Willis's findings in *English Gardens and Landscapes*, pp. 34–9. David Green unearths some important facts about Bridgeman in *Gardener to Queen Anne, Henry Wise*, pp. 72, 148. Laurence Whistler gives an account of his work in association with Vanbrugh in *The Imagination of Vanbrugh* (London, 1954).

[2] See Walpole, *History of Gardening*, pp. 24–5; and Peter Willis, 'From Desert to Eden: Charles Bridgeman's "Capital Stroke"', *Burlington Magazine*, 115 (Mar. 1973), 150–7.

It is probably true that Pope conferred with Bridgeman about the layout of Twickenham, but, as far as we know, his contribution was limited to commissions for specific features and ornaments. The 'Bridgmannick Theatre' which Pope 'turfed' in 1726 with a detachment of workmen from the Prince of Wales's garden at Richmond—'It was done . . . all at a stroke, & it is yet unpayd for, but that's nothing with a Poetical genius' (ii. 372)—appears to have been an imitation of a feature such as Bridgeman designed at Claremont, illustrated in *Vitruvius Britannicus* (1725).[3] It is not identified on Serle's *Plan* (1745), which may suggest that this quasi-formal feature was removed as Pope's design matured.

Because Pope imitated a 'Bridgmannick' feature in his garden at Twickenham, and cited Bridgeman's Stowe as the epitome of his principles in the *Epistle to Burlington*, Pope's taste in gardening has often been identified with Bridgeman's, and the professional is seen as the dominant influence on the amateur gardener.[4] The evidence is too fragmentary and equivocal to allow us to advance far beyond conjecture in characterizing this important relationship, but a careful review of their association reveals a story of friendship during the 1720s, including some documented instances of collaboration, followed in the 1730s (after the publication of the *Epistle to Burlington*) by a falling out apparently beyond reconciliation, that may imply a lack of accord extending to conceptions of garden design. The clues we have tend to confirm the speculation of Walpole that Bridgeman was influenced by Pope rather than the other way round: 'whether from good sense, or that the nation had been struck and reformed by the admirable paper in the *Guardian*, No. 173, he [Bridgeman] banished verdant sculpture, and did not even revert to the square precision of the foregoing age'.[5] In any event, the association of Pope and Bridgeman

[3] See Dorothy Stroud, 'Claremont Woods, Esher', a pamphlet guide (London: Country Life for the National Trust, n.d.), p. 5. Peter Willis discusses 'Bridgemannick elements' in Pope's design in 'A Poets' Gardener', *The Listener*, 72 (24 Dec. 1964), 1009, but states in his dissertation, 'Charles Bridgeman: Royal Gardener' (Cambridge University, 1961, p. 355), that there is no proof that Bridgeman was associated with Pope's garden. For the persistent but erroneous idea that Pope owed the design of his garden to Bridgeman and Kent, see James Boutwood, 'Poet's Essay in the Picturesque: Alexander Pope's Garden at Twickenham', *Country Life*, 143 (7 Mar. 1968), 512.

[4] See Peter Martin, 'Pope and the Garden: A Background, Biographical, and Critical Study' (Ph.D. dissertion, Syracuse University, 1968), p. 100.

[5] *History of Gardening*, p. 24.

casts an interesting light on the relations between amateur and professional garden designers, whose contributions need to be reassessed in this crucial phase of the development of the garden as new evidence comes to light.

We have explored the possibility that Bridgeman worked to Pope's directions at Marble Hill. Of the other places where Bridgeman and Pope might have met during the 1720s only two can be documented in any detail. The first was Down Hall, near Harlow, Essex, previously owned by Matthew Prior, who referred to it as a 'half-way house' to the second, Wimpole, at Arrington, Cambridgeshire.[6] Both were estates of Pope's friend and Bridgeman's client, Edward Harley, 2nd Earl of Oxford (1689–1741), and the possibility exists that Pope made Bridgeman's acquaintance through Oxford. Bridgeman, like James Gibbs and the painters John Wootton and James Thornhill, was one of Oxford's 'Tory Virtuosi', and his name is listed along with the rest as a subscriber to Pope's *Odyssey* (1725). Prior's schemes for building a house at Down Hall came to nothing, but from the summer of 1720 he was exclaiming in letters to Oxford 'how beautiful a situation Down is', and busy with 'commensuration, hortification and edification'. In September he was consulting Bridgeman, already employed by Oxford at Wimpole, and by January he told Oxford 'we have laid out squares, rounds and diagonals, and planted quincunxes at Down'.[7]

Prior and Bridgeman had laid out by the time of his death (Sept. 1721) the beginnings of a garden which conformed to Prior's taste for the 'heroic', 'colored by his long familiarity with the artificial regularities and symmetries of Dutch and French landscape'.[8] Pope enters the scene when Oxford, to whom the property reverted after Prior's death in 1721, was deciding whether to carry out Gibbs's unexecuted schemes for the house, and when further improvements under the direction of Bridgeman in the garden were under discussion. Pope made a visit to Down with Bridgeman over the New Year 1725–6, hoping to see the improvements, but bad weather prevented gardening (ii. 359). Subsequent correspondence between Oxford and Pope shows Pope's keen interest, enthusiastic encouragement, and admiration for 'that

[6] *H.M.C.*, *Bath*, iii. 504 (June 1721).

[7] Ibid., 483–4, 490–2, 505–6 (1720–1). See James Lees-Milne, *Earls of Creation*, pp. 185–205.

[8] Charles Kenneth Eves, *Matthew Prior: Poet and Diplomatist* (New York, 1939), p. 398.

most agreeable Place, Down-Hall' (iii. 114), and Oxford's care to keep his friend informed of progress on his 'Bowling green', and 'wood', with the wish 'that I may enjoy your company both at Wimpole and this place' (ii. 371).

Like the improvements at Marble Hill about the same time, the work at Down Hall followed on a conference between Pope, Bridgeman, and his client. Little can be learned about the design which resulted from this collaboration, of which few traces remain,[9] but it is certain that Oxford welcomed the collaboration of Pope at Wimpole, his principal seat where he employed Bridgeman as early as 1721. Prior pictures Bridgeman there in a well-known passage of his letter to Oxford (1721) describing the activity of his virtuosi: 'friend Bridgeman's devotion has consisted chiefly in contriving how the diagonal may take Waddon steeple exactly in the middle'. Prior writes that he is 'glad Bridgeman has begun so well, he says he will make it the finest and noblest thing in England. The garden side I find he has a mind to be at: he does not open yet, but I think it is rather enlarging than much altering.' Prior's remark is significant for its suggestion of an ambitious plan which appears to be under Bridgeman's direction ('he does not open yet'), and for the statement that he is enlarging rather than altering.[10]

As at Down, visits of Pope and Bridgeman were intended to Wimpole just at the time the layout at Marble Hill was beginning. In October 1724 Pope wrote that a visit to Wimpole had to be postponed:

> I am heartily disappointed, and so is another man, of the Virtuoso-Class as well as I; (and in My notions, of the higher kind of class, since Gardening is more Antique & nearer God's own Work, than Poetry) I mean Bridgman, whom I had tempted to accompany me to you. (ii. 264)

The following year (1725) he cancelled another visit he had planned with Bridgeman to Wimpole (ii. 317). The next spring (1726) Oxford was again inviting Pope to visit Wimpole:

> I am extreamly busie at this place but I will not tell you what I am doing nor of my designs till you come to the place and see it with your own eyes and you shall have

[9] Peter Willis, comparing unsigned, undated plans of Down Hall in the Bodleian and British Museum, asserts that the garden design was becoming 'freer, more suggestive, more enticing' under the influence of Bridgeman. 'A Poet's Gardener', *The Listener*, 72, 1008.

[10] *H.M.C.*, *Bath*, iii. 498–9 (Mar. 1721). See Christopher Hussey, 'Wimpole Hall, Cambridgeshire—I. The Seat of the Hon. Gerald Agar-Robartes', *Country Life*, 61 (21 May 1927), 806, 810–11.

the power to alter and I am sure that will be amending, anything I shall think of. (ii. 376–7)

In 1730 Oxford told Pope he was building 'a New Room', and 'about some plantations'—enough to arouse Pope's curiosity.

These glimpses of Pope and Bridgeman give the impression of a good-natured friendship involving the possibility of collaboration on Oxford's garden designs, at a time when they were collaborating at Marble Hill, when Bridgeman may have been advising Pope at Twickenham, and Pope appears to have been recommending Bridgeman to his friends. At this point we need to consider evidence that points to a difference in outlook between Pope and Bridgeman: some lines in the *Epistle to Burlington* intended as a compliment to Bridgeman, misunderstood as satirical, which Pope refers to in his ironic defence of the poem, *The Master Key to Popery* (1732) as 'a fling at honest Bridgeman'.[11]

In early editions of the poem Pope, thinking perhaps of Bridgeman's masterful integration about 1724 of a formless earlier layout at Stowe,[12] which had included substituting a formal octagonal pond for an ill-placed mount on the southern extremity of the design, introduced the lines illustrating good sense in gardening with the couplet:

> The vast parterres a thousand hands shall make
> Lo! Bridgeman comes, & floats them with a lake. (73–4)

For some reason Bridgeman protested, and in later editions (1735 f.) Pope substituted the name of Bridgeman's client at Stowe, Richard Temple, Viscount Cobham, his intimate friend and owner of the garden Pope regarded as an ideal—proof that satire was not intended.[13] Pope evidently regretted the misunderstanding, but efforts at reconciliation were unsuccessful since Pope

[11] On Pope's recommendations of Bridgeman, see *Correspondence*, ii. 261 (1724), 327 (1725). For the 'fling', see *TE* iii. ii. 183.

[12] G. B. Clarke, 'The Vanbrugh–Bridgeman Gardens. The History of Stowe—VII', *The Stoic* [Quarterly publication of Stowe School, Buckingham, Bucks.] 24 (July 1969), 262–3.

[13] Warburton's note in *Works* (1751), iii. 188 n. summarizes Pope's defence. Elwin–Courthope give the note to Pope, iii. 177 n. Few have been content to accept this explanation at face value: see John Wilson Croker, ed., *Suffolk Letters* (London, 1824), i. 382–3 n.; Laurence Whistler, *The Imagination of Vanbrugh* (1954), p. 68; Peter Willis, 'A Poets' Gardener', *The Listener*, 72 (1964), 1009; Christopher Hussey, *English Gardens and Landscapes* (1967), p. 34; and Kathleen Mahaffey, 'Timon's Villa: Walpole's Houghton', *Texas Studies in Literature and Language*, 9 (Summer, 1967), 217.

refers to the matter in a tone of frustrated condescension in several manuscript variants:

> Bridgeman, unskill'd in wit's mysterious ways,
> Knows not, good man, a satire from a praise;
> Yet he can make a mount, or turn a maze.
>
> I sighed and cursed in bitterness of woe,
> Nay, cursed be Fame with all its noise and show,
> The Fame that made one worthy man my foe,
> If Bridgeman, while his head contrives a maze,
> Knows not, good man, my satire from my praise.[14]

Fame probably refers here to the notoriety of Pope's poem, the *Epistle to Burlington*, resulting from the success of the campaign against it as a libel on Chandos, which may have awakened Bridgeman's suspicion of Pope.

In the *Master Key* Pope ridicules the absurdity of interpreting the lines as satire and makes some interesting comments on the relationship between the professional landscape architect and his client:

> Here we have a fling at honest Bridgeman. I don't wonder to see his name at length, for he is his particular Acquaintance. What a Malicious Representation of one who lives by his profession, as taking pleasure to destroy and overflow Gentlemens fine Gardens!
>
> The vast Parterres a thous[d] hands shall make
> Lo Bridgeman comes, & floats them with a Lake.
>
> As if he should have the Impudence, when a Gentleman has done a wrong thing at a great Expence, to come & pretend to make it a right one? Is it not his business to please Gentlemen? to execute Gentlemen's will and Pleasure, not his own? is he to set up his own Conceits & Inventions against Gentlemen's fine Taste & Superior Genius? Yet is this what the Poet suggests, with intent (doubtless) to take the Bread out of his mouth, & ruin his Wife & Family.

Pope's irony may be directed at Bridgeman's unwillingness to be cited in a poem attacking the taste of 'the Great' and elevating his own above theirs. It certainly exposes the absurdity of supposing that Bridgeman would take 'pleasure to destroy and overflow Gentlemens fine Gardens', and the unlikeli-

[14] A manuscript fragment quoted by Sir James Prior, *Life of Edmund Malone, Editor of Shakespeare, with Selections from his Manuscript Anecdotes* (London, 1860), p. 368, quoted by Mahaffey, 'Timon's Villa: Walpole's Houghton', p. 217; Variant lines in the Chauncey MS. of the *Epistle to Arbuthnot*, E.C., iii. 263 n.

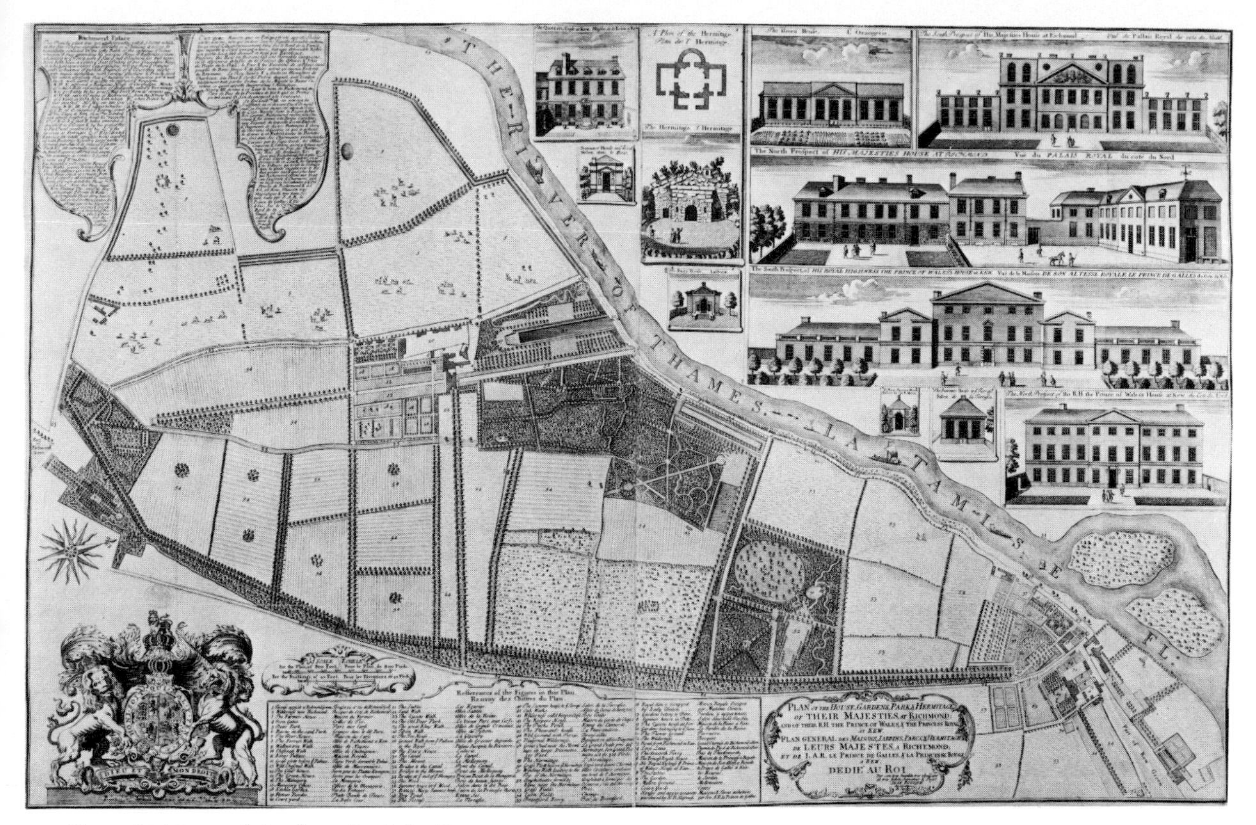

34. Plan of Richmond Gardens. By John Rocque. 1734.

35. Marble Hill House. By Richard Wilson. 1762.

36. Carlton House, Middlesex. By William Woollett. 1774.

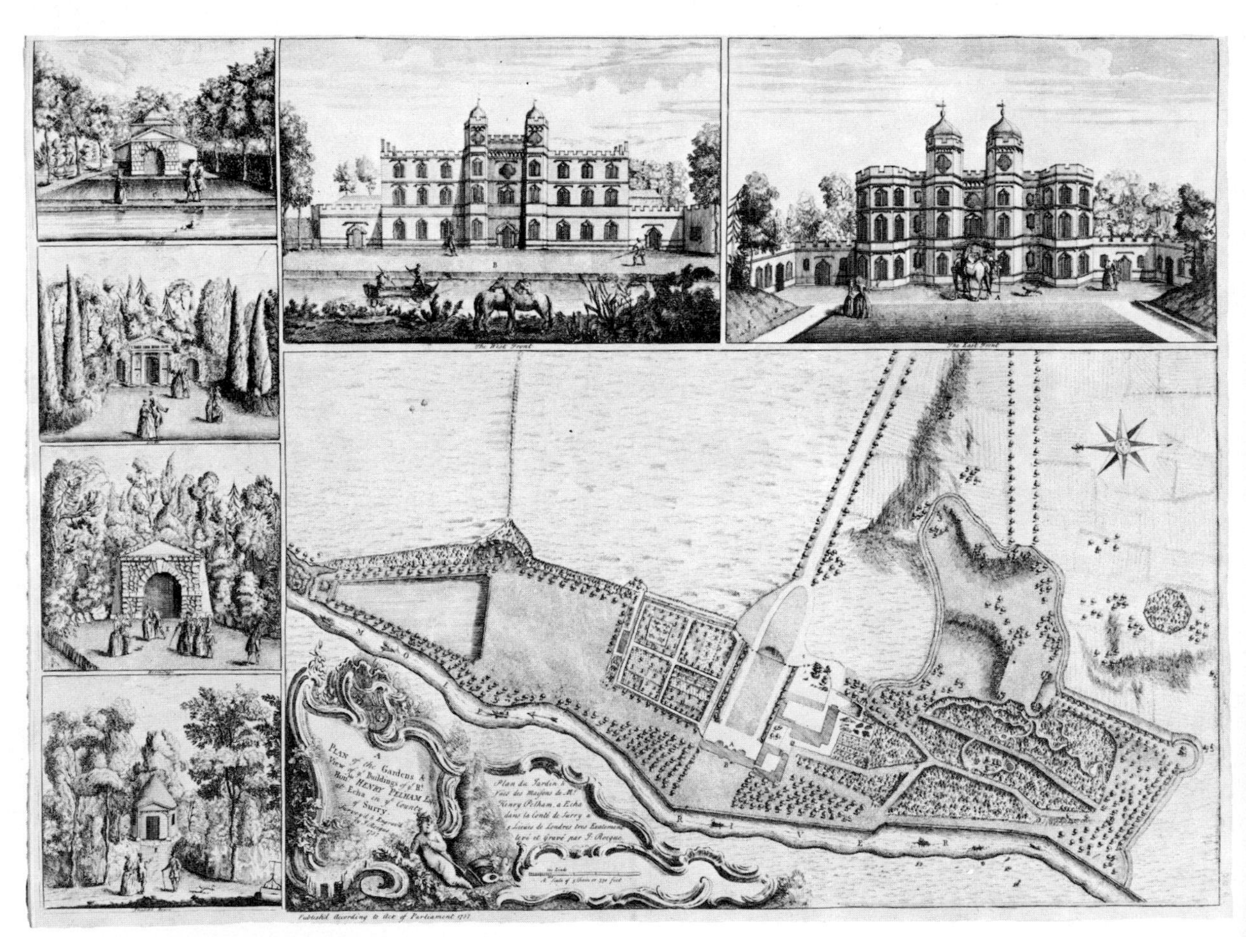

37. Esher, Surrey. By John Rocque. 1737.

hood that he would follow his own invention instead of carrying out the instructions of his client, Cobham, who was himself an experienced garden designer. Pope's defence assumes the existence of the relationship between patron and artist conventional at the time, 'the former superior in every respect to the latter'. Bridgeman was no exception to the rule, even though his status as a specialist garden designer like Le Nôtre was an improvement on that of his predecessors like Wise and Switzer, who were nurserymen-contractors. At the same time the irony glances critically at the subservient status of the professional whom Pope believed the untutored client ought to trust.[15]

Nothing Pope could say in his defence could vindicate him from charges of personal satire against Bridgeman or Chandos once readers began writing their own keys. Stephen Switzer censures Bridgeman in the second edition of his *Ichnographia Rustica* (1742) precisely in terms of Pope's satire on false taste in gardening in the *Epistle to Burlington*, when he identifies the gardens of Timon's villa with Bridgeman's Blenheim where

> Grove nods at Grove, each Alley has a brother,
> And half the platform just reflects the other. (117–18)

He specifically criticizes Bridgeman's management of water, which he compares to Timon's pond (l. 106):

> The same extravagant way of thinking prevailed also to a great degree, in that otherwise ingenious Designer [Bridgeman] in his Plan of Lakes and Pieces of Water, without any regard to the Goodness of the Land, which was to be overflowed: But which he generally designed so large, as to make a whole Country look like an Ocean. (i. 12)

Switzer holds Bridgeman responsible for that 'false sublime' in gardening which is the primary object of Pope's satire throughout the poem:

> This aiming at an incomprehensible Vastness, and attempting at Things beyond the reach of Nature, is in a great measure owing to the late eminent Designer in Gardening ['Mr. Bridgman', identified in a note], whose Fancy could not be bounded. (i. 11)

[15] *Master Key to Popery*, *TE* iii. ii, 183. The possibility of Bridgeman's unwillingness to be cited was suggested to me by Maynard Mack. On Cobham as garden designer, see G. B. Clarke, 'Lancelot Brown's Work at Stowe. The History of Stowe—XIV', *The Stoic*, 24 (Dec. 1971), 21. On patronage see Frank Jenkins, *Architect and Patron* (London, 1961), p. 76. On the status of garden designers, see Hussey, *English Gardens and Landscapes*, p. 36.

Greatness does not consist in size, he observes, again echoing Pope on Timon's villa: 'whereas let the Works be ever so large, unless the Parts cohere in Harmony, there will be but a great many Littlenesses put together' (i. 11).

Switzer's attack on Bridgeman appears to be in large part the expression of professional jealousy. Bridgeman had succeeded in the royal parks and the grand designs of Stowe in realizing Switzer's unfulfilled ambition to design on the French scale of grandeur. His criticism of Bridgeman's management of water is suspect because he criticizes him at Claremont for not making more of the water.[16] At the same time Switzer's highly partisan criticism of a rival is valuable because it appears to sum up accurately the contemporary view of Bridgeman's work, which was associated with the French 'grand Manier', as opposed to Pope's, which was identified with the aesthetics of the picturesque. An informed observer like Philip Southcote distinguishes at Stowe between work 'in the Bridgeman taste' and 'the painting part of the gardens', where we will see that Pope was importantly involved (Spence, No. 1122).

In any discussion of Pope's relations with Bridgeman, the poet's conception of taste as insight which no professional consultant can furnish ought to be taken into account:

> A light wch in yourself y[o]u must perceive
> Jones & Le Nôtre have it not to give.
> For Gibs & Brigman have it not to give.[17]

Thus we must respect the differences between the Bridgeman taste and Pope's taste in gardening, and perhaps we can accept the conclusion of Miles Hadfield about the unsettled question of influence:

> At present Bridgeman as a personality lives more in Pope's correspondence than elsewhere, and one cannot help feeling that Pope's friendship and help, and his great sensibility combined with a practical interest in gardening, must have helped Bridgeman, the consummate surveyor and well-trained gardener, to move towards those wider horizons of which his colleague Switzer was so suspicious.[18]

[16] Laurence Whistler, *The Imagination of Vanbrugh*, p. 153.

[17] Cancelled lines in the Pierpont Morgan MS. (MA 352) of the *Epistle to Burlington*, following l. 28.

[18] *Gardening in Britain*, p. 193.

ii. POPE AND WILLIAM KENT (1684–1748)

Walpole's claim for Pope's influence on the other major contemporary landscape architect, William Kent, has also been questioned, but it can be substantiated. Walpole's statement in the *History of Gardening* that 'Mr. Pope

FIG. 3. Sketch profile of William Kent.
By Dorothy Boyle(?).

undoubtedly contributed to form his [Kent's] taste' (28) is part of his attempt 'to show to what degree Mr. Kent invented the new style, and what hints he had received to suggest and conduct his undertaking' (23–4). Walpole argues that Kent was the first professional to adopt picturesque principles of gardening; Bridgeman had 'banished verdant sculpture' and introduced the sunk fence or ha-ha, but Kent, 'painter enough to taste the charms of landscape, bold and opiniative enough to dare and to dictate, and born with a genius to strike out a great system from the twilight of imperfect essays . . . leaped the fence, and saw that all nature was a garden' (24–5). But he goes on to qualify this claim by observing that 'just as the encomiums are that I have bestowed on Kent's discoveries, he was neither without assistance or faults' (28), and here he makes the claim for Pope's influence on Kent, suggesting that Twickenham was the model for two of his works.

Walpole's irresistible description of Kent as the conquering hero and athletic champion of gardening has been more often remembered than the qualifications, and Kent has been seen ever since through Walpole's eyes as the founder of the landscape garden, 'the friend of nature, the Calvin of this reformation'. Walpole's colourful descriptions of Kent have inflated his importance in the history of gardening. The circumstantial evidence surrounding Kent's gardening career indicates that far from exaggerating Pope's influence on Kent in the *History of Gardening*, as George Sherburn argues, Walpole appears to have underestimated Kent's indebtedness to Pope. Walpole's champion was from the outset Pope's 'bold associate', as William Mason stated it in *The English Garden*, as much under Pope's influence in gardening as under Burlington's in architecture.[19]

Walpole's estimate of Kent reflects the opinions of the best-informed contemporaries, like Joseph Spence and Philip Southcote. Both sized up Kent in less than heroic terms, and linked him closely to Burlington and Pope. Southcote, who employed Kent at Woburn Farm as an architect in the 1740s, observed in 1756 that 'Lord Burlington and Kent were the first introducers of the fine natural taste in gardening' and that both of them 'pretended' to be 'the first . . . that thought of it' (Spence, No. 1121). Southcote credits the introduction of the picturesque in gardening to Pope along with Kent, emphasizing their mutual limitations, and Pope's ambition as a gardener:

> Mr. Pope and Kent were the first that practiced painting in gardening. But Lord Petre carried it farther than either of them, for Kent had little more than the idea of mixing lighter and darker greens in a pleasing manner. (Spence, No. 603)

The image of Kent needs to be modified by the estimate of Joseph Spence, who was choosing his words with care when he remarked that 'Mr. Kent was the sole beginner of the national taste' (No. 1060)—that is to say, Kent

[19] Horace Walpole, *The World*, No. 6 (8 Feb. 1753), in *Works*, 5 vols. (London, 1798), i. 148; Sherburn, '"Timon's Villa" and Cannons', *Huntington Library Bulletin* 8 (Oct. 1935), 132 n. 2; Mason, *The English Garden*, ed. Burgh, p. 23, Book the First, l. 510.

succeeded in making the taste for picturesque gardening fashionable against a strong prejudice still favouring formal design. This is the essence of Walpole's claim for Kent when stripped of its rhetoric; the *History of Gardening* was written to establish Kent's importance in the history of fashionable taste.[20]

The conception of Kent as a diffuser of taste, a popularizer, and crusader for the taste of his patrons and friends, corresponds much more closely to the facts of his career than the image of an original genius or the inventor of a new concept of garden design. Unlike Bridgeman, Kent was not a specialist garden designer; it is questionable whether he can be considered a professional landscape architect at all. He was a coach painter in Hull, who was sent by his patrons to be trained in Italy, where he met the Earl of Burlington. Burlington brought him to England to serve first as a history painter and decorator, and later as an architect. He held official posts on the Board of Works, and as Principal Painter to the Crown. His work in gardening, which was incidental to architectural commissions, for the most part obtained by his patron, cannot be dated before the 1730s, and cannot be traced to more than a dozen places—a meagre achievement compared to Bridgeman's or to Brown's. None of these amounts to an entire layout like Bridgeman's Eastbury, for example; typically, Kent was 'working over other men's foundations', making alterations or siting a piece of garden architecture, and not a single garden plan can be assigned to his draughtsmanship.[21]

Kent's architecture, excepting his garden gothic, was entirely under the dominant influence of his patron, Lord Burlington. This appears to be no less true of his relationship with Pope in garden design. Their association can be dated as early as 1721, after Kent returned from Italy as Burlington's protégé, when they began an intimate and convivial friendship as members of Burlington's circle which lasted until Pope's death: Kent was known to Pope as the

[20] For Walpole's claims for Kent, see William Bowles, ed. *Works of Alexander Pope*, iii. 325. Cf. Walpole's explicit statement of his thesis about Kent in notes to *Satirical Poems by William Mason*, ed. Paget Toynbee (Oxford, 1926), p. 39: 'William Kent, Painter & Architect in the reign of George the 2d was Author of the modern taste in English gardening; or in other words, the First who discovered that the Imitation of Nature was the true Style in gardening, as in all other Arts.'

[21] For Pope's reference to 'Painter Kent', see *TE* vi. 340, l. 2. See Hadfield, *Gardening in Britain*, p. 196; Hussey, *English Gardens and Landscapes*, p. 45. Hadfield states in *Pioneers in Gardening* (London, 1955), p. 58, that Kent was 'practically everything except a gardener'. On Kent's life and works, see Margaret Jourdain, *The Work of William Kent* (London, 1948), and Colvin, pp. 343–6.

'Signior' (iv. 43); he and Pope 'dined together upon Pictures' (iv. 43), paid respect to each other's 'Genius' (iv. 44), and enjoyed some convivial evenings together (iv. 125, 163). Kent assisted Pope with illustrations for the *Odyssey* (1725–6), to which he was a subscriber, and he painted Pope's portrait in 1735. He had visited Pope's garden by about 1725 (see chap. 10) when he made the sketch of the Shell Temple. In the next decade he advised Pope on the architecture of his house, and made his only documented contribution to Pope's garden.[22] Unlike Bridgeman he did not misunderstand Pope's compliment to him in verse, and he put up with Pope's wit on his work at Richmond, Tottenham, and Chiswick. His will records a bequest to Pope.[23]

Walpole's assertion in the *History* that 'the design of the prince of Wales's garden at Carlton-house was evidently borrowed from the poet's at Twickenham' can be substantiated by circumstantial evidence. Carleton House in Pall Mall (plate 36) had been built by Henry Boyle, Baron Carleton, Burlington's uncle, who had been 'Keeper of the Garden of St. James's Palace' (then known as St. James's House) since 1700. In 1709 he obtained a 31-year lease for part of the royal gardens which had been in his custody and improved by him, amounting to 9 acres, 1 rood, 1 perch in extent, running 'along the Skirts' of St. James's Park, north of the Mall, where he built his house opposite Wren's Marlborough House (1709–11).[24]

As we have seen, Pope had made Boyle's acquaintance through Burlington by 1716, became the neighbour of his villa when he moved to Twickenham

[22] See 'The Names of the Subscribers', *The Odyssey of Homer* (1725), vol. 1. For Kent's portrait of Pope and drawing of the Shell Temple, see Wimsatt 14 and 18, *Portraits*, pp. 119, 127. Concerning Kent's contribution to Pope's garden at Twickenham, see letters to Burlington dated 1738: H. Avray Tipping, ed., 'Four Unpublished Letters of William Kent', *Architectural Review*, 63 (May 1928), 180, 182. 'New Works in his [Pope's] garden that I design'd there' probably refer to urns Kent designed. See *Some Designs of Mr. Inigo Jones and Mr. William Kent* (London, 1744), pl. 25: 'Two Vases with Pedestals for Mr. Pope'; and *Correspondence*, ii. 144; iv. 413. Spence's conjecture (No. 602) that Kent designed Pope's mount is unlikely. He apparently confused a lost drawing with a design. See Spence Nos. 603, 1060, 1062.

[23] Pope's compliment to Kent appears in *The Epilogue to the Satires*, *Dia.* ii (1738), l. 67, *TE* iv. 316. For ridicule of Kent see *Imitations of Horace*, Ep. II, i (1737), l. 355, *TE* iv. 224; *Correspondence*, iii. 329 n., 417–18; iv. 323–4. For Kent's bequest to Pope, 'Raphael Head Busto and the Wooden Term and the Alabaster Vase', see Margaret Jourdain, *The Work of William Kent* (1948), p. 90.

[24] On Carleton House, see Horace Walpole, *History of Gardening*, p. 28; 'Carlton House', chap. 8, 'Trafalgar Square and Neighbourhood', *Survey of London*, 20 (London, 1940), 69–76; David Green, *Gardener to Queen Anne, Henry Wise*, p. 91; Hugh Phillips, *Mid-Georgian London* (London, 1964), pp. 55–6; John Macky, *A Journey Through England*, i. 192.

in 1718, and had paid a visit to Carleton House in 1725 during Boyle's last illness—facts which support Sherburn's statement that Pope was 'intimate' with Carleton.[25] After Boyle's death in 1725, the house and gardens passed to his nephew, Lord Burlington, the patron of Kent and Pope, who was the owner until 1732, when it was acquired by the Prince of Wales. Thus it appears that Pope was associated with all the owners of the house during his lifetime, including the Prince of Wales, whom he had earlier advised at Richmond.

Kent's association with the gardens of Carleton House resulted from Burlington's patronage and from his architectural commission for the building of Kew Palace in Richmond for the Prince of Wales soon after 1730. Between 1732 and 1734 the Prince of Wales's part of the royal gardens of St. James's were transformed by Kent in such a way as to attract the attention of an enthusiastic gardener and gossip on the arts, Sir Thomas Robinson.[26] The latter wrote in 1734 to his patron Charles Howard, Earl of Carlisle:

> There is a new taste in gardening just arisen, which has been practised with so great success at the Prince's garden in Town [Carleton House], that a general alteration of some of the most considerable gardens in the kingdom is begun, after Mr. Kent's notion of gardening, viz., to lay them out, and work without either level or line. By this means I really think the 12 acres the Prince's garden consists of, is more diversified and of greater variety than anything of that compass I ever saw; and this method of gardening is the more agreeable, as when finished, it has the appearance of beautiful nature, and without being told, one would imagine art had no part in the finishing, and is, according to what one hears of the Chinese, entirely after their models for works of this nature, where they never plant straight lines or make regular designs. The celebrated gardens of Claremount, Chiswick, and Stowe are now full of labourers, to modernise the expensive works finished in them, even since everyone's memory. If this grows a fashion, t'will be happy for that class of people, as they will run no risk of having time lay on their hands.[27]

The letter clearly indicates that Kent was introducing picturesque principles of design in the garden of Carleton House in 1734. Pope's reputation for

[25] See Pope, *Correspondence*, ii. 289 n.

[26] See *Survey of London*, 20 (1940), p. 74: 'When Carlton House was first acquired from Lord Burlington in 1732, alterations, including the refacing of the garden front with stone, were effected by Flitcroft [Burlington's architect], while Kent improved the grounds, framing bowers and grottos containing marble statues sculptured by Rysbrach.' Cf. Phillips, *Mid-Georgian London* (1964), p. 56.

[27] *H.M.C., Carlisle*, vi. 143–4(23 Dec. 1734).

gardening during the 1720s, the indication that he had laid out another garden in Hampton 'after his own', similarities of scale and appearance between the garden at Twickenham and that at Carleton House as it appears in Woollett's engraving, his intimacy with the Boyles and with Kent, who had visited Twickenham by about 1725, and his increasingly close relations with the Prince of Wales during the 1730s which appear to have involved gardening—all these are circumstances which tend to confirm Walpole's identification of Twickenham as the model for the garden design of Carleton House, and Pope as a formative influence on Kent's earliest work.[28]

Kent's work in landscape design throughout the decade continues to reflect the influence of Pope's precept and example, and to indicate the possibility of direct collaboration. He adopted from the outset the principles of picturesque gardening Pope had practised in the preceding decade at Twickenham. He succeeded Bridgeman in royal gardens, at Kensington, and at Richmond, where, according to Spence (No. 1060) he apparently handled the landscape in a picturesque way. Spence also speaks of Kent's work at Chiswick as marking the beginning of the national taste, and dates the 'first thing done that way *there*', perhaps the cascade, October 1733 (No. 1060).[29]

Kent's work at Chiswick and Carleton House led him in the early 1730s to Tottenham Park, Wiltshire, a house rebuilt to the designs of Lord Burlington between 1730–40 for his brother-in-law, Charles Lord Bruce. Here in July 1734 Pope and Kent were visiting when Pope wrote to Burlington about his rivalry with Kent in the design of garden temples for the park:

It [Tottenham House] is one of the prettiest I ever saw, and one of the best Houses I ever was in, an admirable fine Library, a delicious Park, & extensive Plantations. It

[28] The engraving by Woollett is dated 1774 (Phillips, *Mid-Georgian London*, p. 56, plate 63). Evidence of the friendship between Pope and the Prince of Wales in the 1730s is found in the exchange of visits to Twickenham (iii. 500, 1735), and Kew (iv. 139, 1738); Pope's gift of a Bounce puppy (iv. 48, 1736), and the Prince's of urns (iv. 170, 178, 181, 1739); and Pope's good offices to the Prince, in writing an inscription for the Prince's Bath monument (iv. 170, 176, 1739), and in recommending a Thames waterman (iv. 348, 1741). As Sherburn observes (iii. 448, headnote): 'During the year [1735] royalty was much concerned in constructing grottoes, gazebos, &c., &c. Pope's knowledge of these matters possibly served to increase his intimacy with the Prince of Wales, who in October did the poet the honour of a visit at his house in Twickenham.'

[29] On Kent's work at Chiswick see Sir Thomas Whately, *Observations on Modern Gardening*, 3rd edn. (London, 1801), p. 153; and Rudolf Wittkower, 'Lord Burlington and William Kent', *Archaeological Journal*, 102 (1954), 160, and plate VIII. 2.

wants only a few Temples & ornaments of Building which I am contriving, in defect of better architects (who are a Rare & uncommon Generation, not born in every Family) or rather to prevent a wild Goth, whom I think they call Kent, (from a Country which has ever been held no part of Christendome) I am told this man hath suggested an odd thing, which thro his Violence of Temper and Ungovernable Spirit of Dominion (natural to all Goths) he will infallibly erect; unless I lay a Temple in his way, which he will probably not venture to pull down, after what he has (doubtless) heard of the fate of his Countryman Brennus for sacrilege. However, as I cannot get this done in a day, I fear the owner of this place (who is a man of no Resolution & never Positive in any thing) may drop my design. (iii. 417–18)

The 'Ungovernable Spirit' and the 'Odd thing' are perfectly characteristic of Kent as gardener and garden architect. 'Whenever we find fanciful and witty ideas, disregard of reason and rule, odd escapades', Rudolf Wittkower observes in distinguishing Kent's architecture from Burlington's, 'we can be sure we have the real Kent before us.'[30]

Kent continued his work of this decade in the great Whig gardens, where he introduced picturesque ideas in landscaping his architectural commissions. The most important of these—a garden temple at Stowe, where Twickenham again supplied a model for its situation, and where Kent probably collaborated with Pope—will be considered in detail below (see chap. 8). His sketches for Holkham, Norfolk (1729 f.), where he collaborated with Burlington on the design of a house for Thomas Coke, 1st Earl of Leicester, show the characteristic elements of his picturesque landscape design: plantations in clumps, temples framed in trees, water, and ornamental bridges. Kent's proposals for a house in the manner of Holkham at Euston, Suffolk, for Burlington's friend, Charles FitzRoy, 2nd Duke of Grafton, were accompanied by sketches for the park (where Burlington had designed a wooden bridge as early as 1731) illustrating Kent's ideas of plantation: loosely symmetrical, a mixture of hardwoods and conifers in belts and 'clumps'—'Mr. Kent's passion', which Walpole thought he carried to excess 'till a lawn looks like the ten of spades'.[31]

Robinson's letter quoted above indicates that by 1734 Kent's revision of the

[30] 'Lord Burlington and William Kent', p. 160. On Tottenham, see Wittkower, ibid., pp. 154–5.

[31] On Holkham, see Hussey, *English Gardens and Landscapes*, pp. 45–6, plates 26, 27. On Euston, see Hussey, ibid., p. 156, plates 226–8; Walpole, *Correspondence*, xviii. 255 (to Horace Mann, 20 June 1743); and Arthur Oswald, 'Euston Hall, Suffolk—III. The Seat of the Duke of Grafton', *County Life*, 121 (24 Jan. 1957), 148–51.

Vanbrugh–Bridgeman garden at Claremont, Surrey, laid out for Thomas Pelham, Duke of Newcastle, was under way. Kent designed some garden architecture and a cascade, landscaped the geometrical lake, widened the view of Vanbrugh's belvedere, and rebuilt Vanbrugh's terrace. The last two projects are pictured on Kent's sketches, with a note descriptive of the fate of the formal features near the house: 'a Johns [Sir John Vanbrugh's] level terrace to be taken away'. About 1730 Kent rebuilt a house adjoining Claremont in the Gothic style for Pelham's brother, Henry, at Esher Place in Surrey (plate 37) and laid out the park. As shown in his capriccio sketch (possibly an illustration for Drayton's *Polyolbion*) Kent consulted the genius of the place—the prospect and the windings of the River Mole—and designed the garden architecture shown in his drawing of the hillside south-east of the house, surmounted by a belvedere and grotto.[32] In 1738 Pope praised the place for the reason, I believe, that it realized his poetic–picturesque ideal of stage scene, prospect, retirement, and association:

> Pleas'd let me own, in *Esher*'s peaceful Grove
> (Where Kent and Nature vye for Pelham's Love)
> The Scene, the Master, opening to my view,
> I sit and dream I see my Crags anew! (66–9)[33]

One last landscape attributed to Kent late in this decade, Rousham, Oxfordshire (1738–41), requires more detailed treatment because it is the second place where Walpole claimed Twickenham as the model for Kent's work, a place which he regarded as Kent's finest achievement, and the only design by Kent which still survives in its outlines.

As in the case of Carleton House, Walpole's surmise about Pope's influence at Rousham can be substantiated by circumstantial evidence. Pope's relationship with the Dormer family—Colonel Robert Dormer, Master of Rousham until his death in 1737, his brother General James Dormer (1679–1741), who improved it after his brother's death, and his heir Sir Clement Cottrell (1686–1758), Pope's Twickenham neighbour—appears to have been well established long before his first recorded visit to the house in 1728.[34] As early as 1718 the

[32] On Claremont and Esher, see Hussey, *English Gardens and Landscapes*, pp. 46–7 and n., plates 29–31.

[33] *Imitations of Horace*, *Ep. Sat.*, Dia. II, *TE* iv. 316.

[34] Pope was on dining terms with a member of the family by 1718 (i. 468) but, according to Wimsatt (*Portraits*, p. 40), friendship 'was no doubt solidly established a good many years earlier', and the brothers

house, which was on the way to Stowe and Cirencester and near Middleton, may already have become one of his regular resorts on summer rambles. In the summer of 1725 he had been 'above a Month strolling about in *Buckinghamshire* and *Oxfordshire*, from Garden to Garden' (ii. 314) in the company of John Gay, so that there is reason to suppose he had witnessed the improvements which John Gay alludes to in a letter to General James Dormer (then envoy to Portugal) in a letter dated 1726 (ii. 416). In any event, speaking of his visit in 1728, he writes that 'Rousham . . . is the prettiest place for water-falls, jetts, ponds inclosed with beautiful scenes of green and hanging wood, that ever I saw' (ii. 513).

The garden Pope admired for its waterworks can perhaps be identified with the unsigned, undated plan now preserved in the Bodleian with annotations about waterworks showing the outlines of a formal garden which Kent was to transform at the end of the next decade. The plan has been attributed to Charles Bridgeman, who was at work laying out neighbouring Stowe during the early twenties, and if he was responsible the possibility arises that Rousham was another place where Pope and Bridgeman may have met during the mid 1720s. But the plan, which was drawn 'for Colonel Dormers', shows us a garden which appears to have little enough in common with the mature Twickenham, save for the Bridgmannick theatre on the riverside, and it is interesting to note that this feature appears to have been levelled at Twickenham, as it was at Rousham.[35] Following the contours of the river, the layout is assymetrical and irregular with serpentine walks, but the terraces near the house and the formal management of water are marks of the Bridgmannick taste as yet untouched by the picturesque.

But the subsequent development of the garden by General James Dormer and William Kent appears to have been in perfect harmony with Pope's ideas. Kent's work at Rousham cannot be dated earlier than 1738 when he was

were related to Pope's 'early encourager Sir William Trumbull of Easthampstead'. The family subscribed to both the *Iliad* and the *Odyssey*; and Pope's portrait by Kneller was copied by Worsdale for the family before Kneller's death (Wimsatt 5. 6).

[35] Christopher Hussey attributes the Bodleian plan (Gough drawings, A 4 fol. 63) to Bridgeman in *English Gardens and Landscapes*, pp. 147–8. Peter Willis has written to me (23 Jan. 1971) that the Gough drawing in the Bodleian 'is (to my eye) by Bridgeman and contains all the major elements of what we think of as Kent's work: Venus' Vale with its statuary, and Bridgeman's Theatre are both indicated'.

employed by Dormer to make alterations on the house, even though he was acquainted with General Dormer by 1732 and was soon being described by Pope as 'a happy but plumper copy of General Dormer' (iv. 43) and was referring to the General familiarly as 'bronzo mad' (iv. 150). As usual with Kent, architectural work was accompanied by garden architecture and landscaping, as indicated on another undated plan (plate 38) at Rousham House, showing the plantations which transformed Rousham into a picturesque garden with pronounced similarity to Twickenham.[36]

Records of the clerk of works, White, indicate that coinciding with Kent's commission to alter the garden front of the house, work was proceeding rapidly under his direction in the gardens in accordance with the Rousham House Plan. By the spring of 1738 seventy men were finishing the task of converting the terraces descending to the river from the formal rectangular enclosure north-east of the house into a concave slope to the river, 'The Great Slope', as indicated on the Plan. In the spring of 1738 White wrote: 'the slope will this evening be turfed. The River is pretty clean, the banks everywhere pared. All things thereabouts appear Magnifique.' In November of the same year the Bridgmannick theatre was being rough levelled and replaced by a grove where statues of Bacchus and Ceres were to be placed, a case where the 'laughing Ceres' of Pope's *Epistle to Burlington* (l. 176) literally 'reassumed' the land. It was at this point, White thought, that 'Mr Kent will be most wanted'.[37]

In the next year works were underway in the new garden north of the house along the Cherwell. At the bend in the river, the hinge between the old and new parts of the garden, Kent's seven-arched portico, Praeneste, had been erected, and the 'concave slope from the arcade to ye River' was being turfed in October 1739. At the end of a new grass walk a classical Ionic temple designed by Kent overlooking the river was being erected by the Oxford mason William Townsend, and in November 1739 'planting by Townesend's building' was being discussed. Near by, at the north-eastern extremity of

[36] See Christopher Hussey, 'A Georgian Arcady—I, William Kent's Gardens at Rousham, Oxfordshire', *Country Life*, 99 (14 June 1946), 1084–5. According to Hussey, the Rousham House Plan is 'certainly not' by Kent, 'probably by Bridgeman', but Willis doubts the attribution to Bridgeman. See Hussey, *English Gardens and Landscapes*, p. 149, plate 202; and Willis, letter quoted above, n. 35. The clerk of works, White, who was overseeing these plans, is a possibility.

[37] Manuscript quotations by Hussey, *English Gardens and Landscapes*, pp. 150–1, plate 202.

Elm Walk, the disposition of a statue of Apollo was being discussed in June 1739. The valley between Praeneste and Townsend's building was being improved with a 'new pond', a cascade, a cold bath or grotto, a serpentine rill, and statuary, including figures of Pan and the Venus di Medici, for whom the place was named Venus's Vale. Kent's sketch shows the plantations of 'tall Forest Trees standing in grass' mixed with conifers 'to recall the cypress ilex groves of classical landscape'.[38]

It was this part of the garden which suggested Pope's Twickenham to Walpole: 'I do not know whether the disposition of the garden at Rousham, laid out for general Dormer, and in my opinion the most engaging of all Kent's works, was not planned on the model of Mr. Pope's, at least in the opening and retiring shades of Venus's vale.' Pope was visiting Rousham while these improvements were being planned and carried out, and many of the elements of the composition can be traced to Twickenham or to places like Stowe and Chiswick where Kent and Pope were associated: plantations cut by serpentine walks, the 'cold bath' or grotto, the statuary, possibly the serpentine rill which Christopher Hussey has described as 'the earliest concrete instance of the use of the "serpentine line" applied to garden layout'. But whatever the validity of Walpole's speculation about the source of this passage in the garden, Pope may be responsible for the concept which unites the whole of it, because the layout of the place fulfils to a remarkable degree the possibilities Pope had recognized a decade earlier at Sherborne, Dorset.[39]

Above all, in siting the garden architecture, Kent applied Pope's principle of 'calling in' the country to devise a series of picturesque views similar to those Pope had enjoyed at Sherborne. Here, as at Esher and Sherborne, he opened scenes of the country in a calculated sequence: beginning with views across the Cherwell which could be enjoyed from the house, or from the two

[38] Hussey, *English Gardens and Landscapes*, pp. 150–2, plates 202, 205.

[39] Walpole, *History of Gardening*, p. 29. Pope's *Correspondence* records visits to Rousham throughout the 1730s, and again in 1743: iii. 126 (1730), iii. 410 (1734); iii. 493 (1735); iv. 81 (1737); iv. 188 (1739); iv. 472 (1743). On the serpentine line see Christopher Hussey, *English Gardens and Landscapes*, p. 151; but see Pope's reference in the manuscript of the *Epistle to Burlington* (Pierpont Morgan, MA 352) to what may have been 'a creeping Rill' at Twickenham: chap. 5, n. 62. On Kent's revolutionary concept of garden design at Rousham, see Miles Hadfield, *Gardening in Britain*, p. 197.

green seats at the top of the great slope, or seen from a different perspective from the walk above the arcade; then descending (as at Sherborne) to the 'close Scene' of Venus's Vale and the sound of the cascade; then rising to follow the serpentine walk to Townsend's temple on a neighbouring hill (again compare Sherborne); then to the statue of Apollo at the end of Elm Walk, where Kent had screened the view of the medieval Heyford Bridge to the north with one of his 'clumps'. He improved the perspective beyond the bridge (again as at Sherborne) by Gothic titivation of the 'Ruin'd Temple of the Mill', and, beyond on the horizon, erected a sham ruin shaped as a wide gable with Gothic arches known appropriately enough as 'the Eye Catcher'. Finally the return along Elm Walk was planned to obtain the first 'surprising' view of the portico, and to enjoy from circular seats recessed in its arches framed views of the countryside. Everything that Pope had envisioned at Sherborne was realized in this circumambulation: succession of views, walks along the natural windings of the river, variety of plantation, cascade, statuary, temple on a neighbouring hill, medieval architecture, and sham ruin. These 'perfectly classic' scenes, as Walpole described them, a synthesis of classical architecture and picturesque landscape, appear to derive from the genius of a poet.[40]

The conclusion to be drawn from a survey of Kent's known work in landscape architecture is that Pope was directly or indirectly a dominant influence on his style. Kent's relationship with Pope raises further doubts about his reputation as the founder of the landscape garden. The surprisingly small number of his works, arising usually out of architectural commissions in the Burlington circle, usually limited to landscaping of garden architecture, and consisting of additions or alterations of existing gardens (frequently Bridgeman's), under the influence of Pope's precept and example, and occasional collaboration, indicate that his importance in the movement has been exaggerated. His contemporaries, including Walpole, if we do not misread him, give us the truest estimate of Kent's contribution. They recognized him as the

[40] On the Eye Catcher at Rousham, see Hussey, *English Gardens and Landscapes*, p. 152, plate 215, and Margaret Jourdain, *Work of William Kent*, p. 81. For Walpole's description of Rousham, see Walpole, *Correspondence*, ix. 290 (to George Montagu, 19 July 1760). Cf. *History of Gardening*, p. 29, and *Visits to Country Seats*, Walpole Society 16 (1927–8), p. 26.

first professional gardener to 'practice painting in gardening', the 'sole beginner of a *national taste*', the 'leading executant' of the Palladian movement. The explanation of Kent's career in gardening is that he was a passionate advocate of the new style in garden design, vehement in his opposition to 's[t]rait Walks', and the 'dam'd gusto that's been for this sixty year's past', and charming and dogmatic enough to have his way with his patrons.[41]

iii. AMATEUR AND PROFESSIONAL

Considering Pope's admiration for Bridgeman as a 'man of the Virtuoso-Class' and his respect for Kent's genius, we would not expect his remark on the superiority of the amateur to the professional gardener in his letter to Thomas Wentworth to apply to them: 'I have long been convinced that neither Acres, nor Wise; nor any publick Professors of Gardening, (any more than any publick Professors of Virtue) are equal to the Private Practisers of it' (ii. 309). Neither Bridgeman nor Kent can be compared to Thomas Ackres, a place-seeker and creature of William Benson satirized in the *Dunciad*,[42] or Henry Wise who was identified with the school of Le Nôtre, which Bridgeman began to depart from, and which Kent abandoned. Nevertheless, Pope's remark does apply to Bridgeman and Kent, and cannot be dismissed as mere condescension or snobbery, because it expresses a conviction which rests on different premises.

First of all, Pope's attitude reflects the prevailing conditions of patronage. As we have seen, Bridgeman's social status had improved from that of Wise: payments were made to him *ex gratia*, and he was a member of the St. Luke's Club. Kent suffered criticism but he was never used as badly by his patrons as Vanbrugh, Bridgeman, and Wise by the Duchess of Marlborough at Blenheim. Nevertheless, 'taste remained the prerogative of the man of quality'

[41] On Kent's achievement see Spence, Nos. 603, 1060; Margaret Jourdain, *The Work of William Kent*, p. 46; and Walpole, *History of Gardening*, p. 25. For 'dam'd gusto', see the letter from Kent dated 1719 quoted by Margaret Jourdain, *The Work of William Kent*, p. 46. On 's[t]rait walks', see Thomas Coke to Burlington (1736) in H. Avray Tipping, ed., 'Four Unpublished Letters of William Kent', *Architectural Review*, 63 (May 1928), 210.

[42] David Green deals with the schemes in 1718 and 1727 of 'Benson's protégé Ackres . . . to propose himself as royal gardener, in place of both Wise and Bridgman'. See *Gardener to Queen Anne, Henry Wise*, pp. 142–3, 150 n.

throughout the eighteenth century, and Pope believed that taste was something the patron could not rely on the professional to supply in architecture or gardening.[43] It was better for the untutored patron to depend on a competent professional rather than to disgrace himself. But the true patron and amateur possessed that combination of insight, learning, and (in landscape gardening) understanding of the genius of the place, which Pope defines as taste.

The usual role of the professional was to express the taste of his patron. His position as executant can be seen at its most abject in the relationship between the painter Samuel Closterman and the Earl of Shaftesbury. It can be seen in a different aspect in the opinion of Lord Chesterfield that Burlington had 'lessened himself by knowing . . . too well' 'the minute and mechanical parts' of architecture, things which were properly to be entrusted to professional experts. These conditions are reflected in the treatises on gardening by Switzer and Langley who defer to their patrons, and are timid and pusillanimous about introducing new ideas. Bridgeman, as far as we can tell, was the faithful servant of his patrons; and Kent, for all his flamboyance, was the product of his patrons' taste.[44] All this argues against the convenient historical assumption that new styles in landscape gardening can be identified with the professional designers who carried them out.

It is true that most of the great garden designs of the early eighteenth century are works of collaboration between amateur patrons and professional landscape architects, and it is difficult to balance rival claims. Laurence Whistler makes the reasonable plea concerning exaggerated claims for Vanbrugh's contribution to landscape architecture that 'far too little credit has been given to the professional designers, Wise, Switzer and Bridgeman'; on the other hand, Derek Clifford and others have recognized that far too much has been given to Kent. As for the amateurs, there are the opposing tendencies either to look for the professional ghost behind every amateur, notorious in the case of Burlington and Pembroke, or the snobbish glorifica-

43 On Bridgeman's status, see Christopher Hussey, *English Gardens and Landscapes*, p. 37. On taste, see Frank Jenkins, *Architect and Patron*, p. 80.

44 On Closterman see Edgar Wind, 'Shaftesbury as a Patron of Art', *Journal of the Warburg and Courtauld Institute*, 2 (Oct. 1938), 185–8. Philip Dormer Stanhope, 4th Earl of Chesterfield, *Letters*, ed. Bonamy Dobrée, 5 vols. (London, 1932), iv. 1420 (17 October 1749). On Kent and his patrons, see James Lees-Milne, *Earls of Creation*, p. 17.

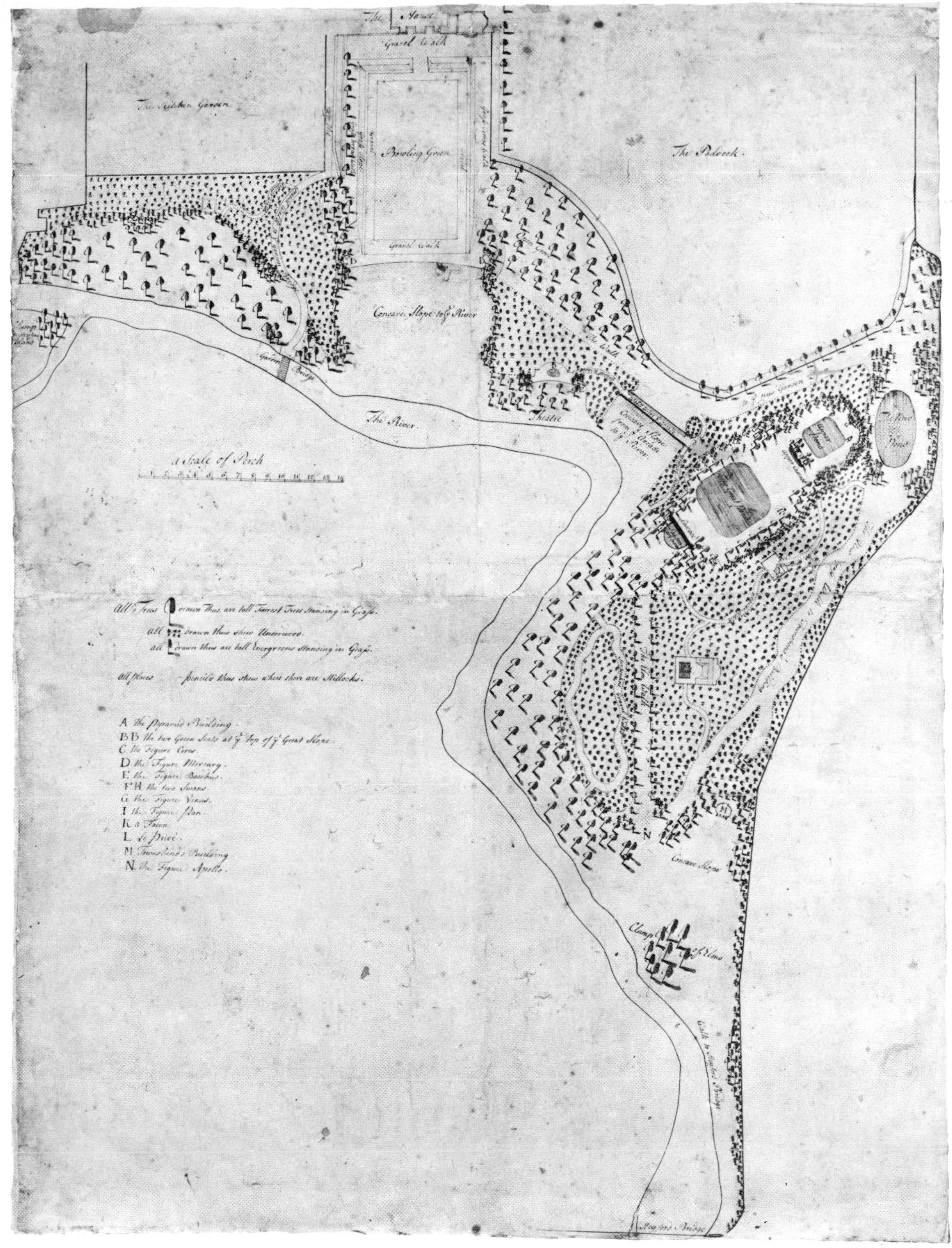

38. Plan of Rousham, Oxfordshire. By White(?). 1738–9.

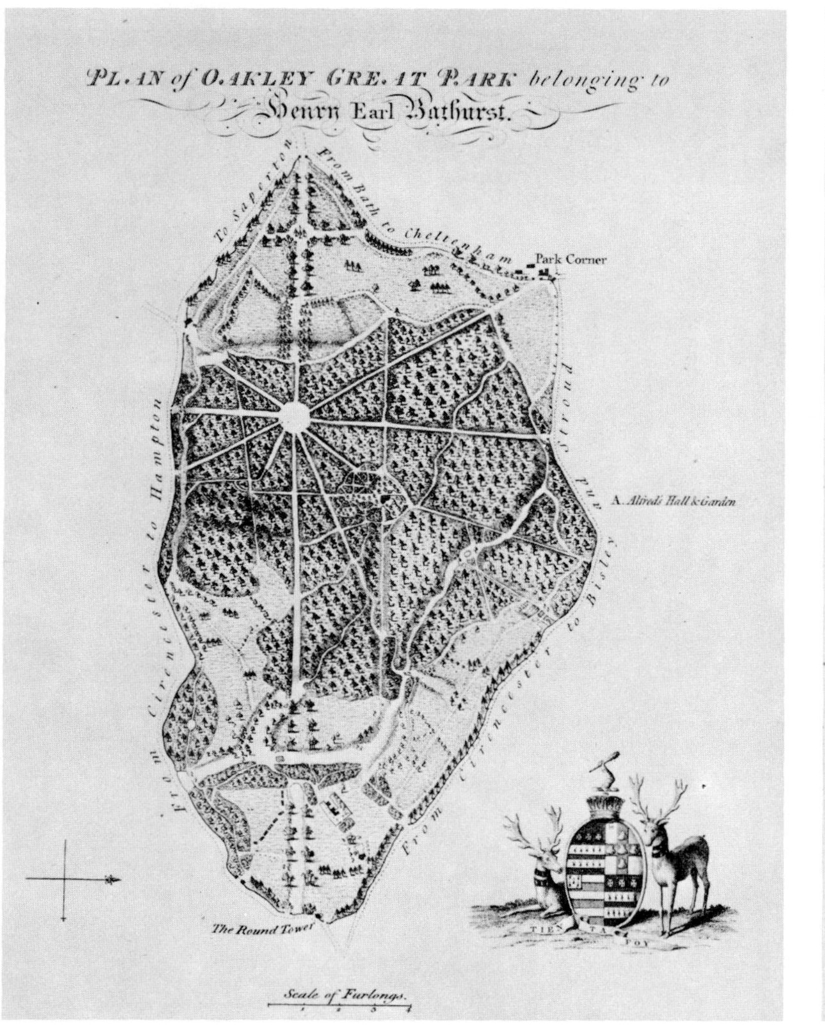

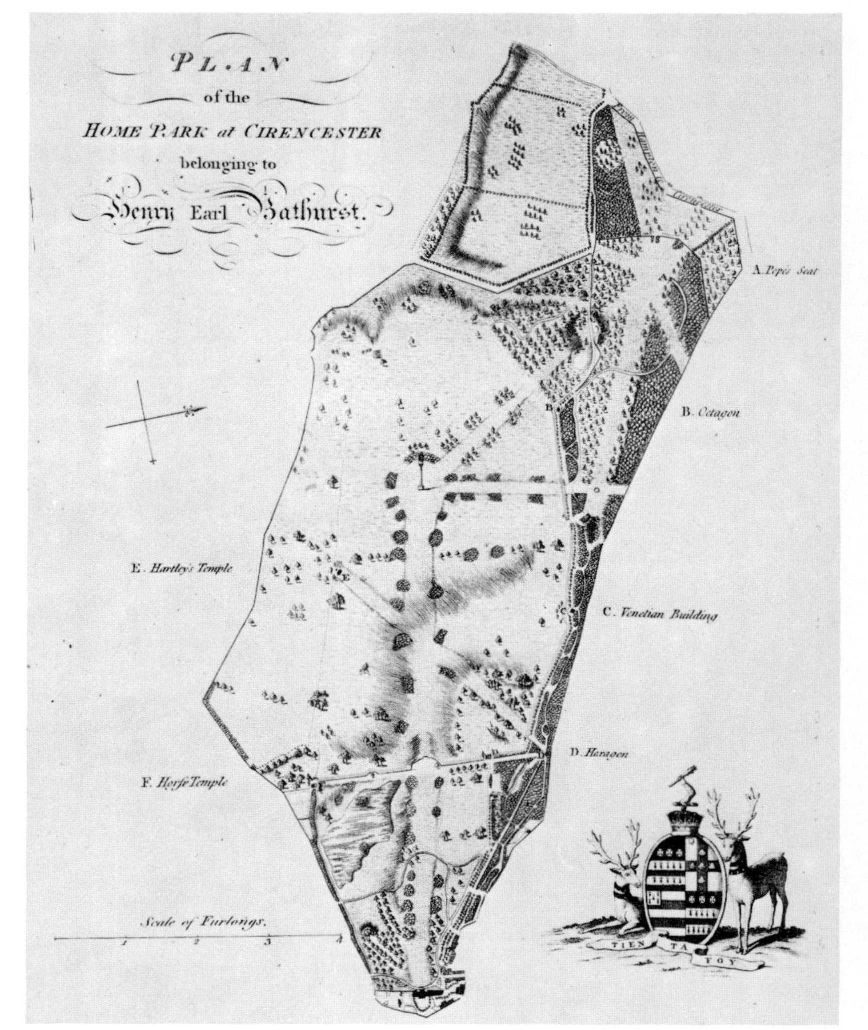

39. Plans of Oakley Great Park and Home Park, Cirencester, Gloucestershire. 1779.

tion of the peer at the expense of the artist.[45] Without exalting the amateur unreasonably, however, it can be argued that the important innovations in landscape design in the early eighteenth century were the work of amateurs, of which Pope is the outstanding example. Evidence of this can be found in a comparison of the gardening careers of Kent and Pope. While Kent was diffusing a national taste at places like Esher, Claremont, and royal parks like Kensington, where, according to Walpole,[46] he lapsed into formula and even planted dead trees, Pope influenced and collaborated with amateurs who deliberately refrained from consulting professional designers, and who contrived gardens which became the mid-century models of the art: George Lyttelton's Hagley, Philip Southcote's Woburn Farm, William Shenstone's The Leasowes, and Henry Hoare's Stourhead—places which together have been described by Christopher Hussey and others as 'England's greatest contribution . . . to the visual arts'.[47]

[45] Whistler, *The Imagination of Vanbrugh*, p. 23; Clifford, *A History of Garden Design* (1962), p. 135; cf. Miles Hadfield, *Pioneers in Gardening*, pp. 58–60; and Rayner Banham, 'Kent and Capability', review of Derek Clifford, *A History of Garden Design*, *The New Statesman*, 67 (7 Dec. 1962), 842.

[46] Walpole, *History of Gardening*, p. 30. Cf. *Works* (1798), i. 148.

[47] Christopher Hussey, 'The Aesthetic Background to the Work of William Kent', Introduction to Margaret Jourdain, *The Work of William Kent*, p. 15. Cf. Nikolaus Pevsner, 'Genesis of the Picturesque', *Architectural Review*, 96 (1944), 139: 'Landscaping is the greatest English contribution to European architecture'; and Fiske Kimball, 'Romantic Classicism in Architecture', *Gazette des Beaux-Arts*, 25 (Feb. 1944), 97: 'It was the landscape garden, the *jardin anglais*, which was the greatest of English artistic inventions.'

8173385 O

8. *Gardening Lords and Vegetable Children: The Landscape of the Greater House*

'I stole the delight of conversing, great part of a day, with some vegetable children of yours . . .' (iv. 94) Aaron Hill to Pope, 11 May 1738

POPE'S reputation as the designer of Twickenham, his friendships with gardening neighbours, and his close association with professional designers led inevitably to visits to country seats where he had an important influence on garden design. Gardening was a primary motive of the tours Pope began to make as early as 1717. In 1719 he stated he had 'no less than five houses, in different counties, through which I make a tour every summer' (ii. 3). Throughout the next decade he continued 'a rambler',[1] enduring the hardships of travel even in winter, inspired by the 'Spirit of Rambling' (iv. 347) until the end of his life. Visits to more than fifty country seats are recorded in Pope's correspondence, extending from Yorkshire in the north, west as far as Devon and perhaps Cornwall, and throughout the home counties.

Pope travelled for reasons of health, friendship, and enjoyment of landscape —'the pleasing prospect of Byberry' in Gloucestershire (ii. 388) or the picturesque ruins of Netley Abbey—but perhaps above all for the sake of gardening. Itineraries were planned to take in 'a famous Seat in [the] neighbourhood',[2] to visit places 'worth seeing' (iv. 347), or to find 'new matter' (ii. 240) for his own gardening and building. Lord Oxford missed Pope's company on a trip through Norfolk in 1732: 'I think you never was in that county it is much different from any that I ever saw & I am sure you would be pleased with some

[1] *The Correspondence of Jonathan Swift*, ed. Harold Williams, 5 vols. (Oxford, 1965), iv. 249 (30 Aug. 1734): 'I am glad to hear Mr Pope is grown a Rambler; because I hope it will be for his Health.' See *Correspondence*, i. 418, 518, iii. 418, iv. 84, 156, 231, 347, 472; and Spence Nos. 51, 657a.

[2] 'A New Pope Letter', ed. George S. Rousseau, *Philological Quarterly*, 40 (Apr. 1966), p. 418.

places' (iii. 325). On a visit in 1721 to Rendcomb, Gloucestershire, the seat of Sir John Guise, sister of Mrs. Edward Blount, Pope 'look'd upon the Mansion, Walls, and Terraces; the Plantations, and Slopes, which Nature has made to command a variety of Vallies and rising Woods; with a veneration mixt with a Pleasure' (ii. 86). A half day spent in 1728 at Dodington Park, Sir William Codrington's estate in Durhams, Gloucestershire, prompted the remark that 'their house is pretty enough, the situation romantic' (ii. 514). One night at John Grubham Howe's place in Stowell, Gloucestershire, in 1728 was sufficient to start him speculating about improvements. Comparing it to Rousham, he thought it 'a fine thing of another kind, where Nature has done every thing, and luckily, for the master has ten children. But it might be made very grand, merely by taking away part of what is there already' (ii. 513).

Little else remains to record many of Pope's visits than such casual remarks: compliments, encouragement, and offers of assistance to those who wished to imitate his own garden at Twickenham.[3] Occasionally Pope's interest in improvements reveals itself more overtly, when he writes to Bathurst in 1725 about his willingness to invest in the improvements of the widow of the Duke of Buckingham, Katherine Sheffield, at Leighs, Essex, another place he considered 'worth seeing':

> The Duchess of Buckingham is at Leighs, wishing (she tells me) to execute your Lordships Schemes, but believing they must be left to the Duke's & your own Riper Judgment, seven years hence. . . . if I live but one year, it would better please me to think an Obelisque might be added to your Garden, or a Pond to hers, with my money, than such a Hospital as Guy's to the City, or such a Monument as Priors to Westminster. (ii. 525)

In 1736 Pope told George Hamilton, Lord Orkney, then owner of Cliveden, Buckinghamshire, which Pope described as 'a delightful palace, on the banks of the Thames',[4] that he was anticipating 'the pleasure of planning & drawing Schemes, as well as of seeing & consulting yours, against the next Planting Season' (iv. 35). In 1735 Pope did a favour for Henry Hyde, Lord Cornbury, obtaining from Philip Miller's nursery at the Physic Garden in Chelsea 'some

[3] See *Correspondence*, i. 211, 409; ii. 126, 176, 314, 393; iii. 68, 125, 237, 406; iv. 407, 483.

[4] *Epistle to Bathurst* (1732), ll. 307–8; *TE* iii. ii, 118–19, and n. See Christopher Hussey, 'Cliveden—I. Bucks.', *Country Life*, 70 (11 July 1931), 38–44; G. C. Taylor, 'Cliveden—II. Bucks.', *Country Life*, 70 (18 July 1931), 68–74.

Cuttings of the Chaumontell, a French Pear, & of the Vingoleuse, & Epine D'Hyver' (iii. 452), which was followed by his advising on the landscape at Cornbury Park in 1739. Cornbury 'urgently' sought him out 'purely to get me to Cornbury for some days, (where I formerly made, and am to make some alterations)' (iv. 189).[5]

Nothing is known about Pope's contribution to Cliveden, Cornbury Park, or many other country seats he visited, but Hyde's urgent request for Pope's advice on gardening seems to have been characteristic, and the basis for his reputation as 'the best gardener in the three kingdoms'.[6] Sherborne, Dorset, is an example of a place where Pope's visits and speculation about improvements were accompanied by collaboration in carrying them out, according to Walpole's reference to 'a Grove of Scotch firs planted by Mr Robert Digby and Mr Pope', amplified in Hutchins' *Dorset* as 'Mr. Pope's plantation on Jerusalem Hill'.[7] But we have fuller records of Pope's contribution to several places which allow us to characterize the nature and extent of his collaborations with those he referred to as 'Gardening Lords' (iv. 454). All of them are examples of 'greater houses', as defined by John Summerson, and their landscape settings figure in what Summerson identifies as the principal architectural issue of the century in the development of the English country-house—the contest between the great house and the villa.[8] The first is Allan Apsley, Earl Bathurst's Cirencester Park, Gloucestershire; the second, Richard Temple, Viscount Cobham's Stowe, Buckinghamshire; and the last, Ralph Allen's Prior Park, Somersetshire.

i. CIRENCESTER PARK: PLANTATION 'IN THE BROBDINGNAG STYLE'

Despite the loss of much correspondence the association of Pope and Allen Lord Bathurst (1684–1775) at Cirencester, Gloucestershire, is the best documented of Pope's collaborations in gardening. It clearly reveals the nature of

[5] See Hussey, 'Cornbury Park, Oxfordshire', *Country Life*, 108 (22 Sept. 1950), 922–6.

[6] Libels on Swift & Pope. B.M. c. 116. 61–4. See *Correspondence*, iii. 399, and n.

[7] Horace Walpole, *Visits to Country Seats*, Walpole Society 16 (1927–8), 47. John Hutchins, *Antiquities of Dorset* (London, 1774), iv. 280. Tradition has it that Brown planted trees in the Deer Park facing the lodge 'to the designs of Pope' (*Visitor's Guidebook* at Sherborne).

[8] John Summerson, 'The Classical Country House in 18th-Century England', *Journal of the Royal Society of Arts*, 107 (July 1959), 552.

his influence on a garden design immense in comparison with Twickenham. Pope's friendship with Bathurst dates from 1716 when he had acquired Sapperton Manor and Oakley Wood, and was beginning to plan his grand design for joining his new estate to the Home Park of Cirencester House (plate 39), which stands on the edge of the town some five miles east of the village of Sapperton—a scheme taking in more than 5,000 acres to which Bathurst devoted a lifetime.[9]

Bathurst, Tory M.P. for Cirencester from 1705, became a financial adviser to Pope and his friends, and was a co-publisher of the *Dunciad*, but gardening was the foundation of his friendship with Pope. As we have seen, Bathurst was the recipient of Pope's letter on Richmond gardeners (ii. 14–15), they collaborated together at Marble Hill, and were indissoluble partners in 'surveying and criticizing' the estates of mutual friends like the Digbys, Carylls, and Blounts.[10] Bathurst was Pope's ideal of a gardener and from the start Pope was closely involved in the planning and design of Cirencester Park.

Pope was visiting Cirencester by the summer and autumn of 1718, when Bathurst offered him the use of a 'silvan seat' or 'Bower' in Oakley Wood (i. 488–9), where Pope translated Homer, enjoyed the autumn colours of his 'Groves' (i. 515), and admired his wood as 'the finest wood in *England*' (ii. 116). A letter to Martha Blount describes his routine there:

> I write an hour or two every morning, then ride out a hunting upon the Downes, eat heartily, talk tender sentiments with Lord B. or draw Plans for Houses and Gardens, open Avenues, cut Glades, plant Firrs, contrive waterworks, all very fine and beautiful in our own imagination. (i. 515)

A year later Pope was 'very curious to know what sort of contemplations employ you', and speculating about the plans Bathurst was making with his friend Erasmus Lewis:

> I wish my self with you both, whether you are in peace or at war, in violent argumentation or smooth consent, over Gazettes in the morning, or over Plans in the evening. In that last article, I am of opinion your Lordship has a loss of me: for generally after the debate of a whole day, we acquiesc'd at night in the best conclusion of which

9 See Hussey, 'Cirencester House—II. The Park', *Country Life*, 107 (23 June 1950), 1883.

10 Robert Digby thought of Pope and Bathurst as 'inseparable' in 1723 (*Correspondence*, ii. 192). In 1725 Bathurst was expected soon to 'survey & criticise these parts' at Holm Lacy, Herefordshire, the estate of his cousin Frances Digby, Viscountess Scudamore (ii. 305).

human reason seems capable in all great matters, to fall fast asleep! And so we ended, unless immediate Revelation (which ever must overcome human reason) suggested some new lights to us, by a Vision in Bed. But laying aside Theory, I am told you are going directly to Practice. Alas, what a Fall will that be? A new Building is like a new Church, when once it is set up, you must maintain it in all the forms, and with all the inconveniences; then cease the pleasant luminous days of inspiration, and there's an end of miracles at once! (ii. 13–14)

The same jocularity, vehemence, and quasi-religious zeal characterized Pope's participation in Bathurst's design throughout his life.

Beginning in 1723 Pope assisted Bathurst in the design of a 'woodhouse' in Oakley Wood, which appears to have been the earliest sham ruin in England (see chapter 10). And his interest in Bathurst's 'Great & Noble Works' (iii. 130) continued throughout the 1730s when Bathurst enticed him to visit with the offer to 'cutt you off some little corner of my Park (500 or 1000 acres) which you shall do what you will with, & I'll immediately assign over to you 3 or 4 millions of plants out of my Nursery to amuse your self with' (iii. 134). In 1732 Pope wished him 'all the pleasure, which if I did not greatly love you I would envy in the Sight of your own Improvements' (iii. 295). And later in that year, when he had almost finished Alfred's Hall, Bathurst wrote to Pope that 'there is enough remaining to employ you for a week at least, and occasion the consumption of a quire of paper in draughts' (iii. 299–300).

In 1734 Bathurst was complaining to Lady Howard that 'Pope endeavours to find faults here, but cannot; and instead of admiring (as he ought to do) what is already executed, he is every day drawing me a plan for some new building or other, and then is violently angry that it is not set up the next morning'.[11] In 1736 Bathurst was awaiting Pope's arrival at Cirencester 'with great impatience': 'The foundation of the building, described in the enclosed plan, will be laid by that time, and one arch up; but I will do no more before you come.' If Pope's visit was impossible, Bathurst was resigned to 'be content with your directions at a distance' (iv. 26). Pope was obliged to put off his Rambles 'at the Expence of writing Letters in folio to Lord Bathurst about his Plans' (iv. 39). The following year Pope wrote to Ralph Allen from Cirencester to say that 'I cannot stay less than a week here, to set some Works of my Lords, and

[11] *Suffolk Letters* (1824), ed. John Wilson Croker, ii. 81.

some Buildings forward, setling Plans, &c' (iv. 84). As late as 1742 he wrote to Burlington that 'the Arbitrary Lord Bathurst demands me' (iv. 409).

Many of these references, and most of the surviving correspondence have to do with architectural ornament, but one letter (1728) describing Pope's visit to Cirencester during Bathurst's absence gives us an insight into his advice on landscape design. He writes of his disappointment in not meeting Bathurst, and speaks ironically about improvements in the park which had been made without consulting him:

my Visit to your House was not wholly void of all Comfort to me: for I saw the Steeple of Ciceter stand on one side over it, and the great Vista in Oakley wood to the said Steeple by being widened beyond its former Hedges, borderd now only with some low thing which I took to be a Box-Edging on either side: Moreover I beheld with singular consolation the Back of the high Wood piercd thro, & every Tree that bore the least pretence to be Timber, totally cut down & done away. Whereby I see with delight not only the bare Prospect you have made, but also another, of the Necessity you are now reduced to, of raising some Building there: And I form to myself yet a third prospect, that you will so unwillingly & grudgingly undertake the said building, that it will be so small & inconsiderable as to oblige you to pull it down again another year, to erect a bigger & more adequate. Nevertheless my Lord (to prove I am not angry, but with a mixture of charity inclind to rectify, what I disapprove) I would not advise you to an obelisque which can bear no Diameter to fill so vast a Gap unless it literally touch'd the Skies; but rather to a solid Pyramid of 100 ft. square, to the end there may be Something solid and Lasting of your works. As to the church Steeple, I am truly sorry for it, yet I would not however pull down the House. I would rather the Reformation began, as reformations always ought, at the church itself; not that I would wish the Body of it entirely taken away, but only the Steeple lower'd: This would bring matters to Some Uniformity. (ii. 517)

The irritable and ironic tone of Pope's letter is an example of the impatience Bathurst complained about to Lady Howard, and it shows that he shared with Kent a 'spirit of dominion' in the argumentation over gardening plans. He expresses his annoyance in the manner of a man who has a proprietary interest in the place, who had appropriated a 'bower' in Oakley Wood, soon acquired a sylvan seat inscribed with his name, and who invested during his lifetime at least £2,000 in Bathurst's improvements.[12] The substance of Pope's complaint

[12] Hussey, 'Cirencester . . . The Park', p. 1880. Pope's seat is illustrated in Hussey, *English Gardens and Landscapes*, plate 91.

has to do with the widening of an avenue in Oakley Wood, probably what is now known as Broad Avenue, the main axis of the design linking Home Park with the lands Bathurst had acquired with the purchase of Sapperton manor in 1716. Pope's early reference to Bathurst 'immers'd' in Oakley Wood (ii. 13) indicates that Bathurst started working from Oakley Wood in both directions, cutting broad rides between solid plantations in the manner of the French forest park, aligning vistas linked by *rond-points* on distant landmarks like Cirencester church.[13]

Pope vehemently objects to the felling of full-grown trees, 'piercing the high wood', replacing the hedge with box, and above all to the unsatisfactory prospect opened in both directions: toward the house, to the east, the odd effect of the steeple of Cirencester church appearing 'to stand on one side over' and above the house; in the other direction the 'bare Prospect' requiring the expense of building a suitable object to terminate the view. Pope's suggestion of a pyramid appears to be an improvement on Vanbrugh's spectacular 60-foot pyramid that had recently been erected at Stowe (*c.* 1726). Bathurst never built a pyramid, but he was scrupulous in consulting Pope in 1736 about avenues and architecture he was designing to terminate the views: 'Now I leave it entirely to you either to come and settle this affair yourself or send the directions' (iv. 25).[14]

Pope's enthusiasm for forest gardening at Cirencester is apparent from his numerous complimentary references to Bathurst's 'Wood' (i. 477),[15] and in his characterization of Bathurst as 'too great an husbandman to like barren hills, except they are his own to improve' (ii. 395), 'never . . . a Florist . . . so much an Enemy to nice Parterres, that he never mows, but grazes them'.[16] He admired the scale of Bathurst's plantations: 'the noble Scenes, Openings, & Avenues of this immense Design' (ii. 82), 'planting a whole Country with

[13] Hussey, *English Gardens and Landscapes*, p. 82; James Lees-Milne, *Earls of Creation*, pp. 47–8; Hussey, 'Cirencester . . . The Park', pp. 1880–3.

[14] Bathurst was designing one building on the Broad avenue 'to answer three walks', 'another building is to be erected afterwards to answer the other diagonal which will also overlook the lake'; and he was levelling a hill in laying out another vista from the house along Elm Avenue where 'an obelisk shall arise on your orders to terminate the view'. *Correspondence*, iv. 25. See Hussey, *English Gardens and Landscapes*, p. 83.

[15] See *Correspondence*, i. 476, 515, ii. 50, 314; and Pope's 'Lines to Lord Bathurst', ridiculing his wood, *TE* vi. 195.

[16] *A Master Key to Popery* (1732), *TE* iii. ii, 181.

Clumps of Firs' (iii. 130), which made him forget his own 'little *Colifichies*' at Twickenham: 'No words, nor painting, nor poetry . . . can give the least Image proportionable to it' (ii. 82).

Christopher Hussey has identified Stephen Switzer's principle of 'Extended or Rural and Forest Gardening' as the basis of the design at Cirencester, and it seems probable that Bathurst and Pope were mindful of his principles when they consulted the Genius of the Place. Bathurst is thought to have been Switzer's client at Riskins, Buckinghamshire, and it is possible that he worked at Cirencester. Switzer dedicated a 1718 printing of the *Ichnographia Rustica* to Bathurst, and published a plan of the layout of his villa at Riskins in the second edition (see chap. 9). He was employed by other friends of Pope, like John Boyle, 5th Earl of Orrery, at Marston, Somerset, and was well acquainted with Pope's works, if not with Pope himself, as we have seen. Pope showed himself to be an uncompromising advocate of his principles at Cirencester.[17]

In 'propagating the Fame' (iii. 295) of Cirencester and Bathurst in his *Epistles on the Use of Wealth* Pope enlarges the meaning of Switzer's theory of design and estate management. The classical principle of utility is stated in the *Epistle to Burlington* (1731):

> Who then shall grace, or who improve the Soil?
> Who plants like BATHURST, or who builds like BOYLE.
> 'Tis Use alone that sanctifies Expence,
> And Splendor borrows all her rays from Sense. (177–80)

Bathurst's practice of forest gardening and Cirencester's 'rising Forests' exemplify the ideal in the following lines:

> His Father's Acres who enjoys in peace,
> Or makes his Neighbours glad, if he encrease;
> Whose chearful Tenants bless their yearly toil,
> Yet to their Lord owe more than to the soil;
> Whose ample Lawns are not asham'd to feed
> The milky heifer and deserving steed;

[17] On Bathurst and Switzer, see Christopher Hussey, *English Gardens and Landscapes*, p. 78. For Switzer's career, see *D.N.B.* On Pope and Switzer, see chap. 4.

Whose rising Forests, not for pride or show,
But future Buildings, future Navies grow:
Let his plantations stretch from down to down,
First shade a Country, and then raise a Town. (181–90)

This would appear to be an idealized picture of Cirencester, where improvements like Bathurst's are celebrated for their usefulness to the needs of man and beast, the nation, and posterity. Unlike Timon's, Bathurst's works are not for 'pride or show', but 'Imperial Works and worthy Kings' (204). At the time of the Prince of Wales's visit to Cirencester in 1738 Pope wrote to George Lyttelton about the education Bathurst could give the Prince in the arts of gardening and architecture 'when Fortune gives him the leading of one':

Above all, the Two great Arts so successfully practis'd by my Lord on other people, and so much more useful to be practis'd on a Prince; that of making him imagine, What is Highway or Common field to all his Subjects, to be His own Walks & Royalities; And that of imposing upon him What was the Work of our own hands but yesterday, for the Venerable Structure of our Ancestours [an allusion, apparently, to Alfred's Hall, the sham ruin in Oakley Wood]. (iv. 142)

In the *Imitations of Horace*, Ep. II, ii (1737) Pope leavens the classical law of utility with the Christian doctrine of the vanity of works for the guidance of the gardener, principles he illustrates again by reference to Bathurst's grand design at Cirencester:

All vast Possessions (just the same the case
Whether you call them Villa, Park, or Chace)
Alas, my Bathurst! what will they avail?
Join *Cotswold* Hills to *Saperton's* fair Dale,
Let rising Granaries and Temples here,
There mingled Farms and Pyramids appear,
Link Towns to Towns with Avenues of Oak,
Enclose whole Downs in Walls, 'tis all a joke!
Inexorable Death shall level all,
And Trees, and Stones, and Farms, and Farmer fall.[18] (254–63)

He had written in 1732 to Bathurst in a more sanguine spirit about 'those Certain Improvements, which Time bestows only on things Inanimate, & which will flourish, when we are gone' (iii. 295). As it happens this prophecy

[18] *TE* iv. 183.

in the case of Cirencester proved inaccurate, and the park exists today almost intact; but the text of Ecclesiastes, the knowledge as Pope puts it in the *Epistle to Burlington* that 'laughing Ceres shall reassume the land' (l. 176), preserved Bathurst from the folly of a Timon whose works violate the laws of nature.

In conclusion, the record of Pope's collaboration at Cirencester indicates that his influence was important in laying out what has been called 'perhaps the most spectacular park in England'.[19] Bathurst, in spite of some annoyance at Pope's impatience, sought out his advice throughout the poet's lifetime, welcomed his visits, his investment in improvements, and active participation in the landscape design. Pope, like Kent, was 'bold enough to dare to dictate', and contemporary reports of Bathurst's conservatism suggest that Pope was a progressive influence at Cirencester.

Christopher Hussey is accurate in his description of the Park as 'a forest on the Fontainebleau and Compiègne model', and Bathurst's contemporaries commented on its formal, French air.[20] But Bathurst's Cirencester was not a literal imitation of the French '*Grand Manier*', with its 'avenues *in vacuo*'. Nor was Bathurst's 'unspectacular' house next to the village an attempt to imitate the splendid isolation of the great Whig houses surrounded by 'square miles of conspicuous waste'. Bathurst, with Pope's assistance, attempted to imitate a classical ideal of magnificence at Cirencester and he succeeded in avoiding 'the barbarous hand of taste/[that] Deforms the grove, and lays the forest waste'.[21]

ii. STOWE: 'THE FRIENDLY GIFT OF THIS *POETICK PLAN*'

Pope propagated the fame of Stowe in the *Epistle to Burlington* even more dramatically than Cirencester when he named it in 1731 the epitome of landscape garden design:

[19] Christopher Hussey, 'Cirencester . . . The Park', p. 1880.

[20] Ibid. See *The Torrington Diaries*, ed. C. Bruyn Andrews, (4 vols., London, 1934–8; reprint New York, 1970), i. 258–9.

[21] See Henry James Pye, *Faringdon Hill, A Poem in Two Books* (Oxford, 1774), pp. 19–20, 22; Ralph Bigland, *County of Gloucester* (London, 1786–95), i. 350; Hussey, 'Cirencester . . . The Park', 107 (23 June 1950), 1881; 'Cirencester House . . . I', *Country Life*, 107 (16 June 1950), 1797; *English Gardens and Landscapes*, p. 80; and W. G. Hoskins, *The Making of the English Landscape* (London, 1955), p. 132.

Still follow Sense, of ev'ry Art the Soul,
Parts answ'ring parts shall slide into a whole,
Spontaneous beauties all around advance,
Start ev'n from Difficulty, strike from Chance;
Nature shall join you, Time shall make it grow
A Work to wonder at—perhaps a Stow. (65–70)

The lines added to the growing reputation of the gardens, gave rise to further publicity in poems, guidebooks, and graphic art, which established the garden as a model of landscape design throughout the century. Unlike Cirencester very little can be determined about the details of Pope's contribution to the design of Stowe, but the role he played in its development is suggested by the opening lines of a poem 'address'd to Mr. Pope' by Gilbert West, entitled *Stowe* (1732):

To Thee, great Master of the vocal String,
O *Pope*, of *Stowe*'s Elyzian Scenes I sing:
That *Stowe*, which better far thy Muse divine
Commands to live in one distinguish'd Line.
Yet let not thy superior Skill disdain
The friendly Gift of this *Poetick Plan*:
The same presiding Muse alike inspires
The *Planter*'s Spirit and the *Poet*'s Fires.
Alike, unless the Muse propitious smile,
Vain is the *Planter*'s, vain the *Poet*'s Toil.
All great, all perfect Works from *Genius* flow,
The *British Iliad* hence, and hence the Groves of *Stowe*.[22]

Pope's 'distinguish'd Line' and West's topographical poem refer to a garden design laid out by Charles Bridgeman in collaboration with the architect John Vanbrugh which had only recently been visited by the muse, but it was subsequently to develop according to a more coherent literary design. It appears that Pope, as much as anyone connected with Stowe, was responsible for the plan which had the effect of changing the entire character of the garden.

Pope's first visit to Stowe is recorded in the summer of 1724, after an important phase in the development of the gardens was completed. In 1720 Richard

[22] *Stowe, The Gardens of the Right Honourable Richard Lord Viscount Cobham. Address'd to Mr. Pope* (London, 1732), pp. 1–2. Published anonymously, it appeared in a later edition (Griffith No. 279) with Pope's *Epistle to Burlington*. Pope had it 'in hand' in Nov. 1731. *Correspondence*, iii. 244 n. See chap. 5, n. 51.

Temple, Viscount Cobham (1675–1749), had employed Bridgeman and Vanbrugh in an ambitious enlargement of the gardens prompted by his elevation to a peerage, his marriage of a fortune, and an interruption in his military career. Bridgeman corrected the weaknesses in an old-fashioned layout by 'inspired geometry . . . [which] tied together the sprawling limbs of the gardens, but also constructed a new central point. . . . The vistas radiating from the Rotunda interpenetrated every sector of the gardens and locked together the whole design'.[23] All this can be seen in Bridgeman's low oblique panoramic view of the gardens dating from the winter of 1719/20, a prospectus of the work which was described by Lord Perceval in a letter to Daniel Dering (August, 1724):

> Yesterday we saw Lord Cobham's house, which within these five years, has gained the reputation of being the finest seat in England. . . . The gardens by reason of the good contrivance of the walks, seem to be three times as large as they are. They contain but 28 acres, yet took us up two hours. It is entirely new, and tho' begun but eleven years ago, is now almost finished. . . . You think twenty times you have no more to see and of a sudden find yourself in some new garden or walk, as finish'd and adorn'd as that you left. Nothing is more irregular in the whole, nothing more regular in the parts, which totally differ the one from the other. This shows my Lord's good tast. . . . Bridgeman laid out the ground and plann'd the whole, which cannot fail of recommending him to business. What adds to the bewty of this garden is, that it is not bounded by walls, but by a Ha-hah, which leaves you the sight of a bewtiful woody country, and makes you ignorant how far the high planted walks extend.[24]

Bridgeman's oblique, asymmetrical design, basically architectural in character —'straight vistas connecting nodal points and formal pools among tightly planted boskets'[25]—was the garden Pope was returning to the following summer 'with fresh Satisfaction' (ii. 314), and continued to visit nearly every subsequent year during summer rambles until his death.

In 1731 he commented to John Knight on further enlargements:

> The Place from which I write to you will be a proof, alone, how incapable I am of forgetting you & your Gosfield; for if any thing under Paradise could set me beyond

[23] G. B. Clarke, 'The Vanbrugh-Bridgeman Gardens, The History of Stowe—VII', *The Stoic*, 24 (July 1969), p. 263.

[24] Quoted by Laurence Whistler, *The Imagination of Vanbrugh*, pp. 182–3. Bridgeman's bird's-eye view is in the Bodleian Library, MS. Gough Drawings, a.4.46, fig. 85 in Whistler.

[25] Hussey, *English Gardens and Landscapes*, p. 106.

all Earthly Cogitations; Stowe might do it. It is much more beautiful this year than when I saw it before, & much enlarged, & with variety. (iii. 217)

Pope is describing the layout which had expanded west and south in the 1720s, enclosing Home Park with a bastion and belt to accommodate a new access road, floating an eleven-acre lake, and more than doubling the area of the gardens. It is this enlarged design which is surveyed in Gilbert West's topographical poem, and illustrated by engravings published with a map of Stowe by Sarah Bridgeman in 1739 (plate 40). 'Poem, engravings and map . . . describe exactly what the gardens of Stowe were like in 1732—that is, at the end of Cobham's first major phase, when Bridgeman's lay-out was complete.'[26]

An outstanding feature of the Home Park perimeter was the sunk fence or ha-ha, the innovation which Bridgeman perfected at Stowe. The Home Park had been 'inclosed in a military Way, with a staked Fence', a turf and wattle embankment derived from methods of fortification. The sloping outer face of the ha-ha and the bank with horizontal stakes are clearly visible in several of Rigaud's engravings (plate 41) which show elegant ladies exchanging glances with cows across the ditch.[27]

The landscape garden fulfilled at this point all of the precepts of Pope's *Epistle to Burlington*. Bridgeman had achieved the rural ideal of 'order in Variety' of Pope's *Windsor Forest*, which underlies Gilbert West's description in his poem. Most of West's poem is a description of 'intermingled buildings' which provides the clearest index of the 'poetick plan' of the Bridgeman–Vanbrugh garden. Vanbrugh was the designer of most of the important garden architecture at this stage in the development.[28] His buildings gave to

[26] G. B. Clarke, 'The Vanbrugh–Bridgeman Gardens', p. 257. See Peter Willis, 'Jacques Rigaud's Drawings of Stowe in the Metropolitan Museum of Art', *Eighteenth-Century Studies*, 6 (Fall 1972), 85–98. Cf. M. J. Gibbon, 'Gilbert West's Walk Through the Gardens in 1731, The History of Stowe—IX', *The Stoic*, 24 (March 1970), 57–9.

[27] G. B. Clarke, 'Military Gardening: Bridgeman and the Ha-Ha, The History of Stowe—VIII', *The Stoic*, 24 (Dec. 1969), 12–14, plate 2.

[28] Laurence Whistler gives Vanbrugh primary credit for the design of the gardens at Stowe in 'their original form': 'a study of the general scheme that contained them [Vanbrugh's garden temples] is enough to indicate that Vanbrugh was the author, and Bridgeman, at Stowe and Eastbury, like Wise at Blenheim, the assistant who reduced bold ideas to a working proposition'. *Sir John Vanbrugh, Architect & Dramatist* (London, 1938), p. 229. He demonstrates Vanbrugh's 'ample contribution' to Stowe in 'The Authorship of the Stowe Temples', *Country Life*, 108 (29 Sept. 1950), 1002–6, 'slightly added to' in an article of the same title from which I take my quotations in *The Stoic*, 14 (Dec. 1950), 176–84.

the gardens a distinct character, which is suggested by Pope's statement in a letter to Peterborough (1732) that 'the two Paradises are not ill connected, of Gardens and Gallantry' (iii. 307). He might well have had the Stowe of Gilbert West's description in mind.

The tonic key of the garden architecture was established by Vanbrugh's splendid Rotunda, after the enclosure of Home Park the focal point of the gardens: 'on Pillars of the Ionic Order, with an Altar of blue Marble, and gilded Statue of the Venus of Medicis' (13 n.). The 'garden of Venus', a rectangular pool and amphitheatre, was surrounded by other buildings designed by Vanbrugh, secluded in closely planted bosquets. These included 'a Private Grotto'; the Temple of Sleep to the south; the 'Rustick Temple' of brick to the north dedicated to Bacchus and, finally, to the south, the Doric Lake Pavilions terminating the main axial avenue, decorated with scenes of pastoral romance.[29]

Vanbrugh's 'heathen temples', as Perceval called them, are entirely in the spirit of a Renaissance pleasure garden. William Kent's earliest works of garden architecture at Stowe dating from 1731 surrounding the ten-acre lake share the same spirit. His first building at Stowe, an austere Palladian temple known as 'Kent's Bastion and Building', featured a 'Roof . . . adorned with a naked Venus', walls painted with Spenserian frescoes by Francesco Sleter, and an inscription on the frieze from Catullus. Kent's ruinous cascade carried 'three Sheets of Water Falls . . . from the Octagon into a large Lake of 10 Acres'. Near by he designed 'the Shepherd's Cove' or hermitage.[30]

All this makes it clear that the gardens of Stowe in 1731 when Pope praised

[29] M. J. Gibbon identifies the grotto with Dido's Cave in 'Gilbert West's Walk', pp. 60–1. Whistler attributes the design to Vanbrugh in 'The Authorship of Stowe Temples' (1950), p. 183. See *A Description of the Gardens of Lord Viscount Cobham at Stow in Buckinghamshire* (Northampton, 1744), pp. 10–11. The motto of Vanbrugh's Temple of Sleep is translated, 'Since all things are uncertain, indulge thyself', in William Gilpin's *Dialogue Upon the Gardens at Stow*, in *A Description of . . . Stow* (London, 1750). For Vanbrugh's Temple of Bacchus, see Gilbert West, '*Stowe*', pp. 9–10, and George Bickham, *The Beauties of Stowe* (London, 1753), p. 11. Vanbrugh's Doric Pavilions are described by Bickham, *Beauties of Stowe*, pp. 2–3.

[30] For the list of Kent's architectural works at Stowe, see Colvin, p. 344. For Kent's Building, or the Temple of Venus, see Sarah Bridgeman, *A General Plan . . . of the Woods, Park and Gardens of Stowe* (London, 1739); Benjamin Seeley, *A Description of Stowe* (1769), p. 9; M. J. Gibbon, 'Gilbert West's Walk', pp. 59–60. Gilbert West (*Stowe*, p. 5) locates the Spenserian frescoes in Kent's Ruin or Hermitage. For Kent's Cascade, see Seeley, *A Description of Stowe* (1744), pp. 2–3.

them as a 'Work to wonder at' were very far from being the 'metropolitan cathedral of English humanist faith', as Christopher Hussey has defined the Whig landscape synthesis. Cobham had not yet gone into opposition; he was not yet the 'absolute Patriot' Pope praised in the *Epistle to Cobham* (1733), and his gardens did not yet reflect 'the ideas of liberal imperialism, Whig humanism, and English idyllic landscape design'. In 1731, when Gilbert West observed of Stowe that 'the same presiding Muse alike inspires/The Planter's Spirit and the Poet's Fires' (1–2), the muse of the gardens was pastoral romance; the garden had not yet moralized its song.[31]

But West's lines were prophetic: Vanbrugh's last building at Stowe, the Egyptian Pyramid (1724–6), was inscribed with lines celebrating Horatian retirement. The Roman imperial theme had been stated by the equestrian statue of George I in armour, prominently placed in the centre of the approach avenue to the north of the house, with an inscription comparing him with Imperial Caesar, and by the statues of royalty and Nelson's Seat in the gardens to the south. The Circle of Saxon Deities, stone statues carved by Michael Rysbrack on pedestals attributed to Vanbrugh, revealed a new attitude to the Gothic and the Whig reading of English constitutional history which is discernible in West's poem:

> Hail! Gods of our renown'd Fore-Fathers, hail!
> Ador'd Protectors once of *England*'s Weal.
> Gods, of a Nation, valiant, wise, and free,
> Who conquer'd to establish *Liberty*! (17)

Finally, and most significant in relation to the future development of the gardens, the building of James Gibbs on the south-west perimeter of Home Park (*c.* 1726), became the model of Kent's Temple of British Worthies in the Elysian Fields, the first and crucial phase of the expansion of the gardens to the east after 1732.[32]

[31] See Christopher Hussey, 'Stowe, Buckinghamshire—I. The Connection of Georgian Landscape with Whig Politics', *Country Life*, 102 (12 Sept. 1947), 529; 'Stowe—III. The Heroic Phase', *Country Life*, 102 (26 Sept. 1947), 626; and *English Gardens and Landscapes*, p. 89. On the 'absolute Patriot', see *TE* iii, ii. 38, and *Correspondence*, iii. 391.

[32] On Vanbrugh's pyramid, see Gilbert West, '*Stowe*', p. 9; Seeley, *A Description of Stow* (1744), pp. 3–4; M. J. Gibbon, 'Gilbert West's Walk', p. 60; and Laurence Whistler, 'Authorship of Stowe Temples' (1950), pp. 181–2. On the statue of George I, see Gilbert West, '*Stowe*', pp. 14–16; Seeley, *A Description*

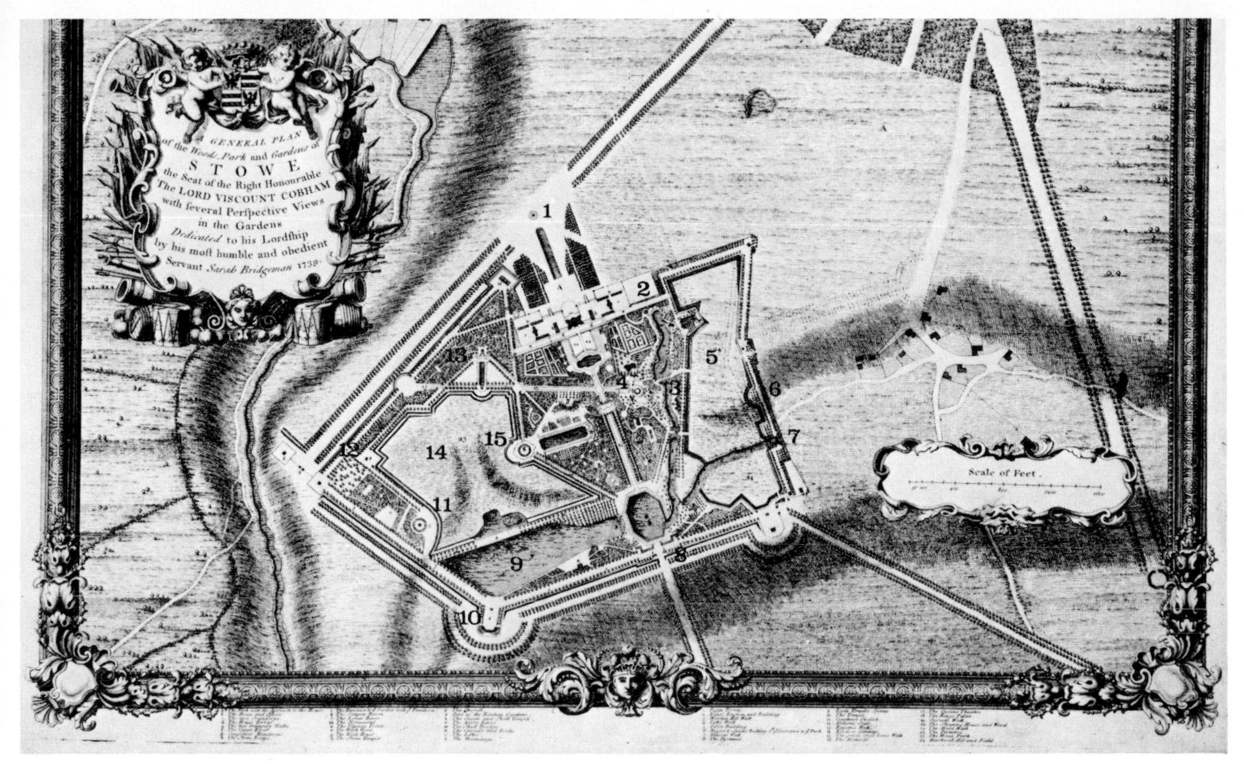

40. Plan of Stowe, Buckinghamshire. After Rigaud. 1739.

1. George I, equestrian statue
2. Grotto and Shell Temples
3. Elysian Fields and British Worthies
4. Temple of Ancient Virtue
5. Hawkwell Field
6. Gothick Temple
7. Palladian Bridge
8. Lake Pavillions
9. Eleven Acre Lake
10. Kent's Temple of Venus
11. Gibb's Building
12. Pyramid
13. Temple of Bacchus
14. Home Park
15. Rotunda

41. The Rotunda at Stowe. By Jacques Rigaud. *c.* 1733.

42. The Alder River and Grotto at Stowe. By Chatelain. 1752.

43. Prior Park, Somerset. Engraved by Anthony Walker. 1752.

Probably James Gibbs's earliest work at Stowe, the open pavilion originally called 'Gibbs's Building' on the west side of Home Park facing the Rotunda, was surrounded by pedestals supporting busts of British worthies by Michael Rysbrack, including Queen Elizabeth, Shakespeare, Bacon, Milton, William III, Newton, Locke, and Hampden. According to West (6), it was inscribed with lines from Virgil's *Aeneid* describing the sacred band of blessed spirits in the Elysian Fields. The choice of heroes indicates, as Michael Gibbon says, that 'the theme was "1688" . . . anti-Stuart and anti-clerical', a distinctly Whig ideology, but one which Tories of the patriot opposition could have approved. It has been plausibly suggested that the 'poetick plan' of this building and Gibbs's employment at Stowe can be related to the visit to Stowe of Pope, Swift, and Gay, in the summer of 1726, three months after Vanbrugh's death, and shortly before Gibbs made his design.[33]

The idea of a Temple of British Worthies appears to derive from a series of essays on this theme in the *Tatler*. *Tatler* 81 (15 October 1709), is an important source of Pope's *The Temple of Fame: A Vision* (1711–15), which Steele saw and encouraged in manuscript. Pope had pursued the theme of British worthies in *Windsor Forest* (1713) and the *Epistle to Addison* (1721); and many of the Stowe worthies in Gibbs's building had been celebrated by Pope in his poetry by 1728. Gibbs's appearance at Stowe might be explained by his prior connection with Bridgeman as one of Harley's Tory Virtuosi, but, as Michael Gibbon points out, 'it seems a little unlikely that Lord Cobham, a "Revolution Whig", would have thought of Gibbs [a Scot, and a Tory patronized by Jacobites] for Stowe without some prompting and encouragement'. 'Perhaps', he concludes, 'this was supplied by the three Tories present on that June day in 1726.'[34]

of Stow (1744), p. 10; Laurence Whistler, Michael Gibbon, and George Clarke, *Stowe, A Guide to the Gardens*, 2nd edn. rev. (Buckingham, 1968), p. 14. Seeley describes the paintings and Latin inscriptions in Nelson's Seat celebrating imperial themes, *A Description of Stow* (1744), pp. 8–9. It is illustrated by Whistler, 'Authorship of Stowe Temples' (1950), p. 183, fig. 11. On the Circle of Saxon deities, see M. J. Gibbon, 'Gilbert West's Walk', p. 61.

[33] On the date of Gibbs's design for the building, now in the Ashmolean Museum, see Whistler, 'Stowe in the Making, Some Original Drawings', *Country Life*, 122 (11 July 1957), 70, fig. 8; and the article which establishes Gibbs as 'one of the prime creators of Stowe', 'The Authorship of Stowe Temples', (1950), p. 180, fig. 12.

[34] On the inspiration from *The Tatler*, and the possible contribution of Pope, Swift, and Gay, see

Gibbs's building was the inspiration for the next important phase in the development of Stowe during the 1730s, when Bridgeman collaborated with Kent in an expansion of the gardens to the east beginning in an area described by a visitor in July 1735 as 'what is call'd the Elysian fields situated in that part of the garden which was lately enclos'd'. Considering Gilbert West's epigraph from Virgil's description of Elysium (*Aeneid* VI. 638–9), his allusion in the poem to 'Elyzian scenes' (l. 2), and his emphasis on the description of the worthies in Gibbs's building (6–9), the idea may have been under discussion when West was writing his poem. In any event, by 1739, when Pope found the gardens much enlarged (iv. 185–6), the landscape and architectural ornament appear to have been essentially complete: Gibbs's worthies had been moved to a 'Monument' designed about 1735 by William Kent. In the centre of Kent's stone screen with niches for busts of worthies a pyramid containing a bust of Mercury, inscribed *Campos ducit ad Elysios*, faced Kent's Ionic rotunda (*c.* 1734) modelled on the Temple of the Sybyl at Tivoli, which was known as the 'Mausoleum', until 1744 when it was dedicated to Ancient Virtue. A sham ruin nearby was dedicated to Modern Virtue.[35]

In the Elysian Fields West's claim that 'the same presiding Muse alike inspires/The Planter's spirit and the Poet's Fires' (1) was fulfilled for the first time at Stowe. The *Aeneid* is the source of the poetic programme: the 'blissful seats of happy Souls below' were imitated in the manner of the sacred landscape at Tivoli. To Virgil's heroic landscape a moral one was added, and once again an essay in the *Tatler* supplied the 'libretto which was to be orchestrated by the architect and garden designer'. Addison's 'vision' of the

Michael Gibbon, 'Gilbert West's Walk', p. 63; and George A. Aitken, ed., *The Tatler* (London, 1898), ii, Nos. 67, 74, 87 (1709). For the worthies in Pope's verse, see *The Temple of Fame*, *TE* ii. 218–19 n., 242–3; *The Epistle to Addison*, *TE* vi. 204; and *The Dunciad* (1728), iii. 211–16, *TE* v. 175.

[35] For the earliest reference to the Elysian Fields, see the anonymous journal, 'An Account of the Journey yt Mr. Hardness & I took in July 1735', quoted by George Clarke, 'Kent and the Eastern Gardens, The History of Stowe—XIII', *The Stoic*, 24 (July 1971), 268. On Kent's Temple of British Worthies at Stowe see Laurence Whistler, 'Stowe in the Making', *Country Life*, 122 (11 July 1957), 69; Michael Gibbon, 'Lord Cobham's Garden Buildings, Part 1 (1715–1737): Vanbrugh, Gibbs, Kent, The History of Stowe—XI', *The Stoic*, 24 (Dec. 1970), 178; and George Clarke, 'Moral Gardening, The History of Stowe—X', *The Stoic*, 24 (July 1970), 118–19. On Kent's Temple of Ancient Virtue, see Seeley, *A Description of Stow* (1769), p. 26; Whistler, Gibbon, and Clarke, *Stowe, A Guide* (1968), pp. 18–19; and Clarke, 'Moral Gardening', pp. 115–16.

landscape of worldly ambition (*Tatler*, No. 123, 21 January 1710), includes temples of Virtue, Vanity, and Honour, which correspond to Stowe's Temples of Ancient and Modern Virtue, and British Worthies. In addition, a strain of political satire was introduced in the Elysian Fields.[36]

Three of the four statues of ancient heroes in the Temple of Ancient Virtue come from Pope's *Temple of Fame*, but their significance is not to be interpreted merely as part of the battle of ancients and moderns; their inscriptions must be read in the context of the Patriotic opposition to Walpole, and the favourite theme of Bolingbroke's periodical, *The Craftsman*—Liberty threatened by Corruption. Hence Homer appears as 'the herald of patriotic virtue'; Socrates 'innocent in the midst of a most corrupted people'; Epaminodas, a type of the soldier and patriot 'by whose valour, prudence and modesty the Theban commonwealth gained liberty and empire'; finally Lycurgus is praised for 'having planned . . . a system of laws firmly secured against all corruption, and for having . . . established in the state for many ages perfect liberty and inviolable purity of manners'. All of these heroes are placed in a temple sacred to patriotic virtue, whose inscriptions urge the patriot 'to be dear to our Country, to deserve well of the public, to Cultivate Justice and Benevolence', that is to say the 'Path [which] leads to the Mansions of the Blessed'—the Temple of British Worthies.[37]

The headless statue amidst the ruins of the Temple of Modern Virtue could be read by the uninitiated according to the theme of *vanitas*. But in terms of the political satire 'the headless statue represented Sir Robert [Walpole] himself, though nothing was explicitly stated', precisely the kind of innuendo that characterizes Pope's satire against Walpole during the 1730s. Likewise, the new statues in the Temple of British Worthies press the oblique attack on Walpole's administration: Gresham and Barnard representing hostile City interests; Drake and Raleigh, figures who reproach Walpole's peace policy with Spain; King Alfred and Edward Prince of Wales, who had appeared in the *Craftsman* as antitypes of George II and his son; Inigo Jones, the English

[36] See Clarke, 'Moral Gardening', pp. 115–16; and Whistler, Gibbon, and Clarke, *Stowe, A Guide* (1968), p. 22.

[37] On the iconography of the Temple of Ancient Virtue, and the relation of the statuary to the opposition poetry of Pope, Thomson, and Richard Glover, see Clarke, 'Moral Gardening', pp. 116–18. For the inscriptions, see Seeley, *A Description of Stow* (1744), pp. 12–16.

Vitruvius, who was responsible for reviving the order of classical architecture; finally, the bust of Pope, inscribed after his death with lines describing him as the opposition poet Lyttelton had urged him to become in 1730.[38] The political satire of Stowe's Elysian Fields is not the work of the professional gardeners Kent or Bridgeman, but of Cobham and his patriot friends who went into opposition after 1733. As we have seen, Thomson's *Liberty* made its contribution; doubtless Cobham's cousin Gilbert West and George Lyttelton had something to say about the choice of heroes and the composition of inscriptions, but the 'presiding Muse' of the Elysian Fields may have been Pope, who was recognized early in the decade as the literary leader of the opposition to Walpole. His friendship with Cobham and visits to Stowe continued until his death. Pope's *Epistle to Cobham* (1733) praised the owner of Stowe for his patriotism; and throughout the decade he continued to celebrate his friend as the 'absolute Patriot' and gardener; in 1734 he read aloud at Stowe one of his *Imitations of Horace*, containing a bawdy allusion to Walpole. Furthermore, Pope was active in what may be called Opposition gardening: in his work for the Prince of Wales at Carleton House, in his design of Alfred's Hall at Cirencester, his satire of Queen Caroline's follies at Richmond with the obtuse choice of worthies, and above all in the dedication of his own grotto to Bolingbroke and the patriot opposition:

> Let such, such only, tread this sacred Floor,
> Who dare to love their Country, and be poor.[39]

The design of the grotto and shell temples at Stowe, at the source of the Upper lake or Alder river (plate 42) just north of the Elysian Fields, suggests that Pope may have had a practical influence on the gardens. Completed about 1742, attributed to Kent, the grotto as illustrated in Châtelain's view

[38] On the satire of Walpole in the Elysian Fields at Stowe, see Clarke, 'Moral Gardening', pp. 116–20.

[39] George Clarke concludes in 'Moral Gardening', p. 119: 'It is hardly an exaggeration to say that, though the Elysian Fields originated in the *Tatler*, they were peopled out of the pages of the *Craftsman*.' For Pope's opposition satire, see Mack, p. 117, and *passim*. George Lyttelton early in the decade in 'An Epistle to Mr. Pope from Rome' (1730) urged him to sing 'the land, which yet alone can boast/That liberty corrupted Rome has lost'. *Works*, ed. George Edward Ayscough, 3rd edn. (London, 1776), iii. 100. On Pope's reading at Stowe, see George Berkeley to Henrietta Howard (27 June 1734), *Suffolk Letters*, ii. 79. Pope's 'Verses on a Grotto by the River Thames at Twickenham', ll. 13–14, *TE* vi. 383.

engraved by Bickham is similar to Pope's in plan, elevation, and ornament.[40] George Bickham gives a description of the building in the *Beauties of Stowe* (1753):

> Imagine you see a small Edifice built with Shells of Mother-of-Pearl ranged with infinite Art, and with the Patience of Penelope. The Inside consists of one Hall, and two Closets, adorned in the most surprising Manner; and, at the same Time, in the most charming Taste. The whole Place is full of Mirrors set in Mother-of-Pearl; by which the Prospects of the Gardens, and of your own Person, are infinitely multiplied. The Place seems divided into a thousand beautiful Apartments; and appears fifty Times as large as it is. And the Sides of the Room are elegantly adorn'd with Landscapes, beyond the Pencil of Titian; with this Advantage, that every View, as you change your Situation, varies itself into another Form, and presents you with something new. On each Side of the Grotto there is a Temple, supported one by four wreathed, and the other by four strait Pillars; all composed, as well as their Domes, of Shells of Mother-of-Pearl of every Size and Colour, and with Pebbles and Flints broken to Pieces, which has a fine Effect. In the Centre within the Grotto is a Marble Statue of Venus, on a Pedestal. (pp. 27–8)

Stowe's grotto corresponds to the basement entrance of Pope's at Twickenham in plan ('one Hall, and two Closets'), elevation (a central arch with windows on either side), and ornament consisting of shells, statuary, and mirrors used to multiply changing views of the garden landscape, a much admired feature of Pope's grotto. The shell temples unmistakably owe their inspiration to Pope's Shell Temple set up in the 1720s.

If the attribution of the grotto and shell temples to Kent can be accepted we have in the Elysian Fields another example, and by far the most important and influential, of Kent's imitations of Twickenham. There is no doubt that Kent followed Pope's principles in landscaping the buildings he designed in the Elysian Fields. It was here that picturesque principles of gardening were introduced at Stowe. Spence recorded Southcote's remark that 'Lord Cobham began in the Bridgeman taste: 'tis the Elysian Fields that is the painting part of his gardens' (No. 1122). Contemporary descriptions and the drawings of Châtelain confirm that here, as at Twickenham, there was the same opening and crowding of shades, the same promiscuous plantations, the same

[40] George Clarke, 'Kent and the Eastern Gardens', p. 269, plate 4.

emphasis on the ruinous, the serpentine, and the picturesque which Gilpin describes in his *Dialogue*.

The Elysian Fields marked a crucial turning-point in the literary and landscape plan of the gardens. 'Soft Kent put the flesh on Stowe . . . Bridgeman jointed the skeleton'—Laurence Whistler summarizes in these words the way Kent's picturesque ideas modified Bridgeman's primarily geometrical designs and eventually 'transformed the whole of the gardens. The hard edges were softened with uneven planting and the straight lines blurred or removed . . . The Octagon Lake was smudged into a "natural" form.'[41]

The change in the poetic plan in the Elysian Fields was no less influential. No longer could the charge be made, even facetiously as in Pope's *Master-Key* (1732), that 'his Ldsps fine Gardens were . . . just such another Scene of Lewdness as Cupids Gardens or Faux-hall [Vauxhall]', or a garden of 'youth devoted to lust', like that in Addison's *Tatler* (No. 120, 1710). The change can be illustrated by a remark of one of the characters in Gilpin's *Dialogue on Stowe* (1748), coming to the Temple of Modern Virtue in the Elysian Fields from the Bridgeman–Vanbrugh garden, where he disapproved of Kent's Temple of Venus, its 'luxurious Couches' and frescoes suggesting the 'loosest Ideas' (3–4). Observing the Temple of Ancient Virtue 'so properly inhabited', Polypthon remarks that 'he was glad to find his Walk grew a little more moral. He expected to have been carried into some Temple of *Pan* or *Priapus*; but was pleased to find himself deceived by so ingenious a Piece of Satyr.'[42]

The theme of heroic virtue became even more explicit in the ornament of Hawkwell Field, the 40 acres enclosed by Bridgeman by 1735 in a major enlargement of the gardens to the east, where Gibbs returned to design a temple of Friendship (1739), the Palladian Bridge celebrating imperial themes, and the Gothick Temple dedicated 'To the Liberty of our Ancestors'.[43]

James Thomson in lines added to the *Seasons* in 1744 pays tribute to the

[41] *The Imagination of Vanbrugh*, p. 180, and *Stowe, A Guide* (1968), pp. 6–7.

[42] See Pope, 'A Master Key to Popery', *TE* iii. ii, 183; *The Tatler*, ed. G. A. Aitkin, iii. 34, 37; and William Gilpin, *Dialogue Upon Stow*, in Seeley, *A Description of Stow* (1750), pp. 3–4, 11.

[43] George Clarke, 'Moral Gardening', p. 119. See 'Kent and the Eastern Gardens', pp. 265–8, 271; Laurence Whistler, 'The Authorship of Stowe Temples' (1950), pp. 176–81; and Seeley, *A Description of Stow* (1769).

'cool judicious art' of Stowe, which he compares to the rhetoric of William Pitt, his companion in the poem on a walk through Stowe's Elysian Fields:

> While there with thee the enchanted round I walk,
> The regulated wild, gay fancy then
> Will tread in thought the groves of Attic land;
> Will from thy standard taste refine her own,
> Correct her pencil to the purest truth
> Of nature, or, the unimpassioned shades
> Forsaking, raise it to the human mind.[44]

It appears to have been Pope's 'friendly gift of this Poetick Plan' in the Elysian Fields, which was to a large extent responsible for raising the gardens of Stowe to the human mind.

iii. PRIOR PARK: 'PROPHETICK HERE, THE MUSE SHALL BUILD THY SEAT'

Prior Park, Somerset, is an example of Pope's continuing influence, practical and poetic, on major landscape designs until the end of his life. As at Cirencester, he played an important role as adviser on the layout of the gardens, and, through his poetry, he influenced its reputation as much as Stowe's. The friendship of Pope and Ralph Allen, Bath civil servant, businessman, and philanthropist, dates from the mid-1730s when Pope was planning to publish his letters, and Allen was planning with his architect, John Wood, to build a large house at Widcombe overlooking Bath—schemes in which they were able to assist each other.[45] Allen gave Pope financial assistance in publishing the *Letters* (1737), and later supplied labour and materials for the enlargement of his grotto in the 1730s. Biographers have taken the view that Allen's generosity was never repaid, and worse, that Pope answered Allen with a notorious act of ingratitude in his will.[46] But there is every indication that Pope repaid his horticultural debt to this rich man with interest, and was largely responsible

[44] 'Autumn', ll. 1054–60, in *Works*, ed. Robertson, p. 170.

[45] See Benjamin Boyce, *The Benevolent Man, A Life of Ralph Allen of Bath* (Cambridge, Mass., 1967), chaps. 5–6; and 'The Poet and the Postmaster: The Friendship of Alexander Pope and Ralph Allen', *Philological Quarterly*, 45 (Jan. 1966), 114–22.

[46] See Boyce, *The Benevolent Man*, pp. 158–9; and Pope's own expression of indebtedness, *Correspondence*, iv. 360.

for identifying Allen and his house, built for motives of social and commercial ostentation, with the highest ideals of architecture. It is scarcely an exaggeration to say that he made of a Timon a Man of Ross. Allen, unlike Cobham, employed no professional landscape architect to lay out the grounds on the untouched site of his house, and it is clear that he consulted Pope throughout the stages of improvement Pope was hoping he would enjoy in 1736:[47] 'first your Schemes, & then the Execution, & then the Completion, of them; for those are three distinct pleasures' (iv. 9–10). Encouragement and offers of assistance appear regularly in Pope's correspondence.[48] He also invited the Allens to visit Twickenham to see his 'finishd works' (iv. 360), and other places like Chiswick and Stowe 'worth seeing' (iv. 347). He arranged for Burlington's gardener to visit Prior Park (iv. 450), sent instructions about building a pine house for raising of pineapples (iv. 429), and passed on advice from John Serle and other local gardeners about plantations of pines (iv. 449), and advice from Burlington about rearing deer (iv. 452).

Between 1737 and 1743 while the gardens at Prior Park were being laid out, Pope's visits to Allen at Bath were prompted by gardening as much as friendship or health. He arranged to be there in the Planting Season (iv. 37); he was prepared to come 'in my own little Chair, which would be highly useful to me . . . in securing my very crazy person from Cold in the works in your Garden, Rock, &c.' (iv. 280); and he looked forward to the long visits to Bath in these years 'where I shall live, read, & plant away my time' (iv. 206). Some indication of the improvements Pope was assisting Allen and his gardener, Isaac Dodsley, in undertaking can be obtained from Pope's letter of May 1740, after a visit of three months:

> It is my firm resolution to inhabit the Room at the end of your Gallery one Fortnight at least in September, & as much longer as I can, to see your Gardens finish'd (ready for Mrs Allen's Grotto & Cascade the following year) I must inquire, next after hers & your health, after that of the Elms we planted on each Side of the Lawn? & of the little Wood-work to join one wood to the other below, which I hope you planted this Spring. (iv. 239)

[47] See Boyce, *The Benevolent Man*, p. 66; 'The Poet and the Postmaster', p. 116. Austin Dobson writes of Allen and Pope that 'on all matters horticultural Pope's word was law'. *At Prior Park* (1912; reprint New York, 1970), p. 11.

[48] See *Correspondence*, iv. 41, 84, 239, 358, 362.

This refers to the woods Pope helped Allen to plant beginning in 1737, as shown on Thomas Thorpe's *Map of Widcombe* (1742), and illustrated in the misleading severely flattened perspective of Anthony Walker's engraving (1752; plate 43). Woods were planted on either side of the precipitous slope of lawn to the north of the house, and later extensive plantations in the park. A path running parallel to the carriage road pictured in Walker's engraving, leading to a 'picturesque old arch', was known as 'Pope's Walk'. Avenues were laid out on the terrace above the house to the south.[49]

It is fitting that the gardens should be described in Defoe's *Tour* (1742) entirely in terms of Pope's ideas of economy and genius of the place in the *Epistle to Burlington*:

> He [Allen] is building for himself a very magnificent House of this Stone . . . and has delightful Gardens laid out with a Profusion of Fancy, yet with great Oeconomy, as to the Expence: for, in short, Mr. Allen is contented with the Situation of his House and Gardens, (and indeed well he may, for it is a very fine one), and, instead of forcing Nature by a great Expence to bend to Art, he pursues only what the natural Scite [*sic*] points out to him, and, by so doing, will make it one of the cheapest, and at the same time, one of the most beautiful Seats in *England*. He levels no Hills, but enjoys the Beauty of the Prospects they afford; he cuts down no Woods, but strikes thro' them fine Walks, and next-to-natural Mazes; and has, by that Means, a delightful Grove always filled with Birds, which afford the rural Ear a Musick transcending all others.[50]

Pope had something to do with the design of a cascade at Prior Park which featured, according to Defoe's *Tour* (1748), the 'Figure of Moses striking the Rock, and the Water gushing out of it, which forms a sort of natural cascade, whence his Bason is supplied'. Its landscape situation is described in a passage attributed to Samuel Richardson:

> The Gardens to this Seat consist of two Terraces, and two Slopes, lying Northward before the House, with winding Walks made through a little Coppice opening to the Westward of those Slopes; but all these are adorned with Vases, and other Ornaments, in Stone-work; and the Affluence of Water is so great, that it is received at three different Places, after many little agreeable Falls, at the Head of one of which is a Statue of

[49] For Thomas Thorpe's 'An Actual Survey of the City of Bath . . . and of Five Miles Round' (1742), and Anthony Walker's engraving of Prior Park (1752), see Boyce, *The Benevolent Man*, pp. 144–5, plates 2–3. On Pope's Walk at Prior Park, see Robert Edward Myhill Peach, *The Life and Times of Ralph Allen of Prior Park, Bath* (London, 1895), p. 113. On the plantations see Boyce, *The Benevolent Man*, pp. 113–14.

[50] Daniel Defoe, *A Tour Thro' the Whole Island of Great Britain*, 3rd edn. (London, 1742), ii. 265.

Moses down to the Knees, in an Attitude expressive of the Admiration he must have been in after striking the Rock, and seeing the Water gush out of it. The winding Walks were made with great Labour; and, tho' no broader than for two or three to walk abreast, yet in some Places they appear with little Cliffs on one Side, and with small Precipices on the other.[51]

By August 1741 it appears that Pope had sent Allen an inscription for this statue, and it is conceivable that he supervised from his chair the disposition of the cascade and rock which he was anxious to see finished in 1740.[52]

Further evidence of Pope's contribution is supplied by Richard Graves's description of Prior Park, where

good use is made of the various rills of water which appear to issue from a rock, stricken by the wand of Moses, (a statue of whom is plac'd above it) and trickling down the precipice, are collected below into a serpentine river, which is ornamented by a fictitious bridge, designed by Mr. Pope, to conceal its termination.[53]

The serpentine stream, a branch of the Lyn, is marked on Thorpe's map running towards Widcombe where it empties into the Avon, and Benjamin Boyce identifies the Bridge among the 'Buildings belonging to Ralph Allen' drawn on a *Survey of the Manours of Hampton, Claverton, and Widcombe*, commissioned after 1758, now in the Bath Reference Library where it is identified as the 'Sham Bridge at the Serpentine River'.[54] It was later replaced by the Palladian Bridge spanning the lake above, a copy of the famous bridge at Wilton by Roger Morris. Graves is no authority ('I do not pretend to great accuracy', p. 61 n.), but it is plausible that Pope, considering his fascination with bridges at Sherborne and his experience at Rousham and Stowe, should have designed the simple bridge of three quoined arches surmounted by pediments to terminate the prospect down river towards Widcombe.

There is little known about Pope's influence on the rest of the garden architecture apart from the 'Pine-house' which he was advising on in 1742 (iv. 429). It is probable that he had something to do with Mrs. Allen's grotto, when he encouraged her in 1740 'to imitate the Great Works of Nature, rather

[51] *A Tour*, 4th edn. (1748), ii. 301–2. According to Boyce, the section on Bath in the 4th edn. was rewritten, 'probably by Samuel Richardson'. *The Benevolent Man*, p. 129.

[52] Pope, *Correspondence*, iv. 239, 280, 360.

[53] 'Trifling Anecdotes of the late Ralph Allen, Esq. of Prior Park, near Bath', in *The Triflers* (London, 1806), p. 65.

[54] See Boyce, *The Benevolent Man*, pp. 114, 247, nn.; plate 10.

than those Bawbles most Ladies affect' (iv. 254). It may be that the building identified on the *Survey* as the 'Gothic Temple in the Woods' (later known as Pope's Grotto), was the grotto Pope had encouraged.[55] It is certainly a mistake to suppose, as Benjamin Boyce does, that Pope would have considered Gothic at Prior Park an aberration. Gothic was a part of the genius of the place (the site of ruins of a medieval abbey, which gave Prior Park its name), and Pope would have encouraged Allen to cultivate the Gothic as he had Lord Digby at Sherborne.[56]

We can conclude with Christopher Hussey that 'the composition of the very beautiful Prior Park landscape . . . is unquestionably due to a master hand',[57] and go on to suggest that the master hand was Pope's. Hussey's is the latest voice to be heard in a chorus of praise for Allen's taste in building and gardening which began, remarkably enough, before he had even started to build or to plant. This extraordinary phenomenon was the result of the influence of Pope's epistles to *Burlington* (1731) and *Bathurst* (1733), and to the portrait of Allen in the *Epilogue to the Satires* (1738). This resulted in the apotheosis of the civil servant and businessman into a saint of eighteenth-century benevolence, one of the central figures in Fielding's morality play, and established the reputation of Allen's house and gardens at Prior Park as an ideal estate.[58]

Allen's motives for building appear to have been a frank mixture of commercial and social ostentation. If his architect, John Wood, is to be believed, the house 'owed its inception to the prejudice against Bath freestone' from Allen's quarries which had been rejected in 1726 by Colen Campbell for the building of Greenwich Hospital. This decision

> brought him to a Resolution to exhibit it in a Seat which he had determined to build for himself near his Works, to much greater Advantage, and in much greater Variety of Uses than it had ever appeared in any other structure.

Wood's original design for Prior Park derives from Campbell's prototype for the great house, Wanstead, Essex, and its derivatives like Houghton Hall,

[55] Ibid., pp. 115–16, plate 10 e.
[56] Ibid., p. 116. On the Gothic at Prior Park, see pp. 115–16, 219–20, 225.
[57] *English Gardens and Landscapes*, p. 52.
[58] *Epilogue to the Satires*, Dia. I (1738), ll. 135–6; *TE* iv. 308.

Wentworth Woodhouse, and Stourhead, which Allen and Wood set out deliberately to outdo in the diameter of columns, size of portico, and length of front. Wood believed that his design, 'wherein the Orders of Architecture were to show forth in all their Glory', had been spoiled by 'humble Simplicity' in the execution, but Allen had not abandoned his conscious rivalry with Whig builders. The wings of the house Allen occupied in 1741 extended a thousand feet, enough to bring 'all Brobdignag before your thought'.[59]

Allen's ambitions to build were well known in Bath in 1734, when Mary Chandler published the poem 'Ev'n Pope approv'd', *A Description of Bath*, which concludes with a tribute to Allen, characterizing his proposed schemes as works of a Man of Ross, the antitype of a Timon:

> Hail, mighty Genius! born for Great Designs,
> T'adorn your Country, and to mend the Times;
> Virtue's Exemplar in degenerate Days,
> All who love Virtue, love to speak your Praise.

A description of his future estate follows—'Prophetick here, the Muse shall build thy Seat'—corresponding well enough to the gardens as laid out so that the passage continued to be quoted in the next decade to illustrate 'the Taste of this Gentleman in his Gardening'. This influential character of the gardens was followed by the definitive portrait of the man in Pope's *Imitations of Horace, Epilogue to the Satires*, Dialogue I (1738):

> Let humble Allen, with an aukward Shame,
> Do good by stealth, and blush to find it Fame. (135–6).[60]

The apotheosis of the estate was not supplied by Pope for Prior Park as it was for Stowe, but there is evidence that Pope inspired Fielding's description in *Joseph Andrews* (iii. 6, 1742):

> I have heard, Squire *Pope*, the great Poet, at my Lady's Table, tell Stories of a Man that lived at a Place called *Ross*, and another at the *Bath*, one Al—Al—I forget his

[59] On Allen's motives for building, see Boyce, *The Benevolent Man*, pp. 98–101; John Summerson, 'The Classical Country House', *Journal of the Royal Society of Arts*, 107 (July 1959), pp. 555–6; John Wood, *An Essay Towards a Description of Bath*, 2nd edn. (London, 1749); and Walter Ison, *The Georgian Buildings of Bath from 1700 to 1830* (New York, n.d.), p. 135.

[60] Mary Chandler's poem is quoted by Boyce, *The Benevolent Man*, pp. 57–8. See Defoe, *A Tour* (1742), ii. 266; and Pope, *TE* iv. 308; *Correspondence*, iv. 93.

Name, but it is in the Book of Verses. This Gentleman hath built up a stately House too, which the 'Squire likes very well; but his Charity is seen farther than his House, tho' it stands on a Hill, ay, and brings him more Honour too. It was his Charity that put him in the Book, where the 'Squire says he puts all those who deserve it.

Pope wrote to Allen in 1743 telling him that Fielding had sent him the books he had subscribed for in which 'he has payd you a pretty Compliment upon your House' (iv. 452). This refers to chapter five of 'A Journey from This World to the Next' in Fielding's *Miscellanies* (1743), where Fielding explains that most of the 'noble Palaces' had been built on the road to Greatness, 'save one greatly resembling a certain House by the Bath' on the Road to Goodness. Finally, in *Tom Jones* the repeated allusions to Squire Allworthy's house are said to derive in large part from Prior Park and its owner. Like Allen, Allworthy

had expended one Part of the Income of this Fortune in discovering a Taste superior to most, by Works where the highest Dignity was united with the purest Simplicity. . . . his House, his Furniture, his Gardens, his Table, his private Hospitality, and his public Beneficence, all denoted the Mind from which they flowed, and were all intrinsically rich and noble, without Tinsel, or external Ostentation.[61]

This is a surprising description of a house which had been conceived of primarily as a commercial venture and a rival to the ostentation of great Whig houses. The identification of the house with the virtue of its owner, the reputation of Prior Park as a place 'where true taste with grandeur meets', as the author of the poem 'Bath and Its Environs' expressed it in 1775, was largely owing to Pope.[62] As long as the reckoning of Pope's debts to Allen continues to show a balance due in the opinion of biographers, one can point to Pope's contribution to the gardens of Prior Park, and to his portraits of Allen and his house. They transformed a businessman into a Man of Benevolence, and a house built for show into a shrine of virtue.

[61] Henry Fielding, *Joseph Andrews*, ed. Martin C. Battestin (Oxford, 1967), p. 235; 'A Journey from This World to the Next', in *Miscellanies by Henry Fielding* (London, 1743), ii. 41–2. See Boyce, *The Benevolent Man*, pp. 125–6, 181–2. *The History of Tom Jones, A Foundling*, ed. Martin C. Battestin, 2 vols. (Oxford, 1974), Bk. VIII, ch. i, vol. i. 403–4. Battestin characterizes Fielding's description of Paradise Hall (Bk. I, ch. iv) as an 'imaginative synthesis' of Sharpham, Hagley, and Prior Park, vol. i. 42.

[62] Anon. (Bath, 1775), quoted by Benjamin Boyce, *The Benevolent Man*, p. 295.

9. 'Practical Poetry': The Landscape of the English Villa

THE gardens and parks of great houses like Cirencester, Stowe, and Prior Park did not realize the full potential of the picturesque ideal of landscape, and grand designs like these were not the most influential models of mid- and late-century garden design in England. Many later visitors apparently agreed with the opinion of George Berkeley, who wrote to Lady Howard in 1734 that Stowe was 'enchanted ground', but, 'charming as Stowe certainly is', he owned 'a partiality for Rowsham': 'One is a most magnificent place, and the other a very pretty one.'[1] The 'cool judicious art' of Stowe admired by Thomson was still too far from nature to satisfy the enthusiasm of a Joseph Warton.[2] 'Can Kent design like Nature?' he asks in *The Enthusiast* (l. 47, 1744):

> Can gilt Alcoves, can Marble-mimic Gods,
> Parterres embroider'd, Obelisks, and Urns
> Of high Relief; can the long, spreading Lake,
> Or Vista lessening to the Sight; can Stow
> With all her *Attic* Fanes, such Raptures raise,
> As the Thrush-haunted Copse, where lightly leaps
> The fearful Fawn the rustling Leaves along. (ll. 5–11)[3]

William Gilpin, who was later to deny that the picturesque can be achieved in garden design, in the *Dialogue on Stowe* (1748) debates the moral utility of the pleasure garden, and finds Stowe licentious.[4] For these reasons, quasi-moralis-

[1] *Suffolk Letters* (1824), ii. 76, 78.

[2] *Autumn* (1744), l. 1046, in *Works*, ed. J. Logie Robertson, p. 170.

[3] Joseph Warton, *The Enthusiast: or, The Lover of Nature. A Poem* (London, 1744). His epigraph is from Martial: *Rure vero barbaroque laetatur*.

[4] Polypthon concludes that Stowe's gardens are 'a good Epitome of the World: They give free Scope to

tic, aesthetic, and philosophical, and also because of the inimitable scale and expense of the English version of Versailles, Stowe was perhaps a work more wondered at than widely imitated in England. Stowe, as we observed in the last chapter, was a paradigm of the greater house, as described by John Summerson, and as such it was destined to be challenged by the English villa, which developed a distinct ideal of landscape, as well as architectural design. In garden design, as in architecture, the outcome of the contest between the greater house and the villa was the same.[5]

The awful progress of the Genius of Gardens described by Robert Dodsley in his poem, *Public Virtue* (1753), is through gardens of a character different from Stowe's.[6] They are places conceived more or less explicitly as villas or retirements like Chiswick, Richmond, or Esher encountered already; or others like Woburn, Hagley, and the Leasowes, which became the most influential models of mid-century taste in gardening, goals of sociable pilgrimage celebrated by poets, journalists, and historians of gardening—'fine examples', as Joseph Warton described them, of 'practical poetry'.[7] Such places frequently define themselves in opposition to greater houses like Stowe, Blenheim, or Houghton. Frequently they are fresh designs on new sites, not fashionable reworkings of older designs; and characteristically, they are laid out by their owners, who pride themselves on doing without professional assistance. They draw or admit inspiration from classical rather than French models; they are conceived to be pastoral Arcadias rather than heroic Elysiums; they are moderate in scale, modest in expense (at least in principle), useful rather than ostentatious, beautiful rather than sublime.

The gardens about to be considered have something else in common which has been generally overlooked, and that is the marked influence of Pope on the theory and practice of their designers. They visited his garden and followed

Inclinations of every Kind; and if in some Parts they humour the Sensualist's debauched Taste; in others, they pay very noble Compliments to Virtue'. Seeley, *A Description of Stow* (1750), p. 28. In *Observations on the Western parts of England, Relative Chiefly to Picturesque Beauty* (London, 1798), Gilpin observes that 'garden-scenes are never *picturesque*. They want the bold roughness of nature' (p. 98).

[5] John Summerson, 'The Classical Country House in 18th-century England', *Journal of the Royal Society of Arts*, 107 (July 1959), 552.

[6] *Public Virtue: A Poem in Three Books* (London, 1753), 'Book the First, Agriculture', pp. 35–6.

[7] *Works of Pope* (1797), ii. 184–5. See H. F. Clark, 'Eighteenth-Century Elysiums', *Journal of the Warburg and Courtauld Institute*, 6 (1943), 171–7; *The English Landscape Garden* (1948), pp. 23–6.

his example at Twickenham, sometimes consulted him and invited his assistance, established and publicized his picturesque principles of garden design, and together fulfilled the poetic and pictorial possibilities of garden design which he had introduced. At Bevis Mount, Hampshire, and Hagley, Worcestershire, Pope was directly involved in the layout of gardens at places conceived of as villas rather than great houses. He 'propagated the Fame' (iii. 295) if he did not contribute directly to three early versions of the *ferme ornée*, an important paradigm of the villa landscape, at Appscourt, Surrey, Dawley, Middlesex, and Riskins, Buckinghamshire; and his ideas influenced the two most famous examples of the kind, Woburn Farm, Surrey, and the Leasowes, Worcestershire. Finally Pope made a contribution to Stourhead, Wiltshire, a garden still to be seen, which perfectly exemplifies his principles of garden design.

1. *Antitypes of the Greater House*

i. BEVIS MOUNT, SOUTHAMPTON

Charles Mordaunt, 3rd Earl of Peterborough and 1st Earl of Monmouth (1658–1735), was the intrepid hero of the Spanish campaign of 1705 who had become, like Cobham, on the accession of George I, one of 'Our Gen'rals now, retir'd to their Estates,/[who] Hang their old Trophies o'er the Garden gates'.[8] In an undated letter to Lady Howard he explicitly characterized the 'odd' and 'out of the way' place (iii. 317) he had leased for £14 *per annum* near Southampton, overlooking Itchin Ferry and the Southampton river as an antitype of the great houses of Marlborough and Walpole: 'Our thoughts are free' he told her:

> I assure you, from the wild romantic cottage where I pass my time I should send few of them [his thoughts] to courts and castles, unless you were in them. *My* Blenheim would not afford lodgings for two maids of honour and their equipage, and yet I cannot forbear wishing that you might somehow or other see my purchase of fourteen pounds a year. Though you had seen the prodigies of Norfolk [Houghton] the day before, I

[8] *Imitations of Horace*, Ep. I, i (1737), ll. 7–8, *TE* iv. 279. According to E. A. Mitchell, *Southampton, Occasional Notes* (Southampton, 1938), p. 83, the motto on the gates of the house in the nineteenth century was *Ostendo non ostento* (I display but boast not).

44. Plan of Bevis Mount. Facsimile by E. Stevens. 1844.

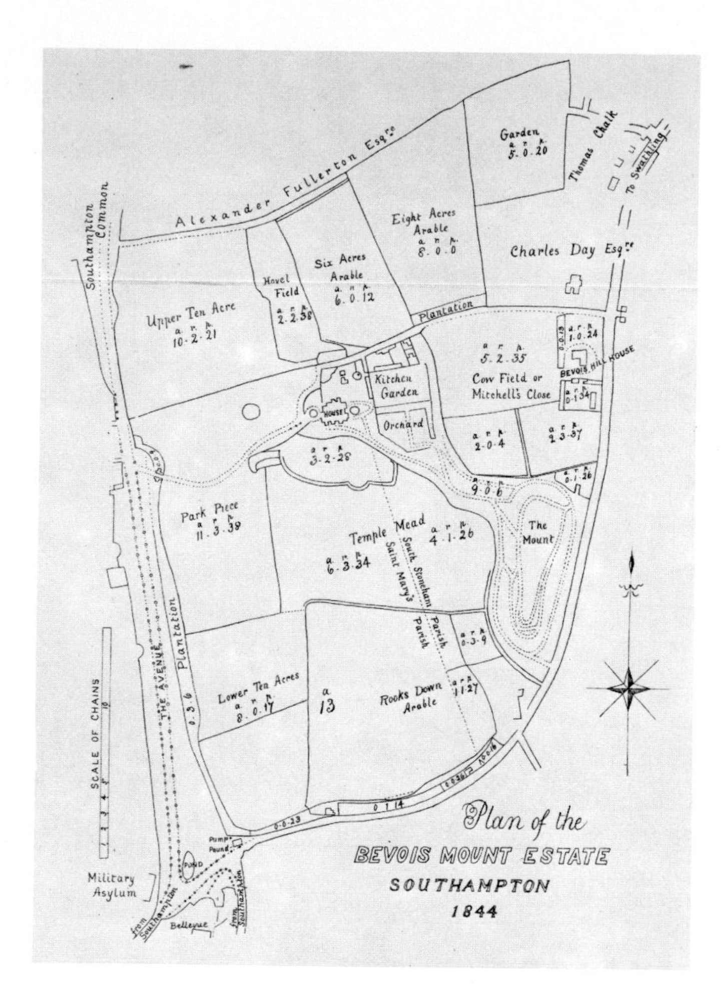

45. Pope's Walk, Bevis Mount, Hampshire. By Thomas Hart. *c.* 1840.

6. Hagley Park, Worcestershire. After Thomas Smith, 1749

should depend upon your partiality to Bevismount, the noble title of my palace, which has put the public to no expense.[9]

'I confess the stately Sacharissa at Stow, but am content with my little Amoret' (iii. 310), Peterborough told Pope in 1732, referring to bathing nymphs involved in the pastoral episode of Damon and Musidora in Thomson's *Summer* (1730–8).[10]

Pope began to make regular visits to Bevis in the early 1730s, and found it delightful.[11] It was a seaside 'Paradise' such as he had admired at Torbay (ii. 176), and he praised the prospect which he described in a letter to Arbuthnot: 'I write this from the most beautiful Top of a Hill I ever saw, a little house that overlooks the Sea, Southampton, & the Isle of Wight; where I study, write, & have what Leisure I please' (iii. 424). He was probably alluding to views from Bevis Mount when he mentioned 'Lord Peterborow's two Hills by Southampton' as examples of picturesque prospects to Spence (No. 608).

A common interest in gardening acquired new impetus at Bevis Mount. Pope was encouraging improvements with wise saws from Cicero in 1732 (iii. 307), which Peterborough answered by saying he 'would dedicate a Temple to Laziness' (iii. 310). The gardens remained unfinished when Peterborough died in 1735, but Pope had promised to complete the gardens after

[9] *Suffolk Letters*, i. 173. Descriptions of Bevis Mount can be found in Rev. Theodore C. Wilks, *The History of Hampshire*, 3 vols. (London, n.d.), ii. 274–5; William Stebbing, *Peterborough* (London, 1890), p. 213; and the fullest account in F. J. C. Hearnshaw, 'Bevis Mount', *Papers and Proceedings of the Hampshire Field Club*, v (1904–6), 114–20.

[10] *Works* (1908), ed. J. Logie Robertson, p. 126 n.:

> Tall and majestic Sacharissa rose,
> Superior trading [*sic*], as on Ida's top
> (So Grecian bards in wanton fable sung)
> High shone the sister and the wife of Jove.
> Another Pallas Musidora seemed,
> Meek-eyed, sedate, and gaining every look
> A surer conquest of the sliding heart;
> While, like the Cyprian goddess, Amoret,
> Delicious dressed in rosy-dimpled smiles,
> And all one softness, melted on the sense. (f. l. 1292, 1730–8)

According to Elwin Courthope Peterborough's allusion is to Waller, x. 187 n.; but Thomson seems more likely the year after the publication of the first collected edition of the *Seasons*, which illustrated the bathing scene in its frontispiece. See W. B. Cooke, 'Thomson's "Seasons"', *Notes & Queries*, 4th series, xi (17 May, 1873), 399.

[11] See *Correspondence*, iii. 424, 430, 436; iv. 33.

the death of his friend. He fulfilled his promise the following year (1736) when he told Allen he was ready to make the journey to Southampton 'if I find I can be of any Use there' (iv. 31), and reported that he found his enjoyment after arrival increased 'by the Employment of planting & improving many Parts of it' (iv. 36). He wrote to Allen that he had been busy in planting for Lady Peterborough and 'imploying much of your Stone in the Ornaments of this place' (iv. 37). After his return to Twickenham, he advised Allen that 'I have some Commissions from Lady Peterborow to you about Bath-Stone, but the Designs are not yet quite setled, & if she speak of it, tell her so' (iv. 41).

The city of Southampton has overrun the gardens, so that the results of these landscape designs must be judged from an anonymous description dated 1753, and drawings and plans dating from the nineteenth century (plate 44), including a view of 'Pope's Walk' (plate 45) at Bevis Mount.[12] The 1753 account describes the Mount, supposedly a Saxon fortification against the Danes, which Peterborough had 'converted . . . into a kind of wilderness':

as it is full of trees and brambles, he cut through them divers circular walks and labyrinths, so very intricate that it is hardly possible to avoid being lost in them. . . . The Mount terminates above, as is feigned of Parnassus, in a kind of fork; and between the two spires is a bowling green, a parterre, adorned with fine Italian marble statues . . . On one side of this parterre, declining gradually from the top of one of the spires to the green, is planted a little vineyard, exposed to the south; on the other side, on the very summit of the spire, stands a very fine summer house, very elegantly built and contrived, with a good cellar under it . . . He intended to rebuild the house [Bevis House, a quarter mile from the Mount], and convert all the grounds lying between it and the Mount into gardens, had he lived a little longer. The beauty of the improvements which his Lordship made in this Mount, is hardly to be conceived. He adorned it with statues, grottoes and alcoves, and diversified it up and down with something new and surprising at every turn.[13]

It may be that Pope's correspondence with Allen (iv. 37) concerned the

[12] William Burroughs Hill in 'Antient Southampton' (a collection of photographs in the central library, Southampton) reproduces pencil drawings of Thomas Gray Hart (1797–1881), an artist known for drawings and water-colours of local scenery who lived in Southampton from 1825. See plate 47, 'Pope's Walk, Bevois Mount—with the tomb of Sir Bevois so spoken of'; and plate 48, 'The beautiful Bevois Mount Park'. F. J. C. Hearnshaw reproduces plans of the estate (1844, 1905) in 'Bevis Mount', pl. fc. pp. 109 and 124. Theodore Wilks mentions a 'Pope's seat' in the gardens, *The History of Hampshire*, ii. 274.

[13] Quoted by Hearnshaw, 'Bevis Mount', pp. 121–2.

paving of this summer house, and that he was responsible for some of the improvements mentioned here.

In 1738 the gardens were much admired by Pope's friends Edward Harley and Aaron Hill (it was here that Hill conversed with Pope's 'vegetable children' and admired 'the increase of [his] flourishing green families', iv. 94). Pococke remarked in 1754 how skilfully 'Beauvoise Hill . . . is taken into the gardens', and in 1755 Horace Walpole 'walked long by moonlight on the terrace along the beach' at a place where 'by the aid of some historic vision and local circumstance I can romance myself into pleasure . . . There are Lord and Lady Peterborough and Pope to people the . . . scene.'[14]

ii. HAGLEY, WORCESTERSHIRE

Stowe was an important influence and a place emulated at Hagley Park, Worcestershire (plate 46), the garden laid out by George Lyttelton, Cobham's nephew and one of his 'cubs' in the patriot opposition. But Lyttelton did not consult professional landscape architects, he was unhampered by an existing garden, and by 1745 he had created a place he was 'as proud of as Ld Cobham of Stowe',[15] a place which rivalled if it did not surpass the fame of Stowe later in the century, and was recognized as a distinct advance in garden art. Thomas Whately, in *Observations on Modern Gardening* (1770), draws a distinction between the garden and the park in a typology of garden design, in which he characterizes Stowe as an example of the first (212–13), and mentions Hagley as a place where 'the excellencies both of a park and of a garden are . . . happily blended' (194). Cobham, the poet James Thomson, and William Kent have traditionally been mentioned as the formative influences on the design of Hagley, but it can be convincingly demonstrated that Twickenham was as important an influence as Stowe in the origin of the layout at Hagley, and

[14] See Edward Harley, 'A Journey Through Hampshire, Wiltshire, and Berkshire to Oxford, 1738', H.M.C., *Portland Papers*, vi. 175; Richard Pococke, *The Travels Through England . . . during 1750, 1751 and Later Years*, ed. James Joel Cartwright, *Travels*, vol. 2, Camden Society, N.S. vol. 44 (London, 1889), ii. 126; and Walpole to Richard Bentley (18 Sept. 1755), in *The Letters of Horace Walpole*, ed. Mrs. Paget Toynbee (Oxford, 1903), iii. 342; Walpole to the Countess of Upper Ossory (11 Aug. 1778), *Walpole Correspondence*, xxxiii. 42–3.

[15] Lyttelton to Doddridge (1745), quoted by Rose Mary Davis, *The Good Lord Lyttelton: A Study in Eighteenth Century Politics and Culture* (Bethlehem, Pa., 1939), p. 167.

that Pope played a direct role in the creation of this synthesis of garden design.[16]

Pope's friendship with Lyttelton dates from the early 1730s when he corrected a poem Lyttelton dedicated to him. Throughout the decade Pope made complimentary references to Lyttelton in his own poetry.[17] Lyttelton visited Twickenham frequently, at least from the time he composed 'Verses Written at Mr. Pope's House' in 1735, which contain lines indicating that he regarded Pope's garden as a model landscape:

> The Muses' green retreat,
> With every smile of Nature grac'd,
> With every art complete.[18]

Lyttelton began to improve Hagley before he came into the estate in 1745, more than a decade earlier than has been supposed.[19] Improvements were in hand in July 1739, when Pope made what appears to have been his first visit,[20] and described his gardening activity to Ralph Allen: 'Among other places,' he writes, 'I have been at Sir Tho. Lyttelton's, where your Pillar is impatiently expected. And where I have designed three buildings' (iv. 190). It may be that the 'rough Dorick Portico' at Hagley, sometimes referred to as 'Pope's

[16] See Gordon Nares, 'Hagley Hall, Worcestershire—I, The Seat of Viscount Cobham', *Country Life*, 122 (19 Sept. 1957), 546–9; Isabel Chase, *Horace Walpole, Gardenist*, p. 56 n.; and Rose Mary Davis, *Lyttelton*, p. 168. Miles Hadfield writes in *Gardening in Britain* (London, 1960), p. 209, that Lyttelton 'was no doubt also greatly influenced by Pope, for evidence of their friendship abounds'.

[17] Pope's corrections of Lyttelton's poem, 'The Progress of Love in Four Eclogues', including 'I. Uncertainty. To Mr. Pope' (1732) in *Works* (1776), iii. 53–72, are discussed by Rose Mary Davis, *Lyttelton*, p. 96, and Howard D. Weinbrot, 'Pope's "Pretty Poem": A Correction to Sherburn, and Corrections by Pope', *Notes & Queries*, 216 (Sept. 1971), 333–4. For Pope's references to Lyttelton, see the *Imitations of Horace*, Ep. I, i (1737), ll. 27–30, *TE* iv. 281; and Dia. I (1738), l. 47 n., *TE* iv. 301.

[18] *Works* (London, 1776), ed. George E. Ayscough, iii. 126.

[19] On the starting-date of Lyttelton's improvements at Hagley, Lyttelton's biographer, Rose Mary Davis asserts that he did not begin laying out Hagley 'in a serious way' until after the death of his wife in 1747, but she takes note of earlier projects, *Lyttelton*, chap. 3, p. 168. H. F. Clark dates them 'about 1751'; 'Eighteenth-Century Elysiums', *Journal of the Warburg and Courtauld Institute*, 6 (1943), 172. The most recent opinion of Gordon Nares is that 'the park and some of its incidental buildings were begun . . . at least by 1743'; 'Hagley Hall—I', *Country Life*, 122 (19 Sept. 1957), 548.

[20] The only visit to Hagley recorded in the correspondence is July–Aug. 1739 (*Correspondence*, iv. 185, 190), but Lyttelton was extending invitations in the 1740s in a way which implies more than one visit (iv. 349). Rose Mary Davis remarks (*Lyttelton*, p. 73), that Hagley was too far from London to be 'an established *rendezvous*', but 'it is probable that Pope was entertained there more than once'.

Building', a feature of a walk known as 'Pope's Walk', was Pope's own design.[21] Joseph Heely gives this description of the building in *Letters on the Beauties of Hagley, Envil, and the Leasowes* (1777):

> Let me remind you, that we are now musing in the midst of Mr. Pope's favourite walk—among those peaceful bowers where he was wont to muse; when a little farther we unexpectedly drop upon a Doric portico, which is honoured with the name of
>
> POPE'S BUILDING: INSCRIBED
> QUIETI ET MUSIS
> To Quiet and the Muses.
>
> This charming seat is on the brink of a steep declivity, the woods in its front and sides forming a very striking area of lawn, where you will observe among the trees, a glimmering of water, and that sturdy ivy-twisted oak I took you to, on emerging from the grot. (i. 204–5)

Heely enthusiastically records the raptures of Pope over the situation of the building on 'his Walk':

> Mr. Pope, who had the honour of being intimately acquainted with the late lord Lyttelton, being often at Hagley, never knew how to contain himself, when he musingly strayed through this part of the park: he used to call it his own ground;—the favourite haunt of the muses;—and would be seen in perfect rapture.—Certainly the bard shewed an extreme delicacy and judgment in his choice: no woods ever more nobly graced the rising hill, or extended themselves so happily down the valley—no lawns ever appeared richer in verdure, in diversity, and in beauty: indeed the whole of what may be stiled *his walk*, which I shall soon make you better acquainted with, is indisputably the pride of Hagley. (i. 168–9)

There may be more of legend than fact in this account, but the circumstances suggest that Pope was the designer of at least one building under construction at Hagley in 1739, and it seems probable he had something to say about its site.

Pococke describes Pope's urn 'on a pedestal and crowned with a double mask, as I suppose of Satyr and Philosophy',[22] and Thomas Whately tells us that the urn was 'chosen by Mr. Pope for the spot' (201). It stood on a rising

[21] Pococke, *Travels* (1756), ii. 234. Thomas Whately refers to the 'Doric Portico which also bears his [Pope's] name'. *Observations on Modern Gardening* (1770), p. 201.

[22] Richard Pococke, *Travels*, vol. i, Camden Society, N.S. vol. 42 (London, 1888), i. 227.

at the east end of the Tinian Lawn, and in 'the stillest watch of night', Whately writes,

it is delightful then to saunter here, and see the grass . . . to catch the freshness of the evening air; a solitary urn, chosen by Mr. Pope for the spot, and now inscribed to his memory, when shewn by a gleam of moon-light through the trees, fixes that thoughtfulness and composure, to which the mind is insensibly led by the rest of this elegant scene. (200–1)

This elegiac, moonlit scene of the memorial is expressive of Pope's sensibility to landscape and his principles of garden design.

Hitherto, Hagley has been more closely associated with James Thomson than with Pope. It was here that Thomson finished revising the *Seasons* in 1743, additions which include the long passage in 'Spring', praising the 'British Tempe' of his patron with its 'bursting prospect' (951).[23] But by this time the spectacular natural situation of Hagley had already been improved by Pope's directions, and was to become one of the most perfect and influential fulfilments of his principles.[24] It was soon to contain everything Pope had advocated at other places with the advantage of a finer natural setting. Like Stowe it acquired an Ionic rotunda, and a Palladian Bridge; its grotto was adorned with a statue of the Venus de Medici, and the requisite antique inscription as Pope had prescribed for his own (ii. 297); its hermitage contained lines from Milton's *Il Penseroso*; a statue of Apollo terminated a walk as at Rousham; on Wichbury Hill within the park the ruins of a Roman camp were 'cultivated', as Pope had suggested at Sherburn: 'cut out into ridings . . . [to afford] many romantick and beautiful scenes within itself, as well as . . . extensive views'. Sanderson Miller supplied a sham ruin, which won him the

[23] 'Spring', ll. 904–62, *Works* (1908), ed. J. Logie Robertson, pp. 37–8. Isabel Chase states that 'Hagley . . . was designed by Lord Lyttelton, the owner, assisted by the poet Thomson', but she supplies no evidence. *Horace Walpole, Gardenist*, pp. 56 n., 109–15.

[24] The reputation of Hagley is attested as early as 1751 when John Brown spoke of Hagley's 'Honour'd Shade' in *An Essay on Satire: Occasion'd by the Death of Mr. Pope* (London, 1745), reprinted with additions in Pope's *Works* (1751), ed. Warburton, iii. xx. Later admirers of Hagley include Richard Pococke, *Travels*, i. (1751), 223–30, *Travels*, ii (1756), 233–6; Walpole to Bentley (Sept. 1753), *Letters*, ed. Paget Toynbee, iii. 185–7; Robert Dodsley, *Public Virtue* (1753), 'Agriculture', canto II, ll. 444–50; Thomas Whately in *Observations on Modern Gardening* (1770), pp. 194–206; and Joseph Heely, who regarded it as a 'school for taste'. See H. F. Clark, 'Eighteenth-Century Elysiums', p. 172. As usual John Byng found fault, but conceded that 'the pleasantest spot is about Pope's Urn'. *The Torrington Diaries*, ed. C. Bruyn Andrews (1934; rpt. 1970), i. 47.

'freedom of Strawberry' in Walpole's estimation; Walpole compared Hagley's serpentine waters and cascades to Milton's Eden, and its picturesque ornament to the prints of Sadeler and the paintings of Nicholas Poussin. Everywhere seats and alcoves opened prospects to the visitor.[25]

II. *The 'Farm-like Way of Gardening'*

In their rival typologies of the landscape garden Whately and Walpole include the farm as one of the distinct early varieties of the landscape garden. Walpole states that Philip Southcote, who began to lay out Woburn Farm, Surrey, in 1735, 'founded the . . . ferme ornée'. This judgement has been generally accepted by modern historians of gardening, one of whom has traced the origin of Southcote's design to Addison's suggestion that a man may make 'a pretty landscape of his own possessions'.[26] But the idea had a professional, more doctrinaire advocate than Addison, and several early practitioners besides Southcote known to Pope, who cast new light on the origins of the ornamented farm in England.

Stephen Switzer claimed in *A Farther Account of Rural and Extensive Gardening* (1728–30) that 'this Farm-like Way of Gardening' was the epitome of the system of 'rural and extensive gardening' he had introduced in earlier works published 1715 and 1718:

> The foregoing Volumes [*Ichnographia Rustica*, 1718] demonstrate, that I was always a Promoter of this Farm-like Way of Gardening, before it was used by any body, in any place, in *Great-Britain*, and must still think it, that it is not only the most profitable, but the most pleasureable of any Kind of Gardening when the Farm is walled or paled in, as is that of Abbscourt . . . it is really the truest and best Way of Gardening in the World, and such as the politest and best Genius of all Antiquity delighted in. (p. 10)[27]

[25] For details of Hagley's landscape, see Thomas Whateley, *Observations on Modern Gardening*, p. 206; Richard Pococke, *Travels*, i. 224–8, ii. 234; Horace Walpole, *Letters*, ed. Paget Toynbee, iii. 186, and *History of Gardening*, p. 15.

[26] Thomas Whately, 'Of a Farm', '*Observations on Modern Gardening* (1770), pp. 161–82; Horace Walpole, *History of Gardening*, p. 33. H. F. Clark, 'Eighteenth-Century Elysiums', p. 171.

[27] *An Appendix to Ichnographia Rustica: Containing A Farther Account of Rural and Extensive Gardening* (London, 1742). This is a pamphlet, separately paginated, bound into vol. iii of the second edition of *Ichnographia Rustica* (1742). In all probability it was written and perhaps published between 1728 and 1730, considering first, the reference (p. 2) to the first edition of *Ichnographia Rustica* (3 vols., London, 1718) as 'the foregoing Volumes . . . publish'd some ten or twelve years ago'; second, the reference (p. 8) to Robert

The publication of Robert Castell's *Villas of the Ancients* in 1729 supplied Switzer with the classical authority he appropriates here:

So much has been already said as to the Beauty of Rural and extensive Gardening, when compared with the stiff Dutch Way, which has been for some time exploded, that as to that Part at least, little need be added; and that this was the Method used by the Romans of old, the curious Drafts and Accounts of the Ancient Villas about that once Mistress of the World Rome, (published by an ingenious Gentleman lately deceased) fully evince. (8)

But in 1715, in the 'Preface' to *The Nobleman and Gardener's Recreation*, Switzer had explicitly avowed the source of his scheme for 'forest or rural' gardening 'from that Magnificence which is easily discoverable from the French Designs, which certainly yet very much excel ours' (xii), and in *A Farther Account* he refers again to French example explicitly with more hope for English emulation:

This Taste, so truly useful and delightful as it is, has also for some time been the Practice of some of the best Genius's of *France*, under the title of *La Ferme Ornée*. And that *Great-Britain* is now likely to excel in it, let all those who have seen the Farms and Parks of *Abbs-court*, *Riskins*, *Dawley-Park*, now a doing, with other Places of the like Nature, declare: In all which it is visible, that the *Roman* Genius, which was once the Admiration of the World, is now making great advances in *Britain* also. (8–9)

Switzer's remarks are significant because of the reference to three English farms 'now a doing' the decade before Southcote's Woburn Farm, and further because Pope can be associated with all three, placing him once again at the forefront of new developments in garden design. Little can be determined about the nature or development of these predecessors of Woburn Farm, which have all disappeared, but the evidence supports Switzer's characterization of them as hybrids of French and Classical ideals. Pope's attitude to these places indicates that the English borrowed from the French the idea of combining a garden or park with a farm, related it consciously to the classical ideal of the villa, and gradually naturalized this mode of garden design by means of a specifically English sensibility to poetic and picturesque landscape. Pope made a distinct contribution to this process.

Castell (d. 1729) as 'an ingenious Gentleman lately deceased'; and third, the reference (p. 9) to the estates of Appscourt, Riskins, and Dawley-Park as 'Farms and Parks . . . now a doing', a statement true of the 1720s.

i. APPSCOURT MANOR, SURREY

Pope was familiar with Appscourt Manor, Surrey, near Walton-on-Thames, 'a farm over-against Hampton-Court', because of its proximity to Twickenham, and his friendship with its owners and tenants. It was being leased by George Dunk, Earl of Halifax, in 1737 to Pope's friends Jeremiah and Anthony Brown (a contributor to the grotto), when Pope gave this description of it in the *Imitations of Horace*, Ep. II, ii (1737):

> If there be truth in Law, and *Use* can give
> A *Property*, that's yours on which you live.
> Delightful *Abs-court*, if its Fields afford
> Their Fruits to you, confesses you its Lord:
> All Worldly's Hens, nay Partridge, sold to town,
> His Ven'son too, a Guinea makes your own:
> He bought at thousands, what with better wit
> You purchase as you want, and bit by bit;
> Now, or long since, what difference will be found?
> You pay a Penny, and he paid a Pound. (230–9)

Pope's choice of the example of Appscourt, a place close to royal gardens widely known to his readers, is significant because of its contemporary reputation as 'a farm', or 'large enclosure', which was particularly cited by Switzer as a model of gardening in 'the Farm-like way'.[28] In the context of Pope's poem Appscourt figures as the type of the classical villa, a modern garden of Alcinous or Sabine Farm, exemplifying the classical doctrine of utility, a place where use confers ownership on its tenant. Its tenant is the anti-type of the mercenary speculator in real estate, who exploits land for profit, like Edward Wortley Montagu (Wordly), notorious for selling his game.

ii. DAWLEY PARK, MIDDLESEX

Dawley Park, the second farm Switzer describes 'now a doing', was the estate, comprising a manor house and about 245 acres, at Uxbridge about four

[28] Warburton's description of Appscourt as 'a farm, over-against Hampton-Court', is in Pope's *Works* (1751), iv. 233 n. Richard Pococke refers to 'the large enclosure of Abscourt' in *Travels* (1757), ii. 261. Pope was invited to Appscourt in 1743, *Correspondence*, iv. 451. Matthew Prior's activity there is described by James Lees-Milne, *Earls of Creation* (1962), p. 196. The history of Appscourt is in Owen Manning and W. Bray, *The History and Antiquities of the County of Surrey*, 2 (1809), 766–7.

miles from Twickenham, where Pope's closest friend, Henry St. John, Viscount Bolingbroke, settled after his return from exile in France in 1725. Judging from a late seventeenth-century engraving by Kip (plate 48) and a map dated about 1722 (plate 47), Dawley's 'extensive formal gardens and plantations, with avenues radiating in all directions over the park', were as French in character when he acquired it as the place he had just left, the Château de la Source, near Orleans, in France. Bolingbroke undertook the improvements to which Switzer refers from 1725 until the place was sold to Edward Stephenson in 1738. From the beginning of his retirement Bolingbroke 'posed as the farmer–philosopher'. 'I am here', he wrote Simon Harcourt in 1725, 'troubling myself very little about any thing beyond the extent of my farm' (ii. 290).[29]

It is probable that Pope encouraged Bolingbroke in the improvements in the farm-like way. Bolingbroke was a frequent visitor and admirer of the garden at Twickenham; his house at Dawley was remodelled by Pope's architect, James Gibbs, after 1724; it is possible that Bolingbroke consulted Bridgeman about the gardens at Pope's suggestion about the same time. According to Spence, Pope discussed landscape and prospects with Bolingbroke (No. 614); he quotes him on the 'Two Paradises of Gardens and Gallantry' (iii. 307), and regarded him as a 'gardening Lord' (iv. 459). Pope was making daily visits to Dawley in 1731 (iii. 193), the year after Swift had inquired in a letter to Bolingbroke about improvements in the gardens—'Pray my Lord how are the gardens? have you taken down the mount, and removed the yew hedges? have you not bad weather for the spring-corn? has Mr. Pope gone farther in his Ethic Poems? And is the head-land sown with wheat?' (iii. 99)—the same year Swift urged Pope to 'contrive new tamgams in your Garden or in Mrs. Howards, or my Lord Bolingbrokes' (iii. 191). All this suggests that an affirmative answer should be given to Sherburn's question as to whether 'Pope's and Martial's admiration for *rus verum barbarumque* affected the gardens at Dawley'.[30]

[29] See Susan Reynolds, ed., *The Victoria History of the County of Middlesex* (London, 1962), iii. 265. Johannes Kip's undated engraving, 'Dawley House, Harlington, in the late 17th Century' (B.M. Maps K. 30.27) is reproduced opposite p. 259. On the Château de la Source, see Sheila Radice, 'Bolingbroke in France', *Notes & Queries*, 177 (28 Oct. 1939), 309; and George Sherburn, *Early Career*, p. 288.

[30] Bolingbroke refers to visits to Twickenham in *Works* (1809), v. 80. See chap. 5, n. 55. On alterations to his house at Dawley, see James Gibbs's MS. Memoir, Colvin, p. 233; and Susan Reynolds, ed., *Victoria*

The intended improvements mentioned by Swift clearly indicate a development towards the informal, but it is doubtful how completely Bolingbroke transformed the French design. Dawley satisfied Switzer, but his idea of a farm was French. Bolingbroke's sister, Henrietta Knight, Baroness Luxborough, declared flatly that Dawley was not a farm: 'its environs were not ornamented nor its prospects good'.[31] There is the suggestion in Pope's playful remarks in a letter to Swift that Dawley was only nominally a farm, in the same sense that its owner, whom he describes reading a letter 'between two Haycocks', was a farmer:

he has fitted up his farm, and you will agree, that this scheme of retreat at least is not founded upon weak appearances. . . . I overheard him yesterday agree with a Painter for 200 l. to paint his country-hall with Trophies of Rakes, spades, prongs, &c. and other ornaments merely to countenance his calling this place a Farm. (ii. 503)

Bolingbroke's own taste, and that of his French wife, besides the natural limitations of a site already developed with severe formality, may have prevented the realization of Pope's picturesque ideals. In any event, it was celebrated for other reasons than landscape design.

Dawley Farm, a poem published in *Fogg's Weekly Journal* (No. 128, 26 June 1731) whose attribution to Pope has been challenged but which perfectly expresses his attitudes, invests the place with all the virtues of a classical villa, and, six months before the publication of the *Epistle to Burlington*, depicts the anti-type of a Timon's Villa. The poem praises the architecture in the classical sense of an entire humanistic environment, and as the expression of the character of its owner:

See! Emblem of himself, his *Villa* stand!
Politely finish'd, regularly Grand!
Frugal of Ornament, but that the best,
And all with curious Negligence express'd.
No gaudy Colours stain the Rural Hall,
Blank Light and Shade discriminate the Wall:

History of the County of Middlesex (1962), iii. 265. On the possibility that Pope recommended Charles Bridgeman to Bolingbroke, see *Correspondence*, ii. 327. George Sherburn, *Early Career*, p. 288.

[31] *Letters Written by the Late Right Honourable Lady Luxborough to William Shenstone* (London, 1775), p. 170.

Where thro' the Whole we see his lov'd Design,
To please with Mildness, without Glaring shine;
Himself neglects what must all others charm,
And what he built a Palace calls a *Farm*. (19–28)

These lines illustrate 'the beautiful Simplicity that appear'd in the House and Gardens', reflecting 'the good Sense, and easy Politeness of its Owner' mentioned in the anonymous introductory letter.[32]

The letter indicates that the poem was occasioned by political attacks on Bolingbroke; the poem praises his virtuous and classical retirement, which is compared to that of an Apollo, or a Virgil. The virtues of the owner as patron and patriot are crowned by his eloquence and hospitality:

His Speech, as tuneful as that Heav'nly Song,
Suspends in Rapture each attentive Guest;
Words more delicious than his gen'rous Feast;
Wit more inspiring than his flowing Bowl;
The Feast of Reason, and the Flow of Soul. (50–4)

The poem attacks the 'mad conduct' of Britain's ill treatment of this man, and its unjust reward of another:

Contraste of Scenes! Behold a worthless Tool,
A dubb'd Plebeian, Fortune's Fav'rite Fool,
Laden with publick Plunder, loll in State,
'Midst dazling Gems, and Piles of massy Plate,
'Midst Arms, and Kings, and Gods and Heroes quaff,
His Wit all ending in an Ideot Laugh. (33–8)

If Pope was the author of these lines which appear to caricature Walpole and Houghton Hall, this lends support to the possibility that he had Walpole in mind in his description of Timon's Villa in the *Epistle to Burlington* published later the same year.[33]

[32] *TE* vi. 452–5. John Butt is 'reluctant to credit Pope with such unpolished verse' (*TE* vi. 455), but the possibility of a collaboration with Swift might explain the unevenness of a poem for which Norman Ault makes a *prima facie* case in favour of attribution to Pope (*TE* vi. 453–5).

[33] On Walpole's knighthood, see J. H. Plumb, *Sir Robert Walpole*, vol. ii, *The King's Minister* (London, 1960), 101–2. For his jewels and plate, see John Morley, *Walpole* (London, 1889), pp. 131–2. For the possibility that Walpole is Timon, see Kathleen Mahaffey, 'Timon's Villa: Walpole's Houghton', *Texas Studies in Language and Literature*, 9 (Summer, 1967), 193–222; and Maynard Mack, *The Garden and the City* (1969), Appendix F.

Like Appscourt, Dawley figures in the satire of mercenary degeneracy and real estate in the *Imitations of Horace*. There is an allusion to a transaction for the sale of Dawley in *The Imitations of Horace*, Ep. II, ii (1737), preceding the lines on Appscourt. Joshua Vanneck had made an unacceptable offer to buy it from Bolingbroke:

> Indeed, could Wealth bestow or Wit or Merit,
> A grain of Courage, or a spark of Spirit,
> The wisest Man might blush, I must agree,
> If vile Van-muck lov'd Sixpence, more than he. (226–9)

In 1738 Pope wrote to Orrery, whom he hoped would buy 'the very best & most commodious House in England, as well as the cheapest':

> it would be more a Comfort to see any English Nobleman of any worth there, than some Child of Dirt, or Corruption; at best, some Money-headed & Mony-hearted Citizen: Such an one as Van Eck has prov'd himself to be. (iv. 136)

Writing to Burlington in December Pope referred to Bolingbroke's continuing difficulties with the sale: 'He has found, that a Great House in this Nation is like a Great Genius, too good for the Folks about it; They are as little worthy of the one, as the other' (iv. 153). Such was the extent of Pope's classical identification of the house with the virtue of its owner.

iii. RISKINS, BUCKINGHAMSHIRE

Riskins, near Colnbrook in the parish of Iver, Buckinghamshire, appears to be the most significant of Switzer's farms 'now-a-doing' in the history of gardening: it inspired some of Switzer's most interesting equivocations, Pope awarded it praise and blame, and William Shenstone honoured it with an *Ode*. In the vicinity of Twickenham, it belonged to Allan Apsley, Lord Bathurst, and served him as a suburban villa from the time he became M.P. for Cirencester in 1705 until he gave the estate in 1735 to his eldest son Benjamin. In 1739 it was purchased by Algernon Seymour, Earl of Hertford, and his wife Frances Thynne, renamed Piercy-Lodge, and celebrated by Shenstone in his *Ode to Rural Elegance* (1750–8). We know more about Riskins than the other early farms because Switzer, who is said to have been employed there by Bathurst, included a plan (plate 49) of it in '*A Farther Account*' with some illuminating descriptive remarks.[34]

Switzer describes the plan in '*A Farther Account*' as 'a regulated Epitomy of a much larger Design portraited and lay'd out, by the Right Honourable the Lord Bathurst at *Riskins* near *Colnbrooke*, upon the Plan of the *Ferme Ornée*, and the Villa's of the Ancients' (9). Switzer's 'imperfect Epitomy . . . a small Specimen of what may be done in a larger Case' (10) emphasizes the French regularity of the design, and obscures any rural informality it may have had. Signs of informality appear on the plan, particularly the serpentine outline of the 'Common Road or Highway', the 'Cart, Coach or Shaise Road round the whole Plantation', and the 'Ah, ha' (N), indicated among the references. But the list of references includes a 'Parterre' (B), 'Terass round the House' (D), 'Avenue' (M), 'Parade' (O), 'Labyrinth' (E), 'Menegarie' (C), and a rigid geometrical frame of diagonals surrounding the straight axis of a canal measuring over 800 feet on the plan. Switzer was doubtful even about the diagonals:

> It may be objected against this Design, and all others of this Kind, that it were better the Fields were more square: Which I grant, but then there can be no diagonal Walks, which are very beautiful in any Villa, however not so very necessary but they may be omitted. (10)

He found the courage to leave in the diagonals, but he regularized an essential feature of Bathurst's design which contemporaries believed he was the first to introduce—a serpentine canal![35] Thus, Switzer's regulated epitomy gives us only as much of Bathurst's design as an apprehensive professional thought fit to expose to prospective clients.

Pope, on the other hand, whose frequent visits to Riskins are recorded from 1723 on, delighted in its daring and could not find superlatives enough

[34] William Bowles interpolates the change of name—'Riskins, now called Piercy Lodge'—in his transcription of Spence, *Anecdotes*, ed. S. W. Singer (London, 1820), p. 12. See Pope, *Works* (1809), iii. 325 n. Christopher Hussey, *English Gardens and Landscapes*, p. 79. For Switzer's employment at Riskins, see Peter Willis, 'Charles Bridgeman, Royal Gardener', Ph.D. dissertation (Cambridge University, 1961), I. xxiii.

[35] Bathurst's cousin, Thomas Wentworth, Lord Strafford, credited him with the first serpentine canal. See B. Sprague Allen, *Tides in English Taste* (1937), ii. 135; and Christopher Hussey, *English Gardens and Landscapes*, p. 83. For Switzer's uneasiness about plans and 'new Schemes in Gardening', see *The Nobleman and Gardener's Recreation* (1715), xxxiii.

to describe the place. The combination of 'the waters of *Riskins*, and the Woods of *Oakley* together . . . would be at least as good as any thing in our World: for as to the hanging Gardens of *Babylon*, the Paradise of *Cyrus*, and the Sharawaggi's of *China*, I have little or no Ideas of 'em, but I dare say Lord B—t has, because they were certainly both very *Great*, and very *Wild*' (ii. 314–15). As usual Pope found something to censure in Bathurst's design. It wanted 'variety', he told Spence in 1728:

> In laying out a garden, the first and chief thing to be considered is the genius of the place. Thus at Riskins, for example, Lord Bathurst should have raised two or three mounts because his situation is all a plain, and nothing can please without variety. (No. 609)

The French atmosphere of Riskins is suggested by Pope's reference to 'his Lordship's *Extravagante Bergerie*' (ii. 314). But the French pleasure garden was also a place which proved Bathurst an 'enemy to nice Parterres' in Pope's *Master Key* (1732), and its farm-like way is indicated by the nursery that supplied trees to Pope in 1725 (ii. 263), and by the livestock Pope was supplying to Benjamin Bathurst in the surprising capacity as cattle agent in 1735 (iii. 504). Switzer states in 'A Farther Account' that 'the Lawns round about the House are for the feeding of Sheep' and that the numerous triangular fields designated on the plan as 'Promiscuous Kitchen Quarters' are 'for sowing of Corn, Turnips, &c. or for the feeding of Cattle'.[36]

The French formality of Riskins prompted facetious exclamations from Pope and his friends in the 1720s about 'how rural we are!' (ii. 302), but in 1739, when it was acquired by the Seymours, the Countess of Hertford wrote that the gardens 'come nearer to my idea of a scene in Arcadia, than any place I ever saw'.[37] Referring to Pope's description of Riskins in his *Letters* (1735) as an '*Extravagante Bergerie*', she says 'the environs perfectly answer that title' (i. 172): the house 'stands in a little paddock of about a mile and a half round; which is laid out in the manner of a French park, interspersed with

[36] Pope, *Master Key to Popery*, *TE* iii. 2, 181. Stephen Switzer, 'A Farther Account of Rural and Extensive Gardening' (1728–30), appendix to vol. iii, *Ichnographia Rustica* (1742), 9. References are to the *Plan of Riskins* following the appendix.

[37] Frances (Thynne) Seymour, Duchess of Somerset, *Correspondence Between Frances, Countess of Hartford . . . and Henrietta Louisa, Countess of Pomfret, Between the Years 1738 and 1741*, 3 vols. (London, 1805), i. 172 (Nov. 1739).

woods and lawns (i. 219–20). Yet the features she admired in the gardens are entirely characteristic of the English taste for the picturesque: a 'cave' and cascade in the ruinous taste reminiscent of Pope's grotto (i. 220–1); 'covered benches . . . little arbours . . . and seats, under shady trees disposed all over the park' with inscriptions by Pope and others (i. 221; ii. 2–3); a 'green-house' on the site of a chapel (ii. 2); and 'one walk that I am extremely partial to . . . rightly called the Abbey-walk, since it is composed of prodigiously high beech-trees, that form an arch through the whole length, exactly resembling a cloister' (ii. 3), recalling Pope's 'idea of planting an old Gothic cathedral . . . in trees' (Spence, No. 619). In addition to these picturesque charms, she discovered at Riskins the virtues of a classical villa: the 'old, but convenient' house, the 'cheap manner' of upkeep, and a sense of retirement (i. 171–2). It cannot be doubted that the place which Bathurst laid out with Pope's encouragement and probable assistance, whose fame he liked to 'propagate' (iii. 295), had already become a model of picturesque landscape design before it figures as Piercy-Lodge in Shenstone's *Ode on Rural Elegance*, composed between 1750 and 1758, dedicated to the Countess of Hertford:

> I see the rival pow'rs [Art and Nature] combine,
> And aid each other's fair design;
> Nature exalt the mound where art shall build;
> Art shape the gay alcove, while nature paints the field.[38] (279–82)

iv. WOBURN FARM, SURREY

Appscourt, Dawley, and Riskins never appear to have gained wide recognition for their innovations in gardening in the 'farm-like way'. Philip Southcote's Woburn Farm, near Weybridge, Surrey, established itself as the first and William Shenstone's The Leasowes, near Halesowen, Worcestershire (plate 50), as the finest, of English ornamented farms. Southcote began and Shenstone completed the integration of garden and farm, which was achieved by a unifying sensibility for the picturesque. It has not hitherto been realized that Pope was an important influence on the theory and practice of Southcote

[38] William Shenstone, *The Works in Verse and Prose*, 3rd edn., 3 vols. (London, 1768–9), i. 121.

47. Plan of Dawley Park, Middlesex. *c.* 1714–22.

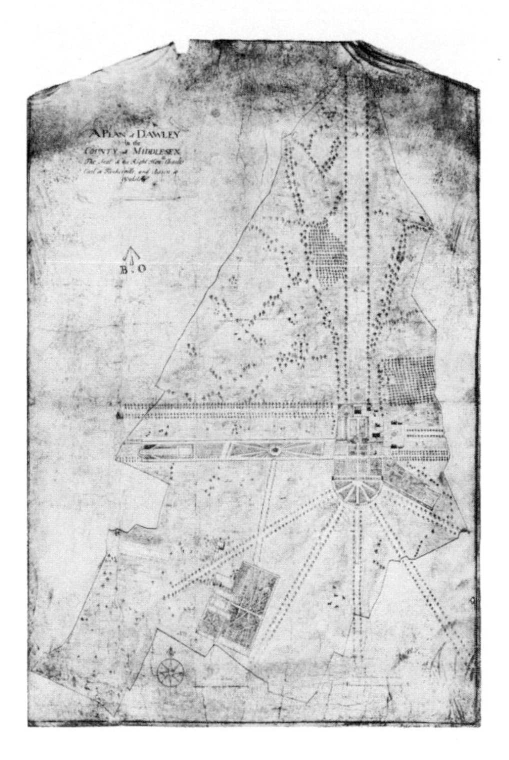

48. Dawley Park, Middlesex. After Leonard Knyff. *c.* 1714.

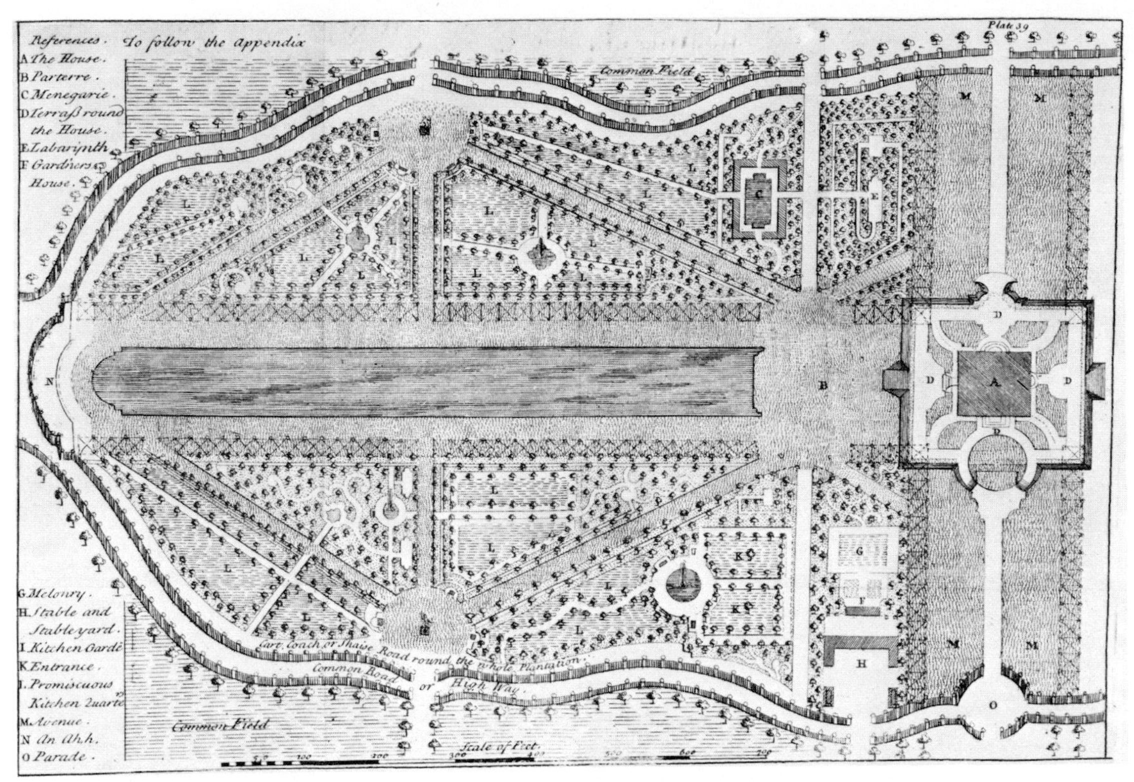

49. Plan of Riskins, Buckinghamshire. 1742.

50. Woburn, Surrey. By Luke Sullivan. 1759.

and Shenstone. It is no exaggeration to say that it was his sensibility they were imitating in these definitive versions of the English *ferme ornée*.

Philip Southcote told Spence that he 'began his garden in 1734' (No. 1126), and he gave this account of his idea for his farm which he said had been inspired by views of 'Fields, going from Rome to Venice' (No. 603):

> All my design at first was to have a garden on the middle high ground and a walk all round my farm, for convenience as well as pleasure: for from the garden I could see what was doing in the grounds, and by the walk could have a pleasing access to either of them where I might be wanted. (No. 1127)

Thomas Whately's description of Southcote's 'belt' at Woburn in *Observations on Modern Gardening* recalls Bridgeman's embankments at Stowe, and the walks Switzer described at Riskins:

> The place contains an hundred and fifty acres, of which near five and thirty are adorned to the highest degree; of the rest, about two-thirds are in pasture, and the remainder is in tillage: the decorations are, however, communicated to every part; for they are disposed along the sides of a walk, which, with its appendages, forms a broad belt round the grazing grounds. . . . This walk is properly garden; all within it is farm. (177–8)

Whately describes how 'the beauties which enliven a garden, are every where intermixed [with] many properties of a farm' (181): a serpentine river, ornamental buildings including an octagon, the ruins of a chapel, a neat Gothic building, a menagerie, seats, alcoves and bridges; picturesque plantations 'massed by the perspective, and gathered into considerable groupes' (180), and gay, extensive, broken, and wooded prospects.

In 1752 Spence described a new walk at Woburn as a '*picture-gallery*' (No. 1134), and he admired Southcote's picturesque composition of a prospect into 'foreground', 'mid-ground', and 'background' (No. 1085). The picturesque effect was not accidental, but the result of the application of principles Southcote made explicit in conversations with Spence, when he acknowledged his debt to Pope. As we have seen Southcote recognized Pope as a pioneer in picturesque gardening (No. 603), and he agreed with Pope's statement that 'all the beauties of gardening might be comprehended in one word, variety' (No. 604). In his numerous remarks on gardening recorded by Spence Southcote reiterates Pope's first principle of gardening, ' 'Tis all painting' (No. 1129), with its corollaries concerning 'perspective, prospect, distancing, and attracting, [which] comprehend all that part of painting in gardening' (No. 1130).

The coincidence is so exact between Pope's and Southcote's views on gardening it comes as no surprise to discover that they were apparently well acquainted through Catholic family connections, and mutual friendships with Spence, Burlington, and Kent. Southcote had visited Pope's garden at Twickenham, and his reference to Pope's plantations around the obelisk to his mother to illustrate the idea of distancing has been quoted earlier (see chap. 5). A remark by Spence about his reaction to the view of the 'farmstead' at Woburn suggests that Pope had often been a visitor to Woburn:

> When I told Mr. Southcote that the sight of his ground near his house was always apt to lead me into a pleasing smile and into a delicious sort of feeling at the heart, of which I had nothing when I was in his much nobler views along the brow of the hill, he said that Mr. Pope had often spoke of the very same effect of it on him. (No. 615)

It seems probable that some of Pope's visits coincided with those of Kent who served Southcote as architect.[39]

Southcote's contemporaries accepted his own claim to be 'the first that brought in the garden farm, or *ferme ornée*' (No. 1125). In his *Travels* (1757) Pococke spoke of Woburn Farm as 'the first improvement in the farm kind' (ii. 260), and Walpole established its reputation permanently with the statement in the *History of Gardening* that 'Mr. Philip Southcote founded the . . . ferme ornée'. But Woburn's art seemed excessive to some observers. In 1752 Spence was happy to find 'Mr. Southcote's rosary that was so close and disagreeable' altered into 'a wilderness of views' (No. 1134). *In Observations on Modern Gardening* Whately finds Woburn too 'licentious' (180): 'the parterre has been rifled for the embellishment of the fields' (179). Although Southcote had committed himself unequivocally to picturesque principles of gardening, Whately declared 'the simplicity of a farm is wanting; that idea is lost in such a profusion of ornament; a rusticity of character cannot be preserved amidst all the elegant decorations which may be lavished on a

[39] Kent designed Southcote's house at Woburn Farm, and 'possibly' a garden temple. See Colvin, p. 345; and John Harris, 'A William Kent Discovery, Designs for Esher Place, Surrey', *Country Life*, 125 (14 May 1959), 1077. On the relations of Southcote and Kent, see Spence, Nos. 603, 1128, 1130, 1139.

garden' (180–2). It was William Shenstone's achievement to perfect the integration of garden and farm at the Leasowes.[40]

V. THE LEASOWES, WORCESTERSHIRE

In 1749 Henrietta Knight, Lady Luxborough, wrote a letter to William Shenstone containing some spiteful remarks about Pope and a compliment on the Leasowes:

> Pope would have died many years ago, had he been obliged to refrain from satire, the sole delight of his little peevish temper. How happy was he to meet with a Timon at his villa! The world furnishes many: but those who would find one, must not seek him at the Leasowes.[41]

She was unaware, and it is still not appreciated, how much Shenstone and the Leasowes owed to Pope. It is possible that they were acquainted during the early stages of the Leasowes's development. Shenstone's theory and practice of gardening derive directly from Pope's; the Leasowes was inspired by Pope's principles of garden design.

It has been clearly established that Shenstone had begun the design of the Leasowes (plate 51) during Pope's lifetime, which makes the possibility of their acquaintance a matter of some consequence. The facts are that he came into his estate, near Halesowen, Worcestershire, next to Hagley, in 1735, leased it to his cousins while he lived in the neighbourhood at Harborough until 1739, when he boarded with his tenants at the Leasowes and took the estate into his own hands in 1743. At the time he wrote: 'I am taking part of my farm upon my hands, to see if I can succeed as a farmer.'[42] The year before he complained he did not have the money 'to exhibit my own designs: It is what I can now do in no other method than on paper' (41). But Richard Graves states that Shenstone had begun improving the Leasowes as early as 1739:

[40] For visitors' remarks on Woburn, see Thomas Gray to Thomas Warton (13 Aug. 1754). *Correspondence of Thomas Gray*, ed. Paget Toynbee and Leonard Whibley, 3 vols. (Oxford, 1935), i. 403–4. Robert Dodsley, *Public Virtue* (1753), Book I, Canto II. William Mason, *The English Garden*, ed. William Burgh (1783), pp. 23–4. Mason states (p. 211 n.) that Southcote was 'the introducer, or rather the inventor of the *Ferme Ornée*; for it may be presumed, that nothing more than the term is of French extraction'.

[41] *Letters . . . by Lady Luxborough to William Shenstone* (London, 1775), pp. 158–9.

[42] *Letters of William Shenstone*, ed. Duncan Mallam (Minneapolis, 1939), pp. 70, xviii. Hereafter cited in the text.

> He had already, on his first coming to board with his tenant at the Leasowes, cut a straight walk through his wood, terminated by a small building of rough stone; and in a sort of gravel or marle-pit, in the corner of a field . . . scooped out a sort of cave, stuck a little cross of wood over the door, and called it an hermitage.

Graves says that at this point there was 'no conception of an whole . . . on any consistent plan . . . giving it its present beautiful and picturesque appearance', but by 1743 Shenstone gave a summary of his numerous works, poetic and horticultural, in a letter to Richard Jago: 'My wood grows excessively pleasant . . . I have an alcove, six elegies, a seat, two epitaphs (one upon myself), three ballads, four songs, and a serpentine river, to shew you when you come . . . I am raising a green house' (51). He was beginning to take jealous notice of Hagley's improvements, to discuss gardening and improvements with his correspondents, and to exclaim about the rural delights of his situation.[43]

It is at least possible that Pope may have been on the scene at the Leasowes at this critical stage of its development. There are cryptic references to Pope in Shenstone's correspondence and poetry at this time: in 1736 a puzzling reference 'to my Pleasure . . . as Pope is in the Country' (4), which may indicate reading, correspondence, or conversation; references in 1740 and 1742 (12, 44) to Pope's literary opinions might derive from conversation, or from hearsay through mutual friends, including Dodsley, Graves, Ralph Allen, or George Lyttelton.[44] Indeed the most likely link between Pope and Shenstone is Shenstone's neighbour and patron, George Lyttelton, who visited the Leasowes in 1736, to whom Shenstone dedicated his first published poem, *The Judgement of Hercules* (1741), containing a flattering allusion to Pope.[45] *Elegy VIII, Written after the Death of Mr. Pope* (1745) describes 'Twitnam's widow'd bow'r' and the effect of Pope's fame on Shenstone's 'early love of poetry and its consequences' (i. 31–2). *Elegy XXIII* and *A Pastoral Ode to Sir*

[43] Richard Graves, *Recollections of Some Particulars in the Life of the Late William Shenstone* (London, 1788), pp. 50–1. For references to Hagley, gardening, and landscape, see *Letters*, pp. 52, 54, 56, 66.

[44] Shenstone visited London several times in the early 1740s, when he could have visited Twickenham. See *Letters*, p. 47 n.

[45] 'Prais'd by that Bard [Pope] whom ev'ry Muse inspires', alludes to Pope's compliments to Lyttelton in the *Imitations of Horace*. See n. 17 above. *The Judgement of Hercules, A Poem Inscrib'd to George Lyttelton, Esq.* (London, 1741), in Shenstone's *Works* (1768–9), i. 234. Hereafter cited in the text.

Richard Lyttelton, in which Pope is personified as 'Pollio', contain further tributes to Pope's friendship with Lyttelton, and his admiration for Hagley (i. 96, 173). The evidence is inconclusive, but it is enough to suggest the possibility that Shenstone met Pope through Lyttelton, perhaps during Pope's visit to Hagley in 1739.

Although it remains uncertain whether Pope met Shenstone or visited the Leasowes, there is no doubt whatever that Shenstone's theory of garden design is closely related to Pope's. Shenstone's *Unconnected Thoughts on Gardening*, a collection of notes on his theory and practice written in 1759, published posthumously (1765) can be fairly described as a paraphrase of Pope's principles as we have them in the *Epistle to Burlington* and in Spence. Shenstone attempts to link his ideas on garden design to the aesthetics of Addison, Hutchinson, and Burke, but the subject of his *Unconnected Thoughts* is 'landskip, or picturesque-gardening' (ii. 111), and his principles derive from Pope's statement that 'all gardening is landscape painting', as Spence noted in the margin of his anecdotes after he visited the Leasowes in 1758: 'Shenstone *therefore* calls it landscape-gardening' (No. 606, italics mine). Shenstone advocates the composition of a succession of varied scenes in the garden 'to form a picture' (ii. 121). He explains 'the art of distancing and approximating' (ii. 124); he recommends Pope's principles of surprise (ii. 128), variety (ii. 112), and genius of the place (ii. 113), which Shenstone conceives of in emotional as well as aesthetic terms: 'whether it be the grand, the savage, the sprightly, the melancholy, the horrid, or the beautiful' (ii. 113). Finally, Shenstone, like Pope, urges the gardener to cultivate the historical and poetic associations of the garden in disposition of ornament and architecture including 'ruinated structures' (ii. 117).[46]

The numerous accounts of the Leasowes, which became by mid-century

[46] Shenstone takes exception to one of Pope's 'rules' of gardening in the *Epistle to Burlington*, when he examines in *Unconnected Thoughts* 'what may be said in favour of that regularity which Mr. Pope exposes':

'No mere slope from one side to the other can be agreeable ground: The eye requires a balance—i.e. a degree of uniformity; but this may be otherwise effected, and the rule should be understood with some limitation.

—Each alley has its brother,
And half the platform just reflects the other.' (ii. 118)

But this is a quibble. Shenstone is in essential agreement with Pope about picturesque principles of design.

the most famous garden of its time, show how Shenstone applied Pope's principles of gardening in practice. Shenstone's layout, which Whately describes as 'literally a grazing farm lying round the house; and a walk as unaffected and as unadorned as a common field path' (162), naturalized and simplified the belt as used at Stowe and Woburn Farm. Dodsley's *Description of the Leasowes* (1765) shows how Shenstone applied the principles of picturesque design to compose distinguishable scenes including distinct foreground, background, and middle grounds, suitably varied with 'inanimates' (ii. 202), presented to view from seats like one on the summit of a hill 'divided . . . into several co[m]partments, each answering to the octagonal seat in the center, to each of which is allotted a competent number of striking objects to make a complete picture' (ii. 301). Dodsley illustrates Shenstone's skill in planning the walks and views according to the principle in *Unconnected Thoughts* that 'when a building, or other object, has been once viewed from its proper point, the foot should never travel to it by the same path, which the eye has travelled over before' (ii. 116). He testifies to Shenstone's virtuosity in catching 'the eye . . . at intervals' (ii. 295) with objects like the Halesowen steeple or the ruined priory, in a word, to his mastery of the picturesque principles of gardening.

Shenstone shows himself indebted to Pope not only in his application of picturesque principles of gardening, but in his use of what Dodsley calls his 'spells' and 'powerful incantations' (ii. 329)—inscriptions on urns, seats, trees, and alcoves dedicated to his friends. Shenstone was evoking in the gardens of the Leasowes the same mood Pope had cultivated at Twickenham. He inscribed a line from Pope's *Eloisa to Abelard* on a bench, and the surrounding scene imitated the melancholy of Paraclete landscape. An urn on Shenstone's 'Lover's Walk' commemorating his cousin, Maria Dolman (d. 1753), bore an inscription much admired by Landor, which derives from Pope's lines on his mother inscribed on the obelisk in his garden at Twickenham (ii. 307).[47] In a letter to Richard Graves (1759) Shenstone comments revealingly on the inscription he was considering for the reverse of this urn:

Now you speak of *our* Arcadia's, pray did you ever see a print or drawing of Poussin's Arcadia? The *idea* of it is so very pleasing to me, that I had no peace till I had used the

[47] A. R. Humphreys, *William Shenstone* (Cambridge, 1937), p. 101.

inscription on one side of Miss Dolman's urn, 'Et in Arcadia Ego'. Mr. Anson has the two shepherds with the monument and inscription in alto relievo at Shugborough [Staffordshire]. Mr. Dodsley will borrow me a drawing of it from Mr. Spence. See it described, Vol. I, page 53 of the Abbe du Bos, 'sur la poesie et la peinture'. (375)

Shenstone's interpretation of Poussin's picture is 'elegiac', as Panofsky describes it, and the inscription associates his garden with Virgil's elegiacal conception of Arcadia.[48]

In his earliest and 'best Scene' (234), Virgil's Grove, which Shenstone laid out during the 1740s, he achieved his most perfect expression of the mood of elegiac melancholy he had inherited from Pope and Twickenham. Dodsley describes the 'beautiful, gloomy scene' (ii. 313) of woods and water designed to evoke the kind of reverie Pope enjoyed at Sherborne, featuring a serpentine stream with 'two little islands', a bridge of one arch, a cascade of natural rock, a grotto with a chalybeate spring (inscribed with lines from Virgil Shenstone considered the definition of a grotto), an obelisk to the memory of Virgil, and a seat dedicated to Thomson (ii. 313–18). As A. R. Humphreys has pointed out, Virgil's Grove was designed to evoke 'the mood of the ancient desiderium, the longing for what has irrecoverably departed'.[49]

Gardening is a dominant theme in Shenstone's poetry, and he shows himself indebted to Pope in much the same way as his garden is indebted to Twickenham. His struggle to free himself from the toils of Pope's poetic influence is dramatized in *Elegy VIII*, but despite his determined efforts to write in a new idiom (blank verse elegies), and his vehement opposition to heroic couplets—'I hate a style, as I do a garden, that is wholly flat and regular, that slides along like an eel, and never rises to what one can call an inequality' (ii. 158)—Pope remained an important influence on his poetry.

Shenstone's ideal of magnificence on the model of the classical villa in opposition to the ostentation of the great house is derived from Pope's *Epistle to Burlington*, but Shenstone has changed the models. In the *Judgement*

[48] Erwin Panofsky, '*Et in Arcadia Ego*: Poussin and the Elegiac Tradition', in *Meaning and the Visual Arts* (1957), pp. 300–1, 312–13.

[49] References to improvements in Virgil's Grove, his 'best Scene', appear in Shenstone's correspondence between 1740 and 1747. See *Letters*, ed. Mallam, pp. 13, 41, 51, 83, 174, 225, 234. To Dodsley's description, cf. Thomas Whately, *Observations on Modern Gardening*, pp. 167–9. See A. R. Humphreys, *William Shenstone*, p. 101.

of Hercules (1741), the 'pride of Stowe' is contrasted to the 'sweets of Hagley' (i. 233).[50] Burlington's Chiswick figures in *Oeconomy, A Rhapsody, Addressed to Young Poets* as a warning against profusion and extravagance:

> Let never bard consult Palladio's rules;
> Let never bard, O Burlington! survey
> Thy learned art, in Chiswick's dome display'd;
> Dangerous incentive! nor with ling'ring eye
> Survey the window Venice calls her own. (i. 288)

In the same poem the character Florelio illustrates the theme of cursed profusion derived from Pope's *Epistle to Burlington*. Everywhere Shenstone describes the Leasowes in terms of the Horatian ideal of virtuous retirement Pope had associated with Twickenham:

> What tho' my roofs devoid of pomp arise,
> Nor tempt the proud to quit his destin'd way?
> Nor costly art my flow'ry dales disguise,
> Where only simple friendship deigns to stray? (i. 83)

Shenstone shows himself most truly the heir of Pope in his conviction that gardening is an expression of a poetic sensibility. His contemporaries regarded the Leasowes as 'a perfect picture of his mind', which raised 'doubt, whether the spot inspired his verse; or whether, in the scenes which he formed, he only realized the pastoral images which abound in his songs'.[51] His sense of the 'intimate relation of poetic and horticultural inspiration'[52] underlies his rebuke to the Muses for forsaking the Leasowes in *Elegy XX* (1745) and *An Irregular Ode, After Sickness* (1749; i. 45, 138). In *Elegy XXIII* he celebrates the change at Hagley from a scene of Saxon regicide to the retreat of poets and the civilized arts of gardening:

> But now, nor shaggy hill, nor pathless plain,
> Forms the lone refuge of the silvan game;

[50] In the *Letters* (p. 460) Shenstone describes his rivalry with Hagley, and the attempt to 'keep my place [The Leasowes] in countenance, so near the pompous piles of Hagley', in terms that recall Peterborough's description of Bevis Mount in relation to the greater houses of Houghton and Blenheim: 'there are few fashionable visitants that do not shew an affection for the little Amoret [The Leasowes], as much as they admire the stately Sacharissa [Hagley]'. See n. 10 above.

[51] Thomas Whately, *Observations on Modern Gardening*, p. 162.

[52] A. R. Humphreys, *William Shenstone*, p. 24.

> Since Lyttelton has crown'd the sweet domain
> With softer pleasures, and with fairer fame.
> Where the rough bowman urg'd his headlong steed,
> Immortal bards, a polish'd race, retire;
> And where hoarse scream'd the strepent horn, succeed
> The melting graces of no vulgar lyre. (i. 95)

'Freedom's hand attires the plain' (i. 96), and now the shades of Thomson and Pope haunt its groves:

> Here Pope!—ah never must that tow'ring mind
> To his lov'd haunts, or dearer friend, return!
> What art! what friendships! oh! what fame resign'd!
> —In yonder glade I trace his [Pope's] mournful urn. (i. 96)

Shenstone makes the interesting statement in a letter to Henrietta Knight (1749) that limitations of human perception justify improvements in gardening: 'It is, I think, owing to the limited Faculties of Men that there is any *need* of Taste, to make alterations in our *Environs*' (143). In his defence of landscape gardening, *Rural Elegance, An Ode* (1750), Shenstone argues that taste is the product of a poetic sensibility, the product of a mind (i. 113, 115) which 'appropriates all we see' in landscape:

> And oh; the transport, most ally'd to song,
> In some fair villa's peaceful bound,
> To catch soft hints from nature's tongue,
> And bid ARCADIA bloom around. (i. 116)

In these convictions Shenstone was the heir of Pope, and his garden, The Leasowes, a lineal descendant of Twickenham.

III. *Stourhead, Wiltshire: Synthesis of Poetic and Picturesque Garden Design*

Stourhead figures in this account not primarily because of Pope's personal contribution to its design (although he made a significant one), but more importantly as a mid-century summary and culmination of the possibilities of landscape-garden art we have been tracing here. Laid out between 1740 and 1760 by Henry Hoare of the London banking family, Stourhead conforms to the architectural ideal of the classical villa, and its landscape is a synthesis of garden, park, and farm, classical and Gothic ornament, literary and pictorial inspiration, public and autobiographical statement. It is important too because the gardens can be seen today essentially unaltered since he eighteenth century, exemplifying the work of an amateur designer unassisted by a professional landscape architect, whose achievement was admired by contemporaries like Shenstone, Lyttelton, and Walpole.[53]

Pope's association with Stourhead may be seen as part of the decisive influence of the Palladian movement and the Burlington circle. Henry Hoare (1677–1725) was related to William Benson, a significant figure in the Inigo Jones and Palladian revivals, and about 1718 he commissioned from Colen Campbell one of his earliest Palladian villas. His son, also Henry Hoare (1705–85), undertook some improvements before he inherited the estate in 1741, and soon afterwards began to lay out his unique lake-centred garden, surrounded by a belt connecting buildings designed by Burlington's architect, Henry Flitcroft, including a Temple of Ceres (1745) and a grotto (completed 1748) at the springs of the river Stour for which the place is named.[54]

The grotto contains the statue of a sleeping nymph with Pope's translation of the pseudo-classical Latin inscription, slightly altered from the version he had intended for his own grotto at Twickenham:

> Nymph of the Grot, these sacred Springs I keep,
> And to the Murmur of these Waters sleep;
> Ah spare my Slumbers, gently tread the Cave!
> And drink in silence, or in silence lave!

Norman Ault admits the possibility that 'these lines were obtained more or less directly from Pope at quite an early date', a conjecture supported by the business dealings of the Burlington circle, including Pope, with Hoare's

[53] In 1765 Horace Walpole called it 'one of the most picturesque scenes in the World'. *Visits to Country Seats*, Walpole Society, 16 (1927–8), 43–4.

[54] See Kenneth Woodbridge, 'The Making of Stourhead: Henry Hoare's Paradise', *The Art Bulletin*, 47 (Mar. 1965), 86, 88, 90, 96. John Summerson identifies Stourhead as one of the prototypes of the Anglo-Palladian villa in 'The Classical Country House', *Journal of the Royal Society of Arts*, 107 (July 1959), 571–2. Hoare's plantations in the garden can be dated as early as 1733. See Kenneth Woodbridge, *Landscape and Antiquity, Aspects of English Culture at Stourhead 1718 to 1838* (Oxford, 1970), pp. 26–7, 42–3. For the temples of Ceres (later Flora), and the grotto, see Woodbridge, 'The Making of Stourhead', pp. 92–3, 96, 99, and *Landscape and Antiquity*, pp. 27–9.

bank, and Pope's visits to Amesbury and Tottenham in the neighbourhood as late as 1743 when the project was in hand. The Stourhead grotto, which Walpole admired in his *History of Gardening* as 'the most judiciously, indeed most fortunately placed grotto', appears to have been modelled on Pope's. Like his, it was a subterranean passage, conceived as a nymphaeum, containing the antique statue and inscription Pope had prescribed for his own. Kenneth Woodbridge attributes the original architectural design to Henry Flitcroft. It was 'a circular domed chamber with equal arms and pedmented arches, an essentially classical building' closely resembling Pope's, and Pococke's description (1754) indicates that its original ornament was similar to Pope's grotto as it emerged from his improvements in the early 1740s.[55]

The significance of Pope's contribution to the grotto can be illuminated by the origins of the inscription he supplied. The probable source of the Latin text he translated, and of the statue modelled for Stourhead by John Cheere, was an engraving of a fountain with statue and inscription (plate 52) in a Roman Renaissance garden, illustrated in Bernard de Montfaucon's *Antiquité Expliquée* (1719), translated into English in 1721. According to Otto Kurz 'the fountain is typical' of the Renaissance attempt 'to re-create works of classical antiquity known only from literature'. Its continuing appeal over a period of three centuries derives from a reverence for classical monuments and the harmonious combination of statue and inscription. Kurz explains that such fountains are 'more than garden ornaments':

> A solemn, one might almost say religious, mood makes itself felt. True, a certain playfulness and antiquarian learning proudly displayed are always present, but at the same time something of the awe surrounding pagan sanctuaries of the nymphs has been preserved. *Nullus enim fons non sacer.*[56]

[55] On Pope's inscription at Stourhead, see *TE* vi. 248, and *Correspondence*, ii. 297. For Norman Ault's comment on the provenance, see *TE* vi. 249 n. Pope visited Amesbury, Wiltshire, in 1743: *Correspondence*, iv. 472. For Horace Walpole on the Stourhead grotto, see *History of Gardening*, p. 32. On the architecture of the Stourhead grotto, see Kenneth Woodbridge, 'The Making of Stourhead', 96. Edward Malins's statement (*English Landscaping and Literature*, p. 52), that the grotto at Stourhead 'is not a grotto like Pope's', overlooks Pococke's testimony (*Travels*, ii. 43), about the original ornament, and the predominance of spar and crystal in Pope's.

[56] See Kenneth Woodbridge, *Landscape and Antiquity*, p. 2. Bernard de Montfaucon, *L'Antiquité Expliqué* (Paris, 1719), 1/2, p. 173, pl. 220. Otto Kurz, 'Huius Nympha Loci', *Journal of the Warburg and Courtauld Institute*, 16 (1953), 174.

This perfectly characterizes Pope's awareness of the numinous implications of his garden and grotto at Twickenham, and the mood of what has well been called the 'sacred landscape' at Stourhead, which, like the fountain itself, was the product of a combination of poetical and pictorial inspiration.

Sacred landscape has been defined as 'an appropriate setting for religious buildings', and it has been suggested that the younger Pliny's description of the source of the river Clitumnus (*Letters*, VIII, 8) may have inspired Hoare's garden design. Pliny's description of 'a holy temple of great antiquity in which is a standing image of the god Clitumnus', and of shrines, temples, statuary, and inscriptions 'picturesquely situated along the river bank' ornamented with a bridge, corresponds remarkably to the earliest features of Hoare's design at the springs of the Stour. The Temple of Ceres, containing a River God in a niche below a Doric portico, was connected by a bridge to the grotto, which was later adorned with the River God's statue. In subsequent development of Stourhead it is clear from the architecture, statuary, and inscriptions which Hoare placed in a planned sequence along the walk surrounding his lake that he conceived of his garden as 'an allegory of Aeneas' journey'. He consciously associated it with the landscape of the underworld and Lake Avernus in Book VI of the *Aeneid*, and with the River Tiber and its associations with the founding of Rome in Book VIII.[57]

Paintings of Claude and his English imitators, John Wootten and Richard Wilson, whom Hoare collected, particularly the series depicting scenes from the *Aeneid*, include architectural features reminiscent of Stourhead. This indicates that pictorial was as important as literary inspiration in the gardens of Stourhead. Paintings may have inspired Hoare's lake-centred design, influenced his choice and spatial interrelationships of architectural features (Temple of Flora, Pantheon [plate 53] Palladian bridge, and temple of Apollo), and probably coloured the atmosphere of the Virgilian landscape.[58]

[57] See Kenneth Woodbridge, 'The Sacred Landscape: Painters and the Lake-garden of Stourhead', *Apollo*, 88 (Sept. 1968), 210–11. See *The Letters of the Younger Pliny*, trans. Betty Radice (Harmondsworth, 1963), viii. 216–17. On the allegory and iconography of the Stourhead garden, see Kenneth Woodbridge, *Landscape and Antiquity*, p. 35, 'The Making of Stourhead', 97–9, and Edward Malins, *English Landscaping and Literature*, pp. 53–5.

[58] See Kenneth Woodbridge, *Landscape and Antiquity*, pp. 31–5; 'The Making of Stourhead', 94–8; and 'The Sacred Landscape', pp. 210, 212.

There is no doubt that Hoare believed with Pope that the principles of plantation are derived from the art of painting. Spence records Hoare's remark that

> The green should be ranged together in large masses as the shades are in painting: to contrast the *dark* masses with *light* ones, and to relieve each dark mass itself with little sprinklings of lighter greens here and there. (No. 1105)

Hoare knew the *Epistle to Burlington* well enough to quote when pointing a moral in a letter to his son, or recommending Capability Brown in 1764 to his son-in-law, Lord Bruce of Tottenham Park, Wiltshire:

> He [Brown] has undoubtedly the best taste of anybody for improving nature by what I have seen of His works, *He paints as He plants* [*Epistle to Burlington*, l. 64]; I doubt not that He will remove the Damps & the too great regularity of your Garden far better to be turned into a park.

He shows his sensibility for the picturesque in a description (1762) of the view across the lake at Stourhead framed by a jagged opening in the grotto, through which is seen the village of Stourton, the country church, and the Palladian Bridge he had recently constructed:

> It [the Bridge] is simple & plain. I took it from Palladios Bridge at Vicenza, 5 arches, & when you stand at The Pantheon the Water will be seen thro the Arches & it will look as if the River came down thro the Village & that this was the Village Bridge for publick use; the View of the Bridge, Village & church altogether will be Charmg Gaspd [Gaspar Dughet, the 17th-century French landscape painter] picture at the end of that Water.

In 1768 the elaborate Gothic cross from Bristol Cathedral which the citizens of Bristol had petitioned to remove in 1733 as a 'superstitious relick' of Popery, was re-erected at Stourhead to form part of the prospect just described. Small stone niches in its intricate canopy contained statues of English Kings from John to Charles I. Three miles north-west of the house on Kinsettle Hill in 1772 a triangular brick structure designed by Flitcroft, Alfred's Tower, was erected on the site where the Danish invaders were said to have been repelled in 878. Thus Hoare consulted the Gothic as well as the classical genius of the place.[59]

[59] On Hoare's quotations of Pope, see Kenneth Woodbridge, 'The Making of Stourhead', p. 102, and *Landscape and Antiquity*, p. 51. Hoare's description of the view from the grotto is quoted by Woodbridge,

Kenneth Woodbridge describes Henry Hoare's gardening at Stourhead as a 'symbol-making activity, giving outward form to inward states' by means of a complex iconography. Pliny and Virgil provided the *ethos* of a sacred landscape in which Hoare could associate his own ambition for establishing his family in a country seat with the heroic story of Aeneas' founding of the city of Rome. Woodbridge suggests that the garden became the vehicle for Hoare's expressions of deeper emotions, of bereavement, compensation for loss, and possibly 'manic' states of the subconscious mind. A Jungian reading of the eighteenth-century landscape garden of a London banker may seem far-fetched, but there is no doubt, as Ronald Paulson says, that by mid-century the English landscape garden had become 'as allusive a structure as the poem'. Derived from the sensibility of poets, coloured by the imagination of painters, it was what has well been called a 'landscape of introspection', which afforded the consolations of philosophy and the pleasures of imagination to its designer.[60]

'The Making of Stourhead', 109. For the Bristol Cross, see Woodbridge, *Landscape and Antiquity*, pp. 58–9, and Christopher Hussey, *English Gardens and Landscapes*, p. 161. For Alfred's Tower, see Woodbridge, 'The Making of Stourhead', pp. 110–11, *Landscape and Antiquity*, pp. 65–6, and Hussey, *English Gardens and Landscapes*, p. 164.

[60] See Kenneth Woodbridge, 'The Making of Stourhead', 108, 99; Ronald Paulson, 'Hogarth and the English Garden: Visual and Verbal Structures', in *Encounters, Essays on Literature and the Visual Arts*, ed. John Dixon Hunt (London, 1971), p. 88; 'The Landscape of Introspection' is John Dixon Hunt's title for a B.B.C. radio broadcast, 'Some thoughts on the developing use of landscapes as metaphors for states of mind in the poetry of the eighteenth century', *Radio Times* (7 Mar. 1968).

Part III. Architecture

10. *Garden Architecture*

THE well-known satirical engraving, 'Taste' (plate 54), until recently attributed to Hogarth, and an unpublished sketch of Pope in his Twickenham grotto (plate 55), illustrate two apparently inconsistent aspects of his taste in architecture.[1] The first, which shows him whitewashing the classical orders of the gate of Burlington House, Piccadilly, identifies him as the reckless apologist for the Palladian revival. The picture of the poet seated in the central chamber of his grotto signifies a devotion to aesthetic principles antithetical to Burlington's uncompromising classicism: a taste for variety, irregularity, for the rustic and the ruinous in architecture, ideas which can be associated with a countervailing movement in contemporary architecture, the Gothic revival, or more precisely as Kenneth Clark reminds us, the Gothic 'survival'.[2] The differences seem irreconcilable between aesthetic norms of regularity and irregularity, between architecture associated with a distinct academic style, and an architecture of mood and association, of national opposed to personal taste, architecture of the house and architecture of the garden. But a third picture of the river front of Pope's Twickenham villa,[3]

[1] Ronald Paulson, No. 277, 'Taste or Burlington Gate' (Jan. 1731/2), plate 321, among 'Prints Questionably Attributed to Hogarth' in *Hogarth's Graphic Works*, 2nd edn. rev. (New Haven, Conn., 1970), i. 299–300, 328. Wimsatt 15 and 16, 'Drawings of Pope in his Grotto, by William Kent?', *Portraits*, pp. 122–5. On 'Taste' see Wimsatt, *Portraits*, pp. 115–19; F. G. Stephens and E. Hawkins, *Catalogue of Prints and Drawings in the British Museum*, Division I, *Political and Personal Satires* (London: British Museum, 1873), 2. 603–5 (No. 1742); F. Saxl and R. Wittkower, 'Lord Burlington's Literary Propaganda', *British Art and the Mediterranean* (1948; rpt. London, 1969), sec. 53; Frank Jenkins, *Architect and Patron* (London, 1961), p. 78; and Kathleen Mahaffey, 'Timon's Villa: Walpole's Houghton', *Texas Studies in Language and Literature* 9 (Summer, 1967), 218.

[2] 'The Survival of Gothic', chap. 1 of Kenneth Clark's *The Gothic Revival: An Essay in the History of Taste* (1928; rpt. Harmondsworth, 1964), pp. 1–16.

[3] An Exact Draught and View of Mr. Pope's House at Twickenham. Peter Andreas (?) Rysbrack *delin.* & *pinx.* Nathanial (?) Parr *sculp.* See Mack, pl. 45, Notes, pp. 307–9.

which shows the arched entrance to the grotto surmounted by the classical portico and façade which Burlington approved, suggests that in the mind of the designer these extremes of regularity and irregularity in architecture were by no means incompatible. The study of Pope's taste in Gothic and Palladian architecture does not lead to the conclusion that it is inconsistent, but that it rests on foundations which transcend differences of style.

Kenneth Clark makes the point that throughout the eighteenth century literary appreciation of Gothic influenced taste in architecture, and cites Pope's well-known passage in the *Preface to Shakespeare* (1725) as an important early example. Indeed, as early as *Windsor Forest* (1713), one can observe what John Summerson calls 'an emotional and dramatic appreciation of decaying Gothic' in Pope's description of New Forest in the time of William:

> The Fields are ravish'd from th' industrious Swains,
> From Men their Cities, and from Gods their fanes:
> The levell'd Towns with Weeds lie cover'd o'er,
> The hollow Winds thro' naked Temples roar;
> Round broken Columns clasping Ivy twin'd;
> O'er Heaps of Ruin stalk'd the stately Hind;
> The Fox obscene to gaping Tombs retires,
> And savage Howlings fill the sacred Quires. (65–72)

The 'naked Temples' and 'broken Columns' give way to the theatrical Gothic of *Eloisa to Abelard* (1717):

> These moss-grown domes with spiry turrets crown'd,
> Where awful arches make a noon-day night,
> And the dim windows shed a solemn light;
>
> . . .
>
> Where round some mould'ring tow'r pale ivy creeps,
> And low-brow'd rocks hang nodding o'er the deeps.
> (142–4; 243–4)

We have already observed how far Pope's interest in the Gothic goes beyond the literary in his visits to Netley and Beaulieu, and Sherborne Old Castle, where he combines antiquarian curiosity with fascination for picturesque landscape. As early as 1717 he was enjoying the melancholy of Oxford architecture where he surrenders to the associative charms of Gothic. His remark in 1739 on a Gothic Cross at Bristol Cathedral indicates that he had a greater appreciation for Gothic than the citizens of Bristol who petitioned for its removal: 'a very fine Old Cross of Gothic curious work in the middle, but spoild with the folly of new gilding it, that takes away all the Venerable Antiquity' (iv. 205).[4]

It is possible to discover in Pope something more than literary or antiquarian appreciation of Gothic, and to understand the aesthetic and architectural values which the early eighteenth century attached to the vague term Gothic from a close scrutiny of Pope's designs for garden architecture. The Shell Temple and grotto at Twickenham, and Alfred's Hall, a building he designed or helped to design for Lord Bathurst in Oakley Wood, Cirencester, Gloucestershire, are all examples of departures in varying degrees from the classical style, architectural experiments violating classical rules which appear to have flourished in the eighteenth-century landscape garden. All are distinct from the essays of scholarship which proliferated in the landscape garden at the same time.[5] Significantly all of these buildings date from 1718–25, the years when Pope was devising his conception of the landscape garden, when he was describing to Jervas his degradation 'into an Architect' (ii. 23), speaking of the presiding genius of the architect as 'Imagination' (ii. 24), and revelling in the 'luminous days of inspiration' (ii. 14) in drawing designs at Cirencester. Except for the grotto these buildings have not attracted much attention; Pope himself dismisses them as follies, 'bawbles', or 'playthings'. But artifacts which can tell us so much about Pope's taste in architecture, and which are fascinating products of his imagination, cannot be ignored.

i. THE SHELL TEMPLE

The Shell Temple (plate 56), was, as we have seen, an integral part of Pope's picturesque landscape design at Twickenham, terminating the central prospect of the garden, and framing views in several directions. It attracts our attention here as an example of picturesque garden architecture, which can be

[4] See Kenneth Clark, *The Gothic Revival*, p. 21; and E.C. x. 549. John Summerson refers to Pope's sensibility to gothic in *Architecture in Britain 1530–1830*, 5th ed. (Baltimore, 1969), p. 237. On the Bristol Cross, see chap. 9, n. 59.

[5] See Margaret Jourdain, *The Work of William Kent* (London, 1948), p. 49.

interpreted as a version of the Gothic. It was completed in June 1725 when Pope described it in the letter to Edward Blount:

> From the River *Thames*, you see thro' my Arch up a Walk of the Wilderness to a kind of open Temple, wholly compos'd of Shells in the Rustic Manner; and from that distance under the Temple you look down thro' a sloping Arcade of Trees, and see the Sails on the River passing suddenly and vanishing, as thro' a Perspective Glass (ii. 296).

Ten years later his fragile structure had collapsed and he was engaged in 'the Rebuilding of the Temple, which I hope', he tells Fortescue in 1736, 'will in Glory equal the First' (iv. 22). Serle's *Plan* (1745) indicates that Pope's hope was realized, and the description of the rebuilt temple in the *Newcastle General Magazine* (1748) adds significantly to the earlier one just quoted.

> In passing out of the grotto [says the Newcastle correspondent] we enter into a Wilderness, and have in view directly before us a Rotundo, or kind of Temple, entirely compos'd of Shells, and consisting wholly of a Cupola, or Dome, supported upon rustick Columns, so as to leave it open every Way to the surrounding Garden.[6]

Serle's *Plan* shows a peristyle of eight columns described in the explanation as 'The Shell Temple'. An undated drawing in the British Museum described as 'Pope's garden at Twickenham' (once attributed to Pope; now assigned to William Kent; plate 56) pictures a bizarre structure which agrees in every detail with the literary descriptions.[7]

The centre of the composition in Kent's wash drawing is a rib-vaulted dome and cupola, supported on square, splayed, rusticated columns peristyle, with corinthian capitals, the drum, cornice, and dome faced with shells. Kent's drawing of the Shell Temple is in all probability architecturally exact since it is characteristic of Kent's garden sketches to introduce fanciful embellishment—like the rainbow, fountain, tripod, and smoking altar here—into scenes which reproduce topography and architecture with care and accuracy.[8]

[6] See Maynard Mack, *The Garden and the City*, Appendix A, pp. 239–40.

[7] John Serle, *A Plan of Mr. Pope's Garden* (1745), 'Explanation', p. 5; and B.M. 1872–11–9–878, 'A View in Pope's Garden at Twickenham', pen and sepia drawing by William Kent, ca. 1725–30. See Binyon, *Catalogue of Drawings*, iii. 174; and Wimsatt 14, *Portraits*, pp. 119–22.

[8] Cf. Kent's drawing of Esher Place with sea horses and Tritons; John Harris, 'A William Kent Discovery: Designs for Esher Place, Surrey', *Country Life*, 125 (14 May 1959), 1076–8; Hussey, *English Gardens and Landscapes*, p. 47, plate 31. Maynard Mack warns (*TE* x. xiii) that 'it would be rash to rely very far upon its [Kent's drawing] details', but even if it is, as he helpfully suggests (xiv), an illustration of the

Since the drawing cannot be conclusively dated it may represent either the original or the rebuilt Shell Temple; but it seems more likely that it depicts the original Temple, soon after its completion in 1725, when an enthusiastic amateur architect would have been proud to hang in the 'little parlor' of his house 'a Picture of the Shell Temple' in black frame, in all probability the drawing under discussion.[9]

There is no evidence to justify descriptions of the drawing as 'a Projected Design by Kent for Pope's Garden' or 'A drawing by Kent for rebuilding' the Shell Temple. Kent's 'works' in Pope's garden cannot be dated before the late 1730s, and were limited to specific commissions. Besides Pope liked to consider himself a rival of Kent in garden architecture; he made fun of his 'odd thing' at Tottenham, and subjected Kent's Hermitage at Richmond to ridicule in a lost dialogue. It is unlikely, in any event, that he would have approved what Walpole called Kent's 'little miscarriages into total Gothic'. Moreover, Pope's temple resembles none of Kent's known garden designs, either half-Gothic or those 'holding fast', as Pope remarked in another context of Kent, 'by the Pillars of sound antiquity' (iv. 140).[10]

The design of the Shell Temple can confidently be attributed to the poet who was speaking about 1720 of the importance of imagination in architecture, and of his ambitions for building at Twickenham (ii. 23–4). It appears to be related to a project inspired by the contemporary notion that Gothic architecture was derived from avenues of forest trees,[11] which Pope described to Spence about 1728:

'wild Paradise' of Pope's 'Preface' to Homer, Kent's book illustrations frequently reproduce identifiable buildings of Burlington's or his own design. See Burlington's bagnio at Chiswick in John Gay's *Fables*, i (1727), xxiv; and a building resembling Kent's seven-arched portico, Praeneste, at Rousham, Oxfordshire, in the illustrations to Thomas Birch's edition of the *Faerie Queene* (London, 1751). See Jeffrey P. Eichholz, 'William Kent's Career as Literary Illustrator', *Bulletin of the New York Public Library*, 70 (1966), 1642; and Margaret Jourdain, *The Work of William Kent*, p. 73, figs. 106, 108.

[9] 'Inventory', p. 255. The allusions to Homer, motifs suggestive of the book illustrations of the 1720s, like the Rainbow which appears in Kent's illustration to Thomson's *Spring* (1730), and Kent's portrayal of himself as a painter are circumstances favouring the earlier date. See Eichholz, 'William Kent's Career', p. 629.

[10] For confusion of Kent's drawing with a design, see Margaret Jourdain, *The Work of William Kent*, pp. 48, 95, fig. 4; Hussey, *English Gardens and Landscapes*, p. 41. For Pope's ridicule of Kent, see chap. 7, n. 23.

[11] Warburton expounds the forest theory in a note to the *Epistle to Burlington*, l. 29 in Pope's *Works* (1751), iii. 268. See Paul Frankl's discussion of Warburton's 'fantasies . . . on the history of architecture'

I have sometimes had an idea of planting an old Gothic cathedral, or rather some old Roman temple, in trees. Good large poplars, with their white stems, cleared of boughs to a proper height, would serve very well for the columns, and might form the different aisles, or peristiliums, by their different distances and heights. These would look very well near, and the dome, rising all in proper tuft in the middle, would look as well at a distance. (No. 619)

Pope's Shell Temple imitates 'some old Roman Temple' rather than an 'old Gothic cathedral', and it was not built of trees apparently, but the forest theory of Gothic architecture strongly influenced his classical design. In the rustication, the curves of the columns, and the titivation of the cupola, the Roman Temple was modified by 'Gothic' irregularity. Kent's drawing and Pope's description indicate that the Shell Temple was planted in trees in the sense that it was situated in the garden to 'look very well near, and . . . at a distance', and to frame views of the garden in all directions. An interesting contrast to the classical rotundas in the gardens at Chiswick and Stowe constructed at the same time, it corresponds perfectly to the aesthetics of picturesque landscape.

ii. THE GROTTO

It has not been recognized in the small library of comment on Pope's grotto that it is, as much as the Shell Temple, a piece of garden architecture. In his facetious references to his 'laborious Bauble' (iv. 253), his 'Plaything' (iv. 254) Pope invited critics to consider the grotto as a folly, and since Johnson's influential verdict ('vanity produced a grotto where necessity enforced a passage') they have invented terms to describe it as various and bewildering as the inventory of minerals in Serle's *Account*. Recently the significance of the grotto to Pope's poetical imagination has been explored by Maynard Mack, but it remains a riddle to students of his aesthetics, and continues to be a symbol of his artistry so fascinating as to eclipse the garden, and to colour our notions of his poetry.[12] But it is possible to make some sense out of it when the

in *The Gothic: Literary Sources and Interpretations Through Eight Centuries* (Princeton, 1960), pp. 391–2, and Appendix 27, pp. 867–9.

[12] Mack, pp. 41–76. See Nikolaus Pevsner, 'Genesis of the Picturesque', *Architectural Review*, 96 (Nov. 1944), 144; E.C. vi. 384 n.; Grace Haber, 'A. Pope—"imployed in Grottofying"', *Texas Studies in Language and Literature*, 10 (Fall 1968), 386; Bonamy Dobrée, *Alexander Pope* (London, 1951), p. 71; Frederick

grotto is re-examined in the light of new evidence as a work of architecture which Pope considered an integral part of the garden, and which changed significantly in the course of its improvement over a period of almost twenty-five years.

Two phases in the development of Pope's grotto can be discerned: the first culminating in 1725, when Pope gave in a letter to Edward Blount the only extended description by the poet we possess; the second, in the year 1740 when his correspondence shows he was working on a major expansion of his design. The grotto Pope describes in 1725 appears to have been a single chamber (Figure 4, Serle's 'Plan of the Grotto', § 3), in the middle of a 'subterraneous way', with porches at either end, eastwards leading to the river front, westwards to the garden.[13] Pope's letter, as noted above in relation to the garden, is primarily a description of the grotto:

> I have put the last Hand to my works of this kind, in happily finishing the subterraneous Way and Grotto; I there found a Spring of the clearest Water, which falls in a perpetual Rill, that echoes thro' the Cavern day and night. . . . When you shut the Doors of this Grotto, it becomes on the instant, from a luminous Room, a *Camera obscura*; on the Walls of which all the objects of the River, Hills, Woods, and Boats, are forming a moving Picture in their visible Radiations: And when you have a mind to light it up, it affords you a very different Scene: it is finished with Shells interspersed with Pieces of Looking-glass in angular forms; and in the Ceiling is a Star of the same Material, at which when a Lamp (of an orbicular Figure of thin Alabaster) is hung in the Middle, a thousand pointed Rays glitter and are reflected over the Place. There are connected to this Grotto by a narrower Passage two Porches, with Niches and Seats; one toward the River, of smooth Stones, full of light and open; the other toward the Arch of Trees, rough with Shells, Flints, and Iron Ore. The Bottom is paved with simple Pebble, as the adjoining Walk up the Wilderness to the Temple, is to be Cockle-shells, in the natural Taste, agreeing not ill with the dripping Murmur, and the Acquatic

Bracher, 'Pope's Grotto: The Maze of Fancy', *Huntington Library Quarterly*, 21 (Feb. 1949), 141–62, rpt. in Maynard Mack, ed., *Essential Articles for the Study of Alexander Pope* (Hamden, Conn., 1964), pp. 104, 118; Robert Carruthers, *The Life of Alexander Pope* (London, 1858), p. 172; Marie Luise Gothein, *A History of Garden Art* (2 vols., London, 1928), ii. 282; Montague Summers, *The Gothic Quest* (London, 1938), p. 20; George Sherburn, *Early Career*, p. 286; Benjamin Boyce, *The Benevolent Man* (1967), p. 88.

[13] See 'A Plan of the Grotto', and 'An Account of the Materials Which Compose the Grotto', in John Serle, *A Plan of Mr. Pope's Garden* (London, 1745), hereafter cited in the text from the reprint in Mack, Appendix C, pp. 259–62. For discussions of the development of the grotto, see Frederick Bracher, 'The Maze of Fancy', pp. 107–14, and Benjamin Boyce, 'Mr. Pope, in Bath, Improves the Design of his Grotto', in *Restoration and Eighteenth-Century Literature*, ed. Carroll Camden (Chicago, 1963), pp. 143–53.

FIG. 4. A Plan of Pope's Grotto. After Serle. 1745.

51. The Leasowes, Worcestershire. Engraving by D. Jenkins. *c.* 1770.

52. The Nymph of the Grot. 1719.

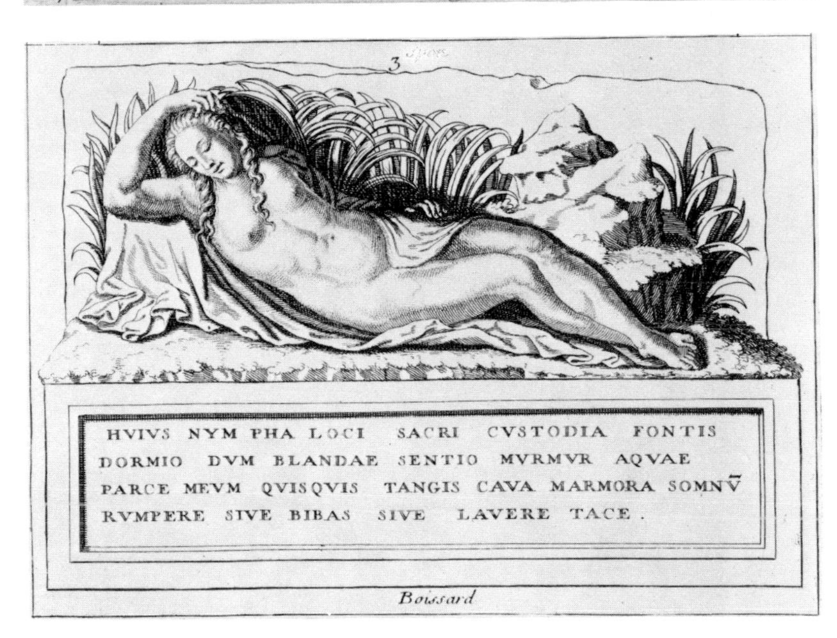

53. View from the Pantheon, Stourhead, Wiltshire. 1765.

56. The Shell Temple in Pope's Garden. By William Kent. *c.* 1725–30.

57. King Alfred's Hall, Cirencester, Gloucestershire. After Thomas Robins. 1763.

Idea of the whole Place. It wants nothing to compleat it but a good Statue with an Inscription, like that beautiful antique one which you know I am so fond of. . . . You'll think I have been very Poetical in this Description, but it is pretty near the Truth. I wish you were here to bear Testimony how little it owes to Art, either the Place itself, or the Image I give of it. (ii. 296–7)

Setting aside for a moment the lamp, looking glass, and *camera obscura*, the idea of the grotto Pope describes is altogether classical. His idea of a grotto, like the gardens he describes in the *Guardian* essay, is derived from poetical descriptions in classical literature: from Homer's grotto of the Naiads in Book XIII of the *Odyssey* and from Virgil's description of the seaside grotto of the Nymphs in Book I of the *Aeneid*. To eighteenth-century landscape gardeners like Pope, and later Shenstone, Virgil's line (*Aeneid* I, 167–8)—'intus acquae dulces, vivoque sedilia saxo, /nympharum domus'—became the definition of a grotto. The 'Acquatic Idea' of Pope's grotto, the 'Spring of clearest Water', and the intended antique statue and inscription—all these things are indicative of the classical nymphaeum. By about 1728 a marble plaque at the garden entrance of the grotto had been inscribed with a line from Horace (*Ep*. I, xviii. 103): '*Secretum iter et fallentis semita vitae*.'[14]

In a letter to Judith Cowper (1722) Pope quoted a line he believed to be hers—'No noise but water, Ever friend to Thought'—to introduce his own lines on 'my Solitude & Grotto' which show how closely he associated his garden and grotto with the classical ideal of retirement.[15] Significantly, Pope's lines on the grotto are in fact a description of the garden. It is evident Pope identified the grotto with the garden, and considered it as much an integral part of the surrounding landscape as the grottoes of Homer and Virgil concealed in coastal landscape.

The 1725 description shows clearly how carefully Pope designed the grotto in relation to the garden: the porch at the eastern end towards the river, 'of smooth Stones, full of light and open', agrees with the measure of formality

[14] For the grottoes in the *Iliad* and *Odyssey*, and a discussion of the 'imaginative affiliation' between Pope's grotto and those described by Homer, see *TE* x. 8–9, and n.; *TE* vii. ccxiv–vi. On the Horatian inscription, see Spence, No. 598, and Mack, p. 111. Two interesting clues to Pope's conception of the grotto are to be found in the tailpiece depicting a subterranean tunnel and walk covered with branches in Sheffield's *Works* (1723), ed. Pope, i. 208; and William Kent's headpiece for Book V of the *Odyssey*, *TE* ix. xiii, pl. 4.

[15] *Correspondence*, ii. 141–2; cf. *TE* vi. 225–7.

of his grass plat, and the genius of the place on the riverside; the porch at the western end, 'rough with Shells, Flints, and Iron Ore' is designed to be compatible with the picturesque irregularity of the garden, to which it leads. Also suggestive of a design calculated to harmonize grotto and garden is the cockle-shell pavement leading to the Shell Temple. Pope's description of the 'Rustic', 'natural Taste' of the ornaments in the grotto corresponds exactly to his concept of garden architecture.

The 1725 letter shows that the grotto is related to the garden in another way than by agreement in conception, decoration, and by picturesque aesthetics of irregularity—that is by its operation as a *camera obscura*. Pope contrived to multiply picturesque effects in his garden 'photographically' in the grotto. He was thus able to enjoy the optical illusions of moving landscape such as Addison had described in the *Spectator* (No. 414), similar to those scenes he described with such skill in the *Odyssey*.[16] Pope's grotto-*camera* may thus be seen to be perfectly adapted in design and function to the classical idea of the *nympheum*, modern optical science, and picturesque aesthetics of the landscape garden.

Pope never abandoned the classical 'idea' of the grotto as he continued to finish and refinish it throughout his lifetime. In 1732 he had 'a Design . . . to make that Basement include a Cold Bath & a fall of Water' (iii. 314). In 1734 he was looking for 'a large Prize of Shells of all sorts' at Calshot Castle in Southampton, probably intended for the grotto.[17] In 1740 the waterworks were being improved (iv. 267) and in 1741 he was planning to add a room (apparently unexecuted) to the wing of the grotto (iv. 352 n.). The Newcastle correspondent was so intrigued by the waterworks in 1747 that he ignored the architecture:

the Stream issuing from the Spring of Water is distributed to a Diversity of Purposes: Here it gurgles in a gushing Rill thro' fractur'd Ores and Flints; there it drips from depending Moss and Shells; here again, washing Beds of Sand and Pebbles, it rolls in

[16] On Addison and the *camera obscura*, see Marjorie Nicolson and George Rousseau, *This Long Disease* (Princeton, 1968), pp. 281–5; and D. F. Bond, ed., *The Spectator*, No. 414 (25 June 1712), iii. 550–1 n.

[17] 'A New Pope Letter', ed. George S. Rousseau, *Philological Quarterly*, 45 (Apr. 1966), 411; and A. J. Sambrook, 'Professor Rousseau on Pope, Another Correction', *Notes & Queries*, 216 (Sept. 1971), 331–2.

Silver Streamlets; and there it rushes out in Jets and Fountains; while the Caverns of the Grot incessantly echo with a soothing Murmur of aquatick Sounds. (239)

He remarks that Pope, in order to 'multiply this Diversity', had placed 'Plates of Looking glass in the obscure Parts of the Roof and Sides of the Cave, where a sufficient Force of Light is wanting to discover the Deception':

> Cast your Eyes upward, and you half shudder to see Cataracts of Water precipitating over your Head, from impending Stones and Rocks, while saliant Spouts rise in rapid Streams at your Feet: Around, you are equally surprized with flowing Rivulets and rolling Waters, that rush over airey Precipices, and break amongst Heaps of ideal Flints and Spar. Thus, by a fine Taste and happy Management of Nature, you are presented with an undistinguishable Mixture of Realities and Imagery. (239)

This carries the 'Acquatic Idea' about as far as it can go, to the point of absurdity it might seem to a modern reader, but the Newcastle correspondent emphasizes Pope's care to conceal his art; and in comparison with the ornate and elaborate grottoes in the Renaissance tradition of the show piece, still popular in Pope's England, Pope's waterworks were naturalistic. His 'watry Cave'[18] must have seemed to Pope as natural as the waterfalls he admired in the gardens of Sherborne in 1724 (ii. 238).

The perfection of the waterworks was incidental to major architectural improvements to the grotto which began in the year 1739/40, and were carried out by the time of Pope's death. Recently plans have come to light which provide substantive evidence about this architectural design, and allow us to compare the grotto as he left it at his death to the 1725 version, and to infer something about its development. Benjamin Boyce has shown that during a visit in 1739/40 to Ralph Allen in Bath, when he began to express an enthusiasm for the 'Scenes of Rocks' (iv. 202) at Clifton, and when it is probable that he visited Allen's quarries at Combe Down,[19] Pope conceived the idea of remodelling his grotto after a mine or quarry. The design thus inspired by geological enthusiasm was executed with the advice and assistance of a geologist, the Reverend William Borlase (1695–1772) of Ludgvan, Cornwall,

[18] A variant reading of 'Verses on a Grotto by the River Thames at Twickenham' (1740), *TE* vi. 382, l. 2, n.

[19] See Benjamin Boyce, 'Pope Improves His Grotto', pp. 144–5, and references to 'Mines' and Allen's 'Quarry' in Pope's *Correspondence*, iv. 227, 230, 239, 247.

kinsman of Pope's Bath physician, Dr. William Oliver, who wrote letters to Borlase in December and January 1739/40 on Pope's behalf asking Borlase for materials and advice. This correspondence gives us the clearest insight we have yet obtained into the nature of Pope's design.

Oliver asked Borlase to supply Pope with minerals, 'three or four Tun, of the finest Spar, Mundick, Copper and Tin Oars, which you shall judge proper for such a work', and invited him to 'add whatever you think will contribute to the Beauty of such a work'. Oliver explained that 'he [Pope] has a mind to make this Passage a beautiful Grotto, adorn'd with all the Several Productions of Nature, which are properly to be found under ground'. Borlase promptly agreed to assist and Oliver in a subsequent letter further specified Pope's intentions: 'If it could be so contrived, he [Pope] could wish to place all the Minerals in their several natural Strata.' 'I suppose', Oliver surmised, 'the Stallactites will be pendulous from the Roof?' Oliver reported that Pope had been much pleased with Borlase's 'letters and proceedings', that he hoped 'a great Improvement of his design from that Taste which he plainly discovers you to be Master of', and 'that you might be fully apprized of the nature of his design, he [Pope] has here given you a Sketch of his Grotto'. The crude ink sketch (fig. 5) which Pope added to the top of Oliver's letter, reproduced by Boyce for the first time, appears to be a rough plan of the Passageway, indicating alterations mainly architectural to the luminous room (Serle's 'Plan of the Grotto', § 3), and the addition of a new room adjacent to it, which was to be constructed by widening the passageway. Borlase played a major role in the execution of this plan: he contributed a large part of the minerals (along with Ralph Allen, he was the principal supplier), and was Pope's authority for the disposition of them.[20]

By the time Borlase's first cargo of minerals had reached Pope at Twickenham (8 March 1740), the geologist had already answered questions Pope had put in the margin of his sketch: '*Quaere* what proper for a natural roof? What for a natural pavement?'[21] He tells Borlase in his acknowledgement that 'the Stalactites are appropriated to the roof, & the Marbles (I think) of various

[20] See the Oliver–Borlase correspondence quoted by Boyce, 'Pope Improves His Grotto', pp. 146–7, pls. I, III; and Thomas Edwards to Richard Owen Cambridge (23 Apr. 1741), quoted by Richard D. Altick, 'Mr. Pope Expands his Grotto', *Philological Quarterly*, 21 (Oct. 1942), 428.

[21] See Benjamin Boyce, 'Pope Improves His Grotto', pl. I.

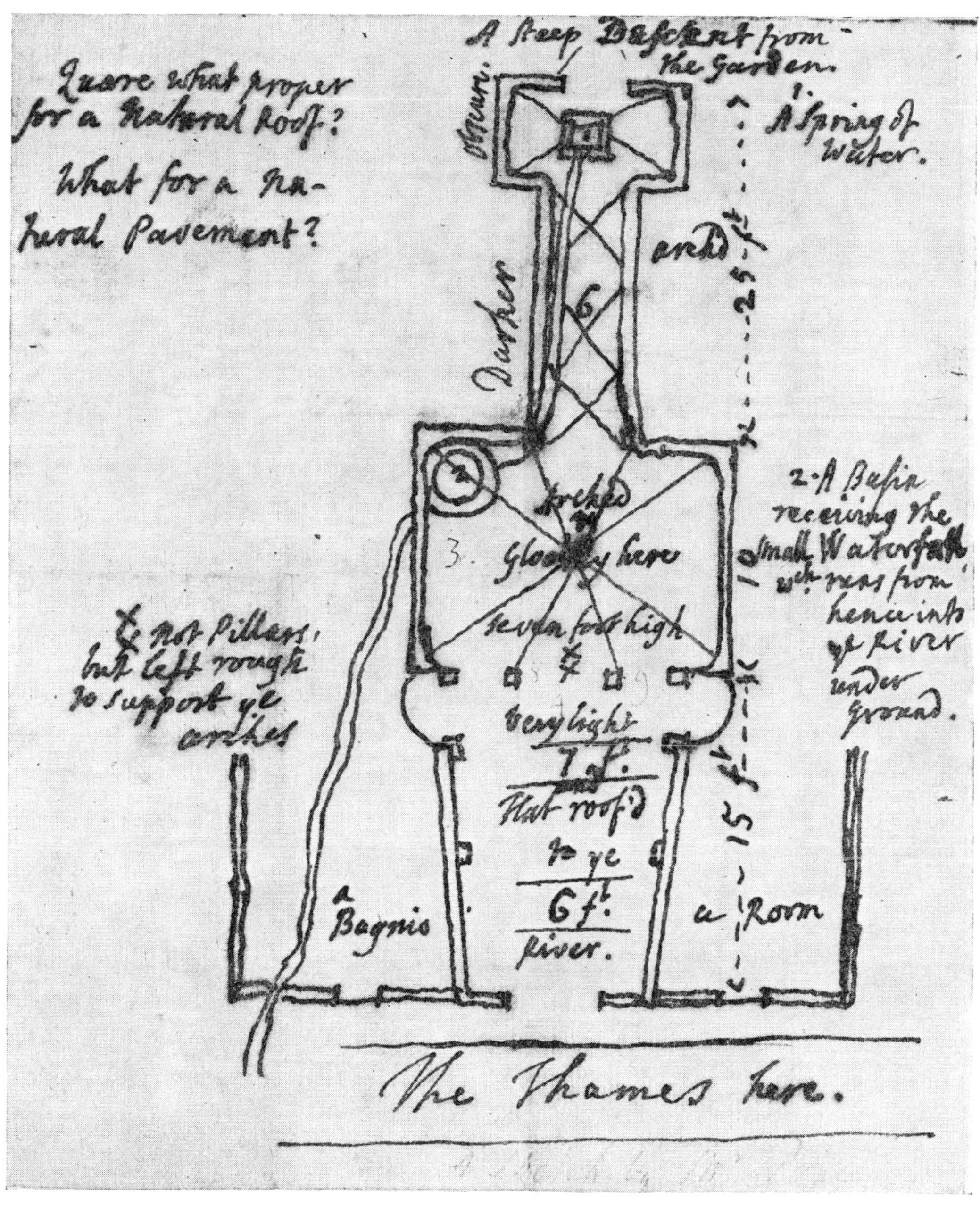

FIG. 5. Pope's Plan of the Twickenham Grotto. 1740.

colours to the pavement' (iv. 229). But he wanted directions about disposition since Borlase's 'Bounty, like that of Nature, confounds all choice':

> It will want nothing to complete it, but Your Instruction as to the Position, and the Direction of the Sparrs & Ores in the Mine, for I would be glad to make the Place resemble Nature in all her workings, & entertain a Sensible, as well as dazzle a Gazing, Spectator. (iv. 228)

It can be inferred from later correspondence that Borlase supplied the necessary instructions and that Pope followed them with great care.

Pope's letter to Borlase of 8 June 1740 when the work was half finished is the fullest description of the grotto during its final stages of development, and it makes an interesting contrast to the earlier account in the letter to Edward Blount. He begins by describing the enlargement of the luminous room (Serle's 'Plan', § 3) according to the sketch mailed to Borlase:

> I have opened the whole into one Room, groin'd above from pillar to pillar (not of a regular Architecture, but like supporters left in a Quarry), by which means there is a fuller Light cast into all but the narrow passage (which is cover'd with living and long Mosse), only behind the 2 largest Pillars there is a deep recess of dark stone, where two Glasses artfully fix'd reflect the Thames, and almost deceive the Eye to that degree as to seem two arches opening to the River on each side, as there is one real in the middle. The little well is very light, ornamented with Stalactites above, and Spars and Cornish Diamonds on the Edges, with a perpetual drip of water into it from pipes above among the Icicles. (iv. 246)

It is obvious that Pope has continued to perfect the picturesque effects of the 1725 design: reflections of light, optical illusions, and waterworks. Indeed, these refinements and improvements carry out intentions Pope had indicated in notes on his sketch, concerning the variation of light in different parts of the grotto and notes on the waterworks, marking a 'Spring', a 'Bagnio', and in the central chamber the little well described on the sketch as 'A Basin receiving the small Waterfall which runs from hence into ye River under Ground'. But an important feature in Pope's architectural design is indicated by the pillars 'not of a regular Architecture, but like supporters left in a Quarry' (iv. 246). Still more clearly the change in design can be seen in Pope's description in the same letter of the refinishing of the grotto.

He had learned from Borlase what constituted a 'Natural Roof', which he had 'managed . . . so as to admit of the larger as well as smaller pendulous [crystals]', and was 'in hopes of some of the Red transparent Spar from the Lead mines, which would vastly vary the colouring' (iv. 246). In placing the minerals Pope carefully followed Borlase's observations, later published in his *Natural History of Cornwall* (1748), on the 'Course of fissures . . . generally east and west in Cornwall'. 'The sides are strata', Pope wrote, 'of various, beautiful, but rude Marbles, between which run the Loads of Metal, East and West, and in the pavement also, the direction of the Grotto happening to lie so' (iv. 246). In the same letter he gives a detailed description of these strata:

> As I procure more Ores or Spars, I go on enriching the Crannies and Interstices, which, as my Marbles are in large pieces, cramp'd fast with iron to the walls, are pretty spacious and unequal, admitting Loads and Veins of 2, 3, or 4 inches broad, and running up and down thro' Roof, Sides, and Pavement. The perpendicular Fissures I generally fill with Spar. (iv. 246)

All that Pope describes here corresponds once again to the account by Borlase in chapter 14 of the *Natural History*, 'Of Lodes, their Properties, Parts, and Inclinations'.[22]

These works in progress were completed by October 1740, when Pope told Oliver he thought that 'the Work is executed in a manner that I think would please' Borlase (iv. 278), and expressed his intention to dedicate parts of the grotto to the geologist. He had contemplated statues to Borlase and Oliver to be placed in the grotto, but he wrote to Ralph Allen, 'I should be prouder of their approbation, if they think I have imitated nature well' (iv. 254). Eventually a marble plaque inscribed in gold letters with Borlase's name was placed over the room Pope dedicated to him (Serle's 'Plan of the Grotto', § 5, known as the Borlase Chamber). Pope's collaboration with Borlase proves that the 'Mine Adventure' of which he spoke frivolously to Allen, comparing it to 'the Adventure of the Bear & Fiddle' (iv. 247), was carried out in a scientific spirit, with the assistance of an authority on natural history. This is what he meant when he said he had 'strictly followed Nature' in the grotto. He carried out meticulously the solemn resolution he made to Oliver after receiving the first cargo of minerals from Borlase: 'The day I receive what

[22] William Borlase, *The Natural History of Cornwall* (Oxford, 1758), pp. 143, 147.

he can send me, I begin my Work, & hope it will be the best Imitation of Nature I ever made. In these sort of works we may pretend to understand her better than in her Animal, much less in her Rational Productions' (iv. 229).[23]

Despite Pope's repeated allusions to finishing his grotto, improvements continued after the *Verses on the Grotto* (1741) were composed to celebrate its completion, and to honour his collaborators. The nature and chronology of these improvements, which may have included substantial additions, cannot now be traced in detail, but from what we can determine about the character of the grotto as he left it, he continued to redevelop the classical nymphaeum as a mine. Our notion of the finished grotto depends almost entirely on John Serle's 'An Account of the Materials Which Compose the Grotto', accompanied by 'A Plan and Perspective View of the grotto', published in *A Plan of Mr. Pope's Garden* (1745). As Doctor Oliver feared, the grotto was practically destroyed after it had fallen into the unphilosophical hands of Sir William Stanhope. Extant sketches are not informative and Serle's 'Perspective View of the Grotto' in the *Plan* 'probably . . . regularizes the prospect'.[24] The eyewitness account of the Newcastle correspondent testifies to the Quarry-like architecture:

> We are presented with many Openings and Cells, which owe their Forms to a Diversity of Pillars and Jambs, ranged after no set Order or Rule, but aptly favouring the particular Designs of the Place: They seem as roughly hew'd out of Rocks and Beds of mineral Strata, discovering in the Fissures and angular Breaches, Variety of Flints, Spar, Ores, Shells, &c. (239)

But Serle's 'Account of the Materials' which has received little attention, must be consulted in order to recover a sense of the aesthetic effect of Pope's grotto.

[23] On the Borlase chamber, see 'William Borlase, St. Aubyn, and Pope: MS. Collections at Castle Horneck, 1720–1772', *Quarterly Review*, 139 (July–Oct. 1875), 384. On Borlase's career, see Marjorie Nicolson and George Rousseau, *This Long Disease*, pp. 261–2. Pope's statement about 'strictly' following nature in the grotto is hearsay from Sir John St. Aubyn, quoted from the Borlase correspondence by Benjamin Boyce, 'Pope Improves His Grotto', 151.

[24] See 'Verses on a Grotto by the River Thames at Twickenham Composed of Marbles, Spars, and Minerals', *TE* vi. 382–3. Pope's references to improvements on the grotto are compiled by Grace Stevenson Haber, 'A. Pope—"imployed in Grottofying"', *Texas Studies in Language and Literature*, 10 (Fall, 1968), 385–403. Oliver's concern for the philosophical fate of the grotto is expressed in a letter to Borlase after Pope's death, 'William Borlase, St. Aubyn, and Pope', *Quarterly Review*, 139 (1875), 385. On the sketches of the grotto, see Boyce, 'Pope Improves His Grotto', p. 153, and Wimsatt 15–16, in *Portraits*, pp. 122–5.

58. Pope's Villa. Engraving by T. Smith. 1748.

59. Chiswick House. By George Lambert(?). 1742.

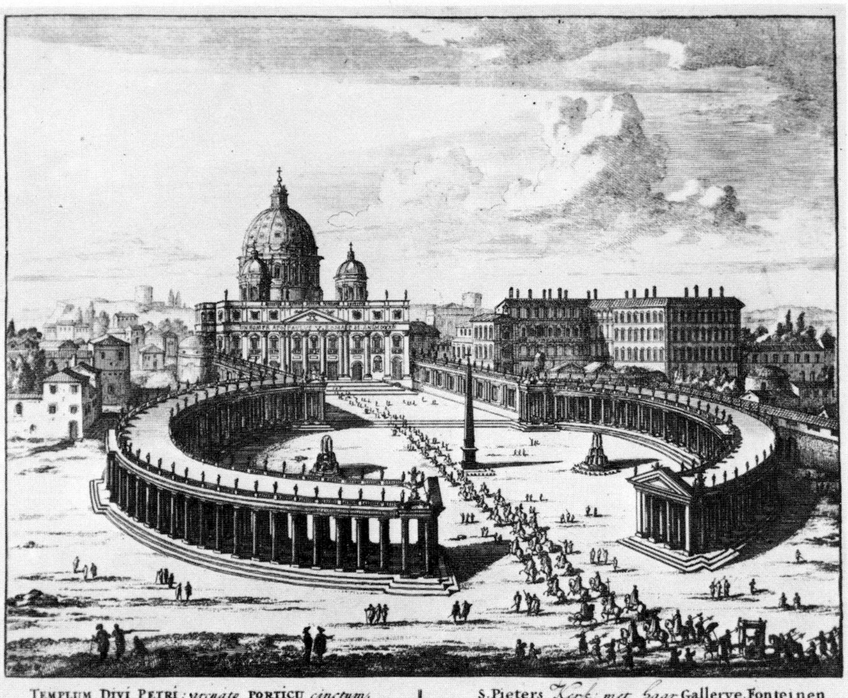

60. St. Peter's, Rome. Engraving by Pieter Schenk, annotated by Pope. *c.* 1700.

61. Theatre and Naumachia at Verona. After Palladio. *c.* 1735.

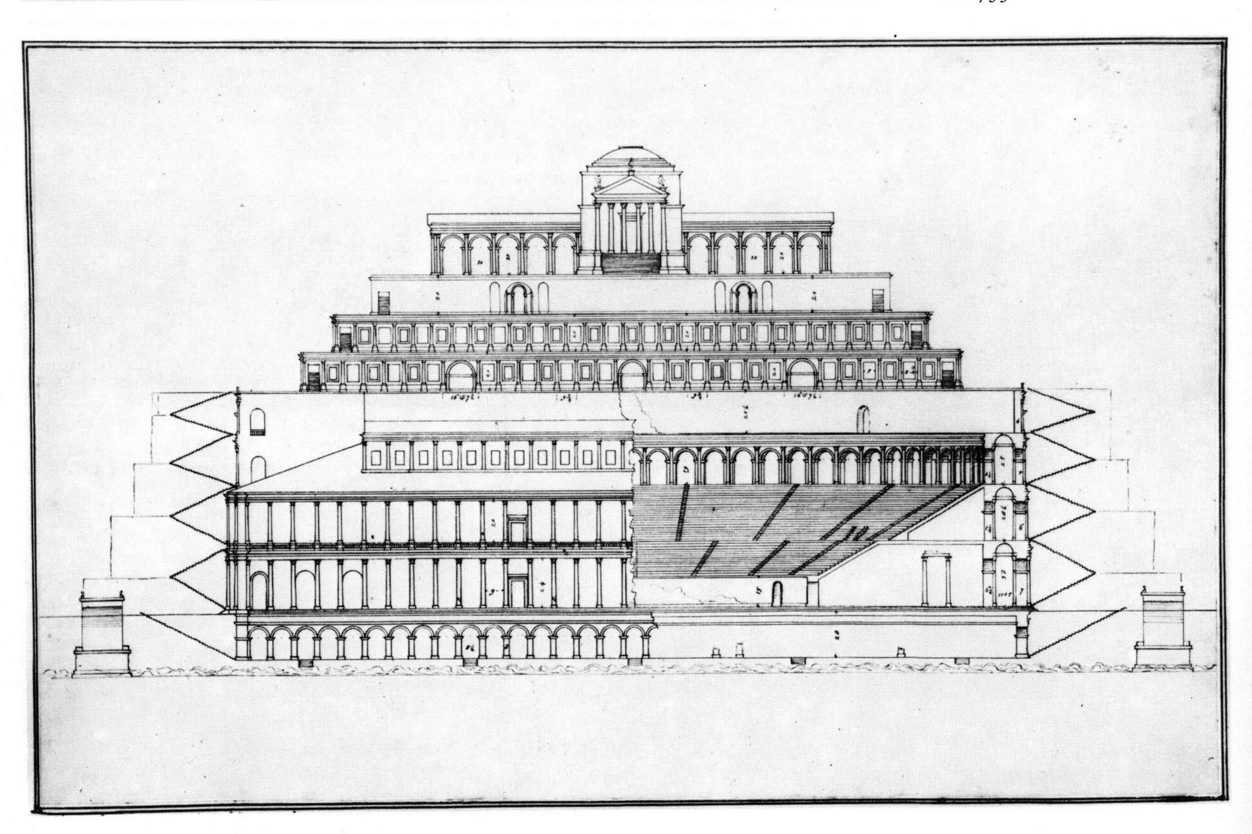

At first glance Serle's 'Account' suggests the grotto was the 'Musaeum' and 'study for Virtuosi' (iv. 262) Pope boasted about to Bolingbroke, rather than an imitation of a mine or quarry. For example the river-front porch ('An Account', Numb. VI) contained much one would expect to find in a *cabinet de curiosités*—'Many Pieces of Coral and petrified Moss, and many other curious Stones from the Island of *St. Christopher* in the *West Indies*; with several Humming Birds and their Nests, from *Antony Brown*, Esq; of *Abbs-Court* in *Surrey*' (261). The rare and exotic minerals here and elsewhere suggest the virtuoso collector's fossilary: 'Mundic, from the *Hartz* Mines in *Germany*; a fine Piece of Gold Ore from the *Peruvian* Mines; Silver Ore from the Mines of *Mexico*; several Pieces Silver Ore from *Old Spain*; *Brazil* Pebbles, *Egyptian* Pebbles and Blood-Stones', 'Several fine Pieces of the Eruptions from Mount *Vesuvius*, and a fine Piece of Marble from the Grotto of *Egeria* near *Rome*, from the Reverend Mr. *Spence*' (260).

But these impressions of Pope's grotto are misleading, and largely derived from the limitations of Serle's inventory, a guidebook intended for tourists.[25] His list is calculated to 'dazzle a Gazing Spectator' (iv. 228) with the rarity of the minerals, and the number and prominence of the contributors. Inevitably it exaggerates the significance of curiosities because it does not discriminate between the gift of an isolated curiosity and the tons of stone furnished by Pope's prime suppliers to his express orders, which determined the character of entire apartments, including the central chambers of the grotto. Moreover, it is a misleading index of Pope's taste since it is probable that a great many, perhaps the majority of the mineral curiosities in Serle's list, were unsolicited gifts from contributors which 'it would have been hard to refuse . . . even when their introduction militated against exact propriety of taste or preconceived plans'.[26]

Where it is possible to read Serle in the light of Pope's intentions as revealed in the correspondence, the 'Account of the Materials' confirms that the grotto at its centre was a studious imitation of a mine, the work of an architect-gardener, and not a collector of minerals. Serle's account of the central

[25] On the guidebook genre to which Serle's *Plan* belongs, see John Harris, 'English Country House Guides, 1740–1840', in *Concerning Architecture: Essays on Architectural Writers and Writing Presented to Nikolaus Pevsner*, ed. John Summerson (London, 1968), pp. 58–74.

[26] Robert Carruthers, *The Life of Alexander Pope* (London, 1858), p. 176.

chambers corresponds very closely to the design Pope described to Borlase, both in the minerals which compose it, and in their disposition. Serle's inventory of minerals in rooms III and V ('An Account', pp. 260–1) shows that they were composed of 'Sparrs & Ores' (iv. 228) supplied by Borlase to satisfy Pope's aesthetic intentions, which are distinct from those of a collector. Pope's requests to Borlase from the outset were for ores and minerals selected for natural beauty rather than rarity. His initial order to Borlase, communicated by Oliver, was predominantly for 'Spar and Mundick, as they are very beautiful so they are cheap, and will make a great Part of the Cargoe'. These minerals are at the farthest remove from geological curiosities. Borlase refers to Spar in the *Natural History* as the 'universal cement' or 'glutten of rock'; and he characterizes pyrite or iron ore, known as Mundic in Cornwall, as the most plentiful and least valuable of minerals.[27]

Repeatedly Pope discouraged Borlase from sending collector's items. 'I would imitate rather her [Nature's] Variety, than make Ostentation of what we call her Riches' (iv. 228). After the arrival of the first shipment from Penzance he writes:

> I shall be satisfy'd if you make your next Cargo consist more of such Ores or Sparrs as are beautiful, & not too difficult to be come at, than of the Scarce & valuable kinds. Indeed the 2 or 300 of Cubes of Mundick which you mention, might find a place luminous enough in one part of my Grotto, and are much the finest Ornaments it can receive. (iv. 228)

Later he insists 'if you will be extravagant, indeed, in sending anything more, I wish it were glittering tho' not curious; as equally proper in such an Imitation of Nature' (iv. 246). Serle's 'Account of the Materials' not only proves that the components of the central chambers of the grotto were common ores and minerals, but gives the fullest description of Pope's disposition of them to imitate the geological strata in a mine. In the luminous room Pope had prominently displayed a geological phenomenon Borlase comments on

[27] See Oliver to Borlase (13 Dec. 1739), quoted by Benjamin Boyce, 'Pope Improves His Grotto', pp. 146–7. See William Borlase, *The Natural History of Cornwall* (1758), pp. 117, 131, 137, where he discusses the question 'whether Spar is not the universal glutten of stones'. Cf. 'An Enquiry into the original States and Properties of Spar, and Sparry Productions, particularly, the Spars, or Crystals found in the Cornish Mines, called Cornish Diamonds', *Philosophical Transactions of the Royal Society of London*, 46 (1749), 256.

in the *Natural History*:[28] 'two sorts of yellow flaky Copper; one shewing, by the different Strata of Metal, that different Masses of Copper will, tho' concreted at different times, unite close into one Globe or Lump' ('An Account', Numb. III, 260). In the adjoining Borlase chamber Serle describes in detail one of the strata Pope had so carefully imitated under the guidance of the geologist: 'Many Pieces of sparry Marble of diverse Colours; and between each Course of Marble, many kinds of Ores, such as Tin Ore, Copper Ore, Lead Ore, Soapy Rock, Kallan, and Wild Lead intermixed, with large Clumps of *Cornish* Diamonds, and several small ones of different Degrees of Transparency' ('An Account', Numb. V, 260).

As this last passage suggests, another value of Serle's account is that it allows us to imagine the aesthetic effect Pope achieved in the central chambers of the grotto; and to appreciate the 'entertainment' which he intended for the 'Sensible' and the 'Gazing Spectator'. The latter was provided for in the overwhelming predominance of Spar in the grotto, the quartz-like crystalline mineral, including Cornish diamonds, incrustations, and stalactites, frequently intermixed with other minerals and ores, which is characterized, according to Borlase, by an 'exceedingly beautiful' variety of form, shape, texture, colour and transparency.[29] Serle's 'Account of the Materials' shows how Pope imitated this variety in the luminous room and the Borlase chamber of his grotto. He had 'stellifyed' (iv. 246) the roof with small and large Cornish diamonds from Borlase, some transparent, some of a green or blackish tinge, with large pieces of red spar to 'vastly vary the colouring' (iv. 246); several groups of Cornish Diamonds incrusted, semipellucid, and shot round a Globe of Yellow Copper; white Spars, interlaced with black Cockle, or shot into Prisms, and, from Ralph Allen's quarries, incrustations of shot Spar 'sprinkled with small Cubes of Mundic, Lead Ore, Kallan, or Wild Iron', and 'several thin Crusts or Films of bright Spar, form'd on a Surface before shot into Protuberances' ('An Account', Numbs. III, V, 260).

How closely this spectacle corresponds to the appearance of a mine can be estimated by comparison with the account Borlase gives of a cave in the tin

[28] See William Borlase, 'Of the Copper Found in Cornwall', *The Natural History of Cornwall* (1758), p. 197.

[29] William Borlase, 'Of the General Basis of Stone, viz. Of Spar, Crystal, and Diamond', chap. 11, *The Natural History of Cornwall* (1758), pp. 117–28.

mine of Pillion Erth in the Parish of St. Just in Cornwall, which he visited about 1740 'on purpose to survey the *Cornish* Crystals in their natural Situation'. The comparison to Pope's grotto is particularly relevant because it seems likely that Pope had read a version of this description when he was planning his expansion of the grotto. Borlase describes the hazardous scramble with a companion down a precipice to the entrance:

> The Cave, to which we were introduced, was not much larger than a common Baker's Oven, and much of that Figure. We had two Candles with us, by means of which we saw the Roof, which might, in the Middle, be about five Feet high from the Floor; in the other Parts not so much. The Roof was the most surprising Piece of Fretwork imaginable, and consisted intirely of Spar shot into *Cornish* Diamonds . . . I could not discern any coveting a Position exactly perpendicular to the Horizon; but in every indifferent Direction they pointed forth very plentifully of several Sizes; sometimes in Groupes and Clusters, sometimes single, now crossing each other, and now standing by each other with parallel Sides: Some were smooth, shining, and clear, others rough and opaque; some vein'd with red, like Porphyry; others speckled thick with the smallest Spots of deep Purple, and a bluish Cast: But the finest of all were those which had innumerable little Diamonds or Sparks (of the clearest Water) stuck upon their Sides, and, by means of the Candle, had a Lustre not to be conceived. We gazed here in this incommodious, but beautiful little Cave, till we could no longer hold up our Heads; and then crept out as we came in, upon our Knees.[30]

It appears from Serle's *Account* that this is the kind of aesthetic effect Pope intended to reproduce in his grotto.

So much for the entertainment of the 'Gazing Spectator'. As for the 'Sensible Spectator' (iv. 228), Pope suggested his entertainment in a letter to Bolingbroke (1740) expressing the 'hope yet to live to philosophize with You in this Musaeum, which is now a Study for Virtuosi, & a Scene for contemplation' (iv. 261–2). The kind of contemplation that could entertain a virtuoso in such a grotto is indicated by Borlase's comments on the other

[30] My quotations are taken from William Borlase, 'An Enquiry into . . . Spar', pp. 275–6, with details introduced from Borlase's letter to Oliver, reprinted in 'William Borlase, St. Aubyn, and Pope', *Quarterly Review*, 139 (1875), 382. 'The Account of the Growth of Cornish Diamonds', which Borlase had sent to Oliver, and which Pope pocketed in Jan. 1740, 'to use', Benjamin Boyce surmises ('Pope Improves His Grotto', p. 148), 'in arranging the promised contributions in his grotto', probably contains Borlase's earliest description of the mine at Pillion Erth which reappeared in all his accounts of the subject: see the undated letter from Borlase to Oliver (1739/40?), reprinted in the *Quarterly Review*, 139 (1875), 382–3; 'An Enquiry into . . . Spar', pp. 275–6; and *The Natural History of Cornwall* (1758), pp. 127–8.

mineral which, along with spar, predominated in the central chambers of Pope's grotto—the iron ore known as mundic in Cornwall. Borlase had generously supplied Pope's demands for mundic, and Serle lists it everywhere in the luminous room and the Borlase chamber of the grotto: 'mundic in small Dice or Cubes', yellow, 'granated' white, purple, and deep blue inclining to black ('An Account', 260–1).

Mundic inspires in Borlase's *Natural History* what can only be described as a physico-theological rhapsody. He is struck by the astonishing variety in the figuration of this commonplace mineral:

> Nature, where-ever we pursue her, has not left herself without testimonies of her regard for colour, shape, and elegance; this will appear from the description of the figured fossils which follow, but in none more conspicuously than in the mundics, in which figure, lustre, gilding, carving, regularity, and finery, are as it were thrown into the scale to make amends for its little intrinsic value. (p. 137)

In annotations on specimens of 'Figur'd Mundics', illustrated by two folio plates, Borlase traces the variety of geometrical designs: 'resemblances of plants and animals, the moldings, casts, and carvings of fancy, the figures of science and erudition . . . enough to surprize us with their regularity and art' (p. 141).

When Borlase tries to account for this variety, he decides that 'natural principles', such as mineral or metallic salts, may explain the geometrical figures, but admits that such principles 'must be very various', and that they do not account for 'those freer strokes of art'. Such cannot be attributed to accident—'a plastick power superintending the congress of fossils, and sporting itself with natural or preternatural representations'. Rather, Borlase concludes, the variety of Nature's works underground must be the work of God: 'the great power which contrived and made all things, needing no delegate, artfully throws the flexile liquid materials of the fossil kingdom into various figures, to draw the attention of mankind to his works, and thence lead them, first, to the acknowledgement, then to the adoration of an intelligent being, inexhaustibly wise, good, and glorious' (pp. 141–2). Borlase's speculations and conclusions are characteristic of the physico-theological attitudes of a scientist who believed that 'Natural History is the handmaid to Providence' ('Dedication', iv). It would not be surprising if the author of the *Essay on Man* shared such physico-theological speculations about the minerals of his grotto with the natural scientist who influenced so radically the design of the grotto. Certainly the design and aesthetic character of the grotto, as Pope left it, were determined mainly by natural science.

If the evidence presented here has been interpreted correctly, we must abandon Pope's playful images of himself as 'Vampire' (iv. 227), Virtuoso-collector (iv. 261–2), or Yahoo burying precious stones underground in the grotto (iv. 359). We must also dismiss the idea of Pope's grotto as a trifle, or romantic extravagance, the notion inspired by Pope's self-deprecating remarks, reinforced by William Mason's elegy, *Musaeus* (1747), which dramatizes Pope repudiating his grotto and early poetry as 'toys of thoughtless youth / When flow'ry fiction held the place of truth', and established once and for all by Samuel Johnson's memorable censure. Nor is it any longer possible to accept the modern interpretation of the grotto as a 'Maze of Fancy', where Pope indulged subversive impulses repressed in his poetry, and abandoned himself to romantic eclecticism.[31]

Considered as a piece of architecture the grotto evolved from the imitation of a feature of classical landscape, literary and topographical—the nymphaeum—to the imitation of a quarry or mine, a plausible development from the classical to the naturalistic.[32] The result was a design in which the aesthetics of the picturesque garden—irregularity and variety—were literally domesticated in architecture. The finished grotto was the architectural equivalent of the picturesque garden, an imitation of 'nature's real and highest art', as Shaftesbury asserted in *Plastics* (1712): 'Thus grottos, caves, etc., the finest imitations of finest gardening. For this is *truth*; the rest *false*.'[33]

Shaftesbury's unpublished categorical statement perfectly expresses the attitude of Pope as a designer of grottoes. In 'Grottofying' (iv. 354), as in

[31] See William Mason, *Musaeus: A Monody to the Memory of Mr. Pope, In Imitation of Milton's "Lycidas"* (London, 1747), p. 17; Samuel Johnson, *Life of Pope*, ed. G. B. Hill (1905), iii. 135; and Frederick Bracher, who expounds the case for romantic eclecticism in 'The Maze of Fancy', in *Essential Articles for the Study of Alexander Pope*, ed. Maynard Mack (1964), pp. 97–121.

[32] See Henry Wotton, *The Elements of Architecture*, ed. Frederick Hard (Charlottesville, 1968), p. 26: 'I finde in some [writers] a curious precept, that the Materials below, be layd as they grew in the Quarrie, supposing them belike to have most strength in their Naturall and Habituall Posture.'

[33] Anthony Ashley Cooper, Earl of Shaftesbury, *Second Characters*, ed. Benjamin Rand (Cambridge, 1914), p. 113.

gardening, Pope was reacting against the Renaissance Mannerist tradition manifest in the excessive refinement and extravagance of the grottoes at Chatsworth and Wilton, or the unbridled allegory of such grottoes as his friend, Aaron Hill, was building at Petty France, Westminster, during the 1730s.[34] It was a tradition which Pope explicitly repudiated: in his censure of the 'labour'd and distant Allegory' of critical interpretation of Homer's grotto of the Naiads; in his attack on 'incongruity of *Ornaments*' in grottoes in the *Epistle to Burlington*, his ridicule of Kent's half-Gothic Merlin's Cave and Hermitage (iii. 329); in his hope that Mrs. Allen would not spoil Prior Park's grotto with 'those Bawbles most Ladies affect' (iv. 254); and finally, in his praise of 'a Grotto of Shells at Crux-Easton', the 'Work of Nine young Ladies': 'Beauty which Nature only can impart, /And such a polish as disgraces Art' (5–6).[35]

Pope's grotto was perhaps the most famous of the eighteenth century. It helped to inspire a 'sub-species of poetry', and it attracted visitors throughout the century.[36] Its influence on grotto design was probably greater than can now be documented but the nature of that influence was clearly in the direction of the classical, the naturalistic, and the picturesque. Without any doubt it helped to establish the taste by which Arthur Young censures 'the regular Works of Art' in a grotto at Clifton in 1772:

> Rustic pillars, the workmanship of nature, (or at least so in appearance) which seems to support a craggy roof, are by no means amiss in a grotto; but this gentleman delights in *the regular works of art*, and accordingly four tuscan pillars are here the supporters of the roof.—A small cascade issuing from broken apertures in a rock, and falling in little sheets on a straggling sea-weed, coral, fossils, &c. is natural. Here is a cascade indeed; but it pours out of the urn of a river God.—Any thing manifestly carrying the appearance of art, in such an imitation of nature, is painful.[37]

[34] On the grotto at Chatsworth, see Christopher Wren, 'Valuation of the Building of Chatsworth' (1692), The Wren Society, vol. 17, *The Work of Sir Christopher Wren, Sir John Vanbrugh, et al.*, A. T. Bolton and H. D. Hendry, eds. (Oxford, 1940), p. 26; Celia Fiennes describes Lord Pembroke's grotto at Wilton in her *Diary* (see Frederick Bracher, 'The Maze of Fancy', p. 98); a detailed description of Aaron Hill's plans for his grottoes is found in a letter to Lady Walpole (May–June 1734) in *Works*, 2nd edn., 4 vols. (London, 1754), i. 251–65.

[35] See *Odyssey*, *TE* x. 8 n.; *Epistle to Burlington*, l. 153 n., *TE* III. ii, 152 n.; the Crux-Easton grotto, *TE* vi. 353–4.

[36] See Mack, 'The Legendary Poet', Appendix E, p. 266.

[37] *A Six Weeks Tour Through the Southern Counties*, 3rd edn., corr. (London, 1772), p. 187.

iii. ALFRED'S HALL

Pope's grotto, even more than the Shell Temple, can be associated with contemporary notions of the Gothic, in its irregularity, and its connection with geological and architectural ruin.[38] In 1741 Pope built a 'Frontispiece' to the grotto, 'a sort of ruinous Arch at the Entry into it on the Garden side' (iv. 343), described in Serle's 'Account of the Materials' as 'various sorts of Stones thrown promiscuously together, in imitation of an old Ruine; some full of Holes, others like Honey-Combs' (259). Pope's appreciation of the Gothic significance of his grotto is suggested by a flight of self-dramatization in a letter (1740) to William Oliver:

> Since his Burial [Pope's, in the Twickenham grotto] he has been seen some times in Mines and Caverns & been very troublesome to those who dig Marbles & Minerals: If ever he has walk'd above ground, He has been (like the Vampires in Germany) such a terror to all sober & innocent people, that many wish a stake were drove thro' him to keep him quiet in his Grave. (iv. 227)

But another piece of garden architecture in the ruinous taste has been attributed to Pope, which has a more direct relation to the Gothic revival. This is the sham ruin known as Alfred's Hall (plate 57), which still stands in the gardens of Cirencester, a building of particular interest because it appears to be the earliest sham ruin that has been traced in the English landscape garden.[39]

Alfred's Hall appears to have been one of those plans which Pope was drawing as early as 1718 at the beginning of his collaboration with Bathurst (i. 515). Pope's supposed authorship of the design of Alfred's Hall is based on the statement of Francis Atterbury, Dean of Westminster, mutual friend and gardening associate of Pope and Bathurst, in a letter to Pope (27 September 1721):

> I am pleas'd to find that you have so much pleasure and (which is the foundation of it) so much health at Lord Bathursts. May both continue, till I see you! May my Lord have as much satisfaction in building the House in the Wood and using it, when built, as you have in designing it! (ii. 85)

[38] See Robert A. Aubin, 'Grottoes, Geology, and the Gothic Revival', *Studies in Philology*, 31 (July 1934), 408–16.

[39] 'Probably the first of mock castles', according to Christopher Hussey, 'Cirencester Park', *Country Life*, 107 (23 July 1950), 1884. Cf. *English Gardens and Landscapes*, p. 81.

The 'House in the Wood' refers to the building under discussion, which replaced a wood house in Oakley Wood, and was later named Arthur's, then Alfred's Hall. Atterbury's attribution is supported by statements of Bathurst indicating that he consulted Pope throughout the erection of the building between 1721 and about 1734, from the outset when he wrote Pope: 'I am resolved to begin the alteration of my wood house, and some little baubling works about it, which you shall direct as you will' (ii. 207). Again in 1732 as the building was nearing completion, when Bathurst told Pope:

> I long to see you excessively, for I have now almost finished my hermitage in the wood, and it is better than you can imagine, and many other things are done that you have no idea of. However, there is enough remaining to employ you for a week at least, and occasion the consumption of a quire of paper in draughts. I will venture to assert that all Europe cannot show such a pretty little plain work in the Brobdingnag style as what I have executed here. (iii. 299–300)

Finally, finishing touches to the Hall seem to be in question when Bathurst writes Pope in 1736: 'you will see that I have brought a great quantity of very good hewn stone from the old house at Saperton to the great centre in Oakley wood. Nothing is wanting but your direction to set the work forward' (iv. 25).

Alfred's Hall, as it stands today, is not the work of a professional architect or an antiquarian. Its irregular castellated walls, its shell of a round tower, broken doorways, and pointed windows are not archaeologically exact or architecturally accurate. At the same time, modern commentators agree with contemporary visitors who recognized it as a successful imitation of the spirit, if not the letter, of medieval architecture. Mrs. Pendarves wrote to Swift not long before its completion that Alfred's Hall had deceived an antiquary: 'My Lord *Bathurst* has greatly improved the wood-house, which you may remember but a cottage, not a bit better than an *Irish cabbin*. It is now a venerable castle, and has been taken by an antiquarian for one of King *Arthur's*, "with thicket overgrown, grotesque and wild".' Edward Stephens's poem, 'On Lord Bathurst's Park and Wood' (1747), makes fun of the idea of an artificial ruin but admires the quality of the sham:

> A lowly pile, with ancient order grac'd,
> Stands, half repair'd, and half by Time defac'd;

> Imbrown'd with Age, the crusted, mould'ring wall
> Threats the beholders with a sudden fall;
> There fix'd aloft (as whilom us'd) we trace
> Imperfect semblance of the savage race.
> This pile the marks of rolling cen'tries wears,
> Sunk to decay,—and built scarce twenty years.

At the end of the century it attracted the 'suff'ring eye' of John Byng, Lord Torrington, whose hostile remarks distinguish Alfred's Hall from the Gothic architecture fashionable after Strawberry Hill. After observing (ironically of the place Pope helped to lay out) that 'Half the platform just reflects the other', Byng says disgustedly: 'It is call'd Alfred's Cave (why I know not) and there is an intention of deceit by old dates; but why shou'd the outside be dirty, and in filthy nastiness? Gothic, and monastic buildings may be kept in taste; and yet as nice as a drawing room.'[40]

Byng wrote when the Gothic revival was well advanced, and fashionable taste no longer craved Gothic ruins filled with topographical and historical associations, but delighted in what has been called 'Rococo Gothic', a neat, light, decorative style of ornamentation. Such are the umbrellas, tents, screens, and eyecatchers which the professional architects like Langley, Kent, and Gibbs introduced to their clients, a style which reached its apotheosis at Strawberry Hill.[41]

Pope's motives in the design of Alfred's Hall, in contrast to those of the professional adapters of Gothic, were those of a poet and landscape gardener rather than an architect. His sham ruin was intended, first of all, to play its part in the landscape garden at Cirencester—to terminate views, and answer avenues. More important, it was designed to inspire melancholy associations, first with King Arthur, later with Alfred, the Saxon King who became in contemporary political satire the type of the virtuous constitutional monarch

[40] On the sham architecture of Alfred's Hall, see James Lees-Milne, *Earls of Creation* (1962), p. 46; Mary Granville Delany to Swift (24 Oct. 1733), in *The Correspondence of Jonathan Swift*, ed. Harold Williams (Oxford, 1965), iv. 199–200. Edward Stephens's poem is quoted by Robert Aubin, *Topographical Poetry in Eighteenth Century England* (New York, 1936), pp. 134–5. John Byng, Viscount Torrington, *The Torrington Diaries*, ed. C. Bruyn Andrews (London, 1934–8), i. 259.

[41] See Kenneth Clark, *The Gothic Revival*, p. 43; John Summerson, *Architecture in Britain*, p. 238; and Barbara Jones, *Follies and Grottoes* (London, 1953), pp. 20–2.

contrasted to George II. Architecture 'as nice as a drawing room' could not achieve these ends.

It is not surprising to discover that one of the early landscape gardeners should have been involved in the Gothic revival. Both movements began at about the same time in England, and were promoted by the same people: those who believed in a genetic connection between Gothic architecture (the architecture of trees, according to the 'forest theory') and natural, unadorned landscape; who recognized in ruined architecture overgrown with trees an aesthetic equivalent to picturesque landscape.[42] But it is surprising to discover that Pope was in all probability the designer of the earliest sham ruin in an English landscape garden, predating Sanderson Miller's castle at Edgehill (1746, usually cited as the earliest) by more than twenty years.

The poetic sensibility to shams and ruins was part of the experience required to educate European taste to understand Gothic as a style rather than a mood, 'an artistic ideal determined by autonomous and determinable principles'. The other part of the experience is only apparently contradictory, the conversion to a strictly classicistic point of view from which the Gothic style as well as the Baroque could be seen 'at a distance' and, therefore, 'in perspective'.[43] Pope's interest in classical architecture, the extent to which he adopted a classicist point of view, is the subject of the following chapters.

[42] On gothic ruins, see Erwin Panofsky, 'The First Page of Giorgio Vasari's "Libro": A Study on the Gothic Style', chap. 5 of *Meaning in the Visual Arts* (New York, 1957), pp. 180–3.

[43] Ibid., p. 184.

11. *Palladian Revival*

At the same time as Pope was building Gothic structures at Twickenham and elsewhere he was giving his support to the movement led by his patron, Richard Boyle, Earl of Burlington, to revive classical architecture as a national taste in England. Thus we find him simultaneously devoted to opposite aesthetic ideals, but there is no sign that he considered them incompatible. At Sherborne, for example, where he had urged the cultivation of Gothic ruins in the gardens, he advised Lord Digby to draw a Palladian veil over the Elizabethan house, originally a hunting lodge owned by Sir Walter Raleigh:[1]

> The Windows & Gates are of a yellow Stone throughout, and one of the flatt Sides toward the Garden has the wings of a newer Architecture with beautiful Italian Window-frames done by the first Earl of Bristol, which, if they were joind in the middle by a Portico covering the Old Building, would be a noble Front. (ii. 236–7)

A study of Pope's taste in classical architecture, and his relationship to the Palladian revival, helps to explain how he was able to reconcile Gothic irregularity with Palladian rules.

i. TOWN HOUSE AND VILLA

Pope's first building project led him straight to the source of the Palladian revival in England. Late in 1717 or early in 1718 his Chiswick neighbour, Richard Boyle, Earl of Burlington, offered him a building site on land north of Burlington House, Piccadilly, one of four sites on Old Burlington Street (now Burlington Gardens) where houses were being built between 1718 and

[1] See Mark Girouard, 'Attitudes to Elizabethan Architecture', in *Concerning Architecture: Essays on Architectural Writers and Writing Presented to Nikolaus Pevsner*, ed. John Summerson (London, 1968), p. 15. For the history of Sherborne, see *An Inventory of the Historical Monuments in Dorset*, Vol. i, *West Dorset* (London, 1952), i. 63–70.

1723 under supervision of Burlington's protégé, Colen Campbell (1676–1729).[2] Campbell, the Scottish architect who had dramatically introduced to Whig gentry the glories of the classical country-house in *Vitruvius Britannicus* (1715), had converted Boyle to a life-long devotion to classical architecture; and his patron was to become the leader of a movement to establish the classical style as interpreted by Palladio and Jones in English architecture. Boyle had engaged Campbell to assist the garden architecture at Chiswick, and to complete the remodelling of Burlington House, which had been begun by his persistent Scottish rival, James Gibbs (1682–1754). At this time Campbell was completing the transformation of Burlington House from the quiet and unassuming Restoration dormers and red brick, into the bold and unequivocal statement of Palladio and Jones in Portland stone. 'The Model of Burlington House', which Pope had among his belongings at Twickenham, probably dates from this period.[3]

It is in this atmosphere of an incipient architectural revival that Pope was considering whether to build in Old Burlington Street in 1718. He speaks of 'the utmost Engagements of business . . . with my Architect' (presumably Campbell, i. 468) early in the year. Rough sketch-plans of a three-storeyed town house, probably referring to the Burlington estate site, appear in the Homer manuscripts at this time.[4] In August Bathurst warned him of the expense of a 'palazotto in London' (i. 488). Finally in October, writing to Burlington from Cirencester, Pope explained his reluctance to build because of financial considerations:

I therfore beg you to know, I have Piqued myself upon being your Tenant in that piece of ground behind Burlington House (which is the Situation I am fond of to the last degree) & that nothing hinderd my being there this Summer, but finding upon the exactest enquiry, the expence Mr Campbell's Proposal would have put me to, to be 200

[2] See F. H. W. Sheppard, ed., *Survey of London*, Vol. 32, *The Parish of St James Westminster, Part Two, North of Picadilly* (London, 1963), 508–17, and Howard E. Stutchbury, 'Nos. 31–4 Great Burlington Street', *The Architecture of Colen Campbell* (Manchester, 1967), pp. 39–44.

[3] On Burlington House, see F. H. W. Sheppard, ed., 'The Third Earl's Ownership of the House', *Survey of London*, 32 (1963), 395–406. See John Summerson, 'The Palladian Movement: Campbell, Burlington, and Kent', chap. 20, *Architecture in Britain*. For Pope's model of Burlington House, see 'Inventory', p. 246.

[4] B.M. Add. MS. 4808, f. 30v. See *Correspondence*, i. 488 n., and *Survey of London*, 32 (1963), 509.

pound above what I am pretty well assured I can build the same thing for. I promise you, my Lord, to build on the same Plan & Front with Lord Warwick's, so as not to clash with any regular design. (i. 516)

Pope's site, No. 32 Old Burlington Street, was adjacent to a site at No. 33 already appropriated by Edward Rich, seventh Earl of Warwick, Addison's stepson. When Pope wrote to Burlington in February 1719 to 'resign the piece of ground intended for me, as not being yet prepard to build, & absolutely unwilling to retard the progress of the rest who are' (ii. 2), Colen Campbell took the lease, and built a house subsequently occupied by Henry Pelham. The plans for Pope's house in Burlington Street have not been identified among the Campbell drawings at the Royal Institute of British Architects, but the elevation for a house on the same site designed for Pelham may derive from the one Pope rejected because of the expense. It is a house of 2½ storeys, five bays, rusticated windows, a balustraded parapet, with a pulvinated frieze below the cornice. Pelham's house did not follow this design exactly, but the astylar front was intended to be part of a regular continuous façade, prototype of much early eighteenth-century street architecture.[5]

After Pope rejected Campbell's stylish Palladian design he leased a house ten miles outside London on the Thames at Twickenham, and employed a rival architect to remodel it, but this did not represent a repudiation of Palladian taste. Indeed, Campbell probably inspired the architectural ambition Pope sought to satisfy at Twickenham. Motifs of the villa in the design of the town house for Pelham's site reflect Campbell's conception of the Anglo-Palladian villa, the potent and influential design Campbell was introducing at this time, which was destined throughout the century to vie with and eventually triumph over the more grandiloquent designs of the 'greater house' he was advertising in *Vitruvius Britannicus*. Between 1719 and 1724 Campbell was responsible for the design of several houses adapted from Palladio's *case di villa* which became prototypes of the English villa. Typically they were

[5] The drawing described in *TLS* ('An English Palladianist', 25 Apr. 1968, p. 440) as 'probably for the proposed house for Pope in Burlington Street', has been catalogued among 'Unlocated & Unidentified Townhouses'. See John Harris, comp., *Catalogue of the Drawings Collection of the Royal Institute of British Architects*, vol. 4, *Colen Campbell* (Farnborough, 1973), No. 50, fig. 149. Campbell's design for Henry Pelham's house at 32 Old Burlington Street is No. 15, fig. 15.

small, situated in the Thames valley suburban to London, and intended to serve as a secondary seat for a wealthy client. Summerson points out that the word 'villa' in the eighteenth century 'was never used with any *architectural* precision', but he insists that 'it is Palladian or nothing', and gives this account of its essential features:

> The English type is square or nearly square in plan, with a symmetrical arrangement of rooms on both axes. The front and back façades are divided into three, the central part having a portico (pilasterwise or in the round), the side parts one window each. The window-rhythm one-three-one is essential to the type. A house of this type has all the formality of a greater house but the window-rhythm renders it totally opposed to the idea of long ranges of intercommunicating rooms. Its accommodation is necessarily modest and its character therefore more in the nature of a retreat than an advertisement of its owner's standing or ability to entertain.[6]

This is the conception which shaped the architecture of the house Pope began to remodel in 1719 with the assistance of the architect James Gibbs (1682–1754).

By June 1719 Pope had occupied his house on the riverside at Twickenham and received a letter from James Gibbs about remodelling it: 'the designes shall be ready for you to approve or disaprove of according as you shall finde them to your purpose, as for making me loose ane houre in your Company, I should always be proud of the honor of spending my tyme so agreeably' (ii. 4). These 'designes', which probably are related to the 'Additions to Alexander Pope's Villa' mentioned in Gibbs's *Memoirs*, cannot now be traced, but something can be inferred from Gibbs's reputation, Pope's intentions indicated in the correspondence, and from an engraving of the house as it emerged from its alterations. Gibbs was a Catholic and a Tory, facts which may have influenced Pope's choice of architect. One of Edward Harley's virtuosi, he was a distinctly Tory architect in the age of Whig supremacy, and he had been bested by his fellow Scot Campbell in the struggle for patronage at Burlington House. Nevertheless, he was a 'prompt snapper-up of Palladian ideas', particularly the idea of the Palladian villa. He designed villas near Twickenham for the Dukes of Argyll and Islay, and his unexecuted

[6] John Summerson, 'The Classical Country House', *Journal of the Royal Society of Arts*, 107 (July 1959), 551–2, 570.

design of a villa for Matthew Prior at Down Hall, illustrated in his *Book of Architecture* (1728) has some claims for precedence over Campbell's villa designs.[7]

It is apparent from the correspondence that Pope was not content to leave everything to his architect, and he wrote exuberantly to Jervas when the remodelling was beginning:

> Alas Sir, do you know whom you talk to? One that had been a Poet, was degraded to a Translator, and at last thro' meer dulness is turn'd into an Architect. You know *Martial*'s Censure—*Praeconem facito, vel Architectum.* However I have one way left, to plan, to *elevate*, and *to surprize* (as *Bays* says.) (ii. 23).

His classical loyalties, and his sense of the daring novelty of Palladian design which had already attracted ridicule,[8] can be observed in a letter to Robert Digby in the spring of 1720 giving the 'best account of what I am building':

> My Building rises high enough to attract the eye and curiosity of the Passenger from the River, where, upon beholding a Mixture of Beauty and Ruin, he enquires what House is falling, or what Church is rising? So little taste have our common Tritons of *Vitruvius*; whatever delight the true, unseen, poetical Gods of the River may take, in reflecting in their Streams my *Tuscan* Porticos, or *Ionic* Pilasters. (ii. 44)

Digby replied wishing Pope enjoyment of 'your new favourite Portico' (ii. 48), and subsequent correspondence is filled with allusions revealing Pope's devotion to Palladio's idea of the villa. In July he complains to Digby about his 'return (Wretch that I am!) to Watergruel and *Palladio*' (ii. 50), a reference to Palladio's *Four Books of Architecture*, which had recently appeared in a trans-

[7] For Gibbs's work on Pope's villa, see Colvin, p. 235, and Bryan Little, *The Life and Works of James Gibbs 1682–1754* (London, 1955), p. 85. On Gibbs, Campbell and the Palladian villa, see John Summerson, *Architecture in Britain*, 197, and 'The Classical Country House', pp. 549, 574–5. Could it be that Gibbs included a rejected design for Pope's villa in his *Book of Architecture* (1728), among the 'numerous designs . . . that remained purely paper schemes', as Bryan Little observes (*James Gibbs*, p. 94)? Plate XLIII, 'A Draught of a House made for a Gentleman in 1720' (xii) coincides in date, and corresponds to the window rhythm of Pope's villa, though differing in its 'uncommon Fronts' (xii).

[8] See *An Epistle to the Right Honourable Paul Methuen Esq.* (1720), ll. 67–70, in *The Poetical Works of John Gay*, ed. G. C. Faber (London, 1926), p. 163:

> While *Burlington*'s proportion'd columns rise,
> Does not he stand the gaze of envious eyes?
> Doors, windows are condemn'd by passing fools,
> Who know not that they damn *Palladio*'s rules.

62. Entrance to Covent-Garden Theatre, London. 1791.

63. Monument to the Fire of London. Engraving by Sutton Nicholls. 1741.

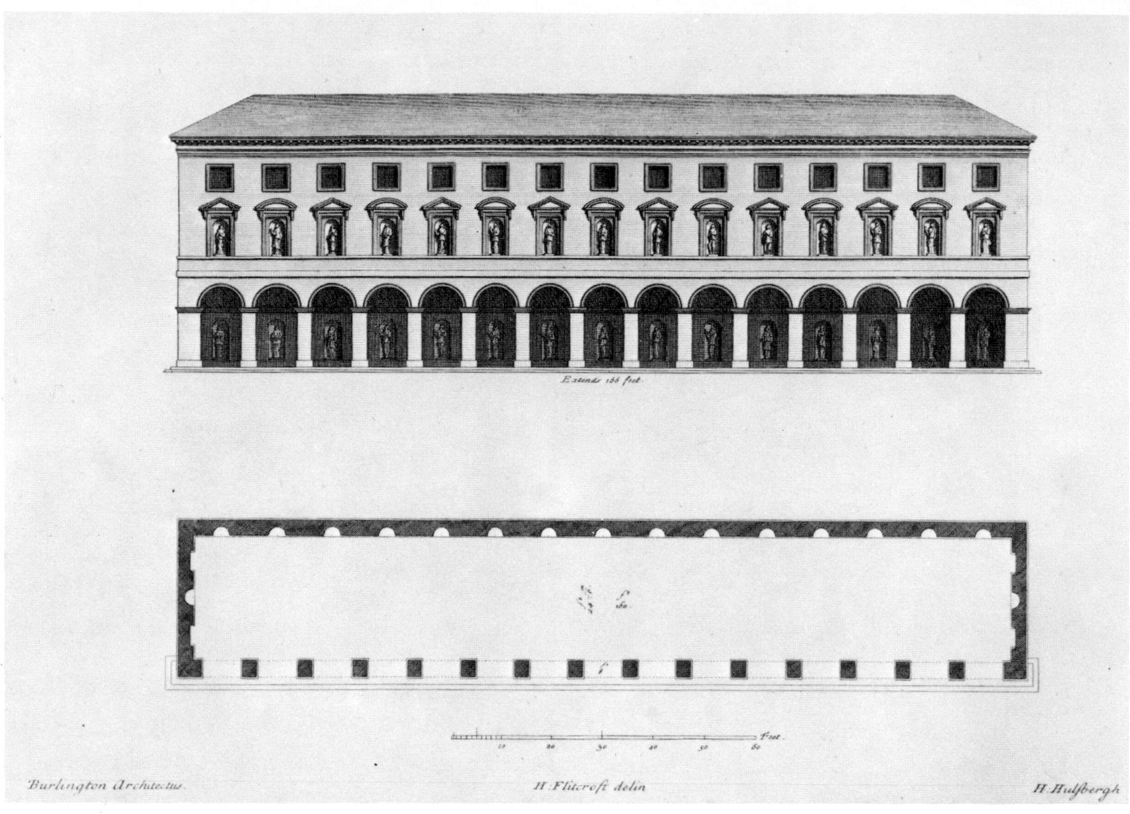

64. Burlington's Westminster Dormitory. By Henry Flitcroft. *c.* 1730.

65. Thomas Ripley's Admiralty Office, Whitehall. By Thomas Bowles. 1727.

lation by Nicholas Dubois.[9] In November Digby is longing to see Pope's 'Villa' (ii. 58); the following year Pope extended an invitation to George Berkeley to 'make trial how you like My Tusculum because I can assure you it is no less yours, & hope you'l use it as your own Country Villa' (ii. 63). Not long before, he had been reading Pliny the Younger's description of his villa (i. 508) which Robert Castell discussed and illustrated in *The Villas of the Ancients*, a folio volume dedicated to Burlington in 1727. By the time Burlington wrote to Pope in 1729 to say he could not call 'at your villa' (iii. 82), the word referred to an architectural ideal, supported by scholarship, and enriched by literary associations.

The engraving (plate 58) of 'The Late Mr. Pope's House at Twickenham' in the *Newcastle General Magazine* (January 1748) indicates that Gibbs's 'designes' gave to Pope's house the essential features of the Anglo-Palladian villa—the threefold division of the façade, the one-three-one rhythm of the windows, and the portico. Maynard Mack has recently described the house as it 'emerged from his extensive alterations':

a dwelling of three storeys and some ten or twelve rooms, whose plan and ornamentation recall in a general way the classicism of Inigo Jones, Palladio, and the north Italian villa. It consisted of a central block, with slightly recessed and lowered wings, the north wing fitted with bow windows framed in Ionic pilasters, the center block rising from grotto-entrance in the basement storey to a balustraded platform at the level of the *piano nobile*, then rising again to a balustraded balcony supported on Tuscan pillars at the chamber-level, and so to a highly decorated cornice topped by a hipped roof.[10]

The rustication and quoins are characteristic of the exuberance of Gibbs's style which offended strict Palladians,[11] but Pope had consulted Burlington and William Kent, successor to Colen Campbell as Burlington's architect, about his portico and façade by the time Rysbrack painted the house.

Pope assured Burlington when he moved from Chiswick to Twickenham in 1719 that 'you shall always have me for your Neighbor, where-ever I live'

[9] *The Architecture of A. Palladio in Four Books, Revis'd. Design'd, and Published by Giacomo Leoni*, trans. Nicholas Dubois (1715–17), one of the manifestos of the Palladian movement. See John Summerson, *Architecture in Britain*, p. 190. Burlington sponsored a second corrected edition by Isaac Ware (1737). See Rudolf Wittkower, 'Giacomo Leoni's Edition of Palladio's "Quattro Libri Dell Architettura"', *Arte Veneta*, 8 (1954), 310–16.

[10] *The Garden and the City*, p. 16.

[11] See Bryan Little, *James Gibbs*, p. 90.

(ii. 2), and Burlington had an important influence on Pope's architecture. Rudolf Wittkower has discovered that Burlington paid for the interior fittings of the poet's house at Twickenham.[12] When designs for improvement of his frontispiece were in progress in the fall of 1732 (the house without the portico can be seen in Tillemans' painting, *c.* 1730), Pope sought Burlington's assistance:

> If you happen to be at leisure enough to day to call on a poor distressed, undetermin'd Designer, whose works lie unfinished for want of a little judgment (the case of many a man) pray come, & take me away with you if you please, for I can do nothing without you. (iii. 515)

He wanted advice about substantial additions to his 'favourite Portico' (ii. 48):

> My Portico is in hand, & by an Expedient of Mr Kents which is here inclosed, the only difficulty we had is remov'd; but I will not proceed till I have your Lordship's Sanction of it. The Basement, if continued no farther on the Sides than the Pillars, would be too thin & want a flight of Steps to spread it: which would spoil a Design I have, to make that Basement include a Cold Bath & a fall of Water. Your opinion of this, as it stands, with relation to its connection to the rest of the Front, will greatly oblige me. (iii. 314)

Burlington was not enthusiastic (iii. 322–3), but he sanctioned the plan and Pope was 'very impatient to be building my Portico' (iii. 329). When building got under way in the spring Pope told Burlington that 'the Zeal of my Portico has eaten me up . . . I cannot proceed in my Stucco-ing, till I see your Lordship & have your directions about the upper Cornish [Cornice] of my house, & the Moldings & members of the Entablature' (iii. 356). In 1734 he had stuccoed his villa, which he was now calling 'Little Whitehall' (iii. 406). Improvements to Pope's 'Outward Façade' (iv. 279) continued into the 1740s under the guidance of Burlington and Kent.

Thus, the design of Pope's villa is directly indebted to Burlington and to Kent and reflects his admiration for Burlington's villa at Chiswick (plate 59) which he expressed in a letter requesting building materials in 1733: 'The Inclosed is the Last Bill I shall draw upon your Lordship for stone, according to the Commands you layd upon me, that there should be nothing Durable in my building which I was not to owe to Chiswick. I am sure there will be nothing to it

[12] 'The Earl of Burlington and William Kent', York Georgian Society, *Occasional Papers Number Five* (York, 1948), p. 9.

Beautiful besides, nor (I believe) in this nation, but what is owed to the Lord of Chiswick' (iii. 341). Burlington's Chiswick House, along with Marble Hill at Twickenham, and White Lodge in Richmond Park, became one of 'the three main prototypes of the English villa—all within a two mile radius', which had immense influence on English country-house design. Boldly original in planning, Chiswick's most striking departure from Palladio and Campbell's imitations was the almost 'toy-like unreality' of its scale. As early as 1727 it was pronounced by a well-informed visitor, Sir John Clerk, to be 'properly a villa and by much the best in Britain'.[13]

Another source of inspiration to Pope as he perfected the design of his villa was Marble Hill House, the Twickenham villa designed and built for Henrietta Howard, Countess of Suffolk, between 1723 and 1729, which was illustrated in *Vitruvius Britannicus* (1725), and served as a model of classical design in Robert Morris's *An Essay in Defence of Ancient Architecture* (1728). Marble Hill reflects in plan, elevation, and interior design the influence on the Anglo-Palladian villa of Inigo Jones. Pope's familiarity with the architecture of Marble Hill during its construction is indicated by his remark to William Fortescue (September, 1724) that 'Marblehill waits only for its roof,—the rest finished' (ii. 257), and his compliment to Lady Howard in 1727 on the completion of a room modelled on Palladio's interpretation of the atrium of a Roman House as described by Vitruvius: 'We [Gay and Pope] think your hall the most delightful room in the world except that where you are' (ii. 436).[14]

Pope's initiation to architecture, like painting six years earlier, was intensive, practical, and stimulating to his imagination. He delighted in his degradation into an architect, and 'the many Draughts, Elevations, Profiles, Perspectives, &c. of every Palace and Garden propos'd, intended, and happily raised, by the strength of that Faculty wherein all great Genius's excel, Imagination' (ii. 24). Rough sketches of architectural plans and elevations appear in the Homer manuscripts, and his competence in architectural

[13] See John Summerson, 'The Classical Country House', p. 573.

[14] See Summerson, ibid., pp. 572–3; Fiske Kimball, 'Burlington Architectus, Part I', *Journal of the Royal Institute of British Architects*, 34 (15 Oct. 1927), 686. On the Jones-Campbell influence on Marble Hill, see W. A. Eden, in *Marble Hill House and its Owners* (1970) by Marie Draper, pp. 19–21. On the hall at Marble Hill, see Marie P. G. Draper, *Marble Hill House, Twickenham, A Short Account of its History and Architecture* (London, 1966), p. 11.

drawing is indicated by his careful design for his family's monument in a letter to Francis Bird (ii. 26). His experience in reading architectural plans is suggested by a note to the *Iliad* (Book XV, l. 67) about the reader's foreknowledge of 'the Facts described': 'The Pleasure in this case is like that of an Architect's first view of some magnificent Building, who was before well acquainted with the Proportions of it.' Thus he acquired enough competence to advise his friend William Fortescue about the proportions of doors and windows, and to oversee some building projects for him.[15] As we have seen he was prepared at any moment to 'lay a Temple' in the way of a 'wild Goth' like William Kent (iii. 417).

But if practical knowledge was necessary to form a taste in architecture, as Pope believed, practice was indivisible from theory. The busts of Palladio and Inigo Jones in Pope's library remind us that study of the Renaissance tradition of architecture underlies even so slight a venture as Twickenham,[16] whose insignificance he was well aware of, as he remarked to Ralph Allen, owner of the Palladian greater house of Prior Park: 'In general they [my Servants] never show the house (which you know is nothing) in my Absence' (iv. 9). A brief consideration of Pope's acquaintance with classical theory of architecture is essential to an understanding of his contribution to the Palladian revival.

ii. 'JUST AND NOBLE RULES'

Pope's improvement of his house illustrates the humanistic devotion of the Burlington circle to classical architectural theory, which was based on a knowledge of Roman antiquities and Vitruvius. Pope's study of classical antiquities was by no means superficial. In preparing the notes to the *Iliad* he compiled a detailed list of authorities on Homeric antiquities and archaeology which he believed indispensable to the translator of Homer. In 1738 he

[15] For Pope's architectural sketches in the Homer autograph, see B.M. Add. MS. 4808, ff. 30^{v}, 200^{v}; 4809, ff. 66^{v}, 67^{v}, 84^{v}, 86^{v}. See Hans-Joachim Zimmermann, *Alexander Pope's Noten zu Homer, Eine Manuskript-und Quellenstudie* (Heidelberg, 1966), p. 61; and James Sambrook, 'Pope and the Visual Arts', in *Writers and their Background: Alexander Pope*, ed. Peter Dixon (London, 1972), p. 151 n. For Pope's note to the *Iliad*, see *TE* viii. 198; his advice to Fortescue, *Correspondence*, iii. 225 (1731), 477–8, 486 (1735).

[16] See 'Inventory', p. 252 n.: 'Palladio and Inigo Jones . . . were probably copies of the busts made by Michael Rysbrack for Burlington's Chiswick House.' See M. I. Webb, *Michael Rysbrack, Sculptor* (London, 1954), pp. 102–4.

spoke to Spence of antiquities as a study 'capable of delighting us after a little application to it':

> I once got deep into Graevius, and was greatly taken with it—so far as to write a treatise in Latin, collected from the writers in Graevius on the old buildings in Rome. 'Tis now in Lord Oxford's hands, and has been so these fifteen years. (No. 557)

Pope's adaptation of Johann Georg Graevius, *Thesaurus Antiquitatum Romanarum* (1694–9), has not been found in the Harleian collection; but a volume of Roman antiquities owned by Pope, *Romae Novae Delineatio* by Pieter Schenk (1660–1718/19), with his measurements and annotations of monuments (plate 60), has survived.[17]

Joseph Spence, who was himself something of an authority on archaeology and antiquities, recorded encounters between Pope and contemporary antiquarians in which Pope held his own with experts. One of these occurred during a conversation about the *Capitoliums* at Rome with Edward Holdsworth when Pope 'answered much more readily and directly than Mr. Holdsworth himself, who was so particularly well acquainted with Rome and its antiquities' (No. 550). On another occasion Pope was able to correct the noted Italian virtuoso, student of antiquities, inscriptions, and the author of *Verona Illustrata* (1732), the Marquis Scipione Maffei (1675–1755), about the buried remains of a Roman theatre in his own city (not the famous amphitheatre). During Maffei's visit to Twickenham in 1736 Pope showed him 'the design of an ancient theatre at Verona':

> The Marquis said 'the artist had done very well, but 'twas all a whim (favola!)'. Mr. Pope begged his pardon, assured him that 'twas a reality, and convinced him that there had been a theatre there from an allowed old writer on the antiquities of Verona. He [Maffei] immediately agreed (and [Pope] mentioned this as a proof of it) that Maffei was a very mediocre man, even in his own way. (No. 561)

The 'design' in Pope's possession was probably a copy by Henry Flitcroft of Palladio's drawing (plate 61) in Burlington's collection at Chiswick.[18]

[17] For Pope's note to the *Iliad*, see Book V, l. 449 n., *TE* vii. 289. On Pope's iconographical bibliography of Homer, see Hans-Joachim Zimmermann, *Alexander Pope's Noten zu Homer* (1966), pp. 37, 202, 390, and 'Werke zur Altertumskunde', in *Bibliographie der von Pope Benutzten Werke*, 404–5. On Pope's treatise after Graevius, see Spence, No. 557 n. On *Romae Novae Delineatio*, see Geoffrey Tillotson, *TE* ii. 237 n. The book is now in the Yale University Library.

[18] George Sherburn, *Early Career*, p. 218. For Edward Holdsworth, see *D.N.B.*, and Spence, No. 1416,

Vitruvius's *De Architectura*, the sole surviving treatise on the architecture of ancient Rome, was regarded by Pope and his contemporaries as the Old Testament of classical architecture. William Trumbull, writing to Pope in 1708 about his incompetence as a critic of poetry, expresses in his analogy the attitude of every educated gentleman of his time:

> There may possibly be some happy genius's, who may judge of some of the natural beauties of a Poem, as a man may of the proportions of a building, without having read *Vitruvius*, or knowing any thing of the rules of architecture: But this, tho' it may sometimes be in the right, must be subject to many mistakes, and is certainly but a superficial knowledge; without entring into the art, the methods, and the particular excellencies of the whole composure, in all the parts of it. (i. 45)

Pope's familiarity with *The Ten Books of Architecture* is indicated by a number of allusions, including his scornful remark (ii. 44) already quoted about the ignorant spectators of his Twickenham villa during its Vitruvian alterations,[19] and his ardent exhortation to the Earl in his *Epistle to Burlington* to 'be whate'er Vitruvius was before' (l. 194). The eighteenth-century man of taste, like Pope or Trumbull, believed that Vitruvius's book contained the secrets of Roman architecture. Here could be found the explanation of the orders, the rules of proportion illustrated by the famous drawing of Vitruvian Man in the third book, the ideals of beauty and utility, and the idea that the rules of architecture are accessible to all educated men.[20]

Vitruvius reached eighteenth-century England sophisticated and enriched by the humanist tradition, particularly the theory and practice of Andrea Palladio (1508–80) and Inigo Jones (1573–1652), whose statues stood in front of Burlington House and Chiswick, and whose busts were in Pope's library at Twickenham. Palladio's *Four Books of Architecture* (1570), which Pope was studying in 1721, illustrated the rules of proportion derived from Palladio's

headnote. On the drawing of the amphitheatre at Verona, see Prunella Fraser and John Harris, *A Catalogue of the Drawings by Inigo Jones, John Webb, and Richard Boyle*, 3rd Earl of Burlington in the Burlington-Devonshire Collection (London: R.I.B.A. typescript, 1960), p. 66. Maffei's account of Palladio's drawing in the Burlington Collection appears in *Osservazioni letterarie* (Verona, 1738), iii. 206. See Spence, No. 561 n.

[19] It was probably a misreading of this allusion to Vitruvius which caused Geoffrey Scott to write in *The Architecture of Humanism* (2nd edn. 1924; rpt. London, 1961), p. 200, that 'Pope satirised him'.

[20] See Rudolf Wittkower, *Architectural Principles in the Age of Humanism*, 3rd edn. (London, 1967), p. 14; and W. A. Eden, *Marble Hill House and its Owners*, p. 3.

study of Vitruvius and his meticulous measurement and drawing of Roman antiquities. Like Vitruvius, Palladio based his rules of proportion on the principle of 'the commensurability of ratios', a symphonic principle of architectural proportion in which by a common standard of measurement—a module such as the diameter of a column—each part of a building can be metrically related to every other part, and all the parts to the whole. It is an organic ideal of architecture, based on a mathematical definition of beauty sanctioned in the Renaissance by analogy to the perfection of human proportions (Vitruvian Man), Platonic cosmology, and the laws of musical harmony. Thus conceived the rules of classical architecture were understood to have absolute validity.

Inigo Jones (fig. 6), the second pillar supporting the English Palladian revival, is currently acknowledged to be the architect who naturalized Palladio and the classical rules in England. In Italy Jones painstakingly studied Roman remains, comparing Palladio's measurements with his own observations. His 'critical appreciation of Antiquity', resulted in buildings like the Whitehall Banqueting House which are entirely Palladian in vocabulary, but speak with an English accent. All parts of the Banqueting House, even the rustication, are subordinated to the module, a single and absolute system of metrical relationships.[21]

How much of Jones's mastery of proportion was appreciated by the Burlington circle cannot be determined; but he was one of the Gods of their idolatry. Burlington's Palladian propaganda included Kent's publication of *The Designs of Inigo Jones* in 1727. In 1716 Pope was 'entertained' at Oxford by Dr. George Clarke's collection of Jones's drawings, 'particularly with the original Designs of *Inigo Jones's Whitehall*' (i. 376), an unexecuted project dear to the Palladians. In 1734 he wrote to Burlington 'I think to morrow to follow the Impulse of my Spirit and walk towards Amesbury, to humble myself before Inigo Jones' (iii. 418).[22]

[21] See Rudolf Wittkower, 'Inigo Jones, Architect and Man of Letters', *Journal of the Royal Institute of British Architects*, 60 (Jan. 1953), 83, 88; and John Summerson, *Architecture in Britain*, pp. 67, 70–1.

[22] Jones's Whitehall designs are now in the Clarke Collection, Worcester College, Oxford. For the possibility that Pope saw Jones's annotated copy of Palladio's *Four Books of Architecture* in Clarke's possesion, see Henry Avril and Peter Dixon, 'Pope and the Architects: A Note on the Epistle to Burlington', *English Studies*, 51 (Oct. 1970), 437–41.

FIG. 6. Design for the Statue of Inigo Jones at Chiswick House.
By William Kent.

Inigo Jones's intended treatise on the orders never appeared, but Pope praised Henry Wotten's *Elements of Architecture* (1628), which can be considered an apology for Jones's architecture. Wotten's book is a delightful recapitulation of the Vitruvian-Palladian architectural ideals of 'Well building . . . Commoditie, Firmenes, and Delight'. It is this tradition (and perhaps specific passages in Wotten)[23] which underlie the 'rules of architecture' which Pope expounded to Spence as an example of 'a sketch or analysis of the first principles of each art with their first consequences [which] might be a thing of most excellent service'. 'All the rules of architecture', he told Spence about 1728, 'would be reducible to three or four heads: the justness of the openings, bearings upon bearings, and the regularity of the pillars' (No. 559). These principles were demonstrable, Pope added, by what he called 'the reasoning of the eye': 'that which is not just in buildings is disagreeble to the eye (as greater upon a slighter, etc.)' (No. 558). The 'well-proportion'd Dome' Pope describes in the *Essay on Criticism* is a product of similar rules:

> 'Tis not a *Lip*, or *Eye*, we Beauty call,
> But the joint Force and full *Result* of *all*.
> Thus when we view some well-proportion'd Dome,
> (The *World*'s just Wonder, and ev'n *thine* O *Rome*!)
> No single Parts unequally surprize;
> All comes *united* to th' admiring Eyes;
> No monstrous Height, or Breadth, or Length appear;
> The *Whole* at once is *Bold*, and *Regular*. (245–52)

According to humanist theory, domes like St. Peter's or the Pantheon in Rome, and St. Paul's in London revealed 'the secret power of Proportion', 'a visible echo of a celestial and universally valid harmony'.[24]

iii. THE BURLINGTON ACADEMY

The Palladian movement attempted to establish the classical ideal of architecture in the public and domestic architecture of England. Inspired by Colen Campbell, led by Burlington, the movement took advantage of what appeared to be favourable conditions for architectural reform. Shaftesbury in *A Letter Concerning Design* (1712) voiced the Whig prejudice against Wren and the aspiration for a 'national Taste'. The influence of Wren was already in

[23] Cf. Wotten's cautions on the '*Orders* of *Columnes*', and his description of the 'harmonie of sight', in *The Elements of Architecture*, pp. 39–44, 53.

[24] See Wotten, *Elements of Architecture*, pp. 118–19, and Rudolf Wittkower, *Architectural Principles*, p. 8. Paul Fussell discusses this passage in *The Rhetorical World of Augustan Humanism* (Oxford, 1965), pp. 180–1.

decline as patronage shifted from the court to the Whig oligarchy, who were alerted to the possibilities of the country-house as a '*national* performance' by Kip and Knyff's *Britannia Illustrata* (1707), and to classical models in Campbell's *Vitruvius Britannicus* (1715, 1717, 1725). Motivated by political ambition and the idea of leisured retirement, a building boom was under way between 1710 and 1740.[25]

Burlington's conversion to Palladianism took place when he was coming of age, and beginning to establish himself after his first trip to Italy (1714–15) as the 'Apollo of Arts' and 'noble Maecenas of the Arts'.[26] 'His Gardens flourish', Pope wrote of his Chiswick neighbour in 1716: 'his Structures rise, his Pictures arrive, and (what is far nobler and more valuable than all) his own good Qualities daily extend themselves to all about him: Whereof, I the meanest (next to some *Italian* Chymists, Fidlers, Bricklayers, and Opera-makers) am a living Instance' (i. 347). Pope is alluding to the circle of artists under Burlington's patronage who he hoped would bring about something like a Renaissance in the English arts. Burlington surrounded himself at Burlington House and Chiswick with the men who were to realize his dreams: Giovanni Battista Guelfi (*fl.* 1715–34), an Italian sculptor; Colen Campbell, William Kent, Georg Friedrich Handel, and finally Pope himself, who was to play a significant role in Burlington's ambitious programme of architectural reform.[27]

Palladian initiatives stimulated, as we have seen, a series of architectural publications on an unprecedented scale, which were widely influential. These included the publication of some of Palladio's drawings in Burlington's collection which was the occasion for Pope's *Epistle to Burlington*. In addition to the imposing folios of drawings by Jones and Palladio dedicated to Burlington, less impressive propaganda included James Ralph's *Critical Review* (1734), 'with a fulsome dedication to Lord Burlington' and uncritical endorsement of everything Palladian.[28] Such books sponsored by Burlington gave rise to a

[25] See John Summerson, *Architecture in Britain*, p. 191.

[26] See Rudolf Wittkower, 'That Great Luminary of Architecture', *The Listener*, 50 (24 Dec. 1953), 1080; F. Saxl and R. Wittkower, 'The Dictatorship of Taste', in *British Art and the Mediterranean* (Oxford, 1948), pp. 53–60; Walpole, *Anecdotes*, iii. 56; and James M. Osborn, 'Pope, the "Apollo of the Arts", and his Countess', in *England in the Restoration and Early Eighteenth Century: Essays on Culture and Society*, ed. H. T. Swedenberg (Berkeley and Los Angeles, 1972), pp. 101–43.

[27] See Rudolf Wittkower, 'Lord Burlington and William Kent', *Archaeological Journal*, 102 (1945), 152.

[28] See Fiske Kimball, 'Burlington Architectus, Part II—Burlington's Influence', *Journal of the Royal*

literature of handbooks and manuals, which put into the hands of builders the rudiments of classical design.

One of the primary ambitions of Burlington was to realize 'a coherent programme for the reform of London's public architecture', the re-creation of 'London's centre of government', and indeed 'the whole public architecture of the realm', and to this end he helped Palladians to infiltrate the Board of Works. Disappointed by William Kent's performance as a history painter, Burlington transformed him into an architect and secured for him a position on the Board of Works. It now appears that Kent's designs, executed and unexecuted during his term on the Works, were completely dominated by Burlington's architectural authority. In the first decade of Burlington's practice 'almost all the characteristic features of English Palladianism appear in buildings erected to his design'.[29]

'The first essay of his Lordship's happy invention' was a temple in Chiswick gardens (1717), which was succeeded by Campbell's 'true Palladian front' for Burlington House with the colonnade now attributed to Burlington himself (1719), and his design of Chiswick villa (*c.* 1725). In 1723 he designed a town house for General Wade at 27 Old Burlington Street (close to Pope's site), which was an almost exact reproduction of one of Palladio's drawings in Burlington's collection. Among country-houses Burlington designed or influenced in this decade Pope praised Tottenham House, Wiltshire, as 'one of the best Houses I ever was in' (iii. 417). Burlington's designs of the 1720s culminate in the Assembly Rooms at York (1731), a public building which included an imitation, archaeologically exact, of the Egyptian Hall of Vitruvius, as interpreted by Palladio.[30]

Institute of British Architects, 34 (12 Nov. 1927), 15; and John Summerson, *Architecture in Britain*, pp. 214–16. On James Ralph's relations with Burlington and Pope, see Wren Society 11 (Oxford 1934), p. 36; and James T. Hillhouse, *The Grub-Street Journal* (Durham, 1928), pp. 71–4.

[29] On the Palladian programme of public building, see Margaret Jourdain, *The Work of William Kent* (1948), p. 46; Fiske Kimball, 'William Kent's Designs for the Houses of Parliament, 1730–40', *Journal of the Royal Institute of British Architects*, 39 (6 Aug. 1932), 734; Colvin, pp. 342, 87; and Rudolf Wittkower, 'The Earl of Burlington and William Kent', York Georgian Society, *Occasional Paper Number Five* (York, 1948), pp. 13–14.

[30] For Burlington's architecture see Colvin, pp. 86–90. On General Wade's House and York Assembly rooms see Rudolf Wittkower, 'The Earl of Burlington and William Kent', York Georgian Society, *Occasional Paper Number Five* (1948), pp. 16–27.

Burlington's development as an architect consists of a steady movement 'towards a simpler, more severe and more dogmatic conception of architecture'. But the York Assembly Rooms, 'perhaps . . . the most revolutionary building by Lord Burlington in existence', excited much hostile comment throughout the century;[31] and Pope may have been expressing the opinion of a minority when he communicated a compliment to Burlington from Hugh Bethel in 1732: 'I hear with pleasure from Mr Bethel, that the finest thing he ever beheld, inspite of Italy, is your Egyptian Hall at York: *And Bethel is an Honorable Man*' (iii. 313).

From the point of view of the architectural historian the Palladian initiatives succeeded triumphantly. But to Burlington and his circle in the heat of the battle the outcome was always in doubt, and considering Burlington's idealism and ambition, his single-minded devotion to architecture, the campaign must have seemed an abject failure. His hopes for a Renaissance of the arts were disappointed: few of his protégés lived up to expectations. The programme for reform of public architecture was scarcely begun. The designs of Kent and Burlington for the Palace of Whitehall and the Houses of Parliament were never executed—Kent's only important public building in London, the Horse Guards (1758), was erected posthumously and gleefully satirized by Hogarth. The truth is that public building in the reigns of George I and II had practically come to a standstill. The little public building that was undertaken was frustrated by political intrigue, lack of financing, incompetence, and litigation.[32]

In domestic architecture the Palladians established a popular fashion in the architecture of the country-house, but the Palladian style was under attack from the time Burlington House was remodelled in 1719, and Burlington's designs were ridiculed for their inconvenience and small scale.[33] The most

[31] Rudolf Wittkower, ibid., pp. 22–3.

[32] See John Summerson, *Georgian London* (1945; rpt. Harmondsworth, 1962), pp. 36, 118; and Frank Jenkins, *Architect and Patron* (1961), p. 69. On the Palace of Whitehall, and Parliament Buildings, see John Summerson, *Architecture in Britain*, p. 201, and Fiske Kimball, 'William Kent's Designs for the Houses of Parliament 1730–1740', *Journal of the Royal Institute of British Architects*, 39 (6 Aug. 1932), 733–55, and 'Designs, 1734–1740, Second Installment', *Journal R.I.B.A.*, 39 (10 Sept. 1932), 801–7.

[33] On the ridicule of Burlington House and Chiswick, see *Suffolk Letters*, i. 385 n., Walpole, *Anecdotes of Painting* (1876), iii. 53–6, and James Lees-Milne, 'Lord Burlington in Yorkshire', *Architectural Review*, 98 (1954), 11–12. See n. 8, above.

famous of these attacks is the engraving after Hogarth, 'Taste' (1732), featuring the gate of Burlington House. Referring to critics of his York Assembly Rooms, Burlington told Pope in 1732 'I despise the whole race of censurers with or without names' (iii. 322), and he had even greater contempt for those who carelessly or ignorantly imitated the Palladian style. Pope referred to such people in a letter to Burlington as 'the Common Enemy, the Bad Imitators & Pretenders' (iii. 188), and he satirized in the *Epistle to Burlington* those who Burlington believed were undermining his scrupulous academic ideal of architecture. A letter from William Kent to Burlington in 1732 characterizes the beleaguered attitude of the Palladians at the time of Pope's *Epistle to Burlington*. Kent is referring ironically to the building of a new theatre in the sacred precincts of Inigo Jones's Covent Garden (plate 62):

as for what you and I do, it may be esteem'd a hundred year hence, but at present does not look like it, by what I see doing in ye Arcad's in convent garding, Inigo thought proper to add a portico of the Tuscan order, but these wise head's have put an Ionick expencive portico in the rustick arches, for an Entrance into the absurd Building they have made.[34]

Burlington's ambitious programme of architectural reform, the difficulties it encountered, and the opposition it aroused, were the occasion for Pope's architectural satire, an important strain in his poetry which dates from the *Dunciad* (1728), and extends through the decade of the 1730s reflecting the vicissitudes of the Palladian movement.

[34] Kent's reference is to the 'great entrance' in the east end bay of the north side of the Piazza to the Covent Garden Theatre designed by Edward Shepherd between 1731 and 1732. See 'Pope-Burlington Correspondence and Kent Letters', Chatsworth MSS., box 143, quoted by F. H. W. Sheppard, ed., *The Theatre Royal Drury Lane and the Royal Opera House Covent Garden*, Survey of London, 35 (London, 1970), 88. See 'Edward Shepherd's Theatre of 1731–2', ibid., pp. 86–8, pl. 41a.

12. *Publick Buildings, Greater Houses, and Villas*

POPE has been called the 'public relations officer' and the 'evangelist' of the Palladian movement,[1] but he is by no means the whitewasher of Burlington's gate pictured in the satirical engraving, 'Taste'. To be sure, Pope believed that Burlington had 'revived the true Taste of Architecture in this Kingdom',[2] and he was in agreement with the ambition of the Palladian movement to reform the national taste in architecture, but he is not a doctrinaire apologist for the Palladian style. He does not share the Palladian prejudice against Wren and Vanbrugh, or Burlington's uncompromising devotion to Palladian architecture. Although he sometimes gets involved in the politics and personalities of architectural controversy, the aim of his satire is to identify Burlington and the Palladian movement with humanistic ideals of architecture rather than to engage in partisan polemic. In the tradition of Vitruvius and Palladio he looks on architecture as a manifestation of virtu, an index of the moral character of the builders, the architect, or the entire nation; and his judgements of builders, buildings, and architects depend as much on ethical as aesthetic principles.

i. NATIONAL WORKS

In *Windsor Forest*, a poem celebrating a Tory peace, Pope endorses Shaftesbury's Whiggish ideal of a national taste in architecture in Father Thames's prophetic allusion to the 'Works of Peace':

> Behold! *Augusta*'s glitt'ring Spires increase,
> And Temples rise, the beauteous Works of Peace.

[1] By Christopher Hussey, 'Introduction' to *The Work of William Kent* (1948) by Margaret Jourdain, p. 20; and Frank Jenkins, *Architect and Patron* (Oxford, 1961), p. 72.

[2] *Dunciad*, III (1729), l. 324 n.; *TE* v. 189.

I see, I see where two fair Cities bend
Their ample Bow, a new *White-Hall* ascend! (377–80)

Shaftesbury had mentioned the rebuilding of the Palace of Whitehall (in ruins since its destruction by fire in the 1690s), along with the Houses of Parliament as one of 'the noblest subjects for architecture', spared from the spoiling hand of Wren.[3] Pope wrote in the belief that the magnificent design of Inigo Jones for the palace at Whitehall would one day be executed, a hope cherished by the Palladians who published Jones's designs.[4] The 'Temples' and 'Spires' refer to the fifty new churches authorized in the reign of Queen Anne. The tone of these allusions to Augusta's 'two fair Cities' expresses the Palladian ambition to build a new Rome in London, based on the Vitruvian ideal of architecture.

In the *Dunciad* (1728) Pope delivered his first stroke supporting a national taste in architecture when Settle prophetically appoints an architect to serve the Queen of Dulness:

B[enson] sole Judge of Architecture sit,
And Namby Pamby be prefer'd for Wit!
While naked mourns the Dormitory wall,
And Jones' and Boyle's united labours fall,
While Wren with sorrow to the grave descends,
Gay dies un-pension'd with a hundred Friends. (iii. 321–6)

It is interesting to discover that Pope's Dunce of architecture, William Benson (1682–1754), was one of the founders of the Palladian movement and its counterpart the Jones revival. He was the designer of Wilbury House, Newton Toney, Wiltshire (1710), 'in the style of Inigo Jones' according to *Vitruvius Britannicus* (1715), and now regarded as 'the earliest evidence of anything in the nature of an Inigo Jones revival'. Benson was not an architect, but a politician (Sheriff of Wiltshire and Whig M.P.), whose influence at Court contributed to the earliest Palladian invasion of the Board of Works in 1718, when Benson succeeded Wren as Surveyor of Works with Colen

[3] Anthony Ashley Cooper, *A Letter Concerning Design* (1732), in *Second Characters*, ed. Benjamin Rand (Cambridge, 1914), p. 21.

[4] E.C. i. 364 n. On the publication of Jones's Whitehall designs by Colen Campbell (1717) and William Kent (1727), see John Summerson, *Architecture in Britain*, pp. 78–9.

Campbell as his deputy, and Vanbrugh and Hawksmoor were displaced. As Pope's note explains, Benson was censured for a 'false and groundless' survey condemning the House of Lords, the Painted Chamber, and the Court of Requests, which resulted in his dismissal in 1719 along with Campbell, swiftly ending the Palladian presence on the Board of Works.[5]

Benson's politics, his incompetence, and his literary enthusiasm for Milton (elsewhere ridiculed by Pope)[6] made him an eligible subject for satire, but Pope's note indicates that he was primarily disturbed by the scandalous treatment of Christopher Wren in this episode: 'In favour of this man [Benson]', Pope's note reads, 'the famous Sir *Christopher Wren*, who had been Architect to the Crown for above fifty years, who laid the first stone of St. *Paul*'s, and lived to finish it, had been displac'd from his employment at the age of near ninety years'.[7] Evidently Pope did not share the prejudice of Shaftesbury and strict Palladians like Burlington against Wren's St. Paul's.[8] His censure of Wren's monument to the fire (plate 63)—

> Where London's column, pointing at the skies
> Like a tall bully, lifts the head, and lyes—

is not a judgement on the architect, but the inscription, 'importing that city to have been burnt by the Papists'.[9] In Pope's mind Wren's architecture, particularly his churches, admirably fulfilled the classical ideal of virtu. It was not important to Pope that his architecture failed to conform strictly to Palladian rules. In Pope's couplet, Wren is linked with John Gay as a pathetic example of the deserving artist unrewarded by a thankless nation.

The Westminster Dormitory in the same prophetic speech by Settle in the *Dunciad* alludes to a more successful Palladian initiative than the abortive invasion of the Board of Works. The reference is to the construction of a new Dormitory designed by Burlington for Westminster School in the pre-

[5] On Wilbury House, see John Summerson, *Architecture in Britain*, pp. 190–1. On William Benson, see *Dunciad*, III (1729), l. 321 n., *TE* v. 188.

[6] See *Dunciad*, IV, ll. 110–12; *TE* v. 352, vi. 395–7.

[7] *TE* v. 188 n.

[8] Anthony Ashley Cooper, *A Letter Concerning Design*, p. 22.

[9] *Epistle to Bathurst*, ll. 339–40 n.; *TE* iii. ii, 121. Pope's attitude to Wren exactly parallels Robert Morris's in *An Essay in Defence of Ancient Architecture* (London, 1728), pp. 25–7, where he remarks on 'the deserving Character . . . of Wren', praises his churches, particularly the 'stupendous' and 'miraculous' St. Paul's, and refers to 'a melancholy Consideration, that he was no more honoured and dignify'd by his Country, nor respected by the unthinking part of Mankind'.

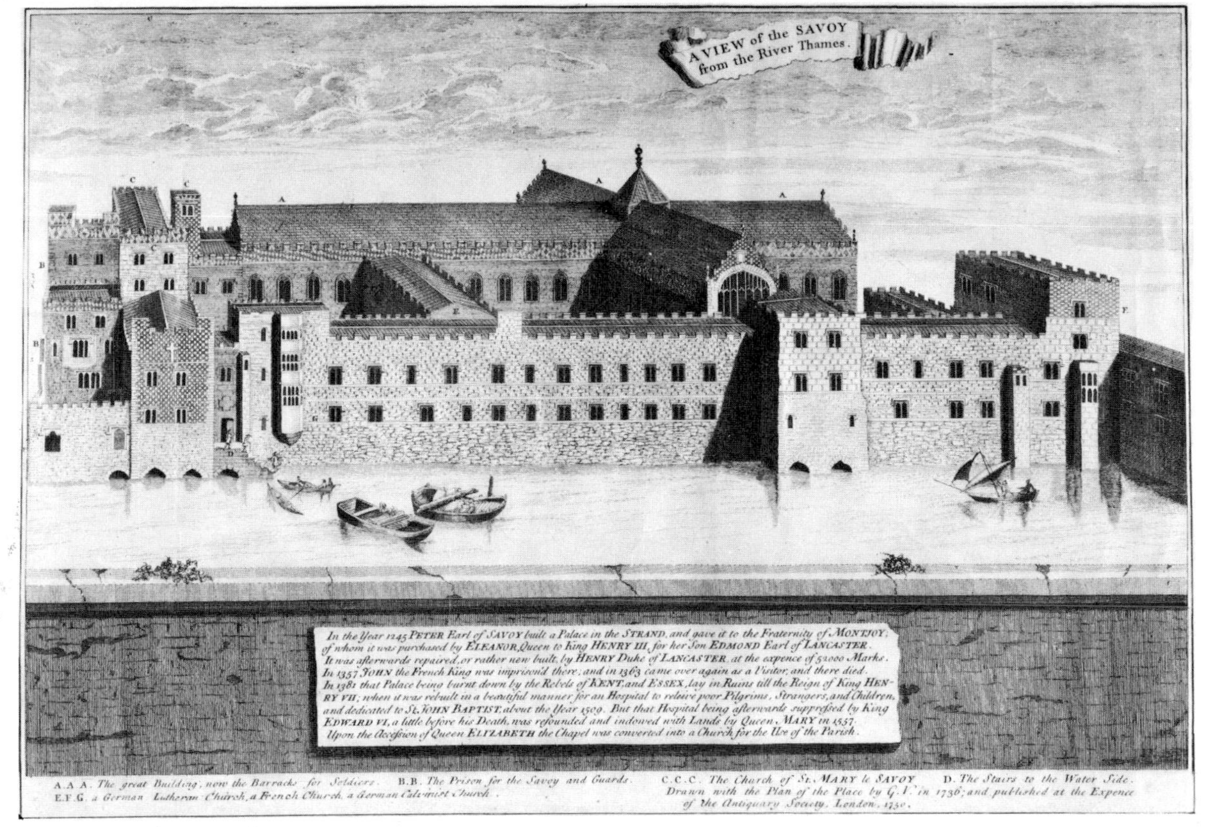

66. Savoy Palace, London. By George Vertue. 1736.

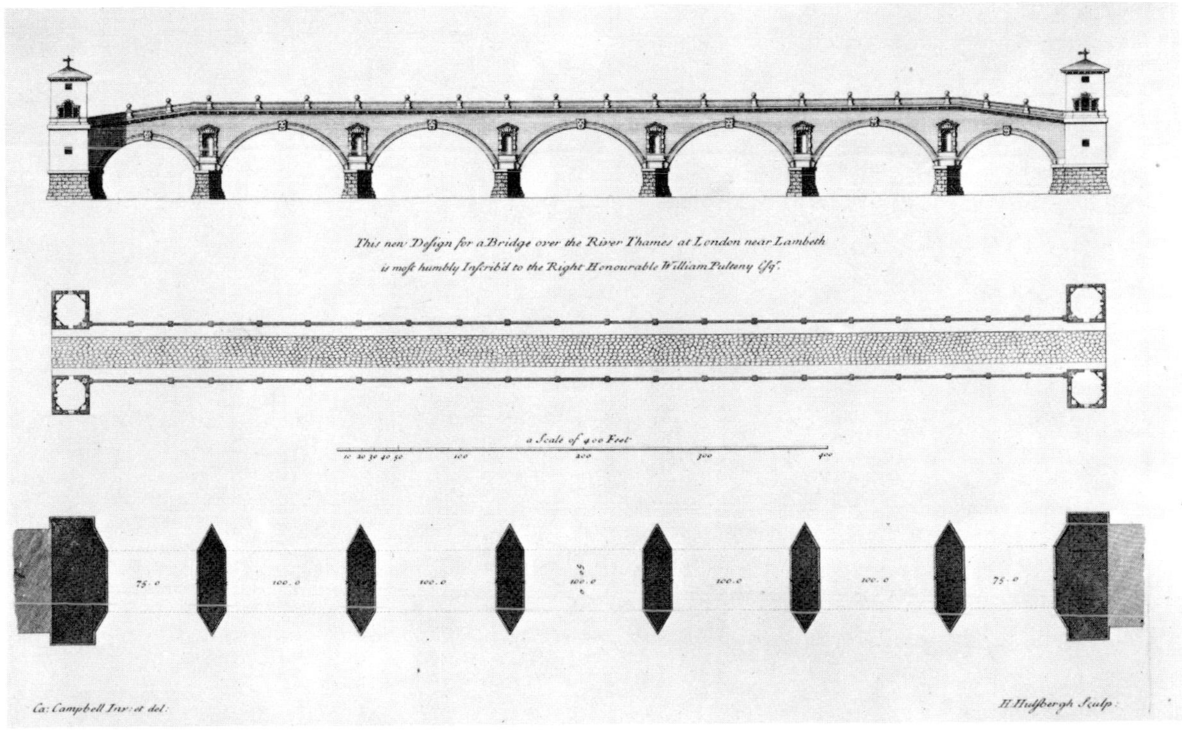

67. Design for a Bridge at Lambeth. By Colen Campbell. 1725.

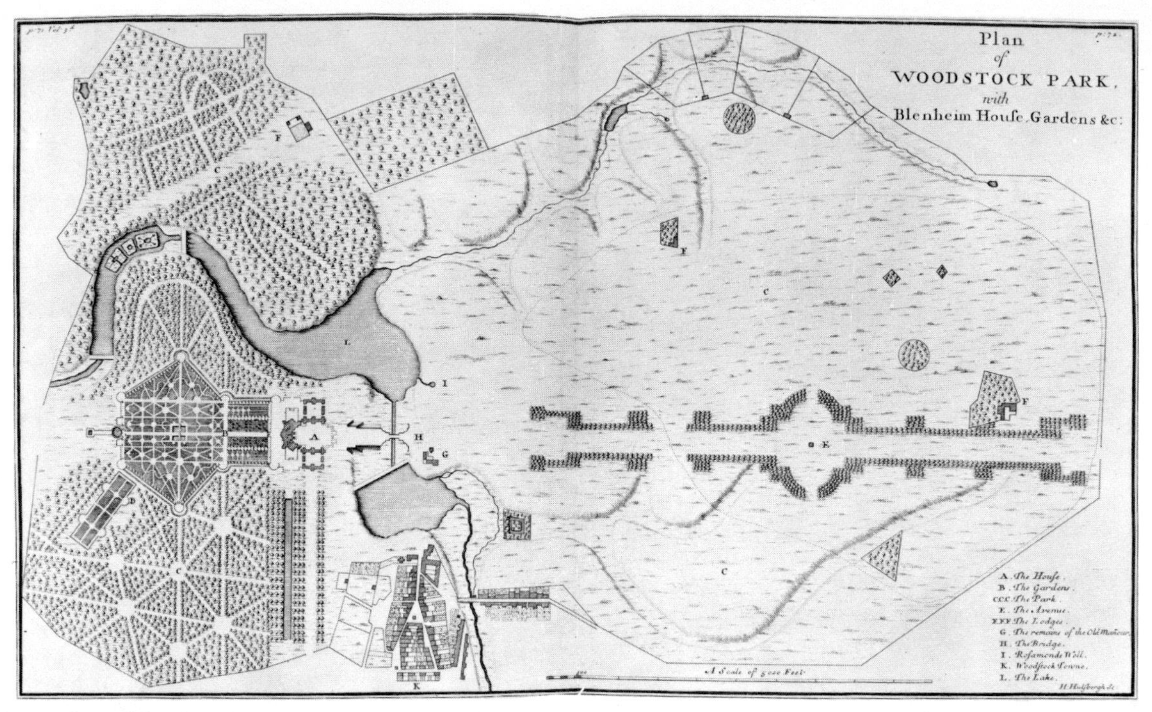

68. Plan of the Gardens at Blenheim, Oxfordshire. By Colen Campbell. 1725.

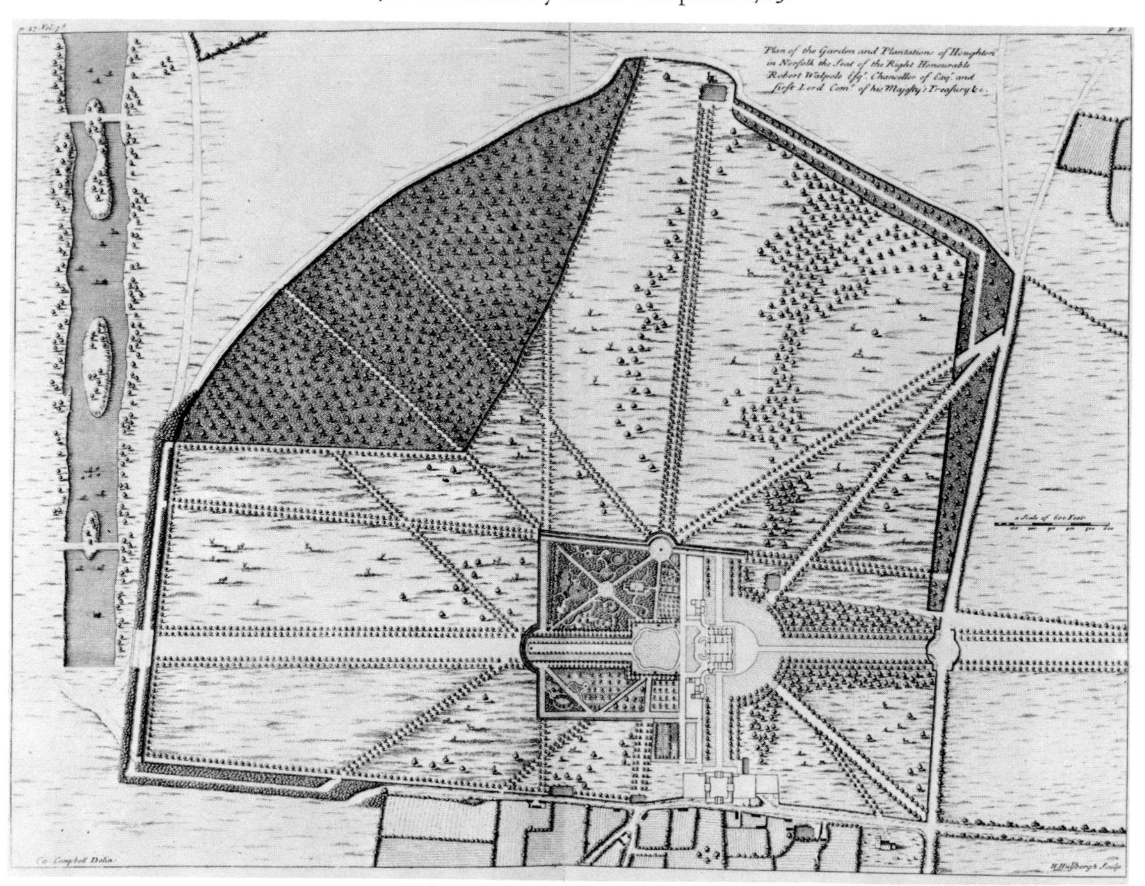

69. Plan of the Gardens at Houghton, Norfolk. By Colen Campbell. 1725.

cincts of the Abbey (plate 64) which was the first Palladian commission for a public building in London, selected by Dean Atterbury in preference to designs of Wren submitted for the same project.[10] The Palladian victory over the school of Wren was soured by delays in the construction to which Pope alludes in references to 'th' unfinished' (1728) and 'naked' (1729) Dormitory Wall, and to faulty execution of Burlington's designs, which did not meet his exacting standards, as Pope's note explains: 'The shell being finished according to his Lordship's design, the succeeding Dean and Chapter employ'd a common builder to do the inside, which is perform'd *accordingly*'[11]—a violation of Palladio's symphonic principle of proportion.

Editions of the *Dunciad* after 1729 substitute for Burlington's Dormitory a building at Whitehall, focus of Palladian hopes for public building: 'See under Ripley rise a new White-hall.' The architect Thomas Ripley (*c.* 1683–1758) had particularly annoyed the Burlington circle when in 1726 through the influence of Walpole he succeeded Vanbrugh in the post of Comptroller of the Works, despite Burlington's 'Great Endeavours' on behalf of William Kent, who was obliged to serve under Ripley in the less lucrative and influential post of Master Carpenter. Ripley had designed one building during his tenure on the Works, the Admiralty building in Whitehall (1722–6; plate 65), which was despised by the Burlington circle. Horace Walpole's plea for his father's architect does little to mitigate the verdict of the modern architectural historian who describes Ripley as a 'nonentity who happened to have Walpole's ear', and the Admiralty as 'scarcely Palladian and nothing but a late and poor specimen of Wren's style, vilely proportioned and adorned with a sort of French quoins which the Palladians had condemned'.[12]

[10] See 'The New Dormitory, Westminster School, 1708–31. Sir Chr. Wren and Lord Burlington Architects', Wren Society 11 (1934), 35–45; and Colvin, p. 87.

[11] *Dunciad*, III (1729), l. 323 n.; *TE* v. 189. The foundation stone was laid by Burlington 21 Apr. 1722, but the inside of the building was unfinished as late as 1733. The workmen were under Burlington's supervision until he lost control after Atterbury's committal to the tower. See 'The New Dormitory, Westminster School, 1708–31', pp. 35–6, 41–2.

[12] See *Dunciad*, III (1742), l. 327; *TE* v. 336. John Summerson discusses the designs for a new Whitehall Palace in *Architecture in Britain*, pp. 78-9, 161–2, 201–2, 214. For Kent's relations with Richard Arundell, Surveyor General of Works in 1726, see F. H. W. Sheppard, ed., Survey of London, *The Parish of St. James Westminster*, 32 (1963), 510. On Ripley, see Horace Walpole, *Anecdotes of Painting* (1876), iii. 49–50; John Summerson, *Georgian London* (1962), p. 113; and *Architecture in Britain*, p. 212.

Once again Pope's satire of Ripley goes beyond mere Palladian prejudice; his judgement of Ripley here and elsewhere cannot be construed as *ad hominem* 'jeers' and 'sneers', as Bateson interprets them.[13] In other references to Ripley Pope characterizes him as a false and obsequious guide to private builders like Walpole, for whom he executed Colen Campbell's designs at Houghton, and as the incompetent spoiler of national works. 'This Man', Pope writes in a note to the *Epistle to Burlington* (l. 18), 'was a carpenter, employ'd by a first Minister, who rais'd him to an Architect, without any genius in the art; and after some wretched proofs of his insufficiency in public Buildings, made him Comptroller of the Board of Works'.[14] The reference to a 'new Whitehall' in the context of a perverse prophecy by the Prince of Dulness, can be read not only as a topical allusion to a vile unPalladian public building, the Admiralty, but as the ironic and unwelcome fulfilment of the prophecy of Father Thames in *Windsor Forest*: 'I see . . . a new *White-Hall* ascend!' (379–80). The building rising before the eyes of Settle and Cibber is not the glorious classical design of Inigo Jones for a royal Palace, but the egregious and contemptible design for an administrative building of a corrupt government designed by an ignorant timeserver, and spoiler of public magnificence.[15]

The reference in the same passage in the *Dunciad* (1729) to the fall of 'Jones' and Boyle's united labours' (iii. l. 324) plays on the irony that while the false judge of architecture, Benson, imagines repairs where none are needed in the House of Lords, glorious national monuments are falling to ruin. The line calls attention to the neglected public buildings of Inigo Jones, and the efforts of Burlington and his circle to restore them, as Pope explains in his note:

> At the time when this Poem was written, the Banquetting-house of *Whitehall*, the Church and Piazza of *Covent-garden*, and the Palace and Chappel of *Somerset-house*, the works of the famous *Inigo Jones*, had been for many years so neglected, as to be in danger of ruin. The Portico of *Covent-garden* Church had been just then [1727] restored and beautify'd at the expence of *Richard* Earl of *Burlington*; who, at the same time, by his publication of the designs of that great Master and *Palladio*, as well as by many noble buildings of his own, revived the true Taste of Architecture in this Kingdom.[16]

Jones's Banqueting House was all that survived of the Palace of Whitehall,

[13] *Epistle to Burlington*, l. 18 n., *TE* iii. ii, 138.

[14] *TE* iii. ii, 137 n.

[15] Cf. *Dunciad*, III, l. 327 n. E.C. iv. 350–1 n.

[16] *Dunciad*, III, l. 324 n., *TE* v. 189.

destroyed by fires in 1692 and 1698.[17] Jones's designs for Somerset House, the London Palace of Charles I's queen, included a chapel (1630–5), and 'a monumental scheme for rebuilding' the Strand front, never executed.[18] Pope satirizes public indifference to the fate of Somerset House and Westminster Hall in *Peri Bathous*, where he ridicules a scheme to erect a theatre at the public expense.[19]

Jones's designs for the Church of St. Paul Covent Garden and the houses on the north and east sides of the square standing on arcades known as piazzas, 'the first and finest of London's long sequence of residential squares', had been vulnerable from the outset to spoliation.[20] The *Weekly Journal* (22 April 1727) indicates Burlington's attitudes to alterations in Jones's design of the Tuscan portico of Covent Garden church, which had been altered during its original construction beginning in 1631:

> The Right Honourable the Earl of Burlington out of Regard to the Memory of the celebrated Inigo Jones, and to prevent our Countrymen being exposed for their Ignorance, has very generously been at the Expence of three or four hundred Pounds to restore the Portico of Covent-Garden Church, now one of the finest in the World, to its primitive Form; 'tis said, it once cost the Inhabitants about twice as much to spoil it.[21]

Kent's complaint about the confusion of the Tuscan and Ionic orders in the Arcade of Covent Garden, quoted in the last chapter, appears to reflect the actions of the 3rd Duke of Bedford, who was 'responsible for permitting the first important deviation from the architectural unity of the portico

[17] See Hugh Phillips, *Mid-Georgian London: A Topographical and Social Survey of Central and Western London about 1750* (London, 1964), p. 31.

[18] John Summerson, *Inigo Jones* (Harmondsworth, 1966), pp. 75–9. On Somerset House, see Nikolaus Pevsner, 'Old Somerset House', *Architectural Review*, 116 (Sept. 1954), 163–7.

[19] *The Art of Sinking in Poetry, A Critical Edition*, ed. Edna Leake Steeves (New York, 1952), pp. 87–8. The editor's conjecture about Somerset House ('Commentary', p. 192), that 'the point of Pope's proposal is directed at its uselessness and the impracticality of keeping it in repair', is surely mistaken. He is satirizing the neglect and abuse of another monument of Inigo Jones's architecture. On Westminster Hall, see Nikolaus Pevsner, *London—I: The Cities of London and Westminster*, 2nd edn., The Buildings of England, 12 (Harmondsworth, 1962), 485–6.

[20] See John Summerson, *Architecture in Britain*, pp. 77–8, and F. H. W. Sheppard, ed., *The Parish of St. Paul Covent Garden*, Survey of London, 36 (London, 1970), 64.

[21] *The Weekly Journal* (Apr. 1727), quoted in *The Parish of St. Paul Covent Garden*, p. 107. See John Summerson, *Inigo Jones* (1966), p. 89.

buildings in the Piazza', and who allowed the building of the Covent Garden Theatre by James Shepherd (d. 1747), an architect despised by the Palladians.[22]

It is interesting to discover that originally (*Dunciad*, 1728), instead of 'Jones and Boyle's united labours', the line read: 'I see the Savoy totter to her fall' (iii. l. 324). Savoy House in the Strand (plate 66) was a Gothic castle built in 1245 by Peter, Earl of Savoy, and restored by Henry VII, which featured a magnificent great hall with a wooden beamed ceiling adorned with carvings of angels clasping heraldic shields. In 1720 this royal building, described in Stow's survey as 'very ruinous', was being used as a barracks for soldiers and a prison, its 'great hall, which had formerly been occupied by kings, was rented to a cooper for storing hoops and barrel-sections, and the rain dripped on them through the unrepaired woodwork ceiling'.[23] As in the reference to Westminster Hall in *Peri Bathous*, Pope's concern for the preservation of national monuments is not confined to classical works of architecture.

Pope's major statement of the idea of 'National Works' in architecture appears at the conclusion of *An Epistle to the Right Honourable Richard Earl of Burlington, Occasion'd by his Publishing Palladio's Designs of the Baths, Arches, Theatres, &c. of Ancient Rome* (1731). In 1730 Burlington had published Palladio's drawings of the principal Roman Baths in a handsome folio with his Italian Preface, *Fabbriche Antiche disegnate da Andrea Palladio Vicentino*, the first of an intended series of publications of Palladio's drawings of Roman antiquities in Burlington's collection. Pope sent to Burlington in April 1731 a version of the *Epistle to Burlington* with 'the Thought . . . of its attending the Book' (iii. 187)—that is, the intended second volume in Burlington's series which never appeared.[24]

The drawings of Roman antiquities were the basis of Palladio's architectural theory in the *Four Books of Architecture* (1570), and the source of his architectural ideals. In the 'Preface' to Book III of the *Four Books* Palladio speaks of the 'publick edifices' of ancient Rome, which exemplify 'the greatness of their souls'. In Roman ruins 'we are able to get at a certain knowledge of the Roman

[22] *St. Paul Covent Garden*, p. 37. Hugh Phillips, *Mid-Georgian London*, p. 140. See chap. 10, n. 34.

[23] John Stow, *A Survey of London*, ed. J. Strype, 2 vols. (London, 1720), i. 212. Hugh Phillips, *The Thames About 1750* (London, 1951), p. 106.

[24] F. W. Bateson, 'Introduction', *TE* iii. ii, xxv.

virtue and grandeur, which perhaps had not otherwise been believed'.[25] These values, moral as much as architectural, are implicit in Pope's allusion in the *Epistle to Burlington* to Burlington's publication of Palladio's drawings of Roman antiquities:

> You show us, Rome was glorious, not profuse,
> And pompous buildings once were things of Use. (23–4)

In the stirring conclusion to the *Epistle to Burlington* with its echoes of the *Aeneid* Pope urges Burlington to extend his ambitions for the architecture of London to the entire Nation:

> You too proceed! make falling Arts your care,
> Erect new wonders, and the old repair,
> Jones and Palladio to themselves restore,
> And be whate'er Vitruvius was before:
> Till Kings call forth th' Idea's of your mind,
> Proud to accomplish what such hands design'd,
> Bid Harbors open, public Ways extend,
> Bid Temples, worthier of the God, ascend;
> Bid the broad Arch the dang'rous Flood contain,
> The Mole projected break the roaring Main;
> Back to his bounds their subject Sea command,
> And roll obedient Rivers thro' the Land;
> These Honours, Peace to happy Britain brings,
> These are Imperial Works, and worthy Kings. (191–204)

Pope addresses Burlington here as the architect who had already been recognized for 'reestablishing the tradition of Palladian architecture in England', and was saluted as 'il Palladio e il Jones di' nostri Tempi'.[26]

Pope's poetry throughout the decade reflects the fate of 'National Works' in Georgian England, and shows how far its architecture remained from the

[25] Rudolf Wittkower, *Architectural Principles in the Age of Humanism*, 3rd edn. rev. (London, 1967), pp. 63–4. Andrea Palladio, *The Four Books of Architecture*, ed. Adolf K. Placzek (1738; rpt. New York: 1965), p. 57.

[26] *TE* iii. ii, 188. On the allusiveness of these lines, see Henry Avril and Peter Dixon, 'Pope and the Architects: A Note on the *Epistle to Burlington*', *English Studies*, 51 (Oct. 1970), 437–41. For the tributes to Burlington, see Colvin, p. 362, and Rudolf Wittkower, 'The Earl of Burlington and William Kent', York Georgian Society, *Occasional Paper Number Five* (York, 1948), p. 10.

Vitruvian-Palladian ideal. Bethel's sermon in the *Imitations of Horace*, Satire II, ii (1734) declaims against the neglect of public works:

> Oh Impudence of wealth! with all thy store,
> How dar'st thou let one worthy man be poor?
> Shall half the new-built Churches round thee fall?
> Make Keys, build Bridges, or repair White-hall:
> Or to thy Country let that heap be lent,
> As M[arlborough] O's was, but not at five *per Cent*. (117–22)

Along with the recurring allusion to the neglect of Whitehall, Pope refers to ill-executed projects like the churches in London and Westminster authorized by acts of Queen Anne and George I, unexecuted schemes for needed embankments along the Thames at Whitehall, and to the long-considered plan to build another bridge across the Thames at Westminster. The fate of all these projects is summarized in Pope's 'very remarkable note' to the passage on 'Imperial Works' in the 1735 and following editions of the *Epistle to Burlington*.[27]

Corresponding to each of the 'Imperial Works . . . worthy Kings' to which Pope urged Burlington to proceed in 1731, the note records the dismal record of achievement. The 'Temples, worthier of God' are identified with the 'new-built Churches' in London and Westminster, some badly sited, which had already started to collapse: 'others', Pope notes, 'were vilely executed, thro' fraudulent cabals between undertakers, officers, &c.' As for 'The Mole projected' and the 'obedient Rivers', the note refers to the long-delayed completion (1723) of an embankment on the Thames breached during a storm in 1707 at Dagenham, Essex, and to unexecuted embankments at Whitehall between Wren's Queen Mary's Terrace (1693) and a quay south of the Duke of Richmond's terrace, where the river had formed a foul delta of mud.[28] Concerning 'public Ways' in the Roman manner of road building: 'Many of the highways throughout England were hardly passable', Pope remarks, 'and most of those which were repaired by Turnpikes were made jobs for private lucre, and infamously executed, even to the entrances of London itself.'

[27] See *Imitations of Horace*, *TE* iv. 63, and n. (l. 119); and *Epistle to Burlington*, *TE* iii. ii, 155–6 n. (ll. 195–204). Details in the next paragraph are derived from these notes.

[28] Montagu H. Cox and Philip Norman, ed., *The Parish of St. Margaret, Westminster*, Survey of London, 13 (London, 1930), 59, 215.

The summons to 'build Bridges' was eventually obeyed in the construction of Westminster Bridge (1738–49) but it was a campaign which illustrated the obstacles in the way of public works, and the frustration of Palladian hopes. At the moment Pope was composing his note, it appeared that the bridge commission was to be given to Thomas Ripley:

> The proposal of building a Bridge at Westminster had been petition'd against and rejected; but in two years after the publication of this poem, an Act for building a Bridge past thro' both houses [1736]. After many debates in the committee, the execution was left to the carpenter above-mentioned [Ripley, l. 18] who would have made it a wooden one.

Between 1726 and 1728 Ripley had submitted designs for timber bridges to commissions appointed to build a bridge across the Thames from Fulham to Putney; in 1737 he was appointed assessor to the Commissioners for the Westminster Bridge, and again submitted a design of his own for a bridge of fifteen arches. Although the design of the Swiss engineer, Charles Labelye (1705–?62) was eventually selected, and the foundation stone laid by the Earl of Pembroke in 1739, it seemed imminent when Pope published his *Epistle to Augustus* (1737) that the first bridge built across the Thames in London since the 12th century was to be a wooden Bridge designed by an architect the Burlington circle regarded as an incompetent creature of Walpole: 'Oh Shame! a *wooden Bridge*! . . . no better perhaps than that at *Fulham*', the *Prompter* exclaimed.[29]

Westminster Bridge, one of two important public works erected in the Georgian period, has usually been attributed to the efforts of the Earl of Pembroke and his circle, but Burlington's party had been advocating the idea since Colen Campbell submitted in 1721 a 'new Design for a Bridge over the River Thames at London near Lambeth' (illustrated in *Vitruvius Britannicus*, iii, 1725, plate 56) to a Committee acting on a petition to Commons chaired by Burlington's friend, William Pultney. Campbell's design (plate 67) is a studied imitation of Palladio's drawings of Roman bridges, probably from Burlington's collection, and it included towers penetrated by Venetian windows in Burlington's manner. It perfectly reflects Palladio's

[29] *Epistle to Burlington*, ll. 195–204 n., *TE* iii. ii, 155–6 n. See Colvin, p. 503; and John Summerson, *Georgian London*, p. 114; *Architecture in Britain*, p. 212.

ideals about the grandeur and dignity of bridges. But Campbell's design went for nothing against the opposition of the City of London, which argued that 'such Bridge, if erected, will prove inconsistent with and destructive of the Rights, Properties, Privileges and Franchises of this City, will be a great prejudice to London Bridge, and to the Navigation of the River Thames, so as to render it dangerous if not impracticable'.[30]

Although Campbell's design sponsored by Burlington was defeated by the City, the Burlington circle can claim some credit for preventing Ripley's design from disgracing the Thames. Pope's long series of allusions discrediting Ripley's architecture culminate in the attack on him as a bridge builder in the *Epistle to Augustus, Imitations of Horace*, Ep. II, i (1737):

> Who builds a Bridge that never drove a pyle?
> (Should Ripley venture, all the World would smile). (185–6)

In the same year Burlington was entertaining the 'Committee of the Bridge' at Chiswick, when Pope wrote to ask for his 'Vote & Interest' (iv. 82) in a candidate for appointment as secretary or clerk to the Commission. From 1737 Burlington was one of the Commissioners appointed to superintend the building of Westminster Bridge. When Thomas Ripley, who was employed as an assessor by the Commission, submitted his design for a bridge, there can be no doubt about how Burlington voted.[31]

Pope's conclusions about the outcome of the Palladian campaign for public works to which he summoned Burlington in 1731 can be read in his allusions to London in 1743 as 'the Land of Perdition' (iv. 423) and 'Jericho' (iv. 441). The grand design of the Palladians for rebuilding London's public architecture had been frustrated. Hopes for a new Whitehall and Palace of Westminster were disappointed with the abandonment of William Kent's designs for rebuilding the Houses of Parliament, a project directly inspired by Burlington's ideals which the Palladians had promoted throughout the 1730s. It was the loss of a unique opportunity:

By the abandonment of the great project for the Houses of Parliament, as earlier by

[30] See Howard E. Stutchbury, quoting the *House of Commons Journals* in *The Architecture of Colen Campbell* (Manchester, 1967), pp. 60–1, fig. 60. For Palladio's preference for stone bridges, see *The Four Books of Architecture*, ed. Adolf K. Placzek (New York, 1965), pp. 62, 68.

[31] Colvin, p. 503; *TE* iii. ii, 156 n.

the abortive issue of the plans for Whitehall, England lost for generations the opportunity of creating on the bank of the Thames a palace worthy of her power and consequence. Of the three great classic buildings proposed for the unrivalled sites afforded by the river, Somerset House alone was to come into being [rebuilt by William Chambers 1776–80]. To imagine the constellation of all three is to appreciate the depth of the artistic loss.[32]

Architecture is pre-eminently one of the arts going out in the *Dunciad* (1742): '*Art* after *Art* goes out, and all is Night' (iv. l. 640).

ii. GREATER HOUSES

The main object of the architectural satire in the *Epistle to Burlington* is not public buildings, but the private builders who were building on an unprecedented scale to advertise their political and financial importance. Among them were ignorant pretenders to taste whom Burlington attacks in the Preface to *Fabbriche Antiche* (1730) for perverting Palladio's art:

> I cannot do less than assert, that the studies of so great a man [Palladio] must be much more valuable, by far the most seasonable gift to our age, of which none other perhaps has ever shown a greater disposition for costly buildings, nor has produced more ignorant pretenders, who have guided others out of the true lines of so beautiful an art.[33]

Pope told Burlington in a letter containing a draft of the *Epistle to Burlington* that he added to his draft of the poem lines attacking the ignorant pretenders to taste: 'Some lines are added toward the End [ll. 23–38, following l. 180 in the first edition] on the Common Enemy, the Bad Imitators & Pretenders, which perhaps are properer there, than in your own mouth' (iii. 188). In the published version of the poem Pope's lines take the following form:

> You show us, Rome was glorious, not profuse,
> And pompous buildings once were things of Use.
> Yet shall (my Lord) your just, your noble rules
> Fill half the land with Imitating Fools;

[32] Fiske Kimball, 'William Kent's Designs for the Houses of Parliament, 1734–40, Second Instalment', *Journal of the Royal Institute of British Architects*, 39 (10 Sept. 1932), 807.

[33] My literal translation of the passage quoted by George Sherburn, '"Timon's Villa" and Cannons', *Huntington Library Bulletin*, 8 (Oct. 1935), 131.

Who random drawings from your sheets shall take,
And of one beauty many blunders make;
Load some vain Church with old Theatric state,
Turn Arcs of triumph to a Garden-gate;
Reverse your Ornaments, and hang them all
On some patch'd dog-hole ek'd with ends of wall,
Then clap four slices of Pilaster on't,
That, lac'd with bits of rustic, makes a Front.
Or call the winds thro' long Arcades to roar,
Proud to catch cold at a Venetian door;
Conscious they act a true Palladian part,
And if they starve, they starve by rules of art. (23–38)

Here Pope condemns the arbitrary and random use of classical designs, which violates the organic nature of classical architecture. The front, which Palladio conceived of as a meticulous composition of harmonic ratios, is pieced together with random ornaments. The Vitruvian principle of *decor* is violated in the application to a church of 'Orders of Pilasters in the Theatrical' style, which, according to Colen Campbell, 'admits of more Gayety than is proper either for the Temple or Palatial Stile',[34] and by introducing pompous arches of triumph into a garden. 'Something previous ev'n to Taste' (l. 42) is violated when builders are proud to catch cold at a Venetian door, and willing to starve by rules of art.

Despite this passage on Burlington's special aversion, the *Epistle to Burlington* is not a Palladian manifesto. Pope's primary emphasis is on false taste as an index of moral character, and on the classical sanctions for architecture—principles of utility and virtue. In remarks to Spence in 1730 he related 'ye Gardening Poem' to the ethical scheme of the *Essay on Man*, and the theme of 'Prodigality [which] flings away all in wrong tastes' (No. 310). In 1735 he grouped the poem with the *Epistle to Bathurst* under the title *The Use of Riches*. The Argument states that 'The Extremes of *Avarice* and *Profusion* being treated of in the foregoing Epistle [*To Bathurst*], this [*To Burlington*] takes up one particular Branch of the latter; the Vanity of Expence in People

[34] Referring to 'A New Design for Tobias Jenkyns', in 'An Explanation of . . . the Plates', *Vitruvius Britannicus*, 2 (1717), 2. On the principle of *decor*, see William A. Gibson, 'Three Principles of Renaissance Architectural Theory in Pope's *Epistle to Burlington*', *Studies in English Literature*, 11 (Summer 1971), 487–505.

of Wealth and Quality.' They have in common a concern with 'the misery of affluence', and the 'Impudence of wealth'.[35]

In this context Timon, the dominating figure of the poem, is not presented as one of the ignorant pretenders to taste, nor is his villa attacked for infractions against Palladian rules. The description of Timon's villa is a study of the character of its owner and the 'Motives of his Architecture' (ii. 24), the example of a man whose false taste betrays radical defects of moral character. Pope denies that this is so in the pseudonymous letter from William Cleland to John Gay (1731) defending the poem against the application of the portrait of Timon to the Duke of Chandos: 'his Reflections are not on the Man, but his House, Garden &c.' Pope asks if bad taste is

> such a *Crime*, that to impute it to a Man must be a grievous Offence? 'Tis an *Innocent Folly* and much more *Beneficent* than the Want of it; for *Ill Taste* employs more Hands, and diffuses Expence more than a *Good* one. Is it a *Moral* Defect? No, it is but a *Natural* one; a *Want of a Taste*. It is what the best good Man living may be liable to: The worthiest Peer may live exemplarily in an ill favoured House, and the best reputed Citizen be pleased with a vile Garden. (iii. 255)

This sounds like plain common sense, but it is really special pleading against the charge of personal satire which Mandeville's argument about private vices and public benefits does little to reinforce. In the logic of the satire bad taste is presented as a crime against natural law and the classical sanctions of architecture—use and virtue—and it reveals a cardinal defect in the moral character of Timon.

According to the 'Argument' of the poem, Timon's 'false Taste of Magnificence' is owing to violation of classical principles of proportion: 'the first grand Error of which is to imagine that Greatness consists in the Size and Dimension, instead of the Proportion and Harmony of the whole.' But the satire emphasizes throughout the moral rather than aesthetic error of violating classical rules of proportion. The monstrous size and disproportion of the house and garden mirror the grotesque self-conceit of its owner: the library reflects his vanity and ignorance, the chapel his vain impiety, the dinner his 'civil Pride' (l. 166). Pride is the operative word in Pope's description of

[35] See *Epistle to Burlington*, *TE* iii. ii, xxi, 129, 132 n. For the 'misery of affluence', and the 'Impudence of wealth', see Spence, No. 293, and *Imitations of Horace*, Satire II, ii (1734), l. 117, *TE* iv. 63.

Timon's villa.[36] It is pride which subverts the classical motive of architecture, use, into ostentation.

Want of taste in the *Epistle to Burlington* amounts to want of virtue, and false taste is presented as a sort of original sin:

> Some Daemon whisper'd, 'Visto! have a Taste.' (16)

A temptation to be resisted:

> Must Bishops, Lawyers, Statesmen have ye Skill
> To build, to plant, judge Paintings wot you will
> Then why not honest Kent our Treaties draw
> Bridgman explain ye Gospel, Gibbs the law.[37]

A visitation on the foolish builder:

> Heav'n visits with a Taste the wealthy fool
> And needs no rod but Ripley with a rule. (17–18)

And a punishment of the proud:

> See! sportive fate, to punish aukward pride,
> Bids Bubo build, and sends him such a Guide. (19–20)

Even good taste is vain because of the vanity of man's works and the uncertainty of the human condition.

The portraits of Villario and Sabinus introduce the important theme stated in cancelled lines of the manuscript:

> Nor waits one Curse alone on the Profuse
> Ev'n when they get [gain?] the Taste, they lose the Use.[38]

Villario's garden approaches the ideal in vain, either because of the owner's ill-health:

> Enjoy them you! the master can no more:
> The Gouty Owner on his Couch is thrown
> And humbly begs you that you walk alone.[39]

[36] See the 'Argument', *Epistle to Burlington, TE* iii. ii, 133; and Christopher Hibbard, 'The Country House Poem of the Seventeenth Century', *Journal of the Warburg and Courtauld Institute*, 19 (1956), 159–74, reprinted in *Essential Articles for the Study of Alexander Pope*, ed. Maynard Mack (Hamden, Conn., 1964), p. 431.

[37] *Epistle to Burlington*, Pierpont Morgan MS. (MA 352), cancelled *marginalia*, l. 20. See E.C. iii. 174 n.

[38] Pierpont Morgan MS. (MA 352), l. 65.

[39] Pierpont Morgan MS. (MA 352), cancelled ll. 74–6.

Or because of the fickleness of his wandering taste:

> Tir'd of the scene Parterres and Fountains yield,
> He finds at last he better likes a Field. (87–8)

Sabinus is cursed by his heir, whose 'fine Taste' destroys a master-piece of garden art:

> Thro' his young Woods how pleas'd Sabinus stray'd,
> Or sat delighted in the thick'ning shade,
> With annual joy the red'ning shoots to greet,
> Or see the stretching branches long to meet!
> His Son's fine Taste an op'ner Vista loves,
> Foe to the Dryads of his Father's groves,
> One boundless Green, or flourish'd Carpet views,
> With all the mournful family of Yews;
> The thriving plants ignoble broomsticks made,
> Now sweep those Alleys they were born to shade. (89–98)

The curse on Timon is not wrought by fate, or taste, or a misguided heir, but by Nature itself, which triumphantly restores what his pride and profusion have violated:

> Another age shall see the golden Ear
> Imbrown the Slope, and nod on the Parterre,
> Deep Harvests bury all his pride had plann'd,
> And laughing Ceres re-assume the land. (173–6)

The case for interpreting the description of Timon and his villa as an attack on Sir Robert Walpole and his country-house at Houghton, Norfolk, has been ably made by Kathleen Mahaffey and Maynard Mack. But there is no disputing Bateson's contention that Timon is a composite portrait, and that one of the houses Pope had in mind was Blenheim. The case can be more strongly stated: Blenheim was the primary source of his description. The 'golden mine of Blenheim' was notorious from the year of foundation in 1705 to its completion in 1720, and its notoriety continued throughout the century. During the 1730s it was frequently mentioned in the same breath with Houghton as the paradigm of the 'Impudence of Wealth', but the circumstantial details of the house and garden of Blenheim correspond more closely to the description of Timon's villa than Houghton, which Pope had never seen. Pope's judgement of Timon's villa clearly reflects the description of Blenheim he wrote after a visit in 1717.[40]

The reference to 'huge heaps of littleness' in the *Epistle to Burlington* (l. 109) recalls a phrase in Pope's letter describing Blenheim: 'I never saw so great a thing with so much littleness in it' (i. 432). The description of Timon's villa as 'a labour'd Quarry above ground' (110) echoes a remark about Blenheim by Pope's friend Charles Talbot, Duke of Shrewsbury, which had become proverbial. The comment of the *Master Key*—'That well known saying of his [Shrewsbury's] fixes this to Blenheim'—is satirical of those who attempted to fix on any one place satire intended for many, but circumstantial details of the house and garden conform more closely to Blenheim than any other single place.[41]

Twice the size, and twice the expense of Houghton, Blenheim was designed by an architect despised by the Palladians, John Vanbrugh, while Houghton was from the start a project of the 'Burlington-inquisition', designed by Colen Campbell with an interior by William Kent. The gardens of Blenheim (plate 68) were the work of Vanbrugh and Henry Wise, gardener to Queen Anne, identified with the formal French style the Palladians repudiated, while the gardens and park of Houghton (plate 69) were the work of his more liberal successor, Charles Bridgeman, whom the Palladians employed. Timon's formal, unnatural, walled gardens, with parterre, terraces,

[40] See Kathleen Mahaffey, 'Timon's Villa: Walpole's Houghton', *Texas Studies in Language and Literature*, 9 (Summer 1967), 193–222; and Mack, 'Sir Robert Walpole and Houghton as "Timon" and His Villa', Appendix F, pp. 272–8. See F. W. Bateson, 'Timon and the Duke of Chandos', Appendix B, *TE* iii. ii, 171–2; and xxvi, 146–8 nn. On the notoriety of Blenheim, see Winston S. Churchill, *Marlborough: His Life and Times*, vol. 6 (London, 1938), 317–19; and David Green, 'Visitors to Blenheim', *Country Life*, 107 (10 Mar. 1950), 648–51. On Pope's visit to Houghton, *A Master Key to Popery* (1732) asserts that 'the Author [Pope] never Saw Houghton', a statement corroborated by Edward Harley's remark in a letter to Pope after a visit to Norfolk in 1732: 'I wished for your company, I think you never was in that county it is much different from any that I ever saw & I am sure you would be pleased with some places.' See *TE* iii. ii, 186, and *Correspondence*, iii. 325.

[41] See *The Master Key*, *TE* iii. ii, 187. Cf. Pope's letter describing Blenheim as 'a great *Quarry of Stones above ground*' (i. 432). 'His building a Town' (*Epistle to Burlington*, l. 105) also appears to allude to Blenheim. See the cancelled couplet in the portrait of Atossa in the *Epistle to a Lady* (1735), an unmistakable reference to Blenheim and the Duchess of Marlborough: 'Thus, while her Palace rises like a Town,/Atossa cheats the Lab'rer of a crown.' F. W. Bateson, 'Who was Atossa?', Appendix A, *TE* iii. ii, 170.

topiary, pond, lake and useless ornament can be more readily 'fix'd' at Blenheim (plate 70) than Houghton (plate 71).[42]

Pope's short account of Blenheim in his letter[43] criticizes proportion more explicitly than the description of Timon's villa, but his conclusions about the implications of these errors is the same. Only the garden front of the south escapes his censure when he looks at the elevations of the building with the 'suff'ring eye' of the Palladian. The garden front seemed to him the best because in its unfinished state it was 'not yet loaded with these turrets' which he found 'finical and heavy' in Vanbrugh's broken and picturesque roofscape. The east and west elevations, containing the residential apartments and long gallery were in Pope's opinion 'intirely spoil'd by two monstrous bow-windows which stand just in the middle instead of doors'. And he criticizes the colonnades and pavilions of the north entrance front:

> As if it were fatal that some trifling littleness should every where destroy the grandeur, there are in the chief front two semicircles of a lower structure than the rest, that cut off the angles, and look as if they were purposely design'd to hide a loftier and nobler piece of building, the top of which appears above them.

Vanbrugh's dramatic composition of mass, recession, and silhouette is lost on Pope's Palladian eye, and he censures at Blenheim the 'grand error' of Timon's villa: mistaking 'Size and Dimension' for 'Proportion and Harmony of the whole'.[44]

Pope judges the inside of Blenheim, the plan, by the same standard of classical proportion, and by the humanist ideals of use and convenience. He objected, 'there are two ordinary stair-cases instead of one great one', violating both proportion and convenience. On the same basis he complains that the great Gallery or library, a room extending 183 feet along the entire west wing is 'spoil'd by two Arches towards the End of it, which take away the sight of several windows'. He admires Vanbrugh's great marble hall on

[42] For Bridgeman's responsibility for the gardens at Houghton, see Walpole, *History of Gardening*, p. 25, and H. Avray Tipping, 'Houghton Hall, Norfolk—III', *Country Life*, 49 (15 Jan. 1921), 71–2. On the garden design of Blenheim, see David Green, chap. 6, 'Earth', *Blenheim Palace* (London, 1951), pp. 62–72, pl. 25. For a detailed comparison between Houghton and Blenheim, see 'Where was Timon's Villa?', Appendix C.

[43] *Correspondence*, i. 432. Sherburn dates the letter Sept. 1717 'with no real assurance' (i. 432 n.). The following year (1718), when Pope spent the summer at Stanton Harcourt near Blenheim (i. 480), seems more likely.

[44] 'Argument', *Epistle to Burlington*, *TE* iii. ii, 133.

the central axis of the house (70 by 45 by 67 feet), a room with side arcades and triumphal arch, Corinthian pilasters supporting a clerestory of arched windows, and a ceiling painted by James Thornhill, and he enjoys the irony that 'the cellars and offices under-ground, . . . are the most commodious, and best contrived, of the whole'.[45]

The principle of convenience underlies this last judgement of Pope's, like his complaint that Blenheim 'is a house of Entries and Passages', and his censure of Vanbrugh's indoor vistas, 'very uselessly handsome'. The same principle explains his criticism of the accommodations:

> There are but just two Apartments, for the Master and Mistress, below; and but two apartments above, (very much inferior to them) in the whole House. When you look upon the Outside, you'd think it large enough for a Prince; when you see the Inside, it is too little for a Subject; and has not conveniency to lodge a common family.

When completed more than ten rooms were appropriated to the owners in the east and south-east wing of Blenheim, but Pope is evidently objecting to the disproportion between the residential apartments and the rooms of state.[46] He sees in the plan of Blenheim a violation of the principle of use, as at Timon's villa, and a sign of the character of its owner. 'I think the Architect built it', he concludes, 'entirely in compliance to the taste of its Owners; for it is the most inhospitable thing imaginable, and the most selfish; it has, like their own hearts, no room for strangers, and no reception for any person of superior quality to themselves.' This statement is an indictment of the owner which amounts to an exoneration of the architect.

There is no foundation for the accepted view that Pope shared Swift's 'ignorant contempt' for Vanbrugh,[47] the architect of Blenheim. The misconception derives from a mistaken interpretation of a line just quoted in the *Epistle to Burlington* introducing one of the 'cursed Profuse':

> See! sportive fate, to punish aukward pride
> Bids Bubo build, and sends him such a Guide. (19–20)

[45] On the dimensions of the Long Library and Great Hall, see David Green, 'Some Blenheim Statistics', *Blenheim Palace* (1951), p. 234, and pl. 19. Cf. *Vitruvius Britannicus* I (1715), pl. 56, plan of the principal floor, M. See T[ipping, H. Avray], 'Blenheim Palace—II', *Country Life*, 25 (5 June 1909), 834–42.

[46] See T[ipping], 'Blenheim Palace—II', pp. 834–5; and David Green and Christopher Hussey, 'Blenheim Palace Re-visited—II. The East Wing', *Country Life*, 105 (27 May 1949), 1246–50.

[47] F. W. Bateson, *TE* iii. ii, 139 n. (l. 20).

70. Blenheim, Oxfordshire. By John Maurer. 1745.

71. Houghton Hall, Norfolk. By Isaac Ware. 1735.

72. Stanton Harcourt, Oxfordshire. By Joseph Farington. 1793.

73. Garden Front of Buckingham House. 1723.

The first editions read 'Babo' like the manuscript, but Pope's *Master Key* indicates that the man intended was George Bubb Dodington, Baron Melcombe (1691–1752), whom Pope satirized as Bubo in the *Epistle to Arbuthnot* (l. 280), in the 1735 and subsequent editions of the *Epistle to Burlington*, and the *Imitations of Horace*.[48] Dodington's house at Eastbury, Dorsetshire was designed by John Vanbrugh, who has consequently been identified as Dodington's contemptible guide. But this ignores the complex architectural history of Eastbury, and the career of Bubb Dodington as a patron of architecture.

Vanbrugh drew the design of Eastbury, published in *Vitruvius Britannicus* (1717), for Bubb Dodington's uncle, George Dodington, who died in 1719 before construction began. Bubb Dodington inherited Eastbury, and, according to Courthope, 'was obliged by the terms of the will to complete the house which Vanbrugh had designed'. Construction began about 1724, but no more than the shell had been completed at the time of Vanbrugh's death in 1726. Subsequently Dodington employed the architect Roger Morris (1695–1749), who finished the house between 1733 and 1738. These facts explain some of Pope's innuendoes in the *Master Key* on the application of the Duke of Shrewsbury's remark about the 'Quarry of Stones above Ground' (iv. 432) to Eastbury rather than Blenheim:

> Were it to be apply'd to a House and not a Castle, I should fancy it must be to one in Dorsetshire of the same Architect; It would be like this Poets Injustice, to reflect on a Gentleman's Taste for a thing which he was oblig'd to build on another Man's scheme—But this Gentleman's Taste is since fully vindicated, by what has been built on his own Directions, that most Genteel Pile in Pall-Mall, which is the Admiration of all Beholders.

'Another man's scheme' is evidently the plan for Eastbury of Bubb Dodington's uncle, George Dodington, and his architect, Vanbrugh, which, Pope argues ironically, it would be an injustice to attribute to his heir—ironic because this costly house (£140,000) of a false patron is an apt model for Timon's villa.[49]

48 For Pope's satire of Bubb Dodington, see *TE* iv. 112, 115, 185, 298, 303, 322, 334.

49 See Laurence Whistler, 'Roger Morris and the Completion [of Eastbury]', *The Imagination of Vanbrugh* (1954), pp. 172–6, and his summary of Eastbury's history, pp. 156–7; E.C. iii. 174 n.; Colvin, pp. 396, 639–40; Pope's *Master Key*, *TE* iii. ii, 188; and Christopher Hussey, 'Eastbury Park, Dorset', *Country Life*, 62 (3 Sept. 1927), 330–7.

The 'Guide' and protégé with whom Pope and the Palladians identified Bubb Dodington was Roger Morris (1695–1749). Morris was a builder-architect associated with the Earl of Pembroke, who was involved in speculative land development of London estates, and had been appointed surveyor in connection with the building of Covent Garden theatre by Edward Shepherd (d. 1747), the architect Pope ridiculed in place of Ripley in the first edition of the *Epistle to Burlington*—' . . . no Rod but S—d with a Rule' (l. 18). Between about June 1731 and November 1732 Morris had been abroad, perhaps in Italy with his patron, whose return is mentioned in a letter from Pope to Burlington: 'Mr Dodington is happily returnd from Italy, without any one Idea of Building more than he set out with, whereby Morris & He continue to admire each other' (iii. 329). Pope's contempt for Dodington as a patron of architecture was shared by William Kent, who wrote to Burlington the same month about 'one wonder more': 'the late great traveller [Bubb Dodington] that . . . is satisfied with what he's built, & wonder's now sence he's come home that his buildings is so perfiect that he cannot alter anything he has done they are so excellent.'[50] Among buildings Dodington was too complacent about to alter to suit Palladian taste one may be Eastbury, 'built after the Design of Sir John Vanbrug with the measures designed by Mr Morris';[51] the other must be Dodington's town house, the 'genteel pile' at the east end of Pall Mall facing Carleton House, rebuilt between 1731 and 1733 probably by Morris. No illustration survives of the house, but it was apparently 'built of rusticated stone in the Italian manner', and Robert Seymour's *Survey of London and Westminster* (1734–5) tells us 'that all the fireplace flues in the mansion were collected into one stack in the vortex of the roof, giving the chimney the appearance of the kiln of a bottleglass factory'—a telling indication of Dodington's taste.[52]

The evidence is sufficient to indicate that in his prose description of Blenheim and in the *Epistle to Burlington* Pope's criticism is not directed at the

[50] 'Pope-Burlington Correspondence and Kent Letters', Chatsworth House MSS., Box 143, quoted by W. A. Eden, in Marie Draper's *Marble Hill House and its Owners* (1970), p. 18. For Roger Morris, see W. A. Eden, ibid., pp. 17–18.

[51] Royal Library, Windsor Castle, Drawings collected by Consul Smith, No. 10570, quoted by W. A. Eden, *Marble Hill House and its Owners*, p. 20.

[52] Quoted by Hugh Phillips, *Mid-Georgian London* (1964), p. 55, figs. 61, 61 a.

architect John Vanbrugh. Pope rebuked Swift for his mean opinion of Vanbrugh, whom Swift had satirized in poems between 1703 and 1707 as a Whig, a modern, and a playwright turned architect. 'You have not the least acquaintance with or personal knowlege of him,' Owen Ruffhead quotes Pope as saying to Swift:

> Vanbrugh is . . . the most easy careless writer and companion in the world. . . . Vanbrugh wrote and built just as his fancy led him; or as those he built for, and wrote for, directed him. If what he did pleased them, he gained his end; if it displeased them, they might thank themselves. He pretended to no high scientific knowledge in the art of building; and he wrote without much attention to critical art.

Pope caused Swift to recant in their joint 'Preface' to the *Miscellanies* (1727); and in conversations with Spence he praised Vanbrugh's character as an 'honest-hearted . . . man', and his 'freer, easier way for Comedy'. John Summerson has remarked on similarities of aesthetic sensibility.[53] Pope's attitude to Vanbrugh, in short, is free of the prejudice of his contemporaries, and corresponds exactly with his judgement in the letter censuring the owner rather than the architect of Blenheim.

In considering Blenheim as one of the models of Timon's villa the difficulty arises that the prodigal character of Timon is opposite to Pope's conception of the owner of Blenheim, John Churchill, Duke of Marlborough. He told Spence that Marlborough's 'reigning passion . . . was the love of money' (No. 368), and that all the inconsistencies of his character could be accounted for by avarice. But Timon and Marlborough are alike in that both are selfish, proud, and inhospitable men who are cursed for want of virtue: Timon's prodigality makes him ridiculous, Marlborough's avarice makes him miserable. Pope described to Spence his suppressed character of Marlborough (apparently composed for the *Essay on Man* during the composition of the

53 Owen Ruffhead, *The Life of Alexander Pope*, in *Works of Pope*, vol. v (London, 1769), 383–4 n. For Swift's satire of Vanbrugh, see *Poems*, ed. Harold Williams, i. 55, 60, 73. For compliments to Vanbrugh see the 'Preface' to the Swift-Pope, *Miscellanies in Prose and Verse*, 3 vols. (London, 1727), p. 9; and Spence, Nos. 118, 483. The line in the *Imitations of Horace*, Ep. II, i (1737), 'How Van wants grace, who never wanted wit!' (l. 289; *TE* iv. 219), is a backhanded compliment ('Observe how seldom ev'n the best succeed', l. 286), which leaves no room for the speculation that 'it refers to the "heaviness" of Vanbrugh's style, architectural and literary, which Pope and Swift are never tired of ridiculing'. E.C. iii. 366 n.

Epistle to Burlington), as the portrait 'of a very great man, who had everything from without to make him happy, and yet was very miserable from the want of virtue in his own heart' (No. 366).

The misery of affluence and the curse of riches is the theme of Pope's suppressed lines:

> Now Europe's Lawrels on his brows behold,
> But stain'd with Blood, or ill exchang'd for Gold.
> What wonder tryumphs never turn'd his brain
> Fill'd with mean fear to lose mean joy to gain.
> Hence see him modest free from pride or shew
> Some Vices were too high but none too low
> Go then indulge thy age in Wealth and ease
> Stretch'd on the spoils of plunder'd palaces
> Alas what *wealth*, which no one act of fame
> E'er taught to shine, or sanctified from shame
> Alas what *ease* those furies of thy life
> Ambition Av'rice and th' imperious Wife.
> The trophy'd Arches, story'd Halls invade,
> And haunt his slumbers in the pompous Shade. (5–18)[54]

Blenheim's 'trophy'd Arches' and 'story'd Halls' are signs of wealth unredeemed by charity, unsanctified by use as much as Timon's marble Hall. Blenheim, even after the building of Houghton, remained the outstanding example of the 'Impudence of wealth' in the mind of Pope and his contemporaries. The treasury spent £240,000 for the building of Blenheim; the total cost has been estimated at £300,000. Pope regarded it as 'a most expensive absurdity' (i. 432), 'the most proud & extravagant Heap of Towers in the Nation' (i. 480), a monument to Marlborough's folly instead of an ornament to the nation.[55] Blenheim was clearly the place Pope was contrasting to Sherborne, Dorset, in 1724:

> When I have been describing his agreable Seat [Digley's Sherborne] I cannot make the reflection I have often done upon contemplating the beautiful Villa's of Other Noblemen, raisd upon the Spoils of plunderd nations, or aggrandiz'd by the wealth of the Publick. I cannot ask myself the question, 'What Else has this man to be lik'd? what else has he cultivated or improv'd? What good, or what desireable thing appears of him, without these walls. (ii. 239)

[54] *TE* vi. 358. [55] See Appendix B.

The inconsistency between the characters of Marlborough and Timon eliminates Blenheim only if we make the unlikely assumption that Pope composed his description of Timon's villa with a single place and a single person in mind. Pope's question remains: 'Why, in God's Name, must a *Portrait*, apparently collected from twenty different Men, be applied to one only?' (iii. 256). The answer appears to be that he had two men primarily in mind: Walpole and Marlborough. Conflation of the character of the one, and the house of the other resulted in one of the most powerful portraits in his satire.

Pope's references to Timon's Brobdingnagian palace and Marlborough's castle as 'villas' are manifestly ironic because he regarded both houses as antitypes of the classical villa, not so much because they violated an architectural ideal exemplified by the small size and perfect classical proportions of Burlington's Chiswick, but because they violated the humanistic ideal of the country-house. The predominance of this ideal over strictly architectural standards is illustrated by Pope's descriptions of two unPalladian houses he characterized as models of the country-house. The first is the medieval manor house with Norman cruciform church and fifteenth-century chapel at Stanton Harcourt, Oxfordshire (plate 72), 'an old romantic Seat of my Lord Harcourt's' (i. 494) where Pope had secluded himself to finish the fifth book of his translation of the *Iliad* in the summer of 1718, the same summer he visited Blenheim (i. 480). His long description of Stanton Harcourt, which appears in letters to Lady Mary Wortley Montagu and the Duke of Buckingham in 1718, shows that Pope considered this ruinous medieval house a match for Pliny's villa, and an antitype of Blenheim: 'the true picture', he told Lady Mary, 'of a genuine Ancient Country Seat' (i. 505).

The house, as Pope describes it, is utterly irregular and unPalladian:

> You must expect nothing regular in my description of a House that seems to be built before Rules were in fashion. The whole is so disjointed, & the parts so detachd from each other, and yet so joining again one can't tell how; that in a poetical Fitt you'd imagine it had been a Village in Amphions time, where twenty Cottages had taken a dance together, were all Out, and stood still in amazement ever since. (i. 505)

The plan confounds Palladian ideas of symmetry:

> One would expect, after entring thro the Porch, to be let into the Hall: Alas nothing less—you find yourself in a Brewhouse. From the Parlor you think to step into the

Drawing room, but upon opening the iron-nail'd door, you are convinced . . . that tis the Pigeon-house. . . . There are upon this Ground-floor in all 24 apartments [26 in 1737], hard to be distinguished by particular names. (i. 505–6)

The elevation of the front, by which Palladio set such store, is an irregular jumble: 'You must excuse me', Pope apologizes, 'if I say nothing of the Front, indeed I don't know which it is' (i. 509), and he goes on to describe chimneys on either side of a porch, a ruinous sloping balcony over the parlour, and the top, 'crown'd with a very venerable tower, so like that of the Church just by, that the Jackdaws build in it as if it were the true steeple' (i. 505).

The whole place is a travesty of classical architecture, and Pope takes great delight in its lack of proportion: 'Our best Room above, is very long & low; of the exact Proportion of a Bandbox. It has Hangings of the finest work in the world, those I mean which Arachne spins out of her own bowells' (i. 506). But he finds in associations—historical, legendary, and antiquarian—inspired by the ruins of the architecture, something more appealing than decorum. He admires the architecture of the medieval kitchen 'built in the form of the Rotunda, being one vast Vault to the Top of the House, where one overture serves to let out the smoak and let in the light' (i. 510). This utilitarian architecture brings to mind fanciful associations with the 'forge of Vulcan, the Cave of Polypheme, or the Temple of Moloch' (i. 510) and local superstitions of witchcraft. He meditates on the reliques of furniture—a 'broken-belly'd Virginal, a couple of crippled Velvet chairs, with two or three mildewd Pictures of mouldy Ancestors' (i. 506), and 'a large Antiquity of Timber . . . either a Bedstead, or a Cyderpress' (i. 506)—and listens to the 'memoirs of the family' related by an old Steward about the 'Adultery-chamber' where 'Lady Francis . . . was here taken in the fact with a neighbouring Prior' (i. 511).

Pope admits to Sheffield that his description of Stanton Harcourt is 'florid' (i. 508), but the appeal to his imagination is primary and he discerns in this ruinous building something closer to the humanistic ideal of architecture than in contemporary great houses like Blenheim. This is particularly clear in his description of the Hall:

The great Hall is high & spatious, flankd with long tables (images of ancient hospitality) ornamented with monstrous horns, about 20 broken Pikes, & a match-lock

Musquet or two, which they say were used in the Civil Wars. Here is one vast archd Window, beautifully darken'd with divers Scutcheons of painted Glass. . . . In this Hall, in former days have dined Garterd Knights & Courtly Dames, with Ushers, Sewers, and Seneshalls; And yet it was but tother night that an Owl flew in hither, and mistook it for a Barn. (i. 505–6)

Pope recognizes in the Hall 'a true image of ancient hospitality' (i. 509), a centre of communal life radically different from the 'marble Hall' of Timon. He sees in its stained glass fragile memorials of the history of a family. The room, like the house itself, is the incarnation of a culture, its history, legends, and folklore. His description was inspired, he says, by 'a generous principle to preserve the memory of a thing that must itself soon fall to ruin' (i. 507).[56]

Pope's attitude to Stanton Harcourt as a house which violates all the classical rules but commands respect, corresponds remarkably to the famous passage in his *Preface to Shakespeare* (1725):

I will conclude by saying of Shakespear, that with all his faults, and with all the irregularity of his *drama*, one may look upon his works, in comparison of those that are more finished and regular, as upon an ancient majestic piece of Gothic architecture, compared with a neat modern building: the latter is more elegant and glaring, but the former is more strong and more solemn. It must be allowed, that in one of these there are materials enough to make many of the other. It has much the greater variety, and much the nobler apartments; though we are often conducted to them by dark, odd, and uncouth passages. Nor does the whole fail to strike us with greater reverence, though many of the parts are childish, ill-placed, and unequal to its grandeur.[57]

This analogy, often cited as one of the earliest eighteenth-century appreciations of Gothic,[58] may have been inspired by Stanton Harcourt; but it is characteristic to find Pope concluding his description of Stanton Harcourt with the assertion that the Gothic house is 'useful' in the classical sense:

Indeed I owe this old house the same sort of gratitude that we do to an old friend, that harbors us in his declining condition, nay even in his last extremities. I have found this an excellent place for Retirement and Study . . . You will not wonder I have translated a great deal of Homer in this Retreat. (i. 507)

[56] On the romanticism of Pope's description of Stanton Harcourt, see Christopher Hussey, 'Stanton Harcourt—II, A Poet's Hermitage in an Oxfordshire Manor House', *Country Life*, 90 (10 Oct. 1941), 674; Geoffrey Scott, chaps. 2–3, *The Architecture of Humanism* (London, 1914); and E.C. v. 129.

[57] E.C. x. 549.

[58] Kenneth Clark, *The Gothic Revival* (1962), p. 21.

Thus Pope assimilates a Gothic manor house into the classical world of retirement; it fulfils his ideal of the villa.

Pope introduced the expanded version of his description of Stanton Har court addressed to John Sheffield, Duke of Buckingham, with a compliment on the superiority of Buckingham House to Pliny's villas:

> I believe, with all the ostentation of Pliny, he would have been glad to have chang'd both his houses [the Tuscan villa and the one at Laurentium] for your Grace's one; which is a country-house in the summer, and a town-house in the winter; and must be owned to be the properest habitation for a wise man, who sees all the world change every season without ever changing himself. (i. 508)

Pope's compliment was occasioned by Sheffield's own description of his house which he had enclosed in a letter to Pope, and which Pope later published in his edition of Sheffield's *Works* (1723) as 'A letter to the D[uke] of S[hrewsbury]'.[59] Characteristically, the house which Pope thought to have excelled the most famous Roman villas was one which scarcely conformed to the canons of classical architecture.

Buckingham House (plate 73), in St. James's Park in the west end of London on the site of the present Buckingham Palace was not the work of a fashionable architect, but a builder, the contemporary of Wren, William Winde (1642–1722). Buckingham house is, according to Summerson, 'the one really convincing prototype' for a large number of country-houses built between 1710 and 1740 by artisans and builders rather than architects. 'The general proportions of Buckingham House with its attic storey, its pilasters at centre and ends of the front, its quadrant colonades and wings flanking a court, set a pattern which was followed for 35 years after its completion in 1705.'[60]

But Pope considered this rather old-fashioned house, so different from Campbell's stylish designs, a match for Pliny's villas because he regarded its owner as a 'wise man' (i. 508), who knew how to enjoy the pleasures of retirement in the heart of the city in a house where he had entertained Pope and his friends at a *convivium poeticum* in 1720. Sheffield's description of his house and way of life in the letter proves the aptness of the inscription on the

[59] *Correspondence*, i. 508 n. *The Works of John Sheffield*, 2 vols. (London, 1723), ii. 275–87.

[60] John Summerson, 'The Classical Country House', *Journal of the Royal Society of Arts*, 107 (July 1959), 548.

garden front of the house, *Rus in Urbe*. From his Salon he could look into 'the pleasantest park in the World' (277), and he enjoyed from his roof 'a far distant prospect of hills and dales, and a near one of parks and gardens' (284). 'The most common shrub in my garden' more excited the Duke's devotion than the view of St. Paul's. Besides the enjoyment of formal gardens, he could obtain prospects of 'the Queen's two parks and a great part of *Surry*' (plate 74):

> On one side of this Terrace, a Wall covered with Roses and Jessemines is made low to admit the view of a meadow full of cattle just under it [no disgreeable object in the midst of a great City] and at each end a descent into parterres, with fountains and water-works. (285)

In addition, the Duke had 'a kitchen-garden full of the best sort of fruit', 'two green houses with a convenient bathing apartment in one of them', and in the other 'a little closet of Books . . . ranked in such a method, that by its mark a very *Irish* footman may fetch any book I want' (285).[61] Neither house nor garden conform to Pope's own taste for the Palladian and the picturesque, but the *modus vivendi* corresponds to his ideal of the villa.

Pope's idea of the villa as a humanistic rather than a specifically architectural concept reflects the architectural imprecision in the use of the word in the period.[62] Pope invested the idea of the villa with humanistic values which transcend aesthetic ones, and reconcile apparently contradictory tendencies of taste. In the gardening chapters we have seen how Pope 'propagated the fame' of Twickenham and many other places in terms of the doctrine of retirement and the ideal of the villa. All the places he praises aspire to the ideal he summarized in lines from Nicholas Rowe's *Jane Shore*, which he used to compliment a house owned by his friend Mrs. Marriot in Sturston, Norfolk (i. 211):

> Far from the crowd and the tumultuous city
> There stands a lonely but a healthful dwelling
> Built for convenience, and the use of Life.

[61] My quotations are from John Sheffield, *Works* (1723), ii. 275–87. Summerson 'found no representation of the garden front', 'The Classical Country House', p. 553, n. 19. But see the tailpiece engraving in *Works* (1723), ii. 274.

[62] See John Summerson, 'The Classical Country House', *Journal of the Royal Society of Arts*, 107 (July 1959), 570.

> Around it, fallows, meads, and pastures fair,
> A little garden, and a limpid brook,
> By Nature's own contrivance, seem dispos'd;
> No neighbours but a few poor simple clowns,
> Honest and true; with a well-meaning priest.[63]

With the idea of 'the use of Life' Pope associates the classical one that use confers ownership.

Pope insists on this idea because he believes that proprietary interest (everything we now associate with real estate values) threatens to destroy the ideal of the villa. This conflict of values is one of the important themes of the *Imitations of Horace*, Ep. I, i (1737):

> Here, Wisdom calls: 'Seek Virtue first! be bold!
> As Gold to Silver, Virtue is to Gold.'
> There, London's voice: 'Get Mony, Mony still!
> And then let Virtue follow, if she will.' (77–80)

The menace was dramatized for Pope with particular force in several instances where villas of his friends, like Bolingbroke's Dawley Farm already discussed, had been alienated by sale to speculators. He gives additional examples in the *Imitations of Horace*, Satire II, ii:

> Shades, that to Bacon could retreat afford,
> Become the portion of a booby Lord;
> And Hemsley once proud Buckingham's delight,
> Slides to a Scriv'ner or a City Knight.
> Let Lands and Houses have what Lords they will,
> Let Us be fix'd, and our own Masters still. (175–80)

The first example refers to the famous manor house of Sir Francis Bacon, at Gorhambury, near St. Albans, which was in Pope's time the property of a Whig M.P. and ridiculed playwright, William Luckyn, who had been elevated to the peerage in 1719—not a speculator, but in Pope's mind a sharp declension from the philosophical owner who preceded him. Helmesley, Yorkshire (now Duncombe Park), one of Sheffield's several retreats, had been sold in 1692 to Sir Charles Duncombe, a London banker, for the sum of

[63] Quoted in a letter to Mrs. Marriot (28 Feb. 1714), *Correspondence*, i. 211.

£90,000, a real estate transaction said to be 'the greatest purchase ever made by any subject in England' at the time.[64]

In the *Epistle to Bathurst* Pope introduces a house which was abused by bad owners before being redeemed by a good one. It is thought that the house Pope had in mind was Edward Harley's Wimpole, previously owned by a City merchant, Sir John Cutler (Cotta in the poem), in whose possession

> Like some lone Chartreux stands the good old Hall,
> Silence without, and Fasts within the wall;
> No rafter'd roofs with dance and tabor sound,
> No noontide-bell invites the country round;
> Tenants with sighs the smoakless tow'rs survey,
> And turn th' unwilling steeds another way:
> Benighted wanderers, the forest o'er,
> Curse the sav'd candle, and unop'ning door;
> While the gaunt mastiff growling at the gate,
> Affrights the beggar whom he longs to eat. (189–98)

Curio, said to be Cutler's son-in-law and heir, the Earl of Radnor, impoverished the estate in a mad zeal for 'his country's cause' (206), before it was acquired by Harley.[65] Between these extremes there is Bathurst, who has

> The Sense to value Riches, with the Art
> T'enjoy them, and the Virtue to impart,
>
> . . .
>
> Oh teach us, Bathurst! yet unspoil'd by wealth!
> That secret rare, between th' extremes to move
> Of mad Good-nature, and of mean Self-love. (219–20; 226–8)

As usual Pope's models do not conform exactly to the ideal: Harley went bankrupt and was forced to sell one of his houses, Down Hall, to a city merchant, George Selwyn.[66]

Feverish speculation in land and the fortunes of real estate in Pope's time led him to the conclusion in the *Imitations of Horace*, Ep. II, ii (1737), that

> The Laws of God, as well as of the Land,
> Abhor, a *Perpetuity* should stand:

[64] See Pope, *Imitations of Horace*, *TE* iv. 285, 181, 143, 69. For Gorhambury, see The Victoria History of the Counties of England, *A History of Hertfordshire*, ed. William Page, vol. 2 (London, 1908), 394–6, plan p. 395.

[65] *TE* iii. ii, 108–9, and n.

[66] *TE* iii. ii, 111. See James Lees-Milne, *Earls of Creation*, p. 204.

Estates have wings, and hang in Fortune's pow'r
Loose on the point of ev'ry wav'ring Hour;
Ready, by force, or of your own accord,
By sale, at least by death, to change their Lord. (246–51)

The conflict between use and proprietary ownership is dramatized throughout the *Imitations* by the example of Pope's villa. In Satire II, vi (1727) he turns Swift's lines to ironic ridicule of the idea of buying the place which he had leased at Twickenham from Thomas Vernon:

Well, now I have all this [House and garden] and more,
I ask not to increase my store;
But here a Grievance seems to lie,
All this is mine but till I die;
I can't but think 'twould sound more clever,
To me and to my Heirs for ever. (7–12)

In Satire II, ii (1734) he again introduces Swift to argue the virtues of proprietary ownership.

My lands are sold, my Father's house is gone;
I'll hire another's, is not that my own,
And yours my friends?

. . .

'Pray heav'n it last! (cries Swift) as you go on;
I wish to God this house had been your own:
Pity! to build, without a son or wife:
Why, you'll enjoy it only all your life.' (155–7; 161–4)

Pope's answer to these arguments is given in the following lines:

Well, if the Use be mine, can it concern one
Whether the Name belong to Pope or Vernon?
What's *Property*? dear Swift! you see it alter
From you to me, from me to Peter Walter,
Or, in a mortgage, prove a Lawyer's share,
Or, in a jointure, vanish from the Heir,
Or, in pure Equity (the Case not clear)
The Chanc'ry takes your rents for twenty year:
At best, it falls to some ungracious Son
Who cries, my father's damn'd, and all's my own. (165–74)

Far better, Pope concludes in Ep. II, ii (1737) to 'enjoy, as well as keep':

> Yes, Sir, how small soever be my heap,
> A part I will enjoy, as well as keep. (284–5)

Thus, his own villa in the *Imitations of Horace* is 'Sacred to social life and social Love', the ideal he applies to Twickenham in Ode IV, i (1737).[67]

Pope's conception of the villa illustrates how thoroughly aesthetic standards are transcended by humanistic ideals of architecture. Like Ruskin, Pope does not regard architecture as an expression of mechanical laws but as the incarnation of human values, and on this basis his taste for Gothic and for classical architecture can be reconciled. Likewise, regular architecture and irregular gardens are harmonized not simply by a 'contrariety betweene *building* and *gardening*', in Henry Wotten's words, but by the humanistic ideal of utility, the idea of an entire environment in the service of human values.[68]

[67] On Twickenham in the *Imitations of Horace*, see *TE* iv. 251 (ll. 7–8 of this passage are Swift's, ll. 9–12 Pope's; see *TE* iv. 248); *TE* iv. 67–9, 185, 151. See chap. 5, n. 56.

[68] See Henry Wotten, *The Elements of Architecture*, ed. Frederick Hard (1968), p. 109.

Part IV. Sculpture

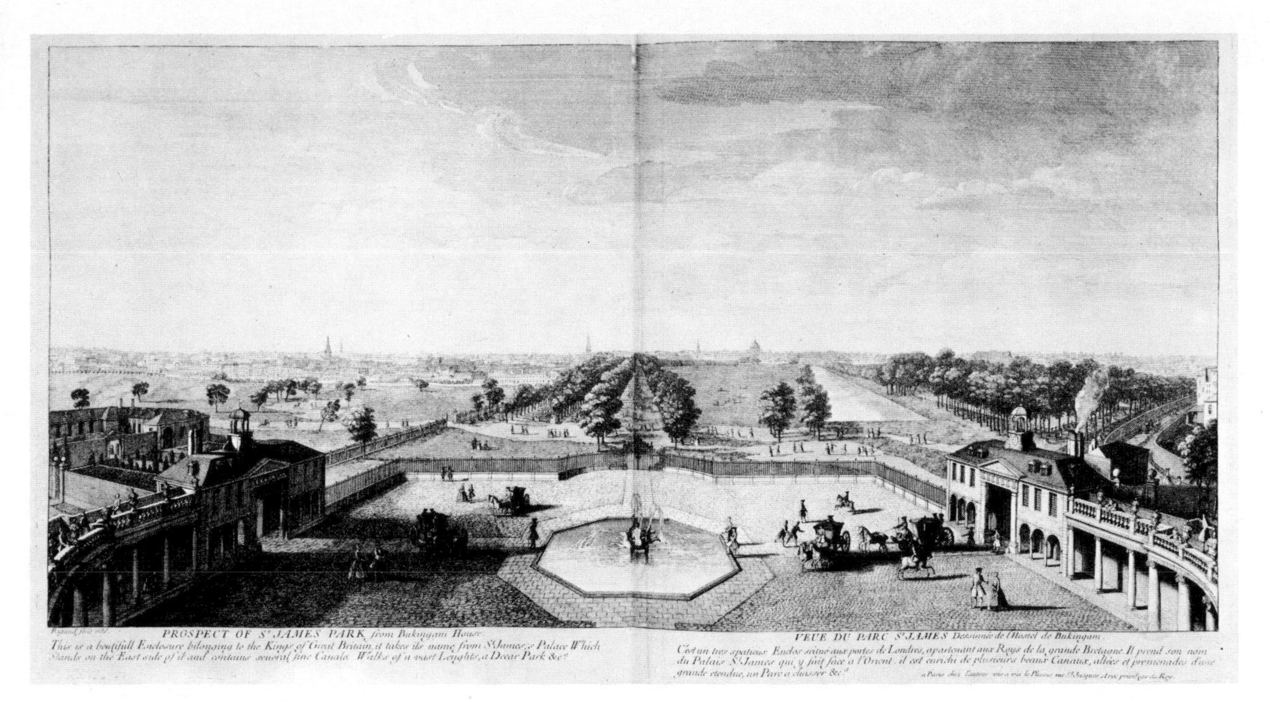

74. View of St. James's from Buckingham House. By Rigaud. 1736.

75. The Diana of Versailles. By Kneller. *c.* 1684–85.

76. Bernini's Fountain in the Piazza Navona, Rome. Engraving by Pieter Schenk, annotated by Pope. *c.* 1700.

13. *Verse and Sculpture*

The verse and sculpture bore an equal part,
And Art reflected images to Art.
Epistle to Addison, 51–2

IN eighteenth-century aesthetics sculpture was considered a paradigm art. Antique statues were regarded as models for ideal imitation by the painter, poet, and sculptor. This doctrine, popularized by Shaftesbury, Richardson, and others, appears in Pope's notes to the *Iliad*, where he repeats the legend that the sculptor Phidias modelled a statue of Jupiter 'from that Archtype which he found in . . . Lines of *Homer*', and asserts that Homer took an idea 'from the Statues of *Daedalus*, which might be extant in his Time'. In Pope's career, however, sculpture is less the paradigm than the sister art, closely related to those previously discussed, and particularly important to the art of funerary monuments, in which Pope was interested not only as a writer of epitaphs, but as designer, superintendent, satirist, and student. Accordingly, this chapter will concentrate on Pope's interest in funerary monuments, after a brief account of the way sculpture figures in Pope's interest in the sister arts of painting, gardening, and architecture. It will conclude with a short discussion of Pope's treatment of sculpture in his poetry.[1]

Monuments make a fitting conclusion to the story of Pope's interest in the arts because they were 'National Works', involving public and private patronage, and the collaboration of all the artists who have so far figured in Pope's career, painters and architects along with sculptors. Pope played a more significant role in the erection of contemporary monuments than his authorship of often anonymous inscriptions and epitaphs would suggest. His important contribution to the establishment of Poets' Corner in Westminster

[1] *Iliad* I, l. 683, *TE* vii. 119 n.; *Iliad* XVIII, l. 488 n., *TE* viii. 345.

Abbey has not been recognized. Moreover, the significance of this activity is of more than antiquarian interest. It reflects Pope's devotion to the movement to celebrate British worthies in accordance with a Renaissance ideal of fame, and it is the pursuit of a poet who sought, in his epistolary verse as much as his epitaphs, to 'preserve a Name', as he puts it in the concluding line of the *Epistle to Jervas*, commemorating the names of the worthy and condemning the unworthy.

1. 'Sculpture *and her* Sister-arts'

The role of sculpture in Pope's campaign to illustrate his fame which we observed in painting, is revealed in the portrait busts of Pope by the leading statuaries of his time, John Michael Rysbrack (1694–1770) and Louis François Roubiliac (1705–62), who carved contrasting images of the poet. The bust by Michael Rysbrack, the Flemish sculptor who arrived in London about 1720 and became the leading sculptor in Britain during the next two decades, was apparently commissioned by Robert Harley, Earl of Oxford. About 1725 Gibbs wrote a letter to Pope (ii. 298) directing him to Rysbrack's studio in Vere Street. By 1730 Pope was speaking facetiously about his 'Head' (iii. 136) in Oxford's library at Wimpole, which can perhaps be identified with the marble bust now at the Athenaeum (Wimsatt, 11. 1, 1725–30), showing the poet in loose contemporary attire in his own hair. The bust, now much admired, was ridiculed by Pope's enemies as a 'misshapen form', 'monstrous Image', and 'hideous Sight'. In the notes to the *Dunciad* (1729) Pope castigates the 'Gentlemen of the Dunciad' who 'went so far as to libel an eminent Sculptor for making our author's *Busto* in marble, at the request of Mr. *Gibbs* the Architect', and answers the attacks in an epigram sent to Oxford the following year:

> Tis granted Sir: the Busto's a damn'd head
>   Pope is a little Elf.
> All he can say for't, is, He neither made
>   The Busto, nor himself. (iii. 100)

This suggests that Pope may have been dissatisfied with his first image in marble.[2]

[2] On Rysbrack's bust of Pope, see Margaret Whinney, *Sculpture in Britain 1530–1830* (Harmondsworth, 1964), pp. 83, 86, and M. I. Webb, *Michael Rysbrack Sculptor* (London, 1954), p. 76. On the identity of

Whatever his opinion of the bust fortuitously involved in the warfare of the Dunces, Pope apparently shared the admiration of his contemporaries for Rysbrack. Plaster of paris busts of 'Poladio and Indigo Jones' in his collection can probably be attributed to Rysbrack, derivatives of the busts and statues carved for Lord Burlington's villa at Chiswick about 1725. In Pope's opinion, Rysbrack's equestrian statue of William III set up in Queen's Square in 1735 at Bristol was one of the redeeming features of the city he visited in 1739 (iv. 204–5). It is possible that Pope and Rysbrack worked together in gardens like Stowe, where Pope's bust attributed to the sculptor was placed in a niche in Kent's Temple of British Worthies in 1734. The possibility of their collaboration on monuments in Westminster Abbey is explored below.[3]

Towards the end of his life Pope sat to the French sculptor Louis François Roubiliac soon after he arrived in London about 1736. Wimsatt dates Pope's sitting between 1737 and 1738, and estimates that all four of the marble busts (1738, 1740, 1741) can be derived from a single terracotta model. The bust of Pope is a characteristic mixture of the sculptor's naturalism and idealization. The bust *ad vivum*, 'more like than any other Sculptor has done', according to George Vertue, reflected Roubiliac's powers of observation. Sir Joshua Reynolds told the story that Roubiliac recognized Pope suffered from headache 'from the contracted appearance of the skin above the eyebrows'. At the same time this 'head of quick intellectual beauty' belongs to the Roman tradition; the classical drapery, the close cropped hair and inscriptions from Horace echo the 'Augustan Spirit'. Horace's eulogy of Homer in the *Ars Poetica*—*Qui nil molitur inepte* (Who never exerts himself foolishly)—is applied to Pope in the inscription on the base of one type (Wimsatt 58) of this bust. Another (Wimsatt 59. 1), dated 1740, is inscribed with the line from Horace's Satire II, i, l. 70, which corresponds to his self-portrait in the *Imitations of Horace* in the 1730s: *Uni Aequus Virtuti Atque Ejus Amicis.*[4]

the Wimpole 'Head', see Wimsatt, *Portraits*, p. 35, and *Correspondence*, ii. 298 n., iii. 100 n. On the bust and the Gentlemen of the Dunciad, see Wimsatt, *Portraits*, pp. 101, 104–5, and *Dunciad* II (1729), l. 134 n., *TE* v. 116 n.

[3] For Pope's busts of Palladio and Jones, see 'Inventory', p. 252, and M. I. Webb, *Michael Rysbrack*, pp. 101–3, figs. 36–7. On Rysbrack's statue of William III in Bristol, see Webb, *Michael Rysbrack*, pp. 140–5, fig. 66, and C. F. W. Dening, *The Eighteenth-Century Architecture of Bristol* (Bristol, 1923), p. 28, pl. 3.

[4] See *Portraits*, pp. 227, 225, 235–7, and 'An Image of Pope', in *From Sensibility to Romanticism, Essays,*

Pope's knowledge of antique statuary was sufficient to enable him to use it ornamentally in gardening and architecture. We have already mentioned his comparison of the 'well-study'd Marbles' in the studio of his painting teacher, Charles Jervas (see chap. 1). He was familiar with many important English collections of statuary, including the Earl of Pembroke's at Wilton, and he commented to Spence (No. 280) on a distinguished collection abroad, which belonged to the Abbé Melchior de Polignac. Pope's familiarity with antique statuary is indicated by his paintings after antique statues of Lucius Verus and Antinous; his remark to Spence 'speaking of comparisons upon an absurd and unnatural footing' (No. 549) in reference to the ivory statues of Polycletes and the Colossus; and his notes to the *Iliad*, Book XVII, where he refers to classical sculpture to explain a simile:

> The whole Comparison is as beautiful as just. The Horses standing still to mourn for their Master, could not be more finely represented than by the dumb Sorrow of Images standing over a Tomb. Perhaps the very Posture in which these Horses are described, their Heads bowed down, and their Manes falling in the Dust, has an Allusion to the Attitude in which those Statues on Monuments were usually represented: There are *Bas-Reliefs* that favour this Conjecture.[5]

His concern with the disposition of antique statuary in gardening is indicated by a letter to John Caryll, who had inquired about a statue of Diana for the gardens of Ladyholt:

> There is but one antique one of Diana, the rest are modern, and but ordinary. And indeed the ancient statue is not in a very gracefull posture. You must have seen it, drawing an arrow out of a quiver over her shoulder, which renders the arm, in some views, so foreshortened as to appear a stump. It is also of a large size, perhaps too large for the area in which you design to place it. I ought to know exactly what the open space is, in which it must stand, for a proportion ought to be observed. (ii. 434)

A copy of the Diana Artemis, then at Versailles, now in the Louvre, had been

Presented to Frederick A. Pottle, ed. F. W. Hilles and Harold Bloom (New York, 1965), p. 56; George Vertue, *Note Books*, Walpole Society, vol. 22 (Oxford, 1934), iii. 105; Joshua Reynolds, quoted by Katharine A. Esdaile, *The Life and Works of Louis François Roubiliac* (Oxford, 1928), p. 49; and F. Saxl and Rudolf Wittkower, 'The Bust in the Roman Tradition', *British Art and the Mediterranean* (1948; rpt. Oxford, 1969), Sec. 68.

[5] *Iliad* XVII, l. 494 n., *TE* viii. 307. See Stephen Larrabee, *English Bards and Grecian Marbles, The Relationship Between Sculpture and Poetry, Especially in the Romantic Period* (New York, 1943), p. 72.

cast in bronze by Hubert Le Sueur for Charles I and placed in the East Terrace garden of Windsor Castle. Kneller made a sketch of the statue during a visit to Versailles in 1684 (plate 75); it was illustrated by Montfaucon in *Antiquité Expliqué* (1719); and a similar one in the Chigi Palace in Rome is described in Richardson's *Account* (1722).[6]

The Kneller paintings on Pope's staircase indicate the importance he attached to '*Picture & Sculpture*'—'two *Arts* attending on *Architecture*', in the words of Henry Wotten. 'A Small Mercury Bronse' was also placed 'Upon the Best Staire Case' at Twickenham, and '4 Busstos Modn with Wood Termes' (unidentified) adorned his hall, which had become in houses of Pope's time a favourite setting for statuary. The legacy to Pope in William Kent's will, 'Raphael Head Busto', would have found a place here. In his library, following the growing fashion for portrait busts, Pope placed a 'Marble Head of Homer', attributed in his will erroneously to Bernini, the 'Marble Head of Sir Isaac Newton, by Guelfi', four marble busts of Spenser, Shakespeare, Milton, and Dryden by the Flemish statuary and rival of Rysbrack, Peter Scheemakers (1690–1721), gifts of the Prince of Wales, and finally plaster of paris busts of Palladio and Inigo Jones.[7] He ridiculed libraries decorated with dismembered antiquities, like Bufo's in the *Epistle to Arbuthnot* 'where Busts of Poets dead / And a true *Pindar* stood without a Head' (235–6), preferring to surround himself in his house and garden with images by contemporary sculptors of 'Heroes, Sages, Beauties' (*Epistle to Addison*, l. 34), notably poets and artists.

The same attitude underlies the advice he offered to Ralph Allen about statuary for the library at Prior Park, when he wrote to him in 1740 from London about business with Johan Van Diest (*c*. 1680–1760), the obscure son of the Dutch landscape painter, Adrien Van Diest (1656–1704):

I shall see Vandiest in a day or two, & concert the best method I can for the Statues

[6] On the Diana, see *Correspondence*, ii. 434 n., and Margaret Whinney, *Sculpture in Britain*, p. 28. For Kneller's drawing, see J. Douglas Stewart, *Sir Godfrey Kneller*, National Portrait Gallery Catalogue (London, 1971), No. 55, p. 46, and the illustration in Bernard de Montfaucon, *Antiquité Expliqué* (1719), vol. i, opp. p. 148, pl. 87.

[7] See Henry Wotten, *Elements of Architecture*, ed. Frederick Hard (1968), pp. 82–3. For sculpture owned by Pope, see 'Inventory', pp. 251–2, 258, and Margaret Jourdain, *The Work of William Kent* (1948), p. 90. On 'The Hall as a Setting for Classical Statuary', see F. Saxl and Rudolf Wittkower, *British Art and the Mediterranean*, Sec. 59. On the cult of British worthies in library busts, see Margaret Whinney, *Sculpture in Britain*, pp. 87–8.

for the Library: I would not neglect seeing him, to prevent any Errors, tho I'm in the midst of my Grand-Workes in the Garden. (iv. 247)

The sacred and profane subjects of Allen's statuary are identified in a note to Allen the following month: 'I've seen Mr Vandiest again. We are quite agreed now about Moses & St Paul; & I hope we shall be as much of one accord concerning Homer & Socrates' (iv. 253). Van Diest is known only as a painter. Perhaps, as Benjamin Boyce says, 'Pope was to work with Van Diest in selecting the manner or attitude' of the statues. Another possibility is that Van Diest was making drawings or designs which would serve as models for the sculptor, who was to be Roubiliac. In any event, Pope wanted to prevent errors in images derived from antiquarian research, which conforms to the practice of the leading engraver of pastiche historical busts, George Vertue.[8]

A year later, in July 1741, Pope was negotiating with Roubiliac about busts of British Worthies for Allen's library, when he wrote to Allen:

I writ to you in a hurry & forgot your desire I should determine you in the Choice of a fourth Head, I agree with your Inclination to have it Sir Walter Ralegh. I went yesterday to the Sculptor's & saw the Heads, that of Milton is near finished, & the other doing. I shall take what care I can of them. (iv. 351)

Pope apparently visited Roubiliac's studio in St. Martin's Lane several times because subsequent correspondence reports 'the Busto's are near done, & the Sculptor will write soon to you' (iv. 354), and confirms Allen's agreement with Roubiliac 'for 20 ll[£] each Head' (iv. 360). Katharine Esdaile's catalogue does not include a bust of Raleigh, but the undated Milton may have been the one executed for Allen at this time.[9]

II. *Funerary Monuments*

'These little rites, a Stone, a Verse, receive'
(Pope's *Epitaph* on Robert Digby, 1727, l. 19)

The various aspects of Pope's interest in sculpture converge in the art of funerary monuments. He made an important contribution to an art which

[8] Benjamin Boyce, *The Benevolent Man* (1967), p. 111. George Vertue, who engraved the busts of Homer for Pope's *Iliad* and *Odyssey*, censured historical portraits 'not done from a genuin [*sic*] picture' See *Note Books*, iii. 51.

[9] *The Life and Works of Louis François Roubiliac* (London, 1928), Appendix A, p. 203.

achieved sufficient distinction in his time to cause George Vertue to remark in 1749 that the 'monuments made and erected in many places especially in the Abby church of Westminster . . . are equal to such done abroad any where'. In Pope's activity many of the significant developments in the art of funerary sculpture of his time are reflected: the revival of interest in antique, particularly Roman statuary and antiquities; the arrival in England of distinguished foreign statuaries; the remarkable rise in popularity of portrait busts; the increasing importance of architects as designers of funerary monuments; and a persistent ambivalence between Baroque and classical style.[10]

Pope's early interest in inscriptions and lapidary art is obvious from his correspondence with Lady Mary, which includes her letter (1718) enclosing three pages of Latin inscriptions she had found on brass tablets, placed on each side of a town-house at Lyons in France (i. 513). He studied and recorded inscriptions on Roman monuments. His careful lettering of title pages in his print hand, and the inscription on his family monument reflects a sensibility to lapidary inscription. In a conversation with Spence (No. 272), he defended Lord Bolingbroke's 'long inscription on the column set up in honour of the Duke of Marlborough at Blenheim' as an imitation of 'the best old inscription style'. His humanistic study of inscriptions is illustrated by his parody of the inscription on the tomb of Pico della Mirandola at Florence by Hercoleo Strozzi, and his imitation of the inscription on Raphael's monument in the Pantheon at Rome for Kneller's epitaph in Westminster Abbey. He was a friend of the Marquis Scipio Maffei (1675–1755), an authority on inscriptions and an associate of L'Académie des Inscriptions in Paris, who visited Pope at Twickenham in 1736.[11]

Pope's study of monumental sculpture is indicated by his annotations on engravings of Roman monuments like Bernini's fountain in the Piazza Navona in Rome (plate 76), and on obelisks at the Papal Palace of Quintus VI, and St. Peter's in Rome; from his study of Montfaucon where he found a Renaissance fountain of the Nymph of the Grot—'a good Statue with an

[10] Vertue, iii. 150. Margaret Whinney, *Sculpture in Britain*, p. 73.

[11] For Pope's print hand, see Geoffrey Tillotson, *TE* ii. 237 n.; *Imitations of Horace*, *TE* iv. 229. For Bolingbroke's Blenheim inscription, see Spence, No. 272 (1735). On Pope's imitations of epitaphs on Pico and Raphael, see Spence, No. 345 (1735), n., and *TE* vi. 297–8, 312–13. For Scipio Maffei, see M. Michaud, *Biographie Universelle* (Paris, 1843–65).

Inscription, like that beautiful antique one which you know I am so fond of' (ii. 297); and again from his correspondence with Lady Mary, which includes her description of the equestrian statue of Louis XIV by Marc Chabry (1660–1727) in the Place de Louis Le Grand in Lyons.[12] On his rambles he remarked on English monuments in the church at Stanton Harcourt (i. 506), and admired at Sherborne, Dorset, 'a noble Monument and a beautiful Altar-piece of Architecture' (ii. 239) erected by Lord Digby.

After his father's death in 1717 Pope designed a simple pedimented wall tablet with a plain Latin inscription which was placed in the North Gallery of the Twickenham Parish Church of St. Mary. Pope's scale drawing of the monument is contained in a letter of instructions to Francis Bird (1667–1731), the most accomplished English statuary in the early decades of the century, noted for his work at St. Paul's, and particularly distinguished for his lapidary inscription. 'Mr. Bird', Pope writes about 1720,

> Pray forward the Monument, as above drawn, as soon as possible. Let it be entirely white Marble. And take a particular care that the Letters of the Inscription be rangd just as they are here, with the Space of two Lines left void in the middle, and the Space of one line at the End, in which Spaces there are future Insertions to be made. (ii. 26–7)

The monument executed to these directions is a good index of Pope's taste. It may be compared with a similar tablet, perhaps also his own design, on the outer wall of the chancel in the same church, 'a Gibbsian frame of intermittent rustication', which Pope put up to the memory of his nurse, Mary Beach (d. 1725). He may also have been responsible for the design of the Obelisk in his garden to the memory of his mother, 'a plain Stone Pillar resting upon a Pedestal', the plinth bearing on its four sides the inscription imitated by William Shenstone at the Leasowes. It would not have been beyond the powers of an amateur like Pope, competent in drawing, who had taken careful notes on Roman obelisks.[13]

[12] See Pope's annotated book of engravings, Pieter Schenk, *Romae Novae Delineatio*, now at Yale, pls. 11, 14, 15 (my numbering); and *The Complete Letters of Lady Mary Wortley Montagu*, ed. Robert Halsband, 3 vols. (Oxford, 1965), i. 436–7, and n.

[13] On amateur designers of monuments, see Katharine Esdaile, *English Church Monuments 1510 to 1840* (New York, 1946), p. 84. For Francis Bird, see Rupert Gunnis, *Dictionary of British Sculptors, 1660–1851*, rev. edn. (London, 1964), pp. 53–5. On the memorial to Mary Beach, see Nikolaus Pevsner, *Middlesex*,

The design of another monument of even more humble design has been attributed to Pope. This is the granite pillar on a pedestal, which Pope's friend William Oliver erected in 1741 in the churchyard of St. Sithney, Helston, Cornwall, in memory of his father. An anonymous writer in the *Quarterly Review* attributes the monument and the inscription to Pope: 'When Dr. Oliver was about to place a monument to the memory of his parents in Sithney churchyard, the poet [Pope] wrote their epitaph and drew the design of a pillar, which was subsequently placed there.' The evidence for this attribution has not been supplied, but Norman Ault states that 'it is wellnigh certain that the [prose] inscription on the west side is Pope's':

> William Oliver, from a filial sense that the blessings he now enjoys were, under the conduct of Providence, owing to the piety and tenderness of his mother and to the goodness and generosity of his father, erected this monument to their memorys. MDCCXLI.[14]

The monuments which Pope set up to the memory of his family and friends are uniformly simple in design and inscription. He stated his intentions for his own monument in his will (12 December 1743): 'As to my body, my will is, that it be buried near the monument of my dear parents at Twickenham, with the addition, after the words *filius fecit*—of these only, *et sibi: Qui obiit anno* 17—*aetatis*—.' These instructions were duly carried out. The monument William Warburton erected to Pope's memory in 1761 at St. Mary's, Twickenham, prominently inscribed with Warburton's name is a good example of a monument 'disgraced with . . . vile names and inscriptions' which Pope satirized in the *Dunciad*.[15]

Pope repeatedly expressed his contempt for the vainglorious monuments and pompous funerals of unworthy men, but he occupied himself throughout his career with the task of commemorating British worthies in verse and stone. He introduces the theme in *Windsor Forest* (299–302) urging the poet George Granville to commemorate English heroes. Like the 'happy Man

The Buildings of England, 3 (Harmondsworth, 1951), 158. On Pope's monument to his mother, see Mack, Appendix A, p. 241, pl. 11.

[14] See Nikolaus Pevsner, *Cornwall*, The Buildings of England 1 (Harmondsworth, 1951), 195; 'MS. Collections at Castle Horneck 1720–1772', *Quarterly Review*, 139 (July–Oct. 1875), 385; and G. C. F. Mead, 'A Pope Inscription', Letter to the Editor, *Times Literary Supplement*, 48 (7 October 1949), 649, where Norman Ault is quoted.

[15] *Dunciad* IV, l. 119 n., *TE* v. 353. See Wimsatt, *Portraits*, pp. 340–3.

who shows the Tombs' in his imitation of Donne (l. 102), Pope points in *Windsor Forest* (311–14) to the tomb of Henry VI in St. George's chapel, Windsor, where he was buried near Edward IV. In the same poem (319–21) he makes the first of numerous references in his poetry to the unmarked grave of a deserving man, in this instance Charles I, who had been buried in the same tomb as Henry VIII without honours. Christopher Wren's plans for a mausoleum and monument to Charles I drawn up in 1678 at the command of Charles II had not been carried out. In epitaphs throughout his career Pope responded to the question he asks in the *Epistle to Addison* (1720):

> Oh when shall Britain, conscious of her claim,
> Stand emulous of Greek and Roman fame? (53–4)[16]

i. JOHN HEWET AND SARAH DREW

The first monument Pope helped to erect, for which he composed his first epitaph, illustrates in an amusing way some of the practical difficulties involved in translating the ambition of commemorating British worthies into stone. This was the 'little Monument . . . of plain Stone' (i. 481), the memorial tablet on the outside wall of the church, which Pope and John Gay prevailed upon Lord Harcourt to erect at Stanton Harcourt in memory of John Hewet and Sarah Drew, described on the inscription as 'an industrious young man, and virtuous maiden of this parish; contracted in marriage who being with many others at harvest work, were both in an instant killed by lightning on the last day of July 1718'. This incident inspired in Pope no fewer than three epitaphs: an obscene one, an 'Eastern' one, and a 'godly one' (i. 495) which Pope submitted to Dean Atterbury 'for your opinion, both as to the doctrine and the poetry; as I am very certain, nothing is either fit for the church or the publick which is not agreeable to your sentiments' (i. 500):

> Think not by rigorous judgment seiz'd,
> A pair so faithful could expire;
> Victims so pure Heav'n saw well pleas'd
> And snatch'd them in Coelestial fire.

[16] See *TE* i. 176–7, 179–80, and nn. For the *Imitation of Donne*, and the *Epistle to Addison*, see *TE* iv. 33, vi. 204.

Live well and fear no sudden fate;
When God calls Virtue to the grave,
Alike tis Justice, soon or late,
Mercy alike to kill or save.

Virtue unmov'd can hear the Call,
And face the Flash that melts the Ball.[17]

Pope's epitaphs elicited from Lady Mary a satirical epitaph on the lovers' good fortune:

Who knows if 'twas not kindly done?
For had they seen the next year's sun,
A beaten wife and cuckold swain
Had jointly curs'd the marriage chain;
Now they are happy in their doom,
FOR POPE HAS WROTE UPON THEIR TOMB. (i. 523)

Pope's 'last cynical reaction' is contained in 'a ribald couplet' sent to Teresa Blount, the older, less sentimental Blount sister:

Here lye two poor Lovers, who had the mishap
Tho very chaste people, to die of a Clap. (i. 349)[18]

The episode reveals Pope as promoter of monuments in a comic light, but the appeal for patronage, attention to decorum in epitaphs, and his ambivalence of attitude are characteristic of his concern with monuments to British worthies throughout his career.

ii. POETS' CORNER IN WESTMINSTER ABBEY

Pope's association with the monuments of poets and artists is an important part of the contemporary cult of British worthies. Soon after the death of the poet Thomas Parnell (d. 1718), whose poems Pope edited in 1721, Pope wrote to the painter Charles Jervas to inquire about Parnell's monument: 'I'd fain know if he be buried at Chester, or Dublin; and what care has been, or is to be taken for his Monument, &c.' (ii. 24–5). In the same letter he

[17] See *TE* vi. 197–9; and *Correspondence*, i. 483, 495–6.

[18] Sherburn dates the letter 1716, but it clearly belongs in the 1718 Stanton Harcourt series. See Norman Ault, *New Light on Pope*, pp. 332–3; and 'Three Epitaphs on John Hewet and Sarah Drew', *TE* vi. 201.

informs Jervas that he is writing an epitaph for Nicholas Rowe (d. 1718), the playwright and editor of Shakespeare: 'I have not neglected my Devoirs to Mr. Rowe; I am writing this very day his Epitaph for Westminster-Abbey' (ii. 25). In the next decade Pope expressed his curiosity about the monument of an acquaintance and subscriber to the *Odyssey*, the portrait painter William Aikman (1682–1731), in a letter to David Mallet: 'Tell me if this was a mere Impulse of your Friendship, to write on a Man, because he deserved it, or is there any body so generous (or rather—so just) to intend him a Monument' (iii. 222). Pope is not known to have contributed either to Parnell's or Aikman's monument, but he was closely connected with monuments to poets which were set up in Westminster Abbey during his lifetime, and with the monument to Kneller.[19]

Addison, writing in the *Spectator* (No. 26, 1711) seems to have been the first to refer to what is now known as Poets' Corner in Westminster Abbey: 'In the poetical Quarter, I found there were Poets who had no Monuments, and Monuments which had no Poets.' The 'poetical Quarter' appears prominently in John Dart's *Westmonasterium*, published about 1724, which included plates of many monuments to 'glorious British Heroes', and Dart's verses, *Westminster Abbey: A Poem*, which speak enthusiastically of 'Briton's Bards' in the South transept (i. xxxviii). He pays homage to the remains of Chaucer, Spenser, Shadwell, Davenant, Rowe, Denham, and, at greater length, to Cowley and Dryden. Dart's text, 'A view of the Monuments . . . in the year 1723' (i. 75), begins with Poets' Corner, lavishly illustrated with plates. He echoes Addison in his assertion that

> this Caemitery of Men of Learning, who honour this Pile (tho' without Tombs to point them out) more than the splendid and more magnificent Monuments of Dead Greatness . . . a plain Proof, that this Church affords Great Characters with no Monuments, and Great Monuments with no Characters. (ii. 61)

Pope was acquainted with Dart, who paid him a compliment in his poem.[20]

[19] See *Westminster Abbey, Official Guide*, rev. edn. (Norwich, 1966), p. 35. After Aikman's death (June 1731) Vertue noted (iii. 51) that 'his body was carryd to Scotland and there was buried—according to his own appointment'.

[20] Joseph Addison, *The Spectator*, ed. D. F. Bond, i. 110 (30 Mar. 1711); John Dart, *Westmonasterium, or The History and Antiquities of the Abbey Church of St. Peters Westminster*, 2 vols. (London, n.d.), i. xxxviii, xl. For Pope's reference to Dart see *Correspondence*, ii. 258. Dart speaks of Pope and Congreve as sons of

iii. JOHN DRYDEN

Pope made his first contribution to Poets' Corner in connection with the monument of John Dryden opened in 1721. In the notes to the *Epistle to Arbuthnot* Pope remarked ironically on the 'magnificent Funeral bestow'd upon him [Dryden] by the contribution of several Persons of Quality'.[21] The lines allude to the Earl of Halifax:

> But still the Great have kindness in reserve,
> He help'd to bury whom he help'd to starve. (247–8)

In epitaphs intended for Nicholas Rowe Pope alluded to Dryden's monument in Westminster Abbey which Halifax had intended but never erected.[22] Pope was not the first to publicize this neglect, but his epitaph to Rowe published in 1720 prompted John Sheffield, Duke of Buckinghamshire, to raise a monument to the poet, and Pope played an important role in its erection.

A letter from Francis Atterbury, Dean of Westminster and Bishop of Rochester, to Pope (August 1720) indicates that the poet was acting as Atterbury's executive in the erection of Dryden's monument. The letter concerns the site of the monument which was erected in the east aisle of the south transept opposite St. Benedict's chapel near the monuments to Chaucer and Cowley:

> I have sent the Officer to view the Place and find, upon his Report, that no Objection lyes against erecting a Tomb, where part of the Screen of the Chappel next Cowley's Monument stands: but there must be a smooth free Stone Wall behind it, both to Support the Tomb backwards, and to remove the Eysore there would otherwise be to those who go into that Chappel to see the Tombs, there: but I do not find, that the Extraordinary Expence of such a Stone Wall will come to so much as Ten Pounds; and such a Trifling Expence therefore is not to be regarded. All Doubts being remov'd (I know not how any came to be entertain'd) I wish you would now hasten the Execution of the Design, for some Reasons which did not occur to me when I saw you last. (ii. 51–2)

The design by James Gibbs consists of 'an elevated base and pedestal supporting a fine Bust of the Poet, by Scheemakers behind which is an arched recess

Homer in his poem, i. xlii. For the history of Poets' Corner, see Arthur P. Stanley, *Historical Memorials of Westminster Abbey*, 5th edn. (New York, 1882), ii. 12–41, and plan, p. 13.

[21] See the *Epistle to Arbuthnot*, l. 248 n., *TE* iv. 113.

[22] *TE* vi. 208.

under an entablature and pediment rising from pilasters'. It was 'first expos'd to publick View' 23 January 1721, bearing Pope's plain Latin inscription, 'being only the name of that Great Poet', which he substituted for a more flourishing couplet:

> This SHEFFIELD rais'd. The sacred Dust below
> Was DRYDEN once: The rest who does not know?[23]

Pope evidently rejected the Latin inscriptions Atterbury sent to him for approval in September, 'which may in a few words say all that is to be said of Dryden, and yet nothing more than he deserves', and ignored Atterbury's suggestion in the same letter: 'If your design holds of fixing Dryden's Name only below, and his Busto above—may not these [lines] be graved just under the Name' (ii. 55). The monument was engraved by J. Cole for Dart's *Westmonasterium* (plate 77), and Dart thought the design 'plain, majestick, and just, equal to the great Imagination of the Patron who erected it, and the Merits of the Poet whose Name it bears' (i. 90). Dart described Pope's inscription as 'a silent Reproach to abundance of others in this Church, by showing how few Words are necessary to express real Merit, and how many are requisite to set off none' (i. 90), and praises the absence of an epitaph in his poem (i. xli).

Gibbs's classical architectural setting for Dryden's bust is conventional, but the participation of an architect in the design of monuments which had been hitherto the work of mason sculptors was an important innovation. Gibbs was the first English architect to take a serious interest in funerary architecture, and between 1720 and 1740 he worked 'in collaboration with the best sculptors of the new generation'. It may be that Gibbs, who was Pope's architect at Twickenham at this time, owed the commission for the Dryden monument to Pope. The identity of the sculptor of the original bust of Dryden has not been determined, but it proved unsatisfactory and was replaced about 1731 by another commissioned by the Duchess of Buckingham from Scheemakers, based on a Kneller portrait.[24] It was probably Scheemakers's bust of Dryden that Pope told Spence about 1729 was 'like him' (No. 57).

[23] The description of Dryden's monument is Edward W. Brayley's, *The History and Antiquities of the Abbey Church of St. Peter, Westminster*, 2 vols. (London, 1818–23), ii. 266. On Dryden's epitaph, see *TE* vi. 237, 209 n.; and *Correspondence*, ii. 51 n.

[24] See Margaret Whinney, *Sculpture in Britain*, pp. 70–1; and Katharine Esdaile, *English Church Monuments*, p. 116.

iv. SAMUEL BUTLER

Pope contributed to another monument to a poet in the Abbey erected in the same year as Dryden's, but the details are obscure. George Sherburn says that Pope 'probably advised Alderman Barber concerning the monument which Barber in 1721 erected in the Abbey to the author of *Hudibras*', who had been buried in the Church-yard of St. Paul, Covent-Garden. Atterbury wrote to Pope in May to say that he had conferred with Butler's intimate friends, the Longuevilles: 'I think there is now no restraint in point of Ceremony to your proceeding with what hast you please in your Epitaph—which I shall be ready to deliver to your Mason, when he calls for it' (ii. 76). Possibly Pope's mason was Francis Bird, who had carved the inscription on Pope's family monument. The designer of the monument to Butler, consisting of a bust 'standing in front of a pyramid, on an inscribed base, having grotesque masks at the sides', has not been identified. Nikolaus Pevsner says that the laureated Roman bust in classical drapery is 'probably by Rysbrack'.[25] The monument placed on the south wall of the east aisle in poets' corner was opened in July 1721.

The Latin inscription on the pedestal of the monument, attributed to Pope by Edmund Curll, pays tribute to the unrewarded genius of 'the outstanding writer of satirical verse among us', and concludes with a compliment to the patron of the monument, Alderman John Barber, a printer and Lord Mayor of London, whose name is offset and carved in letters only slightly smaller than the poet's own. With this 'melancholy Reflection', Pope continues the attack begun in Rowe's epitaph on the nation's neglect of its poets, but his satire later turned on Barber himself, perhaps because of his attempts to persuade Pope to hitch him into verse. He is the Alderman of whom the Goddess Dulness speaks in the fourth book of the *Dunciad* (1742), with the note (l. 131) referring to 'the *Tombs of the Poets*, Editio Westmonsteriensis':

> So by each Bard an Alderman shall sit,
> A heavy Lord shall hang at ev'ry Wit,

[25] See George Sherburn, *Early Career*, p. 277; for the description of Butler's monument, Edward W. Brayley, *History and Antiquities of Westminster*, ii (1823), 263; and Nikolaus Pevsner, *London—I*, The Buildings of England, 12 (Harmondsworth, 1962), 405.

And while on Fame's triumphal Car they ride,
Some Slave of mine be pinion'd to their side. (131–4)[26]

V. MATTHEW PRIOR

Another monument to a poet, Matthew Prior (plate 78), was the subject of correspondence between Pope and Atterbury during the year they were co-operating on the memorials to Dryden and Butler. Atterbury wrote to Pope (27 September 1721) to say that Prior

is buried, as he desired, at the Feet of Spencer; and I will take care to make good in every respect what I said to him when living; particularly as to the Triplet, he wrote for his own Epitaph; which while we were in good Terms, I promised him, should never appear on his Tomb, while I was Dean of Westminster. (ii. 85)

Prior's epigram on Atterbury and the epitaph by Robert Friend finally inscribed on the monument probably explain the disapproval of the monument Pope expressed several years later (1728) to Bathurst:

If I live but one year, it would better please me to think an Obelisque might be added to your Garden, or a Pond to hers [Lady Scudamore's], with my money, than such a Hospital as Guy's to the City, or such a Monument as Priors to Westminster. (ii. 525)[27]

Prior's will had provided £500 'for this last piece of HUMAN VANITY', and Lord Oxford commissioned from James Gibbs a design essentially similar to Dryden's—an architectural setting for a bust, consisting of an elevated base supporting a sarcophagus, but elegantly adorned with figures carved by the Flemish sculptor Michael Rysbrack: a cherub amid festoons of flowers over the bust, two boys reclining on the angular pediment, one bearing an exhausted hour-glass, the other an inverted torch, and full-length figures at the

26 For the inscription on Butler's monument, see *Correspondence*, ii. 76 n; and *Westminster Abbey Official Guide* (1966), p. 41. See Pope, *Dunciad* IV, *TE* v. 54, and n. Cf. Pope's satire of William Benson's monument to Milton: *Dunciad* (1742) IV, ll. 110–12, *TE* v. 352, and n.

27 Pope appears to have objected to Guy's Hospital, as much as to Prior's monument, for reasons other than aesthetic. Thomas Guy (1644/5–1724), bookseller, philanthropist, and successful investor in South Sea stock, provided for the building (1722–5) and endowment of Guy's Hospital in Southwark, which was opened in 1726. Largely because of the calumnies of John Dunton, he had the reputation of a miser, speculator, and usurer, which probably accounts for Pope's animus. See H. C. Cameron, chap. 2, 'Thomas Guy, Founder', *Mr. Guy's Hospital 1726–1948* (London, 1954), pp. 13–34; and Nikolaus Pevsner, *London Except the Cities of London and Westminster*, The Buildings of England, 5 (Harmondsworth, 1952), 400–1.

77. Dryden's Monument in Westminster Abbey. After J. Dowling. 1724.

78. Matthew Prior's Monument in Westminster Abbey. Engraved by Bernard Baron. 1728.

79. John Sheffield's Monument in Westminster Abbey. 1723.

80.

82.

81.

83.

80. Design for James Craggs's Monument in Westminster Abbey. By James Gibbs. *c.* 1723. *Victoria and Albert Museum. Crown Copyright*

81. Model for James Craggs's Monument. By Guelfi. *c.* 1724.

82. James Craggs the Younger. After Kneller. 1720.

83. Craggs's Monument as Originally Sited in the Abbey. 1812.

ends of the sarcophagus of Thalia and Clio, the Muses of Poetry and History. Dryden's monument was outdone principally by the 'brilliant bust' of Prior, carved about 1700 by the French sculptor Antoine Coysevox, and presented to Prior in 1714 by Louis XIV when he was 'plenipotentiary' to France.[28]

It is difficult to understand why Pope would object to a poet's monument in the Abbey unless he shared with James Ralph the view that Prior's 'bust, which is design'd to be the principal figure, is hurt by the whole statues on either side'. More likely he objected to the iconography, particularly the figure of Clio holding a closed book 'in allusion, probably, to the "Account of his own Times", which Prior was composing at the period of his decease'. This was the burden of the long Latin inscription on the sarcophagus and base of the monument, recounting the events of Prior's political career and characterizing his writings, which Pope regarded as a 'Sepulchral lye', as he told Spence in 1736:

> What a simple thing was it to say upon his [Prior's] tombstone that he was writing a history of his own times! He could not write in a style fit for history, and I dare say he never had set down a word toward any such thing. (No. 215)

Pope told Spence, 'I love short inscriptions' (No. 345), and Freind's laboured Latin epitaphs are the subject of Pope's epigram in a letter to Ralph Allen 'To One who Wrote Long Epitaphs' (1736):

> Friend! in your Epitaphs I'm griev'd
> So very much is said,
> One half will never be believd,
> The other never read. (iv. 14)

In addition Pope was probably annoyed by Prior's attacks on Atterbury during the dispute over Westminster Dormitory in 1720, when he wrote lines, 'On Bishop Atterbury's Burying the Duke of Buckingham', satirizing Sheffield's agnostic epitaph.[29]

[28] The description of Prior's monument is Edward Brayley's, *History and Antiquities of Westminster*, ii (1823), 262. See Margaret Whinney, *Sculpture in Britain*, p. 84, and James Lees-Milne, *Earls of Creation*, pp. 202–3.

[29] See [James Ralph], *A Critical Review of the Public Buildings . . . in London and Westminster* (London, 1734), pp. 78–9. For the iconography of the Prior monument, see Edward Brayley, *History and Antiquities of Westminster*, ii (1823), 262. For 'Sepulchral lyes our holy walls to grace', see *Dunciad* (1728) I, l. 41 and n., *TE* v. 65: 'Verse 41 is a just Satyr on the Flatteries and Falsehoods admitted to be inscribed on the walls

vi. JOHN SHEFFIELD

Pope evidently helped to relieve Atterbury's embarrassment about Sheffield's epitaph and he appears to have had something to do with Sheffield's monument erected about 1722 in the north-east aisle of Henry VII's chapel in Westminster Abbey. Pope wrote to Katharine Sheffield about the monument, which was designed by the sculptor from Antwerp, Denis Plumier (1688–1721):

> This Morning I left the Town, I went with Mr. *Jervas* to *Belluchi*'s, but parting in Haste, I had not his Opinion at large; only he assures me, he thinks the Figures will not be too small, considering that those which are nearest the Eye, are, at least, as large as the Life. I can't but be of Opinion, that my Lord Duke's and your Grace's ought to be made Portraits, and as like as possible; of which they have yet, no Resemblance. There being no Picture (as I believe) of the Duke in Profile, it might be well, I fancy, if *Belluchi* copied the Side-Face from that *Busto* that stands in the *Salon*. (ii. 99)

Pope's comments about perspective probably refer to Plumier's figures of Sheffield and his wife on a model of the monument, which Pope was attempting to improve by obtaining a copy of the Duke's portrait bust in the saloon of Buckingham House from the history painter Antonio Belluchi (1654–1726).[30]

Pope may have been acting again as Atterbury's executive in co-ordinating the efforts of the foreign statuaries recently arrived in England, Peter Scheemakers (1691–1781) and Laurent Delvaux (1696–1778), who carried out Plumier's design, but his dealing with Belluchi is the only evidence of his contribution to the monument. The monument features the Duke in Roman armour half-reclining, the Duchess dressed in Georgian costume seated at his feet 'weeping' in the pathetic style, and, in the background on an elevated pedestal, the immense figure of Father Time bearing away medallions portraying the Duke's deceased children. The classical architectural frame and the dominating baroque figure of Father Time carved by Delvaux introduced motifs which became extremely popular and ushered in what has been called

of Churches in Epitaphs.' On Prior's attacks on Atterbury, see H. Bunker Wright and Monroe K. Spears, ed., *The Literary Works of Matthew Prior*, 2nd edn., 2 vols. (Oxford, 1971), i. 550, ii. 993 n.

[30] See George Sherburn, *Early Career*, p. 221.

'the reign of the Roman toga'. The monument was engraved by J. Cole for Dart's *Westmonasterium*; the same engraving appears as frontispiece in volume one of Sheffield's *Works* (1723; plate 79), the other monument to the Duke Pope helped to erect.[31]

vii. JAMES CRAGGS

At an early stage of planning, Buckingham's monument was considered as a model for the monument of Pope's friend, James Craggs the younger, successor to Addison as Secretary of State, who died 16 February 1721. John Knight, a friend of Craggs and his bereaved sister, Mrs. Newsham, who was planning the monument, asked Pope for prints of Sheffield's tomb (ii. 217). It turned out that Buckingham's grandiose monument was not imitated, but Pope superintended the erection of Craggs's monument in the south-west corner of the nave in Westminster Abbey between 1724 and 1727, and may have influenced its design. Giovanni Battista Guelfi (*fl.* 1714–34), whom Burlington had brought to England from Rome about 1715, was commissioned to carve the statue. According to Margaret Whinney, it was 'doubtless because of Pope's connexion with Lord Burlington that Guelfi was chosen the sculptor'. It may also have been because of Pope that James Gibbs was commissioned to design the architectural setting (plate 80) for Guelfi's statue.[32]

Vertue characterizes Guelfi as 'a man of slow speech much opiniated, and as an Italian thought no body could be equal to himself in skill in this Country. Yet all his works seem to the judicious very often defective, wanting spirit and grace. It's thought that Ld Burlington parted with him very willingly.' Pope began with a prejudice in favour of Burlington's protégé, but after three years his patience was wearing thin. He wrote to Mrs. Newsham in July 1724 about Guelfi's progress on the terracotta model (plate 81) of Craggs's

[31] See Nikolaus Pevsner, *London—I*, The Buildings of England, 12 (1962), 402. For the description of Sheffield's monument, see Edward Brayley, 'An Historical and Architectural Account of King Henry the Seventh's Chapel', *History and Antiquities of Westminster*, i. (1818), 62. See Margaret Whinney, *Sculpture in Britain*, p. 80; Katharine Esdaile, *English Church Monuments*, p. 64; and Katharine Sheffield's dedication opposite the engraving of the Duke's monument in *Works*, ed. Pope, i (1723): 'These [his Works] His More Lasting Remains (The Monument of His Mind, and more Perfect Image of Himself).'

[32] On Guelfi, see Rupert Gunnis, *Dictionary of British Sculptors* (1964), p. 183, and Margaret Whinney, *Sculpture in Britain*, p. 80.

statue he was working on in his studio at Burlington House, now preserved in the Soane Museum:

> The Italian sculptor has not yet finished his clay model. Indeed, it is a vast disadvantage as to the likeness, not to be able to see the life. What would not you and I give that that were possible? But at last, by comparing the two other pictures and the print, (together with my own memory of the features of that friend who had often looked so kindly upon me,) he has brought it to a greater degree of resemblance than I could have thought. If you happened to come to town, I could wish you saw the model yet, before the marble be begun: for if you were not satisfied, I would have another sculptor make a model in clay after the pictures, for a further chance of likeness: If the artist were a worse carver than this man, yet it might be a help to improve his Statue in this respect (since all the rest he cannot fail to perform excellently). I am really in pain to have you pleased, in a point that I am sure is a tender one, since it is all you can do for the best of brothers, and I for the best of friends! (ii. 242–3)

In a vain effort to improve the carving of the model Pope had supplied Guelfi with portraits of Craggs, probably by Kneller (plate 82) which he had in his own collection, and which had been engraved by George Vertue and John Simon in 1720.[33]

About a month later, August 1724, Pope writes Mrs. Newsham again to report some progress: 'The model I begin to be satisfied with, and he [Guelfi] is to proceed upon the Statue forthwith' (ii. 246). In October, Pope writes that the marble has been procured, that his cash is sufficient to answer the statuary's demands,[34] and that he has made the Latin inscription for the urn, characteristically, 'as full, and yet as short, as I possibly could'. He was prepared to supervise the statuary closely: 'I will not forget those cautions about the forehead, hair, etc. which we observed when we met on that occasion' (ii. 266).

'It is apparent', J. F. Physick writes, 'that Guelfi followed Gibbs's design closely, even to the folds of the drapery.'[35] About two years elapsed before the

[33] On Guelfi's model of Craggs's monument, see John F. Physick, 'Some Eighteenth Century Designs for Monuments in Westminster Abbey', *Victoria and Albert Museum Bulletin*, 3 (Jan. 1967), 27, 32. On Kneller's portrait of Craggs and engravings after it, see David Piper, *Catalogue of Seventeenth-Century Portraits in the National Portrait Gallery 1625–1714* (Cambridge, 1963), No. 1134, pp. 88–9, and 'Inventory', p. 244.

[34] *Correspondence*, ii. 484 n.

[35] 'Designs for Monuments in Westminster Abbey', *Victoria and Albert Museum Bulletin*, 3 (Jan. 1967), 27, fig. 2.

statue was finished, when Pope wrote to John Knight in October 1727 about moving the statue to the Abbey:

> I went to Burlington-house two days ago, where the statue is boxed up, ready for carriage, by Guelfi: he had sent me two letters in one day about Bird again; that he would not make the box for it, etc. Whereupon I bid him, if Mr. B. did not come for it soon, to take the care upon himself of erecting it. But I since understand Guelfi is fallen sick: so Mr. Bird's care will be the more necessary. I wish to God it were once well set up: it will make the finest figure, I think, in the place; and it is the least part of honour due to the memory of a man who made the best in his station. (ii. 457)

Pope's impatience is obvious: Guelfi was sick, and Francis Bird, who had been hired to transport, erect, and to cut the inscriptions on the urn and base of the statue, was procrastinating. But, finally Pope was able to inform Knight at the end of November 1727: 'At last I have seen the statue up, and the statuary down at the same time' (ii. 463). Some finishing touches still remained to be done on the hands and feet of the statue; the joining of the urn needed improvement; and the inscription on the urn, which Pope had seen 'scored on in the Abbey' (ii. 463), was still to be cut; but Pope's work as overseer was nearly finished. The next month announcements appeared in the *Evening Journal* (14 December) and other newspapers:

> There is now opened in the West-End of Westminster-Abbey [plate 83], a fine white Marble Monument of the late Mr. Secretary Craggs, on which are inscribed these beautiful Lines, which Mr. Pope wrote upon Mr. Addison's *Treatise of Medals*:
>
> Statesman, yet Friend to Truth! of Soul sincere,
> In Action faithful, and in Honour clear!
> Who broke no promise, serv'd no private end,
> Who gain'd no Title, and who lost no Friend,
> Ennobled by Himself, by All approv'd,
> Prais'd, wept, and honour'd, by the Muse he lov'd.[36]

Pope's epitaph, carved by Francis Bird in gilt letters on the urn, flattered the man who had disgraced himself in the South Sea scandal, and was subjected to ridicule and parody.

Despite Guelfi's indifferent carving, the 'graceful and simple' monument

[36] *TE* vi. 282–3. The newspapers printed the text of the epitaph as in the *Epistle to Addison* (ll. 66–72, *TE* vi. 204). I quote the Abbey inscription: *TE* vi. 281–2.

which resulted from this collaboration between poet, sculptor, architect, and mason was 'something of a landmark in English art', and was widely imitated by painters and sculptors throughout the century.[37] Its most important lineal descendant was the monument to Shakespeare in Westminster Abbey (1741), sponsored by a committee on which Pope served with Lord Burlington and Dr. Richard Mead. The Shakespeare monument was the culmination of a decade in which the population of Poets' Corner continued to increase, during which Pope continued to advise on monuments, to write inscriptions and epitaphs for poets, artists, and others, and to sharpen his satire of 'vile names and inscriptions'.

viii. HILL, NEWTON, AND KNELLER

A letter from Aaron Hill to Pope (1731) asking his opinion of a monument he intended to erect in the cloisters of Westminster Abbey to the memory of his wife Miranda, indicates the reputation Pope had acquired as a judge of funerary monuments by the beginning of the 1730s. Hill enclosed a rough sketch (now lost) of his design in the letter which is worth quoting at length to illustrate eighteenth-century taste in tombs:

Give me leave to hope the benefit of your advice, on this mournful occasion. I cannot suffer her to lie unnoticed, because a monument, in so frequented a place as *Westminster-Abbey*, restoring her, to a kind of second life, among the living, it will be in some measure, not to have *lost* her. But there is a low and unmeaning lumpishness, in the vulgar style of monuments, which disgusts me, as often, as I look upon them; and, because I would avoid the censure I am giving, let me beg you to say, whether there is *significance*, in the draught, of which I enclose you an aukward *scratch*, not a *copy*: the flat table, behind, is *black*, the figures are *white* marble.

The *whole* of what you see, here, is but *part* of the monument; and will be surrounded by *pilasters*, arising from a pediment of *white marble*, having its foundation on a *black marble mountain*, and supporting a *coronice* and *dome*, that will ascend to the point of the cloister arch. About half way up a craggy path, on the *black mountain*, below will be the figure of *time*, in *white marble*, in an attitude of *climbing*, obstructed by little *Cupids*, of the same colour; some rolling rocks, into his path, from *above*; some throwing *nets*, at his *feet* and *arms*, from *below*; others in *ambuscade*, shooting *arrows* at him, from *both sides*; while the *Death*, you see in the *draught*, will seem, from an opening between *hills*,

[37] Margaret Whinney, *Sculpture in Britain*, pp. 80–1. Cf. Walpole, *Anecdotes*, iii. 40.

in *relievo*, to have found admission by a shorter way, and prevented *time*, at a distance. (iii. 229)

We do not have Pope's reply to this letter, but it would be surprising if Pope had approved of Hill's grandiose design, or the melodramatic allegory in black and white marble with the figure of Death, which seems to anticipate Roubiliac's highly charged conceptions.[38]

Early in the decade two important monuments in Westminster Abbey to British worthies in the Arts and Sciences, Isaac Newton and Godfrey Kneller, involved Pope for the first time in collaboration with Rysbrack. Newton's monument, designed by William Kent and carved by Rysbrack has been called 'perhaps the finest of all the post-medieval tombs in the abbey'. John Conduitt, who commissioned the monument for Isaac Newton (d. 1727) from William Kent and Michael Rysbrack, was acquainted with Pope. He had asked him to correct the dedication of a work of Newton's published posthumously, and he probably asked Pope to write the 'Epitaph, Intended for Sir Isaac Newton, in Westminster-Abbey' (1730). But Pope's famous contribution to Newton's apotheosis ('Nature, and Nature's Laws lay hid in Night./ God said, *Let Newton be*! and *All was Light*.') was rejected in favour of a long list of Newton's discoveries in Latin, of which Samuel Johnson disapproved.[39]

Pope's epitaph for the monument raised in April 1730 in the south aisle of the Abbey nave to Sir Godfrey Kneller had been still more unfortunate, involving him in disagreeable litigation with Lady Kneller. Pope described to Spence (No. 115) his visit to Kneller on his deathbed, when Kneller showed him 'the plan he had made for his own monument', and got Pope's promise to write his epitaph, but failed to get his consent to remove the monument to Pope's father in the north gallery of St. Mary's Parish Church at Twickenham, which Kneller thought 'the best Place in the Church [for his own

[38] See Dorothy Brewster, *Aaron Hill, Poet, Dramatist, Projector* (1913; rpt. New York, 1966), p. 221.

[39] On Newton's monument, see M. I. Webb, *Michael Rysbrack*, pp. 82–5, and John Physick, *Designs for English Sculpture 1680–1800*, Victoria and Albert Museum (London, 1969), pp. 80–1, figs. 48–50, 53. For Pope's epitaph, see *TE* vi. 317; his relationship with John Conduitt, *Correspondence*, ii. 457–8; and on Newton's apotheosis, see Frank E. Manuel, *A Portrait of Isaac Newton* (Cambridge, Mass., 1968), pp. 151, 265–6. Samuel Johnson wished that 'only the name of Sir Isaac Newton [had] been subjoined to the design upon his monument'. See 'An Essay on Epitaphs', in *Works* (London, 1796), ii. 272. For Margaret Whinney's praise of the monument, see *Sculpture in Britain*, p. 89.

monument] to be seen at a distance'.[40] In 1725 Lady Kneller petitioned the Doctors' Commons for removal of the Pope monument, and Pope based his legal defence on the ground that the proposed design represented a threat to the fabric: 'a vast three-hundred-pound-Pyle', he told Thomas Wentworth, 3rd Earl of Strafford, a parishioner to whom he wrote for support of his case, 'projecting out upon you, overshadowing my Lady Strafford with the Immense Draperies & Stone Petticoats of Lady Kneller, & perhaps crushing to pieces your Lordships Posterity' (ii. 300). He ridiculed Lady Kneller's 'pious Design of making as Large a figure on the Tomb as Sir G. himself':

> One day I mean to fill Sir Godfry's tomb,
> If for my body all this Church has room.
> Down with more Monuments! More room! (she cryd)
> For I am very large, & very wide. (ii. 309)

This appears to be special pleading, because Kneller's drawing, preserved in the British Museum, has no full-length figures. But Pope may have been referring to a more ambitious 'model & designs' by Francis Bird, from whom Rysbrack 'snatched this important commission'.[41]

The monument which Pope thought so large (ii. 213) can probably be identified with Kneller's original design (plate 84) for the 'big hanging monument', which was executed by Rysbrack from a model he made before Kneller died 'by his direction'. It consists (plate 85) of Rysbrack's bust of Kneller, flanked by cherubs, one of whom holds a medallion of Lady Kneller, under a canopy of white marble, inscribed with the imitation of Raphael's Latin epitaph, which Pope thought 'the worst thing I ever wrote in my life' perhaps because of the trouble Kneller's monument had caused him.[42]

[40] Pope quotes Kneller's words in a letter to Thomas Wentworth, 3rd Earl of Strafford, *Correspondence*, ii. 309 (6 July 1725).

[41] For Kneller's drawing of his monument (B.M. 188-7-19-81), see Edward Croft-Murray and P. Hulton, *Catalogue of British Drawings*, i (1960), 395; ii, pl. 181. On Francis Bird's designs for Kneller's monument, see Vertue, iii. 43; and Margaret Whinney, *Sculpture in Britain*, p. 84.

[42] See Nikolaus Pevsner, *London—I*, The Buildings of England, 12 (1962), 422. For Rysbrack's model, see Vertue, *Note Books*, iii. 43. For descriptions of Kneller's monument, see Edward Brayley, *History and Antiquities of Westminster*, ii. 230; M. I. Webb, *Michael Rysbrack*, pp. 51–2; and Margaret Whinney, *Sculpture in Britain*, p. 85. For Pope's low opinion of his epitaph, see Spence, No. 115. Cf. James Ralph in the *Critical Review* (1734), p. 64: 'The epitaph, which is exactly of a piece with the tomb, is as unworthy of Mr. *Pope*'s genius, as the design of that is of *Kneller*'s pencil.'

84. Kneller's Design for his own Monument. *c.* 1723.

85. Kneller's Abbey Monument as Executed. By Gravelot. 1742.

86. Shakespeare's Monument in Westminster Abbey. By Peter Scheemakers. 1740.

ix. GAY AND ROWE

When the Queensberrys erected a monument in the Abbey in 1736 to John Gay, Pope complied with Gay's request in a letter to him (1729) that 'you will, if a Stone should mark the Place of my Grave, see these Words put on it:

> Life is a Jest, and all Things show it;
> I thought so once, but now I know it.

With what more you may think proper' (iii. 20). The lines are more flippant than Atterbury would have permitted, but they were inscribed on the pedestal supporting Rysbrack's winged boy leaning on a portrait medallion of the poet in the south transept. Pope's verse epitaph (1733), 'of Manners gentle, of Affections mild', expresses the same view of Gay as a neglected poet which later appears in the *Epistle to Arbuthnot* (1735).[43]

After a delay of 25 years Pope's epitaph appeared on an Abbey monument to the poet and dramatist Nicholas Rowe erected by his widow after the death of their daughter in 1739. Commissioned from Rysbrack, it features a laureated bust of the poet, a portrait medallion of his daughter, and a full-size seated mourning female figure of Rowe's widow. Pope's revised epitaph takes into account not only the mourning figure in Rysbrack's design, which can be seen standing in his drawing preserved in the Victoria and Albert Museum, but the new situation of the monument now adjoining Shakespeare's rather than Dryden's tomb, to which Rowe's was to have been conductor in the original epitaph:

> Thy Reliques, *Rowe*! to this sad Shrine we trust,
> And near thy *Shakespear* place thy honour'd Bust,
>
> . . .
>
> To these [Rowe and his daughter, d. 1739], so mourn'd in Death, so lov'd in Life!
> The childless Parent and the widow'd Wife
> With tears inscribes this monumental Stone,
> That holds their Ashes and expects her own. (1–2; 11–14)

[43] See Pope's epitaph to Gay, *TE* vi. 349, 352 n., and the *Epistle to Arbuthnot*, *TE* iv. 114. For descriptions of Gay's monument, see Edward Brayley, *History and Antiquities of Westminster*, ii. 259–60, and M. I. Webb, *Michael Rysbrack*, p. 287.

In no other epitaph of Pope's do the verse and sculpture bear the equal part they do here.[44]

X. SHAKESPEARE

Two years before Rowe's monument was finally set up a monument to Shakespeare was erected in the Abbey which represented the climax of the movement to commemorate 'Briton's Bards' as 'British Heroes' in Poets' Corner. The Shakespeare monument had been proposed as early as 1726 by John Rich, manager of the Covent Garden Theatre, was encouraged by James Ralph in the *Critical Review* (1734), and Pope served on a committee with Lord Burlington and Dr. Richard Mead which raised the money for the monument by public subscription. Its erection was assisted by benefit performances of Shakespeare's plays at Drury Lane and Covent Garden, and by 'a present of the Ground' from the Dean and Chapter of Westminster.[45]

Thus, unlike all the earlier monuments to poets Pope had been associated with, which were works of private patronage, the monument to Shakespeare was publicly supported, 'the first great national celebration of Shakespeare', as David Piper observes. This is the point of a satirical couplet Pope is said to have 'proposed should be placed on the vacant scroll under Shakespeare's bust':

> Thus Britain lov'd me; and preserv'd my Fame,
> Clear from a *Barber*'s or a *Benson*'s Name.

Pope insisted, against the objection of Dr. Mead, that the patronage of the public be recognized in the words *Amor Publicus Posuit*. The inscription makes a pointed reference to the delay in erecting Shakespeare's monument (*Anno post Mortem CXXIV*), another of Pope's allusions to the nation's neglect of its poets.[46]

[44] See descriptions of Rowe's monument by Edward Brayley, *History and Antiquities of Westminster* (1823), ii. 260; Margaret Whinney, *Sculpture in Britain*, p. 117; and M. I. Webb, *Michael Rysbrack*, p. 87. For Rysbrack's drawing of Rowe's monument, see John Physick, *Designs for English Sculpture* (London, 1969), pp. 91–3, figs. 59–60. For Pope's epitaph, see *TE* vi. 400. Norman Ault answers the arguments denying Pope's authorship in *New Light on Pope*, pp. 145–55.

[45] See David Piper, '"O Sweet Mr. Shakespeare I'll have his picture", *The Changing Image of Shakespeare's Person, 1600–1800*' (London, 1964), p. 20. On promoters of Shakespeare's monument, see *TE* vi. 395 n.; Vertue, iii. 101; and James Ralph, *Critical Review* (1734), pp. 79–80.

[46] Cf. Pope's satirical epigram: 'After an hundred and thirty years' nap,/Enter Shakespeare, with a loud clap'. *TE* vi. 395, and nn.

The design of the monument, consisting of a life-sized standing figure on an elevated basement, leaning gracefully on a pile of books reared on a pedestal against a finely cut pedimented frame, was by William Kent; the marble statue was carved by Peter Scheemakers, who briefly triumphed over his rival Rysbrack in this commission. The direction of the monument was thus firmly in the hands of the Burlington circle, and Pope's contribution to the design of this famous monument may have extended to matters other than the inscription. As collector and editor he had acquired some knowledge of Shakespeare iconography, a mixture of fact and fiction typical of the time. As early as 1711 he told John Caryll (i. 120) that Shakespeare was one of the votive images of poets he surrounded himself with at Binfield. In his edition of Shakespeare (1725) Pope approved for publication two images of the poet, one spurious, the other composite: the first was a handsome engraving (1721) by George Vertue of a miniature mistakenly called Shakespeare acquired by Edward Harley about 1719, which was promptly denounced by the antiquary John Oldys as 'palmed upon Mr. Pope for an original of Shakespeare'; the second was Vertue's engraving of Shakespeare's Stratford monument, in which Vertue substituted a head based on the Chandos portrait for the effigy at Stratford.

Pope would have been familiar with early heroic busts of Shakespeare as a British worthy: by Rysbrack in Gibbs's Building (1726) and in Kent's Temple of British Worthies (1735) at Stowe; and he owned the marble bust by Peter Scheemakers presented to him by the Prince of Wales in 1735 with those of Spenser, Milton, and Dryden.[47] It may have been on the strength of this bust, which corresponds to the head of Shakespeare on the monument, that Scheemakers was named sculptor over his superior rival, Michael Rysbrack. In any event, the pose of the statue, which Vertue admitted to be 'excellent well dispos'd', bears a direct relation to an earlier Burlington circle commission, Guelfi's standing statue of James Craggs, the Abbey monument with which Pope had been most closely connected.[48]

[47] For descriptions of Shakespeare's monument, see Edward Brayley, *History and Antiquities of Westminster* (1823), ii. 260, and Margaret Whinney, *Sculpture in Britain*, pp. 96–7. On portraits of Shakespeare known to Pope, see 'Inventory', pp. 254, 251, and David Piper, *The Changing Image of Shakespeare's Person*, pp. 10, 14, 18, 36.

[48] On the relation between Craggs's and Shakespeare's monument, see David Piper, *The Changing Image of Shakespeare's Person*, pp. 20, 22.

In May 1741, several months after the monument had been opened, an inscription on the scroll of a version of lines from the *Tempest* (Prospero's 'Our revels now are ended' speech, IV. i) was substituted for the Latin inscription, now placed behind the statue. Margaret Whinney has suggested that the lines were 'perhaps arranged by Pope', but he explicitly disclaimed responsibility in the notes of the *Dunciad* (1743). 'Those most Critical Curators of his Monument', Pope writes ironically,

> deserve our Thanks . . . for exhibiting . . . the first Specimen of an *Edition* of an author in *Marble*; where (as may be seen on comparing the Tomb with the Book) in the space of five lines, two Words and a whole Verse are changed, and it is to be hoped will there stand, and outlast whatever hath been hitherto done in Paper.[49]

Pope also complained that the Latin inscription had been displaced by the corrupt lines from *The Tempest*: 'The Inscription with the Name of Shakespeare was intended to be placed on the Marble Scroll to which he points with his hand; instead of which it is now placed behind his back, and that Specimen of an Edition is put on the Scroll, which indeed Shakspeare hath great reason to point at.' Despite these quibbles, the image of Shakespeare on the Westminster monument (plate 86) does resemble Pope's poet of Nature: he stands in the attitude of an Ancient, dressed to advantage like a Modern, touched with melancholy, urbanely addressing his audience in the 'Conspicuous Scene . . . where Kings and Poets lye'.[50]

III. *'The Faithless Column and the Crumbling Bust'*

The reader of Pope's satire would scarcely suspect that he had been one of the prime movers of monuments to British Worthies in the last twenty years of his lifetime. The *Dunciad* ridicules false 'patrons, who sneak from living

[49] For the lines from *The Tempest*, see *The Works of Shakespear Collated and Corrected . . . by Mr. Pope*, 6 vols. (London, 1725), i. xxiii, 60. See Margaret Whinney, *Sculpture in Britain*, p. 257, n. 22; and Pope, *Dunciad* I (1742), headnote, *TE* v. 267. The 'two Words and a whole Verse . . . changed' refer to the inscription's 'Cloud-cupt' for Pope's 'cloud-capt', 'wreck' for 'rack', and the interpolation of the line, 'And like the baseless Fabrick of a Vision', for 'And like this insubstantial pageant faded'. Cf. *Works* (1725), i. 60, and the lapidary inscription in Margaret Whinney, *Sculpture in Britain*, p. 97, pl. 75.

[50] See *Dunciad* I (1742), headnote, *TE* v. 267–8. For the 'Conspicuous Scene', see *Imitations of Horace*, Ep. I, vi. 50–1, *TE* v. 239. My characterization of the statue is indebted to David Piper, *The Changing Image of Shakespeare's Person*, p. 20.

worth to dead,/With-hold the pension, and set up the head'; attacks 'the practice of tacking the obscure names of Persons not eminent in any branch of learning, to those of the Most distinguished Writers . . . by setting up *Monuments* disgraced with their own vile names and inscriptions'; and satirizes the 'Sepulchral lyes', the 'Flatteries and Falsehoods admitted to be inscribed on the walls of Churches in Epitaphs'. The *Epistle to Bathurst* presents the 'vile image' of a monument to a miser portrayed as a liberal man as an instance of 'the wretched taste of carving large perriwigs on Busto's, of which there are several vile examples in the tombs at Westminster and elsewhere'. In the context of lines in the *Epistle to Addison* quoted above, and the frontispiece of the *Essay on Man* illustrating the vanity of monuments, Pope's attitude seems to bear out the conclusion of Oliver Elton that the Renaissance cult of fame had disappeared by the eighteenth century, and been replaced by a sense of the 'futility of monuments'.[51]

But in Pope's imitation of Chaucer, *The Temple of Fame* (1715), the medieval theme of the vanity of literary fame is replaced by a distinctly Renaissance 'passion for personal glory . . . [and] the hope of a name'.[52] In Pope's temple monuments are everywhere, and monuments to poets are 'predominant in Fame':

> But in the Centre of the hallow'd Quire
> Six pompous Columns o'er the rest aspire;
> Around the Shrine it self of *Fame* they stand,
> Hold the chief Honours, and the Fane command. (178–81)

Homer sits, like Michelangelo's Moses, in an adamant throne. Virgil sits composed and sedate on his golden column looking at Homer with 'a reverend Eye' (202). Pindar rides 'like some furious Prophet' (212) in a Chariot of Swans, 'Emblems of . . . the Sublimity and Activity of his Genius', according to Pope's note (210).

Pope's monuments to literary fame in the poem—Pindar's 'Carr of Silver' (210), Horace's 'polish'd Pillar' (226), Aristotle's 'dazling Shrine' (232), Cicero's 'Roman Rostra' (239)—all are 'describ'd', as Pope remarks in a note

[51] See *The Dunciad* (1742), IV. 95–6, 119 n., *TE* v. 350, 353 n.; *The Dunciad* (1728), I. 41, *TE* v. 65 and n.; and the *Epistle to Bathurst*, 292 and n., *TE* iii. ii, 117. See Oliver Elton, 'Literary Fame, A Renaissance Note', in *Modern Studies* (1907; rpt. Freeport, New York, 1967), p. 65.

[52] See Geoffrey Tillotson, quoting Oliver Elton, *TE* ii. 216 n.

(178), 'in such attitudes as express their different Characters. The Columns on which they are rais'd are adorn'd with Sculptures, taken from the most striking Subjects of their Works; which Sculpture bears a Resemblance in its Manner and Character, to the Manner and Character of their Writings.' The iconographical programme of Pope's monuments to poets is altogether of the Renaissance.[53]

The monumental significance of the statuary in the *Temple of Fame* has been overlooked by critics who, since the eighteenth century, have complained about Pope's stationings of statuary in the poem. Joseph Warton was disappointed by the figure of Hercules, a statue adorning the western front of the temple:

> There great *Alcides* stooping with his Toil,
> Rests on his Club, and holds th'*Hesperian* Spoil. (81–2)

According to Warton, Pope omitted

> the characteristical excellencies of this famous piece of Grecian workmanship, namely, the uncommon breadth of the shoulders, the knottiness and spaciousness of the chest, the firmness and protuberance of the muscles in each limb, particularly the legs, and the majestic vastness of the whole figure.

Pope's note (l. 81) tells us that 'this Figure of Hercules is drawn with an eye to the Position of the famous Statue of Farnese', which may be 'the first time that an English poet "drew" a figure after looking at a specific antique representation of a classical subject'.[54]

Pope's description has been unfavourably compared with James Thomson's lines on the same statue in *Liberty* (1735–6), where the personified figure of Sculpture 'deep digging', 'amid the hoary ruins' of Rome, joyfully turns up the statue of the Hercules Farnese during the Renaissance:

> In leaning site, respiring from his toils,
> The well known hero who delivered Greece,

[53] According to Erwin Ponofsky the Renaissance had a 'retrospective' as opposed to the medieval 'prospective' outlook: 'an attitude not only . . . commemorative but boastful . . . Glorification of intellectual achievements and academic honors has taken the place of pious expectations for the future of the soul.' See *Tomb Sculpture: Four Lectures on its Changing Aspects from Ancient Egypt to Bernini* (New York, 1960), p. 69.

[54] See Joseph Warton, *An Essay on the Genius and Writings of Pope*, 5th edn., 2 vols. (London, 1806), i. 343; and Stephen Larrabee, *English Bards and Grecian Marbles* (1943), pp. 70–1.

His ample chest all tempested with force,
Unconquerable reared. She saw the head,
Breathing the hero, small, of Grecian size,
Scarce more extensive than the sinewy neck;
The spreading shoulders, muscular and broad;
The whole a mass of swelling sinews, touched
Into harmonious shape; she saw, and joyed. (iv. 140–8)

Thomson takes the trouble to give an enumerative description of what Dryden called 'the strength, proportion, and knitting of . . . limbs', and he makes the appropriate academic response to the expression of the statue breathing the hero, but this hardly seems enough to justify the claim that Thomson had 'experienced' the statue, capturing its 'emotional and poetic value'.[55]

In comparing descriptions of statuary in Pope and Thomson critics imply that Pope's response is somehow deficient or inadequate. As in the case of descriptions of landscape, they ignore differences in poetics which account for Pope's rejection of enumerative description; differences in context (Thomson is describing an antique statue, Pope is describing the ornament on the western front of the Temple); and, most important, the radical difference between Thomson's essentially static and Pope's dynamic conception of sculpture. In the *Temple of Fame*, 'the real subject of Pope's descriptions is not statuary but men in action, things in motion'. Following the couplets on Hercules, Pope defies his eighteenth-century critics in the animated description of the relief on the western front of the temple:

Here *Orpheus* sings; Trees moving to the Sound
Start from their Roots, and form a Shade around:
Amphion there the loud creating Lyre
Strikes, and behold a sudden *Thebes* aspire!
Cythaeron's Ecchoes answer to his Call,
And half the Mountain rolls into a Wall:
There might you see the length'ning Spires ascend,
The Domes swell up, the widening Arches bend,
The growing Tow'rs like Exhalations rise,
And the huge Columns heave into the Skies. (83–92)

[55] See Larrabee, *English Bards and Grecian Marbles*, pp. 71, 82; James Thomson, *Works* (1908), ed. J. Logie Robertson, p. 361; and Dryden's translation of Bellori in *A Parallel of Poetry and Painting*, in *Essays*, ed. W. P. Ker (Oxford, 1900), ii. 121.

Dennis ridiculed the 'Motions of inanimate Bodies', but 'transcience, growth, [and] movement' are inherent in Pope's response to sculpture.[56]

In Pope's mind sculpture has nothing to do with Winckelmann's classical stillness and grandeur, or Lessing's frozen paradigm of the visual arts. In the *Essay on Criticism* he identifies sculpture with the revival of the arts in the Italian Renaissance:

> Then *Sculpture* and her *Sister-Arts* revive;
> *Stones* leap'd to *Form*, and *Rocks* began to *live*. (701–2)

Pope's idea of sculpture is virtually opposite to that of Sir Joshua Reynolds later in the century, who repudiated Bernini for the same reasons Pope admired him. In *Discourse* X Reynolds observes that the unique excellence of sculpture is its imitation of ideal beauty, and concludes that sculpture

> is formal, regular, and austere; disdains all familiar objects, as incompatible with its dignity; and is an enemy to every species of affectation, or appearance of academical art. All contrast, therefore, of one figure to another, or of the limbs of a single figure, or even in the folds of the drapery, must be sparingly employed. In short, whatever partakes of fancy or caprice, or goes under the denomination of Picturesque, (however to be admired in its proper place,) is incompatible with that sobriety and gravity which is peculiarly the characteristick of this art.[57]

Pope, on the contrary, regards sculpture as nothing if not picturesque. Filled with surprise, variety, contrast, and irregular grandeur, it is not the art of the ancients but of moderns like Bernini and Roubiliac.[58] The difference between Reynolds's and Pope's idea of the art is essentially the difference between the classicist and the Renaissance humanist.

Ultimately Pope does not think of sculpture, or any of the arts, in terms of the isolated artifact, as the modern formalist does. His conception of sculpture

[56] Geoffrey Tillotson, *The Temple of Fame*, *TE* ii. 239, 242 n.

[57] Sir Joshua Reynolds, *Discourses on Art*, ed. Robert R. Wark (San Marino, 1959), p. 187.

[58] Pope's admiration of Bernini is apparent from his attribution of a bust of Homer in his collection to the sculptor, his notes on Bernini's works at Rome, and his allusion in the *Imitations of Horace*, Ep. II, i, 380–1, to Bernini's bust of Charles I executed in 1636, destroyed in the fire of 1698 at Whitehall Palace, which Pope might have known from the drawings of Jonathan Richardson, or the copy by Francis Bird. See G. W. Beard, 'Alexander Pope', *Apollo*, 57 (Jan. 1953), 4–6; 'Inventory', p. 251; and Pieter Schenk, *Romae Novae Delineatio*, n. 12 above. See Rudolf Wittkower, *Gian Lorenzo Bernini*, 2nd edn. (London, 1966), 'Catalogue', No. 39, 207–8, figs. 47, 48; and Katharine Esdaile, 'The Busts and Statues of Charles I', *Burlington Magazine*, 91 (Jan. 1949), 9–14.

is monumental; an art, like architecture, dedicated to the commemoration of virtue and permeated with elegiac emotion. The ruins of Rome in the *Epistle to Addison* are 'her own sad Sepulchre' (2); the tombs of Virgil, Cicero, and Raphael in the *Epistle to Jervas* inspire mourning, dreams, and repose; the Countess of Bridgewater's tomb in the same poem teaches humility; the monument in *Eloisa to Abelard* brings 'falling tears' (350) to 'some relenting eye' (355). It will be remembered that the monument Pope set up in his garden at Twickenham to his mother was the focal point of the elegiac conception of its design; and the sculpture he planned for the river front was to have been a monument to his own literary career. Pope's frequent identification of his poetic works with his monument is something more than a commonplace. It is the conviction of an artist of the Renaissance.[59]

[59] *Epistle to Jervas*, l. 78, *TE* vi. 158. For the monumental statuary at Twickenham, see chap. 5. For Pope's references to his works as his monument, see 'The Preface to the Works' (1717), and 'The Dedication to the Iliad' (1720), in *Prose*, pp. 295, 326.

Conclusion: '*The Sister-Arts Knit in Harmonious Dance*'

THE modern sceptical outlook on the sister arts is neatly summarized by Margaret Schlegel's petulant question to Leonard Bast in E. M. Forster's *Howard's End*: 'What *is* the good of the Arts if they're interchangeable?' Critics like René Wellek, Ralph Cohen, and William Wimsatt have raised the same question in a more sophisticated form. How different James Thomson's vision of the arts reviving under the Goddess of Liberty in the Whig enlightenment:

> Behold! All thine [Liberty's] again the sister-arts,
> Thy graces they, knit in harmonious dance.

In Thomson's poem, and in the eighteenth-century mind, the arts dwell harmoniously together in the same pantheon. Joined together in a dance led by poetry, the dancers move independently, but in time to the same music. As we have seen, the unity of the arts was an article of Renaissance humanist faith which depended upon common assumptions about art as an imitation of nature, and shared norms of simplicity, naturalness, and utility. It resulted in a conviction that 'poetry, gardening, painting, and architecture were all expressions of a whole mind'.[1]

Faith in the notion of sister arts (as much a commonplace then as the idea

[1] E. M. Forster, *Howard's End* (1921; rpt., New York, 1954), p. 39. On the interrelationships of the arts, see René Wellek, 'The Parallelism between Literature and the Arts', *English Institute Annual 1941* (New York, 1942), pp. 29–63; Ralph Cohen, *The Art of Discrimination* (Berkeley and Los Angeles, 1964), x, p. 247; and William Wimsatt, '"Laokoön": An Oracle Reconsulted', in *Eighteenth-Century Studies in Honor of Donald F. Hyde*, ed. W. H. Bond (New York, 1970), pp. 347–63. James Thomson, *Liberty* (1736), Part V, ll. 683–4, *Works* (1908), ed. J. Logie Robertson, p. 412; A. Lynn Altenbernd, 'On Pope's Horticultural Romanticism', *Journal of English and Germanic Philology*, 54 (Oct. 1955), 477.

of the unconscious mind now) resulted in the kind of fruitful interaction and interchange of the arts which produced the landscape garden. It was a product of poetry and painting as well as architecture and sculpture integrated into a new synthesis, an art of the humanized environment which the century considered 'a science of Landscape', 'entitled to a place of considerable rank among the liberal arts'.[2] The landscape garden combined a mixture of styles and aesthetic norms, Palladian formality and landscape irregularity, which have been explained in terms of eclecticism, 'stylistic chaos', and the spirit of play.[3] Typically, the landscape garden has been seen as the plaything of men like Pope, Walpole, and Chesterfield, all of whom have been characterized as frivolous dilettantes and dabbling amateurs.

But the English landscape garden is important not because 'it was the toy of wits and noblemen—however amusing the extravagances which came of that connection—but because it was a groping after nature, and because it began nearly a century before the date commonly assigned to the romantic revival'.[4] This study has indicated that a sensibility for picturesque landscape rather than mere playfulness or casual stylistic eclecticism underlies Pope's contribution to the landscape garden. The word picturesque is perhaps the most accurate term to 'characterize the unity of all the concurrent movements' of taste in the early eighteenth century.[5] It certainly is the most apt description of Pope's particular aesthetic sensibility to landscape and to the other arts—architecture, sculpture, even music—which holds in suspension and balance opposite aesthetic norms and philosophical attitudes: order in variety, art and nature, reason and emotion. As we have remarked it is consistent with the aesthetic, philosophical, and epistemological ideals of the time. Finally, it is a term which characterizes the imaginative transformation of classical norms

[2] Horace Walpole, 'Notes' on William Mason's 'Preface' to *An Heroic Epistle to William Chambers* (1773), in *Satirical Poems by William Mason*, ed. Paget Toynbee (Oxford, 1926), p. 43. Thomas Whately, *Observations on Modern Gardening* (1770), p. 1.

[3] See Rudolf Wittkower, 'English Neo-Palladianism, the Landscape Garden, China, and the Enlightenment', *L'Arte*, 2 (June 1969), 18; and Johan Huizinga, *Homo Ludens: A Study of the Play Element in Culture* (1938).

[4] See R. W. Chapman, 'The Literature of Landscape Gardening', in *Johnsonian and Other Essays and Reviews* (Oxford, 1953), p. 61.

[5] See Fiske Kimball, 'Art Terms', Letters to the Editor, *Times Literary Supplement*, 45 (8 June 1946), 271.

which is to be found in Pope's translation of Homer as much as in his concept of the garden.

Pope's prophetic eye for the picturesque, besides clarifying the nature of his contribution to the landscape garden, provides a plausible explanation for his influence on eighteenth-century taste and aesthetics. It accounts for the influence he had on the picturesque cult later in the century, which rationalized, exploited, and finally exhausted the possibilities Pope had earlier recognized. Pope's expression of the sensibility of his time was definitive and the century did not escape his influence until Wordsworth discovered a new idiom for a changed sensibility. Wordsworth's point of departure both as a poet and gardener, was Pope's aesthetic of landscape.[6]

The recognition of Pope's endowment with a distinct aesthetic sensibility may help us to escape from the dialectical categories which have so often distorted the interpretation of eighteenth-century taste. It invites us to replace the revolutionary view of the development of eighteenth-century taste from classic to romantic with a more plausible evolutionary view, and to abandon the persistent misconception of this development as a change from a defective, dissociated aesthetic sensibility to a unified, integrated one. Instead of identifying Pope with an absolute and monolithic classicism, projecting on to his work a false classic–romantic antithesis, or an abandoned eclecticism without coherence or integrity, the picturesque aesthetic elucidates his characteristic transformation of classical forms, whether literary or horticultural.[7]

The capacity of the picturesque sensibility to accommodate conflicting aesthetic values clearly reflects the ideas of Shaftesbury and the Whig enlightenment of the early eighteenth century. Liberal Whig ideology enabled the eighteenth-century improver to resolve the apparent contradiction between Palladian formalism and landscape irregularity, and to find sanctions for his designs as readily in the gardens of Imperial China as in the villas of

[6] See Russell Noyes, 'Wordsworth and Landscape Gardening', chap. 3 of *Wordsworth and the Art of Landscape*, Indiana University Humanities Series, No. 65 (Bloomington, 1968).

[7] On dialectical categories and eighteenth-century taste, see R. S. Crane, review of B. S. Allen, *Tides in English Taste*, *Philological Quarterly*, 17 (Apr. 1938), 172; J. Lynn Altenbernd, 'Pope's Horticultural Romanticism', p. 477; and Rudolf Wittkower, 'English Neo-Palladianism and the Enlightenment', p. 30. For arguments urging a spatial rather than temporal view of the development of eighteenth-century taste, see Bertrand Bronson, 'When was Neo-Classicism', in *Facets of the Enlightenment* (Berkeley and Los Angeles, 1968), pp. 1–25.

Republican Rome. The spirit of liberalism encouraged freedom of taste, in accord with a newly won political freedom, and in reaction to the authoritarian orthodoxies of France. Shaftesbury's virtuoso, Addison's man of polite imagination, and Richardson's connoisseur flourished in this atmosphere of enlightened taste in the arts. The new spirit encouraged the virtues of tolerance and a 'detached experimental playfulness of men testing the nature of sensibility and the powers of response'. At the same time it entailed the risks of excess and absurdity which Pope's satire exposed. In Pope's taste in the arts we have noticed both a delight in the freedom, and a sense of the responsibility that freedom implies.[8]

The inconsistencies of Pope's taste, which he describes in the *Imitations of Horace* as 'that eternal Wanderer',[9] have been apparent throughout this survey: between respect for academic history painting, and affection for 'lower' genres of portraiture and landscape; between the Gothic and classical styles in architecture, between his devotion to the picturesque style in gardening, and his tolerance of 'so bad a Taste, as to like all that is good' (ii. 15), which permitted him to praise gardens as different as Chiswick, Cirencester, and Stowe, to declare his respect for Le Nôtre in the *Epistle to Burlington* (l. 46 *n.*), and to find the French walks of Hampton Court 'contemplative' (i. 427).

In Pope's mind the true critic is the man who is not seduced by taste, who balances the claims of the artist, the critic, and the man, to contrive a synthesis of the critical and creative principles. The artist is the exemplary model of the true critic and man of taste: 'Blest' with genius and insight, he has acquired the learning and possesses the good sense, moral integrity, and virtue which combine to produce 'true taste'. He avoids the pedantry of the scholar, the bad manners of the ill-tempered critic, the *je ne sais quoi* of the amateur, and emerges from the dazzling lines of the *Essay on Criticism* as a true virtuoso.[10]

[8] Martin Price, 'The Garden and the Wild: The Picturesque', Chap. XII, vi, *To the Palace of Wisdom* (New York, 1965), p. 387. On the liberal ideology, see Rudolf Wittkower, 'English Neo-Palladianism and the Enlightenment', pp. 18–35. Horace Walpole identified the landscape garden with the constitution: 'the English Taste in Gardening is thus the growth of the English Constitution, & must perish with it'. 'Notes' on William Mason's 'Preface' to *An Epistle to Chambers*, in *Satirical Poems by William Mason* (1926), p. 45.

[9] Ep. II, i (1737), l. 312, *TE* iv. 221.

[10] *Essay on Criticism*, ll. 11–14, 15 n., 560–3, 639, *TE* i. 240, and n., 304–5, 311. On Pope's 'antithetical concept of taste', see William Wimsatt, ed., *Alexander Pope, Selected Poetry and Prose*, 2nd edn. (New York, 1972), p. xxviii, and Austin Warren, *Alexander Pope as Critic and Humanist* (Princeton, 1929), p. 37.

The premisses of his taste are a synthesis of aesthetic and moral values which are those of the Renaissance humanist.

On the whole, humanistic transcends aesthetic significance in Pope's attitude to the arts, but even a portmanteau word like humanism will not resolve conflicts in his response to the arts, which are deeply rooted in his aesthetics and beyond reconciliation. The classical doctrine of the imitation of nature, a fundamental principle of his aesthetics, involves a profound contradiction since Nature itself is paradoxical: on the one hand, 'Unerring Nature . . . one clear, unchang'd and Universal Light' (70–1); and, at the same time, a dynamic teleological process, *natura naturans*.[11] This contributes to his conception of the contradictory nature of the artifact apparent in the contrasts of painting, the opposition between stasis and movement in sculpture, the ordered variety of the garden, the balanced opposites of architecture, and the harmony in division of music. In every instance the artifact, as Pope conceives it, embodies rather than transcends conflict. It contains the opposites composing it, all of the contradictory things comprehended by the terms Nature and Art.

The artifact was inevitably a compromise in Pope's mind between the idea of its inventor and its imperfect realization in the intractable materials of art. As he observed to Bathurst about garden design, it was 'a Fall' (ii. 14) to descend from theory to practice. Because he considered the artifact imperfect, he could never consider a work of art finished; it remained for him in a kind of limbo, suspended somewhere between conception and completion. When was a poem of his own or any of his friends safe from correction? The grotto was 'finished' over and over again; buildings built and rebuilt; strokes stolen in the canvases of finished paintings; the garden planted, rooted up, and replanted: 'My garden, like my Life', he writes to Ralph Allen in frustration in 1736, 'seems to me every Year to want Correction & require Alteration' (iv. 40).

But the cardinal defect of an artifact to an artist like Pope writing in the Renaissance tradition is its impermanence. His indefatigable virtuosoship and his satire are based on a devotion to the 'encouragement and revival of the polite arts' (ii. 51), the belief that the arts are the indispensable bulwark of

[11] *Essay on Criticism*, ll. 70–9, *TE* i. 246–8.

civilization, which the virtuoso-artist has a moral obligation to promote. But this conviction coexists from early in his career with a sense of the futility of arts, which are as transitory as human life, 'mere groping in the Dark' (i. 330). He has constant apprehensions that his ideals are beyond realization, that England, far from emulating classical civilization when

> *Learning* and *Rome* alike in Empire grew,
> And *Arts* still *follow*'d where her *Eagles flew*,

has degraded and disgraced its ideals:

> And learned Athens to our Art must stoop,
> Could she behold us tumbling thro' a hoop.

And he envisions the arts doomed by modern degeneracy and the empire of Dulness in the famous lines from Book IV of the *Dunciad* (1742):

> Thus at her felt approach, and secret might,
> *Art* after *Art* goes out, and all is Night.

This kind of ambivalence is altogether characteristic of the humanist, and it is this attitude which underlies Pope's entire career as a virtuoso.[12]

[12] See Erwin Panofsky, 'The History of Art as a Humanistic Discipline', in *Meaning and the Visual Arts* (1955), p. 2. See Pope, *Essay on Criticism*, ll. 683–4, *TE* i. 317; *Imitations of Horace*, Ep. II, i (1737), ll. 47–8, *TE* iv. 199; and *Dunciad* IV (1742), ll. 639–40; *TE* v. 407.

Appendix A. *Ears of an Untoward Make: the Myth of Pope's Insensibility to Music*

SAMUEL JOHNSON's remark on Pope's *Ode to St. Cecelia* in his *Life of Pope* (1781) summarizes the view of Pope's attitude to music which has prevailed since the eighteenth century:

> Poets do not always express their own thoughts; Pope, with all this labour in the praise of Musick, was ignorant of its principles, and insensible of its effects.[1]

In his *History of Music* (1776) Charles Burney declared that Pope, like Swift and Addison, was an enemy of music. He insisted that 'nothing is more certain than that Pope was by nature wholly insensible to the charms of music, and took every opportunity of throwing contempt upon those who either cultivated, or listened to it with delight'.[2] His *Ode* showed 'the possibility of writing well on what is neither felt nor understood':

> For Pope, who received not the least pleasure from Music himself, by the help of his friends, was enabled to describe its power with all the rapture and sublimity of a great genius, *music mad*. This appears not only in his *Ode of St. Cecelia*, but in speaking of Handel, in the *Dunciad*.[3]

Richard Payne Knight found it 'remarkable that the best versifier in our language should have had no taste or liking for music of any kind',[4] but the idea of Pope's insensibility to music has persisted unchallenged to the present day.

This critical unanimity is surprising because the idea of Pope's obtuseness to music depends entirely upon hearsay evidence and unverified anecdotes about Pope and Handel which distort Pope's attitude to music in general and to Handel in

[1] G. B. Hill, ed., *Life of Pope* (Oxford, 1905), iii. 228.

[2] i (London, 1776), 343 n.

[3] 'Preface', vol. i, 2nd edn., corrected and revised (London, 1789), xv. This statement about Pope was added in the second edition of vol. i. For the bibliography of Burney's *History of Music*, see Roger Lonsdale, *Dr. Charles Burney, A Literary Biography* (Oxford, 1965), pp. 186, 499.

[4] *An Analytical Inquiry into the Principles of Taste*, 2nd edn. (London, 1805), p. 116.

particular. On the subject of Pope and music C. W. Dilke's statement about Pope's biographers is especially apt:

proof that what ought to have been developed has been obscured or passed over; and that what has been preserved in amber is but too frequently the current nonsense of the hour—the babble of ignorance—the falsehood of enemies—the misconstruction of friends.[5]

A careful review of the evidence indicates that Pope had an ear for music, appreciated though he did not study it, and was competent to judge music and musicians independently. His praise of Handel in the *Dunciad* (1742) did not result from coaching by Burlington or Arbuthnot; it clearly reflects his collaboration with Handel on the score of what became the first English oratorio, and his own convictions about the relationship of words and music.

The source of the traditional view about Pope and music can be found in anecdotes related by Handel's earliest but 'often unreliable' biographer,[6] John Mainwaring, in *Memoirs of the Life of the Late G. F. Handel* (1760). Mainwaring tells a story about Pope's attendance at Handel's performance of his own music at Burlington House, a concert such as Gay describes in *Trivia* (1716): 'There *Hendel* strikes the strings, the melting strain/Transports the soul, and thrills through ev'ry Vein' (ii. 497–8).[7] Mainwaring's hearsay anecdote appears to be the sole basis for the unbroken tradition that Pope was 'by nature wholly insensible' to music.[8]

[5] Charles Wentworth Dilke, 'Pope's Writings', *The Papers of a Critic*, 2 vols. (London, 1875), 1: 95.

[6] Paul Henry Lang, *George Frideric Handel* (New York, 1966), p. 16. Charles Burney states that Mainwaring's *Memoirs* 'though written with zeal and candour, are neither sufficiently ample nor accurate'. 'Sketch of the Life of Handel', in *An Account of the Musical Performances in Westminster-Abbey, and the Pantheon . . . in Commemoration of Handel* (London, 1785), p. 2.

[7] John Gay, *Works*, ed. G. C. Faber (London, 1926), p. 76.

[8] For Johnson, Burney and Richard Payne Knight, see nn. 1, 2, and 4 above; Sir John Hawkins, *A General History of the Science and Practice of Music* (5 vols., London, 1776; rpt. of two vol. 1875 ed., Graz, Austria: Akademische Drach, 1969), ii. 859, 912 n.; Thomas Tyers, *An Historical Rhapsody on Mr. Pope* (London, 1782), p. 36; and Joseph Warton, ed., *Works of Pope* (1797), v. 235 n.; S. W. Singer, ed., Spence's *Anecdotes* (1820), p. 312 n.; James Dallaway, ed., *Anecdotes of Painting in England by Horace Walpole*, ii (1876), 270 n.; Edward Dowden, ed., *The Correspondence of Robert Southey, and Caroline Bowles* (Dublin, 1881), p. 245 n.; E.C., iv. 401–2 n.; James Sutherland, ed., *The Dunciad*, *TE* v. 347 n., 442; Robert Manson Myers, *Handel's Messiah, A Touchstone of Taste* (New York, 1948), p. 113; Percy M. Young, *The Oratorios of Handel* (New York, 1950), p. 48; Charles Kerby-Miller, ed., *Memoirs of the Extraordinary Life, Works, and Discoveries of Martinus Scriblerus* (New Haven, 1950), p. 232 n.; Herbert M. Schueller, 'The Use and Decorum of Music as Described in British Literature 1700 to 1780', *Journal of the History of Ideas*, 12 (Jan. 1952), 89 n.; Otto Deutsch, *Handel, A Documentary Biography* (London, 1955), p. 279; Winton Dean, *Handel's Dramatic Oratorios and Masques* (London, Oxford University Press, 1959), p. 197;

The appeal of Mainwaring's story is that it claims to report Pope's own statement, which, as Hawkins says, 'he was honest enough to confess':

> As Mr. Pope was very intimate with his Lordship [Burlington], it frequently happened that he and Handel were together at his table. After the latter had played some of the finest things he ever composed, Mr. Pope declared, that they gave him no sort of pleasure; that his ears were of that untoward make, and reprobate cast, as to receive his Music, which he was persuaded was the best that could be, with as much indifference as the airs of a common ballad.[9]

In a footnote Mainwaring related another anecdote about Pope and Arbuthnot, often conflated with the first and equally influential, which underlies his assertion that 'though Mr. Pope was no judge himself of any productions on this subject, yet he had many friends who well understood them':

> The poet one day asked his friend Dr. Arbuthnot, of whose knowledge in Music he had a high idea, What was his real opinion in regard to Handel as a Master of that Science? The Doctor immediately replied, 'Conceive the highest that you can of his abilities, and they are much beyond any thing that you *can* conceive.'[10]

This harmless question, as reasonable to ask someone trained in music of Handel then as of Boulez now, put the seal on Pope's musical stupidity, and critics ever since have been willing to apply Pope's lines in the *Epistle to Burlington* on music to Pope himself:

> Not for himself he sees, or hears, or eats;
> Artists must chuse his Pictures, Music, Meats. (5–6)[11]

Mainwaring, unlike his readers, was sceptical enough to wonder 'how an ear so perfectly attentive to all the delicacies of rhythm and poetical numbers, should be totally insensible to the charms of musical sounds', and he allowed for the possibility of irony (a 'pretended declaration' by 'one of his [Pope's] satyric turn' at the expense of uncritical admirers of Handel).[12] But with the exception of

Arthur H. Huseboe, 'Pope's Critical Views of the London Stage', *Restoration and Eighteenth Century Theatre Research*, 2 (May 1964), 29; Paul Lang, *Handel* (1966), p. 484.

[9] John Mainwaring, *Memoirs of the Life of the Late George Frederic Handel* (London, 1760; rpt. Amsterdam, 1964), pp. 93–4; Hawkins, *History* (1969), ii. 859.

[10] Mainwaring, *Memoirs*, pp. 189, 93 n.

[11] See n. 8 above. Hawkins makes a substantive improvement on Mainwaring's Arbuthnot anecdote when he supplies Pope's *ipsissima verba*: 'Pope once expressed his sentiments of music to a person now [1776] living [John Christopher Smith, 1712–1795?] in these words: "My friend Dr. Arbuthnot speaks strongly of the effect that music has on his mind, and I believe him; but I own myself incapable of any pleasure from it."' *History of Music* (1969), ii. 912 n.

[12] *Memoirs of Handel*, pp. 94–5.

Richard Payne Knight quoted above, critics have taken Mainwaring's stories at face value. However, Mainwaring's scepticism of the anecdote is confirmed by Pope himself in the answer he gave to Spence in 1744 when asked, 'Did you ever learn anything of music?' To which he replied: 'Never, but I had naturally a very good ear, and have often judged right of the best compositions in music by the force of that' (No. 398). Spence's testimony by itself is sufficient to challenge Mainwaring's, but by 1820, when Spence's *Anecdotes* were first published, the tradition was too strong to yield to first-hand evidence from an unimpeachable source, and the editor, S. W. Singer, makes the astonishing statement that

> Pope does not appear to have been correct in this assertion. He was quite insensible to the merits of Handel, and seriously inquired of Dr. Arbuthnot, whether the applause bestowed on that great composer was really deserved.[13]

The only modern critic to take Pope's remark to Spence into account also expresses disbelief, interpreting it as 'a boast upon which his reported querying of Arbuthnot as to whether the applause bestowed on Handel was really deserved throws much doubt'.[14]

We have no reason to disbelieve the statement Pope made to Spence, a far more reliable source on Pope than Mainwaring. If he did make the apparently contradictory statement Mainwaring reports at second hand, it can plausibly be interpreted as a disclaimer of judgement about an art he had never studied, whatever motives of irony or self-deprecation may have been involved. In any event, the statement appears to have been disingenuous, and not a shred of evidence bears it out. The burden of proof is on those who keep dogmatically insisting Pope was insensible to music.

[13] Joseph Spence, *Anecdotes*, ed. S. W. Singer (1820), p. 312 n.

[14] Charles Kerby-Miller, ed., *Memoirs of Scriblerus*, p. 232 n. For a fuller treatment of this subject, see my article, 'Ears of an Untoward Make: Pope and Handel', *The Musical Quarterly*, 62 (Oct. 1976), 554–70.

Appendix B. *Views of Pope's Villa, A Checklist*

1. Peter Tillemans (1684–1734)
   The Thames at Twickenham with Pope's Villa at Left Centre
   Oil on canvas, $27\frac{1}{4} \times 54$ in., *c.* 1730
   Signed P. Tillemans
   Provenance: Sold by Arthur Tooth and Sons, Ltd., to a private collector, England, 1953
   Literature: *The Connoisseur*, 132 (October 1953), xxii.

2. John Wootton (1682–1765)
   Pope's Villa at Twickenham
   Oil on canvas, at Duncombe Park, Yorkshire, in 1821?
   Literature: 'Duncombe Park: A Brief Catalogue of Pictures', in *Duncombe Park, Rivalx Abbey, and Helmsley Castle*, 2nd edn. (Kirby-Moorside: R. Cooper, 1821), Appendix, p. 32; Spence, No. 109; 'Inventory', p. 254.

3. After Peter Andreas(?) Rysbrack (1690–1748)
   An Exact Draught and View of Mr. Pope's House at Twickenham
   Engraving, $10\frac{1}{4} \times 17$ in., Rysbrack *delin* & *pinx.*, Nathanial (?) Parr sculp. (*fl.* 1730–60)
   c. 1735
   Literature: F.G., 'Pope's Villa at Twickenham', *Notes & Queries*, 8th S., 10 (11 July 1896), 21–2; Mack, 'Notes', pl. 45, pp. 307–9.

4. The Late Mr. Pope's House at Twickenham
   Engraving, $8\frac{3}{4} \times 6\frac{1}{2}$ in., by T[om?] Smith
   Frontispiece to *The Newcastle General Magazine, or Monthly Intelligencer* (January 1748)
   Literature: Mack, 'Notes', pl. 12, p. 284.

5. After Augustin Heckell (1690?–1770)
   The House of the Late Celebrated Mr. A. Pope Fronting the River Thames at Twickenham,/Now in Possession of Sr. Willm Stanhope
   Engraving, $9 \times 15\frac{3}{4}$ in., by James Mason (1710–80?)
   22 April 1749
   Literature: F.G., 'Pope's Villa at Twickenham', *Notes & Queries*, 8th S., 10 (11 July 1896), 21–2. Mack, 'Notes', pl. 5, p. 281.

6. After Augustin Heckell (see No. 5)
   A View of the Late Celebrated Mr. Pope's House, Fronting the River Thames at Twickenham. Printed for Carington Bowles, Next the Chapter House in St. Paul's Church Yard, London. n.d.
   Engraving, $6\frac{7}{8} \times 9\frac{7}{8}$ in.
   Literature: F.G., 'Pope's Villa at Twickenham', *Notes & Queries*, 8th S., 10 (11 July 1896), 21–2.

7. After Augustin Heckell (see No. 5)
   Mr Pope's House at Twickenham, Now in the Possession of Welbore Ellis Esqr
   Engraving, *c.* 1772
   Literature: F.G., 'Pope's Villa at Twickenham', *Notes & Queries*, 8th S., 10 (11 July 1896), 21–2.

8. James Hulett after Augustin Heckell (see No. 5)
   Engrav'd for the *Royal Magazine*: A View of the Celebrated Mr. Pope's House at Twickenham
   Engraving, $6\frac{7}{16} \times 8\frac{3}{4}$ in., by James Hulett (d. 1771)
   Frontispiece, *The Royal Magazine or Gentleman's Monthly Companion* (London: J. Coote), iii (October 1760), 195–6.

9. Robert Sayer after Augustin Heckell (see No. 5)
   A View of the Celebrated Mr Popes House at Twickenham. Vue de le Celebre Mr Pope a Twickenham
   Printed for Robert Sayer at the Golden Buck, Opposite Fetter Lane, Fleet Street.
   c. 1750–60
   Guildhall Library
   Literature: F.G., 'Pope's Villa at Twickenham', *Notes & Queries*, 8th S., 10 (11 July 1896), 22.

10. Robert(?) Carver after Augustin Heckell (see No. 6)
Printed for and sold by Bowles & Carver. The Late Mr. Pope's House at Twickenham. No. 69 in St. Paul's Church Yard, London.
Oval line engraving, $4\frac{3}{16} \times 5\frac{3}{4}$ in., by Robert(?) Carver (d. 1791)
c. 1750–60
Guildhall Library

11. After Augustin Heckell (see No. 6)
Sepia Wash drawing, $11\frac{3}{8} \times 17$ in.
Avery Architectural Library, Columbia University

12. Robert Adam after Augustin Heckell (see No. 6)
View of Pope's House at Twickenham Fronting the Thames
Pen, brown ink, and pencil drawing, $5\frac{1}{2} \times 7\frac{3}{8}$ in., by Robert Adam (1728–92)
C. K. Adam, Blairadam, Kinross-shire, Scotland

13. Attributed to Joseph Nickolls (*fl.* 1720–1748)
Pope's Villa on the Thames at Twickenham Middlesex
After No. 5
Oil on canvas, $17 \times 31\frac{1}{2}$ in.
c. 1755
From the Collection of Mr. and Mrs. Paul Mellon
Literature: *Painting in England 1700–1750: Collection of Mr. & Mrs. Paul Mellon.* Exhibition Catalogue, Virginia Museum of Fine Arts, Richmond, Virginia, 1963 (Kent: Westerham Press Ltd., 1963), p. 44, No. 15; John Walker, 'The Thames Through 18th-Century Eyes: Augustin Heckell and his Imitators', *Country Life*, 146 (3 July 1969), 24–7.

14. Attributed to Charles Knapton (1700–60)
Pope's Villa Looking North West from the River Thames
Water Colour, $14\frac{1}{2} \times 21\frac{3}{4}$ in.
c. 1750
London Borough of Richmond upon Thames

15. Johann Heinrich Müntz (1727–98)
Pope's House with Identification of Some of His Neighbours'
Ink, with grey-green wash, on paper, $7 \times 4\frac{1}{2}$ in.
c. 1756
Sir John Murray, London
Literature: Mack, 'Notes', pl. 3, p. 280.

16. After Johann Heinrich Müntz (1727–98)
A View of Twickenham [with] Lord Radnor's [House] Mr. Hudson's Mr Pope's now Sr. Wm. Stanhope's Lady Ferrer's Mr. Blackwell's
Line engraving, $16\frac{1}{2} \times 22\frac{1}{8}$ in., by John Green (*c.* 1729–57)
1756
W. S. Lewis, Farmington, Connecticut
Literature: Mack, 'Notes', pl. 2, pp. 279–80.

17. Samuel Scott (?1701–72)
A View of Pope's Villa, Twickenham
Oil on panel, 7×14 in.
c. 1759
Mr. and Mrs. Paul Mellon
Literature: Kenneth Sharpe and Richard Kingzett, *Samuel Scott Bicentenary* [Catalogue of] *Paintings, Drawings and Engravings* (London: Guildhall Art Gallery, 1972), No. 46, p. 26, pl. p. 46.

18. Samuel Scott
Pope's Villa, Twickenham
Oil on canvas, $18\frac{1}{2} \times 36$ in.
1759
W. S. Lewis, Farmington, Connecticut
Literature: A Description of the Villa of Horace Walpole . . . at Strawberry-Hill (1774), p. 28; Hilda F. Finberg, 'Pope's Villa, Twickenham', *Burlington Magazine*, 77 (November 1940), p. 170. Mack, 'Notes', pl. 8, p. 282.

19. Samuel Scott
Pope's Villa, Twickenham
Oil on canvas, $19\frac{1}{4} \times 36\frac{1}{2}$ in.
c. 1760
London Borough of Richmond upon Thames
Literature: Hilda F. Finberg, 'Samuel Scott at Twickenham', *Apollo*, 15 (June 1932), 276–8; Elizabeth Einberg, *The Origins of Landscape Painting in England*, Summer Exhibition Catalogue, Iveah Bequest Kenwood (London: Greater London Council Publication 91, 1967), No. 19.

20. Sawrey Gilpin, R.A. (1733–1807)
Mr. Pope's House

Pen and wash drawing, $4\frac{13}{16} \times 7\frac{1}{8}$ in.
1764
From *The Thames from Windsor to London.* Manuscript by William Gilpin with Sketches by his brother Sawrey Gilpin, R.A., No. 24
Victoria and Albert Museum
Literature: Carl Paul Barbier, *William Gilpin: His Drawings, Teachings, and Theory of the Picturesque* (Oxford: Clarendon Press, 1963), p. 35 and n.

21. William Pars (1742–82)
View of Richmond Hill, Twickenham, and Mr Pope's House from the Terrace at Strawberry Hill
Watercolor on paper, $20 \times 14\frac{3}{4}$ in.
1772
W. S. Lewis, Farmington, Connecticut
Literature: Mack, 'Notes', pl. 6, pp. 281–2.

22. Elias Martin (1739–1818)
View of Pope's House at Twickenham
Oil on canvas, $6\frac{3}{8} \times 7\frac{3}{4}$ in.
1773
National Museum, Stockholm
Literature: Algernon Graves, *The Royal Academy of Arts* (8 vols., London, 1905–6), v. 201; Stockholm National Museum, *Paintings and Sculptures of the Northern Schools Before the Modern Period* (Stockholm, 1952), No. 2940, p. 105.

23. William Watts (1752–1851)
Seat of the Rt. Hon. Welbore Ellis, at Twickenham in Middlesex. Published as the Act directs Octr. 1st 1782, by William Watts, Chelsea.
Line engraving, $4\frac{7}{8} \times 7\frac{1}{4}$ in., by William Watts
Plate XLVIII, The Seat of the Right Honourable Welbore Ellis, At Twickenham, in Middlesex. From *The Seats of the Nobility and Gentry, In a Collection of the Most Interesting & Picturesque Views Engraved by W. Watts, From Drawings by the Most Eminent Artists. With Descriptions of Each View.* Published by W. Watts, Kemp's Row, Chelsea, January 1st, 1779
Literature: 'Obituary Mr. W. Watts', *Gentleman's Magazine*, N.S. 37 (April 1852), 420–1.

24. Laurent Guyot after William Watts (see No. 23)
Maison de Plaisance du Tres Honorable Welbore Ellis, At Twickenham in Middlesex./Cette Maison à [*sic*] appartenu au Celebre Pope Poette Anglais W. Watts *del.* gravé par Guyot
Oval engraving on copper in colours, by Laurent Guyot (1756–1806)
c. 1793
Pierpont Morgan Library
Literature: Yves Bruand et Michèle Hébert, *Inventaire du Fonds Français: Graveurs du XVIIIe Siècle*, Vol. XI (Paris: Bibliothèque Nationale, 1970), 'Laurent Guyot', Nos. 302, 409, pp. 112–13, 159–60, 182–3.

25. Samuel Lewis (*fl.* 1774–91)
The Seat of Welbore Ellis Esq.r at Twickenham Formerly Pope's
Coloured drawing, 5 × 8¼ in., S. Lewis *Pinx.t*
1785
London Borough of Richmond upon Thames

26. After Samuel Lewis (*fl.* 1774–91)
The Seat of Welbore Lord Mendip at Twickenham Formerly Mr. Pope's. S. Lewis *del.*
Engraving, 4 × 6 in., F. Cary *sculp.*
From Edward Ironside, *The History and Antiquities of Twickenham* (London: John Nichols, 1797), in *Miscellaneous Antiquities* (in continuation of the Bibliotheca Topographica Britannica), No. VI, pl. vi, p. 81
British Library

27. After Joseph Farington (1747–1821)
Pope's House
Coloured aquatint after watercolour drawing, 7½ × 11¾ in., by Joseph Constantine Stadler (*fl.* 1780–1812)
1 June 1795
From John and Josiah Boydell, *An History of the River Thames*, 2 vols. London: W. Bulmer & Co., 1794–6, ii, opp. p. 4.
Richmond Borough of London upon Thames
Literature: R. V. Tooley, *English Books with Colored Plates* (London: B. T. Batsford, Ltd., 1954), No. 102; Mack, 'Notes', pl. 9, p. 283.

28. William Bernard Cooke (1778–1855)
Drawn and Engrav'd by W. Cooke. for the Beauties of England and Wales. E. W. B. [Edward Wedlake Brayley]*dxt.* Pope's House./Twickenham./

Middlesex./London. Published by Vernor, Hood & Sharpe. Poultry.
Feb. 1, 1807.
Line engraving, $3\frac{7}{8} \times 5\frac{7}{8}$ in., by William Bernard Cooke
From J. Norris Brewer, *The Beauties of England and Wales: or, Original Delineations, Topographical, Historical, and Descriptive, of Each County. Embellished with Engravings.* Middlesex, Vol. X, Part IV (London, 1816), opp. p. 395
W. S. Lewis, Farmington, Connecticut

29. After Samuel Owen (1768/9–1857)
Lady Howe's Villa, Twickenham Drawn by S. Owen Esq.
Engraved by W. Cooke
Engraving, $4\frac{1}{4} \times 6\frac{3}{4}$ in., by William Bernard Cooke (1788–1855)
From William Bernard Cooke, *The Thames*, 2 vols.
London: Vernor, Hood, and Sharpe, 1811, vol. I
Bodleian Library

30. J. M. W. Turner (1775–1851)
View of Pope's Villa at Twickenham During its Dilapidation
Oil on canvas, 36×48 in.
1808
Sudeley Castle, Gloucestershire. The Walter Morrison Settled Picture Trust
Literature: [Edwin Landseer?], 'Mr. Turner's Gallery', *The Review of Publications of Art*, 1 (London: Samuel Tipper, 1808), 155–9; A. J. Finberg, *The Life of J. M. W. Turner, R.A.*, 2nd edn. rev. (Oxford, 1961), pp. 144, 149, 157–8, 184, Appendix ('List of Turner's Oil-Paintings and Watercolours exhibited during his lifetime'), No. 117; *Turner 1775–1851*, Royal Academy Exhibition [16 November 1974–2 March 1975] Catalogue (London: Tate Gallery, 1974), No. 158, pp. 69–70.

31. After J. M. W. Turner (No. 30)
Class I Painting for the Fine Arts of the English School/Pope's Villa./Engraved by John Pye. the Figures by Chas. Heath. from a Picture by J. M. W. Turner, Esqr. R.A. and P.P. in the Gallery of/Sir John Fleming Leicester, Bart.
Engraving, $6\frac{7}{8} \times 9$ in., by John Pye (1782–1874), figures by Charles Heath (1785–1848)
April 1, 1811

From John Britton, *The Fine Arts of the English School; Illustrated by a Series of Engravings . . . of Eminent English Artists* (London, 1812)
W. S. Lewis, Farmington, Connecticut
Literature: A. J. Finberg, *Life of Turner* (1961), p. 184; Adrien Bury, '"Sweete Themmes! runne softly . . ." Paintings and Prints of Twickenham and Richmond in the Collection of the Hon. Mrs. Ionides', *The Connoisseur*, 137 (March 1956), 96.

32. After Robert Havell Jr. (*fl.* 1815–40)
Pope's villa, Twickenham
Coloured aquatint on Card, $7\frac{}{16} \times 5\frac{3}{8}$ in., after drawing by Arthur Havell, Jun.
No. 11 in *The Natuorama: or Nature's endless transposition of Views on the Thames*, London: Havell & Co., n.d. [a panorama]
c. 1823–28
Yale Center for British Art and British Studies
Literature: S. T. Prideaux, *Aquatint Engraving, A Chapter in the History of Book Illustration* (London: Duckworth, 1909), p. 270.

33. Simon Malcho after Lewis Bélanger (1736–1816)
View of the Late Mr. Pope's House at Twickenham Painted by Lewis Bélanger Engraved by S. Malgo
Coloured aquatint, $8\frac{1}{4} \times 10\frac{5}{8}$ in., by Simon Malcho [Malgo] (*fl.* 1763–1781)
c. 1795
London Borough of Richmond upon Thames

34. After William Westall (1781–1850)
W. Westall, A.R.A. *delt.* C. Bentley, *Sculp.*/Pope's Villa, Twickenham. Published 1828 by R. Ackermann, 96 Strand, London
Coloured aquatint, $6\frac{7}{8} \times 10\frac{1}{16}$ by Charles Bentley (1806–54)
From *Picturesque Tour of the River Thames* (London: R. Ackermann, 1828), pl. 10, opp. p. 128
Literature: R. V. Tooley, *English Books with Colored Plates* (London, 1954), No. 502.

35. John Martin (1789–1854)
The Banks of the Thames, Opposite Pope's Villa
Watercolour and body color on brown paper, $11\frac{3}{4} \times 23\frac{5}{8}$ in.
Inscribed J. Martin 1850 lower left
Mr. and Mrs. Paul Mellon
Literature: Algernon Graves, *The Royal Academy of Arts* (8 vols. London, 1905–6), iv. 205; John Baskett and Dudley Snelgrove, *English Drawings and Watercolors 1550–1850 in the Collection of Mr. and Mrs. Paul Mellon* (New York: The Pierpont Morgan Library, 1972), pp. 131, 92–3; William Feaver, *The Art of John Martin* (Oxford: Clarendon Press, 1975), p. 173, pl. 130.

36. W. Thewes
Pope's Villa, an Elizabethan Structure with Modern Additions and Improvements Including Campenella Tower
Colored lithograph, $7\frac{3}{4} \times 13$ in., by W. Thewes, 64 Basinchall St., London
1873
British Library
Literature: British Library, Sale Catalogues of Landed Estates, Middlesex 2.K–2 (1868–83), Maps 137.a.11 (15).

37. C. F. Kell
Pope's Garden, Twickenham with House of Domestic Gothic Architecture
Coloured lithograph, $8\frac{1}{2} \times 11\frac{5}{8}$ in., C. F. Kell lith. Castle St. Holborn, London E.C.
1878
Literature: British Library, Sale Catalogues of Landed Estates, Middlesex 2.K–2 (1868–83), Maps 137.a.11. (16).

Appendix C. *Where was Timon's Villa? Profiles of Blenheim and Houghton*

A COMPARISON of Blenheim, Oxfordshire, and Houghton, Norfolk, the two principal country seats which have been proposed as models for Pope's description of Timon's villa (*Epistle to Burlington*, ll. 99–168), demonstrates that Blenheim conforms far more closely than Houghton. In the following comparison the essential details of Pope's description are followed first by relevant facts about Blenheim, then Houghton.

(1) 'What sums are thrown away!' (l. 100): The cost of Blenheim has been estimated at £300,000, of which £240,000 came from the Exchequer. T[ipping, H. Avray], 'Blenheim Palace—I', *Country Life*, 25 (29 May 1909), 786–98; David Green, *Blenheim Palace* (London: *Country Life*, 1951), p. 137; James Lees-Milne, *English Country Houses, Baroque 1685–1715* (London: *Country Life*, 1970), p. 183. The building accounts of Houghton are lost or destroyed, but one estimate of expenses 'in building, adding, and improving at Houghton' comes to £200,000. See H. Avray Tipping, 'Houghton Hall, Norfolk—I', *Country Life*, 49 (1 January 1921), 21; and John Morley, *Walpole* (London: MacMillan, 1889), pp. 132–3.

(2) 'his building is a Town' (l. 105): The building and courts of Blenheim cover 7 acres with a front of 850′; the front of Houghton is about 450′. See David Green, 'Some Blenheim Statistics', *Blenheim Palace*, p. 234; Colen Campbell, *Vitruvius Britannicus*, 1 (1715), pls. 55–62, 3 (1725), pls. 27–34.

(3) 'all Brobdignag before your thought' (l. 104): Queen Anne gave Marlborough 'the Royal and historic Honor of Woodstock, covering some 22,000 acres'; the park and gardens comprised 2,119 acres. Houghton's park contained 700 acres, a 'design . . . about 12 miles in circumference'. See H. Avray Tipping, 'Blenheim Palace—I', *Country Life*, 25 (1909), 786; Tipping, 'Houghton Hall, Norfolk—III', *Country Life*, 49 (15 January 1921), 71–2; *A Plann of Blenheim*, in

David Green, *Blenheim Palace*, pl. 25, p. 65; and Sir Thomas Robinson to the Earl of Carlisle, H.M.C. *Carlisle*, XV, 6 (1897), 85.

(4) 'His pond an Ocean' (l. 106): The 'Great Bason' at Blenheim was situated at the end of the parterre south of the house. Houghton had 'no water: absolutely none for ornament and all that is necessary for use forced up by art'. See David Green, *Blenheim Palace*, p. 69, pl. 25; Robinson to Carlisle (1731), H.M.C. *Carlisle*, p. 85; and Earl of Ilchester, ed., *Lord Hervey and his Friends* (1950), pp. 70–1.

(5) 'his parterre a Down' (l. 106): At Blenheim the parterre of Henry Wise and John Vanbrugh in the form of a ravelin south of the house extended some 2,500′ in length, 2,200′ in width, with eight bastions 200′ wide, and terraces 1,000′ in length to the north and south. This is about three times the size of the parterre at Houghton. See David Green, *Blenheim Palace*, p. 69, pls. 25, 88; *Vitruvius Britannicus*, 3 (1725), pls. 27–8.

(6) 'a Lake behind' (l. 111): Until Capability Brown enlarged the lake at Blenheim in 1764 the water and canal scheme were ridiculed as meagre, and Vanbrugh's immense bridge was mocked. The plan of Blenheim Park in *Vitruvius Britannicus* (1725) shows the lake to the north-west of the house; the plan of Houghton in the same volume shows a canal (Campbell's invention?) to the west of the house. See *Vitruvius Britannicus*, 3 (1725), pls. 71–2, 27–8; and David Green, *Blenheim Palace*, pp. 49–50, 163, pls. 74–5, 87.

(7) 'behold the Wall' (l. 114): At Blenheim a brick wall 14′ high enclosed the kitchen garden; a wall of rubble and coping surrounded the Great Parterre; near the house there was an 'outboundary wall', another around Woodstock Manor, and an 'enormously costly' wall nine miles in circumference completed in 1729 surrounded the entire park. If the park at Houghton was enclosed by a wall (I don't know that it was) it would have had 'a Circumference of about eight Miles'. See David Green, *Blenheim Palace*, pp. 61, 69, 97, 168, 313–14, pl. 48; and Maynard Mack, quoting Boydell's *Seats of the Nobility* (1779–86), in *The Garden and the City* (1969), p. 309.

(8) 'a Fountain, never to be play'd' (l. 121): Bernini's model for the fountain with four river gods in the Piazza Navona in Rome, a gift to Marlborough from the Spanish ambassador to the papal court about 1710, was not erected at Blenheim until about 1800. Pope owned and annotated an engraving of Bernini's fountain: engraved by Pieter Schenk (1660–1718/19) in *Romae Novae Delineatio*, pl. 12. Nicholas Hawksmoor's proposals in the 1720s for setting it up in a grotto

under Vanbrugh's bridge, or incorporating it in a memorial obelisk for the Duke were rejected by the Duchess of Marlborough. Hawksmoor wrote to the Earl of Carlisle in October 1731: 'the Lake is beautifull, but ye Cascade dos not play all ye rivers are almost dry'. See Geoffrey Webb, *The Letters and Drawings of Nicholas Hawksmoor Relating to the Building of the Mausoleum at Castle Howard 1726–1742*, Walpole Society, 19 (Oxford: University Press, 1931), 127. See David Green, *Blenheim Palace*, pp. 110, 250, 289, pls. 41–2, 69; and 'The Bernini Fountain at Blenheim', *Country Life*, 110 (27 July 1951), 268–9.

(9) 'the Chapel's silver bell' (l. 141): The chapel at Blenheim was completed and consecrated in September 1731, just before the *Epistle to Burlington* was published, and the commission for the Duke's tomb given to William Kent, a sign of increasing Palladian involvement at Blenheim. It had no 'sprawling Saints' (l. 146) by Antonio Verrio and Louis Laguerre, but Laguerre had painted the saloon at Blenheim about 1720. The chaplain at Blenheim, Dean Barzillai Jones, who appears rubicund and portly in Laguerre's fresco, is a plausible candidate for Timon's 'soft Dean' (l. 149). George Sherburn argues that the 'Light quirks of Musick' (l. 143) in the chapel 'might refer to anthems written by Bononcini for Blenheim'. See David Green, *Blenheim Palace*, pp. 160, 269–70, 274, 320, pl. 62; and Sherburn, '"Timon's Villa" and Canons', *Huntington Library Bulletin*, 8 (October 1935), 146 n. Pope's familiarity with the *minutiae* of Blenheim is not unlikely considering his visit in 1718, his rambles in the neighbourhood throughout the 1720s, the notoriety of the house, and the involvement of Pope himself and the Burlington circle at Blenheim. At an early stage Pope was being considered as a person 'who might give a very pretty turn to' the inscription on the Duke's obelisk. In 1723 the Duke of Somerset approached Pope who promised 'to doe his utmost' on condition he should remain anonymous. In the end, Bolingbroke composed a prose inscription, 'imitating the best old inscription style', according to Pope. See David Green, chap. 18, 'Pillar of Truth', *Blenheim Palace*, pp. 168–77; *Sarah Duchess of Marlborough* (London: Collins, 1967), pp. 247–50; and Spence, No. 272 (1735).

Index

This is an index of persons, places, plates, and first references to works cited. Abbreviations: AP for Pope; **P** for plate; q for quotation